In this volume seventeen distinguished historians of early modern Britain pay tribute to an outstanding scholar and teacher. Several present reviews of major areas of debate: of the significance of the regulations which determined the social and legal status of professional actors in Elizabethan England, of Protestant ideas about marriage, of the political significance of the Anglo-Scottish Union, or relations between the Churches of England, Scotland and Ireland under the early Stuarts, and of the riddle of the inner dynamic of the experience of emigration to New England. Case-studies in the social and religious history of the period include the relationship between ideas of cleanliness and godliness, the flowering of the notion of unitive Protestantism in two declarations on behalf of the National Church and provincial preaching at a moment of political crisis in the north of England. Three essays draw on literary evidence to explore attitudes to men of war, and the use of the murder pamphlet as a Puritan conversion narrative and the service provided by scholarly readers for politically influential public figures. Two essays make impressive use of fieldwork to reveal how the churches of James I and VI's two kingdoms were furnished and how the gardens of Sir Nicholas and Sir Francis Bacon illuminate their minds and attitudes. The European dimension is represented by an essay on Nicolas Pithou's history of the Reformation in the city of Troyes.

This very wide-ranging and fascinating collection of essays will appeal both to specialists in the period and to those interested in the social and culture history of early modern Britain.

Religion, culture and society in early modern Britain

Patrick Collinson

Religion, culture and society in early modern Britain

Essays in honour of Patrick Collinson

Edited by

Anthony Fletcher
University of Durham

and

Peter Roberts
University of Kent at Canterbury

CAMBRIDGE
UNIVERSITY PRESS

Published by the Press Syndicate of the University of Cambridge
The Pitt Building, Trumpington Street, Cambridge CB2 1RP
40 West 20th Street, New York, NY 10011–4211, USA
10 Stamford Road, Oakleigh, Melbourne 3166, Australia

First published 1994

Printed in Great Britain at the University Press, Cambridge

A catalogue record for this book is available from the British Library

Library of Congress cataloguing in publication data
Religion, culture and society in early modern Britain: essays in
honour of Patrick Collinson / edited by Anthony Fletcher and Peter
Roberts.
    p.   cm.
Includes bibliographical references and index.
ISBN 0 521 41821 6
1. Great Britain – Civilization – 16th century. 2. Great Britain –
Civilization – 17th century. I. Collinson, Patrick. II. Fletcher,
Anthony. III. Roberts, Peter.
DA320.R47 1994
941.05 – dc20   93-32407 CIP

ISBN 0 521 41821 6 hardback

Contents

Illustrations

Contributors

CHRISTOPHER BROOKE was Dixie Professor of Ecclesiastical History in the University of Cambridge from 1977 to 1993. His many publications include *Oxford and Cambridge* (1988, with Roger Highfield and Wim Swaan), and *A History of Cambridge University: Volume IV 1870–1990* (1993).

ANTHONY FLETCHER has been Professor of Modern History at the University of Durham since 1987. He is the author of *A County Community in Peace and War: Sussex 1600–1660* (1975), *The Outbreak of the English Civil War* (1981) and *Reform in the Provinces: The Government of Stuart England* (1986). He is currently working on a book on gender in early modern England.

MARK GREENGRASS is Senior Lecturer in Modern History at the University of Sheffield. He has published extensively on sixteenth- and early seventeenth-century France and, in particular, on the French Reformation. He is a Director of the Hartlib Papers Project, a major interdisciplinary research project in the humanities, based at the University of Sheffield. He is currently editing Samuel Hartlib's diary, *The Ephemerides* for publication.

SUSAN HARDMAN MOORE is Lecturer in Reformation Studies at King's College London. She is a graduate of Cambridge and Yale, and completed her doctoral work with Patrick Collinson, at Kent and in part at Harvard. Before moving to the University of London, she taught for some years at the Universities of Durham and Edinburgh. She has been a visiting professor at Yale, and a visiting scholar at Princeton Theological Seminary.

MICHAEL HATTAWAY has been Professor of English Literature at the University of Sheffield since 1984. He is author of *Elizabethan Popular Theatre* (1982), *Hamlet: The Critics Debate* (1987), and has edited plays by Beaumont and Jonson as well as *1–3 Henry VI* for the New

Cambridge Shakespeare. He is currently working on an edition of *As You Like It* and a book on drama and society in the early modern period.

LISA JARDINE is Professor of English and Dean of the Faculty of Arts at Queen Mary and Westfield College, University of London. Her most recent book is *Erasmus, Man of Letters: The Construction of Charisma in Print* (Princeton, 1993). She is currently completing a book entitled, *Reading Shakespeare Historically*, and is working with Anthony Grafton and William Sherman on a book on Renaissance readers.

PETER LAKE is Dodge Professor of History at Princeton University. He is the author of *Moderate Puritans and the Elizabethan Church* (1982) and *Anglicans and Puritans?: Presbyterianism and English Conformist Thought from Whitgift to Hooker* (1988).

WILLIAM LAMONT has been Professor of History at Sussex University since 1980, and Dean of the School of Cultural and Community Studies between 1981 and 1986. His Puritan trilogy was reprinted in 1991 under a three-volume title, *Puritanism and the English Revolution*, and his critical edition of Richard Baxter's *A Holy Commonwealth* will be published by Cambridge University Press in 1994.

JOHN MORRILL is Reader in Early Modern History at Cambridge where he has been a Fellow of Selwyn College since 1975. He is the author and editor of fifteen books and his most recent – *The Nature of the English Revolution* – contains twenty of his most influential essays.

PETER ROBERTS is Lecturer in History at the University of Kent at Canterbury and writes on early modern Wales and on the Elizabethan court and stage. He is an honorary fellow of the University of Wales Centre for Advanced Welsh and Celtic Studies at Aberystwyth and editor of the *Transactions of the Honourable Society of Cymmrodorion*.

CONRAD RUSSELL is Professor of History at King's College London. He is the author of *The Crisis of Parliaments: English History 1509–1660* (1971), *Parliaments and English Politics* (1979), *The Causes of the English Civil War* (1990) and *The Fall of the British Monarchies 1637–1642* (1991).

WILLIAM SHEILS is Provost of Goodricke College in the University of York, where he teaches Economic and Social History. He has written books on Puritanism and on the Reformation, and several articles on the church in the early modern period. From 1981 to 1990 he was editor of *Studies in Church History*.

WILLIAM SHERMAN is Assistant Professor of English at the University of Maryland, College Park. His doctoral dissertation on John Dee was directed by Lisa Jardine and Patrick Collinson; and a book based on this research – *John Dee: The Politics of Reading and Writing in the English Renaissance* – will be published in 1994.

HASSELL SMITH is Professor Emeritus in the University of East Anglia where he taught in the School of English and American Studies and directed the Centre of East Anglian Studies. His publications include *County and Court: Politics and Government in Norfolk 1558–1603* (1974) and three volumes of *The Papers of Nathaniel Bacon*.

SIR KEITH THOMAS is President of Corpus Christi College, Oxford, and President of the British Academy. He is the author of *Religion and the Decline of Magic* (1971) and *Man and the Natural World* (1983).

SUSAN WABUDA completed her doctoral thesis under the supervision of Patrick Collinson in 1992. Her monograph *Preaching during the English Reformation* will be published by Cambridge University Press.

GEORGE YULE was Professor of Church History at Ormond College from 1958 to 1978 and Professor of Church History at the University of Aberdeen from 1979 to 1986. His publications include *Puritans in Politics: The Religious Legislation of the Long Parliament 1640–1647* (1981).

Preface

We have sought to gather together friends, colleagues and former students from a wide range of institutions in putting together this tribute to Patrick Collinson on his sixty-fifth birthday. For his academic career has been peripatetic: London, Kent, Sydney, Sheffield and Cambridge are all represented here. We have adopted a broad theme. This reflects the breadth of Patrick's interests and scholarship in the early modern period and it has enabled contributors from different areas of the field to write illuminatingly about topics within their specialist expertise. The flavour of the volume, we believe, represents an appropriate tribute to an historian whose works have enriched our understanding of the period over thirty years. Patrick's own mind has ever been on the move. His supervisor, Sir John Neale, commented at the time of the presentation of Patrick's prodigious PhD thesis on Elizabethan Puritanism in 1957: 'Collinson, I like to think of you spending the rest of your life on this subject.' In one sense he has done this but in another this is very much less than what he has done. For Patrick's later writings show his receptivity to findings from the related disciplines of anthropology, sociology and literature and his unremitting search into the social and cultural implications of religion and religious change in the sixteenth and seventeenth centuries.

It has been a great pleasure to edit this book. It is presented to Patrick Collinson in respect and affection. We honour his distinguished achievement as an historian, his dedication to the subject and his warm generosity towards all those, from undergraduate students to senior colleagues, with whom he constantly shares his learning, experience and enthusiasm.

ANTHONY FLETCHER
PETER ROBERTS

Abbreviations

APC	*Acts of the Privy Council*
BIHR	Borthwick Institute of Historical Research, York
Birthpangs	P. Collinson, *The Birthpangs of Protestant England: Religious and Cultural Change in the Sixteenth and Seventeenth Centuries* (London, 1988)
BL	British Library, London
CJ	*Commons Journals*
CSPD	*Calendar of State Papers Domestic*
CSPI	*Calendar of State Papers Ireland*
CSPV	*Calendar of State Papers Venetian*
DNB	*Dictionary of National Biography*
DWL	Dr Williams Library, London
FL	Folger Library, Washington DC
HJ	*Historical Journal*
HLRO	House of Lords Record Office
HMC	Historical Manuscripts Commission
HRO	Hertfordshire Record Office
JEH	*Journal of Ecclesiastical History*
NRO	Norfolk Record Office
OED	*Oxford English Dictionary*
PRO	Public Record Office
SP	State Papers
SRO	Scottish Record Office
TRHS	*Transactions of the Royal Historical Society*
VCH	*Victoria County History*

Place of publication for books cited in the footnotes is London unless otherwise stated.

Patrick Collinson

Christopher Brooke

'A big man in every way: big in physical frame, and bursting with energy; large in mind and intellectual interests; large in heart and sympathies, wonderfully lacking in any sense of his own importance or any pomposity; finding life, and thought, and gossip (of a superior kind) too much fun, too enjoyable, for there to be room, or time, for narrow-mindedness' or meanness; endowed 'with a kind of natural generosity.' Geoffrey Nuttall's sketch cannot be improved.[1]

Patrick Collinson returned to Cambridge in 1988 as Regius Professor of Modern History after academic experience of quite exceptional variety. His predecessor Sir Geoffrey Elton, for all the continental, cosmopolitan background which has deeply influenced his scholarship, had been nearly forty years in Cambridge by 1988. Patrick Collinson studied in Cambridge and London and taught in Khartoum, London, Sydney NSW, Canterbury UK and Sheffield before accepting an invitation from Downing Street to the Cambridge chair. He is no restless wanderer, but wonderfully adaptable, ready to seek new experience and immerse himself in it body and soul. His return to Cambridge has brought refreshment and the breath of a wider world to the Cambridge History Faculty.

Elton and Collinson were both pupils of Sir John Neale – a unique example of the influence of the London history school by the Cam. Both have made one region of history the centre of almost all their work, Elton the Tudor constitution, from Thomas Cromwell to the Elizabethan parliament, Collinson the religion of Puritans and Protestants in Tudor and Stuart England – and given it great breadth as well as depth by seeing the wider ripples of its continental background and the relation of their theme to every aspect of English life.

---

[1] The reader will quickly see that in preparing this brief prologue I have had invaluable help from Anthony Fletcher, Mark Greengrass, Sybil Jack, John Morrill, Geoffrey Nuttall, Peter Roberts – and Liz Collinson – for which I am deeply grateful.

Patrick Collinson was born in 1929, sprung from a Quaker family – his father had been a missionary in North Africa. His early training lay among Puritans; but his interest in Puritan history only came to hold sway after a remarkable education in the London zoo – which nearly made him a zoologist – and King's Ely, where he was told that he could not be a scientist. At Pembroke College, Cambridge, he read history, scoring a First in Part II and winning his College's Hadley Prize, and was a fervent supporter of CICCU: it was not till he was teaching in Khartoum that he was confirmed as a member of the Anglican communion by Oliver Allison, bishop of the Sudan.

He was over thirty when he married, in his late thirties when his first book was published. It is hard now to imagine Pat or his world without Liz Selwyn and without *The Elizabethan Puritan Movement*. For he is a living example of the truth that an historian and his convictions – and his personality and his home – cannot be severed; though few have attained to his exceptional combination of learning and integrity. He is a man of many friends, warm, kind, thoughtful, encouraging, inspiring; and by the same token he has an infinitely large acquaintance in the sixteenth and seventeenth centuries, and will never allow his acquaintances and their texts to be misrepresented – however courteously he reveals to others the error of their readings.

Behind his first book lay a thesis of legendary proportions and authority, and a scatter of fundamental articles. He laid foundations of exceptional depth and strength which have helped to build many notable structures of learning apart from *The Elizabethan Puritan Movement*. In many respects, the message of his life work is already there; in many more his later work has grown and developed and opened new paths. That first book, in John Morrill's words, 'transformed our understanding of English *Protestantism*. It was very certainly a seminal work in rediscovering the nature of puritanism as a movement rooted in a creative tension with the establishment. Most of Patrick Collinson's own subsequent work is an exploration of the minds of men who were yearning to take over the national church but in various degrees frustrated and having to consider the option of schism . . . When we now explore that mainstream of Elizabethan/Jacobean protestants that conformed but chafed, we call them Collinsonian Protestants, and we all know what we mean'. Our understanding has been transformed most obviously in three ways. First, he wrote in the heyday of Christopher Hill and restored religion and politics to the centre of the picture, where recent fashion had set economics. Next, he rescued Puritanism, in Geoffrey Nuttall's words, 'from being seen, and understood, by hindsight, only through Nonconformist eyes, and [restored] it as a respectable, central, entity in its origins and first century, *within* the Church of England'. Whereas Geoffrey Nuttall's 'major concern was with faith and devotion, and Christopher Hill's with sociology and economics, as expressed in historical circumstances and developments, Patrick has been the true historian, content to portray and elucidate the history, but always aware of the importance of the religious factor in what was undeniably a religious movement'. A third element is his deep knowledge of the European dimension. He has not written on continental movements similar to the Puritans; but he remains 'the least insular of early modern English historians', as Mark Greengrass has put it. 'He writes about the English church in the age of the Reformation with a profound understanding of the issues which were raised on the continent. He knows the debates that European historians have about the Reformation and, equally important, knows which issues are not likely to be worth pursuing very far.'

The 1980s have brought forth three very notable books. 'His major contribution down to 1980', writes John Morrill, 'was to reclaim religious history from denominational history – to jettison a search for the roots of the denominational present in the past . . . for a search particularly of the religious experiences of the past', for the mental world of the preacher in his study and his pulpit and 'the person-in-the-pew'. In his Ford Lectures, *The Religion of Protestants: The Church in English Society 1559–1625* (1982), the whole of the Church of England is deployed on a marvellously rich canvas, in a highly readable book which is yet of the most compelling subtlety and insight. As always, he presupposes some knowledge in his reader; only in his biography of *Grindal* (1979) has he attempted to tell the whole story of one of his leading characters. In the Ford Lectures Matthew Parker, Lancelot Andrewes, George Herbert, John Williams and many others appear alongside his old Puritan friends, deftly introduced to light up many of the threads in his discourse. He does not pause to tell the reader more than a passing word on who these people were: space is thus reserved for 'those precious truths which reside in particulars' in his own words (p. 39). Yet he also makes clear that the evidence he can reveal is a small part of what remains: for example of the 'learned and laborious writing' of the English bishops – 'but who is there prepared to engage seriously with this mountain of extinct divinity? (p. 44). The profusion of riches in the book is so great that even such a gem as Archbishop Sandys' pleading with Burghley to remove his dean to the middle distance – 'the bushoprik of Litchfield wold wel serve the turne' – has been confined to a footnote (p. 10). For all its subtlety, the book does not disguise its author's sympathies. As he contemplates the Jacobean bishops, he concludes 'the most challenging element in these episcopal careers is the emphasis on the reconciliation of puritans and other opponents, as a preferred alternative to forceful suppression: a pointedly anti-Laudian message . . . If these accounts of the Jacobean bishops were only half-true, then Archbishop Laud was indeed the greatest calamity ever visited upon the English Church' (pp. 89–90).

In *The Birthpangs of Protestant England* (1988) the Reformation was sought in the family, in the town, in society at large; and seen too as a cultural revolution. Cultural history has been a major theme of his recent work. 'He has been a keen exponent of historians drawing on the methods and insights of many contiguous disciplines' (John Morrill), developing in Canterbury, Sheffield and Cambridge, for example, 'a deep dialogue' with colleagues in English literature.

One of his greatest gifts is to honour special occasions 'celebrating innumerable quatercentenaries . . . with memorable addresses'. John Morrill 'especially recalls the Nicholas Bacon memorial (1979) . . . A very dull lamp was polished, burnished and shone exceeding bright.' Nicholas Bacon and many others light up *Godly People* (1983), a wonderful treasure house of Patrick's best essays on many themes. My own favourite among his occasional pieces is his *Andrew Perne*, in which he collaborated with David McKitterick and Elisabeth Leedham-Green to commemorate the master of Peterhouse who was not a Puritan, but was everything else, surviving every vicissitude of the Reformation in Cambridge (1991). It is based on a vast store of learning, in which the continental and English movements of the day, and the history of Cambridge, are brought to bear on the puzzling, ambiguous career of the old fox. Patrick does not try to solve the insoluble, but he sets the problem in a new frame; he shows us a man genuinely puzzled on the frontiers of old and new doctrine, yet also a survivor by nature; and he shows how deeply the preservation of Peterhouse and Cambridge entered Perne's motives. It is a striking example of the way in which a small part of English history can be linked to many of the great issues of the day, in unforgettable fashion, a characteristic sketch from the ample store of a great master of historical landscape.

Since 1969 his skills have matured, and his influence has radiated, from Sydney, Canterbury, Sheffield and Cambridge. In Sydney Sybil Jack recalls his efforts 'to give the department a greater sense of corporate identity by holding regular largish parties and smaller dinner parties, with a pleasant level of informality'. He sought out new pastures, and taught 'popular courses on such things as the sociology of religion . . . He also showed himself willing to consider a more democratic departmental structure in which decisions might be made at departmental meetings chaired by someone other than a professor' and in other ways reflected the creative movements of the 1960s and 70s in which he naturally flourished. Especially memorable were the gatherings of early modernists from all over Australia and New Zealand which he and George Yule inspired and led.

In Canterbury, Peter Roberts had devised before his arrival a post-graduate programme on Elizabethan and Jacobean Studies, in which Patrick joined with enthusiasm and inspiration: another collaborator was Michael Hattaway, with whom he was later to work on common ground in Sheffield – 'bringing together literary material and historical evidence on social history topics', in Anthony Fletcher's words. While at Canterbury he suffered a fearful accident which led to the amputation of a leg – and inspired his colleagues with the 'remarkable courage and energy, mental discipline and powers of concentration' he showed in hospital and convalescence, as Peter Roberts recalls: 'his colleagues [in Kent] remember how visits to him in the Kent and Canterbury Hospital were sometimes difficult to arrange because he was likely to be holding a special subject class around his bed'.

In Sheffield he showed once more his eagerness to learn from his environment. 'His democratic, listening, approach was much appreciated. He talked a lot about the Sheffield culture which he was learning . . . The hallmark of effective chairmanship of the department was consultation and painful attempts to bring all together without rushing things. He also had lots of time for students and their problems which they found very impressive' (Anthony Fletcher).

Let us observe him in action in Sheffield and elsewhere, with the aid of Mark Greengrass. 'In meetings, he can be disarming and devastating at the same time. The vigorous nod of his head and infectious laugh can make you nod in agreement with him, even as you inwardly are trying to put the counter-arguments together. Apparently dozing in a seminar, he suddenly emerges from torpor to shape the discussion afterwards and drive it forward with energy and class. At conferences he is wonderful value. He opened the international conference attached to the Hartlib Papers Project, of which he is a director, here in Sheffield last July with an almost sixth sense of what the occasion required and a sure lightness of touch. The result was that the delegates – some 100 or so from 17 different countries – went into the first session of the conference already on their mettle, the intellectual adrenalin flowing.' In *The Religion of Protestants* (p. 244) Pat cites one of his native Suffolkers from the sixteenth century saying 'Come, let's go to Dedham to get a little fire!' – kindled by Mr Rogers, a notable preacher. 'Many of us early modernists have the same response to Patrick – going to him for some intellectual fire' – a quality one does not have to be expert in his own period to identify and enjoy.

If one set to work to portray Pat Collinson in all his stature, one would take one's reader to a view of all his books and to attend his lectures, sit at his feet in seminars and faculty boards; above all, to go with him to church and to visit his family. 'It is difficult to separate Patrick from Liz and the family', Mark Greengrass has said. I am conscious that I can only portray a part of him; let me conclude with one very characteristic encounter. Soon after he had returned to Cambridge, I rang to ask him if he would join with me in writing a history of Emmanuel College. Without a moment's hesitation – or the request for a day or a week's reflection – he said 'yes', and he and I and Sarah Bendall are now embarked on the adventure. He may well have had earlier thoughts of such a task; he loves to say 'yes'; he has a warmth of commitment which is one secret of his great power to encourage and inspire. Yet there was more in it than any of these, and there is more in him than in all we have described. It has been a special delight to spend my last years in harness in his company in Cambridge – where he has learned and taught and inspired with all the experience of the wider world at his command, and with the eagerness which is all his own – and a most singular privilege to open this volume of essays dedicated in his honour, in warm affection and friendship.

1   Nicolas Pithou: experience, conscience and history in the French civil wars

Mark Greengrass

The closing pages of Jean Morély's *Traicté de la discipline & police chretienne*, published in Lyons amidst the first civil war in 1562, contained an interesting suggestion.[1] He completed his critique of the newly agreed French Protestant discipline by proposing that, in each province of the French churches, 'a grave, wise and learned person' should be selected 'who should be entrusted to compile its Ecclesiastical history'. By means of this public record of each Protestant congregation's trials and tribulations the community at large in France would have an 'eternal witness' from which it might draw strength and direction for its future.[2] Morély deliberately avoided saying that it would be written by a pastor; in his view, the active embodiments of the congregation were more likely to come from the laity. The suggestion was one part of a book which placed a *pétard* under the chassis of the freshly framed Discipline of the French Protestant churches. The propositions it contained would be anxiously debated at the fourth National Synod, meeting in Morély's native Lyons in August 1563. A bitter controversy ensued, echoing through the colloquies and synods of French Protestantism during the following decade. But his proposal for ecclesiastical histories, appropriately tamed by the Genevan pastorate, was generally welcomed. The decision was taken: 'que les églises seront adverties de faire un recueil fidèle de tout ce qui est arrivé de plus remarquable par la Providence diuine aux lieux de leur ressort et d'en enuoyer les relations à nos révérends frères de Genève, avec toute la diligence possible'.[3] Thus would 'le chariot triomphale de la vérité de Dieu' (as Morély put it) be proclaimed, the distinctive Protestant perception of God's providence working through history be demonstrated.[4] In provincial synods across

---

[1] I am grateful to Anthony Milton and Penny Roberts for their helpful comments on a draft of this paper.

[2] J. Morély, *Traicté de la discipline & police chretienne* (Lyons, 1562; reprinted Geneva, 1968), 344.

[3] J. Aymon, *Synodes nationaux des églises réformées de France* (The Hague, 1710), I, 47.

[4] J. Morély, *Traité*, 103.

France, local Eusebiuses were put to the task; by May 1565 the results were piling up in Geneva, 'tantae molis' lamented Beza 'ut camelum, nedum asinum possint obruere'.[5]

For the city of Troyes, capital of Champagne, Nicolas Pithou was assigned to the task, probably by the provincial synod held at La Ferté in April 1564.[6] The choice would have pleased Morély, for he was the epitome of the 'grave, sage & docte personnage' whom he had envisaged for the task. Pithou's bulky memorandum was almost certainly already in Beza's hands by May 1565, joining the others which were about to break the camel's back. He doubtless expected to see the published results quite soon; but he was to be disappointed. Like many editors – even of festschrift volumes alas! – Beza was frustrated by late deliverers. At the same time as he was writing to Bullinger about the bulk of the memoirs which had arrived, he was writing apologetically to Pithou: 'Les longs delays desquels on a usé en plusieurs lieux m'envoyer mémoires, m'ont fait retarder jusques à maintenant l'ouvrage que savez: mais j'espère bientôt y mettre la main.'[7] In reality, the famous *Histoire ecclésiastique des églises réformées au royaume de France* only appeared on the shelves fifteen years later, in 1580.[8] By then, however, the climate and context for Protestant history had completely changed. 'Truth's triumphal chariot' no longer had the same drawing-power. A history of French Protestantism which stopped in 1563, had it appeared in the 1560s, might have read as the story of stoic defiance, costly success. So much more had happened by 1580 that it was bound to read more like heroic failure. *L'Histoire ecclésiastique* did not enjoy great acclaim and was not reprinted in the sixteenth century. To Nicolas Pithou, the eventual compilation could not do justice to the measure of his personal experiences. He had provided full, detailed, circumstantial documentation for the congregation of Troyes and what were the results? Thirty-eight succinct paragraphs are dispersed through the first two published volumes, digested highlights (occasionally employing the *ipsissima verba* of his original account) which inevitably lose the freshness, circumstantial detail and passion of the original.[9] Worse, the compiler had made

---

[5] Beza to Bullinger, Geneva, 3 May 1565 (*Correspondance de Théodore de Bèze*, ed. H. and Fl. Aubert, H. Meylan, A. Dufour *et al.* (15 vols. in prog., Geneva, 1973–91), VI, 73.

[6] Referred to in *ibid.*, IV, 61. Cf. *Calendar of State Papers Foreign 1564–5*, ed. J. Stevenson (1870), no. 357, which provides a *procès-verbal* of the synod.

[7] Beza to Nicolas Pithou, Geneva, 22 May 1565 (*Correspondance de Bèze*, ed. Aubert *et al.*, VI, 93).

[8] *L'Histoire ecclésiastique des églises réformées au royaume de France* (3 vols., Geneva, 1580; ed. G. Baum and E. Cunitz, Paris, 1883–9) – henceforth *Hist. eccl.*

[9] The passages are as follows: *Hist. eccl.*, I, 82–3, 101–2, 104–5, 106, 135, 163–4, 333–4, 848–51; II, 461–76. These passages can be compared directly with the equivalent

mistakes. He garbled, for example, the way in which the Protestant *colporteur* from Senlis, Jean de Gannes, having been arrested in Troyes for possessing a bail of heretic books, was subsequently set free in early April 1559. He was probably confusing it with another, rather similar set of events from later that same year, also elaborated by Pithou, of the freeing of the Protestant minister in Troyes, Girard de Corlieu.[10] Pithou was moved to amend the text of his manuscript history at this point, scratching out one passage and recording instead: 'sur quoy je mesbahi com~~m~~ent celuy qui sest meslee de ~~dresser et~~ sen imprimer l'histoire Ecclesiastique des Eglises reformees au Royaume de france racomptant au premier uolume de lade histoire de faict dernier <dict>, que ceulx que le menoient luy donnerent conge, chose de tout contraire a la verite et mesme contre les memoyres quen furent enuoyez pour linserer en lade histoire'.[11] Beyond such matters of detail, however, one suspects that the *Histoire ecclésiastique* disappointed the Eusebius of Troyes in a more general way. Pithou had not envisaged that he was merely contributing a provincial 'case-study' of the Troyen Reformation, a chronicle of local events. Inspired by the classical historians, he had pretensions to write a history which divined the forces of destiny and virtue (or their Protestant equivalents – providence and conscience). This, or something like it, explains why he reworked his initial memorandum on the reformation in Troyes into the remarkable manuscript which he entitled 'L'histoire ecclésiastique de l'église réformée de la ville de Troyes'. In 20 books, 516 folios and over 400,000 words, Pithou detailed the tumultuous history of the Reformation in Troyes, taking it through to 1594. Exactly when he wrote it is impossible to determine although the numerous alterations and intercalations strongly indicate a progression over time. It is likely that he worked from earlier drafts but rewrote or revised the manuscript in detail as time passed. There is no sign that he ever attempted to print the history and it would have offended many of the Troyen elite had he done so. Even now, after a century of attempts and an inadequate selection of published extracts apart, it still remains consultable only in

accounts given in Pithou's manuscript 'L'histoire ecclésiastique de l'église réformée de la ville de Troyes' in Bibliothèque Nationale MS Dupuy 698 – henceforth Pithou. It is thanks to the generosity of Dr Penny Roberts that I have been able to consult her microfilm copy of this manuscript.
[10] *Hist. eccl.*, I, 163; Pithou, fol. 148v.
[11] Pithou, fol. 123. In this, as in succeeding citations, the numerous alterations of the manuscript are provided unless otherwise indicated. Additions to the text are indicated within chevron brackets. Additions within the additions are shown in bold type. Although wearisome for the reader, these alterations provide a precious testimony to Pithou's techniques of composition and the refinement of his historical perspectives.

manuscript.[12] Yet Pithou's history is, quite simply, the most important, detailed, circumstantial account which we possess of what the urban Reformation in France was actually *about*. Written from the perspective of the disinterested observer (Pithou's name appears from time to time in the text, and always in the third person), it nevertheless presents – at least for the periods when he was resident in Troyes – an eye-witness account of its Reformation. Where he was not an observer, he drew on testimonies and affidavits which were available to him as a leading authority in the city, known to defend Protestants in difficulties with the authorities. It was contemporary history, written by someone who was in a privileged, if not unique, position to exploit the new historical methodology which was a distinctive feature of the French Renaissance.

The intellectual milieu of Nicolas Pithou and his brothers reflected the aspirations and interests of their father, Pierre Pithou the elder. He was educated at the university of Orleans at the time when the first effects of new ways of teaching Roman law were being felt.[13] In the hands of a great humanist proponent like Guillaume Budé (who, as canon of the cathedral in Troyes, knew and influenced him), this experience had a transforming impact, particularly on the study and writing of history.[14] The 'niaiseries' of medieval chronicle writing were to be abandoned. Historical sources were to be critically scrutinised, compared and assessed, using the new science of philology. Through the application of this methodology would emerge a rounded and complete historical picture, a broader accompanying reality. Pithou's Protestant contemporary, La Popelinière, wrote of a 'nouvelle histoire' – not, of course, the last time that such a claim would be made for French contributions to historical methodology![15]

Although Pithou's father did not publish anything himself, he influenced the achievements of his sons. He had good contacts with other French humanists in Paris and elsewhere. He transformed the education offered in Troyes through attracting first-rate humanist teachers of Latin and Greek to posts at the local *collège* which his children attended. He

---

[12] C. Recordan, *Le Protestantisme en Champagne* (Paris, 1863), published some fragments (not always accurately transcribed) of the history.

[13] J. Grosley, *Vie de Pierre Pithou: avec quelques mémoires sur son père, et ses frères* (2 vols., Paris, 1756), I, 1–38, provides basic details.

[14] Donald R. Kelley, *Foundations of Modern Historical Scholarship. Language, Law, and History in the French Renaissance* (New York and London, 1970), ch. 3.

[15] G. Huppert, *The Idea of Perfect History. Historical Erudition and Historical Philosophy in Renaissance France* (Urbana, 1970), esp. ch. 2.

was amongst those responsible for the appointment of Jean Lange as its principal and of Nicolaus Stickler as one of the regents in 1539, the latter being also a private tutor to Nicolas for a time.[16] Before they went to college in Paris, Pierre Pithou's sons apparently had a good knowledge of Latin and Greek and some basic awareness of Hebrew. Pierre Pithou also built up an excellent library for which, using his position as *bailli* to the cathedral in Troyes, he acquired copies of unique medieval manuscripts from ecclesiastical libraries. At the same time he amassed a collection of Latin inscriptions.[17]

The influences of this background are everywhere apparent in the scholarship of Nicolas Pithou's distinguished half-brother, Pierre.[18] He used his philological skills, his knowledge of manuscript sources, his unrivalled range of contacts around the humanist milieu of later sixteenth-century France to aid his research into French law and history and transform the study of its medieval past. Pierre, the 'Varro of France' as he came to be known towards the end of his life, kept in touch with Nicolas, corresponding about books and manuscripts as well as sharing his views of contemporary political developments.[19] Nicolas' own scholarship was ultimately less distinguished but his delight in manuscripts and books was as highly attuned. The destruction in 1567 of the library of books collected by Nicolas Pithou and his twin brother Jean is mentioned eloquently in the History: 'un fort grand nombre de livres, tant de l'escripture saincte, que autres qui estoient fort rares et exquis, et fort bien reliez et accoustrez, ensemble tous leurs labeurs depuys vingt ans: qu'ils tenaient plus chers et pretieux, qu'vn bien grand tresor'.[20] The majority were burnt on the orders of the *prévôt* Francoys Mauroy, Pithou's half-cousin, in the provost's courtyard. Yet Pithou's learning was appreciated by many of his contemporaries. Beza, a friend of the Pithou family, wrote a Latin epitaph in his honour after his death, acknowledging his erudition as well as his devotion to

---

[16] G. Carré, *L'Enseignement secondaire à Troyes du moyen âge à la Révolution* (Paris, 1888), 35.

[17] His manuscripts included some Roman law-codes which had been used, with acknowledgement, by Cujas in 1566 in his edition of the Theodosian law-code. These were subsequently edited and published by Pierre Pithou in 1571, beginning with Theodosius. One can reconstruct some elements of Pierre Pithou senior's library from J. Boivin, *Petri Pitheoi vita* (Paris, 1711), and *Les Richesses de la bibliothèque de Troyes* (Troyes, 1951).

[18] See Kelley, *Foundations of Modern Historical Scholarship*, ch. 9; also L. de Rosanbo, 'Pierre Pithou', *Revue du Seizième Siècle*, 15 (1928), 279–305.

[19] This correspondence is scattered through various volumes of Bibliothèque Nationale MSS Dupuy, esp. MSS 688 and 700. I have not had the opportunity to study his surviving letters.

[20] Pithou, fol. 334.

virtue.[21] His historical perspective was particularly appreciated by Simon Goulart, who may have been the compiler of the *Histoire ecclésiastique*. Goulart dedicated the second edition of his Latin history on the life of Justinian to Nicolas Pithou, declaring in its preface that the work had benefited from his view of how the knowledge of the past should be applied to the present in order to draw comfort for the future.[22]

These influences are also to be traced, albeit *sotto voce*, in Pithou's 'Histoire ecclésiastique de l'église réformée de la ville de Troyes'. The first book displays a considerable critical and destructive flair for the legends concerning the early history of the city of the kind which one would expect; 'Je ne puys dire veritablement', 'je n'en ay peu oncques rien apprendre de certain', 'qui est–ce qui ne voit que c'est vn compte faicte a plaisir?'.[23] Medieval chroniclers had created a fabric of myth to buttress the Catholic establishment of the city; Pithou had little difficulty, probably drawing on the researches into provincial history of his half-brother, in dismantling it. The remainder of the work, however, was contemporary history, and that posed the opposite problem to that confronting the humanists who were reconstructing the distant French or Roman past. Their task was to divest the fullness of the past from its fragmentary record; his was to invest the fullness of the present into an inevitably partial account, where, like all observers, Pithou would see what he chose to see. Yet some of the skills of the 'nouvelle histoire' could be applied to contemporary history. Institutional background was fundamental, but it should not dominate the structure; Pithou's history is emphatically *not*, whatever the title might imply, a history of the Protestant church as an institution in Troyes. Social, cultural and linguistic awareness was vital in order to be able to capture the recent past; Pithou's history is distinctive in the degree to which he is able to enable us to relive the events of Troyes. The lessons of the distant past should not be entirely forgotten when it comes to interpreting the present; there are more (uncited, but unambiguous) references to Livy

---

[21] *Bulletin de la Société de l'Histoire du Protestantisme Français*, 20 (1870), 158–9; Beza to Jean Pithou, Geneva, 1 Sept. 1599; the inscription had been written for 'vostre bon frère et nostre commun amy'. Referring to the forthcoming epitaph, the Genevan pastor Charles Perrot wrote: 'Il s'étoit comme enseveli vivant avec vous, ses amis & ses livres, en la méditation de plus louable antiquité' (Grosley, *Vie de Pithou*, I, p. 60). Later, Beza would complain (3 Jan. 1600) that the epitaph had been mutilated by the Paris printers and its editors. Beza had been particularly assisted by Nicolas Pithou towards his scholarly edition of the writings of Tertullian, a manuscript of which was in the Pithou Library ('Lettres de Théodore de Bèze à Nicolas Pithou . . . ', *Bulletin de la Société de l'Histoire du Protestantisme Français*, 32 (1883), 255–6).

[22] S. Goulart, *Iustiniani Avgvsti Historia* (Lyons, 1594; copy in the Bibliothèque Sainte-Geneviève, Paris 1.87, 315), epistle dedicatory, dated 10 February.

[23] Pithou, fol. 1.

than to the Genevan reformers Calvin and Beza in the text. Above all, there was an obsession with precision and factual accuracy. In the successive recensions of the history, evident in the corrections of the manuscript, we can see his efforts to achieve this. 'Plusieurs' becomes 'dix ou douze'; 'un certain personnage' acquires a name when he finally learns it. He is scrupulous about endeavouring to express exactly what he meant. When, for example, he describes the involvement of one of the Catholic city guard in the first civil war, his initial rendition: 'capitaine Belin envoyé de la part des catholiques' becomes, in due course, 'capitaine Belin envoyé de la part du lieutenant Coiffart et ceux de sa faction'; the detail of what has been altered is incidental but its effects on the significance of the incident are important, making it more 'factional' than 'sectarian'. The overall result could hardly be objective; contemporary history rarely is. But it was a vehicle for transferring experience into history which was, one suspects, vital to Pithou – rather in the same way that Primo Levi's cool, clinical account of what he had seen in Auschwitz was, he later recorded, a necessary contribution to his sanity because, quite simply, he felt himself to be a living witness of what he had seen. In his detailed, almost compulsive, narration of the violence perpetrated by citizen upon citizen in and around Troyes, the accounts of barbarous acts of cruelty and killing of men, women and children, each coolly pinned down to the written page as carefully as butterflies in a collection – Pithou was testifying to what he had experienced and been touched by. In the process he was able, for himself, to put it into some sort of perspective.[24] La Maconne, 'pauvre femme de la religion', was killed on the steps of a church because she refused to kneel before a statue; her body was dragged to the bridge over the Seine and dumped there. The town's lieutenant, the sieur Desbordes, came to investigate the incident, and ordered her body to be fished out of the river. Yet, when he was told of 'la qualité de lade femme' and of the reasons for the incident, he instructed the watch to throw the body back in.[25] Huguenot life was cheap in Troyes, at least if you were not a Pithou. There was the woman cut into four pieces and her mutilated body arranged in the form

---

[24] The detail of religious violence in Troyes, provided by Pithou, does not (in general) conflict with the interpretation offered by D. Crouzet, *Les Guerriers de Dieu* (2 vols., Paris, 1990). Its analysis needs to be undertaken, however, in the context of an urban study of Troyes in the sixteenth century, the nature of its Protestant community and in relation to other similar urban studies. This has been successfully undertaken by Dr Penny Roberts in her recent doctoral thesis, 'A Town in Conflict: Troyes during the French Wars of Religion' (University of Birmingham PhD, 1992). I am grateful to Dr Roberts for her permission to cite this thesis in the preparation of this article.

[25] Pithou, fol. 231.

of a cross around that of her husband; or Guillaume Venet, a child about ten or twelve years old, who bragged to a cloth weaver in the Catholic town guard of the money in his purse, only to be led down a side-alley and killed for his pains; or another child, about the same age, shot for being heard to repeat the Lord's Prayer in French; or the woman, about to give birth, who was killed, along with her child. In the case of the latter incident, Pithou was careful to report that there were no independent eye-witnesses to the event but only the later testimony of the perpetrator. Yet his account of this, in itself, was yet one more painful encounter with the vaunting, bragging, gloating which Pithou's *History* carefully records as part of the trauma. During the first civil war the Catholic soldiery in Troyes, for example, 'se promenerent tout le long du iour de ce iour parmy la ville, avec les tabourins sonnans, portantz au col de fort grosses patenostres, au bout desquelles pendoit vn gros crucifix de bois, qu'ilz presentoient a baiser a tous ceux qu'ilz rencontroient. Ceux qui en faisoient la moundre difficulté, estoient chargez de coups et grandement outragez'.[26] Such brutality, such behaviour is 'barbare' to Pithou – 'les barbares auroient horreur de les ouy reciter'.[27] Putting it all in the past meant committing it to history for its better comprehension by others who had not experienced it directly. The same point was made in the introduction to the *Histoire ecclésiastique*: 'attendu que l'histoire est le seul moyen par lequel la mémoire des choses passées estant conservée, l'homme peut cognoistre ce qu'il n'a oncques veu ni ouy, voire sans aucun danger, & trop mieux, bien souvent, que si luy-mesme l'avoit ouy ou veu'.[28]

Implicit throughout Pithou's 'Histoire ecclésiastique de l'église réformée de la ville de Troyes', of course, is its Protestant sense of history. Superficially, this was dictated by a retrospective picture of Providence at work. God was a 'merveilleus ouvrier, et qui par sa sainte providence scait bien admener toutes choses (contre l'oppinion des hommes) au point qu'il a determiné'. When the Protestant minister in Troyes was saved from the mob in 1562, partly through the unanticipated thoughtfulness of the 'bons hommes' of the city guard who shut the gates of the city and let him escape without the pursuit of the Catholic crowd behind him, Pithou's comments are entirely conventional: 'Par ainsy nostre dieu laisse monstra en l'issue et retraite de ce pauure ministre, des

---

[26] *Ibid.*, fol. 226v.
[27] *Ibid.*, fols. 241, 270; in the case of the latter incident, Pithou is scrupulous to record that there were no independent witnesses but that the evidence came from the testimony of the perpetrator somewhat later.
[28] *Hist. eccl.*, I, 1.

tesmoinages et signes fort mermarcables, de sa faveur paternelle, et providence admirable envers les siens.'[29] Even with the depressing turn of events in Troyes during the first civil war, as the Protestants lost any degree of political protection which they had enjoyed as well as their own optimism, Pithou felt compelled to record:

qu'il sembloit proprement au iugement humain, que dieu voulust entierement ruiner et confondre cest pauure Eglise. Car les meutres, qui se commirent en icelle durent ce temps, par les ennemys de la verité, furent telz, et si grands, que mal-aisement les pourroit on reciter, tant il se trouva de corps morts de ceux de la religion, sur le pavé, et en l'eau, qui avoient esté inhumainement tuez et massacrez . . . Mays quoy que Satan, comme victorieux et triomphans de ceste pauure Eglise, si est ce que au plus fort de ses triumphes, et au milieu de tant de miseres et de calamitez, qui pour lors y regnoient, nostre bon Dieu ne laissa point les siens, sans quelques signes et marques evidents de assistance et bonte paternelle envers les siens eux.[30]

At the same time, Pithou firmly rejected any sense that human invocation to God to operate in and through history could be effective.[31] When it was attempted, it was an open door to tyranny and abuse.[32] The response amongst the peasantry of Champagne around Troyes to the poor harvest of the previous year, compounded by a severe drought during the following winter months, was to organise mass 'processions blanches' towards the end of Lent 1556. The villagers marched on the town, ostensibly to pray at the shrines of Sainte-Heléne and Saint-Mâtie in the cathedral.[33] Children, dressed in linen and barefoot, took part in separate processions. Wine barrels were opened and available to passing penitents in both the villages and the streets of Troyes. Penitential rituals were re-enacted; in one procession, a poor young man, playing the part of Jesus carrying the cross of Calvary and virtually naked, was beaten (some said to death). When the pilgrims arrived in Troyes, they were initially welcomed. Candles, tabernacles, statues and images were erected in the city and its citizens (including those from the elite) joined in.[34] Pithou

---

[29] Pithou, fol. 230v.

[30] Ibid., fol. 256v.

[31] Cf. D. Crouzet, Les Guerriers de Dieu, I, 640–8, which has much influenced the following analysis.

[32] Pithou provides a summary account under the year 1557 of a treatise entitled 'Plaidoyer faict par un certain Advocat de Paris, a l'encontre de quelques gens qu'il appelle pseudochrestiens' – one which he had perhaps composed himself. It is a commentary on the classical story of Umma Pampiliùs who invented gods for his superstitious people to worship (with apparent success) and how this was an invitation to tyranny.

[33] F. Lebert, Les Processions blanches au XVIe siècle (Meaux, 1918); Pithou, fols. 87v–9v.

[34] 'Les filles de meilleures et plus apparentes maisons de la ville estoient de la partie, voyre mesme quelques personnages de reputation, et qui estoient tous des plus sages et myeulx aduisez de la ville . . . ' (Pithou, fol. 89).

could not resist some comparisons with the sacrifices undertaken in classical Rome before pointing out that their efforts were in vain and 'une servirent que d'irriter Dieu de tant plus. Car de faict le ciel fut tellement fermé, que depuis le caresme iusques au temps de l'iuer, il n'y eut . . . aucune pluye, synon la veille et le iour qu'on appelle la feste Dieu.' Worse, as the importunity of the pilgrims increased and the possibilities of disruption in the city grew worse, the city fathers were forced to close the gates and mount guards on the streets. For Pithou, such processions were both pathetic and odious. They encouraged immorality (their promiscuity, drunkenness and near nudity open encouragement to 'orgies'); by exploiting the superstitions of ignorant people, they perpetrated a cruel trick on their participants, encouraging them to believe wrongly that God was the one who would redress their wrongs. But God, according to Pithou, does not work through history like this. There would be no supernatural solutions. History was about the laws of nature, including human nature, the good and evil in us. As if to reinforce the point, Pithou described how it was through human agency that the processions were dispersed:

Car comme ces desordres et pauuretez se renforcerent de plus en plus il [God] esmeut si bien les coeurs des catholiques de ceux de la religion romaine que voyant qu'il n'y auoit point de bout en ces processions, ils y aduiserent de pres pour la crainte qu'ilz eurent, que quelques boute feux meslez parmy ces troupes, n'apportassent quelque dommage irreparable a la ville.[35]

With fears spreading that the city would be set on fire (as it had been in 1524) the processions were halted by the authorities and dispersed. The Protestant community, Pithou carefully notes, continued its meetings throughout this season, in disdainful and dangerous isolation.

So Pithou's explanatory framework for Troyes during the civil wars contains no comets, strange portents, monstrous births or divination. When there were 'tonnerres horribles, orages et tempestes', such as accompanied a meeting of the lieutenant from Troyes, the sieur Desbordes and the duc de Nevers in the autumn of 1562, Pithou took pains to record the superstitious reactions of the Protestants' superstitious and guilty adversaries. Instead the history is a demythologised and desacralised one of the plots, machinations and duplicities of the Protestant community's enemies and the stoic courage and patience of its adherents. In the case of the politics, Pithou's account is best understood on two levels. At one level it is a history of what actually happened; at another, it is a metahistory of the fears and suspicions generated on

---

[35] *Ibid.*, fol. 89v.

both sides. By 'metahistory' I mean the powerful anxieties which were created by an amalgam of what had happened in the past and what might happen in the future, all conspiring in an emotive combination of language and gesture to influence the outcome of the present. His superficially confusing account of the critical events of April 1562 to January 1563 is a complex attempt to reconstruct both the history and the metahistory of what happened during those months. The chronology unfolded rapidly, each event leaving its legacy, beginning with the massacre at Vassy (the Protestant community sponsored from Troyes close by the city) in March 1562, and ending with the appointment of the duc de Guise as governor of Champagne in succession to the duc de Nevers in January 1563. In his interpretation of these months, Pithou was inevitably partisan and one-sided.[36] In his evocation of the metahistory, however, he is invaluable. He describes for us (for example) the hatreds of the Protestants for the cathedral *official* Nicolas Tartrier, already known and feared for his interrogation of suspected Protestants. He evokes the individual quarrels and hatreds amongst the royal officials of the town which fed into these events, especially that between the *lieutenant particulier*, Me Philippes Belin, the *lieutenant général*, Noel Coiffart, and the *président* of the local court, Mesgrigny, so embittered that Coiffart refused to look at his colleague on the bench or stand when he entered the chamber.[37] Intermingled in the account are the fears of Condé's raising of troops from the town as well as the duc de Guise's political machinations (through his agent Escavolles).[38] Pithou recreates the *frisson* of fear in the city after the news of other massacres elsewhere, comprehending the apprehensions of the Catholics as often as he presents those of the Protestants. His *History* gives us the language of anxiety, the gestures of sectarian fear. Take, for example, the meeting in the council chamber of the city in October 1562. The Catholic merchant and councillor Jean Tartrier was heard to say 'Que le plus prompt et expedient moyen pour s'en asseurer estoit de les embrocher tous comme des alouettes.' This was followed by Christophe Angenoist who, towards

---

[36] The necessary detailed analysis of the events of 1562, analysing Pithou's picture of events in comparison with other sources, is provided by Penny Roberts in her thesis (ch. 5).

[37] One suspects more than a little personal animus in Pithou's account of Philippes Belin, who had purchased his office in 1558 from M. Antoine Bazin, and whom Pithou dismissed as a 'simple advocat' who had little legal experience (*ibid.*, fol. 114). Had Pithou himself entertained hopes of purchasing that office himself?

[38] See, for example, his description of Catholic fears of Protestant troop-raising in Lent 1562; 'ce qui causa vn tel effroy entre les catholiques que la plus part d'eux se ~~tint~~ <contiennent> serrez en leurs maison, ou ils demourent toute la nuict en transe'.

the close of a long speech, accompanied the same sentiments with a sinister Gallic shrug: 'dist pour toute conclusion, avec vn <crucillement> et branslement de teste, Hault et court, Hault et court, ~~sug~~ voulant signifier par ces mots, qu'il les failloit pendre'. Pithou describes the inception of a secret council of hard-line Catholic notables within the city's ruling groups around September 1562, subverting its constitution from within, manipulating and steering events towards a forcible exclusion of Protestants from the city; 'Menez le dehors', like beggars, for 'le mist de hors' had become a convenient euphemism for Protestant elimination, one of many sanitised expressions which Pithou records for religious cleansing.

For both sides, however, decisions were being taken in the civil war by their adversaries without regard (as they saw it) to propriety or consti-tutional norms. Pithou was particularly concerned that the majesty of the law should provide an anchor in a storm of anxieties. The legal profession (he was a practising attorney) was 'louable et honorable et servant grandement en une republique', an instrument for good 'selon dieu' so long as it was not corrupted by avarice or ambition. His objection to the proposed introduction of an Inquisition in France in 1557 was precisely on the grounds that it would encourage both.[39] His unconcealed dislike for Nicolas Tartrier, the *official* of Troyes, drew on similar fears and reflected the Gallican tendencies of his family and other leading Paris *avocats*. One of the themes of his *History* was that of the importance of the civic constitution of Troyes, and the need for its protection. After a careful description of the elective procedures of the mayor and aldermen of the city, Pithou then described the attempt to postpone the elections in 1562 by the *lieutenant criminel* Escavolles on the grounds of fears of imminent popular sedition and a commission which he pretended to have in his pocket, but which he was not able to produce.[40] The *History* emphatically rejected the proposition that he, Pithou, was anything less than a good citizen of Troyes and a loyal subject of the king of France. The Huguenots were amongst 'les myeux avisez et affectionnez au repos public'. When, towards the end of 1562, the Protestants began to be called 'Huguenots' in Troyes and 'rebelles de la majesté du Roy' Pithou recalled that they 'ne voulurent accepter ces tiltres tant magnifiques et honorables et en remercierent bien humblement leurs concitoyens catholiques, les supplians de les vouloir garder et retour pour eux, d'autant qu'ilz leur convenoient trop myeux, et leur debvoit cet honneur appartenir'.[41] Given, however, that

---

[39] *Ibid.*, fol. 101.   [40] *Ibid.*, fol. 197v.   [41] *Ibid.*, fol. 262.

the framework of law was threatened both nationally and locally, Pithou accepted that there was no alternative to securing a measure of protection from a grandee as the key to survival for the movement.

Pithou's history makes very little of his connections with Condé, his *entrée* into the favour of Coligny's brother d'Andelot in the 1560s and then, later, his protection amongst the clients of Antoine de Crussol, who named him *bailli* and governor of the county of Tonnerre on the French border in Champagne in 1572. His *History* does, however, give us precious testimony of how a Protestant church attempted to win the battle for the 'arrière-boutique' of a powerful grandee or a figure at court.[42] His account of the Protestant failure at Troyes in 1562 hinges on the collapse of such protection. The church deputed to the prince de Condé at Orleans, requesting 'vn seigneur de marque' and reinforcements to sustain them during the first civil war. Condé initially agreed and then, some hours later, mindful of promises he had made to his nephew the duc de Nevers, governor of the province of Champagne, he countermanded these instructions.[43] Thereafter, and for the remainder of the first civil war, the efforts of the Troyen Protestants were directed to hold on to the favour of the duc de Nevers. Although initially favourable to their cause, he was gradually weaned away under the influence of his secretary (Blaise de Vigenaire) and the lieutenant of his *gens d'armes* (the sieur Desbordes).[44] His servants assumed authority in his name, invoked that of others including the king and exploited the power of rumour and ridicule. At a critical juncture, Vigenaire told the duke that the Protestants were reported in the city to be wanting to set fire to it; worse, that the Protestants were laughing at the duke behind his back, saying that his recent injury from falling off his horse was 'a cause de l'extreme grosseur de ses chausses, qui estoient les plus grosses qu'on veit oncques, si embourrees et enflees de poil que a les voir vous eussiez proprement dict que c'estoient deux tabourins <chose Incroiable a ce qui ne les auoit veues>'.[45] There was perhaps no speedier way to sacrifice the *appui* of an aristocrat than to treat his loins with levity. In any case, the influence of the governor of the province was rapidly being eclipsed by the more local power-brokers who knew only too well how to assume royal authority in and around the city in order to advance their own (and their family's)

---

[42] *Ibid.*, fol. 194v.
[43] *Ibid.*, fol. 209v.
[44] *Ibid.*, fol. 194v. Vigenaire 'avoit l'oreille de son maistre et le manioit a sa discretion'.
[45] *Ibid.*, fol. 223v.

position.[46] For some of these (such as the Dintevilles), active and entrepreneurial in the royal interest, Pithou had much respect. Others (such as the provincial clients of the Guises, the duc d'Aumale and the cardinal de Lorraine – the seigneur de St Phalle or, later, St Pol) he saw as the proscribers and excluders by force of the Protestant population in the province, all standing to gain personally from the imminent prospects of religious cleansing.[47]

The authority of the king was the fragile protection upon which Troyes' Protestants depended in the wake of the edict of pacification of 1563. Pithou inevitably became involved in the legal representations to ensure that the congregation was not denied its benefits. This entailed, however, an uphill struggle against 'l'impunité de ces meschants, la nonchallance du Magistrat, et le peu de conte qu'on faisoit d'administrer iustice'.[48] The duc d'Aumale, who was one of the commissioners of the edict, assigned them a place of worship at Aix-en-Othe, some thirty kilometres to the west of Troyes. The majority of the congregation could hardly make the journey to and fro in one day on a regular basis and thus, in practice, this decision consigned the Protestants of Troyes to progressive depletion and eventual extinction. Reversing it became one of Pithou's main objectives but he was faced with hostility from amongst a majority of the notables of the city. Even the *procureur du roi* was heard to remark of the Protestants in the wake of the edict that 'il les falloit tous envoyer au marché au bled, Qui estoit autant, que s'il eust dict, qu'il les falloit tous fayre pendre'.[49] So their efforts, orchestrated by Pithou, were directed more towards members of the royal court. These began during its visit to the city in March 1564. Remonstrances were prepared which documented some of the supposed injustices of the local notability during and after the civil wars. Pithou had a predictably stormy encounter with the duc d'Aumale ('fort desagreable'). Unused to his authority being so overtly questioned, Aumale quickly lost his temper with Pithou: 'Vous mentez paillard, vous mentez, ie vous feray attacher a ceste fenestre'; on being told that the Protestants represented a good proportion of the households of the city who would not have their rights so cavalierly dismissed, Aumale reached for his dagger 'comme faisant contenance de le vouloir fraper, adiousta qu'il le feroit pendre'. Pithou's icy reply to the duke assured him 'que la Iustice n'auoit accoustumé de

---

[46] For the distinctive voice of the leaders of Champagne's nobility, whose position was enhanced by the province's vulnerable frontier position, see the excellent thesis by Laurent Bourquin, *Noblesse seconde et pouvoir en Champagne aux XVIe et XVIIe siècles* (Doctorat d'histoire, l'Université du Maine, 1991).

[47] Pithou, fol. 213v.

[48] *Ibid.*, fol. 289 (1563).   [49] *Ibid.*, fol. 290.

fayre pendre de si gens de bien que luy, et que s'il le faisoit, ce seroit vne pauure recompense des services que feu son pere auoit faict du passé, en leur maison'. This self-assurance and astute reference to past fidelity left the duke somewhat at a loss for a reply and, perhaps ominously, Pithou heard him turn to members of his entourage and inquire: 'Qui est il? Qui est il?' before the audience was brought to an inconclusive conclusion. Pithou's subsequent description of the manoeuvres to secure a favourable hearing before the queen mother is a precious evocation of the various back-eddies and counter-currents that operated at the court in civil war France. There were efforts to blacken his name, attempts by various members of the Troyes city council to forestall their accusations, disputes at the heart of the privy council between the chancellor and others, deputations from prominent Huguenot notables' wives to influence members of the queen mother's entourage, not to mention shrewd political games played by the Protestant aristocrats at court and the even more consummate political artistry of the queen mother, too complex to be given its just desserts here. When, however, the affair came before the privy council there was little to be gained from it. Pithou was left to wait upon the secretary of state Morvilliers to obtain a copy of the council's reply to their remonstrance. When Pithou told him that he thought the problems for the Protestants of Troyes and the whole civil war stemmed from the failure to enforce the edict of January 1562 justly, Morvilliers reminded him angrily of the fragility of the protection afforded by any edict:

On scait bien comment ceste ~~edict~~ tollerance des deux religions que vous appelez Edict, a esté bastie. Ca esté vne chose forcee, et laquelle la Royne, et les principaux et plus anciens Catholiques, conseillers de la couronne, qui n'estoient alors les plus forts, furent contrains laisser passer, de peur de pis. Esperans que sa maiesté uenue en aage, se feroit obeir, et ne le soufriroit iamays. Cela vous a esté accordé par provision seulement, et le Roy estant en bas aage. Asseurez vous que luy qui a puissance de relever les mineurs, des contracts qu'ils ont faictz, scaura bien quelque iour, estant venu en aage s'imparter ce mesme benefice, en vne affayre d'vne telle Importance, ou il y va totalement du faict de la religion catholique, et de l'estat de tout son Royaume.

Pithou's reply consisted of an allusion to the integrity of royal law and the congruence between such justice and the Protestants' cause. It was this belief which sustained his subsequent and renewed attempts to represent the Protestants of Troyes in 1565 before the queen mother in yet another, ultimately vain, attempt to modify the local application of the terms of 1563. The same belief sustained Pithou such that, despite the massacre of St Bartholomew, he did not cut off his ties with Troyes entirely or with royal service.

Against the crimes, follies, misfortunes and injustices of mankind, stood, in Pithou's historical framework, the power of conscientious objection, stoic courage. Pithou was fascinated by the importance of witnessing to the inner truth of conscience and its energising effect on others. Perhaps this was bound to be a theme of significance to a practising *avocat*.[50] One of his objections to the wealth and pretensions of the old church was that it stifled the expression of conscience in a public context.[51] The origins of the Reformation did not lie in any mystic process, no bewitchment or enchantment, but in the hearts and consciences of mankind whose witness to truth had an inevitable captivating effect on others. In a long passage, Pithou describes the pact, arrived at between the tanner Pierre Boissonnet and a box-maker Blaise Chantefoin, that neither would let the other die polluted in the old faith. Boissonnet became ill shortly thereafter, and, despite the death-bed pressures of his wife, the local parish priest, his brother and others, he spat out the Host, defied the efforts of the household to administer the last rites and instead endlessly repeated to himself the three words: 'In domino confido'. Pithou relates how, at the last, Boissonnet upbraided Chantefoin for not witnessing to his conscience and staying with the pact which they had agreed, urging him to watch out for similar temptations in the future and not to give in so easily.[52] Amongst several similar accounts in Pithou is that of the arrest and interrogation of the minister Corlieu, seized in the upper rooms of the inn where he was lodging in November 1559. He was interrogated several times, twice a day and pressed to reveal his friends and acquaintances. Each time he 'respondoit qu'il ne pouuoit dire en saine conscience et usoit de ceste responce a tous les interrogatz qui luy estoient faictz concernantz le faict d'autruy'.[53] In due course, some paper and ink was smuggled in to his prison cell and he wrote out his confession of faith, asking for it to be presented to the judges. Pithou's account piously ends with the judges being suitably impressed by the 'gentillesse de son espit, sa doulceur et debonnairette naturelle' to the extent that 'il toucha si vifvement le coeur de l'ung d'eux nommé Maistre Jean Davalus, quil luy eschappa de dire (bien qu'il feust grand

---

[50] This is the point implicitly made in Donald R. Kelley, *The Beginning of Ideology* (Cambridge, 1981), 58–70.

[51] 'Depuis que les ecclesiastiques eurent rendue ferme et accesser leur domination barbare et tyrannique sur les pauures consciences, il ne fut plus question en leur endroict que de s'enricher, remplir leurs bourgs aux depends du peuple, et de le charger d'infimes exactions' (Pithou, fol. 16v).

[52] *Ibid.*, fol. 112v.

[53] *Ibid*, fol. 145.

catholique) qu'il vouldroit qu'il luy eust couste deux cents escus et que Corlieu feuste en liberte'. In due course, after torture by the *prévôt* (where his 'constance' also made its mark) he was put in a cart to be taken to Paris for sentencing but, on the way, he talked to his guards about faith to such effect that they released him, thanking him for having enlightened them.

The *History* also contains an account of Pithou's own witness to conscience and confirmation (if not conversion), which he dates to 1559. The account is long and of particular interest. He describes himself as 'ce personnage, sur lequel principalement on se reposait allors ansi du tout, des affayres d'icelle' before explaining that, nevertheless, 'si ne desistoit il point toutefoys de se polluer et peantrer [puanter?] par foys contre sa propre conscience, parmy les abominations et ordures de la papauté'.[54] What did it matter, he had argued to himself if he went 'quelquefoys auec les autres baiser le babouin, c'est a dire fayre l'hommage a la beste les dimanches'? He merely did not want 'd'estre congnu et remarqué parmi tels que a la verité il estoit au dedans'. In essence, as he put it, 'il postposoit la crainte de Dieu a celle des hommes et a la perte de ses biens, comme aussy a la verité tous <les> autres n'en faisoient pas moins'. During a serious illness, however, the failure to match his outward behaviour to his inner convictions led to a serious emotional crisis. 'La souvenance d'une telle et si grande offence se representoit en sa maladie a toutes heures deuant ses yeulx' to the effect that 'sa propre conscience luy servoit allors comme dun bourreau, pour le fayre mourir cent et cent foys le iour.' He called on his legal training to explain further: 'Il estoit la comme vn poure criminel estendu sur la torture attendant l'issue de son proces', awaiting 'une attente horrible et miserable du iuste iugement de Dieu'. He hallucinated in his delirium ('flotoit et chanceloit tantost d'vn costé, puis d'vn autre') until the arrival of the minister Corlieu to whom he made his confession 'comme une anathomie des passions de son ame'. As soon as Corlieu 'eut appliqué a ce mal les passages de l'escripture saincte propres pour ce faict', the effects were both emotional and physical. He promised openly to abstain from the 'abominations de la papauté, et se rengeoit en lieu ou il luy seroit permitz de l'inuoquer, seruir et adorer en toute pureté et liberté de conscience'. The verses of Psalm 30 'ainsy qu'il es couche en rithme francoise, luy vent en memoyre avec le chant icelluy' and, as he recovered he felt a final huge sweat overcome him 'avec laquelle la fieubure qui estoit fort aigree et argente se termina'.[55] It was on the basis of this experience that he

[54] *Ibid.*, fol. 131v.
[55] *Ibid.*, fol. 133 (Ps. 30.2 'O Lord my God, I cried unto thee, and thou hast healed me').

determined to come out of his religious closet and allow his conscience its liberty. When he felt he could no longer do so in Troyes, he would leave the city for temporary and self-imposed exile.[56] He departed in the year following his conversion experience in 1560, returning from Geneva in 1561.[57] He left again in the second civil war in 1567 and was to be found in Zurich and Basle before returning after the peace of Saint-Germain.[58] In the wake of the St Bartholomew massacres, his appointment as *bailli* of Tonnerre provided him with a secure, rural retreat from which he was able to continue to protect the Protestant community of Troyes, which he visited at regular intervals.[59]

The 'outer' and the 'inner' person should be at one; the significance of this theme for the Pithous was doubtless strengthened by their experience of closet heterodoxy in the 1550s. Their father's household had been one of quiescent, conformist, 'nicodemite' evangelism. His father had entertained heterodox religious opinions and (according to Pithou) been encouraged by the outspoken preaching of the Franciscan Friar, Pierre Morel in Troyes from 1545 to 1547; he was again, albeit briefly, emboldened by the preaching of the new bishop of Troyes, the wayward Antonio Caracciolo, in 1551. But his father justified his continued attendance at the Mass on the grounds that he went to hear the psalms, prayers, scripture and the Lord's Prayer being read 'et autres telles choses <bonnes> quon y dict et chante, quoy qu'il y ait du vin meslé'.[60] Morel, the dominican friar Guerrapin (whose preaching in 1552 against purgatory turned out to be nothing more than 'vn feu de paille'), the extraordinary tergivisations of Antonio Caracciolo, both in 1551–2, and then again in 1561–2, form a strong theme to the earlier part of Pithou's *History*, an explanatory framework for his own 'conversion' arising from

---

[56] G. Huppert, *Les Bourgeois Gentilshommes* (Chicago, 1977), comments (p. 160): 'None of the Pithou, so far as I know, chose more than token exile.' The judgement is rather harsh in respect of Nicolas.

[57] This is what he says in his history but there is, however, no record in the *Livre des Habitants* of his arrival in Geneva at this time.

[58] *Correspondance de Bèze*, ed. Aubert *et al.*, X, 209–10; XI, 153.

[59] Grosley, *Vie de Pithou*, I, 56; for a legal commission which he carried out at *bailli* of Tonnerre on behalf of the Crown to adjudge the precise delimitation of the frontier between France and Lorraine in *c.* 1580–1, see M. Dannrouther, 'La forêt de Passavent (Haute-Saône). Lettre de Nicolas Pithou au sujet d'une rectification de frontière entre la France et la Lorraine', *Bulletin de la Géographie Historique et Descriptive*, 16 (1901), 186–93. In fact, he spent some time after 1572 in shelter in Montbéliard.

[60] Pithou, fol. 77v; according to J. Roserot de Melin, *Antonio Caracciolo, évèque de Troyes* (Paris, 1923), 300–1, there was a treatise (which one of the Pithous had perhaps written) entitled *Le Calendrier qui dispense l'homme fidele et lui permet de se trouver à la messe et aux vespres catholiques à cause des Psaumes, des Prieres de l'Evangile, de l'Oraison dominicale et autres telles choses bonnes qu'on y dit et chante quoiqu'il y ait du vice meslé*.

his family experience; in the same way, abjuration forms an important backdrop to the later part of the *History* which, in turn, also reflects the Pithou family's own religious divisions after the massacre of St Bartholomew.[61]

Pithou's experience was, therefore, of a world where many individuals had 'quelque sentiment', 'quelque cognoissance' of Protestantism but were too frightened to make it public. The result was a division which, so the *History* implies, led to and was at the heart of the individual and collective madness of the civil wars. Repeatedly, Pithou describes the behaviour of the town's citizens as in the grip of a 'frenzy', 'mad', no longer whole human beings. There are individual stories, too, which develop the theme, most notably the sad case of the physician and Pithou's close neighbour in the *marché au blé*, M. Jean Collier. He was an 'homme docte et experimenté en son art' who had been noted for providing his services free to the poor of the city. He had married against his family's wishes and eventually migrated for a time to Geneva. When he returned to Troyes in the 1550s he was quickly noted as a suspected heretic, imprisoned and taken to Paris for investigation before the *parlement*. There, he was tortured until his brother, a good lawyer, successfully orchestrated his defence and acquittal. He told his brother to act as though he were mad. He then argued before the court that, because his brother had lost his mind, his testimony was of no value. His brother played the part so well that he was acquitted by the judges and he returned to Troyes.[62] So feigned madness was the only way to sustain a dissimulation. Sadly, the effects of the process (including his torture) did disturb his mental balance, causing a 'mal phrenetique'. Pithou attempted to counsel him with uplifting words of God's mercy but to no avail. After several scenes of domestic disorder, he eventually committed suicide, throwing himself from an upper window crying 'Osiana filio David'.[63] Feigned madness, the reader is led to conclude, leads to real madness, where no man is his own. 'Fleschir aucunement le genoul devant Baal' results in 'vn coeur double' and leads us to the heart of the politique debate during the civil wars. The tempest of the civil wars so devoured reason, Pithou suggests, because those in authority and

[61] Nicolas' half-brother, Pierre Pithou, experienced the massacre in Paris at close quarters. The majority of the household where he resided were butchered whilst he escaped in his shirt across the roof-tops to shelter in a friend's house. The following year he abjured before the curé of St-Paul, Simon Vigor, subsequently corresponding with his half-brother under the pseudonym 'De la Masure' (e.g. Bibliothèque Nationale MS Dupuy 688, fol. 67 (5 Jan. 1579).

[62] Pithou, fol. 63.

[63] *Ibid.*, fol. 93.

influence were not being honest with themselves and others. We enter the world of the sieur de Rieux, of Pierre d'Espinac, of M. le recteur Rozé and the others who swallow the tablets which make them hallucinate when they take to the stage of the Estates General in the *Satyre Menippée*. The famous *Satyre*, composed (at least in part) by Nicolas' half-brother Pierre, enjoys some traits in common with the *History*. Both works explore the metahistory of the civil wars, the anxieties which had fuelled the conflict. Both works occasionally contain similar Champagne colloquialisms.[64] And, for both authors, the only solution to the civil wars was that presented by the disinterested urban notable, of the *Satyre Menippée*, the 'rond et entier' sieur d'Aubray.

The 'Histoire ecclésiastique de l'église réformée de la ville de Troyes' inevitably reflected the social milieu of its author. Nicolas Pithou belonged indisputably to the *gratin* of municipal families who came to dominate Troyes' political and intellectual life in the sixteenth century.[65] The family's merchant origins were already fading by the early sixteenth century.[66] The family's town house faced the *marché au blé* in the exclusive Belfroy *quartier* to the west of the city.[67] On the basis of wealth partly acquired through his father's first marriage to a daughter of Jean Bazin, *lieutenant particulier* of the *bailliage* of Troyes (there would be Bazins among the senior royal officials of Troyes throughout the sixteenth century), he acquired *seigneuries* at Savoie, Bierne and Changobert to the south of the town not far from the river Seine. Nicolas Pithou affected to believe that he was descended from a Miles de

---

[64] E.g. among other examples, 'pour amuser nos ennemis à la moustarde' (*La Satyre Menippée*, ed. C. Read (Paris, n.d.), 83); compare Pithou, fol. 213 'tout le monde en alloit a la moustarde'.

[65] Kuno Böse, 'Städtische Eliten in Troyes im 16. Jahrhundert', *Francia*, 11 (1983), 341–63, identifies a core elite of twenty-six families, mainly of mercantile origins who strove to dominate the municipal council in the first half of the sixteenth century. Cf. F. Binet, 'Etudes sur quelques familles de la bourgeoisie troyenne au XVIe siècle', *Positions des Thèses. Ecole des Chartes* (1945), 51–8. These merchants exploited the constitution of the town council. Established in the reign of Louis XI, it was composed of a mayor, eight *échevins* and twenty-four *conseillers* and the electoral arrangements gave the merchants both sufficient access to municipal office and adequate possibilities for oligarchic rule to maintain their position in normal times (F. Bibolet, *Les Institutions municipales de Troyes aux XIVe et XVe siècles* (Troyes, 1945–58)).

[66] Grosley, *Vie de Pithou*, I, 1–14, for Pierre Pithou senior and also the entry in E. Haag, *La France protestante* (10 vols., Paris, 1846–59; 2nd edn, incomplete, 6 vols., Paris, 1877–88; 1st edn reprinted in 10 vols., Geneva, 1966)

[67] According to calculations made by Penny Roberts, the tax rolls for Troyes in 1553 revealed that the Belfroy *quartier* housed just over 19 per cent of the population but contributed 38 per cent towards the tax raised.

Pithou in 1300.[68] He certainly aspired to noble status, carefully adding the title 'sieur de Changobert' after each mention of his name in the revision of his manuscript history; other phrases in the history, however, recall the proximity of his merchant past.[69] At the same time, the family's marriage patterns during Nicolas' lifetime reinforced its connections with the Troyen notability whilst branching out to embrace some filiation with the rich and influential world of royal officialdom in the capital, three days' ride away in Paris. Pierre Pithou's second marriage had been to Bonaventure de Chantaloé, niece to a *président aux enquêtes* and also to a *conseiller* of the *parlement* of Paris. In time, all of Nicolas' kin of his generation who married, provided themselves with partners comfortably close to the *crème* of the Troyen mercantile elite.[70]

Pithou's Reformation was thus inevitably 'magisterial'. To the east of Troyes lay the *quartier* Saint-Jacques, home of the royal prisons, the old *cité* stronghold, the cathedral of St Peter and St Paul as well as a large number of the churches, abbeys and the Franciscan convent. It has been calculated by Penny Roberts that 77 per cent of the clergy in the tax rolls of 1570 were registered in the *quartier* of Saint-Jacques.[71] This was where the town's brothels were to be found, and the majority of its poor artisan cloth workers. Of the populace at large, represented by the east-end of the city, Pithou was characteristically contemptuous. It was a 'multitude effrenee', a 'populace obstinee et endurcie', 'opinants, seditieux, bouillant, estant gens de nulle obeissance, de sorte qu'il seroit fort difficile de reprimer leurs audaces et violence', to be feared precisely because it had no conscience.[72] Not that rich and poor, east-end and west-end of the city should be delineated too sharply – sixteenth-century cities did not work like that, and wealth, like poverty, was something of which Pithou was conscious only in combination with other things. Although sophisticated modern analyses have attempted to prove that the reality was otherwise, Pithou himself did not present the process of

---

68 Grosley, *Vie de Pithou*, I, 40. *Biographie universelle*, XXIII, 420. According to Grosley (*Vie de Pithou*, I, 80), Nicolas wrote a dedicatory Latin verse to Jérôme de Barat, *Grand blason d'Armes* (1581) which contrasted the ephemeral misery of the civil wars with the enduring values of noble heritage.

69 When, for example, he recounted the myth that the city of Troyes had begun its existence as three castles, held by three brothers, he continued: 'Voila ce que disoient ces bonnes gens. Vous en prendra la marchandise pour le pris qu'elle me couste ~~sans~~, sans uouloir rien gaigner sur icelle ny m'obliger a la garendie' (Pithou, fol. 7).

70 Nicolas Pithou himself married Perrette de Vassan, a merchant's daughter, a solid, albeit hardly spectacular alliance. His half-sister Jeanne married Jean de Nevelet, sieur de Dosches, one of Troyes' municipal notables whilst his half-brother Antoine married Jeanne de Hault and eventually became *maire* of Troyes in 1610.

71 Roberts, 'A Town in Conflict', 29.

72 Pithou, fols. 119v, 160, 217v.

reformation as powered by the steam of fiscal resentment or driven by dismay at economic distress.[73] Pithou's refined social perception was all mediated through a lens where the pressures for heterodoxy amongst those who perceived themselves as the godly were complex in origin and focused by the collective anxieties of the authorities.

In any case, to get to the *quartier* Saint-Jacques, Nicolas Pithou had to walk down the rue Moyenne, the 'petit Genève' of Troyes;

d'une assez belle et grande estendue. ~~Elle estoit~~ Ceste rue estoit pour lors peuplee ~~fut~~ et remplie de menuisiers et autres artisans ~~de la religion en sorte que'ils s'en trouvent bien peu d'autres en ville~~ tous braues hom*m*es gens fortz et robustes de bon esprit ~~et adroietz aux armes~~ <et affectionné a la religion> et de la Religion.[74]

Far from being the 'via media' that its name suggests, this was where war took to the streets with a vengeance in 1562. In 1558, Pithou's wife and his half-sister had already escaped a possible confrontation there.[75] In 1560, a procession of children organised by the clergy of the parish of Saint-Jean down the street led (or so Pithou represents it) to stone-throwing and intimidation of its residents.[76] They responded by throwing tiles off the roofs and barricading themselves in with barrels and carts. A few months later, there was renewed tension and violence surrounding the desecration of a statue of the Virgin Mary on the corner of an alley leading off the rue Moyenne, the Huguenots 'en leurs maisons com*m*e l'oiseau sur la bra*n*che attendant lheure qu'on les allast piller et saccager, ou leur fayre quelque meschant tour' as another procession wound its way down the street.[77]

Pithou's attitude to the Protestant artisans of Troyes was undeniably ambiguous. They were 'braues hommes', who took their consciences seriously. His history documents their individual acts of defiance and

---

[73] Henry Heller, *The Conquest of Poverty. The Calvinist Revolt in Sixteenth-Century France* (Leiden, 1986), esp. ch. 5. It is not, of course, a full rejection of Heller's argument to say that Pithou was not consciously aware of the pressures in quite the way that he claims they operate behind the Reformation.

[74] Pithou, fol. 160, etc. Cf. his comment in August 1562 that the rue Moyenne was, to the municipal officers, 'le lieu qu'ilz redoutoient le plus, pour estre de facile garde, les maisons fort serrees, et pour la plus part ~~tenues~~ habitees de menuisiers, et autres artisans, tous bons hom*m*es, et de la Religion' (fol. 228).

[75] *Ibid.*, fols. 117v–18. They were visiting some suspect Protestants detained in prison when the wife of a Catholic merchant, Jean Haillart, 'grosse grasse et en bon point', pursued them into the rue Moyenne crying 'aux fagots, aux Lutherien*n*es . . . les battans a grands coups de bec'. Fortunately, 'toutes leurs boutiques estoient allors fermees et ces artisans este alles s'escatre[?] hors la ville, a cause que ce jour la, com*m*e estoit le 25 iour de fevrier on celebroit la feste Sainct Mathias'.

[76] *Ibid.*.

[77] *Ibid.*, fol. 168v.

bloody-mindedness in the fact of the municipal and legal authorities. Like Crespin's *Histoire des Martyres*, Pithou scrupulously records their professional status and social background, almost as a reminder to himself and others that extraordinary things, through God's providence, could come from, and happen to, ordinary men and women. 'Jeanne Fournet, servante de Girardin[?]' refused to reveal to the authorities what she knew of the Protestant meetings at her master's house; the torture of 1555 left her permanently crippled.[78] Guillaume de Marisy, 'orfeuvre de son mestier, autant doux et paisible que aucun autre qui se trouvast en la ville' was knocked down dead in the street outside his house for singing a Marot Psalm in 1559, although he was hardly yet of the faithful.[79] The *menuisier* of the rue Moyenne, Claudin Collot, 'ieune homme, fort dispos et bien delibere', was forced to kill someone in cold blood who was about to stab him in one of the street disturbances of the rue Moyenne in 1560.[80] Pithou's own half-sister Ambroise risked prosecution and worse by refusing to attend Mass in 1562. She resisted giving birth to her child under the family roof in order to avoid the pressure for a prudent Catholic baptism. Instead, to Pithou's discreet admiration, she accepted the offer from a Catholic nurse to look after her during the birth and took up the skills of a tapestry-maker to keep her family alive.[81] These were individuals who did not have much *science*; but they had *conscience* enough. That was the challenging and perplexing part about it for Pithou. He recounts the story of the artisans taken for questioning and torture from Troyes to Paris in 1556 for holding an illegal Protestant assembly. Before the magistrates of the *parlement* they declared that they had only been reading some edifying books to one another, eating some food together and giving thanks to God before and after, as all good Christians should. The magistrates presented a book to the one who was suspected of being a minister. 'Ce fut ~~pitie~~ vne grande pitié de luy voir manier ~~il~~ car il ne peut oncques venir a bout ~~????~~ de y lire vne seule ligne a droit. Aussy a la verité il estoit fort mal exercé a ce mestier'.[82] The magistrates were so convinced by this display of manifest ignorance that the charges were false that they released all of them. *Non-science* had served God's purposes; conscience had proved the victor. When it came to narrating the fact that the founding minister of the Troyes Protestant church was a carder from Meaux, of low extraction, whose knowledge of languages did not extend beyond French, Pithou's perplexity is all too apparent in the successive attempts he has to write the passage:

---

[78] *Ibid.*, fols. 82–3v.   [79] *Ibid.*, fol. 123.
[80] *Ibid.*, fol. 161.   [81] *Ibid.*, fols. 256–61.   [82] *Ibid.*, fol. 99.

Ce personnage estoit ~~cardeur et drapeur de son mestier~~ <de bas estat, ascavoir cardeur de laine et tisserant de draps **n'ayant connoiss*a*nce quelconque des scie*n*ces humai*n*es ny d'autre langue que de la france Mays il avoit>** grandement poufité en la lecture <et Intellige*n*ce> des escriptures sainctes <et si estoit> plein de zele et de l'esprit de dieu <~~ainsy qu'il~~> ~~bien qu'il n'eust aucunes lettres latines~~.[83]

Yet, especially before the founding of the Protestant consistory, Pithou felt out of place in the company of these artisans – and they in his. After the arrival of Poncelet in the city, Pithou resolved to go and introduce himself. He arrived unannounced to the prayer-meeting which artisans from the city had been holding regularly for over a year (and of whose existence Pithou was, until then, evidently unaware) in the suburb village of Bréviandes. His appearance: 'troubla ~~fort~~ et effroya grandement ces pauures artisans co*mm*e aussy leur presence et reco*n*tre ~~appr~~ causa vne merveilleuse crainte a Pithou De sorte qu'ilz com*m*encoient d'entre en deffia*n*ce les vns les autres ~~dautant quilz ne seauoient pas quils embrassoient vne mesme religion~~ <pour ne scavoir de quelque boy*s* il*s* se chauffoient>.'[84] Such initial encounters of the suspicious kind would be overcome; but behind Pithou's misgivings were the fears that these artisans of the New Jerusalem were notoriously unpredictable, liable to take the law into their own hands, easily led astray. There was no knowing, for example, how they would react when faced with the 'folle arrogance' of a false prophet like the apothecary Halvert.[85] A group of artisans was, in fact, excluded from the Protestant congregation in Troyes 'pour aucun bon regard' (as Pithou said in an uncharacteristically vague fashion), although they continued to meet as a separate conventicle until its existence was revealed to the authorities towards the close of 1556.[86] Some of the intemperate artisans amongst the Troyes Protestants were undoubtedly responsible for acts of iconoclasm, which Pithou deplored.[87] And there were those on the streets of Troyes who,

[83] *Ibid.*, fol. 66v. The passage in bold is an addition to the intercalation.

[84] *Ibid.*, fol. 67 (an additional small folio added to the original).

[85] He was originally from Provence, arriving in Troyes in 1553 to echo the critique of Calvin's theology which, at the same time, convulsing Geneva; 'ils desgorgeoient ordinairement des blasphemes villains et execrables contre la saincte et sacree maiesté diuine s'efforceant par ses propos ordinaires, fayre dieu autheur du mal et de la corruption de nostre nature, n'attribuant a l'homme nulle volu*n*té, non plus que si c'estoit vne pierre' (*ibid.*, fol. 72v).

[86] 'En mesme temps, quelques ~~ge~~ artisans et gens de mestier, ~~qui~~ lesquels pour aucun bon regard n'estoient admiz en l'assemblee chrestie*n*ne, furent descouuertz en vne assemblee qu'ilz auoient faite pour prier Dieu' (*ibid.*, fol. 97v).

[87] The destruction of the Virgin Mary on the rue Moyenne in 1560 was the result of those elements in the church 'qui ne regardoient plus loing que leurs affections bouilla*n*tes les co*n*duisant, y penserent admener vne ruine et dissipation totale' (*ibid.*, fol. 168).

like the minister Corlieu, writing from the prisons in Paris in 1559 to his former congregation, cried out for 'Jerusalem, Jerusalem'.[88] In 1562, there would be hot-heads in the congregations who wanted to use the urban contingent of Protestant troops, raised to help Condé, to influence the municipal politics of Troyes. Pithou describes approvingly how their captain went into the street 'en chausse et en pourpoint' and sword in hand, to reason with them and, 'auec vn maintien gay et ioyaulx', dissuaded them gently from starting what might turn into a blood-bath on the streets of the town. Pithou was impressed and relieved. It was the kind of authority he did not possess.[89] Crowds were not to be trusted; Pithou was proud of his native city but of its people he had no illusions. So when it came to the mass congregation held by the Protestants of Troyes at Pentecost 1562 in the fields outside the town, the climax (as it would turn out) of the popular Troyen reformation, Pithou's description was one of cautious surprise. 'C'est vne grande excellent [sic] et beauté, de voir si belle compagnie' he wrote,[90] depicting the large gathering of 8,000–9,000 worshippers who gathered at that time, including some from the households of the ducs de Guise and Nevers. The weavers spread out the 'toilles de chasse du Roy' which they had manufactured to make 'vn grand pavillon' and provide some shade from the sun. Like a modern pop-concert, however, there were the inevitable rowdies who disturbed the good order, the lackeys (or so he suspected) from the disorderly noble households. The early history of the French Reformation still tends to be written in a very 'constitutional' way, determined by the formation of churches along orthodox Genevan lines and the establishment of its synodical and colloquial structure. Pithou's history is precious testimony of the kinds of social tensions, the creative and chaotic atmosphere which had made the Discipline so apparently necessary to the leading figures of the French churches.

By 1564, when Nicolas Pithou was beginning to write his first memorandum, these tensions were coming to be a thing of the past, at least as far as the internalities of the Protestant community in Troyes were concerned. By then, Pithou was the leading elder of the church, guardian of the die stamp which produced the *méreaux* for the congregation, the tokens which individuals of good standing were given and which they were required to produce before receiving

---

[88] *Ibid.*, fol. 157.
[89] 'Ainsy fut moderee par ceste prudence et bon aduis la collere et furie de ce peuple que de soy n'estoit que trop bouillant' (*ibid.*).
[90] *Ibid.*, fol. 213v.

communion.[91] The *méreaux* were symbols of the moral discipline, enforced through conscience and the right regulation of a church and commonwealth, to which Nicolas Pithou felt attracted. His history reproduced approvingly the letter he received from Beza in 1566 on the right usage of games of chance.[92] At about the same time, he published a treatise which he had composed with his twin brother, Jean Pithou, on Christian marriage, the most extensive equivalent of *Hausvaterliteratur* produced by a French Calvinist in the sixteenth century.[93] The theme of moral discipline, the public encouragement of conscientious living within the context of a properly framed commonwealth, was also the subject of the *Traité de la police et du gouvernement de républiques* which his twin brother published in Lyons, possibly with his assistance, and probably around the same date.[94] Henceforth, Pithou would contemplate not a New Jerusalem amidst the ignoble barbarism which his *History* recounts in France but a New World and the noble savages of North America, as related by Martin Frobisher.[95]

Revolution, if it were to occur, would come from the forces ranged against the Reformation. Pithou already foresaw gloomily the dangers towards the close of 1562, as more and more Protestants from the city were forced to take up exile, were proscribed or found themselves the objects of intimidation and worse. Pithou had imagined a moral reformation in Troyes in which a godly, conscientious magistrature fulfilled its leading vocation. Instead, what came to pass was a city where all order and police was 'in confusion'. Force 'was the mistress'. 'Justice slept, using silence or, rather, connivance, to curry favour with an enraged populace.' The result was 'the pinnacle of all these troubles'

---

[91] *Ibid.*, fol. 308, introduced at the Easter communion of 1564 to exclude all the 'gens de vie dissolue et desbouchees'.

[92] *Correspondance de Bèze*, ed. Aubert *et al.*, VII, 59–61.

[93] *L'Institution du Mariage Chrétien*. Grosley, *Vie de Pithou*, I, 81, gives a brief summary of the work and describes it as published in Lyons in 1565 by Nicole; but Nicole was a Paris printer. H. L. Baudrier, *Bibliographie lyonnaise* (13 vols., Lyons, 1895–1921), VII, 437, says that it was published by Senneton frères in Lyons in 1565. To date, I have not managed to locate a copy of either the Lyons or the Paris edition of this work.

[94] Lyons, n.d. – copy in Bibliothèque Municipale Toulouse Réserve, 251 (N). I believe that Nicolas Pithou also wrote the *Instruction pour tous états, en laquelle est sommairement déclaré comme chacun en son état se doit gouverner et vivre selon Dieu* (Lyons, 1566) but I have not so far located a copy of the work or attempted to verify its authorship.

[95] N. Pithou, *La Navigation du capitaine Martin Frobisher Anglais, ès regions de west & Nordwest en l'année MDLXXVII* (n.p., 1578). Pithou's preface presents the opportunities afforded by Frobisher's voyage as indications of God's providence 'à fin que par la communication de sa saincte parolle ces barbares soyent approvoisez, rangez & admenez à raison'. The treatise had presumably been communicated to him through his half-brother Pierre who by this date was (I think) in the service of the French ambassador in London, Michel de Castelnau.

when 'the principal leading magistrates' including the mayors, the aldermen and the majority of the town council 'attisoient sans cesse la fureur, qui desia n'estoit que par trop embrassee en ces meutriers'. Those who should have set aside their individual prejudices and particular grudges in favour of protecting and advancing the public weal, instead 'n'oublierent rien de ce qu'ils s'aduiserent pouvoir servir a l'entiere ruine et extirpation de leurs concitoyens de la religion'. A pessimistic Nicolas Pithou concluded: 'Brief, vous eussiez proprement iugé que l'estat de ceste pauure ville de Troyes, estoit pour lors reduit en une pure et vraye democratie, c'est a dire en vn gouvernement ou le peuple a plain pouvoir de souveraine puissance, par la seule connivence de feux, qui debvoient refrener et retenir l'insolence effrenee de ce peuple.'[96]

Such fears would be echoed again, later in the *History*, when Pithou narrated the events of the Catholic League in Troyes. Why God allowed such things to happen, Pithou's *History* could not explain. What it could do was provide for its author some sense of a perspective on a life's experience which had brushed so close (as Nicolas Pithou said in his will) to 'tant de périls et dangers, et estranges misères et calamités par lesquelles il lui a pleu me faire passer en la fleur de mon aage'.[97] In the Epistle Dedicatory to his selections from St Bernard, published at the height of the popular League in Troyes, he wrote of the 'peines, des chagrins & des malheurs qui avoient rempli sa vie'. 'Les pertes que j'ai faites dans ma famille', he continued, 'la mort de mes meilleurs amis, le dérangement de mes affaires domestiques m'avaient amené au point de ne pas même oser espérer de soulagement ni d'adoucissement à ma cruelle situation.'[98] In the writings of St Bernard, the Boethius of the Church Fathers, Pithou recommended the consolations of piety, quietness and patient waiting upon events. The work implicitly reminded its readers that the Protestant Reformation had not turned its back on the Fathers of the Church as historical reservoirs of experience to be drawn on in present dilemmas. It was on such reservoirs which Pithou drew when he came to formulate his will, signing it in Troyes on 3 August 1595. Reflecting the perplexity which had led him to write his *History*, the last section of which he was perhaps just completing, he wrote:

---

[96] Pithou, fol. 269v.
[97] E. Berthe, 'Le testament de Nicolas Pithou', *Bulletin de la Société de l'Histoire du Protestantisme Français*, 15 (1866), 108–10.
[98] N. Pithou, *Thesaurus à monumentis D. Bernardi Claræv. abbatis primi* . . . (Geneva, 1589), He dedicated the book to his twin brother Jean and his nephew Pierre Nevelet. For details on the publication see P. Chaix *et al.*, *Les Livres imprimés à Genève de 1556 à 1600* (Geneva, 1966), 125.

Quant au bien que Dieu m'a donné icy, peut-estre il ne s'en trouvera, à beaucoup près de ce qu'on pense, mais si on considère combien de tems et d'années j'ai été agité, çà et là, à cause de la religion, et soubs plus de trente-quatre ans sans faire aucun gain ni proffit, deppendant [*dépensant*(?)] le mien peu à peu, on trouvera matière d'admirer la grande bénédiction et Providence de mon Dieu envers moy en cet endroit et luy en rends grâces.[99]

[99] Berthe, 'Le testament de Nicolas Pithou'.

2 Elizabethan players and minstrels and the legislation of 1572 against retainers and vagabonds

Peter Roberts

Two official measures of 1572 which restricted the movement of the strolling players are generally regarded by historians of the English stage as marking an epoch in its history.[1] According to one of the most recent authorities, the proclamation of 3 January, reviving the existing laws against unlawful retaining, and the statute 14 Elizabeth, c. 5, for the relief of the poor and against rogues and vagabonds, were two of the seven 'most decisive acts taken by the central government toward the London theatre during the reign of Elizabeth I'.[2] While the cumulative effect of the new regulations was indeed to redefine the social and legal status of the players, the relationship between the measures has not been fully understood: the standard work on the common players, for example, considers the proclamation as a 'prelude' to the act and confuses the provisions of two quite distinct pieces of legislation.[3] To appreciate their significance for the fortunes of the players in particular, the proclamation and the act should be examined in the context of the precautions taken by the Elizabethan regime against disorder and sedition in the aftermath of the first major crisis of the reign.

Vagrancy and excessive retaining were perennial problems of Tudor

My interest in this subject was first aroused while teaching a course on the English Renaissance with Patrick Collinson. More recently, my understanding of what happened in parliament in 1572 has been enhanced by conversations with Sir Geoffrey Elton and Dr David Dean. It would be an ill return for their kindness to saddle these scholars with any responsibility for my reading of the evidence.

[1] It was 'an early step in the progress of the professional players from strolling entertainers . . . to permanently established repertory companies'. Andrew Gurr, *The Shakespearean Stage, 1574–1642* (Cambridge, 1980), 28–9.

[2] Scott McMillin, 'The Queen's Men and the London Theatre of 1583', in *The Elizabethan Theatre*, ed. C. E. McGee (Port Credit, Ontario, 1988), x, 9. The other significant dates are taken to be: the letters patent to Leicester's Men in 1574, that to Edmund Tilney as Master of the Revels in 1581, the formation of the Queen's Men in 1583, the privy council order of 1589 for a licensing commission for plays, and that of 1597 for the dismantling of all playhouses.

[3] Muriel C. Bradbrook, *The Rise of the Common Player: A Study of the Actor and Society in Shakespeare's England* (1962), 53.

government; they could lead to disorderly assemblies at any time, but in the years between 1568 and 1572 they were perceived to threaten the security of the realm. The privy council became alarmed at the increase in vagrancy even before the outbreak of the rebellion of the northern earls in the autumn of 1569. The danger signals began in 1568 with the arrival in England of Mary, Queen of Scots, who was to become a rival focus of loyalty for Elizabeth's disaffected Catholic subjects. Conciliar orders were sent out against the circulation of rumours and seditious books by malcontents who flitted about the countryside inciting the people to rebel. A system of watches set up for most of the English shires on 21 June 1569 led to the rounding up of 13,000 masterless men in the following months.[4] The publication in the following year of the papal bull excommunicating Elizabeth appeared to justify the paranoia of the Protestant regime. On the outbreak of a rising in Norfolk the deputy lieutenants were instructed to make special provision for suppressing vagrants, rumour mongers and assemblies. In the same year watches were authorised in London to discourage common assemblies at interludes, gaming houses and cockpits.[5] Though subversive ballads circulated during these times of emergency, only occasionally are they associated with the strolling minstrels and interluders.

In 1571 William Cecil was exercised about seditious rumours being spread abroad in Lancashire, where the earl of Derby and his family failed to maintain the observance of Protestant services in his household and in the local churches. An exhaustive list of those 'devoted to the earl' in three counties was drawn up by Cecil, who evidently had cause to question Derby's allegiance to the queen and the established church. One Kent, 'a mynstrell or such like' and servant to the earl, had lately railed against the officers of Chester for not permitting the ringing of church bells on All Saints day. The retainers of other members of the Stanley family were also behaving suspiciously: one had been used as a messenger between known recusants, while another had been summoned from Staffordshire to teach the Lord Strange's son to dance! Among those in the service of Sir Thomas Stanley were a blind astrologer, described as a seditious person who wandered up and down the country, and a seaman 'all cladd in yellow'.[6] Notwithstanding the suspicious behaviour of a few eccentrics, the strollers were generally

[4] PRO SP 12/80, 81, *passim*; *APC*, n.s., VIII (1894), 52, 72–3. P. Aydelotte, *Elizabethan Rogues and Vagabonds* (Oxford, 1913), 66.
[5] Aydelotte, *Elizabethan Rogues and Vagabonds*; N. Williams, 'The Rising in Norfolk, 1569 and 1570', *Norfolk Archaeology*, 32 (1961), 78.
[6] Hatfield House, Cecil Papers 159/15–17; HMC, *Calendar of Salisbury at Hatfield MSS*, part I (1883), no. 1754.

perceived by the authorities to pose a greater threat to public order than to political security. The Elizabethan regime had no cause to repeat the orders issued by the Marian council in 1556 to suppress strolling players and pipers who disseminated sedition and heresies throughout the land.[7] Mystery plays were to be suppressed by Elizabethan bishops and towns, but secular drama was not used in this reign as a medium to spread Catholic propaganda.

The rebellion of 1569 highlighted the dangers posed to stability and the rule of law by illicit retaining as well as masterless men. In 1571 the Council in the North was instructed to investigate armed retainers and to seek out any offenders who might have been pardoned after the rebellion.[8] The inquiry was extended to the whole of the country in the proclamation of 3 January 1572, and the sense of renewed danger in the wake of the Ridolfi plot and the duke of Norfolk's disgrace is conveyed in its preamble. The maintenance of innumerable 'unordinary servants' by badges and liveries hindered justice and undermined the loyal service of the queen's officers and tenants 'by stirring up and nourishing of factions, riots and unlawful assembles, the mother of rebellion'. Only household servants were to be exempt from the penalties of the law, and 20 February 1572 was stipulated as the date from which these were to be imposed.[9] It must have been during this breathing space of seven weeks between the promulgation and the date of commencement that the earl of Leicester's company of players petitioned their lord for permission to be accounted members of his household.[10] They already wore his livery and so this formal recognition was necessary to qualify them for exemption from the laws against retaining. Leicester had in 1565 been licensed for life to retain 100 persons who were not in the queen's service, besides his household servants and officers serving under him. If, as we

---

[7] Report of the 'Select Council' to King Philip, 7 May 1556; PRO SP11/8/50, 51; *CSPD 1547–1580*, 82.

[8] J. Strype, *Annals of the Reformation . . .* (Oxford, 1824 edn), I, part 2, 346; A. L. Beier, 'Vagrants and the Social Order in Elizabethan England', *Past and Present*, 64 (1974), 3–29. Paul Slack, *Poverty and Policy in Tudor and Stuart England* (1988), 124.

[9] *Tudor Royal Proclamations*, ed. P. L. Hughes and J. F. Larkin, II (1969), no. 582. PRO SP12/83/38, 90: the draft contains minor corrections in what appears to be the very regular hand of Sir Thomas Smith, who was already functioning as the queen's secretary before his formal appointment. The Council in the Marches of Wales received special instructions on 11 January to publish the proclamation in each of the Welsh shires. *A Calendar of the Register of the Queen's Majesty's Council in the Dominion and Principality of Wales and the Marches . . . 1569–1591*, ed. Ralph Fleney (1916), 96–7.

[10] Longleat, Marquess of Bath MSS, Dudley Papers III/125, printed in E. K. Chambers, *The Elizabethan Stage* (4 vols., Oxford, 1974 edn), II, 86. Chambers does not make it clear that this is a copy, in which 'your Lordshippes *commoditie*' has been corrected rather crudely to '*convenience*'.

must assume, the players' bid was successful, they became attached to his establishment at Wanstead, Essex, if not at Leicester House in London.[11] Their status in law would thereby be secure, and this three months or so before parliament met to discuss the fate of Mary Stuart and Norfolk and to address the vexing problem of vagabondage.

In December 1571 the privy council expressed its concern to the lord mayor and bishop of London that the throng of beggars in the streets had swollen so much that it was impossible to distinguish the poor and impotent from rogues and vagabonds. Parliament had discussed the problems of poverty and vagrancy in 1571 but a bill introduced into the Commons had been unacceptable to the Lords. By the spring of 1572 the situation in the capital had become desperate. A commission set up on the queen's accession to inquire into felonies expired in March 1572, when the privy council sent Sir James Croft, comptroller of the royal household, to consult with the mayor and common council about a problem that encroached on the court itself.[12] They were to devise remedies for poor relief and the control of sturdy beggars, and this seems to have been the most immediate initiative which led to the regulations enacted in parliament as well as by the City in this year. Two months later the privy council instructed the court of aldermen to arrange for householders ('housekeepers') who staged plays and interludes in open spaces on their own property to be licensed to do so and placed in sureties to avoid such performances in times of divine service. Such shows for the recreation of the people 'maye tende to repress vyce & extoll vertuwe' and thereby draw them away from worse exercises. The alderman replied that it was undesirable to hold such 'conventicles . . . whereof the greatest number are of the meanest sort' in the hot weather, and they sued for a temporary suspension of the order.[13] In this they seemed to have succeeded, for plays were indeed banished for a time out of London, as we learn from the entry for 1572 in William Harrison's 'Chronology', 'lest the resort unto them should ingender a plague or rather disperse it, being already begonne'.[14] Thus did the privy council and the City fathers express the polarised attitudes to public shows that

---

[11] *Calendar of Patent Rolls, Elizabeth I, III: 1563–66* (1960), no. 1058. Along with the licence Leicester received a pardon for all infringements of the laws against unlawful retaining.

[12] *APC*, n.s., VIII, 1571–5, 52, 72–3.

[13] Chambers, *The Elizabethan Stage*, IV, 269.

[14] BL Additional MS 70984, fol. 257; *Elizabethan England*, ed. L. Withrington and F. J. Furnivall (n.d.), appendix, 268. The original MS, missing for over a century after Furnivall consulted it in Derry diocesan library, was purchased by the British Library in 1991.

were to characterise their transactions on the conditions of playing in London for the remainder of the reign.

The City was loath to surrender its jurisdiction to the queen's council in this as in other matters, and it was against this background that the debate took place in the Commons in the last days of May over whether minstrels and other wanderers in the country should be classified as vagabonds. A reconstruction of the making of the relevant section of this measure will reveal the legislative intention and the significance of the changes made to the crucial clause on vagabondage during its passage in the lower house. The bare outline supplied by the official journals can be supplemented by some illuminating extracts from the surviving private diaries kept by parliamentarians.

In this, the first of the major Elizabethan statutes to address the problems of poverty, the poor, deemed to be dangerous, were marginalised and, though the genuinely indigent were to be treated differently from the able-bodied and work-shy, mendicancy was made a criminal offence. A progressively severe scale of penalties was prescribed: a vagrant who refused to be taken into service could be whipped and branded in the ear for the first offence, adjudged a felon for the second and sentenced to death without benefit of clergy for a third. Vagabonds are defined as those who, without land, master or craft wherewith to sustain a livelihood, wander about the countryside without proper warrant. Apart from proctors collecting alms for invalids, students who went begging without permission from their universities, perpetrators of illicit games, fortune tellers and bogus sailors claiming losses at sea, a number of itinerant occupations were classified as vagabondage for the first time. These included the strolling entertainers of the English countryside: minstrels, jugglers, interlude players, bearwards and fencers.[15]

The traditional form of minstrelsy was in decline in Reformation England but the strollers continued to flourish and these would include players of instruments as well as of interludes. Even those troupes who enjoyed the nominal patronage of the great depended on the ability to wander in the country in the summer months to eke out a living, and so they were explicitly exempted from the provisions of the act. Those who did not benefit from such sponsorship were now, in common with the other migrants, deemed to be vagabonds and made subject to the full penalties of the law – unless, that is, they obtained licences to travel from the country magistracy. There had been previous attempts by the

---

[15] 14 Elizabeth, c. 5: *Statutes of the Realm*, IV, 590–8. E. M. Leonard, *The Early History of English Poor Relief* (Cambridge, 1900), 69–72. Glynne Wickham, *Early English Stages, 1300 to 1600*, II, part I (1963), 107.

Elizabethan regime to regulate plays, their contents and performance, but this was the first step taken to control the movement of the actors, and it betokened a change in the official attitude to acting for a living, as distinct from amateur acting.[16] It has been represented by historians of the stage and of the poor laws as an attempt to encourage higher standards among the actors. These authorities agree on the significance of the act for the emerging 'profession of players': it was not hostile but protective and salutary.[17] It protected in particular the companies organised under the patronage of lords like Leicester. Viewed in this perspective, the act becomes the first of the seminal events of this decade which fostered the growth of the English stage. With the letters patent of 1574 Leicester's Men acquired a royal warrant for their privileges, and in 1576 their enterprising leader, James Burbage, erected the first permanent London playhouse, the Theatre in Shoreditch.[18]

Speaker Bell remarked at the start of the session of 1572 that one of the reasons for calling parliament was 'for punishment of vagabonds.'[19] The writs went out on 28 March and parliament met on 8 May. A bill for the punishment of vagabonds and for relief of the poor was introduced into the upper house on 12 May.[20] The bill received its second and third readings on 15 and 17 May and was delivered to the Commons two days later. The lower house began by reading a new bill *pro forma* on the same subject on 14 May; this was to be superseded by the Lords' amended version of the measure it had rejected in 1571 in what now became an official bill, given its first reading in the Commons on 20 May.[21] We do not know how much had been salvaged from the aborted bill of 1571; nor can we identify its draftsman, though it is likely that Burghley had a hand

---

[16] A proclamation of 16 May 1559 had continued the practice of the previous two reigns of prohibiting the performance of plays and interludes without permission: a prior licence had to be obtained from the civil authorities or, within the shires, from the lords lieutenant or two justices of the peace. *Tudor Royal Proclamations*, ed. Hughes and Larkin, II, no. 458.

[17] C. J. Ribton-Turner, *A History of Vagrants and Vagrancy* (1887), 110–11; W. Bridges-Adams, *The Irresistible Theatre* (2 vols., 1957–64), I, 93; Bradbrook, *The Rise of the Common Player*, 37; Gurr, *The Shakespearean Stage*, 28–9.

[18] Chambers, *The Elizabethan Stage*, I, 308–10; II, 383–400.

[19] *Proceedings in the Parliaments of Elizabeth I*, ed. T. E. Hartley (Leicester, 1981), 339.

[20] Little can be gleaned from the bare entries in the *Lords Journal* except that after its first reading it was committed to the archbishop of Canterbury, the earls of Huntingdon, Rutland, Pembroke and Hertford, the bishops of London, Worcester, St Davids and Bangor; the Lords Grey, Evers, St John of Basing and St John of Bletsoe, Justice Harper and Christopher Wray, serjeant at law. Sir Simonds D'Ewes, *The Journals of all the Parliaments during the Reign of Queen Elizabeth* (1682), 198.

[21] *Ibid.*, 165. A summary of the readings is given in G. R. Elton, *The Parliament of England, 1559–1581* (Cambridge, 1986), 269–70.

in it, at least in formulating the clause that was to be the main bone of contention between the houses. As early as 1566, possibly in preparation for an ill-fated bill introduced into the Commons in that year, William Cecil had jotted down notes on 'Exposition of a vagabond: fensers, berewardes, mynstrells, pedlars, tynkers.'[22] The list may be taken to reveal Cecil's own attitude, and if it is a less than sure guide to the scope of the measures against vagabonds which came before parliament in 1566 and 1571, it could well represent an earlier recension of the clause defining vagabondage in the Lords bill of 1572. This originally read:

& all Fencers, Bearwardes, Common Players in Enterludes & Minstrels, not belonging to any Baron of this Realme or towardes any other honorable Personage of greater Degree; all Juglers, Pedlars, Tynkers and Petye Chapmen, *players of enterludes belonging to gentlemen not having* Lycense of two Justices of the Peace at the leaste, whereof one to be of the Quorum, wher and in what Shier they shall happen to wander . . . shalbee taken, adjudged and deemed Roges, Vacaboundes and sturdy Beggars.[23]

The italicised phrase was later removed by the Commons and the list of those eligible for licences enlarged. Of the itinerants listed in this section, the only ones not on Cecil's list are the players and jugglers. At this stage in its formation the bill recognised three categories of common players of interludes: those belonging to nobles, those belonging to gentlemen and those without any such attachment. In the first category not only the players but fencers, bearwards and minstrels who enjoyed noble patronage were to be exempt from the penalties now imposed for vagrancy and they thus acquired a protected status in law. The restrictions placed on the movement of all other players held a special implication for those sponsored by commoners, for these were to be accounted vagabonds if they wandered without licence. It amounted to an indirect form of control over the households and retinues of the gentry, and it was to that extent related to the measures against illicit retaining. The licensing provision in this clause appears to be based on that established in an act of 1552 (5 & 6 Edward VI, c. 21) requiring every pedlar, tinker and petty chapman to have a licence from two justices of the peace in the shires in which they travelled.[24] In the original Lords bill of 1572 only two other types of wanderers, jugglers and players kept by gentlemen, were added to this provision.

The bill from the Lords was read for the first time in the lower house on 20 May, and it provoked a lively debate which is recorded in some

---

22 PRO sp12/41/76; Leonard, *Early History*, 68.
23 The original act with list of amendments in the HLRO.
24 *Statutes of the Realm*, IV, 155.

telling detail in Thomas Cromwell's journal.[25] It was the matter of vagrancy, rather than the provisions for poor relief, which mainly concerned the speakers, who drew attention to the 'diversitie in roges'. Ralph Sekerston, burgess for Liverpool, thought the bill too partial to London and other great cities and lacking in provision for small boroughs like his own. He censured bishops, lords and gentlemen for keeping so few servants, 'which breedeth vagabondes'. As he warmed to his subject, Sekerston grew more indiscreet. 'A gentleman's apparell shall nowe be worth a 100^{lis} and but a boy to attende him. Besides bishopps and other priestes troble us with their childrine. And as for Courteors they care not for us, nor we care not for them.' If this was to aim the blunderbuss at the target of the ills of the commonwealth, the suggestion that the rise in vagrancy and the curbs on retaining household servants were connected may not have been so wide of the mark. Even so, it was a remarkable outburst, revealing of social tensions which rarely surfaced in the Commons. Francis Knollys considered the speech perverse and castigated the member for Liverpool for his levity. Other members dilated more respectfully on the causes of the problem and advanced their individual remedies. Thomas Norton proposed three amendments, objecting in particular to the fact that minstrels were 'by the bill appointed roges though they goe not aboute, "which I would have reformed"'. Knollys warned against a counsel of perfection: the house should be careful lest the bill 'be not hindered for smale scruples'; it should rather be approved, 'because the last parliament it went from us, and is nowe retourned to use [sic] by the Lords'. Mr Serjeant Lovelace spoke in favour of initiatives to be taken within the counties for searching out vagabonds. Roger Slegge, burgess for Cambridge (described in the bishops' report of 1563 as 'of godly religion') 'would have those minstrels onely punished which wander abroade, not which keepe a continuall habitation'. While being opposed to the imposition of a uniform regulation on the whole country – for each county knew best its own affairs – he argued for the extension to borough officers of the authority given to the justices of the peace in the shires.[26] This referred to the provisions for poor relief as well as those against vagabondage, but had Slegge's advice been followed the licensing authority vested in the magistrates might have been enlarged so as to restrict even further the freedom of movement of minstrels and players alike. If parliament had legislated for towns as well as shires, the subsequent history of the playing companies and the playhouses would have been very different. As it was, city and town corporations would continue to

[25] *Proceedings*, ed. Hartley, 366–7.   [26] *Ibid.*, 367.

exercise their own civic rights to control the itinerants' presence within their walls.

After the bill's second reading in the Commons on 22 May, it was committed to Sir Henry Gates, Serjeant Lovelace, Christopher Yelverton, Thomas Cromwell himself, an indefatigable committee man, Thomas Heywood, Sir Thomas Bowyer and Lewis ab Owen. Cromwell and Yelverton were notable Puritans and most of the committee were lawyers. They were to meet the following morning but later on the same day another bill, of unknown provenance, 'to avoid the multitude of rogues and vagabonds', and presumably proffering different remedies, was read for the first time.[27] The most pressing parliamentary business of these last days of May was the petition of both houses to the queen to execute Norfolk without further delay and to put Mary Stuart on trial. On 24 May the Commons requested a conference with the Lords both on this matter and 'touching some Amendments to be had in the Bill of Vagabonds'.[28] At 8 o'clock in the morning of 28 May the 'committees' from both houses were given an audience by Elizabeth 'on the great cause'. What transpired at the meeting in Star Chamber between the committees of the two houses to confer about the vagabonds bill is not clear, but the Lords' representatives would have had an opportunity to register their views on the provisos which came before the Commons for their second reading later that day. The proviso for the minstrels in Wales was rejected and the others ordered to be engrossed. On 29 May the alternative bill surfaced again and was rejected after a second reading, before the official bill and its provisos were given a third reading and – an unusual procedure – committed again.[29] The debate during the third reading was contentious: both Francis Alford and Thomas Wilbraham, who 'made an excellent argument both wise and eloquent', spoke against it. Sir Francis Knollys spoke at length both for and against different parts of the bill, while Sir James Croft objected to one part of it. Cromwell informs us that 'Much argument *pro et contra* was made aboute minstrels.' The point raised by Norton and Slegge at the first reading was still unresolved: it had apparently not been among the amendments discussed at the conference with the Lords, and this may have been the reason for the bill's recommittal 'to be better considered of'. This time the committee consisted of Knollys, Croft, Wilbraham, Miles Sandys, Robert Mounson, John Marshe, Thomas St Poll, Bowyer again and 'Mr Cromwell'. This is unlikely to have been the diarist, who notes that he

---

[27] D'Ewes, *Journals*, 213; *CJ*, I, 97.

[28] *CJ*, I, 98. D'Ewes, *Journals*, 214.

[29] *Proceedings*, ed. Hartley, 384; *CJ*, I, 99; D'Ewes, *Journals*, 220.

was absent from the house the next day, but rather Francis Cromwell, alias Williams, of Huntingdonshire.

As if to compensate for the lacuna in Cromwell's diary, the entry in that kept by Fulk Onslow, the clerk of the Commons, happens to be particularly full for 30 May. Knollys reported that the committee had 'travailed much' in reforming the branch of the bill against vagabonds, which was read again, 'wherein in the newe alteration of these wordes "minstrelles", whether they should be contained within the said bill or not, great argument arose'.[30] The amendment to the crucial clause, in the form that was to be interlineated in the engrossed bill, read as follows:

& all Fencers, Bearewardes, Common Players in Enterludes & Minstrels, not belonging to any Baron of this Realme or towardes any other honorable Personage of greater Degree; all Juglers, Pedlars, Tynkers and Petye Chapmen; *which said Fencers, Bearwardes, Comon Players in Enterludes, Mynstrels, Juglers, Pedlars, Tynkers & Petye Chapmen, shall wander abroade and have not* Lycense of two Justices of the Peace at the leaste, whereof one to be of the Quorum, wher and in what Shier they shall happen to wander . . . shal bee taken, adjuged and deemed Roges, Vacaboundes and sturdy Beggars.[31]

The italicised section indicates what the committee advised should be substituted for the original phrase 'Players of Enterludes belonging to gentlemen not having . . . '.

The revision to the clause thus enlarged the category of itinerants eligible for licences, which in the original drafting was restricted to jugglers, pedlars, petty chapman and players kept by gentlemen. It may have been an element of ambiguity in the phrasing of the catalogue of mendicants that provoked the debate on 29 May. There is certainly an ambiguity in the entries in the journals. In Onslow's account 'these wordes "minstrelles"' is clearly an abbreviation: in this instance the private journal is less full than the official record. The entries in both the *Commons Journal* and D'Ewes are more explicit about the reception by the house on 30 May of the committee's proposed amendment: 'Upon the question it was resolved . . . That the wordes Minstrells, Bearwards, Pedlars &c. shall not be put out in the Bill, but stand still in the same, qualified by Licenses of the Justices of the Peace in such sort, as upon the Committee hath been considered and agreed upon.'[32] The implication of this notation is that what had been at issue on the previous day was whether not only the minstrels but the other itinerants listed should be removed from the clause altogether. In considering the objections voiced

[30] *Proceedings*, ed. Hartley, 312–13.
[31] HLRO, original act and amendments.
[32] *CJ*, I, 99; D'Ewes, *Journals*, 220.

during the third reading, the committee had not been unanimous in its recommendations but had devised a compromise which at least the Commons could put to the vote, and this is what was done on 30 May. The debate now turned on whether all the itinerants listed should be subject to licensing by the justices of the peace in the shires. Onslow records the disposition of members of the committee and the others who spoke to the motion.

Wilbraham to have them [the amended words] left out. Sir James Croftes to the same effect. Cromwell to have them within the bill; Marshe to the same effect. Sir Owen Hopton with the minstrelles. Sir Frauncis Knowles neither with them nor against them. Sandes with the minstrelles. Snagge much talk and to no purpose. Sir Nicholas Arnold against them. Sampoll [St Poll] against them.

Recorder of London, a longe tedious talke nothing touching the matter in question. He took a theame *Res ipsa dabit consilium*, whereupon he replied still but to little purpose. Sackford, Master of the Requests, against them. St John, Gargarve, Mounson, Edgecome, Popham against them. Aylworth to no purpose.

In the ende it was agreed by the more number they should be within the bill, and so the House brake up.[33]

Knollys remained neutral during the debate, but of the other members of the committee whose opinions are recorded, three appeared to be in favour of the amendment and four against (Bowyer's view is not given). Onslow's notes, however, need to be read carefully. Those named as speaking 'to have them' (that is, the words 'minstrels etc') omitted from the clause were evidently opposed to the extension of the licensing system, which would in fact relieve the lot of the ordinary minstrels and other itinerants included in the revised formulation. It follows that these speakers were not necessarily on the same side as those described as being 'with the minstrels'.

Thus it was that not only minstrels but the other itinerants listed in the amendment were in the event not excluded from the rigours of the penalties against vagabonds, but rather brought within the licensing system.[34] It is noteworthy that the debate was not characterised by Puritan hostility to these itinerant entertainers. Many of those reported as being in favour of the amendment can be identified as Puritans, but it looks as if it was as lawyers, rather than as moralists, that most of them spoke and voted on this issue of public order. Knollys, perhaps the most ardent Puritan of them all, was 'neither with them nor against them'. Of the committee men, Miles Sandys, brother of the archbishop of York,

---

[33] *Proceedings*, ed. Hartley, 312–13.
[34] The amendment also added 'tinkers' to the list; they had presumably been inadvertently omitted from the original bill.

owed his seat in parliament to Puritan patrons: he had opposed the vagabonds bill of 1571 as 'over sharp and bloody',[35] and would not subject the minstrels to the severity of the present measure. Croft, a crypto-Catholic and Knollys' adversary in the royal household and on the privy council, opposed the amendment, and yet he was later known to have kept a company of players.[36] William Fleetwood, the earnest recorder of London who was to be the scourge of rogues and players in the City in later years, seemed to be of the opinion that the question of definition, if left alone, would resolve itself. He failed to make an effective speech, while his predecessor in that office, Thomas Wilbraham, now attorney to the court of wards, opposed the amendment in committee and debate. Owen Hopton, lieutenant of the Tower and accounted a follower of Leicester, was 'with the minstrelles'.[37] Thomas St Poll, one of the most active country gentlemen in mid-Elizabethan parliaments, was earnest in religion and a hunter of recusants yet not in favour of draconian measures against vagrants in general. 'Considering there is diversity in roges', he had earlier spoken in support of granting bail to the less serious offenders, but on the second committee he was all for extending the severity of the law against minstrels. The voting disposition of these speakers permits no facile generalisation to be made about the predilections of Puritans or courtiers on the question of the freedom of movement to be allowed to the travelling entertainers.[38]

In the original bill interlude players, like minstrels, were listed among the itinerants who were to be classed as vagabonds, and only those players attached to gentlemen's households were eligible for licences to travel. In the revised form the phrase 'players belonging to gentlemen' disappears; all those not sponsored by noblemen are now described as 'common players of interludes' and made subject to the licensing provision. Players were evidently subsumed in the formula 'minstrels, bearwards, pedlars &c.' and so their position must have been discussed during these proceedings without leaving a more specific trace in the records than an et cetera. Since by this period travelling troupes often consisted of both interluders and instrumentalists, whether these were

[35] *The History of Parliament: The House of Commons, 1558–1603*, P. W. Hasler (3 vols., 1981), III, 341–4.   [36] See below, n. 60.

[37] He is misrepresented in the biography of him in *History of Parliament*, ed. Hasler, II, 336–7, as being in favour of removing 'minstrels' from the bill. Leicester's enemies accounted Hopton one of the earl's followers, but after 1588 he served on the High Commission and was thought to be too sympathetic to his Catholic charges in the Tower.

[38] The religious dispositions of most of the named speakers are identified in their biographical entries in Hasler though according to a definition of Puritanism which tends to reflect the views of Sir John Neale and to which Patrick Collinson would not necessarily subscribe.

designated musicians or minstrels, it was increasingly difficult to draw distinctions between them[39] and it may be that this point was raised in debate as one of the objections to the clause. At any rate, the amended clause put minstrels and players on a par before the law and tempered the severity of the original provision by holding out the prospect of a warrant for their activities.

As to its wider significance, the revision has been interpreted by historians of the theatre as in effect depriving the gentry of a significant form of patronage. Thus Glynne Wickham claims that 'baronets [recte knights] and gentlemen were stripped of their rights to maintain companies'.[40] In so far as the House of Commons was dominated by the gentry, it would appear at first sight to be passing a self-denying ordinance, but in fact what was removed from the bill was an explicit statement that even players kept by gentlemen were not allowed to travel without licence. In the new formulation there is no prohibition on interluders being retained by either gentlemen or corporations, and their movement in the shires is to be supervised by such members of the gentry as served on the commissions of the peace. Players maintained by noblemen are still excluded from the licensing provision, so that the peers' rights of patronage were not affected by the Commons' tinkering with the clause. Even so, the amendment was not promoted with any confidence that it would be acceptable to the upper house. When on 30 May it was put to the vote and passed by a majority, the Commons was careful to specify a condition: 'That if the Lords shall not agree to that qualification [the licensing provision], then this House will not be so bound by the said resolution, but that they may alter and change the same at their Liberty and pleasure, if they shall so think good.'[41] Had the clause been left unamended and the Lords insisted on retaining this part of the bill as they had originally framed it, the licensing of interluders would have extended only to those 'belonging to gentlemen'. As it was, these words were left out of the revised formula, but had the vote gone the other way, this restriction would presumably have been retained and the bill passed in its original form. The surviving provisos to the bill were further considered on 2 June; one of them, for prisoners in the Marshalsea, was rejected and that for John Dutton allowed and passed.[42] It was at this stage that the amendments to the clause were interlined in the engrossed bill without recasting the whole, and the final provisions

---

[39] In the letters patent of 10 May 1574, Leicester's Men are authorised to use their instruments as well as to perform their plays. Chambers, *The Elizabethan Stage*, II, 87–8.
[40] Wickham, *Early English Stages*, 107.
[41] D'Ewes, *Journals*, 220.
[42] *Ibid.*, 221; *CJ*, I, 99.

were stitched on to it in a schedule. After the complete bill was given its final reading it was returned to the Lords, who on 4 June gave it their second and third readings, approving the provisos and amendments without a murmur of dissent.[43] Patrons of companies of players, including privy councillors like Leicester, were evidently satisfied that their rights of sponsorship or retaining had not been touched by the revision. Within a few days, however, what looks to have been an official bill to prohibit retainers and household servants from acting as justices of the peace and high constables passed the Commons but failed to make any progress in the Lords before parliament was prorogued on 30 June.[44] On that day the 'acte for the Punishment of Vagabondes, and for Relief of the Poore and Impotent' received the royal assent. It was a tentative and temporary measure that was intended to last for no more than seven years but was in the event revised, and renewed in part, by the poor law of 1576 (18 Elizabeth I, c. 3).

Three provisos in the act of 1572, including two of those tacked on at the end, were to have a direct bearing on the legal position of players. It was stipulated in one of these provisos that the justices of the peace in the shires were not to encroach upon the jurisdictions of the towns in respect of any of the other provisions. In the event the civic authorities were to enforce their own inhibitions, quite independently of the act, on the visits and performances of strolling troupes. A proviso in the body of the act acknowledged that licences granted under the great seal by the lord keeper were not affected by its provisions. This was of course a prerogative power that superseded the authority of mere magistrates to issue warrants, and it was to be exercised in favour of Leicester's company of players in 1574.[45] The last proviso confirmed the historic rights of the Dutton family in Cheshire to issue licences to minstrels within the county. This privilege was secured for John Dutton of Dutton, probably by his brother-in-law, George Calverley, who sat in parliament as burgess for Chester in both 1571 and 1572. Within two years Dutton and Calverley were to fall out in an acrimonious family quarrel which led to a case in Star Chamber. Calverley countered a charge of assault levelled against him by Dutton by accusing his brother-in-law of

---

[43] D'Ewes, *Journals*, 200. *Pace* Leonard (*Early History*, 69–70), who claims that there was a 'dispute' between the two houses 'as to the definition of the word "vagabond"'.

[44] The bill was introduced on 7 June, engrossed after its second reading on 9 June and sent to the Lords with what D'Ewes calls 'Bills of no great moment' after its third reading on 10 June. D'Ewes notes that 'the reason why so few Statutes received Life' was because parliament was called chiefly to consider the fate of Mary, Queen of Scots. D'Ewes, *Journals*, 222–3, 225; *CJ*, I, 101; *Proceedings*, ed. Hartley, 395, 397, 401.

[45] Chambers, *The Elizabethan Stage*, I, 280–1.

conspiracy to murder him and his own wife in order to be free to marry Calverley's widow, and of employing 'a notable conjuror' to bring about these ends by black magic.[46] Notwithstanding this fracas, the Dutton family was able to perpetuate their traditional protection of minstrelsy in Cheshire in the poor law code of 1597 and its continuation in 1601.[47]

A 'proviso for Welsh minstrels' was rejected by the Commons during the second reading of the provisos for the bill against vagabonds on 28 May. The journals are silent as to the nature of the debate, but it may have been decided that no separate provision was required for Wales because the special needs of the principality had already been addressed on previous occasions. A licensing system for minstrels and bards had operated since the reign of Henry VIII to sustain quality among an order that continued to occupy a more exalted position in Wales than minstrelsy did in England. The custom of *clera*, of wandering minstrels who begged for their living, was enshrined in Welsh society, and many of the *uchelwyr*, the gentry of Wales, for all the process of anglicisation that had set in since the union with England, were not disposed to relinquish their traditional role of patrons. A bard or harpist might be formally attached to the household of an *uchelwr*, but he was also expected to visit other houses on 'circuit' in search of a livelihood. The custom was liable to abuse and to intrusion by the uninitiated, while the bardic order itself was in crisis by the later sixteenth century.[48] In 1568 the Council in the Marches investigated the movements of 'vagrants and idle persons naming themselves minstrels, rhymers and bards', who had lately grown into an intolerable multitude. These hangers-on pestered the gentry in their houses so that bards and musicians 'expert in tongue and cunning' were discouraged from the exercise and practice of their craft, 'and also not a little hindered in their livings and preferments'. The Council at Ludlow was concerned not only to control vagabondage but to create the proper conditions for the bardic order and Welsh harpists to thrive. In consequence twenty-one gentlemen known for their patronage of these traditional skills as exercised by the professionals were commissioned to organise an eisteddfod at Caerwys, Montgomeryshire, a historic centre for such assemblies.[49]

---

[46] PRO Star Chamber 5/D1/13 (Feb.–March, 1574); *History of Parliament*, ed. Hasler, I, 532. For the origin of the minstrelsy rights of the Duttons, see George Ormerod, *History of the County Palatine and City of Chester* (3 vols., 1819), I, 475, 484.

[47] Cf. the acts 39 Elizabeth, c. 4, 43, Elizabeth, c. 9: *Statutes of the Realm*, IV, 899–902, 973–4. In 1601 the confirmation of Dutton's privilege was made provisional on his producing legal proof of his hereditary right to license minstrels.

[48] G. D. Owen, *Elizabethan Wales: The Social Scene* (Cardiff, 1962), 36.

[49] HMC, *Report of MSS in the Welsh Language I: The Welsh MSS of Lord Mostyn* (1898), 291–2.

Two of the commissioners of 1568 sat in the parliament of 1572 for Welsh constituencies, but the member who was responsible for proposing the proviso for Welsh minstrels was no doubt Lewis ab Owen, knight of the shire for Anglesey, who served on the committee set up on 22 May after the bill's second reading.[50] That neither commission nor statute succeeded in the event in curbing the wanderings of those Welsh minstrels and bards who were not of the 'allowed & advanced skill, sobrietie and good behaviour', emerges from the petition which a new generation of gentlemen-patrons addressed to the Council in the Marches in 1594. The lord president, the earl of Pembroke, was asked to sanction another eisteddfod to be held at Cearwys to maintain standards through contests of skills.[51]

This excursus on the Welsh minstrels and bards prompts the question: could there have been a comparable impulse behind the legislation of 1572 to regulate English minstrels and players so as to safeguard quality and standards? If any such argument was advanced during the debates of 29 and 30 May, it has left no trace in the journals. During the earlier readings of the bill, two members had suggested that a distinction be made between wandering minstrels and sedentary ones: these latter would have included the London waits, and it was these that Thomas Norton, as the City remembrancer, probably had in mind.[52] That was the full extent of the concern expressed for the livelihood of the minstrels in any capacity or for the service they provided. A contemporary commentator was prepared to draw even finer distinctions. Thomas Whythorne was so confident of his status as a professional musician that he expressed his scorn for the traditional wandering minstrels who had to seek out their audience, be it private or public. 'Also to banketers, revellers, mummers, maskers, dancers, tumblers, players and suchlike, they sell also the sounds of their voices and instruments.' Whythorne approved of the recent restraint placed on the vagabond life which some of them followed, going so far as to advise magistrates to give these strollers licences as minstrels rather than musicians, and so observe the strict letter of the statute. He insisted that there were degrees of difference between those who lived by making music, just as there were gradations in the professions of the law and the church. Minstrels occupied the lowest rank in this hierarchy.[53] There is no evidence in this

---

[50] *History of Parliament*, ed. Hasler, III, 162. The two members who had served as commissioners in 1568 were John Gruffydd of Caernarfon and John Lewis Owen of Merioneth.
[51] *HMC Mostyn MSS*, 293–4.   [52] See above, n. 25.
[53] *The Autobiography of Thomas Whythorne*, ed. J. M. Osborn (modern spelling edition, 1962), 191–2.

period of any ranking among stage players as there evidently was among musicians, or of a comparable antipathy to the less accomplished strollers by the players who sought to improve the conditions of their craft. No gradations of quality were recognised apart from that which was reflected in the patronage of the leaders of society. It may have been an unspoken assumption that the itinerant entertainers sponsored by the nobility would be of superior skill to those in the service of the gentry, but the priorities of the legislators were clear – to curb disorderly elements in the commonwealth while at the same time enhancing social distinctions and privileges. Parliament protected the rights of the noble patrons and only incidentally those of the favoured players.

It would be a mistake to antedate the emergence of the acting 'profession' by suggesting that the more accomplished players somehow sought an official recognition as superior practitioners of their craft. There is nothing in the record to point to any lobbying by the companies to gain exemptions, or to patrons like Leicester actively intervening on their behalf, during the making of the legislation. If, as one authority on the history of the acting companies has intimated, the act of 1572 'gave warrant to their quality',[54] it was an unlooked-for consequence; to claim that this was the legislative intention in 1572 is to reason, *post hoc, ergo propter hoc.*

The author of the most recent study of 'the business of playing' concedes that the act 'contained provisions one might easily construe as being inimical to the welfare of the playing profession'.[55] It is certainly true that it afforded only a limited recognition of the existence of a profession: the references are always to individual players, who may or may not be attached to a household or entourage, and never to the fact that they were or could be organised as companies. William Ingram goes on to reaffirm the consensus among historians of the theatre, that 'such official restriction on playing was salutary as well as punitive'. The greater security enjoyed by the sponsored actors may well have acted as an incentive for the more enterprising among them to organise them- selves in more autonomous touring companies. One plausible scenario for the emergence of a 'profession' is, therefore, that having secured through patronage the right to travel in the countryside, the favoured companies took the initiative in seeking greater economic independence and a permanent base in the London playhouses. However, as Professor Ingram recognises, the patent granted to Leicester's Men in 1574 could

---

[54] Gurr, *The Shakespearean Stage*, 29.
[55] W. Ingram, *The Business of Playing: The Beginnings of the Adult Professional Theater in Elizabethan London* (Ithaca and London, 1993), 120.

not have been in response to the act of 1572, since they were not subject to its provisions.[56] The restraints that the pioneers of the London playhouses, under the leadership of James Burbage, had to overcome were those imposed not by parliament but by the City authorities.

The version of the history of the Elizabethan stage that traces a pattern of evolution for the emergence of 'a profession of players' (and which has subscribed to a Whig view of progress) is currently being revised by historians of the English theatre.[57] When that new history has been fashioned the significance of the statute of 1572 may be seen in a quite different perspective. The rest of this essay is concerned with the less ambitious task of reviewing some of the evidence for the impact of the legislation on the players who fall within its purview, especially those who looked to 'gentlemen' for patronage.

Strolling players sponsored by knights and gentlemen, far from being proscribed in 1572, continued to exist, though admittedly in fewer numbers. J. T. Murray lists fifteen such companies in the period 1558–72 and ten in the years 1573–97. The numbers of troupes maintained by towns increased in the same periods from seven to eleven. In his will in 1581 Alexander Houghton of Lea, Lancashire, bequeathed his collection of musical instruments and playing costumes to his brother Thomas.[58] If he were not minded to keep players, these effects were to be given to Sir Thomas Hesketh, whom Houghton urged to take his two players, Fulk Gyllome and William Shakeshafte, into his service, or else to help them to some good master. Similarly, Sir William Holles of Haughton, Nottinghamshire (d. 1591), as a mark of hospitality, kept a company of stage players who performed masques and plays for him at festival times and on days of solemnity. His grandson, Gervase Holles, relates how

In the summer time they usually acted abroad in the country; and old Alderman Fotherby [of Nottingham] has tolde me that he hath heard them act many times, alwais at the end of the play praying (as the custome then was) for the Queene's Matie, the Councill and their right worshippfull good Maister, Sir William Holles.[59]

As an hospitable and law-abiding man, Sir William would no doubt have had little trouble in ensuring that his actors had a sufficient warrant

---

56 *Ibid.*, 121.
57 See, as well as Ingram, Scott McMillin in *The Elizabethan Theatre*, ed. McGee, 1–17.
58 J. T. Murray, *English Dramatic Companies, 1558–1642* (2 vols., 1910), II, 77, 113; Chambers, *The Elizabethan Stage*, I, n. 2.
59 Chambers, *The Elizabethan Stage*, I, n. 2; *Gervase Holles, Memorials of the Holles Family, 1493–1656*, ed. A. C. Wood (Camden Soc., 3rd ser., 55, 1937), 42.

from his fellow justices to wander in the shire. Even Sir James Croft is known to have retained a troupe of actors after the act was passed: 'Maister Comptroller's players' made a single visit to Gloucester in 1574-5.[60] Though the paucity of the evidence precludes any confident conclusions to be drawn about the impact of the measures of 1572 on the fortunes of the players themselves, there are few signs that knights and gentlemen felt discouraged thereby from keeping player-servants.

The first comment on the poor laws of 1572 and 1576 to appear in print is found in William Harrison's *The Description of England*. Harrison's gloss on the clause defining vagabondage suggests possible reasons for the inclusion of some of the itinerants: the begging students were 'pretensed scholars', and as for bearwards, their bears were a danger especially to children, some of whom had even been devoured 'whose parents knew not what was become of them'.[61] In his 'Chronology' Harrison records his own hostility to the players as well as the bearwards, though the entry under 1572 refers to the banning of plays in London because of the plague rather than to the legislation of that date.[62] (In other sections of the manuscript he expressed his disapproval of the Puritan activists in parliament.) One modern commentator finds significance in the juxtaposition, in the list of vagabonds, of players with scholars from the universities, whom after all Sir Thomas Smith allowed within the ranks of gentlemen, 'so that it is evident that no particular mark of opprobrium was cast on the actor's quality'.[63] However, in the light of Harrison's remark on the 'scholars', it is clear that to be placed in the same category with them was not necessarily to keep good company.

For all the distinctions drawn by the legislators, a stigma came to be attached to players of interludes of all kinds, even those not touched by its provisions, as a result of the act against vagabonds. Contemporary critics were indiscriminate in their condemnation of the practitioners of 'so infamous an art', and to Philip Stubbes all players were beggars. 'Are they not taken by the lawes of the Realm for roagues and vacabounds? I speak of such as travaile the Cuntries with playes & enterludes, making an occupation of it, and oght so to be punished, if

[60] Murray, *English Dramatic Companies*, II, 82.
[61] *The Description of England, by William Harrison*, ed. Georges Edelen (Ithaca, 1968), ch. 10, 180-6. This was first published as part of Holinshed's *Chronicles* in 1577.
[62] See above, n. 14.
[63] William Ringler, 'The First Phase of the Elizabethan Attack on the Stage, 1558-1579', *The Huntington Library Quarterly*, no. 4 (1942), 392-4. *De Republica Anglorum by Sir Thomas Smith*, ed. Mary Dewar (Cambridge, 1982), 72.

they had their deserts.'[64] Critics of the stage were not on the whole respecters of persons and the published tracts against the stage spared neither sponsored players nor patrons. Stephen Gosson, the apostate playmaker, was especially virulent in denouncing the strollers: 'We have infinite poets, and pipers, and such peevish cattle among us in England, that live by merry begging, maintained by alms, and privily encroach upon every man's purse.' He deplored the protection afforded them by the law, and his advice to the City fathers was to curb the players by undermining the patronage which they received mainly, if not exclusively, from the court nobility. 'If their letters of commendation were once stayed, it were easy for you to overthrow them.'[65]

Urban oligarchies continued to exercise their own control over migrants in general and the itinerant entertainers in particular, and there were occasions when these were called on to respect the definitions laid down by parliament in 1572. The evidence for the reception of visiting companies of players in provincial cities and towns has not always been correctly interpreted by historians of the stage. In this context the ordinances devised by the common council of Gloucester in 1580 are the most complete to have survived. The reasons advanced in them for restricting attendance at plays echo those to be found in the records for London, particularly the order of 1574: the need to protect the apprentices from idleness, extravagance and a dissolute life. In Gloucester, the mayor was given exclusive authority to regulate the times and places of playing; the number of performances that a visiting troupe could give was limited according to the rank of its patron. Thus on every visit the queen's players (that is, before the formation of the Queen's Men in 1583, the old court interluders) got the lion's share of three plays over three days; those belonging to peers could perform twice in two days; one performance was vouchsafed to 'any other subiects players under the degree of a Baron of the parliament and beinge allowed by the statutes and Lawes of the Realme to keape or have players'. In commenting on these ordinances, Peter Greenfield erroneously concludes that this last condition represented a misreading of 14 Elizabeth,

[64] *Philip Stubbes's Anatomy of the Abuses in England*, ed. F. J. Furnivall (1877–9) part 1, 144–5. In 1577 John Northbrooke lamented the laxity in executing the laws against vagabonds of 1572 and 1576: *A Treatise against Dicing, Dancing, Plays and Interludes, with Other Idle Pastimes* (1840 edn), 76.

[65] Stephen Gosson, *The School of Abuse* (1579), sig. B1r, E7v, E8r, cited in Bradbrook, *The Rise of the Common Player*, 71. William Ringler, *Stephen Gosson: a Biographical and Critical Study* (Princeton, 1942), 53–82. The City failed in its attempts to neutralise the patronage of the court, and achieved only a limited success in controlling the conditions of playing within its jurisdiction.

c. 5.[66] It is in fact a precise reference to the licensing provision of this act as it had been continued in 1576, and the travelling companies involved would have had to obtain the warrant of two justices of the peace in every shire before arriving at their destination. They would also have been armed with a letter of recommendation from their patron to identify them to their hosts and to the authorities of town and shire alike. After the award of the letters patent to Edmund Tilney as Master of the Revels in 1581, the right of the civic authorities to control conditions of performance within their jurisdictions was qualified by his power to approve plays and to grant permission to favoured companies, 'for her majesty's better service', to perform in any city or town in the realm.[67]

Stephen Gosson was not the only turncoat playwright to criticise the players and the permanent London playhouses. The anonymous author, now thought to be Anthony Munday, of *A Second and Third Blast of Retrait from Plaies and Theatres* (1580) dared to censure noblemen who allowed their servants to travel for sustenance to gentlemen's houses.[68] Examples of this practice, whereby the retainer system could be extended without heavy charge being incurred by the lord, are hard to find.[69] The surviving records have not yielded up a single instance of a lord's company of players visiting his clients among the gentry, and there is only one recorded case dating from this reign of an alleged infringement of the act of 1572 by a gentlemen's troupe.[70] This is in every sense a singular case and merits close attention.

In 1583 Thomas Potter, a justice of the peace of Kent, complained to Sir Francis Walsingham that the servants of Sir Walter Waller of Groombridge had proclaimed an interlude at Brasted on 13 May without sufficient warrant. Potter had forbidden them to perform, warning them

[66] Peter H. Greenfield, 'Professional Players at Gloucester: Conditions of Provincial Performing', in *The Elizabethan Theatre*, ed. McGee, 78. The prohibitions of the act of common council of London, 6 Dec. 1574 were of course more complex and more concerned with issues of public order, health and morality. Chambers, *The Elizabethan Stage*, IV, 273–6.
[67] W. R. Streitberger, 'On Edmund Tyllney's Biography', *Review of English Studies*, n.s., 29, no. 113 (1978), 20–1. Tilney sat in parliament in 1572 as burgess for Gatton, but did not take part in the debates on the 'minstrels etc.': *History of Parliament*, ed. Hasler, III, 509.
[68] Ringler, *Stephen Gosson*, 71–82.
[69] In 1594 the court book of Norwich records the arrival of a troupe of musicians armed with a letter of commendation from Sir Arthur Hevingham to the mayor; one of them was his liveried retainer but as for 'the rest, they were retained with him but yesterday'. W. L. Woodfill, *Musicians in English Society from Elizabeth to Charles I* (Princeton, 1953), 66.
[70] The other examples cited by Chambers of players of any kind being prosecuted under the terms of the acts against vagabonds all date from James I's reign. Chambers, *The Elizabethan Stage*, I, 304 n. 1.

that they stood within the danger of the statute against rogues and vagabonds.[71] When he exhorted them to leave 'that wandering trade of life, but to employ themselves to some more commendable exercise', the players took umbrage at this slur on their only means of livelihood and refused to abandon it unless he gave them £100 a year for their maintenance. They were threatened with the stocks but were apparently spared imprisonment by temporising with the constable, offering to pawn their playing apparel while they made contact with their patron. When Waller appeared on the scene he proceeded to abuse Potter with great oaths and was in turn rebuked by the latter's companion, one Studely, a visiting preacher from London. On being warned that his behaviour warranted a report to the privy council, Waller vaunted his faithful service to the earl of Leicester and to the queen 'in Court, in the country and in the field against her enemyes'.[72] The vituperative exchange did not turn into an affray; it was reported to the privy council but did not become a Star Chamber matter. Waller was summoned to appear before Walsingham, he excused himself on a pretext, and Lord Cobham was delegated to try to reconcile the parties.

The players are identified by Potter as William Senock (or Sevenocke, clearly a Kentish man), their leader, who lived in Speldhurst with his wife, his brother John, one John Smith, Alexander Pearson, a musician, who admitted he was not Waller's servant but lived in London, Thomas Jones, a London tailor, and two boy minstrels, Richard Maugham and John Mathew. They are described variously in Potter's letters as vagrant minstrels and players of interludes, and whatever their exact relationship with the patron who took up their cause with such vehemence, their names must be added to the list of known Elizabethan actors and instrumentalists. By the example and maintenance of Waller, it was alleged, the countryside around was swarming with minstrels and players coming out of London and Middlesex and the Puritan Potter was concerned to prosecute them under the act as rogues and not merely as vagabonds. In 1582 William Senocke had been imprisoned for six months at the White Lion in Surrey by Sir Thomas Browne and 'Mr Cowper the counseller' for posting a seditious rhyme against ministers on the church door at Dorking. The one verse cited in Potter's letter to Walsingham is innocuous enough, but it serves to show that the hostility of some churchmen to players and minstrels was

---

71 PRO SP12/160/48, SP12/163/44. It is significant that in the charges the words 'players' and 'minstrels' are used interchangeably.
72 This is spelled out in one of the documents as seven years in Leicester's service, five at court (in what capacity is not known), three in Ireland with men kept at his own charge and fourteen on the commission of the peace (SP12/163/44i).

reciprocated.[73] It may have been the circulating of such ballads which prompted the attack on these itinerants in parliament in the first place.

The players never got around to performing their play (we are not told what their repertory was) but the episode had a drama of its own which exposed a division of loyalties in the local community. In his denial of the charges Waller made much of the fact that no performance had actually taken place and he told Walsingham that if there was any substance to them he should have been tried at common law. Twenty-two inhabitants of Brasted, including the constable, signed a 'testimonial' on behalf of Waller's men declaring that they had been his household servants for many years; they had not played an interlude but had been maliciously detained as rogues by Mr Potter.[74] The Secretary no doubt read this document in the light of Waller's reputation for intimidation. In 1577 Lord Bergavenny had complained to Burghley that he oppressed poor men and his retainers flouted the law, 'but because he was a justice of the peace, these matters were slipt over'.[75] By 1583 Waller had ceased to be a justice, a demotion that, haughty character that he was, had evidently cut him to the quick and exposed him to the present charges. It particularly rankled with him that Potter was a gentleman of the first head; he had not been able to work his malice when Waller himself was a magistrate, and he now acted factiously against his servants, who wore his livery and not clothes of many colours as was alleged.[76] His household servants should be free to travel in the country on his business without being accounted wanderers, and they should not be adjudged rogues for 'having skill in musick, being requested by my frendes or appointed by myself do use other instruments or sing or exercise any other musicall pastyme'. Potter was perverse in his reading of the law and, 'to seeme wonderfull wize and to be accompted a nyce myncer att the wordes of a penall statute', in fact abuses it and slanders its makers. In response to Waller's claim that the men should have been indicted at Quarter

[73] Ye mynisters gluttons
that love laced muttons
your arses make buttons
as I understande
I holde you a Testar
beffore the feaste of Easter
you wyll not so pester
thys reallme of England.
SP12/163/44iv.

[74] SP12/160/48i.

[75] 8 April 1577: *Queen Elizabeth and her Times*, ed. Thomas Wright (2 vols., 1838), II, 51–3.

[76] Potter's vices, according to Waller, were inherited: his father had been pilloried and punished for perjury, while his grandfather had been a tanner, 'which all be such barres for gentility' SP12/163/44ii.

Sessions, Potter pointed out that they were not bailable under the terms of the act, and besides sureties for their good behaviour had not been forthcoming. A letter had been produced by one of the players from Kentish justices 'written in the plural number' but signed only by Sir Thomas Cotton, since the other justice approached, Sir Christopher Allen (as he told both Potter and William Lambarde), had refused to subscribe his name.

Not surprisingly, perhaps, Potter's version of events differs markedly from Waller's and, although it is not substantiated by any independent source, the circumstantial details he provides have an air of verisimilitude. He denied that he knew the players to be Waller's household servants: only one of them had claimed to be so retained by him, and besides the state of his finances hardly enabled him to support his family and countenance, let alone 'such an idle charge' of servitors.

Waller countered with the somewhat contradictory charges that his accuser was guilty both of stinting on hospitality and of infringing the laws against excessive retaining that had been so recently renewed by proclamation.[77] It was a rather desperate defence, calculated no doubt to distract attention from his own record in that regard and to cloak his resentment that the statute against vagabonds had been interpreted so narrowly by such a 'precise gentillman'. The proper working of the licensing system set up by the act depended on close co-operation between the county gentry and it broke down in this case under the strain of a petty faction. Waller's men had failed to obtain a valid licence that would have released them from the penalties imposed in the act of 1572. His protection availed them little once his past caught up with him and he was no longer on the bench.

Lord Cobham failed to reconcile the recalcitrant parties in 1583 and two years later he had occasion to bring another aspect of Waller's hospitality to Burghley's attention, when a search had to be made for Catholic fugitives who had been sheltered by Waller and his wife. Thomas Potter seems to have had the last word in the exchange when he submitted a deposition to the privy council on indiscreet remarks made by his old enemy to the effect that the Paget brothers, Lord Henry and Charles, who were then exiled in France, intended to join Parma in the Netherlands.[78] Waller's own service in that theatre of war under Leicester's command may have saved him from further investigations of serious charges at home, at least until the earl's death in 1588. In 1589, however, his lieutenant, Thomas Morgan, complained to Walsingham

[77] 19 April 1583: *Tudor Royal Proclamations*, ed. Hughes and Larkin, II, no. 664.
[78] Cobham to Walsingham, 28 Sept. 1585: PRO SP12/182/50.

that Waller had dishonoured the order of knighthood by abandoning his men in time of need. He was to survive all these disgraces and a constant lack of funds to sit in parliament for Steyning in 1593.[79]

The scene which disturbed the peace in the streets of Brasted on 13 May 1583 was a psychodrama exposing the latent religious tensions in Kentish society, a clash of cultures as well as of personalities with ramifications which reached beyond the county boundaries. Potter was evidently a 'precisian' with decided views on the playing of interludes, while his opponent may have had closer connections with Leicester's patronage of the players than the evidence for the dispute reveals. In the same year as this altercation Waller's name is linked with John Brayne in the latter's legal suit with his brother-in-law and business partner, James Burbage. Brayne and his co-defendant in the action, Roger Myles, who were alleged to be greatly in debt, claimed they 'had a proteccion under Sir Walter Waler, knight'.[80] The phrase is tantalisingly ambiguous: it either hints at a relationship of patronage or else, taken in context, it may signify that Brayne's credit is limited because of his association with a notorious debtor. In either case, it uncovers hitherto unsuspected connections within the circle of Leicester's players and clients.

The penalties prescribed for vagabondage in the act of 1572 and renewed in that of 1576 were not uniformly or efficiently applied, and it may be that the justices sometimes baulked at imposing the more savage sentences. A proclamation of 14 December 1576 deplored 'the want of the good execution' of these laws, ordered the expulsion of all masterless men from the capital and prescribed more thorough searches to be made in the counties around.[81] There is some evidence from sources other than critics like Whythorne that the licensing procedure set up by statute was abused in practice. In 1593 a draft bill was submitted to parliament to tighten the provision of 14 Elizabeth, c. 5, for the granting of licences to pedlars and petty chapmen. The act had 'not donne soe much goode to the commonwealth as it was intended', because it had not been duly executed, with the result that these wandering tradesmen had actually increased in numbers. The objection to them, apart from their deceitful trading, was that they were accessories to cutpurses and other malefactors, and 'carriers of Lettres and Messengers from one trayterous

---

[79] *History of Parliament*, ed. Hasler, III, 565–6. His service in both Ireland and the Netherlands was blighted by debt: *APC*, n.s., XIII, 1581–2, 141–2; n.s., XIV, 1586–7, 35.

[80] PRO C24/226/10 *ex parte* Burbage, cited in Ingram, *The Business of Playing*, 213.

[81] *Tudor Royal Proclamations*, ed. Hughes and Larkin, II, no. 622. The surviving Quarter Sessions rolls for Middlesex indicate that the justices enforced the most extreme penalties of the law on vagabonds in 1575–6 and 1590: Leonard, *Early History*, 70–1 n. 2.

and disloyall Subiecte to another'. They displayed their wares in church porches and yards on the Sabbath in the time of divine service, contrary to God's laws and the queen's. Having no certain place of abode, they were freed from all forms of taxation, and the unfair competition impoverished the mercers, grocers and linen drapers in most of the market towns in the realm. The remedy proposed was that these Tudor travelling salesmen should not be allowed to sell the same wares as the established tradesmen without a licence obtained from *all* the justices in open sessions within the shires.[82]

The suspicion that these itinerants acted as messengers of sedition, although it may have been present when the clause was originally devised, failed to make an impression on parliament in 1593. Nothing further is heard of the fate of this private bill – it does not seem to have been considered by either house – and there was no comparable attempt to revise the licensing provision of 1572 as it applied to the wandering entertainers until parliament in 1597 repealed all previous acts against rogues, vagabonds and sturdy beggars and enacted new regulations. In the act 39 Elizabeth I, c. 4, the clause of the original act which defined vagabondage was revised so as to bring within its scope all fencers, bearwards, minstrels, players, jugglers, tinkers, pedlars and petty chapmen. The only players to be exempted were to be those belonging to peers of the realm, under whose 'Hand and Seale of Armes' they were authorised to play.[83]

Thus the licensing system was finally dropped; no commoner could henceforth sponsor a troupe of players under warrant and the status of those players who did not enjoy the protection of a noble patron was finally compromised. If this was an index of the increasingly aristocratic nature of society, the legislative intention was not immediately realised. When in the first year of James I's reign the act was continued, it was necessary to add an explanation of the crucial clause. It was declared that since 1597 the act had been variously interpreted because of a certain ambiguity in the wording. To dispel all doubts it was now enacted that no authority given by any nobleman to any persons (that is, players) should be construed to discharge them from the punishments prescribed

[82] HLRO, *HMC, Appendix to Third Report* (1872), 9.
[83] *Statutes of the Realm*, IV, 899–902. Licensing by justices could be suspended in times of emergency by conciliar action, and this happened in 1593, when the privy council forbade plays enacted by common players within five miles of Cambridge and Oxford. The vice-chancellors were instructed that neither the mayors nor any other justices 'may give them lycense to the contrary', *APC*, n.s., XXIV, 427–9. It was not only the incidence of the plague that occasioned this ban, but the undesirability of exposing the students to the 'leuwd example' and vanity of most of the plays, and the distrust of large gatherings.

in the act.[84] In the absence of evidence for the implementation of the act of 1597, or for the making of that of 1604, we cannot be sure what lay at the root of the confusion, but the circumstances perhaps suggest that letters of commendation from patrons had been abused in courts of law in ways redolent of the customs of livery and maintenance.

The statutory monopoly of the nobility to maintain players was to be short-lived, as King James transferred the patronage of the leading companies to himself and to members of his family. Parliament returned to the subject of players in 1606, when it was enacted that blaspheming and swearing in 'stageplayes, Interludes, Maygames, Shewes and such like' were to be punished by a fine of £10. It was the first and indeed only time that parliament legislated on matters relating to the contents and performance of plays.[85] For the most part it had been concerned with problems of order in the commonwealth, and since 1576 increasingly with questions of conduct and civility.[86] Throughout this period the conditions of playing in the London playhouses by the established companies had been decided by the privy council and the City authorities. The regulation of the activities of the players was only incidentally the concern of parliament, but the narrowing of the base of patronage allowed by law over three decades can be traced in the history of the attempts to amend and to implement a single clause in the act of 1572.

---

[84] 1 James I, c. 7: *Statutes of the Realm*, IV, 1024–5.

[85] 3 James I, c. 21: 'An acte to restraine Abuses of Players'. *Statutes of the Realm*, IV, 1097.

[86] Joan Kent, 'Attitudes of Members of the House of Commons to the Regulation of "Personal Conduct" in Late Elizabethan and Early Stuart England', *Bulletin of the Institute of Historical Research*, 46 (1973), 41–71.

3   Cleanliness and godliness in early modern England

Keith Thomas

Wee can suffer no uncleannesse in our bodies, but incontinent we wash it away, neither can abide it in our garments, but without delay, we remedie it: yea, the smallest uncleannesse in the vessells that serve us for meate and drinke makes our very food loathsome unto us.

> *The Workes of Mr. William Cowper* (1529), 732.

Dear Johnny, . . . Keep thy hands and clothes clean; think of what I have sometimes said to thee, *All cleanly people are not good, but there are few good people but are cleanly* . . . Our bodies are the Temple of the Holy Ghost, therefore due honour is to be given to them . . . I would have thee always wear gloves, but [*i.e.* except] when it is not convenient.

> Elizabeth Walker, wife of the rector of Fyfield, Essex,
> to her grandson, 1689; [Anthony Walker],
> *The Holy Life of Mrs Elizabeth Walker* (1690), 291–2.

This world is all over dirty. Everywhere it is covered with that which tends to defile the feet of the traveller. Our streets are dirty and muddy, intimating that the world is full of that which tends to defile the soul, that worldly objects and worldly concerns and worldly company tend to pollute us . . . We can't go about the world but our feet will grow dirty. So in whatever sort of worldly business men do with their hands, their hands will grow dirty and will need washing from time to time, which is to represent the fulness of the world of pollution.

> Jonathan Edwards, *Images or Shadows of Divine Things*,
> ed. Perry Miller (New Haven, 1948), 94, 128–9.

In mid-nineteenth-century Britain it was widely assumed by reformers and moralists that physical cleanliness was the route to virtue as well as to health; and that soap was an instrument of moral piety. In Charles Kingsley's fantasy for children, *The Water-Babies* (1863), the grimy, little chimney sweep, Tom, only gets to heaven after he has been symbolically cleansed of his dirt in the cool, clear water of the river and learned that water babies have to 'work very hard and wash very hard' if they are to avoid the fate of the efts (or water newts), who, because they are 'stupid and dirty', lose out in the Darwinian struggle; their brains and bodies deteriorate; they 'hang about in dirty ponds, and live in the mud, and eat

worms, as they deserve to do'.[1] Assumptions of this kind underlay the
enormous investment in sewage, waste disposal and water supply which
was so conspicuous a feature of the Victorian age. In the eyes of many
sanitarian reformers the improvement of ventilation, drainage and
public health was a religious duty, a form of moral crusade.[2]

How far back did this association between cleanliness and godliness
go? And how important had it been in the early modern period as a
determinant of people's attitudes to their bodies, their clothes and their
living quarters? To answer those questions adequately would require
more substantial treatment than can be attempted here. But perhaps
even a superficial survey will help to draw attention to a minor strand in
that complex fabric of English Protestant life which the writings of
Patrick Collinson have so richly illuminated.

It is sometimes said that in the Tudor and Stuart periods people were
largely indifferent to cleanliness. Lawrence Stone tells us that 'this was a
time when personal and public hygiene was largely disregarded. Men and
women rarely, if ever, washed their bodies, and they lived in the constant
sight and smell of human faeces and human urine.'[3] These statements
are not altogether untrue, but they are distinctly misleading. For people
in the sixteenth century were not indifferent to these matters. They had
a conception of bodily cleanliness, but it was different from Professor
Stone's.[4] In particular, they did not usually think that it was necessary to
bath or to wash all over.[5] In polite society it was customary on getting up

---

[1] Charles Kingsley, *The Water-Babies* (1863), 347–9.
[2] See, e.g., Charles E. and Carroll S. Rosenberg, 'Pietism and the Origins of the
American Public Health Movement', *Journal of the History of Medicine*, 23 (1968);
Charles E. Rosenberg, 'Florence Nightingale on Contagion', in *Healing and History*, ed.
Charles E. Rosenberg (New York, 1979); Anthony S. Wohl, *Endangered Lives. Public
Health in Victorian Britain* (1983), 6–7.
[3] Lawrence Stone, *The Family, Sex and Marriage in England 1500–1800* (1977), 159.
[4] The essential starting-point is now Georges Vigarello, *Concepts of Cleanliness. Changing
Attitudes in France since the Middle Ages*, trans. Jean Birrell (Cambridge, 1988), though
the English story differs in some respects from the French one. Equally indispensable
are Richard L. Bushman and Claudia Bushman, 'The Early History of Cleanliness in
America', *Journal of American History*, 74 (1987–8), and the articles by Ginnie Smith
cited in notes 112 and 132. Though not concerned with personal cleanliness, Mark
Jenner's DPhil thesis, 'Early Modern Conceptions of "Cleanliness" and "Dirt" as
Reflected in the Environmental Regulation of London, *c.* 1530–*c.* 1700' (Oxford
University, 1991), raises the discussion of this whole area to a new level and its
publication is eagerly awaited.
[5] For representative advice on washing, see Andrew Boorde, *A Compendyous Regyment or
a Dyetary of Helth*, ed. F. J. Furnivall (Early English Text Soc., 1870), 248, 300; Sir
Thomas Elyot, *The Castel of Helthe* (1541; New York, 1937), fol. 93; Thomas Coghan,
The Haven of Health (1584), 6; Francis R. Packard *et al.*, *The School of Salernum* (New
York, 1920), 76; *Manners and Meals in Olden Time*, ed. Frederick J. Furnivall (Early
English Text Soc., 1868), 8, 22, 73, 81, 258, 316, 338; and, for practice, Lodewijck

in the morning to wash the hands and face, to clean the teeth and comb the hair, and at meal times to wash the hands (after eating as well as before, for until the later seventeenth century most people used a knife at the table but no fork). The feet might be washed weekly or monthly.[6] Opinion about the merits of washing the head varied. In 1653 the diarist John Evelyn resolved to do so once a year. But the most usual practice was summed up in the popular proverb: 'wash thy hands often, thy feete seldome, but thy head never'.[7]

As for bathing, that might be useful as a means of treating certain complaints, whether at home or in the mineral waters of a spa. But it seems to have been less usual as a method of keeping the body clean than it had been in the later Middle Ages.[8] Public baths had largely disappeared, partly in response to fears of plague and syphilis, partly because of their association with prostitution.[9] Total immersion in water, whether hot or cold, was regarded as a potentially dangerous procedure. 'If any will enter into the bath for cleannesse sake,' declared an almanac-maker in 1649, 'let the moon be in Libra or Pisces.'[10] Piped water was an expensive luxury. Swimming was recommended in Elizabethan times as the best way 'to purge the skin from all external pollutions or uncleanness'.[11] But quite a lot of people were drowned when trying to wash in rivers and ponds.[12] There are occasional records of baths being taken for hygienic reasons. Samuel Pepys mentions in 1665 that his wife went off to 'a hot-house to bath herself, after her long being within doors in the dirt, so that she now pretends to a resolution of being hereafter very clean

---

Huygens, *The English Journal*, ed. A. G. H. Bachrach and R. G. Collmer (Leiden, 1982), 40; Margaret Pelling, 'Appearance and Reality: Barber-Surgeons, the Body and Disease', in *London 1500–1700*, ed. A. L. Beier and Roger Finlay (1986), 93–4.

[6] The regulations for the royal household of William III and Mary envisage the weekly washing of the king's feet; *A Collection of Ordinances and Regulations for the Government of the Royal Household* (Soc. of Antiquaries, 1790), 386.

[7] *The Diary of John Evelyn*, ed. E. S. de Beer (Oxford, 1966), III, 53; William Vaughan, *Naturall and Artificial Directions for Health* (1602), sig. Ei^v.

[8] Cf. Thomas Wright, *A History of Domestic Manners and Sentiments in England during the Middle Ages* (1862), 259; *Manners and Meals*, ed. Furnivall, 182–3.

[9] This subject needs more investigation, but meanwhile see Vigarello, *Concepts of Cleanliness*, 21–37; Peter Thornton, *The Italian Renaissance Interior, 1400–1600* (1991), 319; and A. Cabanès, *La Vie aux Bains* (*Moeurs Intimes du Passé*, 2nd ser. (Paris, n.d. [1911]), 253–8); and for a medical opinion hostile to 'hot houses' in time of plague, T. Phayer, *The Regiment of Life* (1545), sig. Mviii.

[10] *Neve 1649. Mercurius Annalis* (1649), sig. B4^v.

[11] Nicholas Orme, *Early British Swimming 55 B.C.–A.D. 1719* (Exeter, 1983), 117.

[12] Pelling, 'Appearance and Reality', 93–4; Frank W. Jessup, *Sir Roger Twysden 1597–1672* (1965), 33. Two Presidents of Corpus Christi, Thomas Jackson and Edmund Staunton, narrowly escaped drowning in this way; Thomas Fowler, *The History of Corpus Christi College* (Oxford Hist. Soc., 1893), 185; Samuel Clarke, *The Lives of Sundry Eminent Persons* (1683), 160.

– how long it will hold, I can guess.' He was right, for there is no record of her ever doing it again.[13] Late medieval royal palaces had been equipped with bathrooms ('stews') and in the seventeenth century many aristocratic houses had their 'bathing rooms' or 'sweating closets'. Other households may have had tubs or basins, though the evidence is scanty.[14] Sir Hugh Plat, propounding 'a delicate stove to sweat in', remarked in 1609 that he knew that 'many gentlewomen, as well for the cleering of their skins as cleansing of their bodies, do now and then delight to sweat'.[15] In general, bathing was regarded either as a sophisticated form of sensual indulgence or as a medical procedure to be undertaken for some specific therapeutic purpose and only after consultation with a physician. Francis Bacon recalled a bishop who used to bath twice a day, but he 'was somewhat a delicate person'.[16]

The normal toilet was a dry one: brushing or rubbing down with towels and changing the clothes next to the skin. 'Every one that can will have plentiful changes both of linen and woollen garments; for if they have not, experience does shew that the excrements and breathings of the body will generate vermin.'[17] Even then the emphasis was on the linen which could be seen – cuffs and collars – rather than that which could not. The inventory of Dr Busby, the great seventeenth-century Headmaster of Westminster School, reveals that he had only two shirts ('shifts'), but no fewer than fifteen pairs of cuffs.[18] In the seventeenth century people changed their clothes with increasing frequency, but personal cleanliness was defined primarily in terms of visibility. It meant clean clothing rather than clean skin.

Yet by 1800 assumptions had changed. External appearance remained important and the introduction of cotton fabrics made clothes easier to wash. But clean clothes were no longer regarded as an acceptable substitute for clean bodies. Many persons now thought it also desirable to bath regularly or at least to wash themselves all over. During the eighteenth century the sales of commercially produced soap more than

13 *The Diary of Samuel Pepys*, ed. Robert Latham and William Matthews (1970–83), VI, 40.
14 L. F. Salzman, *Building in England down to 1540* (1952), 130, 276, 277, 397; *The History of the King's Works*, ed. H. M. Colvin (1963–82), I, 246, 550; II, 697, 926, 934, 974, 998, 1000; III, 317; IV, 27, 136, 310; V, 157, 269, 275, 412–13; Peter Thornton, *Seventeenth-Century Interior Decoration in England, France and Holland* (1978), 315–21; *Diary of John Evelyn*, ed. de Beer, IV, 118; *Diary of Samuel Pepys*, ed. Latham and Matthews, V, 161; Friends of the National Libraries, *Annual Report for 1988*, 29; Peter Earle, *The Making of the English Middle Class* (1989), 298–9.
15 Sir Hugh Plat, *Delightes for Ladies*, ed. G. E. and Kathleen Rosemary Fussell (1948), 97.
16 *The Works of Francis Bacon*, ed. James Spedding, Robert Leslie Ellis and Douglas Denon Heath (1857–9), vii, 130.
17 Thomas Tryon, *A Treatise of Cleanness* (1682), 6.
18 G. F. Russell Barker, *Memoir of Richard Busby* (1895), 123.

doubled.[19] What part, if any, did religious ideas play in bringing about this change? How far had washing come to be regarded as a moral duty as well as a practical convenience?

The link between cleanliness and religious observance went back a very long way. As an eighteenth-century writer remarked, 'a great part of the religion of the ancient heathen, as well as of the Jews, consisted in washing'.[20] For the Greeks, the Jews and the Muslims, water possessed a sacred, purifying role. By washing their hands or by total immersion, people prepared themselves for prayer and sacrifice. The Essenes, an extreme case, bathed three times a day. Such forms of cultic purification were to be found in many Eastern religions. Essentially, they were symbolic rituals of separation. But already in Old Testament times bodily cleanliness was coming to be associated with moral integrity. Clean hands went with a pure heart.[21]

Early Christianity, by contrast, stressed the need for internal purity of mind rather than the outward purification of the body. For Christ nothing was intrinsically unclean. All depended on the moral state of the person concerned: 'To eat with unwashen hands defileth not a man.' Only sin did that.[22] In medieval English the very term 'cleanliness' originally implied not a physical state but moral purity.[23] Some early Christians were notoriously dirty on principle. They showed their contempt for the flesh by shunning the luxury of warm baths and allowing their bodies to be tormented with lice.[24] In the twelfth century one religious writer elaborated upon the 'marvellous mystery' of smelly, greasy, matted and verminous beards, with saliva dripping down them, as a revelation of 'interior cleanness, that is divine virtue.[25] The indifference of holy men to their personal appearance indicated that their minds were on higher things than the comforts of hot water and clean clothes. For them, the odour of sanctity was no mere figure of speech.[26]

Yet though such extremes of Catholic asceticism would provide rich

---

[19] B. R. Mitchell, *Abstract of British Historical Statistics* (Cambridge, 1962), 265.

[20] C. Lucas, *An Essay on Waters* (1756), I, 152.

[21] Psalms 24.4; *The International Standard Bible Encyclopedia*, ed. Geoffrey W. Bromiley (Grand Rapids, 1979–88), *s.v.* 'clean and unclean'.

[22] Matthew 15.20. Cf. Mark 7.1–23; Romans 14.14; William Burkitt, *Expository Notes . . . on the New Testament* (1703), sig. Ff2.

[23] *Oxford English Dictionary*, *s.v.* 'cleanliness'; A. C. Spearing, 'Purity and Danger', *Essays in Criticism*, 30 (1980).

[24] William Edward Hartpole Lecky, *History of European Morals* (1913), II, 105, 108, 109–11; Johannes Zellinger, *Bad und Bäder in der altchristlichen Kirche* (Munich, 1928), ch. 3; J. N. D. Kelly, *Jerome* (1975), 93, 97, 274.

[25] Burchard de Bellevaux, *Apologia de Barbis*, in *Apologiae Duae*, ed. R. B. C. Huygens (*Corpus Christianorum Mediaevalis*, 62, Turnhout, 1985), 148, 159.

[26] For a fine example of this tradition in seventeenth-century Russia, see Y. I. Krizhanich's attack on Westerners whose 'carnal cleanliness' led them to wipe the floor

material for later Protestant satirists, they were never in the mainstream of medieval religion. The leaders of the early church condemned the sexual and luxurious associations of the Roman baths, but they were seldom against bathing for reasons of health or cleanliness.[27] The monastic orders indeed were notable for their rules about daily washing and periodic bathing.[28] Moreover, the rituals of the church preserved the ancient association between religious purity and physical cleanliness. Just as the Jews had to be ritually clean before engaging in prayer, so the Catholic priest ceremonially washed his hands when celebrating Mass and guests at formal banquets washed theirs before grace was said. Even in the eighteenth century, the Knights of the Bath were ceremonially bathed as part of their rite of initiation, 'to denote the inward purgation and future purity of the mind'.[29] Within the religious orders bathing customarily took place on the eves of great festivals, while foot-washing established itself in lay as well as ecclesiastical contexts as an activity appropriate for Saturday nights.[30] On Sundays clean clothes were conventionally worn to church. 'When we are to come to the house of God, we prepare our bodies, in regard of the company we come unto, we wash our selves, and change our apparell, and see that it be clean.'[31] In Francis Bacon's words, 'cleanness of body was ever esteemed to proceed from a due reverence to God'.[32] Physical cleanliness was not proof of spiritual purity, but it was something which might well accompany it.

Of course, ceremonial purification is not the same thing as hygienic cleansing: the water of baptism is not a substitute for washing the baby's hair. But the baptismal ceremony preserved the notion of sin as something that could be washed off. 'The blood of Christ washeth away sinne, as water doth bodily filthinesse', declared a Jacobean preacher.[33] Conversely, there was a longstanding metaphorical association between

---

after a guest had spat on it: 'it should not be asked who has the cleanest floor or bedding, but who has the clearest conscience'; W. H. Parker, *An Historical Geography of Russia* (1968), 106–7.

[27] Zellinger, *Bad und Bäder*; Cabanès, *La Vie aux Bains*, 130–1, 139–40, 151–3; Henry Chadwick, in *Monks, Hermits and the Ascetic Tradition*, ed. W. J. Sheils (Studies in Church History, 22, Oxford, 1985), 16.

[28] Zellinger, *Bad und Bäder*, ch. 4; Cabanès, *La Vie aux Bains*, 141–6; David Knowles, *The Monastic Order in England* (2nd edn, Cambridge, 1963), 465–6.

[29] John Anstis, *Observations Introductory to an Historical Essay upon the Knighthood of the Bath* (1725), 69 and *passim*.

[30] Zellinger, *Bad und Bäder*, 73ff.; Cabanès, *La Vie aux Bains*, 131–2, 140–1.

[31] John Angier, *An Helpe to Better Hearts* (1647), 220.

[32] And also 'to society, and to ourselves'; *Works of Francis Bacon*, ed. Spedding *et al.*, III, 377.

[33] Robert Horne, *Points of Instuction* [*sic*] *for the Ignorant in Life and Death* (1613), sig. A6.

dirt and evil. Heaven was sweet-smelling, but Hell was notoriously a foul and stinking place.[34] Filth was a symbol of sin.

The Reformation led to the closure of many holy wells and mineral baths because of their association with the worship of saints. It also coincided with the shutting down of public stews and bath houses. Yet in some ways it reinforced the traditional association between godliness and cleanliness. Protestant theologians firmly repudiated the old ascetic tradition, denouncing the austerities of the medieval saints and maintaining that it was 'intolerably ridiculous' to think that men could please God by being 'nasty and sordid' in their persons and 'unclean and filthy in their cloathing'.[35] They saw an analogy, not a polarity, between the physical and spiritual states of believers. Christianity, they said, required 'purity, not only of soul but [also of] body'.[36] The supposed dirtiness of monks and nuns ('a race of filthy animals', Edward Gibbon called them) was emphasised in much later Protestant polemic. By the nineteenth century it would become habitual for the English to assume that they, like other Protestant peoples, were infinitely cleaner than the inhabitants of Catholic countries.[37]

In Protestant thought the underlying assumption was that the body had been given to man by God and that it should therefore be kept free from pollution by mud, sweat and bodily emissions, 'the outwarde cleansing and washing away of the filth of our bodies, being the savour of sinne raigning in us'. It was 'a brutish thing' to have one's 'handes spotted, face besmeared, [and] countenance disfigured'.[38] Clean clothes symbolised moral purity: 'In fairest weedes are cleanest thoughts and purest minds.'[39]

This theme was taken up with enthusiasm by some of the Puritan wing of the Church of England. The Elizabethan Philip Stubbes reflected that, 'as the filthines and pollution of my bodie is washed and made clean by

---

[34] Cf. Piero Camporesi, *The Fear of Hell*, trans. Lucinda Byatt (Oxford, 1990), 15, 60–2 and ch. 5.

[35] John Edwards, *Sermons on Special Occasions and Subjects* (1698), 264.

[36] *Ibid.* Cf. Bishop Shaxton's contemptuous description of Catholic relics as 'stinking boots, mucky combs, ragged rochets, rotten girdles . . . filthy rags'; *Visitation Articles and Injunctions*, ed. Walter Howard Frere and William McClure Kennedy (1910), II, 59.

[37] Edward Gibbon, *The History of the Decline and Fall of the Roman Empire*, ed. J. B. Bury, III (5th edn, 1912), 208; Arthur Dent, *The Ruine of Rome* (1603), 265; Martin Lister, *A Journey to Paris* (2nd edn, 1699), 19; Richard Ford, *Gatherings from Spain* (1846), 141–2; Hazlitt, 'The Plain Speaker', in *The Collected Works of William Hazlitt*, ed. A. R. Waller and Arnold Glover (1902–6), III, 169, 170, 176–7; George Gilfillan, in *The Poetical Works of William Lisle Bowles* (Edinburgh, 1855), II, viii ('Foreigners were then as they are still, more depraved in morals and filthier in personal habits than we').

[38] [Edward Topsell], *The Reward of Religion* (1596), 162.

[39] *Records of Early English Drama. Norwich 1540–1642*, ed. David Galloway (1984), 314.

the element of water; so is my bodie and soule purified and washed from the spots and blemishes of sin, by the precious blood of Jesus Christ . . . This washing putteth me in remembrance of my baptism.'[40] Edward Topsell agreed that God required 'the outwarde cleansing and washing away of the filth of our bodies, being the savour of sinne raigning in us'.[41] Noting that the Jews had required priests and people to wash before drawing near to God, the Jacobean Richard Bernard concluded that 'God required of his people cleanlinesse. Our Christian profession is pure and holy, which outward cleannes well befitteth, and seeing it is of good report, we are to observe it.'[42] Since godly Protestants were encouraged to think of themselves as in the sight of God at all times, not just when they went to church, it followed that they should always be presentable. The nonconforming divine, John Angier, liked to see his flock neat and clean: 'he shamed some out of their slovenliness with friendly rebukes'.[43]

It was partly because of the importance that puritanical moralists attached to physical cleanliness that they were so hostile to the use of perfumes, powders and other cosmetics, which they saw, not just as an interference with God's handiwork, but as an undesirable alternative to washing.[44] They were against men's long hair for the same reason, stressing that, 'without diligent care', long hair would become 'a fit harbour for lice and vermin'. (They were particularly unimpressed by the example of the native Irish, who had very long hair, which they used as a napkin for wiping their hands after eating.)[45]

During the Interregnum some sectaries revived the early Christian ascetic tradition of indifference to the body. In 1659 Solomon Eccles burst stark naked into Aldermanbury church, 'and not only so, but he was shamefully beshit, so that none could lay hands on him'. A Ranter

---

[40] Philip Stubbes, 'A Perfect Pathway to Felicitie', in *Philip Stubbes's Anatomy of the Abuses in England*, ed. Frederick J. Furnivall (1877–9), 215.

[41] [Topsell], *The Reward of Religion*, 162.

[42] Richard Bernard, *Ruth's Recompence* (1628), 255.

[43] *Oliver Heywood's Life of John Angier*, ed. Ernest Axon (Chetham Soc., 1937), 84.

[44] Thomas Tuke, *A Treatise against Painting and Tincturing* (1616), sigs. B3ᵛ–4; Samuel Wesley, *Poems on Several Occasions*, ed. James Nichols (1862), 545 ('in self-defence, they stench to stench oppose'). The Scottish Catholic, John Leslie, contrasted English 'cleannes by washing' with French and Spanish 'unsavery painting'; *A Treatise of Treasons against Q. Elizabeth* (1572), fol. 144.

[45] Thomas Hall, *The Loathsomenesse of Long Haire* (1654), 47; J[ohn] B[ulwer], *Anthropometamorphosis* (1653), 59; Vaughan, *Naturall and Artificial Directions*, sig. Eii. The parliamentarian Col. Hutchinson offended the godly by his long hair, 'curling into loose great rings at the ends', but his wife stresses that he was careful to keep it clean; *Memoirs of the Life of Colonel Hutchinson Written by his Widow Lucy* (Everyman's Library, n.d.), 18, 96.

named Nathaniel 'pretended to be a sign of Presbyterian ministry, that as he did stink in the nostrils of people, so should they; for he went always beshit, for he was called *Shitten Nat*; he eat his own dung, and stank that none would come nigh him'.[46] After this early, enthusiastic stage, however, the Quakers concentrated on avoiding 'the defilements and spots of the world'.[47] Believing that, when 'the inside would be made clean, . . . then the outside would be made clean also',[48] they became celebrated for the neatness and cleanliness of their dress and appearance. In York the Friends sent agents to their members' houses in 1697 to ensure 'that all things may be kept as clean as may be amongst us'.[49] The American Quaker, John Woolman, criticised the practice of dyeing clothes because it concealed the dirt: 'Real cleanliness becometh a holy people', he declared; 'hiding that which is not clean by coloring our garments seems contrary to the sweetness of sincerity.'[50] When William Cobbett visited America in 1818, he noted that 'the Philadelphians are cleanly, a quality which they owe chiefly to the Quakers'. In Philadelphia gaol the prisoners were required to wash daily and to bath in summer because 'cleanliness is connected with health, and health with morals'. Charles Lamb wrote in 1821 that

The very garments of a Quaker seem incapable of receiving a soil; and cleanliness in them to be something more than the absence of the contrary. Every Quakeress is a lily; and when they come up in bands to their Whitsun conferences, whitening the easterly streets of the metropolis, from all parts of the United Kingdom, they show like troops of the Shining Ones.[51]

But it was not only Quakers and Puritans who linked cleanliness and godliness. George Herbert, the Anglican poet, urged his reader to

Affect in all things about thee cleanliness,
. . .
Let thy minde's sweetnesse have his operation
Upon thy body, clothes, and habitation.

---

[46] Lodowick Muggleton, *A Looking-Glass for George Fox* (reprinted 1756), 100.
[47] Arnold Lloyd, *Quaker Social History 1669–1738* (1950), 70.
[48] William C. Braithwaite, *The Second Period of Quakerism* (1919), 505.
[49] David Scott, *Quakerism in York, 1650–1720* (Borthwick Papers 80, York, 1991), 36 n. 115.
[50] *The Journal of John Woolman*, with introduction by Frederick B. Tolles (Secaucus, N.J., 1961), 220. Perhaps for similar reasons, he was also against 'the wearing more clothes in summer than are needful'; Amelia Mott Gummere, *The Quaker. A Study in Costume* (New York, 1901; 1966), 51.
[51] William Cobbett, *A Year's Residence in America* (Abbey Classics, n.d.), 22; Thomas Clarkson, *A Portraiture of Quakerism* (3rd edn, 1807), I, 211; Charles Lamb, 'A Quakers' Meeting', *Essays of Elia* (World's Classics edn, 1901), 68.

Herbert stressed that the country parson's clothes should be 'clean, without spots, or dust or smell; the purity of his mind breaking out, and dilating itself even to his body, clothes and habitation'.[52]

Even earlier, the Jesuit martyr, Robert Southwell, declared that the rooms of a house should be 'kept clean and handsome' because 'God is delighted in cleanness, both bodily and ghostly, and detesteth sluttish-ness as a thing which he permitteth as a punishment of sin and one of the scourges of hell'.[53] An unknown Catholic ballad-writer sang of Jerusalem that

> Within thy gates nothing doeth come
> that is not passinge cleane;
> Noe spider's web, noe durt, noe dust,
> noe filthe may there be seene.[54]

Since the association between bodily and spiritual purity was an ancient theme in Judaeo-Christian thought, it is not surprising that cleanliness should have been linked to godliness in several distinct religious milieux in early modern England. Religious justifications for physical cleanliness long antedate 1786, the year when the founder of Methodism gave a new proverb to the English language. In a sermon on dress, John Wesley declared that 'Slovenliness is no part of religion . . . "Cleanliness is indeed next to godliness." '[55] This was a theme which Wesley had developed on earlier occasions. Not only did his hymns encourage Methodists to seek to be washed 'white as snow' in Jesus' 'cleansing blood', but in 1769 he urged them to 'take pattern by the Quakers': 'avoid all nastiness, dirt, slovenliness, both in your person, clothes, house and all about you. Do not stink above ground . . . Clean yourselves of lice . . . Do not cut off your hair, but clean it, and keep it clean.'[56] Wesley also attached importance to the availability of adequate privies for visiting speakers: 'I particularly desire wherever you have preaching – namely, that there may be a little house. Let this be got without delay. Wherever it is not, let none expect to see me.'[57]

---

[52] 'The Church-Porch', in *The Poems of George Herbert* (World's Classics, 2nd edn, 1961), 17; 'A Priest to the Temple', in *The Remains of . . . George Herbert* (1836), 7.

[53] Robert Southwell, S.J., *Two Letters and Short Rules of a Good Life*, ed. Nancy Pollard Brown (Charlottesville, 1973), 43–4.

[54] 'Hierusalem, my happie home', in *Old English Ballads 1553–1625*, ed. Hyder E. Rollins (Cambridge, 1920), 166.

[55] *The Works of John Wesley*, III: *Sermons iii (71–114)*, ed. Albert C. Outler (Nashville, 1986), 249 (sermon 88), and again at 392 (sermon 98, 1786).

[56] *Hymns and Spiritual Songs* (3rd edn, 1754), 12, 17, 62, 76; *The Letters of John Wesley*, ed. John Telford (1931), v, 133. His brother Samuel also extolled 'constant, cheerful cleanliness'; *Poems on Several Occasions* (1862), 653.

[57] *Letters of Wesley*, ed. Telford, v, 134.

Yet Wesley did not claim to have coined the phrase about cleanliness being next to godliness. On the contrary, he attributed it to 'a pious man'.[58] Who was that 'pious man'? He did not say and no one subsequently has been able to find out. The latest editor of Wesley's works suggests that it might have been one of the ancient Jewish Midrash commentators. The evidence for this attribution is rather slight.[59] But it would not have been all that surprising if the ancient association between physical cleanliness and ritual purity had resurfaced in Hanoverian England.

So religious pressures for cleanliness undoubtedly existed. Yet they were not a notably conspicuous element in Protestant teaching and they certainly cannot be given sole credit for bringing about a change in people's personal habits. For most of these moralising injunctions related primarily to visible cleanliness, particularly clean clothes and clean houses. The Puritans and Quakers said very little about the desirability of washing all over. In the early modern period religious teaching may have helped to make people more conscious of the need to clean their visible parts, but it did less to suggest that bodily cleanliness was more than a matter of visibility.

Moreover, although religious writers urged people to be clean, many of them stressed that they should not be *too* clean. They shared the widespread notion that there was something effeminate and undesirable about excessive cleanliness. The Puritan William Perkins noted that what some called 'cleanliness' was really a facade for personal pride and vanity.[60] His colleague Richard Bernard explained that, though it was bad to be 'sluttish' and 'nasty', it was also wrong to 'spend too much time in trimming, washing and starching', so as to be 'curiously neate': the goal, agreed John Dury, should be 'cleanliness without curiosity'.[61] Isaac Watts urged children to wash their hands and faces, and to keep their clothes clean, but he also thought that some children took cleanliness too far and were 'foolishly nice'.[62] When in 1662 the godly Richard Baxter married Margaret Charlton, who came from a gentry family, socially rather above him, he was disconcerted by having to adapt to higher standards: 'I had been bred among plain, mean people, and I thought

[58] *Sermons iii (71–114)*, ed. Outler, 392.
[59] *Ibid.*, 249 n. 6 and 392 n. 29. The passage in Rabbi Phinehas ben Yair's commentary on the Song of Songs (*Midrash Rabbah*, i, i, 9) does not seem very close.
[60] *The Workes of . . . William Perkins* (Cambridge, 1608–9), I, 545; repeated by Robert Abbot, *Milk for Babes* (1646), 254.
[61] Bernard, *Ruth's Recompence*, 255; John Dury, *The Reformed School* (n.d. [1650]), 31.
[62] Isaac Watts, *Catechisms* (2nd edn, 1730), 187 (kindly shown me by Dr Ian Green). Cf. *Tudor School-Boy Life. The Dialogues of Juan Luis Vives*, trans. Foster Watson (1908), 47.

that so much washing of stairs and rooms, to keep them as clean as their trenchers and dishes and so much ado about cleanliness and trifles, was a sinful curiosity, and expense of servants' time.' In his view, the drive to hyper-cleanliness in the household used up time which would have been better spent reading some good book.[63]

All religious teachers agreed that it was wrong to put the cleanliness of the body above the welfare of the soul. Bathing, particularly in warm water, long retained undesirable associations with decadent Romans, brothels and sexuality;[64] for similar reasons the puritanical British refused to accept the French *bidet* when it became popular in the eighteenth century.[65] In the nineteenth century George Eliot, describing the dirty cottages and children of the Midland villages, remarked that 'pious Dissenting women . . . thought that salvation depended chiefly on predestination, and not at all on cleanliness'.[66]

The example of Protestant Scotland reminds us that godliness was no guarantee of cleanliness. Most English travellers who went north of the Tweed in the seventeenth and eighteenth centuries came back with lurid reports of the extreme dirtiness of Scottish living conditions and people. Arrangements in Edinburgh for the disposal of human excrement were notoriously inadequate and the inhabitants were said to live 'buried in filth'.[67] Samuel Pepys remarked that 'so universal a rooted nastiness hangs about the person of every Scot (man and woman), that renders the finest show that they can make nauseous, even among those of the first quality'. One eighteenth-century wit observed that 'It is the ostentation of a Scotsman to let the world know he has a handkerchief.' Another

---

63 *Richard Baxter and Margaret Charlton*, ed. John T. Wilkinson (1928), 137. Cf. *The Practical Works of Richard Baxter* (1707), 1.230.

64 Seneca, *Epistulae Morales*, lxxxvi; George Hakewill, *An Apologie* (1630), 398, 400.

65 Jean-Pierre Goubert, *The Conquest of Water*, trans. Andrew Wilson (1986), 88–90. Cf. Stone, *The Family, Sex and Marriage*, 486.

66 George Eliot, *Felix Holt, the Radical* (1866), ed. Fred C. Thomson (Oxford, 1980), 7. Cf. Havelock Ellis's picture of a pious young woman, sitting in her undrained hovel, 'with rings of dirt about her neck, turning over with dirty hands Brown's Dictionary to see whether the newly elected minister was "sound" in his doctrine'; *The Nineteenth Century* (1900), 141–2.

67 *An American Quaker in the British Isles. The Travel Journals of Jabez Maud Fisher, 1775–1779*, ed. Kenneth Morgan (British Academy, 1992), 58; Cf. HMC, *Report on Manuscripts in Various Collections*, VII (1914), 390–1, 394; *Epistolary Curiosities*, ed. Rebecca Warner (1818), I, 24; CSPD 1639, 341; *Letters and Papers Illustrating the Relations between Charles the Second and Scotland*, ed. Samuel Rawson Gardiner (Scottish Hist. Soc., 1894), 136–7; Sir Anthony Weldon, 'A Perfect Description of the People and Country of Scotland', in *Secret History of the Court of James the First* (Edinburgh, 1811), II, 75–6, 87–8; [Thomas Kirke], *A Modern Account of Scotland* (1679), 4, 6, 10; Joseph Taylor, *A Journey to Edenborough*, ed. William Cowan (Edinburgh, 1903), 134–5.

remarked that, if you set a louse on the table, it would head northwards for its mother country.[68] When all allowance has been made for ethnic stereotyping, it is hard not to conclude that the early modern Scottish people, however godly, were not particularly cleanly.

But the most important reason for discounting the influence of religion unaccompanied by other forces is that if we examine the preachers' arguments in favour of cleanliness we find that they were strongly coloured by more secular considerations. For when Richard Bernard urged the importance of physical cleanliness, he explained that to be cleanly was not just pleasing to God. It was also 'healthfull to us' and 'delightsome to others'. When Isaac Watts commended 'a degree of cleanliness' he justified it as 'necessary to my own health as well as to keep my clothes from spoiling and to render my company agreeable and inoffensive to others'. When John Wesley urged people to keep their clothes clean, he went on to say that cleanliness was 'more conducive to health than is generally consider'd'. And when the author of a nineteenth-century etiquette book observed that cleanliness was akin to godliness, he added that care of the person was the beginning of good manners.[69] So there were two non-religious reasons for cleanliness: manners and health.

First, good manners. The sixteenth and seventeenth centuries saw a great proliferation of books on good behaviour, so-called 'civility'. There were various reasons for this. There was the Renaissance rediscovery of classical Roman codes of elegance and urbanity, disseminated in translations of prescriptive works by Italian and French writers. There was the political importance of the royal court, at which it was necessary to cultivate the art of pleasing others in order to get on. There was the growth of trade, the greater complexity of society and the mounting pressure of population, each of which required greater self-discipline than those attempting to live and work together harmoniously. All these circumstances encouraged men and women to be more conscious of the effect which their bodily comportment could have on others.[70]

---

[68] *The Letters and Second Diary of Samuel Pepys*, ed. R. G. Howarth (1933), 139; Horace Bleackley, *Life of John Wilkes* (1917), 323; *The English Travels of Sir John Percival and William Byrd II*, ed. Mark R. Wenger (Columbia, 1989), 187.

[69] Bernard, *Ruth's Recompence*, 255; Watts, *Catechisms*, 187; John Wesley, 'Advice to the People Called Methodists', in *Sermons on Several Occasions* (Bristol, 1760), 149; T. L. Nichols, *Behaviour* (1874), 16.

[70] Norbert Elias, *The Civilizing Process. The History of Manners*, trans. Edmund Jephcott (New York, 1978); Anna Clare Bryson, 'Concepts of Civility in England *c.* 1560–1685' (Oxford University DPhil thesis, 1984); Fenela Ann Childs, 'Prescriptions for Manners in English Courtesy Literature, 1690–1760, and their Social Implications' (Oxford University DPhil thesis, 1984).

Prominent in this new discourse of civility was the stress on personal cleanliness, not for hygienic reasons, but in order to avoid offending others by unpleasant sights or smells. It was this which gave bodily cleanliness a place among the 'small morals' or even, as the marquis of Halifax believed, made it part of morality itself.[71] Though a Scot, the philosopher David Hume was sure that cleanliness was a virtue because 'it naturally renders us agreeable . . . , and is a very considerable source of love and affection'. Negligence in this area was a fault because of 'the uneasy sensations which it excites in others'.[72] This theme ran through scores of manuals on good behaviour, from Erasmus' early sixteenth-century treatise, advising small boys to keep their teeth and nails clean, to Lord Chesterfield's letters to his son in the mid-eighteenth century, which stressed that a particular attention to cleanliness was 'but common decency, in order not to offend people's eyes and noses'. 'In your person you must be accurately clean; and your teeth, hands, and nails should be superlatively so.'[73]

School regulations accordingly required pupils to arrive with their faces washed, their hair combed and their shoes clean.[74] The young Philip Sidney was urged by his father to 'delight to be cleanly, as well in all parts of your body as in your garments; it shall make you grateful in each company – and otherwise loathsome'; while the great scientist, Robert Boyle, when a boy at Eton, was praised by his tutor in a letter to his father for his 'neatnes in aparelling, kembing and washing'.[75] Well-to-do women spent much time on lotions designed to make their faces and teeth white and their breath sweet-smelling.[76]

Yet the ideal of cleanliness set out in this literature of civility had some obvious limitations. First, it was much concerned with the need to show deference and respect to one's social superiors. The rules of the royal

---

[71] *The Works of George Savile, Marquis of Halifax*, ed. Mark N. Brown (Oxford, 1989), III, 71.

[72] David Hume, *A Treatise of Human Nature* (1739–40) (Everyman's Library, 1911), II, 304.

[73] Erasmus, *De Civilitate Morum Puerilium*, trans. Robert Whitsinton (1540), sigs. A7ᵛ–8, B3ᵛ; *The Letters of Lord Chesterfield to his Son*, ed. Charles Strachey (1901), I, 343; II, 87 (also I, 173, 243, 332).

[74] E.g. Foster Watson, *The English Grammar Schools to 1660* (1908; 1968), 133, 135, 136; John Sargeaunt, *Annals of Westminster School* (1898), 37; Sir H. C. Maxwell Lyte, *A History of Eton College* (4th edn, 1911), 139, 140; Edward Coote, *The English Schoole-Master* (1627), 57; *Samuel Hartlib and the Advancement of Learning*, ed. Charles Webster (Cambridge, 1970), 119, 149; Charles Hoole, *A New Discovery of the Old Art of Teaching Schoole* (1660), 33–4.

[75] H. R. Fox Bourne, *Sir Philip Sydney* (1891), 28–9; *The Lismore Papers*, ed. Alexander B. Grosart, 2nd ser., 3 (1888), 223.

[76] Carroll Camden, *The Elizabethan Woman* (1952), ch. 7; Neville Williams, *Powder and Paint* (1957).

court stressed that persons attending the king should be especially clean and neat, just as servants were warned to direct their stinking breath away from their masters.[77] At school, children 'of the poorer sort' were forbidden to be 'sordidly or uncleanly habited or kept, to the offence of others of better quality'; a young scholar was expected to behave 'in such a civill manner that he may be a companion for his betters'.[78] People washed and dressed up when they went to church because they thought they owed God the same kind of outward reverence which they displayed towards their social superiors. During the rest of the week, however, bodily cleanliness was a form of respect not to God but to man.

Secondly, there was a clear implication that cleanliness was a form of social distinction by which people staked out a claim to respect and preferential treatment. It was an attribute of higher social status. Just as a gentleman should 'passe and excell others in gentleness and sobre lyfe', it was said, 'so oughte he also in civilitie of outwarde thinges, as in cleane wearing of his garmentes, being therein an example to others of cleanelynes'.[79] Cleanliness was an important social marker, distinguishing the elite from their inferiors. In the late 1530s Lady Lisle's son, James Basset, was sent to the College of Navarre in Paris, where the Rector sought 'to bring him up in cleanliness and good manners pertaining to a gentleman'.[80] Lord Chesterfield told his son two centuries later that 'nothing looks more ordinary, vulgar, and illiberal than dirty hands, and ugly, uneven, and ragged nails'; the ends of the nails should be kept 'smooth and clean, not tipped with black as the ordinary people's always are'.[81] A late Victorian commentator recalled that the custom of washing all over every day had taken root 'because it became one of the signs of class. It was adopted as one of the habits of a gentleman, and afterwards spread rather lower.'[82] As Somerset Maugham would observe, the morning tub had grown into a decisive social shibboleth.[83]

Thirdly, all the emphasis in the literature of civility was on appearance rather than reality. Hence the ostentatious display of white collar and cuffs and the incessant changes of clothing, however dirty the body beneath. 'Our nicer gentlemen' changed their shirts twice a day, Defoe

---

[77] N.W., *The Refin'd Courtier* (1663), 48; *Manners and Meals*, ed. Furnivall, 136.
[78] Watson, *The English Grammar Schools to 1660*, 136; Samuel Harmar, *Vox Populi* (1642), sig. B2. Cf. Bryson, 'Concepts of Civility', 98–9.
[79] *The Institution of a Gentleman* (1555), sig. Iv.
[80] *The Lisle Letters*, ed. Muriel St Clare Byrne (1981), IV, 498.
[81] *Letters of Lord Chesterfield*, ed. Strachey, II, 88.
[82] Philip Gilbert Hamerton, *French and English. A Comparison* (1889), 255.
[83] Cited by George Orwell, *The Road to Wigan Pier* (1959), 131.

tells us in the 1720s.[84] Hence also the concern to eliminate unpleasant smells, whether of dirty bodies or bad breath, by the extensive use of perfumes, toothpastes and cosmetics. One Jacobean writer advised those who had been eating onions to take away the smell by drinking beer, an interesting reversal of modern practice.[85] In later seventeenth-century houses there was much concern to separate the different smells of cooking, young children and bodily waste. 'The affectation of cleanness', wrote Roger North in 1698, 'hath introduc't much variety of rooms, which the ancients had no occasion for, who cared not for exquisite neatness.'[86]

The main object was to avoid making a bad impression upon visitors or superiors. That was why housewives devoted so much attention to polishing and cleaning the contemporary equivalent of the front room.[87] It was also why even the most elegant gentlemen could be extremely filthy once they were off-stage. When Charles II's courtiers stayed in Oxford, 'they were neat and gay in their apparell, yet they were very nasty and beastly, leaving at their departure their excrements in every corner, in chimneys, studies, colehouses [and] cellers'.[88] In the nineteenth century, an Indian visitor thought that Hindu standards of cleanliness were much higher than those of the British, because in England all the emphasis was laid on externals; unlike the Hindus, an Englishman thought it better not to wash his mouth at all than to do so in public.[89] The laws of civility also required higher standards of cleanliness for women than for men. As the manuals explained, 'Cleanliness in women doth please men wel: and husbands do oftentimes abhorre their wives for

[84] Daniel Defoe, *The Complete English Tradesman* (Oxford, 1841), II, 232. Margaret Cavendish boasted that her husband, the duke of Newcastle, changed once a day and also whenever he took exercise or became overheated; *The Life of... William Cavendish, Duke of Newcastle* (Everyman's Library, n.d.), 141. For more on shirt changing, *Boswell's Life of Johnson*, ed. George Birkbeck Hill, rev. L. F. Powell, V (2nd edn, Oxford, 1964), 60.

[85] Char[les] Butler, *The Feminine Monarchie* (Oxford, 1608), sig. A7ᵛ.

[86] *Of Building. Roger North's Writings on Architecture*, ed. Howard Colvin and John Newman (Oxford, 1981), 126. On the rebuilding of Hampton Court in the 1660s to avoid smells, see *History of the King's Works*, ed. Colvin, IV (2), 141. For the growth of spatial specialisation, see Ursula Priestley and P. J. Corfield, 'Rooms and Room Use in Norwich Housing, 1580–1730', *Post-Medieval Archaeology*, 16 (1982); and Peter Clark, *The English Alehouse* (1983), 197.

[87] On the emergence of the parlour, see Frank E. Brown, 'Continuity and Change in the Urban House: Developments in Domestic Space Organisation in Seventeenth-Century London', *Comparative Studies in Society and History*, 28 (1986).

[88] *The Life and Times of Anthony Wood*, ed. Andrew Clark (Oxford Hist. Soc., 1891–1900), II, 98.

[89] Tapan Raychaudhuri, *Europe Reconsidered. Perceptions of the West in Nineteenth Century Bengal* (Delhi, 1988), 304.

sluttishe apparell.' However, 'this kind of care is not seemly but among women . . . a man that is too curious is worse then he that is too careless'. Ladies, themselves, allegedly often preferred a man 'all sunburnt, and covered with sweat and dust, that is returned from the war, or from hunting'.[90]

Yet overall the requirements of civility and good manners were a powerful incentive to external personal cleanliness, luring the socially ambitious and shaming the recalcitrant. For it was a disgrace to be lousy; and employment was more readily available to those who were neatly turned out.[91] Along with these social pressures, however, there were also medical considerations. Between the sixteenth and nineteenth centuries it was widely held that bubonic plague and other diseases were caused by the corruption of the air, partly through the uncontrollable influence of the heavens, but primarily by noxious exhalations from stagnant water, decaying rubbish, dead animals, human excrement and other forms of putrefying matter. This was the concept of miasma. The most obvious evidence of miasma was a bad smell; and it was axiomatic that the cause of bad smells was dirt. Dunghills, privies, slaughter-houses, stagnant gutters and filthy houses all gave off unpleasant odours and were therefore regarded with suspicion, particularly during epidemics, when local authorities reacted with a vigorous campaign of street cleaning and urban purification.[92] Even at normal times, householders were expected to sweep the streets daily in front of their dwellings and arrangements were made for their waste to be carried away.[93] It was accepted that disease came from 'living uncleanly and sluttishly' and that cleanliness was 'a special preservative against infection'.[94] Early modern towns devoted much more energy to keeping the urban environment clean than is generally appreciated. If they did not succeed, it was because of inadequate technology for water supply and waste disposal, not because of indifference.

A similar concern to avoid smells and putrefaction for reasons of health

---

[90] Nicholas Faret, *The Honest Man: Or, the Art to Please in Court*, trans. E[dward] G[rimestone] (1634), 357, 359–60; Lewes Lavaterus, *The Book of Ruth Expounded*, trans. Ephraim Pagitt (1586), fol. 92ᵛ.

[91] Thomas Mouffet, *The Theater of Insects*, in Edward Topsell, *The History of Four-Footed Beasts*, revised by J[ohn] R[owland] (1658), 1102.

[92] Paul Slack, *The Impact of Plague in Tudor and Stuart England* (1985), 45; and, more generally, Oswei Temkin, 'An Historical Analysis of the Concept of Infection', in his *The Double Face of Janus* (1977).

[93] J. H. Thomas, *Town Government in the Sixteenth Century* (1933), ch. 6. There is a penetrating analysis in Jenner, 'Early Modern English Conceptions of "Cleanliness" and "Dirt"'.

[94] Slack, *Impact of Plague*, 27; *Cyvile and Uncyvile Life* (1579), sig. Giiᵛ.

was shown aboard ship, in military camps, in schools and similar institutions, all of which had their rules about sweeping, cleaning and the disposal of waste. Within the household, there was much stress on the desirability of keeping kitchens and dairies spotless and making sure that pans, drinking vessels and bed linen were clean and sweet. Books on household management emphasised that it was the woman's duty to 'keep all at home neat and cleane', and that 'cleanness in houses, especially in beds', was 'a great preserver of health'. 'Cleanlinesse be such an ornament to a housewife,' thought Gervase Markham, 'that if shee want any part thereof, shee loseth both that and all good names else.'[95] The early Hanoverian physician, George Cheyne, ruled that, 'in order to preserve their health', every one should strive for 'cleanness and sweetness in their houses, cloaths, and furniture'.[96] Poverty and inadequate technology meant that this goal was not always achieved, but the hygienic value of a sweet-smelling environment was widely accepted. 'Most people', observed Thomas Tryon in 1682, 'take care that their furnitures are daily brushed and rubbed, and their very floors washed, as though they were to eat their food on them.'[97] The amount of energy, particularly female energy, which in the early modern period went into scrubbing floors, boiling clothes, scouring pots and pans and polishing furniture is incalculable.[98]

The medical arguments for keeping the body clean were at first less conspicuous than those for environmental cleanliness. Tudor doctors stressed that 'the cutting of the heer, and the paring of the nailes, cleane keping of the eares and teethe, be not onely thynges comely and honest, but also holsome rules of phisick'.[99] Washing the mouth warded off toothache, while keeping the head clean was an obvious protection against lice. In the mid-eighteenth century Chesterfield told his son that 'a thorough cleanliness in your person is . . . necessary for your health'. Wesley agreed: 'Cleanliness . . . is . . . more conducive to health, than is generally considered.'[100]

[95] Sir Thomas Smith, *De Republica Anglorum*, ed. Mary Dewar (Cambridge, 1982), 58; Tryon, *A Treatise of Cleanness*, 5; G[ervase] M[arkham], *The English House-Wife* (1631), 196. Cf. *The Arundel Harington Manuscript of Tudor Poetry*, ed. Ruth Hughey (Columbus, 1960), II, 30; [Thomas Salter], *A Mirrhor Mete for all Mothers, Matrones, and Maidens* (1579), sig. cviij.

[96] George Cheyne, *An Essay of Health and Long Life* (6th edn, Dublin, 1725), 9.

[97] Tryon, *Treatise of Cleanness*, 6.

[98] Earle, *Making of the English Middle Class*, 222; *Kalm's Account of his Visit to England . . . in 1748*, trans. Joseph Lucas (1892), 12–13, 62, 326–7; Mary Collier, *The Woman's Labour* (1739), 12–16.

[99] William Bulleyn, *A Newe Booke Entituled the Government of Healthe* (1558), fol. xxxiii.

[100] *Letters of the Lord Chesterfield*, ed. Strachey, I, 343 (and II, 87); Wesley, *Sermons on Several Occasions*, 149.

But doctors moved only slowly to the view that people ought regularly to wash all over. There was a large literature on the medical value of baths, but total immersion still tended to be thought of as a form of treatment rather than as a routine method of keeping clean. Most Tudor and Stuart doctors regarded water not as a neutral substance, but as something dynamic and penetrating which could have a powerful effect upon the permeable body, for better or worse. Washing in cold water was a risky procedure which should not be embarked upon by those unused to it, while hot baths opened the pores and were notoriously debilitating.[101] Doctors were aware that in the ancient world and among the Turks bathing was 'as usual as eating and sleeping', but they pointed out that 'the Romans, going barelegged, and their waies dusty, had need of often washing', while the Turks, who slept in their clothes, would have been 'subiect to lice and wormes, if it were not for their often bathing'; besides, their diet was different.[102] Even so, Francis Bacon thought that the Romans had grown soft through their use of baths, while an English visitor to Turkey noted in 1667 that 'often bathing makes both men and women to decay betimes'.[103] So when Peter Chamberlen FRCP proposed to erect public bath houses in London in 1648, it is not surprising that the Royal College promptly vetoed the idea, on the grounds that they would be physically and morally harmful, 'effeminating bodies, and procuring infirmities, and . . . debauching the manners of the people'.[104] Physicians long continued to argue that 'the washing of the hands and face in cold water constantly without any respect to seasons or a consequence, is not an argument for equally serving the whole body'.[105]

But during the later seventeenth century medical opinion on the subject of bathing seems to have shifted; and public bath houses returned to London.[106] It is sometimes said that the reason for this was a growing understanding of the mechanism of perspiration, thanks particularly to the quantitative observations of the Italian physician Sanctorius (1561–1636).[107] As the volume of the bodily waste discharged invisibly through the skin came to be appreciated, washing seemed increasingly

---

[101] Vigarello, *Concepts of Cleanliness*, 9–17.
[102] *Works of Francis Bacon*, ed. Spedding *et al.*, II, 578; Edward Jorden, *A Discourse of Naturall Bathes* (1631), 2; *ibid.* (2nd edn, 1632), 3.
[103] *Works of Francis Bacon*, ed. Spedding *et al.*, II, 578; Sonia P. Anderson, *An English Consul in Turkey. Paul Rycaut at Smyrna, 1667–1678* (Oxford, 1989), 211. More generally, see Vigarello, *Concepts of Cleanliness*, 9–17.
[104] Peter Chamberlen, *A Paper Delivered . . . for Bathes and Bath-Stoves* (1648), 2.
[105] James Sedgwick, *A New Treatise on Liquors* (1775), 355.
[106] Bryant Lillywhite, *London Coffee Houses* (1963), 95–7.
[107] An English translation of his *Medicina Statica: Or, Rules of Health*, was published in 1676.

important as a means of ensuring that perspiration was not obstructed.[108] But the need to keep the pores open had been stressed in medical literature long before the publication of Sanctorius' studies[109] and the reasons for the new emphasis on this point remain unclear.

By 1700, however, there was emerging an influential school of medical writers who recommended baths as a form of personal hygiene. They did so in conscious opposition to the prevailing use of drugs by the chemical doctors, urging instead a return to classical ideas of a regimen of healthy living. Prominent in this regimen was regular bathing, which was portrayed as a necessity, both therapeutic and hygienic, a cure for innumerable diseases and a help to long life. The leader of this school of thought, Sir John Floyer, declared that if the English could only be brought to understand the value of a bath, they would all want to have one in their houses.[110]

During the course of the eighteenth century, most medical writers recommended that baths should be both hot and cold, according to the time of year and the constitution of the patient.[111] But though hot baths, whether of water or steam, had their supporters as a means of relaxing the body, opening the pores and assisting perspiration, the majority opinion favoured the more accessible and more invigorating tonic of a cold bath, which would harden the flesh, tone up the body and quicken the circulation. The influential physician, George Cheyne, observed in 1724 that 'the necessity of a free perspiration to the preservation of health is now known to every body and frequent washing the body in water cleanses the mouths of the perspiratory ducts from that glutinous foulness that is continually falling upon them'. He advised everyone who could 'to have a cold bath at their house to wash their bodies in' and 'constantly two or three times a week, summer and winter, to go into it'.[112]

The fashion for cold bathing did not necessarily reflect a desire to keep

---

108 See, e.g., Sir John Floyer, *An Enquiry into the Right Use and Abuses of the Cold, and Temperate Baths in England* (1697), sigs. b4ᵛ, C5; [Thomas Guidott], *An Apology for the Bath* (1705), 2; George Cheyne, *An Essay of the True Nature and Due Method of Treating the Gout* (7th edn, Dublin, 1725), 45; John Quinton, *A Treatise of Warm Bath Water* (Oxford, 1733), I, 46–8; C. Lucas, *An Essay on Waters* (1966), I, 202, 211.

109 E.g., Elyot, *Castel of Helthe*, fols. 46ᵛ, '45' (47).

110 Sir John Floyer, *Medicina Gerocomica* (1724), xiii–xiv.

111 E.g., Sedgwick, *New Treatise on Liquors*, ch. xvii; Lucas, *Essay on Waters*, I, 199–232; Richard Reece, *A Practical Dictionary of Domestic Medicine* (1808), *s.v.* 'baths'. Vigarello, *Concepts of Cleanliness*, chs. 7 and 8, charts parallel developments in France.

112 Cheyne, *Essay of Health and Long Life*, 55, 52–3. On the vogue for a cool regimen see Ginnie Smith, 'Prescribing the Rules of Health: Self-help and Advice in the Late Eighteenth Century', in *Patients and Practitioners*, ed. Roy Porter (Cambridge, 1985), and 'Physical Puritanism and Sanitary Science', in *Medical Fringe and Medical Orthodoxy*, ed. W. F. Bynum and Roy Porter (1987).

clean, for some of its advocates thought that the same effect could be achieved by bathing in cold air. But during the eighteenth century it became increasingly common for medical writers to stress the connection between good health and frequent washing, and to lament 'the shameless disuse of bathing, hot and cold, that prevales in our days'.[113] In his deeply influential *Domestic Medicine* (1769 and repeatedly reprinted), William Buchan stressed 'the continual discharge from our bodies by perspiration' and declared that 'few virtues were of more importance to society than real cleanliness'.[114] In polite society bathing became more fashionable at the very end of the century, when Beau Brummell, in deference to the new ideas, prohibited perfumes for men and recommended washing all over instead.[115] The slow change from cleanliness defined in terms of external appearance to cleanliness defined as the state of the body underneath was justified essentially in terms of health. When in the early nineteenth century the philosopher Jeremy Bentham came to examine the term 'cleanliness', he described it as 'the absence of practices by which disease or the apprehension of disease is produced'.[116] 'Without cleanliness', explained an early nineteenth-century tract for children, 'we could not enjoy health.'[117]

So it was considerations of health and civility which did most to propel the British people in the direction of more frequent and more thorough washing of their bodies. Of course, the change was slow: as late as 1801 a doctor declared that 'most men resident in London and many ladies, though accustomed to wash their hands and faces daily, neglect washing their bodies from year to year'.[118] Moreover, people's readiness to accept the change depended very much upon their social position. Long before the days of George Orwell, it was axiomatic that the lower classes were dirtier than their superiors and that they smelt more strongly.[119] They had fewer social aspirations and they could not afford

[113] Lucas, *Essay on Waters*, I, 202.

[114] William Buchan, *Domestic Medicine* (2nd edn, 1772), 124–31. Cf. James Hanway, *A Journal of Eight Days Journey* (2nd edn, 1757), II, 119–20; Smith, 'Prescribing the Rules of Health', 269–70.

[115] Captain Jesse, *The Life of George Brummell* (new edn, 1893), 47–8.

[116] Jeremy Bentham, *Deontology*, ed. Amnon Goldworth (Oxford, 1983), 358–9.

[117] Anonymous, *History of the Robins Designed for the Instruction of Children* (Dublin, 1821), I, 137.

[118] Robert Willan, cited in M. C. Buer, *Health, Wealth, and Population in the Early Days of the Industrial Revolution* (1926), 129.

[119] Brents Stirling, *The Populace in Shakespeare* (New York, 1949), 65–73, urges that this view was peculiar to the playwright. But cf. George Gascoigne, *The Steele Glas*, ed. John W. Cunliffe (Cambridge, 1910), 170; M. G. Smith, *Pastoral Discipline and the Church Courts: The Hexham Court 1680–1730* (Borthwick Papers, York, 1982), 38; Orwell, *Road to Wigan Pier*, 129–30.

frequent changes of clothes. Neither could they pay for expensive perfumes or for servants to boil and carry hot water for the laundry.[120] It is not surprising that in the 1690s a social observer discovered that the higher Londoners were socially, the oftener they changed their clothes and the more soap they consumed.[121] When the middle classes visited the cottages of the poor, they frequently recoiled because they found the smell intolerably 'noisome and offensive'.[122]

The poor were dirty primarily from necessity rather than choice. But there is evidence that they regarded some forms of cleanliness as objectionable affectations. A speaker in an Elizabethan dialogue noted that in the countryside, 'if any other gentlewoman bee more fine or delicate', 'shee is misliked among them, and called a cleane-fingered girle, as though that were a great ignomy'.[123] In the same way the dirt of the labourer was often perceived as a mark of masculine virility. A Tudor writer observed that 'plaine people in the countrey, as carters, threshers, ditchers, colliers and plowmen, use seldome tymes to washe their handes, as appereth by their filthynes, and as very fewe tymes combe their heads, as it is sene by floxe, neites, grese, fethers, strawe and suche like which hangeth in their heares.'[124] In popular belief dirt could be protective. Eighteenth-century doctors found themselves up against 'a vulgar notion, familiar only to common people, that a frequent change of linen has a tendency to weaken newborn children' by robbing them of 'nourishing juices'; and it was a long lasting notion that it was dangerous to wash a child's hair.[125] 'Dirty things', like lice and millipedes, were thought to have therapeutic value.[126] One medical practitioner lamented that 'the people in general seem to delight in stench and personal dirt and filth'; another remarked that 'the peasants in most countries seem to hold

---

[120] On the cost of piped water, see Jenner, 'Early Modern English Conceptions of "Cleanliness" and "Dirt"', 324.

[121] John Houghton, *A Collection for Improvement of Husbandry and Trade*, 133 (15 Feb. 1695).

[122] Clarke, *Lives of Sundry Eminent Persons*, 158; *The Journeys of Celia Fiennes*, ed. Christopher Morris (1947), 204; Daniel Defoe, *A Tour through England and Wales* (Everyman's Library, 1928), II, 63; Thomas Ruggles, *The History of the Poor* (1794), II, 289–90; Edmund Gosse, *Father and Son*, ed. James Hepburn (1974), 74–5.

[123] *Cyvile and Uncyvile Life*, sig. KI.

[124] Bulleyn, *A Newe Booke Entituled the Governement of Healthe*, fol. 'xxx' (xxxii).

[125] 'A Physician' [William Cadogan], *An Essay upon Nursing and the Management of Children* (1748), 12; Vaughan, *Naturall and Artificiall Directions*, sig. EI'; Michael Underwood, *A Treatise on the Disorders of Childhood* (1797), III (2nd pagination), 30.

[126] Charles E. Rosenberg, 'Medical Text and Social Context', *Bulletin of the History of Medicine*, 57 (1983), 30. Cf. Françoise Loux, *Le Jeune Enfant et Son Corps dans la Médecine Traditionnelle* (Paris, 1978), 201–5, and Françoise Loux and Philippe Richard, *Sagesses du Corps* (Paris, 1978), ch. ix.

cleanliness in a sort of contempt'.[127] 'The lower classes of most countries seem to be actually fond of dirt', sighed John Stuart Mill in 1874.[128]

It would be a long time before the new definition of personal cleanliness was readily embraced by the whole of the population. Nevertheless, it is clear that well before 1800 the attitudes of the upper and middle classes to washing all over had begun to change. The primary reasons appear to have been the changes in medical opinion which favoured regular bathing, and the changes in manners and fashion which made personal cleanliness increasingly essential to social acceptability.

Yet the influence of religious ideas should not be underrated. For the stress on the importance of physical health was itself a religious idea. As Richard Baxter explained, it was men's duty to keep their bodies in the condition 'fittest for the service of the soul'; disease was to be avoided because it 'hindered from the contemplation of heavenly things, and from the service of God'.[129] The quest for physical cleanliness sprang from a sense that the body was sacred and should be protected from the pollutions of the world. In 1744 the poet John Armstrong defended

> The warm ablution just enough to clear
> The sluices of the skin, enough to keep
> The body sacred from indecent soil.
> Still to be pure, even did it not conduce
> (As much it does) to health, were greatly worth
> Your daily pains.[130]

The eighteenth-century movement in favour of regular cold baths had an obvious ascetic ingredient. It was associated with a regimen of austerity, self-denial and sexual restraint. Characteristically, its supporters favoured cold houses, hard beds and a simple diet based on sparing recourse to meat and alcohol. They wished to subdue the passions, to purge themselves of gross matter and to make their bodies into what the late seventeenth-century Behmenist, Thomas Tryon, called 'unpolluted temples for the holy spirit of God to communicate with'.[131] Tryon was an early advocate of cold bathing and scrupulous

---

127 James Graham in 1790, cit. Smith, 'Prescribing the Rules of Health', 271; Buchan, *Domestic Medicine*, 126.
128 John Stuart Mill, *Essays on Ethics, Religion and Society (Collected Works*, x), ed. J. M. Robson (1969), 394.
129 *Practical Works of Richard Baxter*, I, 212; *The Workes of . . . Elnathan Parr* (4th edn, 1651), 310.
130 'The Art of Preserving Health', in *The Poetical Works of Armstrong, Dyer and Green* (Edinburgh, 1858), 40.
131 Smith, 'Prescribing the Rules of Health', 270 and *passim*.

cleanliness, believing that 'all kinds of uncleanness contradicts the whole course of nature, and in the highest degree opposeth God's law'.[132] Dissenters and Quakers were prominent in the movement thereafter, puritanically rejecting what Richard Baxter called 'inordinate flesh pleasing'.[133]

But asceticism could cross religious boundaries. Sir John Floyer was a High Churchman whose campaign for cold bathing was meant to provide medical backing for the revival of baptism by total immersion. Similarly, George Cheyne could not imagine how cold bathing 'should have ever come into such disuse, especially among Christians, when commanded by the greatest lawgiver that ever was, under the direction of God's holy spirit to his chosen people, and perpetuated to us in the immersion at baptism'.[134] The Spartan discipline of cold bathing also appealed to those many eighteenth-century polemicists who revived classical arguments against 'luxury' and 'effeminacy'.

John Wesley, the man who explicitly linked cleanliness to godliness, was much influenced by these associated currents of thought. His *Primitive Physick*, a domestic guide to medicine, urges a plain diet, preferably with water as the only drink, and culminates with a section on the virtues of cold bathing.[135] It is hard to doubt that it was the moral implications of cleanliness which made it so important in Wesley's eyes. For him, as for so many after him, cleanliness was important because it was associated with such other qualities as self-discipline, regularity and hard work. Dirt, he remarked, was 'a bad fruit of laziness', whereas cleanliness was 'one great branch of frugality'.[136]

This link between dirtiness and idleness was an old one in Protestant moralising. In his *Characters* (1608) the Calvinist Joseph Hall described the 'slothfull' man as 'a standing poole; [who] can not chuse but gather corruption: he is decried . . . by a drie and nastie hand, that still savors of the sheet; a beard uncut, unkembed; an eye and eare yellow with their excretions; a coat, shaken on, ragged, unbrush't; by linnen and face

---

132 Thomas Tryon, *Tryon's Letters, upon Several Occasions* (1700), 120. Also *idem.*, *Wisdom's Dictates* (1691), 102; Ginnie Smith, 'Thomas Tryon's Regimen for Women', in The London Feminist History Group, *The Sexual Dynamics of History* (1983).
133 *Practical Works of Richard Baxter*, I, 212; David Harley, 'Religious and Professional Interests in Northern Spa Literature, 1625–1775', *Bulletin of the Society for the Social History of Medicine*, 35 (1984). Cf. Max Weber, *The Protestant Ethic and the Spirit of Capitalism*, trans. Talcott Parsons (1930), 171, 266.
134 Cheyne, *Essays of Health and Long Life*, 52. I am very grateful to Dr Mark Jenner for the chance to read his unpublished paper on 'Sir John Floyer and the Politics of Cold Bathing'.
135 [John Wesley], *Primitive Physick* (5th edn, Bristol, 1755), 119–22.
136 *Letters of Wesley*, ed. Telford, v, 133; *Sermons on Several Occasions* (Bristol, 1760), 149.

striving whether shall excell in uncleanlinesse'.[137] The theme became increasingly pronounced as time went on. 'Cleanliness and industry generally accompany each other', declared the author of an eighteenth-century tract for apprentices. Lord Kames thought that 'industrious nations . . . , all the world over, are the most cleanly . . . the English are indebted for their cleanliness to the great progress of industry among them in later times'.[138] Cleanliness, moreover, was prized, not just as an end in itself, but because the application and self-discipline needed to achieve it were admirable qualities for a productive and docile labour force. Hence the great concern of later middle-class reformers to teach cleanliness to the poor. As Bishop Berkeley wrote of the Irish in 1750, 'A little washing, scrubbing, and rubbing, bestowed on their persons and houses would introduce a sort of industry, and industry in any one kind is apt to beget it in another . . . You shall not find a clean house inhabited by clean people, and yet wanting necessaries; the same spirit of industry that keeps folk clean being sufficient to keep them also in food and raiment.'[139]

Cleanliness was thus seen as conducive to good order and virtue.[140] It also fitted the values of a middle-class world of respectability and conspicuous consumption. As William Hazlitt would write, 'a people that are remarkable for cleanliness, will be so for industry, for honesty, for avarice, and *vice versa*'. And he continued: 'The more any one finds himself clinging to material objects for existence or gratification, the more he will take a personal interest in them, and the more will he clean, repair, polish, scrub, scour, and tug at them without end, as if it were his own soul that he was keeping clear from spot or blemish.'[141]

Above all, physical cleanliness symbolised the control of the passions and the bodily functions. It could be regarded as an almost indispensable precondition of salvation, because 'the neglect of the body certainly brings on the neglect of the soul'.[142] One Victorian doctor remarked that, before a man could be made into a good Christian, 'his house must be

[137] Jos[eph] Hall, *Characters of Vertues and Vices* (1608), 123–4.
[138] J. H. Conway, *Moral and Religious Instructions* (1767), xlvii; Henry Home, Lord Kames, *Sketches of the History of Man* (Dublin, 1774–5), II, 10.
[139] George Berkeley, *A Word to the Wise*, in *The Querist* (1750), 75–6.
[140] James Raine, *A Memoir of the Rev. John Hodgson* (1857), I, 78; Joseph Farrar, *Baths and Bathing* (4th edn, Bristol, 1890), 26–9; Temkin, *Double Face of Janus*, 468; Richard L. Schoenwald, 'Training Urban Man', in *The Victorian City*, ed. H. J. Dyos and Michael Wolff (1973). II, 683; Karl Figlio, 'Chlorosis and Chronic Disease in Nineteenth-Century Britain', *Social History*, 3 (1978), 189 n. 75.
[141] Hazlitt, *Collected Works*, ed. Waller and Glover, VII, 176–7.
[142] Conway, *Moral and Religious Instructions*, xlviii.

made clean and the impurities by which he is surrounded removed'.[143] Immorality was seen as rooted in physical pollution.

The history of bodily cleanliness is a very difficult subject. As the philosopher Thomas Fowler wrote in 1887, the habit of cleanliness is one 'of very complex origin, arising partly from the discomfort of dirt, partly from the desire to set off one's personal appearance to the best advantage (love of distinction), partly from love of health or fear of disease, and partly also, in more cultivated men, from self-respect and a kind of homage to the human body'.[144] Even earlier, a contributor to the *Spectator* magazine in 1714 concluded that cleanliness was many things: it was 'a mark of politeness'; it rendered us 'agreeable to others' and 'easy to our selves'; it was 'an excellent preservative of health'; and, finally, it bore 'a great analogy with purity of mind' and naturally inspired 'refined sentiments and passions'.[145]

Certainly, changes in the conception of what bodily cleanliness was cannot be entirely attributed to any single factor. Sociologists who follow Norbert Elias in explaining new concepts of personal hygiene in terms of changes in the structure of society underrate the importance of changing medical ideas.[146] Historians who attribute them all to medical ideas ignore the fact that the rules of cleanliness are not always the same as the rules of hygiene; it is not because we think that they will damage our health that we object to dirty shoes on the carpet.[147] Anthropologists who accept the definition of dirt as matter out of place underrate the special feeling of repugnance inspired by bodily emissions and putrefying matter which make them seem more disgusting than, say, a book misplaced on the library shelf. Dirt may be matter out of place, but all matter out of place is not dirt.[148]

In the end there is something visceral about concepts of dirt and cleanliness. As Freud suggested, they reflect disgust for bodily excretions, particularly for their smell.[149] The greater this sense of loathing, the greater the concern to avoid bodily pollution. Even in the

---

[143] Dr Hector Gavin, cit. Wohl, *Endangered Lives*, 8.
[144] Thomas Fowler and John Matthias Wilson, *The Principles of Morals* (Oxford, 1894), II, 59n–60n.
[145] Thomas Tickell, in *Spectator*, 631 (10 Dec. 1714).
[146] Smith, 'Prescribing the Rules of Health', 282. Cf. Elias, *The Civilizing Process*, 159.
[147] Goubert, *The Conquest of Water*, 51, 109–10. Cf. Vigarello, *Concepts of Cleanliness*, 140, 228.
[148] Hence my omission here of any consideration of the issues raised by Mary Douglas, *Purity and Danger* (1965). Contrast Edwyn Bevan, *Hellenism and Christianity* (1921), ch. 8 ('Dirt'), 146.
[149] Sigmund Freud, *Civilization and its Discontents*, trans. Joan Riviere (1930), 66n–67n. Also C. R. Hallpike, *The Foundations of Primitive Thought* (Oxford, 1979), 160 n. 4. This is not to deny that different cultural traditions will express this disgust in different ways.

seventeenth century, this concern sometimes became a neurosis; as in the case of one woman whose doctor noted that she could not stop washing her clothes, however clean and new: '[She] will not suffer her husband, child, nor any of the household to have any new clothes until they wash them for fear the dust of them will fall upon her. Dareth not go to the church for treading on the ground, fearing lest any dust should fall upon them.'[150]

It is no coincidence that so many of those who proclaimed the religious importance of cleanliness should have found the body repellent and been hypersensitive to the polluting nature of bodily waste. For them, the very essence of dirt was bodily emission. As William Prynne put it:

> What is the belly but a filthy sinke,
> Jakes which engenders nought but dung and stink?
> So Noysome that its scent offends the smell,
> Corrupts the aire, even when the body's well.

'Looke what filthy excrements issue out of the nose, eares, pores and other passages', urged John Downame, 'and judge what the fountaine it selfe is from which proceed such loathsome streames.' Richard Baxter thought the human body was 'vile', 'a silly loathsome lump of dirt', with 'loathsome excrements within'. Thomas Tryon considered that the smell of human excrement was more offensive and more dangerous to health than that of the excrement of other animals.[151] Such attitudes had a long history in Christian thought and were certainly not unique to Puritans or sectaries. The Caroline bishop and crypto-Catholic, Godfrey Goodman, considered that 'of all the noysome sents, there is none so rammish and so intollerable, as is that which proceedes from man's bodie . . . I will not speake of his filth issuing from his eares, his eyes, nostrils, mouth, navill, and the uncleane parts.' George Herbert, who laid such stress on cleanliness, shared the same disgust for bodily processes:

> Look on meat, think it dirt, then eat a bit,
> And say withall, 'Earth to earth I commit.'[152]

John Wesley's own reference to what he called 'nastiness' suggests that he too had a highly developed sense of disgust.[153] Like Florence

---

[150] Michael MacDonald, *Mystical Bedlam* (Cambridge, 1981), 154.

[151] William Prynne, *Mount-Orgeuil* (1641), 182; John Downame, *The Christian Warfare* (4th edn, 1634), 407; *Practical Works of Richard Baxter*, I, 372, 214; *Tryon's Letters upon Several Occasions*, 120.

[152] Godfrey Goodman, *The Fall of Man* (1616), 77; Herbert, 'The Church-Porch', in *Poems*, 8. For medieval examples, see G. R. Owst, *Preaching in Medieval England* (Cambridge, 1926), 341, and Chaucer, 'The Pardoner's Tale', lines 534–6.

[153] *Letters of Wesley*, ed. Telford, v, 133.

Nightingale after him, he conceived of filth as 'contamination . . . embodying an absolute moral otherness'.[154]

For those who thought in this way, life was a repulsive 'process of respiration, consumption, excretion, and decay', in which people were 'moving dunghills' and the greatest source of pollution was the human body itself.[155] Disgusted by their own bodily functions, they vainly sought to overcome the intrinsic limitations of the human condition. In ranking cleanliness next to godliness, they proclaimed their yearning for a purity of which human beings could, alas, never be capable.

[154] Rosenberg, 'Florence Nightingale on Contagion', 122.
[155] Nancy Tomes, 'The Private Side of Public Health: Sanitary Science, Domestic Hygiene, and the Germ Theory, 1870–1900', *Bulletin of the History of Medicine*, 64 (1990), 522; Smith, 'Prescribing the rules of Health', 271.

4 Blood is their argument: men of war and soldiers in Shakespeare and others

Michael Hattaway

'As at Turwin I was a demi-soldier in jest, so now I became a martialist in earnest.'[1] This remark, taken from Thomas Nashe's *The Unfortunate Traveller*,[2] might help us to recognise a categorical shift, a change from an historical moment when fighting was a chivalric sport or form of group-specific behaviour to a moment when fighting was an occupation – from a moment when a fighter was regarded as a gentleman-amateur to one in which he was a professional or 'martialist'. The opposition of the two terms corresponds to the opposition made by Michel Foucault between the 'homme de guerre' and the professional 'militaire', an opposition which is central to this essay. Nashe's noun 'martialist' is cited only from 1576 in *OED* and is not current in English: its appearance suggests that war in the period was changing from something familiar in the order of things to an object of inquiry.

In what follows I want to argue that a reading of the Shakespearean canon might lead us to conclude that at the end of the sixteenth century the age of the 'soldier' had passed and the age of the 'martialist' had arrived. Because, perhaps, of the recognition of a tradition of pacifism established by Erasmus, More and others,[3] 'martialists' are constructed in Shakespearean texts as suspect figures, often, despite the victory at Lepanto in 1571, demonised in the figure of the 'cruel Turk'.[4] Shakespeare, perhaps in revulsion against the blood and violence plays of

---

[1] An abbreviated and early version of this paper appears as 'L'Homme de guerre chez Shakespeare', *L'Homme de guerre au xvie siècle*, ed. Gabriel-André Pérouse, André Thierry and André Tournon (Saint-Etienne, 1992), 325–35.

[2] Cited from *An Anthology of Elizabethan Prose Fiction*, ed. Paul Salzman (Oxford, 1987), 228.

[3] See the anti-militarist sentiments in the chapter 'Of Warfare' in Book 2 of the *Utopia*; and, generally, Robert P. Adams, *The Better Part of Valor: More, Erasmus, Colet and Vives on Humanism, War and Peace 1496–1535* (Seattle, 1962).

[4] See *Othello, passim*; Simon Shepherd, *Marlowe and the Politics of Elizabethan Theatre* (New York, 1986), 142–56; and Thomas Becon, 'The Policy of War', *Early Works*, ed. J. Ayre (Parker Soc., 1843), 239–40; Paul A. Jorgensen's *Shakespeare's Military World* (Berkeley, 1956) offers useful material on images of war and its representation, but does not investigate ideology.

Greene etc.,[5] which were in the main performed by the Admiral's and Queen's Men under Henslowe, does not offer us a discourse that allows us to identify with military power. This may also distinguish him from Spenser, from passages in Marlowe and from the tone of Chapman's Homer.[6] From a general aversion to the warlords who appear in the early history plays, he moves towards a more telling scrutiny of the private lives of the great warriors, Othello, Alcibiades, Coriolanus, often implying a connection between, to use Othello's word, their 'occupation' and their emotional being.

To begin, let us consider three well-known lines from the first part of Marlowe's *Tamburlaine* (c. 1588) which quickly became a commonplace in the theatre of the English renaissance. They define what Bertolt Brecht called a 'gestus', a striking and significant theatrical image.[7] Near the beginning of the play there is a moment when the hero proclaims that a career will open to him by virtue of his talents:

> Lie here, ye weeds that I disdain to wear:
> This complete armour and this curtle-axe
> Are adjuncts more beseeming Tamburlaine.

> (*1 Tamburlaine*, 1.1.237–9)

Before our eyes, Tamburlaine, the Scythian shepherd, fashions himself as a martialist and conqueror of the world. It is not only a moment when a man fashions himself as a martialist but – and here's the rub – a moment when a man translates himself from shepherd to conqueror by proclaiming his military talents, and marks the occasion by defying the sumptuary laws that the Tudors imposed to maintain status divisions in the society over which they ruled.[8]

I should like to suggest that a reading of the Shakespearean canon – as of the Marlovian one – does not allow us simply to endorse or acclaim the sheer bravura represented by Marlowe's hero. Why? First, because Tamburlaine is a theatrical dream – or a prince's nightmare: Shakespeare does not trade in such simplified figures and they seem to reflect no social

---

[5] See plays like Greene's *1 Selimus* (1592?), the anonymous romance *The Famous History of Captain Thomas Stukeley* (1596?) which narrates the story of the adventurer Stukeley (1525?–78) who fought in France, became a privateer, and died at the Battle of Alcazar, and Peele's *The Battle of Alcazar* (1588–9) – on these two latter plays, see A. R. Braunmuller, *George Peele* (Boston, Mass., 1982), 66–8.

[6] On parallels between Chapman's *Iliads* and *Henry V*, see Gary Taylor's edition of that play (Oxford, 1982), 52–5.

[7] Michael Hattaway, *Elizabethan Popular Theatre* (1982), 3.

[8] N. B. Harte, 'State Control of Dress and Social Change in Pre-Industrial England', in *Trade, Government and Economy in Pre-Industrial England*, ed. D. C. Coleman and A. H. John (1976), 132–65.

reality. There are no examples of charismatic low-born military geniuses in Shakespeare's England. That notwithstanding, it is also the case that the aristocracy of the period could not endorse their authority simply by their military prowess. It was all too obvious that this group which claimed to occupy the role of the military caste palpably derived their material wealth from the land as well as commercial ventures, and that it was in a state of crisis. Moreover, it was Tudor policy to wean 'the landed classes from their ancient habits of violence'.[9] In *Coriolanus* the patricians live by a code of valour which serves to legitimise their authority: war sustained the hierarchy of the Roman state but certainly not that of King James the peacemaker, and Shakespeare subjects both the code and the cult of valour to a probing scrutiny (see below).

The causes for this crisis are multiple: I should like to offer two considerations. The first is ideological and a paradox: although it is possible to describe the Renaissance as an age of the individual[10] – an age, at least, when individualism or alienation was a common literary theme – it is also important to realise that it is an age of the nation-state in which the interests of the individual needed to be subordinated to those of the polis or at least those of the group. This explains the parables of the body politic which are studded throughout the work of Shakespeare, and, conversely, is perhaps why Edmund Spenser was not able to write a book on the subject of courage, one of the Aristotelian virtues which were to define the structure of *The Faerie Queene*.

In the context of war – for it is necessary to define war before describing the man of war – Shakespeare writes chronicles where the principal actors tend to be nations rather than great men: he is a writer of political rather than mere chronicle-history plays. As his career progressed, from, say, *Henry VI* (1590?) to *Henry V* (1599), narrative becomes more and more deeply embedded in analysis: the latter play is, despite being constructed around the figure of a 'hero', a far more complex political document than the former. Even at the beginning of his career, however, Shakespeare laid down an agenda that was shot through with politics, with, in effect *Realpolitik*, as when he portrays the death of the heroic Talbot in *1 Henry VI*, a death caused by perfidy on the part of aristocratic politicians. He continued it in another key in *Henry V* where the French, playing at chivalric champions, are brought down by English

⁹ Lawrence Stone, *The Crisis of Aristocracy, 1558–1641* (Oxford, 1965), 121; see also C. L. Barber, *The Idea of Honour in the English Drama, 1591–1700* (1957); Jonathan Dollimore, '*Antony and Cleopatra*: Virtues under Erasure', in *Radical Tragedy* (Brighton, 1984), 204–13.

¹⁰ David Aers, 'Reflections on Current Histories of the Subject', *Literature and History*, 2, 2 (1991), 20–34.

mastiffs, the latter fighting not for honour but for political need. Pistol's motto 'Holdfast is the only dog' (1.3.48) gives a keynote for this sequence. It is evident in *Troilus and Cressida* (1601) which concludes with the massacre of Hector, the incarnation of chivalry, by Achilles and his Myrmidons. In the words of Montaigne (in 'Whether the captain of a place besieged ought to sally forth to parley', a meditation on 'virtue' and 'craft') craft (*finesse*) triumphs over virtue: the Greeks and the English know that military valour can triumph over chivalric honour. (This reverses the customary identification of the English with the Trojans.)

In reality, moreover, during the reign of Elizabeth it was at court rather than on the field of battle that honour was won. The device *Tam Marti quam Mercurio*[11] reflects a residual ideology and not a reality – Don Armado in *Love's Labour's Lost* is an inevitably comic version of the counterfeit man of war who haunts the court.[12] The preliminary matter of William Segar's *Honour Military and Civil* (1602) suggests an unfashionable attempt to build up esteem for the military. During the years that Shakespeare was writing his history plays, the queen despatched military expeditions to France, Portugal, the Low Countries and Ireland,[13] but although these were regarded, according to the bishops, as 'holy wars',[14] it was scarcely a time of glamorous military (as opposed to naval) success, and militias[15] (i.e. non-professional citizen forces, service in which was compulsory) and trained bands (more professional groups) were often resented by those who had to pay for and attend their musters.[16] They were held in low social esteem,[17] and men who covered themselves with glory, the earl of Essex, for example,[18] were considered threats to the order of the kingdom. (It was the navy – and the wind – and not the English army which destroyed the Spanish armada in 1588.) The queen had no successor, and any military hero was dangerous. King James, committed to peace, was not going to allow

---

[11] This was the device of the poet George Gascoigne; Segar, in his penultimate chapter of *The Book of Arms*, 'The Author's Intention', is quite defensive about his praise of arms, admitting the necessity of learning for a gentleman (see pp. 66–7).

[12] I am suggesting that the *miles gloriosus* constituted an actual social type; see Jorgensen, *Shakespeare's Military World*, 82–3.

[13] C. G. Cruickshank, *Elizabeth's Army* (Oxford, 1966 edn), 13–16.

[14] Jonathan Dollimore and Alan Sinfield, 'History and Ideology: The Instance of *Henry V*', in *Alternative Shakespeares*, ed. J. Drakakis (1985), 212–13.

[15] The word 'militia' designating a body of troops appears first in *OED* only in 1590 (*OED*, sb. 3a).

[16] Lindsay Boynton, *The Elizabethan Militia, 1558–1638* (1967), 25–30.

[17] J. W. Fortescue, 'The Soldier', in *Shakespeare's England*, ed. S. Lee and C. T. Onions (2 vols., Oxford, 1916), I, 112–26, at 121–6.

[18] G. B. Harrison, *The Life and Death of Robert Devereux, Earl of Essex* (1937), chs. 9–12.

soldiers a high profile: one of his 'first legislative acts was to repeal the 1558 statutes for the taking of musters and the keeping of horses and armour',[19] although after 1613 military activity had to increase because of fear of another Spanish invasion.

Unemployed soldiers like Pistol in *Henry V* – England did not have a standing army until 1660[20] – also posed a problem,[21] and many satirical portraits of this type are to be found in the plays of the period. The military profession was not flourishing – the queen could not even pay her soldiers,[22] and taxes to raise moneys for war weighed heavily upon the lower orders and were detested, as we see in *2 Henry VI*. The crisis of the aristocracy was above all a crisis for the man of war.

My second thesis is material and a commonplace: England, and London especially, was developing as a commercial and administrative centre. Much has been written on bastard feudalism, a system under which ties of duty were transformed into financial bonds, the cash nexus. (We are reminded of this social change by considering the etymology of the word *militare*, which, in low Latin, meant 'feudal service', and which in earlier times explained to the knight the spirit which is to guide all his actions.)[23] Shakespeare takes note of the centralisation in *1 Henry IV* where he demonstrates that, for reasons of state, the gallant Hotspur must deliver up the sums of money he has won through ransom to the king's exchequer. In the absence of a viable taxation system, the spoils of war had to feed the king's purse. Glory in this context has become a means and not an end. Conversely, Henry IV, 'The vile politician Bullingbrook' (*1 Henry IV*, 1.3.241), dreams of becoming a Christian warrior, a crusader, perhaps having been pricked by his conscience after his involvement with the murder of Richard II. For these two antagonists, Hotspur and Bullingbrook, military glory turns out to be a dream.

A particular nightmare, the 'civil butchery'[24] of the Wars of the Roses, haunted the Elizabethans. Too many men had suffered, in their native

---

19 Boynton, *The Elizabethan Militia*, 209.
20 Ian F. W. Beckett, *The Amateur Military Tradition, 1558–1945* (1991); J. A. Sharpe, *Early Modern England, a Social History 1550–1760* (1987), 101–3; Derek Hirst, *Authority and Conflict: England 1603–1658* (1986), *passim*; a foreigner, Frederick, duke of Wirtemberg, noted in 1592: 'The soldiers . . . are excellent, but they do not willingly go of foreign service. When soldiers are wanted, and idlers are seen lounging about, they give them money, and then they are bound to serve whether they like it or not', W. B. Rye, *England as Seen by Foreigners in the Days of Elizabeth and James the First* (1865), 50; Becon argues implicitly for a standing army, 244–5.
21 Lucy de Bruyn, *Mob-Rule and Riots* (1981), 62.
22 See Fortescue, 'The Soldier', 121–2.
23 F. W. Cornish, *Chivalry* (1901), 13.
24 The phrase occurs in *1 Henry IV*, 1.1.13.

land, the scourge of the search for glory on the part of the nobility. A series of works on civil war had been written during the last decade of the sixteenth century.[25]

One can, moreover, describe precisely how the ideology of honour[26] was changing. It has been claimed that until Kett's Rebellion in 1549, the espousal of an honour code by the nobility had a subversive potential – as we can see from *Henry VI*, Shakespeare's chronicle of the Wars of the Roses, but obviously a political comment on his own age. After this rebellion, in reaction perhaps, caste solidarity among the nobility generated new ideas concerning honour and obedience which stigmatised dissidence as an activity which was fit only for the lower and ignorant orders. The state had come to possess a monopoly of honour and legitimised violence.[27]

Shakespeare stressed not what is won in war but what is lost: he is always conscious of war's cost. In *Henry V* the chorus proclaims 'they sell the pasture now to buy the horse' (2 pr. 5), and Mountjoy's description of the violation of Peace occupied a prominent position in the resolution of the play. Figures bathed in military glory survived only in myth – remember Sir Philip Sidney – and the ceremonial tilts that celebrated the queen's accession appeared to be infused by nostalgia.[28] Dramatic texts, however, demonstrate that actual combat obeyed no rules and that old narratives were being overwritten by new technology: Marlowe, rather self-consciously, inserted details from Paul Ive's *Practise of Fortification* (1589) into *2 Tamburlaine* (3.2.55–92) as if to explain away the fantasies encoded in Tamburlaine's never-ending military victories. In *1 Henry VI* a base Walloon stabs the Lord Talbot in the back, and a little boy, in charge of a cannon, annihilates the earl of Salisbury. In *Henry V* Fluellen asserts that 'mines is not according to the disciplines of war' (3.3.4). Chivalry, in fact, served propaganda and not power. It has even been suggested that one of the reasons for this lack of prestige for the military is that developments in weapons and therefore in strategy were advancing so swiftly that the practice of warfare declined: war was avoided as a consequence of the 'military revolution'.[29]

---

[25] See Marlowe's translation of the first book of Lucan's *Pharsalia* (1593) and plays by Thomas Lodge, *The Wounds of Civil War* (1594), and Robert Wilson, *The Cobbler's Prophecy* (1590?).

[26] Julian Pitt-Rivers, 'The Anthropology of Honour', in *The Fate of Shechem* (1977).

[27] *Rebellion, Popular Protest and the Social Order in Early Modern England*, ed. Paul Slack (Cambridge, 1984), 13. Slack cites Mervyn James, *English Politics and the Concept of Honour 1485–1642*, Past and Present, Supplement No. 3 (1978).

[28] Frances Yates, *Astraea* (1975), 88–111.

[29] Boynton, *The Elizabethan Militia*, 4; however, Frank Tallett, *War and Society in Early Modern Europe 1495–1715* (1992), claims that changes in the field of tactics and weaponry

A confrontation between myth and reality is the theme of *Hamlet*. The hero is visited by two mythic beings: one, from the feudal past, the ghost of his father and the other, from a more distant classic age, the brutal martialist Pyrrhus (Neoptolemus, son of Achilles).[30] (In a magnificent production in 1988, in Avignon, Patrice Chéreau placed the ghost on horseback, an image at once frightening and anachronistic.) In Hamlet's mind's eye, these two figures appear as monsters, unnatural beings. There is no place for military revenge during the reign of Claudius, a good diplomat, who maintains peace by means of a strategic deterrent (*Hamlet*, 1.1.70–9). The third soldier in the play, Fortinbras, also appears to the audience as a monster.[31] For him, personal revenge is all, and it is a question left to prove whether Denmark will prosper under his rule.

In former times war could be deemed to serve not only politics but justice: I am thinking of the trial by combat.[32] In Spenser, an interminable succession of duels perform the role of theodicies, and William Segar, in *The Booke of Honor and Armes* (1590), while admitting that duels 'are in this age either rarely or never granted',[33] could set out the rules of noble and ceremonial combats of this kind. In Shakespeare we again encounter a kind of realism: duels in his plays are often a question of might against right. I have already mentioned Hector: let us also remember the armourer Horner in *2 Henry VI*, who, dead drunk, is vanquished by his apprentice (2.3). On this occasion it is a question of power against impotence – right does not come into it. This sequence constitutes a typical subplot, a demonstration, in this context, that the combats of the nobility are *not* duels played out under the eye of God but only combats played before the spectators, in the presence of the people who suffer the effects of the predations of those a rank above them socially. Duels in the theatre deconstruct the aphorism with which Segar begins his *Booke of Honor and Armes*: 'The cause of all quarrel is injury and reproach, but the matter of content is justice and honour.'[34] In the theatre this secularisation of the duel makes these combats more exciting: you do not know who is going to win. Prince Hal defeats

were much less significant than has been previously argued, and did not amount to a military revolution.

30 Michael Hattaway, *Hamlet: The Critics Debate* (1987), 89–90.
31 Brecht's sonnet 'On Shakespeare's Play *Hamlet*', in *Poems*, ed. J. Willett and R. Manheim (1976), 311.
32 Keith Thomas, *Religion and the Decline of Magic* (Harmondsworth, 1973), 143, 260–1; see also Catherine Belsey, 'Tragedy, Justice, and the Subject', in *Literature and Power in the Seventeenth Century*, ed. F. Barker *et al.* (1981), 166–86.
33 William Segar, *The Booke of Honor and Armes* (1590), sig. A2v.
34 *Ibid.*, sig. A2r.

Hotspur by virtue of his strength and skill and not by right (*1 Henry IV*, 5.4): it is a military and not a moral victory.

At the beginning of his career, Shakespeare tended to defamiliarise the figure of the warrior. In the fourth act of *1 Henry VI*, Talbot plays his role in couplets, between inverted commas, as it were. His adversary, Joan of Arc, la Pucelle, is perhaps a monster, a witch, or at least a figure who, like her adversary, comes out of dream or myth.[35] Shakespeare seems to be a populist, and the valour of Talbot creates a mythic 'feast of death' in opposition to the machinations of the politicians. In the most recent notable production of the play, that of *The Plantagenets*, directed by Adrian Noble at Stratford in 1988, we did not witness the anti-Lancastrian prejudice that appeared in the work of most of the play's directors since Brecht, and the spectators were invited to applaud the romantic and physical bravura of both Talbot and la Pucelle. But Shakespeare is always impartial, and, in the third play of the trilogy, he gives us a man of war totally constant to his 'mystery' and totally efficient. This is the monstrous Clifford, the complete martialist, who kills the young Rutland and, along with the ferocious Margaret of Anjou, displays a napkin soaked in the blood of the child to his father, the duke of York, before killing him too (*3 Henry VI*, 1.3–4).

Now Talbot was fighting for his country, Clifford was fighting for his faction: the Henry VI plays can be read as an exposition of the difference between patriotism and nationalism, the former an individual's love of country, place or race, his loyalty to kin or language, the latter a desire to serve something far more artificial, the state or, as it was termed in the Renaissance, the nation. Thomas Becon, writing in 1543, gives us a useful definition of patriotism: 'I think there is no man so far estranged from civil humanity which knoweth not how much every one of us is indebted to our native country . . . but also allured into the love and desire of the same even by a certain inspiration both of God and nature'.[36] By implication Henry VI is thinking what is his country when he sees a father who has killed his son and a son who has killed a father. There is a great difference between these deaths and the Horatian vision of sweet and decorous death for the fatherland:[37] the scene is a demolition of the notion of fatherland.

Civil war was a particular cause: it is also possible to argue that the Reformation had torn apart the identification of country and nation. Becon, in his treatise *The Policy of War*, feels it necessary to establish the

---

[35] *1 Henry VI*, ed. Michael Hattaway (Cambridge, 1990), 21–7.
[36] Becon, 'The Policy of War', 232.
[37] 'Dulce et decorum est pro patria mori' (*Carmina*, 2.2.13).

identity of the two before he goes on to argue that wars are won only by the just and defeats visited upon only the unjust. The difficulty of his first task is registered when he argues, slightly desperately and with a flurry of double negatives, that

if any nation be estranged from the unnatural affection toward their country, certes I think England, I mean the inhabitants thereof, may justly contend with any country for the alienation of this vice. It doth me good, yea, it maketh me seriously to rejoice even at the very heart, to see how glad my countrymen are to serve the commodities of this our country, England.[38]

The appropriation of patriotism to the cause of nationalism creates a potent and subtle weapon – as the present state of Eastern Europe reminds us today. The 'Elizabethan concept of order' entailed loyalty to nation rather than country.[39] And, as we know to our cost, it is a common legitimation of war: Henry V has no compunction in using patriotic sentiments for nationalistic ends.

Now I argued that this was an age of emergent capitalism. Shakespeare, however, seems to have in advance demonstrated the inadequacy of Marx and Engels' theory of the necessary disappearance of nationalism: 'National differences, and antagonisms between peoples, are daily more and more vanishing, owing to the development of the bourgeoisie, to freedom of commerce, to the world-market, to uniformity of the mode of production, and in the conditions of life corresponding thereto' (*The Communist Manifesto*, 1848). The concentration here on the economic at the expense of the political has wrought untold misery, as recent history has proved. For this was not only an age of economic take-off but of colonisation or imperialism, and these ideologies destroy 'country'.[40] 'What ish my nation?' asks McMorris (*Henry V*, 3.2.122), thinking about Ireland, colonised by the English, its language destroyed.

In *Henry V* we have a rare example of Shakespeare using the babble of foreign tongues, demonstrating the realities of both fatherland and empire. Generally national antagonists speak the same tongue – a necessity on the stage. Examples are the Romans and Volscians in *Coriolanus* and the Greeks and Trojans in *Troilus and Cressida*. The effect of this is to deconstruct both country and nation and suggest that these wars between states are wars between *tribes*, smaller groups without a territory of their own. This itself, I consider, generates a pacifist reading. Trevor Nunn's Stratford production of *Coriolanus* some years ago was

[38] Becon, 'The Policy of War', 235.
[39] For an example, see *ibid.*
[40] There is no instance of the word 'fatherland' (the word was translated from the German only in 1672) or an English equivalent of 'patrie' in Shakespeare.

justified neither in identifying the plebeians with the proletariat nor the Volscians with noble savages, victims of Roman imperial aggression. We can go further and suggest that the tribalism of *Henry V* is a register of the limits of centralised rule.

To turn now from the figure of the warrior and warlike groups to discussions of the causes of war.[41] A convenient starting-point is provided by William Segar in Chapter 3 of *Honour Military and Civil*, 'Of war, and the causes thereof'. He takes discord and dissension as given, argues with Cicero that these are ended by persuasion by men and by force by beasts. He concedes, however, that 'each man hath war within himself', and, having invoked Aristotle's proof 'that some men are by nature born to command, others to obey', reviews a number of imperialist ventures from ancient times and concludes that 'peace is not the only end of war, yet no doubt the chiefest and most necessary cause thereof'.[42] His argument rather desperately converts a political argument into a moral one.

Shakespeare's analysis of the causes of wars, the Hundred Years War and the Wars of the Roses, is far more complex, a *political* analysis that takes into account not only the history and balance of power in Europe but the conflict between social groups and classes within the kingdom. Few would now be able to present Henry V as England's 'ideal king' – but it is equally reductive to depict him merely as a cunning politician who followed the pragmatic advice of his father.[43] On his death-bed, Henry IV advises his heir to have as his 'course to busy giddy minds with foreign quarrels' (*2 Henry IV*, 4.5.213–14). The dauphin's insult, the gift of tennis balls, gives the young king a perfect *casus belli*. For Henry V, as for Machiavelli,[44] and, much later, for Carl von Clausewitz, war was a rational instrument of the national political interest.[45] By means of war Henry can at the same time confirm glory on England and control his state. Shakespeare, however, seems sceptical of this claim. Long passages of the play involve Pistol and his crew, and for them war is occasion for

---

[41] For a general survey, see J. R. Hale, 'Sixteenth-Century Explanations of War and Violence', *Past and Present*, 51 (1971), 3–26.

[42] Segar, *Honour*, 4.

[43] H. Holderness, 'Agincourt 1944: Readings in the Shakespearean Myth', *Literature and History*, 10 (1984), 24–45.

[44] J. A. Mazzeo, *Renaissance and Revolution* (1967), 121-2.

[45] *Clausewitz on War*, ed. Anatol Rapoport (Harmondsworth, 1968), 12; Philip Edwards interprets *Henry V* as propaganda for the conquest of Ireland: *Threshold of a Nation* (Cambridge, 1979), 74–86; David Hopkins, 'Ben Jonson and *Henry V*', *Notes and Queries*, 30 (1983), 148 cites 'To Sir Philip Wroth' as a poem which criticises 'Once more into the breach . . . ' (*Henry V*, 3.1.1); see also James A. Freeman, *Milton and the Martial Muse: Paradise Lost and the European Tradition of War* (1980).

pillage, an opportunity for individual advancement – as we see in 4.4 in which Le Fer is captured.

This concept of war, war as strategy, is embedded in the provocative title of Becon's revisionist treatise, *The Policy of War* – 'policy' turns out to be God's policy and not Machiavellian *Realpolitik*. At the opening of this text, however, Becon adumbrates two further concepts: war as eschatology – to which the end of the play conforms – and war as cataclysm.[46] I should like to suggest that Shakespeare offers us these three interpretations of war in the same play. As I have already stated, for the king – and equally for the archbishop of Canterbury[47] – war against France is a matter of strategy but, as we know, he wins at Agincourt a magnificent victory over the French. Of the French, 10,000 soldiers were killed, against 29 English:

> O God, thy arm was here,
> And not to us, but to thine arm alone
> Ascribe we all. When, without stratagem,
> But in plain shock and even play of battle
> Was ever known so great and little loss
> On one part and on th' other? Take it God,
> For it is none but thine.

> (*Henry V*, 4.8.104–9)

Non nobis, domine – the opening, of course, of Psalm 115, which is glossed by the Geneva Bible as follows: 'a prayer of the faithful oppressed by idolatrous tyrants'.[48] The French are scarcely tyrants in this play and there is no mention of idolatry.

How might we resolve this contradiction? In 1976 in a Royal Shakespeare Company production of the play at Stratford, the director Terry Hands found an enlightening solution. When Alan Howard, who was playing the king, spoke these lines, he and his soldiers dropped suddenly to their knees. They were in the presence not of a miracle generated by a good god, but of action by a partisan and cruel deity, or perhaps of a true *deus absconditus*. Becon had argued that cataclysmic wars were the consequence of the visitation upon the wicked of God's wrath: the notion of the 'scourge of God' is a common 'cause' for war in Renaissance texts.[49]

> . . . Miracles are ceased,
> And therefore we must admit the means
> How things are perfected

[46] Becon, 'The Policy of War', 238.   [47] See his moral reversal at 1.2.79ff.
[48] *The Geneva Bible* (1560), fol. 26or.   [49] Becon, 'The Policy of War', 240, 248.

says Canterbury near the beginning of the play (1.1.67–9), and yet there can be no 'admission' of the means whereby this battle was won. The text, in other words, may align itself with the way in which theological explanations of war were steadily losing ground in the sixteenth century.[50] Shakespeare and all writers for the theatre are constrained by their medium to concentrate on what Aristotle would term the efficient and not the final causes of wars. It is man's strategy and not God's. Becon, however, quotes Proverbs 21.31 on the title page of his treatise: 'The horse is prepared against the day of battle, but the Lord giveth the victory',[51] a claim that war is the revelation of final causes.

As for the third concept of war, war as cataclysm, that is the one endorsed by the private soldiers who understand nothing of what is going on. Henry claims that his cause is just and his quarrel honorable. 'That's more than we know', retorts private Michael Williams (Henry V, 4.1.124).

Another fact to note is that almost all the great men of war in the canon of Shakespearean texts are shown either in the company of their fathers (sometimes of their sons) or as being very aware of their fathers. I am thinking of Talbot's son, of Richard III, son of the duke of York, of Henry V, son of Bullingbrook, of old and young Hamlet, of course, of old and young Fortinbras, of Coriolanus and his son who mammocks butterflies (1.3.72). This tendency to portray two generations of soldiers is perhaps a means of marking the decadence of chivalric militarism. And, without erecting an overambitious psychological theory, I might claim that the presence of the father creates, in the warrior, a wounded, defective personality, given to uncontrollable acts of aggression.[52]

Now in the sixteenth century, violence was generally discussed in the context of anger, and anger came from the heating of blood in the heart.[53] Blood, however, was associated not just with anger but with the libido, and Shakespeare, it seems to me, is well aware of the connection. It is hinted at in Williams' remark that none 'can charitably dispose of anything, when blood is their argument' (Henry V, 4.1.142–4). In comedies like Love's Labour's Lost we watch how Venus disarms Mars:[54]

---

[50] Hale, Past and Present, 51 (1971), 'Sixteenth-Century Explanations', 9.

[51] The Geneva text reads '. . . but salvation is of the Lord'.

[52] Sigmund Freud, Civilization, Society and Religion, vol. XII of The Pelican Freud Library (Harmondsworth, 1985), 322–3.

[53] Seneca, De ira, and Robert Burton, The Anatomy of Melancholy, ed. Floyd Bell and Paul Jordan-Smith (New York, 1948), 1.2.3.9, p. 233.

[54] See too the tale of the subjugation of conquering Alexander by Campaspe in Lyly's Campaspe, and the fate of Lyly's braggart soldier Sir Tophas who, disarmed by love, saves his self-esteem by a Latin conceit, 'Militat omnis amans, et habet sua castra Cupido' (Endymion, 3.3.52–3) – 'Every lover is a warrior and Cupid has his own camp.'

in the histories and tragedies this same blood serves to inflame Mars.
Henry V urges on his men thus:

> But when the blast of war blows in our ears,
> Then imitate the action of the tiger.
> Stiffen the sinews, conjure up the blood,
> Disguise fair nature with hard-favoured rage.

(3.1.5–8)

Coriolanus, of course, was the cognomen to a man named Martius, and
his prowess is constantly associated with images of sexuality:

> The breasts of Hecuba
> When she did suckle Hector looked not lovelier
> Than Hector's forehead when it spit forth blood
> At Grecian Sword, contemning.

(1.3.42–5)

THIRD SERVINGMAN But when they shall see, sir, his crest up again and the man
in blood, they will out of their burrows like conies after rain, and revel all
with him.

(4.5.215–17).

It is difficult not to suggest that Shakespeare has anticipated Freud who,
in 'Why war?', wrote 'A lust for aggression and destruction is certainly
among [the motives which incite men to war]: the countless cruelties in
history and in our everyday lives vouch for its existence and strength. The
satisfaction of these destructive impulses is of course facilitated by their
admixture with others of an erotic and idealistic kind'.[55]

In the case of Henry V, it seems to me that his energy and *élan* stem
specifically from what Freud called sublimation.[56] Let us recall the
speech of the king before the walls of Harfleur:

> How yet resolves the Governor of the town?
> This is the latest parle we will admit.
> Therefore to our best mercy give yourselves,
> Or like to men proud of destruction
> Defy us to your worst. For, as I am a soldier,
> A name that in my thoughts becomes me best,
> If I begin the batt'ry once again

---

[55] Freud, *Civilization*, 357. The destructive instinct arises when the death instinct is
'directed outwards, on to objects. The organism preserves its own life, so to say, by
destroying an extraneous one' (*ibid.*).

[56] Sigmund Freud, *Introductory Lectures on Psychoanalysis*, vol. I of *The Pelican Freud
Library* (Harmondsworth, 1973), 390.

I will not leave the half-achievèd Harfleur
Till in her ashes she lie burièd.
The gates of mercy shall be all shut up,
And the fleshed soldier, rough and hard of heart,
In liberty of bloody hand shall range
With conscience wide as hell, mowing like grass
Your fresh fair virgins and your flow'ring infants . . .
What is't to me, when you yourselves are cause,
If your pure maidens fall into the hand
Of hot and forcing violation? . . .
        in a moment look to see
The blind and bloody soldier with foul hand
Defile the locks of your shrill-shrieking daughters . . .

(3.3.81–115)

Three images of rape in thirty-five lines – and note, in this connection, the phallic passages in the first Pistol scene.

In other plays by Shakespeare we find further remarkable links between militarism and sex. The French court in *All's Well that Ends Well* is a place where war is considered as a sport.[57] It is a totally masculine world, and it seems to me that the king's malady, the *fistula*, is a metaphor for sexual impotence or for lack of feeling that must be cured by a woman, the faithful Helen.[58] Like Henry V and Coriolanus, the young Bertram, the young 'blood' of the play, is an emotional eunuch. Concerning the virgin Diana it is said that he 'fleshes his will in the spoil of her honour' (4.3.16). It is a frightening example of a militarised libido. (There is a secondary meaning that derives from hunting.)

Finally Coriolanus: he is a patriot – or does he wish to please his mother, who, like him, regards valour as honour? His mother Volumnia, like Lady Macbeth and Lady Macduff, like Cleopatra, finds herself possessed by a single idea of man's role: manhood is measured only by virility and military courage.[59] The great Roman matrons are transformed into '"mankind" women' (4.2.16). In this milieu, Virgilia has lost her voice, her being: 'My gracious silence, hail' (2.1.175). She represents a centre of resistance to all war propaganda.

Moreover, for the patricians war is at once a sport – Coriolanus says that Aufidius is 'a lion / That I am proud to hunt' (1.1.233–4) – and an

[57] R. B. Parker, 'War and Sex in *All's Well that Ends Well*', *Shakespeare Studies*, 37 (1984), 99–113.
[58] However, see F. D. Honeger, *Medicine and Shakespeare in the English Renaissance* (1992), 297.
[59] See D. W. Harding, 'Woman's Fantasy of Manhood', *Shakespeare Quarterly*, 20 (1969), 245–54.

erotic activity. Again we think that a sublimated libido erupts under the form of valour. Coriolanus seeks Aufidius with as much ardour as Cleopatra shows when she is seeking Antony, and let us hear Aufidius speaking of his enemy:

> Let me twine
> Mine arms about that body, where against
> My grainèd ash an hundred times hath broke,
> And scarred the moon with splinters . . .
> Know thou first,
>   I loved the maid I married; never man
> Sighed truer breath; but that I see there here,
> Thou noble thing, more dances my rapt heart
> Than when I first my wedded mistress saw
> Bestride my threshold . . .
>   Thou hast beat me out
> Twelve several times, and I have nightly since
> Dreamt of encounters 'twixt thyself and me –
> We have been down together in my sleep,
> Unbuckling helms, fisting each other's throat –
> And waked half dead with nothing

(4.5.107–27).

For Volumnia too combat is erotic: 'If my son were my husband I should freelier rejoice in that absence wherein he won honour, than in the embracements of his bed, where he would show most love' (1.2.2–5): in fact she rejoices in his wounds (2.1.120ff.).

As for the plebeians, it seems that they have been seduced by war:

1 SERVANT Let me have war, say I. It exceeds peace as far as day does night: it's sprightly walking, audible and full of vent. Peace is a very apoplexy, lethargy; mulled, deaf, sleepy, insensible; a getter of more bastard children than war's a destroyer of men.
2 SERVANT 'Tis so, and as war, in some sort, may be said to be a ravisher, so it cannot be denied but peace is a great maker of cuckolds.

(4.5.228–35)

For critics of the left, this passage is an embarrassment: in the production by Helene Weigel of the version of the play by Bertolt Brecht, these lines were reassigned to two drunken Volscian officers.[60] But we might note that, once more, it is a question of eroticism. For the greater part of the people war is the cause of famine and inequality. But Shakespeare seems to be invoking what Mikhail Bakhtin calls 'material bodily lower

---

[60] See *Coriolanus*, ed. P. Brockbank (1976), 87–8n, 261n.

stratum'.[61] War is a veritable aphrodisiac – but whereas for the patricians war can bring eternal glory, for the plebeians it is just a question of an ephemeral pleasure.

But, finally, what can be said about the character of Coriolanus? Without doubt he is a superb martialist. Aufidius offers us a catalogue of his virtues and his faults: what is lacking is the possibility that, quite simply, he detests the people, that he is a patrician militarist who cannot abide anyone who does not want to sacrifice himself. Clausewitz said that war is a continuation of politics:[62] politics is also a continuation of war.[63]

There is one problem: we do not know how Shakespeare supervised the *mis en scène* of the defeat of the Romans before the town of Corioli. Is it the case that the soldiers are truly cowards, or were they treated like lambs for the slaughter with the result that they decided to save themselves? Like Macbeth, Coriolanus is 'Bellona's bridegroom' (*Macbeth*, 1.2.54): once more Shakespeare suggests that a man married to war is going to be blind to any virtue that is not military valour. Although his 'nature' cannot 'move from the casque to the cushion' (*Coriolanus*, 4.7.43), he must undergo a rite of passage, like many other tragic heroes, and this rite, I believe, nurtures in him a tendency to theatricalise himself.

If there is an Aristotelian recognition, it begins in the scene with his mother:

> Would you have me
> False to my nature? Rather say *I play*
> *The man I am.*

(3.2.14–16)

> Like a dull *actor* now
> I have forgot my part and I am out,
> Even to a full disgrace.

(5.3.40–2)

> Behold, the heavens do ope,
> The gods look down, and this unnatural *scene*
> They laugh at.

(5.3.183–5)

---

61 Mikhail Bakhtin, *Rabelais and his World*, trans. Hélène Iswolsky (Bloomington, 1968), 368ff.; see also Michael D. Bristol, 'Lenten Butchery: Legitimation Crisis in *Coriolanus*', in *Shakespeare Reproduced*, ed. Jean Howard and Marion F. O'Connor (1987), 211.

62 *Clausewitz*, ed. Rapoport, 119.

63 See Michel Foucault, *Discipline and Punish: The Birth of the Prison (Surveillir et punir)*, in *The Foucault Reader*, ed. Paul Rabinow (Harmondsworth, 1985), 185.

His *virtus* is not something essential, but an instrument of the state.

Shakespeare gives Coriolanus only one soliloquy – it is therefore difficult to anatomise his personality. But I think that one can get one fix on his character by thinking of his role as a Roman warrior. Consider these passages:

> You common cry of curs! Whose breath I hate
> As reek o' th' rotten fens, whose love I prize
> As the dead carcasses of unburied men
> That do corrupt my air: I banish you!
> And here remain with you uncertainty!
> Let every feeble rumour shake your hearts!
> Your enemies, with nodding of their plumes,
> Fan you into despair! . . .
>   Despising
> For you the city, thus I turn my back.
> There is a world elsewhere!
>
> (3.3.120–35)

3 SERVANT Where dwell'st thou?
CORIOLANUS Under the canopy.
3 SERVANT Under the canopy?
CORIOLANUS Ay.
3 SERVANT Where's that?
CORIOLANUS I' th' city of kites and crows.
3 SERVANT I' th' city of kites and crows? What an ass it is.

> (*Coriolanus*, 4.5.38–45).[64]

Coriolanus plays his role under the dome of the heavens, but also under the 'cover' of the theatre, the cockpit. But it also seems to me that here we recognise a nostalgia for another city, for the celestial city, a city where his *virtues* would be legitimated by God. He cannot understand the Roman city: the body politic described by Menenius at the beginning of the play. He is aware of his own body, but it is striking how often Coriolanus is described as a thing:

> As weeds before
> A vessel under sail, so men obeyed
> And fell below his stem: his sword, death's stamp,
> Where it did mark, it took; from face to foot

---

[64] Stanley Cavell noted 'Christian stirrings and murmurings under the surface of the words' '"Who Does the Wolf Love?": *Coriolanus* and the Interpretation of Politics', in *Shakespeare and the Question of Theory*, ed. P. Parker and G. Hartman (1985), 246.

He was a *thing* of blood, whose every motion
Was timed with dying cries

(2.2.105–10)

                   He leads them like a *thing*
Made by some other deity than nature,
That shapes men better

(4.6.91–3)

Michel Foucault has noted that after the Renaissance the conception of the body was changed into something that could be modelled or constructed: the man of war (*l'homme de guerre*) was changed into the soldier (*le militaire*).[65] Menenius speaks in the parable of the belly of the 'arm, our soldier' (1.1.121), suggesting that the soldier was a mere unsentient instrument. Coriolanus, however, begins to understand that his passion for the valour of the warrior, his pursuit of absolute power over his soldiers, his cult of the man-machine has cost him dear. For the man of war turned martialist the world is a veritable waste land. Perhaps he dreams of becoming a knight in another world, a Christian world like the one created by Spenser. But, as I have argued, the world of the man of war, of Spenser's 'gentle knight' was, in 1608, long gone.

---

[65] Foucault, *Discipline and Punish*, 186; there is, of course, no mention of uniform in Segar's chapter 'Of Apparel' (*Honour*, 2812–19) – the word is first recorded in *OED* only in 1748; see Cruickshank, *Elizabeth's Army*, 91–101. *OED* also records the way which, in the age of Shakespeare, 'army' meant usually a band of men mustered for a particular occasion. Only in 1647 was the word applied to the whole of the parliamentary forces.

5   Pragmatic readers: knowledge transactions and scholarly services in late Elizabethan England[1]

Lisa Jardine and William Sherman

In 1595, after his Oxford studies and continental travels, Henry Wotton entered the service of the earl of Essex.[2] Amongst the earliest tasks he undertook was an English synopsis and intellectual analysis of a Spanish work 'the which was lately Imprinted and Written (as it is supposed) by *Antonio Peres* [Perez], sometimes Secretary to the King of *Spain*, and now residing in *London*', the *Pedacos de Historia* (or *Relaciones*, as the work became known in its later editions).[3] This 'scholarly service' rendered to Wotton's new master appropriately exploited his considerable intellectual talents – his fluent Spanish, his knowledge of European affairs, his training in methodical analysis. Together with his *The State of Christendom*, it established Wotton as the kind of scholar who could provide Essex with knowledge profitable to the enterprise of government. Pearsall Smith argues that *The State of Christendom* was written in 1594, and that, in the terms of the present paper, it was designed to draw Wotton to the attention of Essex, as a scholar with the kind of 'intelligence' which would be valuable in the service of a prominent political figure.[4] This kind of activity, crossing as it clearly does both disciplinary and professional boundaries, and hovering between the private and the public realm, we call a 'knowledge transaction'; the working relationship established between noble employer and his professional reader is what

[1] This piece of work is the product of collaborative research which will ultimately be incorporated in Anthony Grafton, Lisa Jardine and William Sherman, provisionally titled *Politics in the Margins*. We are grateful to Paul Hammer for making available to us his PhD thesis, '"The Bright Shininge Sparke": The Political Career of Robert Devereux, 2nd Earl of Essex, c.1585–c. 1597' (Cambridge PhD thesis, 1991). Without Paul's invaluable help on the Essex circle, the Essex secretaries and Tudor history in the 1590s in general, we would never have been able to make sense of the scholarly readers we deal with.

[2] On Wotton, see L. Pearsall Smith, *The Life and Letters of Sir Henry Wotton* (2 vols., Oxford, 1907).

[3] G. Ungerer, *A Spaniard in Elizabethan England: The Correspondence of Antonio Perez's Exile* (2 vols., London, 1976), II, 280.

[4] It is interesting to note, therefore, that the semi-fictional context for the work is advice sought from a young exile abroad on the part of an English Lord. See Pearsall Smith, *Life and Letters*, I, 241–99.

we call in our title, 'scholarly service'. In this essay we shall argue that knowledge transactions and the private service relations they establish between scholars and those who employ them form a vital part of our understanding of the intellectual and political life of England in the 1580s and 1590s.[5]

Let us begin by looking a little further at our notion of 'scholarly service', still in the company of Henry Wotton. Five years before he successfully gained employment with the earl of Essex, Wotton sought to establish a similar service relationship with Lord Zouche. On 20 November 1590 he wrote to Zouche, who was then at Altdorf. At this date Wotton was resident in Vienna. He had, in fact, procured lodgings with the Imperial Librarian, Dr Hugo Blotius. His study there opened out on to the Library itself, to whose treasures he enjoyed unrestricted access. Wotton begins his letter with a report on general political news, the kind of foreign intelligence which he calls his 'plain kind of service':

The Assembly at Franckfordt is dissolved without anything done, and much disagreement between the Palatine agent and the Bishop of Wirtsburg. I heard the Venice ambasador's secretary tell an Italian so much with wonderful joy. Other important matter we have none. As the times alter, this my plain kind of service shall be very ready to let your Honour know it.

At this point the focus of the information he has been compiling sharpens, and Wotton indicates that he is consciously in competition with other news gatherers:

The secretest debates about the Empire I have good means to learn by the gentleman with whom I live yet, and he hath given me promise of meeting in half way, for exchange of the like out of England. I will always take care to write that which I think is least known unto your Honour. What the Intelligentiary Letters of Augsburg, Lyons and Venice bring, Mr. Osborn[6] I know fails not to advertise. My duty and best diligence shall be bestowed upon that which no money or charges can come unto.

He proceeds to detail some of the varied kinds of material he has gathered:

Concerning the model of the Emperor's lust-house, your Honour may trust me with it.[7] I hope to send withal a view of all the present Almaigne princes, their

---

5 On the particular resonances of the term 'private' in the period see W. Sherman, '"A Living Library": The Readings and Writings of John Dee' (Cambridge PhD thesis, 1991), in press as *John Dee: The Politics of Reading and Writing in the Renaissance* (Amherst, Mass., 1994).
6 See Hammer, '"The Bright Shininge Sparke"'.
7 See L. R. Shelby, *John Rogers: Tudor Military Engineer* (Oxford, 1967).

Courts, chief affinity, riches and strength, and their inclinations, as they lean to this or that extremity, not otherwise than they are found this year 1590. I have lighted upon a notable man, and good books in that kind of argument; what else I can with labour come unto that belongs to the state-life, or may any way delight your Honour, I am bound to be right willing and glad to perform. There are certain mathematical authors to be sold here, in my opinion wonderful good cheap, whose names and price I have thought good to set down *a basso delle lettere*. If it please your Honour to have them, upon conference with Pretorius, how he finds them priced elsewhere, I will upon word received lay out the money, and take order for the conveyance; if not, there is no harm done. The books rest till I hear from your Honour.[8]

What is of interest to us here is the combination which Wotton offers Zouche of both 'intelligence' (information about contemporary politics and events: the plat of the Emperor's summer house; the political state of affairs in Frankfurt), and what we would term 'learning' – books, and intellectual debates. The scholar, Wotton, offers these together as the knowledge transaction he negotiates with the person he regards as his potential patron. They apparently form a 'package' of skills which the young Wotton believes will enhance his prospects of service with Lord Zouche.[9] The correspondence (of which we only have Wotton's side) shows Wotton trying to construct a relationship of mutual obligation and indebtedness between himself and Lord Zouche, by contracting promises of future knowledge he can acquire for him, further books he can obtain, desirable pieces of information he might be able to lay his hands on.

A glimpse of the correspondence from three months later reveals that the close relationship between 'learning' and 'intelligence' had intensified and become a still more explicit part of what Wotton offered to Zouche in the way of service. Their exchange continues to deal primarily in books, with the two men acting as each other's agent in the continental book trade:

Your Honour's books which I delivered very safely, trussed up to the merchant, upon conference with him, I thought convenient to stay a while, till his next sending of certain wares upon the river towards Nuremburg . . . The sum is not great, and if your Honour would allow me leave to be so bold, I would crave the employing of it in a better use for me there, because here (I thank God) I want

---

8 Pearsall Smith, *Life and Letters*, I, 245–6.
9 The package is remarkably similar to the following, by Francis Bacon: 'The sovereignty of man lieth hid in knowledge; wherein many things are reserved, which kings with their treasure cannot buy, nor with their force command; their spials and intelligencers can give no news of them, their seamen and discoverers cannot sail where they grow' ('Mr. Bacon in Praise of Knowledge' (BL Harleian MS 6797, fol. 47), *The Works of Francis Bacon*, ed. J. Spedding, R. L. Ellis and D. D. Heath (14 vols., 1858–74), VIII, 125–6).

no money for as far as my affairs go. At my being in Altorph, I remember myself to have dealt with Glasianus [Professor of Oratory at Altdorf] for a Polybius in Greek, which he signified unto me he could well help me unto: if by his means I might procure me a copy of that author ancienter than MDXXX (because I have Perot's edition of that year already), I should be very glad and most earnestly entreat your Honour at his visiting of you, to motion it unto him in my behalf. I desire the bare Greek without the Latin version, if it be possible.

But Wotton had at his disposal – and was able to offer – books and manuscripts with a much higher (specifically political) value:

We have here in his Majesty's library notable discourses of military matters, and in that sort a book of especial estimation, written in Italian, having many experiences of fortification and the like. If your Honour have a fancy to it, I will cause it to be written out, which I desire to hear in the next, because the book is in quarto and of a reasonable quantity. If in any other particular state-point you crave the like, no doubt whatsoever the argument be, amongst 9,000 volumes (whereof the most part are manuscript) we shall find some author to please your Honour. For my part my chief care and charges are bestowed in Greek and Dutch writers and secret letters of the Empire, of which, in my profession, I have some that might make a great man beholding to me; but I will not flatter myself so far. Whatsoever it be, or can become unto by exchange of those I have, or gain otherwise, shall ever be, and most worthily are, only at your Honour's commandment.[10]

Here the focus sharpens to allow something close to bare-faced bargaining for patronage: Wotton has access to 9,000 volumes, amongst which there is bound to be found information of political or tactical value to Zouche. Some of the manuscript material is possibly politically sensitive: 'I have some that might make a great man beholding to me.'

Wotton offers Zouche his service in a variety of related knowledge transactions: the providing of local knowledge; detail of the availability of scholarly books (a transaction in which he and his master participate more symmetrically, since each helps the other in book acquisition); the obtaining and organising of detailed textual material relevant to state-craft, including transcription, abridgement, compilation; the processing of written material on secret matters of diplomatic or political interest. This kind of 'intelligence' plainly embraces both sensitive and innocuous, scholarly and political knowledge, and elides the functions of information gatherer and spy. As a version of 'scholarly service' – secret counsel from an informant with a scholarly training in synthesising knowledge from a range of sources – it suggests the possibility of real scholarly influence in the political domain. It sets in a different

---

[10] Pearsall Smith, *Life and Letters*, I, 255–6.

light, for instance, that infamous and illfated liaison between scholar and political master in the Essex circle – between Essex and Henry Cuffe.[11]

By the 1590s, we are suggesting, scholarly readers are providing a highly specific (though not yet institutionally regularised) form of private service for politically involved public figures. Already in 1581, in his *Positions*, Richard Mulcaster emphasises the value of such service, in terms which take for granted its status as recognised *employment* for academics (we shall come in a moment to the question of 'hire' which Mulcaster raises):

For *readers* of yeares, of sufficiencie, of continuance, methinke I durst enter into some combat that it were beyond all crie profitable, and necessarie, to haue whom to follow, and of whom to learn how to direct our studies . . . They that haue bene acquainted with cunning *readers* any where will subscribe to this I know.

Priuate studie tied to one booke led by one braine . . . cannot compare for iudiciall learning with the benefit of hearing one, nay of repeating to one vpon interrogatories after reading, to trie his iudgement, his keeping, and remembrance: which one hath red, and digested all the best bookes, or at the least the best bookes in that kinde, whereof he maketh profession . . . Whose seruice, for the benefit that comes from them will saue their whole hire in very bookes, which the student shall not so much neede, when his *reader* is his librarie . . . And therefore that great sufficiencie doth still call for great recompence to be tyed a stake for it all ones life time.[12]

Towards the end of Elizabeth's reign, efficient knowledge gathering was an integral part of the activities of those jostling for power, and scholarly readers and their 'knowledge transactions' had become a recognised part of these bids for influence in political decision making.[13] There is a nice example of the way this kind of service functioned from the *employer*'s end, in the surviving correspondence of Francis Bacon. In a 1593 letter, the earl of Essex requests a specific research task from Bacon:

The Queen did require of me a draft of an Instruction for matter of intelligence, seeming willing now she hath sworn me one of her Council to use my service in that way . . . The places are Rheims and Rome. Mr. Phillips hath known Mr. Secretary's courses in such matters; so as I may have counsel from you and precedents from him. I pray you, as your leisure may serve, send me

---

[11] See A. Grafton and L. Jardine, ' "Studied for Action": How Gabriel Harvey Read his Livy', *Past and Present*, 129 (1990), 3–50, at 6–8.

[12] Richard Mulcaster, *Positions Wherein those Primitive Circumstances be Examined, which are Necessarie for the Training vp of Children* . . . (London, 1581), 254–5. We are extremely grateful to Warren Boutcher for providing us with this quotation at exactly the appropriate moment.

[13] See Hammer, ' "The Bright Shininge Sparke" '.

your conceipt as soon as you can; for I know not how soon I shall be called on. I will drawn some notes of mine own which I will reform and enlarge by yours.[14]

Wotton, in one of his commonplace books, describes scholarly reading of this kind suitable for responding to questions on military matters:

In reading of history, a soldier should draw the platform of battles he meets with, plant the squadrons and order the whole frame as he finds it written, so he shall print it firmly in his mind and apt his mind for actions. A politique should find the characters of personages and apply them to some of the Court he lives in, which will likewise confirm his memory and give scope and matter for conjecture and invention. A friend to confer readings together most necessary.[15]

This, then, provides a context for looking at some surviving late sixteenth-century exercises in reading, which might qualify as 'scholarly services'. These include Gabriel Harvey's famously copious marginal annotations, in his extensive library of books on subjects ranging from oratory to military battle formations.[16] But before we turn to Harvey's marginal annotations, what were the financial and professional implications of this kind of scholarly reading? We need some kind of answer to this question, in order to account for the fact that traditional Tudor history has found no trace of this knowledge support system, which, we are suggesting, extended beyond the circle of officially retained (and publicly remunerated) secretaries residing at Leicester house (subsequently Essex house).

In the *Apology* he produced after the disgrace of the earl of Essex, Francis Bacon wrote of his service to Essex in the early 1590s:

I applied myself to him in a manner which I think happeneth rarely among men; . . . neglecting the Queen's service, mine own fortune, and in a sort my

---

[14] *The Letters and the Life of Francis Bacon*, ed. J. Spedding (7 vols., 1861–74), I, 251 = *Works*, ed. Spedding, Ellis and Heath, VIII, 251.

[15] Pearsall Smith, *Life and Letters*, II, 494.

[16] The present piece of work on Harvey's annotations is a companion piece to one recently completed by Tony Grafton and Lisa Jardine on marginalia from the period 1580–90, in Harvey's copy of Livy's *Decades*. See Grafton and Jardine, ' "Studied for Action" '. There is actually evidence amongst the marginalia of a Harvey connection with Essex. Harvey's copy of Richard Davies, *A Funerall Sermon Preached the xxvi Day of November . . . at the Buriall of the Right Honourable Walter Earle of Essex and Ewe* (London, 1577), now in the library of St John's College, Oxford, bears the following inscription on its title page: 'Ex dono nobilissimi domini, Robert Devereuxii, Comitis Essexii'. At the end of the volume are the initials 'R.E.' (see V. F. Stern, *Gabriel Harvey: His Life, Marginalia and Library* (Oxford, 1979), 208). But that connection is not necessary to the argument here, which suggests a type of activity, not a particular relationship with Essex.

vocation, I did nothing but advise and ruminate with myself to the best of my understanding, propositions and memorials of anything that might concern his Lordship's honour, fortune, or service.[17]

To the modern reader, the intensity of such an account of Bacon's devoted private service suggests an indecorous level of emotional involvement. But this is because the services thus rendered take place beyond the public domain, within the intimate space of the noble employer's household. Because of its 'private' nature, all reference to material reward is couched in a coded language of friendship and exchange, mutual obligation and indebtedness. The contractual bases of the service (who has contracted to offer what services to whom, in return for what) are all but invisible; they leave minimal traces in the sphere of 'business'.[18] The question we need to ask here is, how were those who provided such services rewarded? In other words, if service lay somewhere between rank-equal friendship and servant's hire, how did the individual convert his 'credit' with his master into 'profit' (the means to survive materially)? How did he turn his credit with one master into the kind of 'worth' which would gain him further employment in other households?[19]

The well-documented case of Antonio Perez, the Spanish secretary who fled to England in the 1590s, offers the beginnings of an answer to this question. Throughout his period in England, during which he provided Elizabeth and her ministers with intelligence on Spanish affairs, Perez's upkeep appears to have been primarily the responsibility of the earl of Essex. When the support of Perez became an undue financial burden, Essex sought support from the queen, who (according to a report of Anthony Bacon's) agreed to make a

[17] *Letters and Life*, ed. Spedding, I, 106. Lady Bacon wrote to Anthony Bacon in 1594: 'Some do think that yor Brother and yow make to great a note of the Earles favo^r' (Ungerer, *A Spaniard*, I, 221).

[18] Even in the period itself, private service could attract criticism from contemporaries precisely on grounds of a dangerous closeness between the parties. See the infamous letter from Lady Bacon to Francis concerning his relations with Perez, with whom he was linked by bonds of mutual service to Essex (*ibid.*, 219–20). According to Alan Bray, the relationship of *service* between a noble master and a servant of only slightly lesser rank, in the later sixteenth century, was regularly expressed as one of extreme intimacy (A. Bray, 'Homosexuality and the Signs of Male Friendship in Elizabethan England', *History Workshop Journal*, 29 (1990), 1–19). See also L. Jardine, 'Twins and Travesties: Gender, Dependency and Sexual Availability in *Twelfth Night*', in *Erotic Politics: Desire on the Renaissance Stage*, ed. S. Zimmerman (1992), 27–38; J. Barrell, 'Editing Out: The Discourse of Patronage and Shakespeare's Twenty-Ninth Sonnet', in J. Barrell, *Poetry and Politics* (Manchester, 1988), 18–43.

[19] 'Debt', 'credit' and 'profit' are terms freely used in the period by those in exactly the kind of service relationship which we are describing. See, for instance, Wotton's letters to Zouche. That such services were paid for is confirmed by the Mulcaster passage above.

contribution.[20] But no direct settlement was made on Perez himself, either in land (which as a foreigner he could not, in any case, hold), or in terms of grants or pensions. Instead, settlements in land to precisely the amounts pledged by Elizabeth were settled on two of Essex's household servants (lesser gentlemen, quite suitably entitled to handle the earl's money, and one of whom Essex had put in charge of overseeing Perez's mobile household during his stay in England).[21] We have to presume that they passed the monies raised on the properties to Perez; but without Anthony Bacon's letter, this financial transaction between Essex and Perez would be invisible. In other words, the 'hire' did not necessitate exchange of money between master and 'friend', but passed indirectly through those whose service relationship was socially unambiguous.

Another curious document, this time relating to Francis Bacon, provides further evidence of there being an arrangement available which circumvented the awkwardness of supporting financially those whose service could not be publicly acknowledged without compromising the secrecy or intimacy of the bond. In the first 'Life and Letters' volume of the *Complete Works*, James Spedding transcribes a set of accounts for 1593–5, itemising 'Money paid by Mr. Anthony Bacon to his brother Francis and to Sir Anthony Standen.'[22] Spedding identifies these sums as

---

[20] The arrangement is reported in a letter from Anthony Bacon to his brother Francis in December 1594: 'The occasion was verie fitlie ministred by my Lo. [Essex] himself by aduertysing to Sr Perez that the Queen had signed at ij of the clocke, and had giuen him a hundred poundes lande in fee simple and 30 li in parckes, which for her quietnes sake and in respecte of his frende he was content to accept without any further contestacion' (Ungerer, *A Spaniard*, I, 222–3: no. 109; see also *Letters and Life*, ed. Spedding, I, 324).

[21] Ungerer, *A Spaniard*, I, 223. See also no. 199 for further details. On Meyricke's role as financial go-between between Essex and Perez, see Ungerer, *ibid.*, 189.

[22] *Letters and Life*, ed. Spedding, I, 322. The items in this set of accounts run: '1593 A part ce qui a este paye a Mons. Senhouse. / Le 21ᵐᵉ de Septembre, a Mons. Francois Bacon £5 / 11 de Septembre, 93, a Pierre pour Mr. Fr. Bacon £20 / 26 d'Octob. 1593, a Pierre £20 / 30 d'Octob. /93 a Mr. Fr. Bacon £1 / 31 d'Octob. /93, a Kellet pour Mons. Fr. Bacon £23 / 18 de Novem. 93, a Ashpoole pour Mr. Fr. Bacon £4 / 6 de May, /94, a Pierre pour Mr. Fr. Bacon £10 / 11 de Juillet, /94, a Mr. Fr. Bacon £60 / 31 de'Aoust, /94, a Mr Fr. Bacon £100 / 9 Septemb. /94, a Mr. Fr. Bacon £50 / 29 Janvier, /94, a Mr Trott pour Mr. Fr. Bacon £30 / 8 Mars, /94, a Rich. Grome pour Mr. Fr. Bacon £10 / 14 d'April, a Kellet pour Mr. Fr. Bacon £44 / 14 Juin, /95, a Mons. Sugden par son homme £50 / £373'. During the period August 1593 to at least April 1594, Anthony Bacon was laid up with chronic gout, first at his home in Gorhambury and then at Redbourne. During this period Anthony Bacon continued to operate as 'controller' for the network of continental spies he operated on behalf of the earl of Essex. 'From [Gorhambury], [Anthony] Bacon could continue to receive the streams of intelligence which came to him from Scotland and the Continent. On the other hand, he needed someone whom he could trust to convey this sensitive information to the earl of Essex, who was generally resident at Court. It was precisely this function which [Anthony] Standen came to share with Francis Bacon during what proved to be Anthony Bacon's long sojourn in Hertfordshire. Receiving confidential dispatches from his friend, he

'debts' apparently incurred by Francis Bacon with his brother Anthony, and he adds the following note:

It is not often, I suppose, that a relation of debtor and creditor like this continues long even between the best of friends without making their intercourse more or less uncomfortable; especially when the lender has so good an excuse for objecting to fresh demands as that of not being able to lend more without embarrassing himself, and placing himself under fresh obligations to other acquaintance. It is worth recording therefore that in all this correspondence I find no trace of disagreement between these brothers. Not a word of reproof, expostulation, reluctance, or impatience drops from Anthony; . . . and the fact deserves notice, . . . as affording a strong presumption that *he* at least, who had the best means of judging and was every way so much interested, did not disapprove of the course which Francis was taking, or suspect him of prodigality or carelessness.[23]

The reason for Anthony Bacon's uncharacteristic reasonableness over these 'debts', we suggest, is that the sums which passed from Anthony to Francis, via discreet intermediaries (who signed the papers acknowledging receipt of the money),[24] or occasionally in person, were actually payments for the delicate private services which we know from other sources he was conducting during this period – namely, the transmission of highly sensitive material between Anthony Bacon and the earl of Essex.[25] Since the concept of 'hire' is singularly inappropriate to a relationship not just of social peers but of brothers, the money is acknowledged in the form of an 'indebtedness' – a bond of obligation forged by the transaction.[26]

conveyed them to Essex in private meetings in the earl's chambers at Court. [Standen] became, therefore, one of his patron's frequent and privileged companions, intimate at once with the earl's greatest secrets and his person' (Paul Hammer, 'An Elizabethan Spy who Came in from the Cold: The Return of Anthony Standen to England in 1593', *Historical Research*, 65 (1992), 277–95). Anthony Standen was employed as an intelligencer on the continent, first by Burghley, and then by Essex – the changeover in patronage took place during the period of these accounts.

23 *Letters and Life*, ed. Spedding, 1, 322–3. In thinking about the implications of 'obligation', 'debt', 'hire' and bonds versus money transactions we have been given invaluable advice by Craig Muldrew.
24 *Letters and Life*, ed. Spedding, 1, 322.
25 One might note that in Shakespeare's *King Lear* it is precisely such 'private service' which Kent offers Lear, when, in disguise, he re-contracts himself to the service of the king: '*Lear.* What services canst thou do? *Kent.* I can keep honest counsel, ride, run, mar a / curious tale in telling it, and deliver a plain / message bluntly' (1.iv.33–6).
26 As we saw above, Francis Bacon was performing other 'private services' of a specifically knowledge transaction kind for Essex during exactly this period. So it is quite possible that the payment is *actually* made by the earl of Essex (whom both Standen and Francis Bacon regard as their 'Lord' in this period), but is made *via* Anthony Bacon. Since Anthony provides the money, there is *really* a debt to him, which represents an obligation between him and the earl of Essex. If Essex never paid up for

Francis has use of the money (reward for his service), but it is registered as a debt to Anthony (a bond of mutual obligation between them).[27] The key concept, in other words, is the one of 'obligation', or 'indebtedness' in the *broad* sense of a mutual bond, on the basis of the exchange of service and reward.[28]

Recent work on the scholar John Dee suggests that much of the mystery surrounding his role in Elizabethan intellectual and political life derives from the marginality – and often invisibility – of scholarly service relationships.[29] Although Dee was fastidious about recording in his diary the details of his transactions with prominent members of the government and court circles, the economics of these knowledge transactions are not presented in terms familiar to the modern reader. They are not expressed in terms of remuneration, but rather as future *expectations*, promises of friendship and pledges of support at times of need. This package of promises adds up to Dee's 'credit' – what he is 'worth' in the public eye as a consequence not just of his cultivated intellectual credibility, but of his backing and connections. The tokens of reward through which services rendered can be traced within this kind of credit system are more often gifts of food or jewellery (notionally, 'gifts') than currency. Intellectual services of this kind, with which Wotton provided the Lord Zouche, or with which Harvey provided Edward Dyer, Philip Sidney and the younger Thomas Smith,[30] or Cuffe provided the earl of Southampton, or Anthony and Francis Bacon the earl of Essex,

such transactions (relying on more social kinds of credit and debt to bind Anthony Bacon to him), this might begin to explain the chronic and continuing money shortages of the Bacon brothers. On the proliferation of bonds, and absence of hard currency in England in the period, see J. C. Muldrew, 'Credit, Market Relations and Debt Litigation in Late Seventeenth Century England, with Special Reference to King's Lynn' (Cambridge PhD dissertation, 1990).

[27] Francis Bacon could, apparently, borrow further money on the basis of his 'credit' with Anthony and Essex. See, e.g., Ungerer, *A Spaniard*, I, 222. The 'debts' will only be discharged, as far as we can judge, upon the death of one of the parties, or some unsatisfactory termination of their relationship. See the memorandum of October 1594, in which Francis totals his debt to Anthony on paper 'after a fit of the stone' (*Letters and Life*, ed. Spedding, I, 322). When Lord Zouche was on the point of returning to England, Henry Wotton wrote to him acknowledging a 'debt' incurred towards him (i.e. monies received in exchange for the private services described in the correspondence): 'I do most humbly crave to know . . . when your determination is to draw towards England, that I may provide some convenient means to pay your Honour those thirty crowns, to whom I am besides in debt as much as my soul can compass' (Pearsall Smith, *Life and Letters*, I, 292).

[28] For a legal version of 'debt' in this period which appears to square with the picture we have reconstructed, see J. H. Baker, *An Introduction to English Legal History* (London, 1979), 266–71, 282–7 (especially the discussion of 'debt on an obligation', 269–71).

[29] See Sherman, *John Dee*.

[30] See Grafton and Jardine, ' "Studied for Action" '.

masquerade as exchanges under the rubric of male friendship, but are covertly acknowledged as 'knowledge transactions', with a fee, a material benefit, attached to them. There was, apparently, a living (or part of a living) to be made, during the 1580s and 90s, by providing intellectual service for members of an outer circle of Elizabeth's government.

In 1597, John Dee presented Edward Dyer with a reading of his own *General and Rare Memorials Pertayning to the Perfect Arte of Navigation* written twenty years earlier, in 1577. He did so in response to a specific request for advice on a political matter in a letter from Dyer (now lost). The reading Dee proposed adapted his existing printed text for a specific government-directed purpose. Dyer had requested Dee's scholarly advice on 'Her Ma.ties Title Royall and Sea Soveraigntie in St Georges Chanell; and in all the Brytish Ocean; any man[er] or way next envyroninge, or next adioyninge vnto, England, Ireland and Scotland, or any of the lesser Iles to them apperteyning.'[31] Dee responded by providing Dyer with a reading 'route' through his own work, designed to extract the information requested.[32] Dee's reading instructions are prefaced by a direct announcement of an understood service relationship with Dyer: 'I thank yor Wurship highly, that you still contynue yor true love & good will toward me: and allso remayne firmly perswaded of my constant redines, to do any thing of service, or pleasure, unto yor Wurship, that doth, or shall lye in my power, to performe.'[33] His response to Dyer's question, concerning 'Her Ma.ties Title Royall and Sea Soveraigntie in St Georges Channell: and in all the Brytish Ocean', was pragmatic and precise, and took the form of what Dee termed a 'directed reading'. He was to look back at Dee's published discussion of territorial waters (and Dee courteously furnished a copy of the original book), and adapt it to the current question:

---

[31] BL Harleian MS 249, fols. 95–105.

[32] Sherman, ' "A Living Library" ', 289–99. Early in their career, both Gabriel Harvey and Edmund Spenser aspired to this kind of relationship with Dyer, or so the phrasing of remarks in the so-called Harvey letter book, and amongst Harvey's marginalia, suggest. In a letter transcribed in the letter book, Spenser [Immerito] writes: 'The twoe worthy gentlemen, Mr. Sidney and Mr. Dyer, have me, I thanke them, in sum use of familiaritye; of whom and to whome what speache passith for your creddite and estimation, I leave yourselfe to conceyve, havinge allwayes so well conceyvid of my unfainid affection and good will towardes yow' (BL Sloane MS 93, fol. 53r). 'Two outstanding courtiers thanked me for this political and historical inquiry: Sir Edward Dyer and Sir Edward Denny. But let the project itself – once fully tried – be my reward. All I want is a lively and effective political analysis of the chief histories: especially when Hannibal and Scipio, Marius and Sylla, Pompey and Caesar flourished' (Harvey's Livy, 277). There is further evidence of Harvey's personal contact with both Dyer and Essex on fol. 422v or Harvey's Chaucer (BL Additional MS 42518).

[33] Sherman, ' "A Living Library" ', 289–90.

There, in the 20th page of that boke, (against the figure, 9, in the margent) begynneth matter, inducing the consideration of her Ma:^ties Royall Sealimits . . . And herevppon, in the 21st page, both in the Text, and allso in the Margent, is pregnant matter conveyned . . . Then, peradventure, the Consequences of the matter, will lead you on, to reade the 22, 23, 24, 25, 26, and vnto the middle of the 27 page . . . Afterward you may pass ou[er], to the 37 page: and there (in the .15th. lyne, from the ende of that page) you may begin againe, to reade . . . and so you may hold on, till you haue attentifely, red ouer the 38th page, wholy, and so much of the 39th, as will bring you, to the Conclusion of that extraordinarie discourse: (almost abowte the middest of that page,) ending with this worde, *Opportuntie* . . . Returning againe, to yor present purpose; Yt will not be impertinent to your Consideration, to procede consequently, in reading of the 54th, 55, 56, and 57 pages . . . Yet, a little more, your paynes takinge, will gete you some more matter, here & there, till you co[m]me to the end of the boke. The Marginall Notes, sometimes, are of great moment.34

In the summer of 1597 the privy council was engaged in the escalating conflict between the English Merchant Adventurers and the merchants of the Hanseatic League. During these months England's commercial relations with northern Europe had degenerated: the Merchant Adventurers were accused of monopolising trade and of harassing the Hanseatic merchants in England. In August 1597, Emperor Rudolph II issued a decree which effectively banned trade with the English merchants. During the next months the interested parties exchanged diplomats at a furious pace. To support the English negotiators and buttress the English claims, the government clearly consulted outside experts. Several of their reports survive in the State Papers: an anonymous paper offered 'reasons to prove the Merchant Adventurers cloth trade on the River Elbe', and Laurence Thompson produced a comprehensive treatise entitled, 'Assertio veritatis de legitima interceptione Ansiaticarum Navium, contra anonymum calumniatorum'. Dee's advice to Dyer belongs alongside such advice – scholarly services rendered to the Elizabethan government.35 The Dee/Dyer exchange offers a glimpse of the complicated workings of knowledge transactions along a submerged chain (from academic margins to political centre) of scholarly service.

A more fully documented example of scholarly services survives in the case of Gabriel Harvey, though the 'credit' arrangements are equally obscure today. Harvey was a 'reader' (in something like Mulcaster's sense) for a group of individuals which included Sir Philip Sidney,

34 *Ibid.*, 290.   35 *Ibid.*, 297–8.

Thomas Preston and the younger Thomas Smith.[36] Jardine and Grafton recently reconstructed a possible context for a set of readings carried out in 1580, when Harvey was officially employed as a secretary by the earl of Leicester. Here we shall be looking at some further knowledge transactions of Harvey's from around this period: readings of legal texts, centred on the year 1579–84. We suggest that in this period of comparative public visibility (for an academic!), Harvey's services might well have been sought for 'knowledge transactions' of the kind we have been describing. He became a fellow of Trinity Hall, Cambridge, in late 1578, commenced study of the civil law and gained his Bachelor of Law degree in 1584. Harvey and Spenser's joint publications date from 1579–80 – publications which in the present context look very like carefully-judged samples of informed opinion, for the non-specialist reader, of the kind we showed Wotton offering Zouche at the beginning of this essay.[37] In autumn 1580 Harvey entered the earl of Leicester's official service, briefly, as a secretary.[38]

The volumes from this period on whose marginalia our treatment of Harvey's particular kind of reading, or 'knowledge transaction', is based are:

Ioachim Hopperus, *In veram Iurisprudentiam Isagoges ad filium Libri octo* . . . (Cologne, 1580)[39]

Nicolaus Vigelius, *Iuris civilis totius absolutissima Methodus* . . . (Basle, J. Oporinus, 1561)[40]

---

36 Grafton and Jardine, ' "Studied for Action" '.
37 See the epistle dedicatory to the *Shepheardes Calender* (London, 1579), and *Three Proper and Wittie, Familiar Letters: Lately Passed betwene two Universitie Men: Touching the Earthquake in Aprill Last, and our English Refourmed Versifying . . . Two Other very Commendable Letters, of the Same Mens Writing: Both Touching the Foresaid Artificiall Versifying, and Certain Other Particulars* . . . (London, 1580; entered Stationers' Register, 30 June 1580).
38 Spenser was a confidential emissary in Leicester's service in 1579; when he left for Ireland, as secretary to Lord Grey, in August 1580, Harvey apparently took his place. See Stern, *Gabriel Harvey*, 68. During his residence at Leicester house Harvey would have been a conventional secretary, presumably receiving a stipend; when *not* part of a noble household we argue that he becomes a 'scholarly reader' of the type we are discussing, and his employment enters the realm of 'private service'.
39 BL, London c.60.e.14. 'Gabrielis Harveij, 1580' on title page. Contains the *Elementorum iuris, sive principiorum iusti et iniusti*. At the bottom of p. 449, Harvey indicates that he reread the Hopper in 1581: 'Bis in die. Aureum vnius diei pensum. 1581. gabriel haruejus. J.C.'
40 Folio. Gonville and Caius Library, Cambridge H.6.12, title page: 'Gabrielis Harueij. 1580. Mense Aprile.' 'Arte, et Virtute.' Not in Stern. A note on the final endpaper indicates a 1581 reading for this volume also: 'In Vigelij methodo iuris Pontificij, Lugduni apud Junctam excusa 1581' (and a number of notes in the body of the text refer to Vigelius' *Methodus iuris Pontificii*). We are grateful to the Master and Fellows of Caius College for permission to consult this volume.

Ioannis Freigius, *Paratitla seu synopsis Pandectarum iuris ciuilis* (Basle, [1583]).[41]

Within the 'knowledge transaction' context of service which we have been describing, Harvey's annotations in these volumes signpost the text for two distinct stages of directed reading. The first provides a reading 'route' or 'path' through the text (of the Vigelius), to facilitate another reader's speedy grasp on the contents. The second is 'pragmatic', in something like the specifically legal Ciceronian sense, in that its purpose is systematically to accumulate legal material to be produced (on behalf of someone else) to answer a particular legal question.[42] But this second kind of reading also contains the possibility of something more like our modern understanding of 'pragmatic' – available for immediate

---

[41] Private collection, deposited in the Princeton University Library, title page: 'Gabrielis Harueij. 1583. Arte, et Virtute.' We are grateful to the owner, and to Princeton University Library, for allowing us access to this volume. In a fuller version of this paper, a further group of volumes are obvious candidates for inclusion: Duarenus, *De sacris ecclesiae ministeriis ac beneficiis libri VIII. In quibus quicquid ad plenam Iuris Pontificij cognitionem necessarium est, breviter ac dilucide explicatum continetur* (Paris, 1564), where on sig. a6ʳ Harvey writes, 'Duarenus: Vigelius: Speculator [on ecclesiastical law]: all thre in 8°; & worthy to be fayerly bouwnd togither jn on volume' (Stern, *Gabriel Harvey*, 209–10, 271). This volume is dated 'Mense Februario. 1580'. 'Prima cursoria, et perfunctoria lectio'; Joachim Mynsinger, *Dn. Iochachimi Mynsingeri . . . in tres libri II. Decretalibus* . . . (Helmstadt, 1582) (Caius Library H.4.31(2)), title page, 'Pre. vjˢ. Londini. Gabrjelis Harueij. 1582. GH.'; Justinian, *D. Iustiniani Imp. Institutionum libri IIII* . . . (Lyons, 1577) (Emmanuel College Library, Cambridge, 324.8.62), title page, 'x lj Gabrielis Harueij. / 1579. G.H. mense Martjo CIƆ IƆ LXXXIX.'; Joannis Oldendorpius, *Loci communes iuris ciuilis* . . . (Lyons, 1551) (BL Bagford 5991), title page inscribed 'GH. Iuris regulae: pluribus locupletatae pragmaticis Sententijs. J.C. Gabriel Harvejus. Gnomae, et Aphorismi Pragmatici', and at end of index, 'gabrielis harvey, et amicorum. 1579. Disce: doce: age' (Stern, *Gabriel Harvey*, 229) [not yet seen]; Cicero, *M. Tullii Ciceronis Epistolae ad Atticum ad M. Brutum, ad Quinctum Fratrem* (Venice, 1563) (BL c.60.f.9), at end of letters, sig. cc3ᵛ, 'Relegi has politicas pragmaticasq[ue] epistolas in aula Trinitatis, multo, quam unq[uam] antea, accuratius; et plane, ut Liuij verbo utar, deliberabundus. Mense Julio, sole in Leonis corde flagrante. 1582. gabriel harueius, aulae Justinianae socius'. Unfortunately a later owner has excised the entire text of the ad Atticum letters (presumably because they were already heavily annotated), and added his own notes to the ad Brutum and ad Quinctum Fratrem letters, in which few Harvey notes occur. Cicero, *Topica* (Paris, 1550) (All Souls, Oxford, a-II-4(3)), final page (sig. E5ᵛ), Gabriel Harvejus. Calendis Februar. 1570', 'Multo etiam diligentius, 1579 iamtum aliquanto studiosius iuri ciuili incumbens.' We are grateful to Walter Colman for providing us with a transcription of the marginalia in this volume.

[42] In Cicero's *De oratore* Antonius advises the orator not to fill his head with legal detail, but to employ someone to get it up for him: 'Itaque illi disertissimi homines ministros habent in causis iuris peritos, cum ipsi sint pertissimi, et qui . . . pragmatici vocantur' ('This is why, in the lawcourts, those who are the most accomplished practitioners retain advisors who are expert in the law (even though they are very expert themselves), and who are called "pragmatics"'). See also Quintilian, *Institutiones oratoriae*, 12.iii.4. Standard Renaissance Latin dictionaries give this technical definition of the 'pragmaticus' (We are grateful to Warren Boutcher for this observation).

application to practical action (in political life).[43] Throughout his
marginalia, Harvey plays on these competing senses of 'pragmatic', and
refers to himself regularly as 'pragmaticus'.[44]

'The civil law is written by the watchful' ('Jus Ciuile Vigilantibus
scriptum est'), notes Harvey on the title page of Vigelius. The attentive-
ness of the compiler of civil law compendia facilitates access, and
provides the would-be practitioner with an invaluable tool. Harvey's legal
annotations are above all preoccupied with this 'methodical' aspect of
legal studies: knowledge of the law itself is evidently less important to him
than a clear grasp on the most up-to-date retrieval processes. Vigelius'
Method (as its title advertises) reduces the civil law to a set of key
headings or 'places', systematically ordered, so as to provide just such an
information retrieval system. Harvey pronounces on its effectiveness at
the top of page 4: 'The use of this method is unparalleled, both for the
most ready knowledge of universal law, and also for the fastest practical
access in the lawcourt. And lawyers are much in need of a more ready
instrument, both in study, and for action.'

To understand how such a method works, we can conveniently follow
an example which Harvey himself picks out – bracketing it in the text and
adding a marginal note. At the end of the first, general preface, against
one of Vigelius' worked examples, Harvey writes: 'Hence the scope of
any case whatsoever can be comprehended within its ready embrace.
Which [case] otherwise might seem to be excessively broad, and in no
way resolvable. And the judgement itself, regarding any doubtful legal
question whatsoever, may hence readily be arrived at.'[45] Vigelius'
example shows how a question arising from a legal nicety is satisfactorily
and speedily resolved by referring it promptly to its appropriate heading,
and scanning the entries under it. The problem is: a husband and wife
make their wills in the same document, in which they jointly appoint
their heirs. After the husband's death, the wife changes the will. The
question is: does the wife's later will make the previous one, made with
her husband, void? The substantial issue is: are there grounds on which
the wife's will ought to be disallowed? The key distinction on which the
case turns is: whether the later will was an emended will made in the
absence of the husband, or whether it was an entirely fresh will,
superseding the previous one (the husband being deceased). According
to Vigelius, the obvious appropriate head under which to pursue this

---

[43] On the endpaper of the Vigelius volume Harvey identifies his use of 'pragmatic' with
Vigelius' use of 'orator' ('quos plaerunque oratores uocat').
[44] See, for instance, Grafton and Jardine, ' "Studied for Action" '. Harvey plays similarly
on the word 'action', which can be taken generally, or in the more strict sense of a legal
action.   [45] Vigelius, *Methodus*, 6.

distinction comes in chapter 12, book ix, of his work: 'Where immediately at the beginning occur the words: "Concerning alteration of the wishes of a testator, and posterior wills".' The crucial distinction is nowhere made, and 'where the law makes no distinction we ought not to distinguish', so that in the present case, the wife's later will simply supersedes (and makes void) the earlier joint will.[46]

When we turn to chapter 12, book ix, of Vigelius, we find that the methodical presentation of material 'immediately at the beginning, under the title, "De mutata uoluntate testatoris, testamento posteriore"' is actually a reading route through Justinian's *Institutes* and *Digest*, and the *Codex*. Here is the entry:

Inst. [II] tt. 17 posteriore quoque. usque ad alio autem. ex eo autem ff. [*Digest*] lib. 28. tt. 1. l. 21. j. tt. 2. l. 7. l. 9. in prin. fin. tt. 3. l. 1. l. 2. l. 3. sed etsi stante. [actually, sed et si sit ante.] l. 11. l. 12. fin. l. 16. tt. 5. l. 45. in prin. l. 51. l. 52. l. 90. tt. 6. l. 14 si suo. lib. 29. tt. 1. l. 36. fin. lib. 34. tt. 44. l. 22. tt. 9. l. 12. lib. 36. tt. 1. l. 29. lib. 37. tt. 11. l. i. non autem omnes. si quis in duob. l. 11. plane si. lib. 38. tt. 6. l. j. penult. c. [*Codex*] tt. 22. l. 6. tt. 23. l. 20. l. 21. si quis autem. l. 27. l. 1. si haeres.

Taking the *Institutes* reference, for example: 'Inst. [II] tt. 17 posteriore quoque. usque ad alio autem. ex eo autem ff.' tells us to go to the second book of the *Institutes*, title seventeen, and begin reading at 'posteriore quoque' ('Again, an earlier will is broken by a second will properly made'), down to 'alio autem'. Then begin reading at 'ex eo autem' ('But a will cannot be rendered ineffective merely because the testator later wishes it so') and read to the end of the title. Sure enough, this gives us a running narrative of precisely those portions of the title relevant to this particular case concerning the validity of a later will.[47] Given a particular project, the *Methodus* provides a reading strategy which directly and purposefully addresses its solution.[48]

At the end of the first preface, at the bottom of page 6, Harvey echoes Vigelius by providing his own methodical reading routes, to make the best possible use of the volume as a whole for a specified purpose:[49]

---

[46] *Ibid.*, 5–6.
[47] See J. A. C. Thomas, *The Institutes of Justinian: Text, Translation and Commentary* (Amsterdam and Oxford, 1975), 131–3.
[48] This kind of instruction for reading in response to a specific technical question uses the same general procedure as Dee gave to Dyer. In both cases a reading route is recommended by a combination of page or paragraph references and word cues.
[49] The body of Vigelius' *Methodus* is practically unmarked; the procedural prefaces, by contrast, are heavily annotated. Similarly, Harvey's octavo copy of Justinian's *Institutes* is entirely unmarked in the body of the text. We suggest that this is because all his scholarly reader's attention is focused on *preparatory* manoeuvres, before the task at issue (which is, indeed, gaining speedy access to the contents of the civil law).

In each part, look closely at its distinguished preface, below. These should be referred above all to the praise of the Law (this applies to the fifth preface and the third); or to the partition and summarising of the Law (this applies to the first preface, which also treats the topic of the academic practice of the Law); or to the interpretation of the Law (this applies to the preface to the reader, the fourth preface and the seventh); or finally to the juridical practice (the second preface and the sixth), together with the tractate concerning legal reasoning, and the paradoxes, which are above all directed at forensic practice, and ought to be linked with the practical prefaces by being read consecutively). These are all, indeed, distinguished prefaces, and particularly useful if read in this order.

The route to be taken depends on the question asked – the kind of knowledge transaction sought via Harvey as scholarly reader inter-mediary. Throughout the text, Harvey's marginal notes keep the reader's attention on the narrative possibilities which he has advocated. They effectively turn the book into a new work – part printed text, part manuscript – with Harvey as its co-author (in the absence of Harvey himself from the reading), or guide (if he sits at the shoulder of the participant in the knowledge transaction). At the top of page 17, for example, is a note reminding the reader of the preferred route for preparing a 'praise of the law': 'The reading of the civil law, as it is most useful, so it is most sweet; after the fashion of the most beautiful and most joyful spectacle. See especially below, in the vivid preface to the fifth book.' Sure enough, the preface to book five begins: 'If someone could look down on the universal deeds and actions of men from some elevated place, without a doubt he would be seized with the greatest pleasure, on account of the marvellous diversity and accomplishment of human events. The reading of the civil law seems to me no less joyful than that spectacle.'[50] On the endpaper to the volume, Harvey reduces his reading route instructions to the two 'applied' objectives (interpret-ation and practice), and expands these to include other works by Vigelius:

Vigelius's prefaces above all, partly on the interpretation of the law (the preface to the reader, the fourth preface and the seventh); partly on legal practice (the second and the sixth). Which if read together (along with the method of judging

---

[50] Vigelius, *Methodus*, 282. This example clearly shows that Harvey's notes for the reader's guidance are written *after* he has read through the volume, rather than (as we might expect), as he reads. See also, at the top of p. 101, where Harvey cross-references the preface to part 3 for its defence of private ownership against Plato's advocating of communality: 'For private ownership, against Socrates's communal ownership; see the elegant and intelligent preface to part 3' ('Pro rerum proprietate, contra communionem Socratis; ecce elegans, et prudens praefatio in parte[m] 3'). For this passage in the preface see Vigelius, *Methodus*, 153.

forensic cases) are worth more than anything else in directing judgement, whether for readier knowledge of the law, or for more expeditious legal practice. In either case, more certain. And it will be useful to join with the methodical prefaces the one to the method for legal controversies [*Methodus Iuris controuersi* (1579)], and the one to the repertory of the law [*Repertorium Iuris* (1581)]. To the methodical prefaces should be added the preface to the Method of ecclesiastical law [*Methodus vniversi iuris pontificij absolutissima* (1579)]. To both the methodical and the practical [routes], the preface to the Method for the rules of the law of either kind. Which three erudite, and intelligent prefaces are altogether pertinent to the most expeditious method of the law, and its practice.[51]

Prominently placed in the volume, these instructions, we suggest, define the scholarly transaction, as the reader commences his reading.[52] Handed to someone who wants a good grasp of the civil law (whether as a general theoretical grounding in politics and diplomacy, or for practice as a civilian advocate), Harvey's Vigelius offers a reading strategy which builds on the foundations of the scholarly reader's own expert mastery of Roman law – a ready route, or *methodus*, tailored to the needs of either a politician or a practitioner in the law courts. Or simply the needs of someone who wishes to *know* about such activities. As Harvey writes at the end of part 1 of Vigelius: 'This first part is above all useful and most essential to the politician or courtier. The remainder is more particular to lawyers or pragmatics, apart from book 2 of part 1, which properly also belongs to the [practice of the] law.'[53] As this passage reminds us, Harvey's honed down method for scanning contemporary legal handbooks offers a further service: that of providing prompt access to *matter* for pleading (a kind of advocate's handbook).[54] Armed with such systematised compendious knowledge, the reader becomes a 'pragmaticus' – one furnished with the kind of 'intelligence' which will allow him to serve as counsellor to a man in office. Hopperus' *Elementa*

---

[51] This note indicates a date later than 1580. On the endpaper Harvey begins a note. 'In Vigelij methodo iuris Pontificij, Lugduni apud Junctam excusa 1581 . . . '. This note appears to be contemporary with notes in Harvey's copy of Duarenus, *De sacris ecclesiae ministeriis*. This volume is dated 'mense Februario. 1580'. 'Prima cursoria, et perfunctoria lectio'. If the date is old style, its reading comes after the Vigelius; if new (which seems likely, since the hands of the Vigelius date and the Duarenus match closely) the first 'perfunctory reading' precedes the Vigelius by two months.

[52] Seasoned students of Harvey's marginalia always turn to title page and end sheets for their first 'taste' of a new volume.

[53] Vigelius, *Methodus*, 96.

[54] For some further annotations in Elizabethan law texts, showing the existing apparatus for those trained in or training for the legal profession, see L. A. Knafla, 'The Law Studies of an Elizabethan Student', *Huntington Library Quarterly*, 32 (1969), 221–40.

Iuris and Freigius's *Synopsis Pandectarum* are both works which assist the accumulation and classification of legal material. Harvey's annotations weave the contents of these volumes (and a number of others) together, creating a mesh, as it were, with which to trawl for material:

Give me your blessing, oh best and most prudent Hopperus, with those your renowned books, the golden foundations of the whole of the law. Which have been so solidly and illustriously built that who would not rejoice to apply their attention most sharply to this magnificent and distinguished study. There is nothing in the entire study of the law which draws me to it more happily, or instructs me copiously. Preserve me, most outstanding Hopperus, who has taught me the art of advancing in this most excellent profession with dexterity and maturity. Three analyses above all bring everything together in an outstanding fashion: Freigius's method of general logic; Hopperus's particular legal method; Vigelius's and Maranta's most special pragmatic method. Together, finally, with Bodin's strict political method.[55]

In a later annotation, on the final endpaper, these running remarks on pragmatic reading are rendered crisply as advice to the reader: 'Hopperus expounds political method; Freigius logical method; by the most compelling strategy. The two to be conjoined for Analysis; together with the practical method of Genesis of Bucherellus's and Lancelottus's *Institutes*. Whose shortcomings Speculator will make up; from the practice of the Court of Arches.'[56] While elsewhere he is more precise in specifying an orderly way of collating the material from the various volumes in his inventory of essential sources:

[sideways down page] Vigelius's Repertory of the Law, a small book, but the best of all. After these Elements of the Law, and with the Rules of the Law, logically digested in Freigius's *Paratitla*. These three, Eudromus's handy weapon, above all when joined with Decius on distinctions, And the problems of Gribaldus greatly sharpen the intellect.
[sideways the other way] First and last, Gothofredus's Institutes, which are more full than the laws themselves. But these seem more probable and lively by this civil method, above all in the following order: after Gothofredus of persons, Hopperus of persons; after the former of things, the latter; after the former of actions, the latter of actions. Together with Freigius's rules in their place.[57]

---

55 Fol. *7ʳ.
56 Harvey became Doctor of Law in 1586, and some time after this began to practise in the court of arches the London court to which the civilian advocates were attached (see Baker, *Legal History*, 147).
57 Hopperus, 100. On the title page to the volume, Harvey singles out the Gothofredus: 'Colligenda Gothofredi Opuscula'.

The reading technique which these notes suggest is one in which the would-be civilian sets a group of legal compilations on the table together, and cross-refers amongst them under titles; a fairly obvious way of reading for a lawyer – witness the *Digest* itself – but one which Harvey extends to *contemporary* abridgements and epitomes.[58]

One of the aims in the notes seems to be to graft the works of individual authors seamlessly into a purpose-built, composite volume. Hopperus, Vigelius and Freigius are verbally bound together in a series of notes like the following (in the Vigelius):

Hopperus is half the soul of Justinian, and Vigelius is the other half. The one the Hercules of the law; the other its Theseus. Both my inseparable leaders and companions.[59]

Hopperus and Vigelius, as it were the Theseus and Hercules of our [English] law. In spite of what is maintained to the contrary by ancient or modern jurists. Together with Freigius's logical analysis and Bodin's political analysis. Neither of which true Jurisprudence ought under any circumstances to be without.[60]

Matching such notes, a note on the flyleaf before the title page of Harvey's copy of Freigius' *Paratitla seu synopsis Pandectarum iuris ciuilis* (1583) brings the *Paratitla* together with the *Elementa Iuris*:

The logical and material method of these [texts] ought to be supplemented from the Justinian Questions, from the *Paratitla* of the Pandects, from the Analysis of Counsel of Zasius, and above all from the Logic for Lawyers itself. Which is above all essential, to the letter. Only Freigius's Dialectical Analysis of the Law takes on this task, as for Genesis does Vulteius above all; and now also finally Althusius [*Iurisprudentia Romana methodice digesta*].
The civilian method itself is more clearly set out by Hopperus, in book 4 of the Elements, and book 4 on the Pandects.
The pragmatic method is more subtly laid out by Nicasius in his Institutes, Decius and Dynus in the Rules of either Law, Bartholus in his Digest, Baldus in his Codex, Durandus in his *Speculum iuris*, Maranta in his golden practice.

This note echoes precisely, in tone and content, notes in the Hopperus volume (and no doubt in the Vulteius, Althusius and Nicasius, if these

---

58 Many of the authors and titles he suggests in his annotations are obscure, and some we cannot as yet trace. They are presumably contemporary textbooks, some of which have not survived. A late note on fol. *5ᵛ suggests that Harvey's original aim was to become a legal professor, not a practitioner: 'Saepe rogare; rogata tenere; retenta docere; Hae tria discipulu[m] faciunt superare magistrum. Eheu, quam breuibus pereu[n]t ingentia causis?'

59 Vigelius, *Methodus*, 13.

60 Sig. **4ʳ. Some of these notes date from 1590, since they include references to Vigelius' *De uera Iurisprudentia* of that date. See 263: 'Hopperi Vera Iurisprudentia ad Regem. Extant tande[m]: et habeo.'

survived), suggesting, indeed, that the volumes sit together before the scholarly reader and his advisee, on the table, to be compared and collated.[61]

For a reader of the 1580s, Roman Law is far more than an academic discipline. For Harvey and the circle he served, it was the essential background to those key texts for contemporary political thought – the letters and political writings of Cicero. And it is in this context that we find, scattered through the marginalia, notes with a good deal more vitality than those we have looked at so far.

Harvey first read and annotated his copy of Cicero's *Topica* in 1570, but in 1579 he went through it again, this time in the context of his studies of the civil law. His annotation at the end of the text reads:

> Gabriel Harvey / February 1570/1.
> Much more thoroughly, 1579.
> when I was already leaning considerably more seriously towards the study of the civil law.[62]

At the top of the same page he has written the instruction: 'Now turn to Agricola's golden places of dialectical invention, which I would always wish to be joined together with Cicero's *Topics*. Together with at least one of the most carefully selected logic texts for jurists, for perfect readiness.' While on the title page, below his customary monogram, he writes:

I.C. ☉ .
No book on the Roman language more suitable, or more necessary to the acute dialectician, or to the fluent orator, or finally to the skilled jurist.[63]

---

[61] See Hopperus (502): 'Juris periti no[n] multi: iuris subtiles pauci: iuris prudentes, vt Hopperus, et Vigelius, paucissi[mi]. Nemo argutus J.C. sine Nicasio in Institutiones: Decio, et Dyno in Regulae: Bartholo in Digesta: Baldo in Codicem: Vigelio in Jus cont[rouerium?] co[n]uersum: Speculatore in forum. [sideways the other way] Vt hic summa Institutionu[m]: ita summa Pandectaru[m] in libris 4. de iure ciuili priuato. Quod meu[m] adamantinum fundamentu[m] totius iurispru[dentis] ciulis.' See also, in Duarenus, *De sacris Ecclesiae ministeriis*, fol. 6ᵛ: Thre notable Abridgments, or Methods of yᵉ whole Canon Law: more effectual in this kind, then any on special Traict Syntaxewn Summarys: Duarenus: Vigelius: Speculator: all thre in 8º; & worthy to be fayerly bownd togither jn on volume: as also Lancelots Institutions, & yᵉ Alphabetical, or memoratiue Compendiu[m] of Petrus Rauennas, jn 4º; woold hansomly be combined in on fayr book, *kath' avto*. My Art memoratiue of yᵉ Canon Law: yᵉ like of yᵉ Ciuil, jn on other booke, compiled of Sigonius, Hopperus, & Gothofred[us]: with Logica J.C. tanq[uam] Anima vtriusq[ue] corporis. The Two Soueraigne Titles, de verb[orum] sig[nificatione], et de Reg[ulis] Juris.'

[62] Cicero, *Topica*, 74.

[63] And see also, once again contributing to the 'mesh' of linked volumes discussed above: 'Ad ciuilem Topicoru[m] vsum, forensemq[ue] argumentoru[m] praxim, malim

At the end of the dedicatory epistle to Harvey's (now much mutilated) copy of the *ad Atticum* letters he writes with the same kind of energy and enthusiasm: 'These letters are extremely political, and above all, pragmatic. Nor indeed is anything else of Cicero's of so much importance to the Commonwealth.'[64] While at the end of the volume he notes: 'I reread these political and pragmatic letters in Trinity Hall, much more carefully than at any time before, and weighing them very carefully. July 1582. gabriel harvey, fellow of Justinian's Hall.'[65] It is notes such as these, we suggest, which recall us to the vital and intellectually invigorating political atmosphere of the 1580s and 1590s, in which the private services of scholarly readers were called upon by those moving like Harvey in the ambit of the earl of Essex, and those moving in other post-Leicester/ Walsingham groups, like the competing Burghley circle. It is notes like these, also, we believe, which suggest that Harvey had considerable *expectations* of these knowledge transactions – that he expected that they would gain him office and influence. Such expectation comes through in a tone which the modern reader is bound to construe as personal vanity and 'vaunting ambition' – the undisguised bid for attention, the assumption that scholarly service will be followed by raised personal worth, stored up credit and, ultimately, entry into the household of someone who attaches value to such services. Harvey's obtrusively autobiographical 'readings' do contrast strongly with the more detached pragmatism of John Dee's reading instructions to Edward Dyer. One might want to suggest that Dee's success (at least in the short term – Dee too ended his life out of court favour) contrasts with Harvey's long-term lack of preferment – Harvey continually advertises the possibility of service, while Dee sometimes executes the required task for a political master.

On the heavily annotated flyleaf preceding the first title page of the

Ciceronem topicum doctorem, quam ipsum Aristotelem, aut alium aliquem illius temporis magistrum, seu Graecum philosophum, seu Latinum scholasticum. Nec vero, quod permagni aestimandum arbitror, vllum exstat antiqui iuris ciuilis, et veteris illius prudentiae forensis vel certius testimoniu[m], vel locupletius monumentu[m], praesertim cum Ciceronis etiam libris de Legibus. Nullum turpius hodiernoru[m] Jurisconsultorum dedecus, quam quod tales ignorant iuris ciuilis fontes. Huc ad unguem recentioru[m] dialectica Jurisconsultorum, praesertim Freigij, Vigelij, et Hotomani. Nec Hegendorphinum aspernor, nec Cantiunculam contemno, nec reijcio Oldendorphum, nec vllum despicio iurisprudentem dialecticum: cui cogniti etiam Euerardus, Apellus, Latomus, Omphalius, Bellonus, aliquot alij nouitij. Sed paucos malo perfecte digestos, quam multos imperfecte delibatos. Vnus, aut duo, tresue exquisitissimi, instar omnium. Eadem decies repetita placebunt optima. Nunq[uam] nimis, quod nunq[uam] satis. gabrielharueius, 1579' (5, after dedicatory epistle).

64 Cicero, *ad Atticum*, sig. A4^r.
65 Cicero, *ad Atticum*, sig. cc3^v.

Hopperus, Harvey has written, 'My Trinity Hall diet, and exercise. My Caesarian perambulation, G.H. A crucial text.' Between pages 449 and 502 of the volume he records the circumstances of his own first, exploratory reading more precisely:

Twice in one day. The golden task of a single day.
1581.
Gabriel Harvey. civilian advocate.[66]

The golden task of a single summer's day: Gothofredus's Institutes, packed with legal information; and this fourth book of the Elements together with the rules of the law, reduced to the same order by Freigius.

On page 373 of the Hopperus, Harvey records an early application of his 'pragmatic' training. Against the title, 'De usu supradictorum', he writes, 'a recent problem set at Trinity Hall'. And at the top of the page: 'The problem set for Peter Withipole, bachelor of laws and fellow of this Hall. Withipole respondent. I and Gardiner opposing. Great expectations; a competent outcome. Withipole himself somewhat more skilled in the law.' Here we glimpse Harvey for a moment acting as academic civilian himself, in strong contrast to the steadily directive marginal annotations which preserve for us Harvey, scholarly reader, reading the law for and on behalf of others.

We are arguing here that these last marginal notes of Harvey's, reviving the lively relationship between the Elizabethan scholar and his chosen field of expertise, are, in their autobiographical vigour, unusual. From the variety of marginal notes from the period we have begun to excavate a more directed use of dialogue between reader and text – one deliberately calculated to turn the text into a work co-authored by professional reader and original author for the use of another, to a particular purpose. We have begun to show here how attention to the mechanics of pragmatic reading makes visible new types of intellectual work, within social and political frameworks, which emerge during Elizabeth's reign. By focusing on varieties of textual mediation we gain insight not just into the intellectual productions of these readers as authors, but into the social and professional economy of their textual transactions.

---

[66] 449. This is written against a passage in Hopperus which reads, 'Ius ciuile est, quod maxime omnium contractum, cuiusque proprium est ciuitatis, vt supra probauimus; et ex quibus fontibus tota haec diuisio ortus sui principatum duxerit ostendimus.'

6   The gardens of Sir Nicholas and Sir Francis Bacon: an enigma resolved and a mind explored

Hassell Smith

> God Almighty first planted a Garden. And indeed it is the purest of
> human pleasures. It is the greatest refreshment to the spirits of man;
> without which buildings and palaces are but gross handyworks: and a
> man shall ever see that when ages grow to civility and elegancy, men
> come to build stately sooner than to garden finely; as if gardening were
> the greater perfection.[1]

With unsurpassed eloquence Sir Francis Bacon captures the significance
of gardening for the human spirit and proclaims its challenge to artistic
creativity. Yet as a garden designer Francis Bacon is an enigmatic figure.
The problem arises because the ideal garden which he described in his
essay *Of Gardens* (1625) owes nothing to the garden he created at
Gorhambury. As Sir Roy Strong has remarked: 'his detailed specification
for a royal garden is oddly surprising after his own at Gorhambury'.[2] The
latter, planned in 1608, was a water-garden which, as will be shown,
comprised a series of streams, palisaded ponds and islands which
provided a setting for flowers, statues, a rock, a grotto, an arbour and a
banqueting house. It has been suggested that he drew inspiration from
the water parterres created for Henry IV at Fontainebleau, Gaillon and
Saint-Germain-en-Laye, even perhaps from Salomon De Caus, whose
work at Richmond and Hatfield may well have coincided with that of
Francis at Gorhambury.[3] By contrast the garden which he depicts in his
essay had no water features other than conventional fountains. 'Pools',
he wrote, 'mar all, and make the garden unwholesome, and full of flies
and frogs.'[4] Nor does he advocate statuary. Indeed, far from reflecting
early seventeenth-century mannerist ideas, his essay looks back to the
early and mid-sixteenth-century garden planning at Nonsuch,
Theobalds and Kenilworth. Nor do these contrasting garden styles

---

[1] *The Works of Francis Bacon*, ed. J. Spedding, R. L. Ellis and D. D. Heath (14 vols.,
1858–74), VI, 485.
[2] R. Strong, *The Renaissance Garden in England* (1979), 135.
[3] *Ibid.*, 126–7.
[4] Spedding, *Works*, VI, 490.

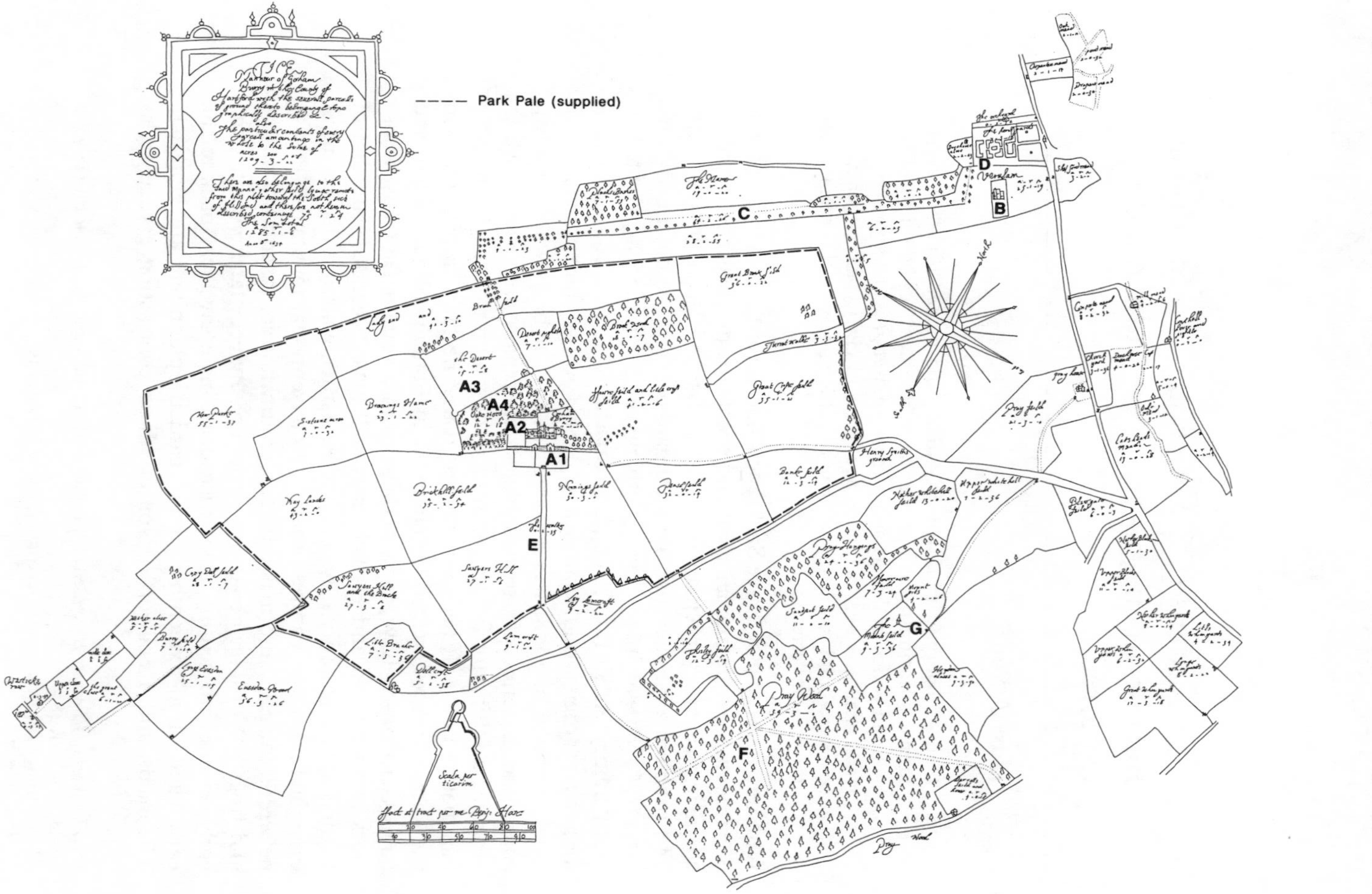

Figure 1   The manor of Gorhambury in 1634

appear to reflect stages in Bacon's development as a garden designer since the backward looking design presented in the *Essay* was published almost two decades after he had laid out his water-garden at Gorhambury.[5]

Initially, this essay attempts to resolve these apparent contradictions by reconstructing the entire garden layout at Gorhambury as it appeared at Bacon's death in 1626 and by exploring the stages through which it had evolved. That this has not already been done is surprising since Francis Bacon's contribution to early seventeenth-century garden design is widely recognised, and sources for such a reconstruction have been available for many years, most of them in print.[6] The fact that Gorhambury neither figured among English gardens which were visited by foreign travellers nor fell within the remit of the parliamentary surveyors in 1649 may help to explain why its gardens (as distinct from its gardener) have escaped serious investigation. Only indefatigable tourists and antiquaries seeking classical manifestations in the English countryside such as Aubrey, Evelyn, Pennant and Nichols have preserved some impression of this lost landscape. Of these only Aubrey and Evelyn can have glimpsed the lingering vestiges of its splendour since, in 1632, six years after Bacon's death, the Gorhambury estate was acquired by his friend and secretary Thomas Meautys[7] who precipitated the destruction of both park and gardens by letting them as grazing land to tenant farmers in what must be judged one of the most vandalistic acts of the age.[8]

An estate map of 1634[9] (Fig. 1) shows two quite separate gardens. One,

[5] I am grateful to Mr Michael Riviere, Professor Robert Ashton, Dr Tom Williamson, Dr Victor Morgan and Mrs Anthea Taigel for advice and constructive criticism in the course of preparing this essay, to members of the Feilden condominium at Stiffkey Hall for their hospitality, friendship and help on numerous occasions, to Lady Verulam for kindly allowing me to see artifacts in Verulam House and to undertake fieldwork in the park, and to Ms Mavis Wesley and Mr Philip Judge for providing respectively secretarial and cartographic support. I am also grateful to the Leverhulme Trust for an Emeritus Fellowship which has facilitated much of the research for this essay.

[6] Since preparing this essay Paula Henderson has published her article on 'Sir Francis Bacon's Water Gardens at Gorhambury', *Garden History*, 20, ii (1992), 116–31. I have seen no reason to revise the views advanced in this essay.

[7] The story of Thomas Meautys' acquisition of the Gorhambury estate is long and involved. It has been pieced together by Mr L. M. Munby who had kindly allowed me to consult his manuscript.

[8] HRO, Gorhambury Collection, Schedule of Records, p. 14; MS 1 A 83/7, an undated survey of Gorhambury estate in which the gardens and park are described in agricultural terms. It has been dated incorrectly in pencil to *c.* 1600, but was compiled shortly after Bacon's death and bears all the marks of being prepared *c.* 1630 for either the sale or lease of the property.

[9] HRO, D/EV P1. Inscribed 'Map of the manor of Gorhambury 1634'; signed: Benjamin Hare.

which is adjacent to Gorhambury House, comprised a series of four enclosures (A1–4 on Fig. 1); the other, called The Pondyard (D on Fig. 1), provided a setting for Verulam House (B on Fig. 1), as did a wide avenue with counter- or side-walks (C on Fig. 1), which extended for about a mile and which created a spectacular approach to this house.[10] This avenue remains intact, somewhat lengthened and recently replanted. Sadly, both houses have been demolished (except for a fragment of Gorhambury House) and their gardens totally obliterated, although the earthworks of the pondyard have survived, perhaps not incorrectly described as 'fishponds' by the Ordnance Survey.[11] Nonetheless, the layout of both these gardens can be substantially reconstructed from surviving documentation.

The Pondyard

This is, of course, Francis Bacon's famous water-garden. His planning notes have survived[12] and are sufficiently detailed to have tempted Sir Roy Strong and others to reconstruct its layout (Fig. 2).[13] There is, however, further evidence about the composition of this garden which merits consideration: notably its layout as represented in the 1634 estate map, a field survey made shortly after Bacon's death,[14] the remaining earthworks[15] and John Aubrey's account of what he saw in 1656.[16]

[10] This avenue is not accurately shown on the 1634 map although the site is marked with a single row of trees. This is undoubtedly because it had been newly planted shortly before Francis Bacon's death. It is described in a survey of c. 1630 as 'newlie sett with rowes of trees from the park gate at windmill hill to Verulam house' (HRO, Gorhambury Collection MS, 1 A 83/7).

[11] O/S 1:2500, Herts., sheet XXXIV.10.

[12] The Letters and Life of Francis Bacon, ed. J. Spedding (7 vols., 1861–74), IV, 76–7. I have used this source throughout my discussion of the water-garden.

[13] Strong, Renaissance Garden, 129. The first such plan was produced by J. C. Rogers in 1936 ('The Manor and Houses of Gorhambury', Transactions of the St Albans and Hertfordshire Architectural and Archaeological Society, 4 (1936), 123). A similar reconstructed plan has been produced recently by Paula Henderson (see n. 6 above). All three authors are in substantial agreement about the interpretation of these notes.

[14] HRO, Gorhambury Collection, MS 1 A 83/7. For the dating of this MS see note 8 above.

[15] O/S 1:2500, Herts., sheet XXXIV.10. Surveyed in 1878, published in 1898. These earthworks are in a remarkable state of preservation. They appear to have been remodelled in the second half of the eighteenth century since at least one sluice contains brickwork of that period. It was probably at this time that all traces of Francis Bacon's mannerist features were removed.

[16] 'Brief Lives' Chiefly of Contemporaries, Set Down by John Aubrey between the Years 1669 and 1696, ed. A. Clark (Oxford, 1898), 79–81. For an appreciation of John Aubrey's observations and fieldwork, see H. Welfare, 'John Aubrey – the First Archaeological Surveyor', in From Cornwall to Caithness. Some Aspects of British Field Archaeology: Papers

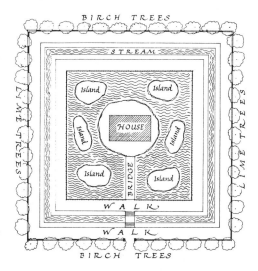

Figure 2   Diagram based on Francis Bacon's description of a pond with islands and a house at Gorhambury (1608)

Conflicting though it be, all this evidence must be considered, and if possible reconciled, in any attempt to reconstruct this garden. The 1634 map shows that the pondyard occupied an approximately rectangular area of seven acres, four of which were laid out with a series of ponds and moat-like features (D on Fig. 1 and Fig. 3). Their earthworks are still intact and confirm the accuracy of the early seventeenth-century surveyor as does John Aubrey's estimate that his lordship's ponds 'doe containe four acres'.[17] The map also shows a series of islands and platforms (A, B, C, D and E on Fig. 3) on one of which stood a substantial rectangular building. Undoubtedly this layout, as Bacon indicated in his planning notes, was modelled out of earlier water-features which may have served either as fishponds or as a source for a water supply to Gorhambury House, or for both purposes.

The garden revealed by this cartographic and archaeological evidence differs greatly, however, from the one which Bacon's planning notes have prompted historians to reconstruct.[18] These state that the ground was 'to be inclosed square'; that most of it was 'to be cast into a laque'; that

Presented to Norman V. Quinnell, ed. M. Bowden, D. Mackay and P. Topping (British Archaeology Reports, British Series, 209, 1989), 17–28. M. Hunter, *John Aubrey and the Realm of Learning* (1975).

[17] Aubrey, *'Brief Lives'*, ed. Clark, 80.

[18] The most recent writer on Bacon's water garden is of the view that he did not lay out his ponds 'according to his original plans' (Henderson, 'Bacon's Water Gardens', 121).

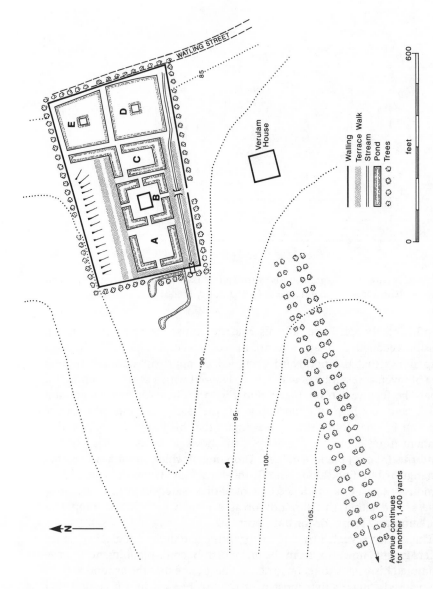

Figure 3 Reconstructed plan of the water-garden and avenue at Verulam House

in the 'middle of the laque where the howse now stands' there was to be 'an Iland of 100 [feet] broad; An in the Middle thereof . . . a howse for freshnes' or a stylish banqueting house. As well as this central island six more islands were to be 'sett in fit places'. These comprised:

> An Iland where the fayre hornbeam standes with a stand in it and seats under Neath.
> An Iland with Rock.
> An Iland with a Grott.
> An Iland Mounted with flowres in ascents.
> An Iland paved and with picture.
> An Iland with an arbor of Musk roses sett all with double violetts for sent in Autumn, some gilovers which likewise dispers sent.[19]

Access to the 'Middle great Iland', we are told, was to be by a 'fayre bridg'; the other islands were to be approached by boat.

These notes seem to suggest that he planned a smaller and more regular water-garden than the one he built. Although they give no overall dimensions, they appear to indicate a single pond which was small enough to give access to the central island via a bridge. But the more one ponders this layout the more improbable it becomes. To propose a single pond which was small enough for a central island to be approached by a bridge, while six other islands, disposed in what can have been no more than a moat, were to be approached by a boat, was, surely, to produce a water-garden of paddling pool proportions. Or, in fairness to Francis Bacon, could it be that historians have incorrectly interpreted his planning notes, especially since he is explicit that he intended to convert an existing set of fishponds (the pondyard) into 'a place of pleasure'?

Such considerations prompt the thought that some of the discrepancies between plan and achievement may be more apparent than real since they may arise from the difficulties inherent in attempting to reconstruct a complicated artifact from a purely verbal description; the more so since Bacon's notes were intended, not to describe this garden, but to memorialise himself about it, and to that extent may be incomplete or less than explicit. They certainly contain ambiguities which can be read as suggesting that he intended his water-garden to embrace such other ponds and islands as already existed in the pondyard. When he wrote 'in the middle of the laque where the howse how stands' he could have been using the phrase to differentiate one lake from another rather than implying a garden with a single lake. Similarly his note about 'an Iland where the fayre hornbeam standes' would appear to be identifying

---

[19] *Letters and Life*, ed. Spedding, IV, 76–7.

another extant island, possibly at site A or C (Fig. 3). Likewise, when he mentions 'a fayre bridg to the Middle great Iland' he may be differentiating it from the two other substantial islands located at A and C rather than from a group of smaller ones standing in the same lake.

Such reinterpretations suggest that the discrepancies between the garden which Bacon planned and the one he built may be less real than they appear; that it may be profitable to attempt to reconcile his planning notes with the cartographic and archaeological evidence, thereby providing, with some assistance from John Aubrey, a comprehensive picture of the garden he built. We have already seen that he planned seven islands and that in fact he provided five by using the platforms within the existing fishponds and probably adding the small islands in each of the large ponds. The three available platforms were each about 100 feet square and so would have provided adequate space for the larger island layouts suggested in his notes (see above p. 131). Each of these islands was then to be embellished with 'a fayre Image to keepe it, Tryten or Nymph etc.'. He proposed to enclose the entire site (about seven acres) with a brick wall. Outside it were to be 'sett fayre straite byrches on 2 sides and lyme trees on 2 sides, some x foote distante from the Wall', so that, seen from the garden, 'the wall may hide most of the shaft of the tree and onely the tufts appear above'. Unsuitable terrain and the absence of brick footings, even of any brick debris surrounding the site, suggests that in the event he paled it – a modification which would have left his planting scheme intact. Inside, the walls were to be 'plashed' with fruit trees planted on a raised terrace walk twenty-five feet wide, and encompassing the entire garden. A turfed retaining bank then sloped down to a 'fyne littell stream', 1½ yards wide, which ran 'upon gravell' and 'fyne peppell' thus making 'the whole residue of the ground an Iland'. These terraces and the stream are still discernible on the south side of the site, albeit the terracing is shallow; to the north the ground rises more sharply, thereby providing natural terracing but also precluding the possibility of a stream. Within these terraced walks the series of ponds (the 'lake' as he called them) were to be palisaded ('a fayre hedge of Tymber woorke till it towch the water') and enclosed with a 'fayre raile with images gilt rownd about it'. These ponds, according to Aubrey, were 'pitched at the bottomes with pebbles of severall colours, which were work't in to severall figures, as of fishes'.[20] The 'howse for freshness' or summer house stood on the largest island or platform as is clearly marked on the 1634 plan. It had 'an upper galery open upon the water, a tarace above that and a supping roome open under that; a dyning roome,

---

[20] Aubrey, *'Brief Lives'*, ed. Clark, 81.

a bedd chamber, a Cabanett and a Roome for Musike'. According to
Aubrey it was built in classical style, paved with black and white marble,
covered with Cornish slate, and neatly wainscotted.[21]

These gardens undoubtedly dictated the unusual location of Verulam
House since, in order to overlook them, it stood outside the park and
uncomfortably close to Watling Street, then the main thoroughfare from
St Albans to Redbourne (Fig. 3). Although little is known about this
building (it was demolished in 1666), a sketch in the estate map of 1634
and a vivid description of it by Aubrey suggest that it was fanciful both in
conception and execution. It was conceived, so Aubrey tells us, as 'his
lordship's summer-howse: for he sayes (in his essay) one should have
seates for summer and winter as well as cloathes'.[22] Its layout and
architectural detail suggest that Bacon indulged his personal predilections as did his contemporaries when building lodges for hunting,
entertainment or retreat.[23] The significance of Verulam House in the
context of this essay is that visitors approached it from Gorhambury
House via a magnificent avenue flanked by side-walks. This feature,
which extended for a mile, was terraced into the scarp of the hillside
running east from the water-garden. Bacon may well have intended this
carefully engineered ceremonial avenue to frame the house, since
calculations suggest that it could have been seventy feet wide with side-
walks each extending to a further thirty feet.[24] The scale and grandeur of
this feature amazed Aubrey who observed it from the leads of Verulam
House when its trees were reaching maturity:

From hence to Gorambury in a straite line leade three parallell walkes: in the
middlemost three coaches may passe abreast: in the wing-walks two may. They
consist of severall stately trees of the like groweth and heighth viz. elme, chesnut,
beach, hornebeane, Spanish-ash, cervice-tree etc whose topps . . . doe afford
from the walke on the howse the finest shew that I have seem, and I sawe it about
Michaelmas, at which time of the yeare the colour of leaves are most varied.[25]

In another passage he referred to the tops of these trees as affording 'a
most pleasant variegated verdure, resembling the workes in Irish-stitch',
and he was at pains to show diagrammatically how Bacon achieved this

[21] *Ibid.*, 79.
[22] *Ibid.*, 79.
[23] E.g. Sir Thomas Tresham: New Bield; Sir Charles Cavendish: Bolsover Castle;
Thomas Howard, Viscount Bindon: Lulworth Castle; Sir Thomas Cecil: Wothorpe
Hall; perhaps even Sir Roger Townshend: Raynham Hall.
[24] The survey of *c.* 1630 (HRO, Gorhambury Collection, MS 1 A 83/7) gives the area of
this avenue as seventeen acres. Since it was *c.* 1,700 yards in length it must have been
48 yards or 144 feet wide. The map of 1634 suggests the total width was about 115 feet.
[25] Aubrey, *'Brief Lives'*, ed. Clark, 79–80.

effect by planting a sequence of eight species in a strictly repetitive pattern. Terrain contributed to this magnificent tree-top view since the avenue proceeded from the house up a gentle and uniform slope – 'the way easily ascending', as Aubrey puts it, 'hardly so acclive as a deske'.[26] Surely a supreme example of nature and art in harmony.

Gorhambury House garden

If Francis Bacon's water-garden has proved to be both more extensive and more compromised by previous landscapes than historians have allowed, his garden at Gorhambury House is remarkable for having passed entirely unnoticed. This is surprising since the estate map of 1634[27] shows this garden to have been one of the most extensive in early Stuart England.[28] It consisted of three separate enclosures (A1, A2, A3 on Fig. 1) which jointly extended to almost twenty-seven acres. The first enclosure (A1), a rectangular court of about three acres, was bounded to the south, east and west by a herber or walk of arching trees.[29] The entire court appears to have been turfed,[30] its sweeping lawn presumably being broken by gravel paths or pavements which led to two ornamental gates in its north wall, one giving access to the house, the other to the detached long gallery which Sir Nicholas Bacon had added in the 1570s.

[26] *Ibid.*, 79.
[27] Rogers, 'Gorhambury', 35–112, map no. 2. This article presents a great deal of information on both Gorhambury House and its gardens. It deserves better acknowledgement than it has so far received.
[28] It is not easy to obtain data concerning the size of Tudor and Stuart gardens. Nonsuch, at the time of Lord Lumley, appears to have been somewhat over sixteen acres (J. Dent, *The Quest for Nonsuch* (1970), 112). Of the gardens at Theobalds Roy Strong writes: 'the most important impression it made on every visitor was one of size; it was said that one could walk for two miles through its pleached arbours and covered walkes. The area it occupied far exceeded that of any early Tudor palace garden and was not to be surpassed until Wilton in the 1630s' (Strong, *Renaissance Garden*, 56). The gardens built at Raglan Castle by the 3rd earl of Worcester probably did not exceed twenty acres (E. H. Whittle, 'The Renaissance Gardens of Raglan Castle', *Garden History*, 17, i (1989), 92). Those at Campden House, Gloucs., extended to about twenty-five acres (P. Everson, 'The Gardens of Campden House, Chipping Campden, Gloucestershire', *Garden History*, 17, ii (1989), 113). Wimbledon House, to judge from Robert Smythson's plan of 1609, was probably under twelve acres (Strong, *Renaissance Garden*, 61). Thorpe's plan of the gardens at Burghley has been published but unfortunately with no scale shown (E. C. Till, 'The Development of the Park and Gardens at Burghley', *Garden History*, 19, ii (1991), 129).
[29] This walk is not shown on the 1634 map which is essentially an estate survey. It is, however, shown as being extended in an undated seventeenth-century sketch map prepared with a view to renovating the park (HRO, Gorhambury Collection, MS 1 B 10). This map was almost certainly prepared for Sir Harbottle Grimston after he had purchased the entire property in 1652 (Rogers, 'Gorhambury', 68).
[30] The 1634 map, which is colour-coded, shows this court as an area of grassland.

Of the main garden beyond this entrance court (A2 on Fig. 1) we know comparatively little. The 1634 map suggests that it was divided, in mid-Tudor style, into several courts. One, walled and extending to about three acres, lay to the west of the house; others undoubtedly lay to its north and south, the former possibly containing an orchard garden.[31] To the east, since the house almost certainly had no integral service-court, stood a group of stables and out-buildings. By 1656 these courts had so decayed that Aubrey could only tell us that 'the garden is large, which was (no doubt) rarely planted and kept in his lordship's time'. He did, however, observe the gateway leading from the orchard garden into Oak Wood grove: 'here is a handsome dore, which opens into Oake-Wood; over this dore in golden letters on blew are these six verses'.[32] These he failed to record, leaving it to the traveller Thomas Pennant, perhaps not the best authority but presumably drawing upon extant records, to do so over 100 years later. Pennant also recorded that a statue of Orpheus stood above these verses and that a small banqueting house which still stood in the orchard was adorned with great 'curiosity' having the Liberal Arts beautifully depicted on its walls 'with the heads of Cicero, Aristotle and other illustrious antients and moderns who had excelled in each'.[33] We know from other sources that a terrace ran round one walled court – probably the privy garden to the west of the house – and that at least one fountain embellished it.[34]

The great garden gave access to a grove of oaks (A4 on Fig. 1) where, according to Aubrey, the trees were already 'very great and shadie' in 1656. Their maturity suggests that Francis Bacon did not plant them, although, as Aubrey continues, 'His Lordship much delighted himselfe here: under every tree he planted some fine flower, or flowers, some whereof are there still viz. paeonies, tulips'.[35]

Oak Wood led, in turn to a wilderness or 'desert' (A3 on Fig. 1) as it was known to Bacon and his contemporaries. It lay within a rectangular enclosure of fifteen acres, walled on all sides,[36] and with summer-houses

31 The gate into Oak Wood is in this north court (see Fig. 1). Pennant, for what his testimony is worth, described this gate as leading out of the orchard (T. Pennant, *Journey from Chester to London* (1782), 225).

32 Aubrey, *'Brief Lives'*, ed. Clark, 82–3.

33 Pennant, *Journey*, 224–5; *The Progresses and Public Processions of Queen Elizabeth*, ed. J. Nichols (1823), II, 58–60.

34 *Letters and Life*, ed. Spedding, IV, 52; University of Chicago, Joseph Regenstein Library, Redgrave Collection MS 4091.

35 Aubrey, *'Brief Lives'*, ed. Clark, 83.

36 There is some ambiguity about the extent of the walling. The 1634 map, which presents the great garden walling in red, shows none. The survey of *c.* 1630 records 'the desarte grounde incompassed with a Brick wall and the walks and hedgerowes rounde about the said desarte', HRO, Gorhambury Collection, MS 1 A 83/7. This would suggest that

or belvederes standing, bastion-like, at each corner. This garden, which seems to have survived longest, certainly caught Aubrey's attention. He describes it, with some exaggeration, as 'a place as big as an ordinary parke'; and he marvelled at the summer-houses: 'at severall good viewes, were erected elegant sommer-howses well built of Roman architecture, well wainscotted and cieled; yet standing, but defaced, so that one would have thought the Barbarians, had made a conquest here'.[37] The layout of this 'desert' remained sufficiently intact for him to attempt a description: 'the west part . . . is coppice-wood, where are walkes cutt-out as straight as a line, and broade enoug for a coach, a quarter of a mile long or better'. The eastern part, he sadly records, 'now is a large ploughed field'. He must therefore have been relying upon local recollections when he wrote: 'this eastern division consisted of severall parts, some thicketts of plumme-trees with delicate walkes, some of rasberies. Here was all manner of fruit-trees that would grow in England; and a great number of choice forest-trees; as the whitti-tree, sorbe-, cervice-, etc. eugh [sic]. The walke[s] both in the coppices and other boscages, were most ingeniosely designed.'[38]

This rather muddled account is unambiguous on one point: this 'desert' or wilderness garden was divided into several sections. To the west stood long, straight, tree-lined walks and arbours which by 1656 had degenerated through years of neglect into nothing more than coppiced woodland. East of this came an area of 'thicketts' planted with fruit trees and bushes set amidst 'delicate walks'. Bacon himself confirms this planting pattern and explains the thickets when he wrote in 1608: 'some profite of the desert ground by Roses, frute, phisike herbes etc.'.[39] Moving further eastwards the thickets appear to give way once more to coppice ground, this time remnants of former handsome walks lined with small forest trees and possibly fruit trees as well, although Aubrey is unclear as to whether the latter lined these walks or grew amidst the thickets.

Students of garden history may have been struck by the similarities between these gardens and those which Francis Bacon depicts in his essay *Of Gardens*. The ideal 'prince-like' gardens, he tells us, 'ought not well to be under thirty acres of ground'; those at Gorhambury covered

the walks and hedgerows lay outside the 'desert'. The 1634 map, however, shows no walks or coppice woodland outside this desert. It may therefore be that only the central part of the desert, planted, as we shall see, with a variety of fruit, roses and herbs, was walled. This might reduce the walled area to six or seven acres.

[37] Aubrey, *'Brief Lives'*, ed. Clark, 83.
[38] *Ibid.*
[39] *Letters and Life*, ed. Spedding, IV, 86.

almost twenty-seven acres (excluding Oak Wood). The ideal garden should be in three parts: 'a green in the entrance; a heath or desert in the going forth; and the main garden in the midst'.[40] Such was the basic structure at Gorhambury. The entrance green should extend to four acres; that at Gorhambury ran to at least three. It should have on either side 'a covert alley, upon carpenter's work . . . by which you may go in shade into the garden'. That at Gorhambury had arbours on either side. The main garden, according to the Essay, should be a square of twelve acres bounded on all sides with an arboured terrace and enclosed by an elaborate hedge which provided hanging spaces for cages of birds and 'some other little figure, with broad plates of round coloured glass gilt, for the sun to play upon'. Size apart, such a garden does not appear to have much in common with its counterpart at Gorhambury which was walled and sub-divided into courts. But Bacon is reticent about the layout of, and features in, his ideal main garden: 'for the ordering of the ground within the great hedge, I leave it to variety of device'. He suggests it should be open and airy with broad side alleys of fruit trees; the centre-piece should be a mount thirty-feet high and 'some fine banqueting-house'. Thereafter he is most explicit about the features he does not advocate: no topiary images – 'they be for children'; no knots – 'they be but toys'; emphatically no ponds or pools. He is not enthusiastic about statues, but fountains are acceptable as is a small pool provided 'the water be in perpetual motion'. Our sources are equally reticent about features in the main garden at Gorhambury. As we have seen they refer to an orchard, a banqueting house, terracing and at least one fountain; we can infer from the limited water supply to the house that there were no ponds, but beyond this we know too little about both gardens to infer either similarities or dissimilarities.

It is quite otherwise with the heath or 'desert' garden. Here both Bacon's essay and our sources are sufficiently explicit to reveal two very similar and outstandingly unusual gardens. Both are huge – fourteen and fifteen acres respectively; both are walled on all sides, and both are divided into three quite distinct sections. The centre-piece of the ideal garden was to be a six-acre area of heath 'framed, as much as may be, to a natural wildness'. This was to comprise randomly planted thickets of sweet briar, honeysuckle and wild vine underplanted with violets, straw-berries and primroses; these were to be interspersed with 'little heaps, in the nature of mole-hills (such as are in wild heaths)' planted with herbs and flowers and some of them topped with 'standards of little bushes'

---

[40] *Works*, ed. Spedding, Ellis and Heath, VI, 488–92, for this and all subsequent quotations relating to Bacon's ideal garden.

such as 'roses, juniper, holly, berberries, . . . red currants, gooseberry, rosemary, bays, sweet-briar; and such like'. 'Side grounds' flanked this artificial heath. Each extending to four acres, they were to be laid out with alleys, some designed to provide full shade 'wheresoever the sun be', others were to be framed for shelter 'that when the wind blows sharp, you may walk as in a gallery'. Some alleys were to be set with 'fruit-trees of all sorts' but clearly those intended for shelter would require close-growing and well-foliaged shrubs and small trees. Finally, at each outer corner of these side-grounds was to be 'a mount of some pretty height, leaving the wall of the enclosure breast high, to look abroad into the fields'.

The similarities between Bacon's ideal 'desert' and the real one at Gorhambury need no underscoring. They are sufficiently striking to remove any lingering doubt that a close relationship existed between these hitherto unrecognised gardens at Gorhambury House and those depicted in the *Essay*; that the latter, far from being either a piece of literary fancy or prompted by his uncle's garden at Theobalds (as Reginald Blomfield and Conyers Read respectively have suggested)[41] was either inspired by his gardens at Gorhambury House or was a blueprint in literary style for the layout of those gardens. In either case this relationship means that his *Essay* provides one of the most detailed contemporary descriptions of a great Jacobean garden. It also means that the discrepancy between the type of garden he advocated and the one he built can be resolved since he would appear to have laid out two gardens, each of which he considered appropriate to its use: the grand garden, conservative in style, served as a setting for the great house; the water-garden, mannerist and experimental in style – a *joie d'esprit* – served to amaze and entertain his guests at his summer retreat. All of which would suggest some revision of his contribution to garden design and perhaps even of the concept of a prevailing fashion in design. This is, however, to outrun what has been established, since a *relationship* between the great gardens at Gorhambury House and those described in the *Essay* does not necessarily imply that Francis built these gardens. There remains the possibility that they had already been constructed by the time he inherited the property in the early seventeenth century. In which case his role as a planner and builder (as opposed to a publicist) would be diminished and it would be necessary to reattribute the Gorhambury House gardens. When, then, were they built?

The *Essay* published in 1625 provides a sufficiently stylised view of these gardens to suggest that it post-dated them; that Bacon conceived

[41] R. Blomfield and F. Inigo Jones, *The Formal Garden in England* (1892), 35; Conyers Read, *Lord Burghley and Queen Elizabeth* (1960), 123–4.

his ideal garden as an improved version of the one he 'trimmed and dressed' at Gorhambury; that, like any critical scholar, had he had the opportunity to start again he would have done differently. He seems particularly anxious to impose some geometry on the irregular layout at Gorhambury. The grove of oaks which contributed to that irregularity does not figure in the *Essay*. The unshapely main garden is transposed into a square which relates geometrically to the desert garden so that the side-walks or alleys in the latter could be extended to flank the main garden and indeed to join up with those in the entrance court (Fig. 4). These continuous side-alleys, besides giving access to all the gardens, provided an unrestricted view through gateways and arches until, like his grand avenue, they reached vanishing point.

Whatever can be inferred about dating from the *Essay*, there are other indications that these gardens must have been laid out by the late 1590s. Stylistically, as has already been suggested, they belong to the mid-Tudor period. The wilderness must certainly have been laid out by the turn of the century since by 1608 it was sufficiently mature for Bacon to calculate that the sale of its crops – rose petals, herbs and fruit – would yeild sufficient revenue to contribute materially towards the alleviation of his dire financial circumstances.[42] His notes also show that Gorhambury Park, having been leased to tenant farmers in the 1590s, was still in their occupation in 1608.[43] The wilderness (together presumably with the other gardens) must therefore have been laid out prior to the lease-making since thereafter no land would have been available for expansion on the scale required by its layout.

Although by 1597 Francis Bacon's interest in gardening had been recognised by his peers at Gray's Inn,[44] it is unlikely that he could have been responsible for laying out the Gorhambury House gardens at that date, as a glance at his family circumstances will show. Sir Nicholas Bacon had purchased Gorhambury Park (an ex-monastic property) from his brother-in-law Sir Ralph Rowlett in 1561.[45] Here, between 1563 and

---

[42] *Letters and Life*, ed Spedding, IV, 86.

[43] *Ibid.*, 81. For the leasing of the park see below, p. 142.

[44] D. Jacques, 'The "Chief Ornament" of Gray's Inn: The Walks from Bacon to Brown', *Garden History*, 15, i (1987), 45. He may also have been responsible for the garden layout at Twickenham Park which he had rented in 1595 (M. Girouard, ed., 'The Smythson Collection of the Royal Institute of British Architects', *Architectural History*, 5 (1962), 36).

[45] H. C. Andrews, 'Notes on the Rowlett and Jennings Families', *Miscellanea Genealogica et Heraldica*, 5th ser., 10 (1936), 88–96; M. K. McIntosh, 'Sir Anthony Cooke: Tudor Humanist, Educator, and Religious Reformer', *Proceedings of the American Philosophical Society*, 119, iii (1957), 241. Sir Ralph Rowlett married Margaret, a daughter of Sir Anthony Cooke. Sir Nicholas had married her sister Anne.

1568, he built a substantial quadrangular house, making some additions (notably the famous long gallery) in the early 1570s. By the time he died in 1579 he had established his older sons Nicholas and Nathaniel on estates adequate to the lifestyle of county gentlemen,[46] but he had not managed to make similar provisions for his younger sons Anthony and Francis – 'poore orphans without a father', as he described them in his will.[47] He therefore settled the Gorhambury property, which consisted of little more than the park, the house and some adjacent parcels of land, on Anthony with the stipulation that his widow, Anne, Lady Bacon, should have the right to live in the Hall and to remain possessed of half its stuff. Francis received even less, having to make do with some marshlands in Essex and Kent, the manor of Marks in Essex and the reversion of Gorhambury at Anthony's death.[48] Although Anthony died in 1601, Lady Anne continued to live at Gorhambury until her death in 1610; only in 1602 did she renounce her share of the estate to Francis thereby giving him full possession and freedom to indulge his passion for gardening.[49]

Even had his mother and brother permitted him a free hand earlier (and there is no evidence that they did) his personal circumstances would have prevented him from building what must have been one of the largest gardens in England. In the first place he did not live at Gorhambury, but divided his time between Twickenham Park, which he had leased for twenty-one years in 1595, and the family chambers in Gray's Inn.[50] Secondly he was by no means sure that he would inherit the estate from Anthony who by 1600 was threatening to break the entail and to sell the property. Thirdly, down to the early seventeenth century his small inheritance and his failure to gain a lucrative government post left him heavily in debt and overmortgaged to the point where he had to sell what property he had as city money-lenders pursued him through the courts for defaulting over repayment of loans.[51]

Similar considerations make it impossible to attribute these gardens to Anthony or his mother. While the property remained in Anthony's possession and her occupation it was effectively in the hands of an

---

[46] A. Simpson, *The Wealth of the Gentry, 1540–1660* (Cambridge, 1961), 91–6; A. Hassell Smith and G. M. Baker, *The Papers of Nathaniel Bacon of Stiffkey*, I (Norwich, 1979), xxxvii–xli.

[47] Smith and Baker, *Bacon Papers*, II (1983), 27.

[48] C. L'Estrange Ewen, 'Francis Bacon and the Money-Lenders', *Baconiana*, 3rd ser., 21 (1934), 239; Simpson, *Wealth of the Gentry*, 103.

[49] Strong, *Renaissance Garden*, 120; Girouard, ed., 'Smythson Collection', 36.

[50] HRO, Gorhambury Collection, MSS I A 2 & 3.

[51] For the financial plight of Anthony and Francis, see L'Estrange Ewen, 'Francis Bacon and the Money-Lenders', 238–53; Simpson, *Wealth of the Gentry*, 103–5.

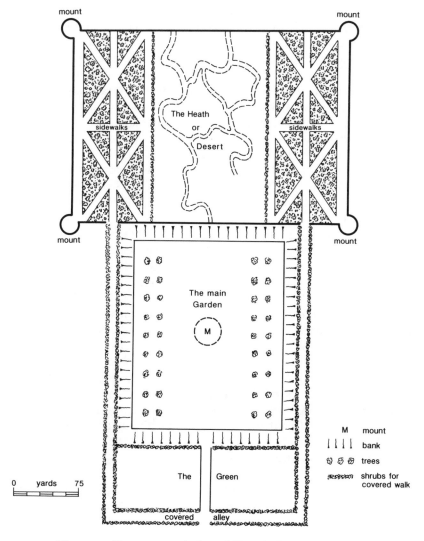

Figure 4 Reconstructed plan of Francis Bacon's ideal garden for a palace

impecunious absentee owner whose only impact on the estate was to haemorrhage it to pay debts he incurred in the course of his dissolute life in France as a special agent, first to his uncle William Cecil, Lord Burghley, and then to the earl of Essex. On one occasion alone he sent home for £500.[52] In vain the steward 'begged him to study the balances he was sending annually, and to come home'.[53] Gradually, outlying property had to be sold, the park let and Lady Anne, by then a crazed old woman, disposed of her jewellery to meet the insatiable demands of her son.[54] 'He shall have none of me', she is reported to have stormed in 1594, 'he have undone me, and nobody else but he.'[55]

Thus, by a process of elimination, we must conclude that the extensive gardens at Gorhambury House were laid out by Sir Nicholas Bacon between 1563 and 1573 when he was building, and subsequently improving, his new courtyard house there. If this be so, then these gardens were contemporary with, or even slightly earlier than, those at Theobalds for which his brother-in-law, William Cecil, Lord Burghley, was so justly famous. Such a conclusion may add a footnote to the history of garden design, but within the context of this essay the reconstruction of these gardens and their attribution to Sir Nicholas Bacon is intended to enhance our appreciation of this great Elizabethan statesman, the author of the Anglican *Via Media*, who, despite his bulk, his oft-quoted aphorisms and the plaudits of posterity, has remained a shadowy figure.[56] This is because the loss of his personal and political papers has made it difficult for historians to discern the mind behind the man and the influences which moulded that mind. Or at least it had, until Professor Collinson's penetrating and sensitive study in the *Historical Journal* for 1980.[57] It is that essay which has stimulated this attempt to extend our understanding of the mind-set of Sir Nicholas through his activities as a garden designer and builder.

His penchant for building is undeniable: a house and garden in Noble Street, London;[58] Redgrave Hall, gardens and park in Suffolk;

---

[52] *Letters and Life*, ed Spedding, I, 323–4.

[53] Simpson, *Wealth of the Gentry*, 102.

[54] *Ibid.*, 102, 105; HRO, Gorhambury Collection, MSS I H 29 and 30; I M 14 and 14A; I L 19 and 20. L'Estrange Ewen, 'Francis Bacon and the Money-Lenders', 239.

[55] *Letters and Life*, ed. Spedding, I, 311.

[56] R. Tittler, *Nicholas Bacon: The Making of a Tudor Statesman* (1976), is the only serious attempt at a biographical study.

[57] P. Collinson, 'Sir Nicholas Bacon and the Elizabethan *Via Media*', *HJ*, 23 (1980), 255–73.

[58] C. L. Kingsford, 'On Some London Houses of the Early Tudor Period', *Archaeologia*, 71 (1921), 32–8. I am grateful to my colleague, the late Mr Alan Carter, for drawing my

Gorhambury House, gardens and park in Hertfordshire; Stiffkey Hall and gardens in Norfolk; Cursitors Inn, off Chancery Lane;[59] the Chapel of Corpus Christi College, Cambridge; a speculative range of tenements in Fetter Lane[60] and Botesdale School in Suffolk.[61] For such large-scale enterprises, as Mark Girouard and others have reminded us, gentlemen-builders usually turned to London master craftsmen and 'surveyors' in the Royal Works for the preparation of their plans. Sir Nicholas, however, true to his yeoman stock, seems to have been more self-reliant and to have done his planning 'in house' – a fact which may help to explain why so little of his building has survived! But this is to presume upon our story.

The house in Noble Street seems to have been his first building enterprise. A survey plan suggests that he converted and renovated two properties which stood on adjacent sites. Perhaps foreshadowing his later interests, he added a detached garden loggia with a gallery above which ran for seventy feet along one side of a small enclosed garden.[62] By 1545 he had begun to build Redgrave Hall having purchased the park and its decayed hunting lodge, formerly a property of the abbot of Bury St Edmunds, from the Crown.[63] Evidence suggests that part of the medieval lodge was incorporated into the new hall and that, like his peers, Sir Nicholas turned to a London stonemason, John Guybon, to provide a plan and to supply teams of carpenters and masons. The house was a modest structure, symmetrically arranged round three sides of a court, but typical of its period in that chimneys, staircases and ranges of service rooms were disposed as convenience and tradition dictated to its rear and

attention to this reference. J. Stow, *A Survey of London*, ed. C. L. Kingsford (Oxford, 1971), I, 304. SRO (Ipswich), MS HA 2508/1435 is a survey plan of the house (probably made before Bacon extended it in the 1540s) together with a rough plan showing the proposed extensions and alterations. See also Smith and Baker, *Bacon Papers*, II, 38, 41, 76 and 114 where it appears that Sir Nicholas is again renovating this house in 1578.

[59] C. Kitching, 'The Cursitors Office (1573–1813) and the Corporation of the Cursitors of Chancery', *Journal of the Society of Archivists*, 7 (1982), 78–84. I am indebted to Mrs Catherine Hall for drawing my attention to this article.

[60] Smith and Baker, *Bacon Papers*, I, 31, 35, 36, 37, 38, 40, 42, 60, 64, 71, 75, 114, 121–4.

[61] In 1561 he acquired the chapel of St Botolph in Botesdale which he converted to a grammar school and against which he built a schoolhouse. Simpson, *Wealth of the Gentry*, 27; J. Simon, *Education and Society in Tudor England* (Cambridge, 1966), 309; N. Pevsner, *Suffolk* (1974), 104.

[62] Kingsford, 'Some London Houses', 34; SRO (Ipswich), MS HA 2508/1435. See n. 58 above.

[63] Detailed building accounts for Redgrave Hall have survived (University of Chicago, Regenstein Library, Bacon Collection MS 990). These accounts form the basis of an article by E. R. Sandeen ('The Building of Redgrave Hall 1545–1554', *Proceedings of the Suffolk Institute of Archaeology*, 29 (1961), 1–33). In what follows I have drawn upon Dr Sandeen's article unless otherwise stated.

side. Since Bacon had married the daughter of a Suffolk merchant and had close associates in mercantile circles,[64] this house may well have been the model for the mid-century 'E' type house adopted by such rising merchants as Edmund and Paul Withipoll at Christchurch Mansion, Ipswich, and William Clifton at Barrington Court, Somerset.[65] It is impossible to assess the influence respectively of Bacon and Guybon on its design, but the absence of a porch and of any external decorative features, coupled with the fact that it was rubble-built and stuccoed, suggests that it was not a stonemason's masterpiece. The gardens may well have reflected the hand of Bacon. They comprised two smallish rectangular walled enclosures which lay to the rear and side of the house (see Fig. 5).[66] Their walls were battlemented and embellished with turrets or pinnacles, probably of cut brickwork after the style of the near-contemporary garden walls at Stutton Hall, Suffolk.[67] The enclosure to the rear (c. 160 × 160 feet) was separated from the house by a wide passage and laid out in part as an orchard with fruit trees planted in alleys,[68] in part as a garden with a central pond encompassed by a brick terrace. The court to the west (c. 60 × 60 feet) served as the privy garden and, as at Noble Street, was bounded on one side by a detached loggia with a timber-built gallery above.[69] Sir Nicholas also appears to have built garden features in the park. He paid out substantial sums for the cutting and palisading of a pond[70] as well as for a mount[71] which seems likely to have been built on high ground beside the park pale, a site now occupied by an eighteenth-century summer house in classical style and

---

[64] In 1540 he had married Jane, the daughter of William Ferneley of West Creeting (Suff.) (Tittler, *Bacon*, 33). For his merchant connections, see Simpson, *Wealth of the Gentry*, 34–6.

[65] Edmund and Paul Withipoll began to build their house (now Christchurch Mansion) in 1548 (N. Pevsner, *Suffolk* (1974), 198). Barrington Court, built by a former Norwich and London merchant is now dated to the 1550s (*VCH Som.*, IV (1978), 115).

[66] The basic layout of these gardens is shown in two contemporary maps prepared for the laying of water courses to the house and to garden features (BL Additional MS 14850; SRO (Ipswich), MS HA 2508/1435, endorsed 'The conduyt at Redgrave').

[67] University of Chicago, Regenstein Library, Bacon Collection, MS 990 *sub* Masons, 8 March, 5 Edw. VI, 'paid to [the masons] when they began to Hewe their brick'; *sub* Brickburners, March, 5 Edw. VI, 'to Pearson for making pavement and battlement pieces'. For Stutton Hall see Pevsner, *Suffolk*, 449.

[68] University of Chicago, Regenstein Library, Bacon Collection, MS 990 *sub* Labourers, 21 Nov., 5 Edw. VI.

[69] *Ibid.*, *sub* Labourers, 7 Oct., 4 Edw. VI. The rear of this gallery and loggia is shown in a seventeenth-century painting of Redgrave Hall which is reproduced in D. du Maurier, *Golden Lads: A Study of Anthony Bacon, Francis and their Friends* (1975), facing p. 80.

[70] University of Chicago, Regenstein Library, Bacon Collection, MS 990 *sub* Labourers, 17 Oct., 5 Edw. VI.

[71] *Ibid.*, various refs. *sub* 7 Edw. VI and 1 Mary.

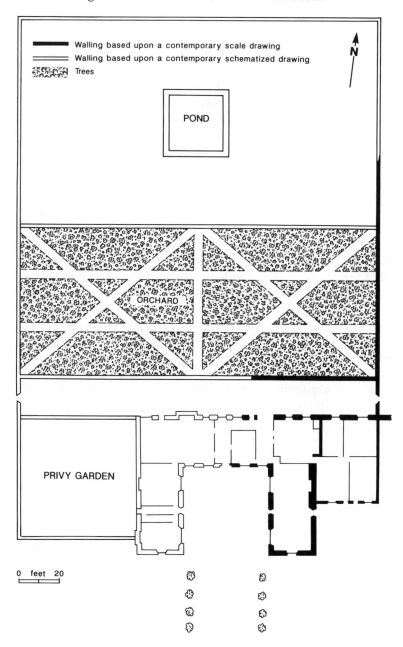

Figure 5 Reconstructed plan of the house and gardens at Redgrave Hall

which commands extensive views over the countryside. All of which suggests a fairly typical early or mid-Tudor garden layout.

Sir Nicholas began his third major building – Gorhambury House – in 1563. By this time his first wife, Jane, had died and for nine years he had been married to Anne, the cultured daughter of Sir Anthony Cooke, who was himself building at Gidea Park, about twenty-five miles from Gorhambury.[72] This marriage, together with his appointment as lord keeper, had catapulted Sir Nicholas out of his mercantile social milieu and into an aristocratic and wider intellectual one in which the study of the classical writers as a guide to all aspects of human endeavour was only sometimes second to the study of holy writ. William Cecil became his brother-in-law as did Thomas Gresham, Thomas Hoby and Francis Killigrew. As lord keeper and an influential privy councillor he moved with the court from one prodigy house to another, or at least from one building site to another since most of these houses were in various stages of construction or reconstruction. By 1563 he was well into his 'second age' and he might be expected to have adopted the building processes, style and symbolism appropriate to his status.

Undoubtedly he did; for Gorhambury House manifested an awareness of French-style Renaissance planning and architectural features. It was a single-courtyard house,[73] the main range rising above the wings while the entrance range, comprising a loggia with gallery above, was set low as at Anet, Bury-en-Blésois and Ecouen;[74] this main range and both wings were raised on a podium or well-lit basement which accommodated many of the domestic offices;[75] other services were located some distance

---

[72] *The Book of Architecture of John Thorpe*, ed. J. Summerson (Walpole Society, 40, 1966), 90; McIntosh, 'Anthony Cooke', 247–8.

[73] The house has frequently been described as having two courtyards (*VCH Herts.*, II (1902), 394–5; Tittler, *Bacon*, 66–7; J. A. Gotch, *Early Renaissance Architecture in England* (1914), 98–9), but the second court (now entirely demolished) was almost certainly added to the rear either by Sir Francis Bacon or, more likely, by Sir Harbottle Grimston in the later seventeenth century. It does not appear in the 'bird's eye' view of the house drawn by Benjamin Hare for his 1634 estate map (see Fig. 1); it has little architectural relationship to the main court (see plan: *VCH Herts*, II, 395) and it would have been unusual in a sixteenth-century double courtyard house for the main court to be located before the secondary or service one. The detached long gallery was added subsequently by Sir Nicholas Bacon to provide better accommodation for the queen and her court.

[74] A. Blunt, *Art and Architecture in France 1500–1700* (1957), 8–51; J.-A. du Cerceau, *Les Plus Excellents Bastiments de France*, ed. D. Thomson (Paris, 1988). For the relationship between the main range at Gorhambury and its wings and entrance range, see the bird's-eye sketch in the 1634 map (HRO, D/EV P1).

[75] The remaining fragment of the house (now in the care of English Heritage) shows a deep and well-lit basement throughout the main range and the surviving part of the west range. An eighteenth-century engraving shows basement windows in the rest of the west range (Bodleian Library, Gough Maps 11, fol. 36) while an eighteenth-century water-

from the house thereby ensuring that its external facades remained relatively uncluttered;[76] the walls, built in brick and flint, were rendered to look like stone,[77] while the entire court was paved in Newcastle stone supplied from London;[78] its porch, of course, has long been recognised as a fine piece of Renaissance architecture in the French style.[79] Gorhambury House, nonetheless, was a modest affair, mean in size,[80] its walls devoid of architectural ornament, whether antic or classical, its courtyard elevations unrelieved even by an oriel window and with structural defects of such magnitude that by the eighteenth century most of it had to be demolished.[81] Porch apart, it lacked architectural finesse, suggesting that its designer had little appreciation of three-dimensional planning or any sense of recession and the juxtaposition of mass. In short it seems to have been planned by a surveyor rather than an architect; by someone who thought functionally and two dimensionally after the manner of a land surveyor laying out his fields or a yeoman building his barn.

Or could it be that in designing this modest structure, which shows considerable awareness of architectural trends yet at the same time eschews many of the architectural conventions of both mid-Tudor England and the continent, Sir Nicholas was fashioning his house to

colour in the Gorhambury Collection shows basement windows on the front facade of both east and west ranges (du Maurier, *Golden Lads*, plate facing p. 160). For the introduction into England of basements as service areas, see M. Girouard, *Robert Smythson and the Elizabethan Country House* (1983), 59.

[76] HRO, Gorhambury Collection, MS 1 A 83/7. This survey of *c*. 1630 refers to wood, barn, stable and carpenters' yards as proximate to the house. The 1634 map also shows the gable-end of a detached building near the house (see Fig. 1).

[77] Rogers, 'Gorhambury', 45.

[78] Huntington Library and Art Gallery, MSS HM 41757–9. Two undated 'reckonings' for paving the court. They are among a group of draft building contracts, all of which appear to be in the hand of John Osborne. Since he did not become secretary to Bacon until *c*. 1568 they undoubtedly relate to work undertaken at Gorhambury in the early 1570s when the long gallery was built.

[79] J. Summerson, *Architecture in Britain 1530–1830* (6th edn, 1977), 47.

[80] Approximate calculations of the ground-floor areas of some near-contemporary houses are as follows:

Redgrave Hall	*c*. 6,000 sq. feet	(Sir Nicholas Bacon)
Gorhambury House	*c*. 9,000 sq. feet	(Sir Nicholas Bacon)
Gidea Park	*c*. 10,000 sq. feet	(Sir Anthony Cooke)
Stiffkey Hall	*c*. 10,500 sq. feet	(Sir Nicholas Bacon)
Ingatestone Hall	*c*. 11,000+ sq. feet	(Sir William Petre)
Hill Hall	*c*. 11,000 sq. feet	(Sir Thomas Smith)
Wimbledon House	*c*. 12,000 sq. feet	(Sir Thomas Cecil)
Hardwick Hall	*c*. 12,000 sq. feet	(Countess of Shrewsbury)
Wollaton Hall	*c*. 13,500 sq. feet	(Sir Francis Willoughby)
Longleat house	*c*. 18,000 sq. feet	(Sir John Thynne)
Bisham Abbey	*c*. 13,000+ sq. feet	(Sir Thomas Hoby)

[81] Rogers, 'Gorhambury', 85–6.

reflect the *mediocria* manifested in both his statesmanship and the *sententiae* with which he would shortly embellish his long gallery?[82] Either way one is struck by the contrast between this modest house and the colossal scale of its associated gardens. Certainly at first glance the great geometric wilderness manifests little *mediocria*. What, then, were the sources of inspiration for these gardens, and what do they reveal about the intellectual development of their designer? Clearly they represent a dramatic shift from the medieval *hortus conclusus* Sir Nicholas had built at Redgrave. In scale they are comparable with those at Hampton Court and Nonsuch, especially as the latter were being developed by John, Lord Lumley.[83] In basic layout, too, they had close affinities with Nonsuch where the great garden and privy garden gave way to an extensive orchard and wilderness. But, here the similarities end. For the gardens at Hampton Court and Nonsuch were flamboyant, designed to display heraldic devices and pieces of sculpture set amidst topiary and intricate garden knots. Those at Gorhambury, in contrast, were chaste and sombre. They appear to have been devoid of heraldic devices or symbolic topiary and knots.

They also appear to have been conceived as part of a larger and carefully contrived landscape. It was as if, having decided to build in an ex-monastic deer park, Bacon regarded the entire site, and even beyond the pale, as an extended garden whose 'natural' landscape he respected and, where possible, improved. He sited his house at the highest point, overlooking gentle valleys to the north and south, with its southern aspect commanding extensive views to Prae Wood and the rising ground beyond (F on Fig. 1). Where this ground plateaued he laid out woodland with walks or alleys radiating from a central point to provide dramatic glimpses of distant countryside. This point was marked, not by a monument or piece of sculpture, but by a huge snake-like reservoir which he built to supply water for the house. One alley led to a mount,[84]

---

82 Here I am adopting the concept of 'self-fashioning' borrowed from S. Greenblatt (*Renaissance Self-Fashioning* (1980)) and developed with regard to mid-Tudor architecture in Maurice Howard's essay 'Self-Fashioning and the Classical Moment in Mid-Sixteenth-Century English Architecture', *Renaissance Bodies: The Human Figure in English Culture c. 1540–1660*, ed. L. Gent and N. Llewellyn (1990).
83 For Nonsuch gardens, see J. Dent, *The Quest for Nonsuch* (1981), 112–33.
84 The mount is attributed to Sir Francis Bacon by the Ordnance Survey (see O/S 1:2500, Herts., sheet XXXIV.14, where the surveyors have described it as 'Lord Bacon's Mount'). Both this and the alleys are more likely to have been the work of Sir Nicholas since in 1608 Francis records giving instructions for a 'plott to be made of my poole; and the Waulk through Pray wood and the stand thear on the hill for prospect' (*Letters and Life*, ed. Spedding, IV, 52). This reads like stock taking prior to improvements especially since the 'pool' or reservoir had been built to supply water to the house and so must date from the time of Sir Nicholas. The surveyors have marked this feature as 'camp'.

crowned with a stand or gazebo, which stood at the eastern end of this plateau where, like its counterpart at Redgrave, it provided panoramic views over the park and surrounding countryside (G on Fig. 1).

The park, much of which lay between the house and Prae Wood, was divided into hedged and tree-lined fields (see Fig. 1), but with gaps in the hedges so that the deer could roam freely.[85] These closes may have been medieval in origin, Sir Nicholas merely incorporating them into his landscape scheme. Whether old or newly created, Sir Nicholas located and shaped his formal gardens so that they appeared to be integral with these closes (A1–4 on Fig. 1). He further integrated gardens and parkland by siting the 'desert' some distance from his house so that it could dramatically straddle a gentle valley on the north side of the park. Abutting the privy garden he replanted a grove of ancient oaks (A4 on Fig. 1), part of which he had cleared to make way for the 'desert' and walled gardens.[86] No doubt he intended these oaks, some of which still stand,[87] to be a 'natural' feature within his parkland scheme, but they also served to provide a visual barrier between the walled garden courts, roughly aligned to the house, and the 'desert' which was aligned to the contours of the valley across which it lay – a clever device to obscure the compromise between the dictates of a geometrical layout and those of the local terrain.[88] The park also contained several arbours and at least one water feature, or, in the words of the seventeenth-century

It has recently been surveyed and identified as a reservoir by Dr J. Hunn of the Herts. Archaeological Trust. I am grateful to him for drawing my attention to this feature.

[85] HRO, Gorhambury Collection, MS 1 A 83/7, fol. 1r and v.

[86] *Ibid.*, fol. 1. Over the doorway which led into oak wood and painted in blue and gold (as were the *Sententiae* in Bacon's long gallery) were the following verses:

> Horrida nuper eram aspectu latebraeque ferarum,
> Ruricolis tantum numinibusque locus.
> Edomitor faustò huc dum forte supervenit Orpheus
> Ulterius qui me no sinit esse rudem;
> Convocat, avulsis virgula virentia truncis,
> Et sedem quae vel Diis placuisse potest.
> Sicque mei cultor, sic est mihi cultus et Orpheus:
> Floreat O noster cultus amorque diu!

Aubrey, 'Brief Lives', ed. Clark, 82–3; *The Progresses and Public Processions of Queen Elizabeth*, ed. Nichols, II, 58–9.

[87] Mrs Anthea Taigel, an historic landscape consultant, examined and girthed the standing oaks. At least two had measurements of over seven metres which led her to suggest that they could, if growing in a grove, have been planted in the second half of the sixteenth century.

[88] I am grateful to my colleague Dr T. Williamson for suggesting this explanation of the alignment of the 'desert'.

land surveyor, 'a watering place inclosed and tarassed about with brick'.[89]

This emphasis upon features which lay outside the formal garden, upon embellishing the landscape so that it becomes a 'suitable garden format', has resonances with park landscaping in the late medieval period at, for instance, Somersham, Stow, Bodiam and Kenilworth; resonances with some of the horticultural if not religious concepts of John Beale and John Evelyn in the seventeenth century and with the ideas of Stephen Switzer in the early eighteenth century.[90] Others too, were experimenting with this type of landscaping in the second half of the sixteenth century: for instance Sir William Drury at Hawstead (Suffolk), Sir Thomas Gresham at Osterley (Surrey) and possibly Sir William Cecil at Theobalds.[91] Clearly it is part of an English tradition which draws its inspiration from a variety of intellectual, philosophical and cultural roots. Furthermore, students of Renaissance garden design will have sensed resonances with contemporary Italian villa landscapes: the emphasis on sweeping vistas; on variety within those vistas; the integration of *villa* and *vigna* which is suggested by the hedged closes within the park and by the relationship of the formal gardens to those closes; and the creation of woodland alleys designed to provide unexpected and dramatic views from Prae plateau.[92]

Thus at Gorhambury we may be witnessing a native tradition being revived and stimulated by ideas about gardens and their landscaped settings which derived from Italian Villa gardening (disseminated by travellers like Sir Nicholas' brother-in-law Sir Thomas Hoby)[93] and

[89] HRO, Gorhambury Collection, MSS 1 A 83/7, fol. 1, and 1 B 10, undated map (endorsed 'Gorhambury Park with its old inclosures') probably of the late seventeenth century.

[90] For Somersham (Cambs.), Stow (Lincs.), Bodiam (Suss.) and Kenilworth (Warws.), see C. C. Taylor, 'Somersham Place, Cambridgeshire: A Medieval Landscape for Pleasure?', in *From Cornwall to Caithness*, ed. Bowden, Mackay and Topping, 211–24. I am indebted to Mr Christopher Taylor for drawing my attention to the aesthetic treatment of these late medieval parks. For the ideas of Beale, Evelyn and Switzer, see *Culture and Cultivation in Early Modern England: Writing and the Land*, ed. M. Leslie and T. Raylor (Leicester, 1992), esp. 130–222; P. H. Goodchild, ' "No Phantasticall Utopia, But a Reall Place". John Evelyn, John Beale and Backbury Hill, Herefordshire', *Garden History*, 19, ii (1991), 105–27.

[91] For Hawstead Park, see R. Hoppitt, 'A Study of the Development of Parks in Suffolk from the Eleventh to the Seventeenth Century' (University of East Anglia, PhD thesis, 1993), 266–71. For Osterley, see Henderson, 'Bacon's Water Gardens', 118. For Theobalds, see Strong, *Renaissance Garden*, 53–4.

[92] For this, see J. Dixon Hunt, *Garden and Grove: The Italian Renaissance Garden in the English Imagination 1600–1750* (1986), esp. chs. 3 and 7.

[93] 'A Booke of the Travaile and Liefe of me, Thomas Hoby, with Diverse Things Woorth the Notinge', ed. E. Powell (*Camden Miscellany, Volume the Tenth*, Camden Society, 1902), 3–130.

from the study of the classical sources which inspired those gardens. Or at least from some of them, for, as we have seen, the gardens at Gorhambury eschewed more of the classical repertoire than they adopted. More specifically, as in the case of Tudor gentlemen farmers, Sir Nicholas (himself of yeoman stock) may have been stimulated by writers like Pliny, Virgil and Columella, who emphasised the horticultural aspects of gardening and the self-sufficiency it promoted.[94] He undoubtedly owed a great deal to Seneca who, in his *De Vita Beata*, had justified the garden as a means of enrichment for the stoic (as opposed to pleasure for the Epicurean) by reconciling wealth and comfort 'with the doctrine of virtue achieved by living according to nature'.[95] For surely Gorhambury and its gardens were a manifestation of Sir Nicholas Bacon's stoic philosophy. His greatest pleasure derived from involvement in creating those gardens: *Laborare est orare* might have been carved upon their portals. For him gardening, horticulture and agriculture were inter-related and challenging activities which provided intellectual, moral and physical refreshment. Hence the integration of all three within the Gorhambury landscape. Like the elder Pliny and Virgil he regarded gardening as a utilitarian activity, hence the emphasis upon fruit and herbs in the planting scheme for the 'desert'. Above all he designed these gardens as a place for retreat, for solitude, for private discourse with friends, for that *negotium animi* which his contemporary, the Flemish classicist and neo-stoic, Justius Lipsius, extolled in his *De Constantia* (1584) as being one of the great attributes of the stoic garden.[96] Hence, just as his long gallery served as a memory theatre of classical (and mainly stoic) aphorisms rather than as a portrait gallery of courtly contemporaries and bogus ancestors,[97] so his gardens were devoid of amusing hydraulics, cunning conceits, heraldic devices, knots, statuary and symbolic topiary. Emphatically they were not designed to entertain, least of all to entertain the Court. Like the house, they incorporate aspects of both continental and English planning traditions; but most striking is what they eschewed of both; for these gardens are first and foremost a manifestation of his

---

[94] M. Morford, 'The Stoic Garden', *Journal of Garden History*, 7, ii (1987), 156–8. For the impact of classical literature on English agricultural practices, see J. Thirsk, 'Making a Fresh Start: Sixteenth Century Agriculture and the Classical Inspiration', in *Culture and Cultivation*, ed. Leslie and Raylor, 15–34.

[95] Morford, 'The Stoic Garden', 158. For the influence of Seneca upon Bacon's intellectual development, see Collinson, 'Sir Nicholas Bacon', 258–60.

[96] Morford, 'The Stoic Garden', 163–70.

[97] For the decoration in the long gallery at Gorhambury, see E. McCutcheon, *Sir Nicholas Bacon's Great House Sententiae* (English Literary Renaissance Supplements, 3, Amherst, 1977).

moral and philosophical attitudes, of his participation in the 'Commonweal' debate.

By the time Sir Nicholas had completed Gorhambury in 1569 he had become interested in the application of new ideas to the design of houses and gardens. In this 'third age' of his intellectual development his building activities manifest an awareness of concepts such as centralised and axial planning, proportions derived from harmonic ratios and the architectural integration of house and garden.[98] From the late fifteenth century first in Italy and then in France practising architects had been experimenting with these concepts. By the 1560s their achievements, or at least their idealised versions of them, could be studied in England through a growing number of published architectural treatises. As early as 1512 Alberti's *De Re Aedificatoria* had been translated into French but it was between 1550 and 1570 that works by practitioners and publicists such as Serlio, Palladio, Du Cerceau, de L'Orme, Vredeman de Vries and Pietro Cataneo (to mention only some) were published.[99] To judge from the building activities of the English aristocracy during the first decade of the Elizabethan *Pax*, they occasioned widespread interest and discussion. They provided the stimulus whereby the gentleman-patron aspired to become the gentleman-architect. The achievements of Roger Pratt were a far cry, but at least by the 1560s architecture had become a subject of gentry discourse; in an aristocrat's library books on architecture jostled with treatises on theology, astrology, militia training, navigation, gardening and hawking.[100] No record of Sir Nicholas' library has survived, but a copy of Serlio's *De Architectura* is listed among books he presented to the University of Cambridge Library in 1574.[101] In any event, in days when books and manuscripts circulated freely, his neighbours were well stocked: Sir Thomas Smith had at least ten books on architecture in his library; Sir Thomas Knyvett had even more, while Sir William Cecil acquired a stock by purchase and through gifts.[102]

---

[98] R. Wittkower, *Architectural Principles in the Age of Humanism* (1967).
[99] For the availability of pattern books in England, see Summerson, *Architecture in Britain*, 54–6.
[100] L. Gent, *Picture and Poetry 1560–1620: Relations between Literature and the Visual Arts in the English Renaissance* (Leamington Spa, 1981), contains a useful, but not exhaustive, appendix on 'Books on Art, Perspective and Architecture in English Renaissance Libraries 1580–1630'; S. Jayne, *Library Catalogues of the English Renaissance* (Berkeley and Los Angeles, 1956); A. T. Friedman, *House and Household in Elizabethan England: Wollaton Hall and the Willoughby Family* (1989), 29–35.
[101] Cambridge University Library, University Archives, Grace book Δ, fol. 332a.
[102] P. J. Drury, '"A Fayre House, Buylt by Sir Thomas Smith": The Development of Hill Hall, Essex, 1557–81', *Journal of the British Archaeological Association*, 136 (1983), 120; D. J. McKitterick, *The Library of Sir Thomas Knyvett of Ashwellthorpe c. 1539–1618*

Crucial to an appreciation of Renaissance architectural concepts and of their application to the design of houses and gardens were the mathematical arts, as John Dee was at pains to stress in his preface to Henry Billingsley's translation of *Euclid's Geometry* (1570).[103] Dee, following Vitruvius, emphasised the necessity for the architect to have knowledge of 'Geometrie, Arithmetike, Astronomie, Musike, Anthropographie, Hydragogie [and] Horometrie'.[104] Evidence suggests that Sir Nicholas both encouraged the study of the mathematical arts and participated in their practical application. Among the seventy-three books he presented to Cambridge University Library in 1574 at least twenty-nine were subsequently catalogued under 'Astronomia', 'Cosmographia', 'Geometria', 'Musica' and 'Arithmetica'.[105] He employed Thomas Blundeville, a scholar whose 'breadth of accomplishment ran to truly Renaissance proportions', and a friend of John Dee and William Gilbert, as a mathematical tutor to his children.[106] He also had close associations with Leonard Digges, a friend of John Dee and a mathematician and land surveyor of European reputation, who wrote two treatises on mensuration.[107] The second of these, published posthumously by his son Thomas Digges, carried a dedication to Sir Nicholas Bacon which recalled 'the great favour your Lordship bare my father in his life time, and the conference it pleased your honour to use with him touching the sciences Mathematical, especially in geometrical mesurations'.[108] His mathematical interests may well have contributed to his decision to use Roman inscriptional capitals for the *Sententiae* with which he decorated the walls of his long gallery. Undoubtedly these Roman capitals evoked a variety of symbolic resonances,[109] but as has been pointed out by one historian of lettering, 'they are illustrations of the Renaissance interest in the importance of

(Cambridge, 1978); J. A. Gotch, 'The Renaissance in Northamptonshire', *Transactions of the RIBA*, n.s., 6 (1890).

[103] F. Yates, *Theatre of the World* (1969), 20–41.

[104] *Ibid.*, 26.

[105] See n. 101 above. For the recasting of the university curriculum at Cambridge with emphasis in the first year on cosmography, arithmetic, geometry and astronomy, see Simon, *Education and Society*, 252–3.

[106] E. G. R. Taylor, *The Mathematical Practitioners of Tudor and Stuart England* (Cambridge, 1954), 173; Tittler, *Bacon*, 58–9; T. Blundeville, *M. Blundevil, His Exercises* (1594), preface.

[107] Girouard, *Smythson*, 9; Taylor, *Mathematical Practitioners*, 166–7; *DNB sub* Digges, Leonard.

[108] L. Digges, *A Geometrical Practise Named Pantometria, Divided into Three Bookes, Longimetria, Planimetria, and Stereometria . . . Framed by Leonard Digges, Gent. Lately Finished by Thomas Digges his Sonne . . .* (1571).

[109] McCutcheon, *Bacon's Sententiae*, 10–11.

proportion and in mathematics and in the Platonic idea of perfect form'.[110]

His building activities in his 'third age' undoubtedly manifested these interests. From about 1568 his environmental planning reveals a growing interest in geometrical and axial layouts. Alberti's advocacy that 'the garden was the province of the architect', that it should be treated as an extension of the house, that both should be conceived in terms of Renaissance harmony and proportion expressed by means of geometry, had been much practised in Italy since the late fifteenth century.[111] By the mid-sixteenth century it had become a feature of chateaux building in France where the axial layout of house and garden combined with the geometric use of canals was well exemplified at Anet and Saint-Germain-en-Laye. In 1568 Sir Nicholas applied these ideas in a modest way at Redgrave where he added an avenue and canal to the park landscape. The avenue, which was axial to the main range of the house and which extended for 600 yards to the southern park pale, crossed the canal at its mid-point and at right angles to its line of flow. To achieve this it was necessary to rechannel a meandering stream and, no doubt, control its flow with sluices. He entrusted the supervision of this work to his friend and fellow-builder, Edmund Withipoll of Ipswich, in the process leaving a description of what he was trying to achieve in prose which lacks the usual concision and precision of his recorded oratory. 'I have enformed [Withipoll]' he told his son Nicholas, 'howe I wold have that part of the Ryver made, Over the which my Bridge shall go . . . My desyer is that the bridg may stand iuste in the mydest betwene both heedes of that parte of the Ryver that the bridg doth go over, and so shall the mydest of that water be iuste agaynst the mydest of my house as the bridge is.'[112] This layout was destroyed in the eighteenth century when the valley through which the stream flowed was dammed by Capability Brown to create a landscaped lake, but part of the submerged causeway leading to the bridge can still be discerned by aerial photography, while a late seventeenth-century painting of the house shows the avenue of trees, by that time well matured.[113] At Gorhambury, a few years later, Sir Nicholas added a similar avenue or 'walke' which appears to have been axial to the

[110] N. Gray, *A History of Lettering* (Oxford, 1986), 140–7; N. Gray, *Lettering on Buildings* (New York, 1960), 16–17.
[111] Strong, *Renaissance Garden*, 15.
[112] Sandeen, 'Redgrave Hall', 23 and 27.
[113] This painting is in the possession of Mr P. J. Holt-Wilson. I am grateful to him, through the good offices of Dr and Mrs W. R. Cordeaux, for allowing me to see it. It has been reproduced by Dr E. R. Sandeen in his article on the building of Redgrave Hall (*ibid.*, n. 63).

house and which also extended for about 500 yards to the park pale[114] (E on Fig. I). Here, however, terrain and location of the house prevented the avenue being laid out in association with a water feature. It may well be that the 'desert' at Gorhambury also belongs to this phase of his garden planning since its geometrical layout distinguishes it from that of the main garden.

The necessity to build Stiffkey Hall (1576) for his second son Nathaniel provided the occasion for Sir Nicholas to apply geometric layouts and harmonic ratios within an integrated scheme rather than tinkering with existing layouts. We know a good deal about this project through the papers of Nathaniel Bacon. They show that Sir Nicholas planned the house and gardens from his study at York House in London and that his secretary, John Osborne, drafted the 'plats'.[115] He appears to have indulged his neo-platonic philosophy by designing an ideal scheme which required the purchase of adjacent property before it could be implemented.[116] Once this property had been acquired he had the site surveyed according to his own idiosyncratic requirements through a series of questionnaires directed to his son. These reveal his concern about the dimensions of the site and the nature of the terrain. They also suggest, by now not surprisingly, that he was preoccupied with the garden layout.[117] Once this remote-control survey had been completed, he produced further plats which he despatched to Nathaniel so that they could be checked against the realities of the site and, if necessary, modified.[118] By such processes the ideal plan became compromised. It was further compromised in the process of building by shortages of cash,[119] the unavailability of dressed stone,[120] the limitations of the local craftsmen who could only work within the vernacular tradition,[121] his son's failure to complete the house and possibly even to appreciate the

---

[114] He almost certainly added this walk-way when he built the long gallery in the early 1570s since it appears in the 1634 map as axial to both the house and gallery rather than to the house alone.

[115] Smith and Baker, *Bacon Papers*, I, 90, 263; NRO, MS Raynham deposit 6/50 is a draft first-floor plan of the house in Osborne's hand.

[116] The property involved was a barn belonging to Thomas Barker. For the negotiations over the purchase of this site see Smith and Baker, *Bacon Papers*, I, 84, 95, 112, 120, 243.

[117] *Ibid.*, 110, 113, 163–4, 172–3.

[118] *Ibid.*, 187.

[119] *Ibid.*, 90, 196, 219–20.

[120] *Ibid.*, 170–1, 196, 224, 226. The house was built of flint and brick. Even the window mullions were of moulded brick.

[121] The building accounts for the second phase of building are extant (FL, MS E.b 2), these show that, with rare exceptions, the craftsmen employed were drawn from the parishes within an eight mile radius of Stiffkey (A. Hassell Smith 'Labourers in Late Sixteenth Century England: A Case Study from North Norfolk', *Continuity and Change*, 4, i (1989), 37–42).

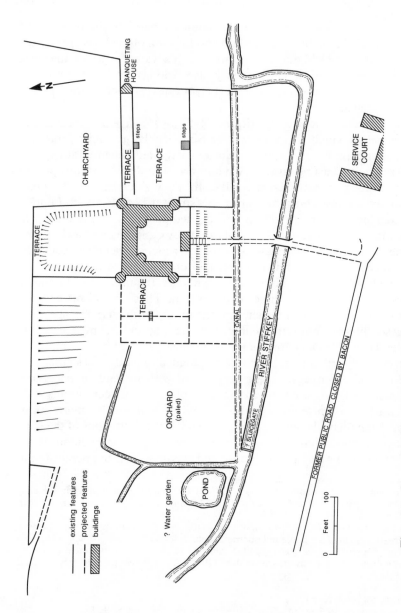

Figure 6   Plan of Stiffkey Hall and gardens

principles which underlay his father's plan. All of which makes it difficult, but not impossible, to deduce that plan.

Like Smythson at Wollaton (but several years earlier) he attempted to combine the house, courts and gardens in a unified and symmetrical scheme (Fig. 6).[122] His inspiration, as Sir Roy Strong suggests for Smythson's plans at Wollaton, may have been derived from French garden design at Ancy-le-Franc Anet and Verneuil, albeit views of these gardens only became widely available in 1576 when Du Cerceau published them in his *Les Plus Excellents Bastiments de France*.[123] As at Redgrave, he incorporated water features into the geometric layout by straightening the course of the river Stiffkey and converting it to a canal by cutting a new channel for the main course of the river.[124] This canal, which bounded the gardens to the south, was then bisected by a carriageway which was aligned axially to the house. He also cut a canal to frame the west side of 'the great west garden' and to provide the core feature of a water-garden.[125] Archaeological evidence suggests that the house was approached via a flight of steps traversing a series of shallow terraces which produced an effect similar to, albeit less dramatic than, that which his nephew Sir Thomas Cecil was to build at Wimbledon a decade later.[126] He was at great pains to exploit the sloping site to the east of the hall by laying out a magnificent flight of terraces which still survive and which descended from the churchyard wall to the canal[127] – an aspect of his planning which involved so much earthmoving that it was probably never completed as he intended,[128] but which was directly in the tradition of Italian Renaissance garden design. The terrain west of the hall prevented Bacon from creating there a mirror image of these terraces; instead he seems to have laid out this area as a huge square court corresponding roughly in size to the area of the courts to the north, south and east of the house. Its composition is obscure since it was heavily disturbed by farm buildings in the nineteenth century but terracing to its north and east gave way successively to an

---

[122] Strong, *Renaissance Garden*, 56–7.

[123] De Cerceau, *Bastiments de France*, ed. Thomson.

[124] Smith and Baker, *Bacon Papers*, I, 196; NRO, MS Hammond deposit 20.1.87 (S117A).

[125] Smith and Baker, *Bacon Papers*, II, 21.

[126] The archaeological evidence is based on observations made when a trench for a water main was cut to the south of the house. For Wimbledon House, see Summerson, *Architecture in Britain*, 74–6; C. S. Higham, *Wimbledon Manor House under the Cecils* (1962).

[127] For an account of the detailed layout of these terraces, see my entry for Stiffkey in T. Williamson and A. Taigel, 'Some Early Geometric Gardens in Norfolk', *Journal of Garden History*, 11, i and ii (1991), 94–7.

[128] See below, p. 158.

orchard which was paled and laid out in alleys and then to a water-garden.[129]

It has been suggested that, 'at least as far as the floor plans were concerned', he designed this house 'as a deliberate mathematical conceit'. 'The house and its courtyard', writes Dr Airs, 'form a square with the inner towers exactly placed on the diagonals.' The latter also draws attention to the frequent application within the plan of the ratio 2:1.[130] Furthermore, according to an extant plan, the great hall and courtyard were laid out using ratios of $1:1\frac{1}{2} \times 2$ and 3:4:5 respectively.[131] This is not the place for a discussion of the house, but its apparent mathematical planning prompts some consideration as to whether Sir Nicholas aspired to create similar ratios within his garden layout. A glance at an archaeological survey of Stiffkey gardens suggests not (Fig. 6). But, bearing in mind the gulf between the Platonic ideal and the real, it is worth considering the compromises which were forced upon Sir Nicholas by the constraints of the site. The most promising location for the house lay in the vicinity of the churchyard where the ground rose quite steeply from the river's flood-plain. This meant that if he built there he could only achieve an integrated relationship between the house and the garden courts if he treated the churchyard as one of those courts. Hence the obtrusion of the hall's north-eastern turret into the south-western corner of the churchyard. That decision made, the south side of the churchyard (c. 255 feet) dictated the length of the garden court to the east of the house. If the area of this court was to be twice that of the house, then the width of the latter needed to be 127 feet. Hence, presumably, Sir Nicholas' decision to build a courtyard-house measuring c. 127 × 127 feet; a decision which may explain why he planned a residence which was considerably larger than those of most county magnates and even larger than his own at Gorhambury for a younger son who had no political aspirations. In the event the amount of in-fill which would have been required to raise the eastern end of the terrace caused him, or more likely his son, to shorten it and so to compromise the ratios. A similar problem arose from the proximity of the river since it prevented the entrance court from being a square equal to that occupied by the house. Sir Nicholas appears to have responded to this by increasing the area of the court to the north of the house by as much as that to the south had to be truncated, thereby

---

[129] Williamson and Taigel, 'Geometric Gardens in Norfolk', 97.

[130] M. Airs, 'The Designing of Five East Anglian Country Houses', *Architectural History*, 21 (1978), 63.

[131] NRO, MS Raynham deposit 6/50. The dimensions of the great hall are given as 51 × 23 feet.

maintaining a ratio of 2:1 between the area of both courts and that of the house.

If the reader's credulity has been strained by this rationalisation of Sir Nicholas' attempt to achieve mathematical ratios within an integrated layout at Stiffkey, it can perhaps be restored by a glance at his plan for the chapel at Corpus Christi College, Cambridge.[132] In 1578 he had agreed to provide £200 for this building, but when the Master and Fellows produced their plan he rejected it. Instead he provided one, elegant in its simplicity, which was again drawn by his secretary John Osborne, but which undoubtedly embodied his own architectural aspirations. In this plan the chapel appears as an unadorned rectangular building with windows symmetrically placed and it is laid out to the ratio of 1:1½ × 2 – proportions already in use in the great hall at Stiffkey and commonly applied to public rooms by Renaissance architects.[133]

It was intended originally that this essay should discuss Sir Nicholas Bacon's building activities. In the event, Clio, the muse of history, beckoned its author to a prospect from which the gardens appeared more exciting than the buildings which accompanied them. As a result a hitherto unknown facet of Sir Nicholas' manifold accomplishments has been discussed and some new insights gained into the role of Sir Francis Bacon as a garden designer. Essentially, however, this essay has confirmed (if such was necessary) the features of Sir Nicholas Bacon's personality which Professor Collinson delineated in his essay in the *Historical Journal*. There he tells us that 'Bacon's stoicism has two enduring monuments: the *sententiae* painted and perhaps incised on the walls of the long gallery . . . [and] Gorhambury itself, which the Queen called a "little house".' To these two monuments we might now add a third: the gardens and parkland which the lord keeper laid out to complement that house. He also argues that the *via media* pursued by Sir Nicholas in religion and politics was a matter of 'policy', his 'moderation' shifting and adapting to the changing religious and political scene in both England and on the continent. This same probing mind, unwilling to

---

[132] Corpus Christi College, Cambridge, MS volume of miscellaneous documents 1400–1700, no. 41. The plan is printed in E. R. Sandeen, 'The Building of the Sixteenth-Century Corpus Christi Chapel', *Proceedings of the Cambridge Antiquarian Society*, 55 (1961), plate 5.

[133] *Ibid.* Dr Sandeen suggests that this plan may have been drawn by John Osborne (p. 26). The latter's unmistakable handwriting on the plan confirms that this surmise is correct. Although a gentleman of minor status it is unlikely that he was more than the draughtsman since the house he subsequently built at Wattisfield, Suff., does not suggest a man of great architectural pretensions. Sandeen's surmise that Sir Nicholas 'has a strong . . . claim to partnership in the creation of the chapel's design' is surely an understatement. As in the case of Stiffkey he designed and Osborne drafted.

become trapped in a 'time-warp', is manifest in his developing views on garden layouts and their relationship with the house. Redgrave, Gorhambury and Stiffkey each reveal a different phase of Sir Nicholas' intellectual development as he endeavours to reconcile new ideas about garden design, the practicalities of the situation, his philosophical predisposition and the need to interpret classical precepts within an English gardening idiom. This essay may also have something to tell us about the generational differences between Sir Nicholas and his son Francis. In many ways they were profound: Sir Nicholas created gardens where none existed before. Sir Francis adapted and improved, or, as he told the queen, 'trimmed and dressed' them. Sir Nicholas was a planner and an engineer, Sir Francis an artist, scientist and plantsman. Yet for both, gardening was a passion; an essential element of their psyche. For Sir Nicholas it was an act of regeneration; for Sir Francis an integral part of his scientific interests. There can be no doubt that when the latter extolled gardens as 'the greatest refreshment to the spirits of man', Sir Nicholas, to borrow a phrase from Professor Collinson, 'would have said Amen to that'.

7   The Protestant idea of marriage in early modern England

Anthony Fletcher

Patrick Collinson concluded a recent tautly argued review of the historiography of the Protestant family by saying that 'the doctrine and, so far as we can observe it in the field, the practice of early Protestantism in respect of marriage and domestic matters generally was not a total novelty, if novel at all'. In view of this it may appear consciously challenging to entitle a contribution to this book 'The Protestant idea of marriage'. Yet his essay is full of sensitive comment on the questions that are left open after students of the conduct books have variously interpreted them on the one hand as embodying new values, even as giving shape to the family in its modern form, and on the other as repeating time-honoured or at least earlier advice. The Reformation, Collinson declares in a memorable phrase, 'riveted home patriarchy', but Protestantism, he also believes, 'deepened the emotional quality of family life'. Within the conduct books he sees a discrepancy between 'a stress on patriarchy amounting to a kind of benevolent despotism' and attitudes towards wives and children 'which encouraged affection and respect for their personal autonomy'.[1] Others also have seen an historical problem here. Lawrence Stone saw one but closed it off with a schematic formulation of the development of the family which has not convinced many.[2] Susan Amussen talks of the 'double messages' of the conduct book writers in her analysis of the texts.[3] The purpose of this essay is to explore whether the advice on marriage given by a group of Puritan clerics in the period from the 1590s to the 1640s really is rent by inconsistency.

We can begin with the concept of patriarchy. From the Hebrew society of the Old Testament until the sixteenth century, the family had been at the centre of a system of institutionalised male dominance over

[1] *Birthpangs*, 62–3, 70, 93.
[2] L. Stone, *The Family, Sex and Marriage in England 1500–1800* (1977); for typical critiques, see M. Ingram, *Church Courts, Sex and Marriage in England 1570–1640* (Cambridge, 1983), 137–44; and K. Wrightson, *English Society 1580–1680* (1982), 103–4.
[3] S. D. Amussen, *An Ordered Society* (1988), 41–7.

women and children which extended outwards from the household to society in general.[4] The conduct book writers, steeped in scripture, lived and breathed all this. Patriarchy was a scheme of gender relations that men found, though they probably never thought of it quite like this, was in constant need of repair. And there is good reason to think that many Englishmen felt some unease about the security of their hold upon the gender order at times between the 1560s and the 1660s. Conduct books can be seen in this respect as one of a series of discourses designed to bolster patriarchy at a time when it was believed to be under some degree of threat.[5] They can also be seen as a product of the Reformation and of an evangelistic impulse for reform. Martin Luther found it inconceivable that a woman should choose not to marry. Marriage and motherhood was her inescapable vocation; to deny it was to fight her natural sex drive, seen as more powerful than a man's. It also flouted the divinely imposed order which made women subject to men. Luther, as his copious table talk makes clear, was no feminist. Martha, the obedient wife busy at home, not Mary her sister devoted to Christ's teaching or Mary the Virgin Mother of Christ, was his ideal woman. His was a sanctification of marriage that domesticated women and that fitted well with the conservative thinking of the time about their proper role.[6] The Reformation, more generally, was a revolt against an alternative tradition in Christianity to the patriarchal one, a tradition which distrusted sex and enjoined its members not to marry. With the abolition of monasteries and clerical celibacy, the patriarchal family was stressed more forcefully than ever before as the nucleus of the church and of society. What the Reformation did not do, it should be noted, was in any sense modify the fundamental presumption of patriarchy, namely that it is the order of creation.[7]

The English conduct book writers, themselves from the first generation of married pastors, saw it as their task to model the patriarchal family afresh for this new world. It was entirely predictable that they should do so. In the Puritan circles in which they moved there was constant talk about the godly household. Its premise was that the family could only exist as a hierarchy. Its main features were the absolute authority of the male head, the subordination of women and the

---

[4] G. Lerner, *The Creation of Patriarchy* (Oxford, 1986).
[5] I cover this subject fully in 'Men's Dilemma: The Future of Patriarchy in England 1560–1660', *TRHS* (forthcoming).
[6] M. Wiesner, 'Luther and Women: The Death of Two Marys', in *Feminist Theology: A Reader*, ed. A. Loades (1990), 123–34; *Birthpangs*, 65.
[7] R. Radford Ruether, 'The Liberation of Christology from Patriarchy', in *Feminist Theology: A Reader*, ed. Loades, 138–48.

disciplined upbringing of children. Its purpose was that it should act as a bedrock of evangelisation. 'If ever we would have the church of God to continue among us', wrote Richard Greenham, 'we must bring it into our households and nourish it in our families'.[8] 'The family is a seminary of the church and commonwealth', declared John Downame, 'and as a private school, wherein children and servants are fitted for public assemblies.'[9] Samuel Ward traced all 'scandals and enormities' in the commonwealth to parental neglect of religious education and discipline of children and servants.[10] 'First reform your own families and then you will be fitter to reform the family of God', Edmund Calamy told MPs in a sermon of 1642. 'You are like to see no general reformation till you procure family reformation', warned Richard Baxter in a treatise of 1655.[11] Classical ideas, transmitted by sixteenth-century humanists, certainly contributed to this spiritualisation of the household. William Perkins cited Aristotle as his source for the image of the family as the 'seminary of all other societies' which, righteously governed, was 'a direct means for the good ordering both of church and commonwealth'.[12] But the main impetus came from a moral ethic that is distinctly Protestant. The Reformation was at the same time a religious movement and a social movement. Gender relations, it has been shown persuasively, were at the crux of it in the German city of Augsburg. So too were they in the conception of moral and religious reform propagated by English Puritan divines. Lyndal Roper's conclusion that a 'politics of women's role in marriage and the household' was a key to the successful implementation of the German Reformation can be applied equally to the Reformation in England in the decades between the 1560s and the 1650s.[13]

In the early sixteenth century tracts on marriage tended to focus on matters of common law and theological interpretation, while also containing hints that the clergy who used them could pass on about the actual conduct of marital relations. William Harrison's *Commendations of Matrimony*, published in 1528, is typical of this genre. Richard Whitford's *A Work for Householders* provides rules for the conduct of the household dominated by directions for prayer and explanations of the creed and commandments. Heinrich Bullinger's *The Christian State of Matrimony*, translated for the English market by Miles Coverdale in 1541, established

---

8 Cited in C. Hill, *Society and Puritanism in Pre-Revolutionary England* (1964), 443.
9 Cited in J. Morgan, *Godly Learning* (Cambridge, 1986), 142–3.
10 Cited in M. Todd, *Christian Humanism and the Puritan Social Order* (Cambridge, 1987), 100.
11 Cited in Hill, *Society and Puritanism*, 444–5.
12 Todd, *Christian Humanism*, 96–117.
13 L. Roper, *The Holy Household* (Oxford, 1989), 5.

the new genre of the practical domestic conduct book, although considerable space was still given to the legal and ceremonial aspects of marriage. The lay hunger for advice and instruction on the management of family life is evident from the fact that this went through nine printings between 1544 and 1575.[14]

The normal starting-point for the conduct books with which we are concerned in this essay was a marriage sermon. There must have been numerous such sermons that were never printed. Alice Thornton, for example, refers in her autobiography to the sermon at her wedding: 'Mr Siddall made a most pious and profitable exhortation to us showing our duties and teaching us the fear of the Lord in this our new estate of life.'[15] The first such sermon to reach the press was one by Henry Smith which he entitled *A Preparative for Marriage*. It was published in 1591 and went through three more editions that year. 'Silver tongued Smith', as he was called, clearly did little to rearrange his wedding day text which is not well organised. Much material was lifted from Smith's tract by Robert Cleaver, who published *A Godly Form of Household Government* in 1598. This saw eight more editions by 1630. Cleaver, also known for his sermon on keeping the Sabbath, co-authored the later editions of this very popular conduct book with John Dod, one of that select band of Puritan diviners whose nonconformist ministry was preserved from the prying eyes of the ecclesiastical court officers by the patronage of the Puritan gentry. Dod lived in the comfortable seclusion of the Dryden and Knightley manor houses at Canons Ashby and Fawsley respectively from 1608 until the end of the 1630s. There could be no better place to write and these were productive years for him. 'I thank God I have no intermission of my peace', he wrote to Sir Robert Harley in December 1639.[16] *A Godly Form of Household Government* was well written and comprehensive. It proved one of the most popular of the conduct books.[17] The 1614 edition was dedicated to three JPs and their wives living in the Midlands who, it was said, already practised the precepts set out in the manual. They are not named but we can guess that Sir Erasmus Dryden and Sir Richard Knightley were probably two of them. Gentry who pretend to be 'sound professors of the gospel', insisted Dod

---

[14] C. L. Powell, *English Domestic Relations* (New York, 1917), 106–16; L. B. Wright, *Middle Class Culture in Elizabethan England* (Chapel Hill, 1935), 205–6; K. M. Davies, 'Continuity and Change in Literary Advice on Marriage', in *Marriage and Society*, ed. R. B. Outhwaite, (1981), 61, 79.

[15] *Autobiography of Alice Thornton*, ed. C. Jackson (Surtees Society, 62, 1875), 81.

[16] P. Collinson, *The Religion of Protestants: The Church in English Society 1559–1625* (Oxford, 1982), 279–80.

[17] Wright, *Middle Class Culture*, 211–14.

and Cleaver in their Preface, talk in vain of discipline 'unless they will begin this most necessary discipline in reforming their own houses'.[18]

It was in the 1620s and 1630s that the market for advice literature was at its height and that the genre really came into its own. This was when Nehemiah Wallington, that quintessential London Puritan artisan, went to buy his copy of William Gouge's *Of Domestical Duties*. He was recently married and was feeling the weight of 'the charge of so many souls'. 'Every one of us', he recorded in his diary, 'may learn and know our duties and honour God every one in his place where God has set them.' The articles for his family 'for the reforming of our lives', which he later drew up, were signed by his three servants and his apprentice as well as by his wife. Here, prompted by Gouge's work, was the holy household in action.[19]

The central texts of this period are, in chronological order of first editions, William Whateley's *A Bride Bush* in 1616, Gouge's *Domestical Duties* in 1622, Matthew Griffith's *Bethal* in 1633 and Daniel Rogers' *Matrimonial Honour* in 1642. Gouge and Griffith are the two most comprehensive writers in their treatment of all aspects of the management of the household including control of servants as well as children. Both books are 528 pages in length. Gouge's account was by far the more popular of the two since it avoided excessive biblical quotation and was well arranged, with a table of contents, index and cross-references. New editions appeared in 1626 and 1634 and the text also appeared in Gouge's *Works*, which itself went through four printings. Whateley confined himself to the relationship between husband and wife and dealt with this more deeply and more thoughtfully than anyone had done before. His hard practical sense and use of personal experience shines through on every page.[20] This was the man whose vigorous preaching during his ministry at Banbury earned him the title of the 'roaring boy'. His father had been an Elizabethan major of the town, one of those Puritan aldermen who fought the cause of moral reformation in the manner that stirred local factionalism.[21] Whateley's foreword explains that the book grew from a marriage sermon in around 1612 which a friend, to whom he lent a copy, took the liberty of publishing. Whateley's philosophy was that many married people complained about marriage who should

---

[18] J. Dod and R. Cleaver, *A Godly Form of Household Government* (1614), sig. A2.

[19] P. S. Seaver, *Wallington's World* (1985), 79.

[20] Wright, *Middle Class Culture*, 220–3; Powell, *English Domestic Relations*, 136–8. It is worth noting that Rogers' *Matrimonial Honour*, though not published until 1642 was completed by the end of 1634: T. Webster, 'The Godly of Goshen Scattered: An Essex Clerical Conference in the 1620s and its Diaspora' (Cambridge PhD thesis, 1992), 307.

[21] *Birthpangs*, 137–8.

complain about themselves. His book was a 'direction' for the married, specifying the duties of each partner and if these duties were followed, he promised, they would help some who neglecting them found marriage 'a little hell'.[22] Daniel Rogers' *Matrimonial Honour* is one of the most attractively written of the conduct books since his approach is human and down to earth.[23] It has only received less attention from commentators than Gouge for the reason that it is much more limited in scope than Whateley and because its author was a less colourful and controversial character.

There are further shorter and less well-known works whose prefaces testify to the strong public demand for this type of literature in the decades before the Civil War. John Wing published a revised version of a marriage sermon he had given during his ministry at Sandwich in 1620 after he had crossed the Channel to be pastor to the Protestant congregation at Flushing. He dedicated it to Matthew Peake, mayor of Sandwich and the jurats there, saying he had been prompted to publish by friends including other Puritan clerics. He decried the output of profane, idle and impure ballads and playbooks which his earnest treatise had to compete with.[24] Thomas Gataker, the minister of Rotherhithe, was so popular as a wedding day preacher among the Puritan gentry that he found himself with a stock of sets of notes, three of which from the weddings of Robert and Dorothy Cooke, Sir Robert and Lady Brilliana Harley and John and Elizabeth Scudamore he was persuaded to put into print. Wing's and Gataker's productions, though not advice books in the full sense, take us closer to the occasion with which the genre originated than the compendious tomes of Dod and Cleaver or Gouge. In these Puritan circles the sermon was as much the centrepiece of the wedding ceremony as of any other act of worship. We can imagine the hushed congregation listened intently. The Bible was rich in texts which provided the basis for a disquisition putting the emphasis, as the preacher wished, on male authority in the household or on the mutual duties of husband and wife. Wing chose Proverbs, chapter 12, verse 4: 'a virtuous woman is the crown of her husband'; Gataker selected Colossians, chapter 3, verses 18 and 19, for the Cooke marriage: 'wives submit yourselves unto your husbands, as it is comely in the Lord, husbands love your wives and be not bitter to them'; for the Harley marriage he turned to Proverbs, taking chapter 18, verse 22: 'he that findeth a wife, findeth

---

[22] W. Whateley, *A Bride Bush* (1623), preface.
[23] Powell, *English Domestic Relations*, 138–9.
[24] J. Wing, *The Crown Conjugal or Spouse Royal: A Discovery of the True Honour and Happiness of Christian Matrimony* (1620).

good, and obtaineth favour of God'.[25] Whatever the particular slant suggested by the chosen text, the overall content of these publications was predictably similar to that of the weightier books with which we are concerned and they can conveniently be discussed in the same context.

The celebrated fracas between William Gouge and his congregation at Blackfriars provides an entry to the question of a discrepancy in the message of the conduct books.[26] When Gouge first set out his ideas on domestic relationships from his pulpit some of the wealthy city wives in his pews were furious with him. They objected to his argument that the doctrine of a wife's subjection involved 'the restraining of her from disposing the common goods of the family without or against her husband's consent'. He was prepared to modify his position on this in so far as special circumstances, such as the absence of a husband or the proper ownership of goods prior to a woman's marriage, were concerned. There was also dispute about what Gouge called 'some other particular duties of wives'. He is not specific but he almost certainly refers to some of his sharper comments on the proper forms of reverence and obeisance, which he thought wives should show their husbands 'at suitable partings or sitting or rising from table' and perhaps to his demands that they should at all times he mild and modest, humble and cheerful even if a husbandly reproof was manifestly unjust. These were issues, according to Gouge, which came 'too near to the quick and pierceth too deep' but we may suspect that it was he who was unrealistic and outdated in some of what he was urging.[27]

In general Gouge was not prepared to budge in this debate with his more assertive female parishioners and the reason, when we look at it in the round, is obvious. His biblical fundamentalism made it impossible for him to do so. In charge of the pulpit in a parish which was a hotbed of Puritan dissent, yet the friend of influential gentry like Sir Robert Harley, Gouge had reason to be on the defensive about social order. In *The Alchemist* in 1612 Ben Jonson had satirised the Blackfriars house-holders as 'sober, scurvy, precise . . . that scarce have smiled twice since the King came in'.[28] At the heart of social order was gender order. Gouge must have been fully aware of the unease all around him, an unease which showed itself in the drama of the period, in proclamations about

---

[25] T. Gataker, *Marriage Duties Briefly Couched together out of Colossians 3: 18 & 19* (1620), *A Wife in Deed* (1623), *A Good Wife God's Gift* (1624); J. Eales, *Puritans and Roundheads: The Harleys of Brampton Bryan and the Outbreak of the English Civil War* (Cambridge, 1990), 15, 19.

[26] For previous accounts, see *Birthpangs*, 71; Amussen, *An Ordered Society*, 44–7.

[27] W. Gouge, *Domestical Duties* (1622), preface.

[28] Cited in Eales, *Puritans and Roundheads*, 62.

women's dress and concern about their sexuality, in a virulent pamphlet debate about the nature of women.[29] It was his highest duty to expound scriptural patriarchy. Yet, at the same time, here was a man who clearly cared deeply about the personal happiness of his parishioners, to whom he dedicated his book, and who in his own experience of marriage knew about the give and take of a working relationship between a man and a woman. Gouge writes as one who understood that married people had to work hard at learning to live together harmoniously. He is quite candid that there was almost always going to be a difference between theory and practice. Thus he admits that he will take the wife's duties first and put the argument in terms of the uttermost a wife was bound to 'in her subjection under which God hath put her'. This was the case 'whether her husband exacted it or no'. But, coming to the husband's duties, he went on in this apology at the opening of the book, 'I showed that he ought not to exact whatsoever his wife was bound unto . . . but he ought to make her a joint governor of the family with himself and refer the ordering of many things to her discretion and with all honourable and kind respect to carry himself towards her.'[30] In other words, Gouge modifies quite remarkably his account of the authority the husband could exercise with his statements of what should happen: 'I so set down a husband's duties as if he be wise and conscionable in observing them, his wife can have no just cause to complain of her subjection.' What we get in *Domestical Duties* is an account in which duties and failings on both sides are 'parallel'd and laid over one against the other'. In its arrangement and visual effect, as well as in its detailed content, his book is a practical do-it-yourself guide for both parties in a successful marriage. At the same time no man could fault it as a manifesto of the patriarchal system. Deeply sensitive to the accusation heard on some London streets that he was a 'hater of women', Gouge found a way out of the dilemma in which the female deputation placed him, a way which was both human and intelligent. We can take it as read, as a starting-point for the discussion of the content of this advice literature as a whole, that other authors, though they probably never faced this dilemma in so sharp a form, were capable of being similarly mentally agile.

Male authority, in the account given by the conduct books, was based both on God's direction and on nature. 'Thy husband is by God made thy governor and ruler', wrote Whateley. Female inferiority was simply the result of 'God's appointment in the ordering of higher and lower places'.[31] Her husband was the woman's head, said Gouge, and 'by

[29] Fletcher, 'Men's Dilemma'.
[30] Gouge, *Domestical Duties*, Epistle Dedicatory.   [31] Whateley, *Bride Bush*, 192.

virtue of his place carrieth the very image of Christ'.[32] Gataker quoted liberally from scripture about women's inferiority and made extensive reference to the Fall: 'woman was an instrument to draw the man on into evil' he reminded his readers.[33] Wing stressed the huge penalty still to be paid by women: 'The time was when it was natural to your sex to be so excellent but she that first enjoyed it destroyed it, altering the property and losing the prerogative belonging to you all; you must therefore go to that God who made her so good to make you anew because now you are so bad.'[34]

The clerical prescriptions were also suffused with the notion of the Great Chain of Being: 'All advancement in place', insisted Whateley, 'doth carry with it a bond to more virtue than that which is called for of them which are set in a lower room.'[35] 'A man must entreat his wife with gentleness and softness', Henry Smith told his readers, 'not expecting that wisdom, nor that faith, nor that patience, nor that strength in the weaker vessel which should be in the stronger.'[36] It was not that every man was mentally and emotionally stronger than every woman: male and female characteristics were seen to overlap within individuals. But the Fall was the proof of women's ultimate flaw, a basic imperfection from which only men could save them. This was why a woman's 'affecting mastership', as Gataker put it, in the home was so very dangerous: 'a course that bringeth commonly disgrace and contempt upon both parties yea utter ruin oft of the family and of their whole estate'. A woman must 'learn to know her place and her part and to fashion her mind and her will, her disposition and her practice accordingly', Gataker's admonition continued, 'yea though she be herself of a greater spirit and in some respects of better parts'.[37] Whateley drew upon the physical makeup of male and female bodies as further evidence of what God and nature intended. The print of government appeared in man's 'very face which is more stern and delicate than the woman's'. Men should 'not suffer this order of nature to be inverted'.[38]

The duties of submission were reverence and obedience. Reverence was a matter of words, gestures and behaviour. Whateley, citing biblical precedent, criticised excessive familiarity. Shortened names like Tom, Dick, Ned and Will were fine for servants but a woman should call her

---

[32] Gouge, *Domestical Duties*, 269.
[33] Gataker, *Marriage Duties*, 8–9.
[34] Wing, *Crown Conjugal*, 62.
[35] Whateley, *Bride Bush*, 30.
[36] H. Smith, *Preparative to Marriage* (1596), 53.
[37] Gataker, *Marriage Duties*, 10–11.
[38] Whateley, *Bride Bush*, 97–8.

husband husband.[39] Gataker too disliked 'gross terms' used in a too familiar way. This concern with the style in which husband and wife related to each other was a question of example. In the 'little commonwealth' of the household they were set in authority together over children and servants. But the young, learning their social duty, needed to see that the head of the household was firmly in control. A wife's duty, explained Gataker, showed itself in a willingness 'to be directed and advised by him for her self, her attire, her behaviour, her carriage, her company, the marshalling and managing of domestical affairs'.[40] When it comes to work and the actual running of the home, all the writers assume there will be a partnership but the partnership is clearly to be an unequal one. The conventional roles are several times set out, emphasising the distinction between tasks indoors and out of doors. Man and wife, Henry Smith tells them, should see themselves like the cock and the dam: 'the cock flyeth abroad to bring in and the dam sitteth upon the nest to keep all at home'. This is what God ordered, he reflects, what the 'nature, wit and strength' of the two sexes fits them for.[41] Whateley was highly practical about it all. They should each in their own sphere 'be content to unite their pains for their profit' he believed. Husband and wife should be 'as two oxen that draw together in one yoke'.[42]

This agreement about a wife's basic responsibilities in general terms reflected contemporary practice and popular assumptions. Women were to educate and discipline the young children of the house, to cook, clean and organise, or in many cases among the readers of the conduct books manage the servants who did these things.[43] This role could provide a good deal of scope for independence and decision making but much depended upon who held the purse strings. Whateley was liberal about this, arguing that, because 'two eyes see more than one, two hands despatch more business than one', wives should be fully involved in the family's financial affairs.[44] Gouge appears restrictive at one point, defining the area where a husband's consent was needed to include 'ordering and disposing the goods, cattle, servants and children of the family, entertaining strangers and ordering the wife's going abroad'. Yet he later advised husbands not to be too exacting towards their wives and

[39] Ibid., 199–200.
[40] Gataker, Marriage Duties, 14–16.
[41] Smith, Preparative to Marriage, 43.
[42] Whateley, Bride Bush, 83–4. See also Amussen, An Ordered Society, 43–4.
[43] R. A. Houlbrooke, The English Family 1450–1700 (1984), 106–10; J. A. Sharpe, 'Plebeian Marriage in Stuart England: Some Evidence from Popular Literature', TRHS, 36 (1986), 75–7.
[44] Whateley, Bride Bush, 86.

not to restrain them over details of running the house such as furnishing, provisioning, control of maids and the bringing up of children while they are young. He also recommended that wives should receive an allowance to enable them, at their own initiative, to show the fruits of faith by works of charity.[45]

Such hints as the conduct books contain about real partnership in day to day domestic management are vitiated time and again by warnings about the necessity for obedience and recommendations to husbands about the manner in which they should give reproof when they found it necessary. Wives, one is left feeling, are given little room for discussion or questioning of decisions without appearing shrewish. In so far as a problem with bad husbands is recognised at all, the only advice is to accept the situation with stoic resignation.[46] But there is an assumption that the women of the house will not always come up to scratch. Dod and Cleaver suggested rewarding 'good and dutiful' behaviour and showing patience when a wife was 'shrewish and wayward' so that 'she wax not worse'. A husband should reprehend his wife as seldom as possible but 'admonish her often'.[47] Gouge, taking a similar line, called for mildness in reproof, stressing the weakness of those under the husband's authority: 'glasses are tenderly handled, a small knock soon breaks them'. 'Sweet and pithy persuasions' should be mixed with the husband's precepts. A wife's reputation should be protected by ensuring that her ignorance was not proclaimed before children, servants or strangers. Gouge found continual chiding too common a fault in husbands and he thought it necessary to lecture them on the body language they displayed in giving reproof. 'His authority over her and eminency above her may not make him forget the near conjunction and union between them', he declared. At the same time he was scathing about some husbands who, forgetting the gravity and sobriety that attached to their household role, were for ever, with their wives in their laps, 'colling, kissing and dallying with them'. This showed 'more lightness, fondness and dotage than true kindness and love'.[48] Wing was rather harsher than either of these writers, seeing a place for a mild kind of punishment. It was proper, in his view, for a man to humble his wife when he was justly angry by depriving her for a while of 'some favours and kindness which formerly she hath more freely enjoyed'.[49]

What all these writers insisted upon and others supported was that on

[45] Gouge, *Domestical Duties*, 292, 370–2, 409.
[46] E.g. Gouge, *Domestical Duties*, 317–23.
[47] Dod and Cleaver, *A Godly Form of Household Government*, sig. L4.
[48] Gouge, *Domestical Duties*, 374–92.
[49] Wing, *Crown Conjugal*, 47–8.

no account should a husband use physical force as punishment. We can detect a new attitude here. Sixteenth-century writers like Harrington and Whitford had accepted that wife beating was lawful and passed no further comment.[50] Gouge, Smith and Wing all emphatically rejected it as a servile form of punishment suitable only for children and servants. Gouge put the argument under three heads. First there was no specific warrant in scripture for husbands to subject wives to corporal punishment. Secondly common sense forbade it: 'can it be thought reasonable that she who is the man's perpetual bedfellow, who hath power over his body, who is a joint parent of the children, a joint governor of the family, should be beaten by his hands?'. Thirdly their 'near conjunction and very union', the whole nature of their relationship, made it inappropriate.

Gouge saw the absurdity of the holy household being ruled by a master who could chastise his yoke fellow. He thought there could be occasions though when a husband, believing that his wife deserved a whipping, could properly 'refer the matter to a public magistrate'.[51] Whateley argued by contrast that there were extreme circumstances when a husband should beat his wife, who should submit to his 'just blows'. He comes to the point after maintaining that husbands married to forward and 'sturdy spirited' women should win them by skill rather than offer them violence. He knew he was on tricky ground, that many saw wife beating as 'too imperious in him, too servile in her'. But after a long passage about the extremes of a woman's foolish behaviour in defying her husband's authority, he concluded that correction for 'palpable wickedness' was acceptable. What other remedy had the husband faced with a wife who estranged herself, whose wilful cursing and swearing, whose railing upon him, attacked the centre of his being as master of the household, when reproof had failed and so had withdrawal of wanted kindness and trust? Given the patriarchal premises, the argument had a certain logicality. 'Doubtless', declared Whateley, weary with his own lengthy discussion, 'many a man's case is so desperate that there is no other remedy.' The beating should be delivered with 'loathness and unwillingness, grieved countenance and lamenting words', accompanied by earnest entreaties to reform. No wife, he conceded, would be persuaded easily to submit, but she must follow the Apostle's direction of subordination even in this, receiving the 'just blows' patiently and fruitfully with the intention to reform the faults that had procured them.[52]

[50] Davis, 'Continuity and Change', 68.
[51] Gouge, *Domestical Duties*, 394–7.
[52] Whateley, *Bride Bush*, 99–116, 123–5, 210–16; Amussen, *An Ordered Society*, 42–3.

We can see Whateley's determined defence of wife beating as a mark of the intensity with which he believed in the enforcement of the patriarchal imperative. As a system of gender relations patriarchy did of course rest in the last resort on force. But the irony is that the whole impetus of the conduct books as a genre was directed towards securing the foundations of patriarchy by discourse, in the Foucauldian sense, rather than by violence. Whateley's stance made no more sense in Jacobean England than the Augsburg Council's approval of wife beating had done in the 1540s. The reality of marital disputes in Germany at that time, it has been shown, 'bore little relation to the model of dispassionate exercise of just authority which the Council proposed'. Correction of wives did not proceed in a measured orderly fashion. On the contrary husbands and wives fought with whatever objects came to hand.[53] From what we know of early modern England the reality was little different.[54]

The conduct book writers knew their whole Bibles inside out. Whereas their fiercest patriarchal strictures by and large took their source from the Old Testament, they were at the same time able to propound a doctrine of mutuality in marriage which was based upon a close reading of St Paul's epistles, particularly Colossians, chapter 3, verses 18 to 20, Gataker's text for the Cooke marriage, and Ephesians, chapter 5, verses 21 to 33. We need to summarise the findings of the latest biblical scholarship about these household tables as a basis on which to assess the modernity of the Puritan prescriptions. New Testament scholars are not agreed about the origins of these codes of relationships between people in a household, but it is likely that Paul was drawing upon ethical material inherited from his Jewish heritage. The basic argument is that the wife's duty is submission and the husband's is love. The Ephesian household table pursues an analogy between two different kinds of relationship, that between husband and wife and between Christ and the church. It has been argued that what Paul was seeking to do here was set out a new approach to marriage which would effectively reform the patriarchal structure of his day: 'husband and wife are called to a mutual self-giving that is to be total and rules out the idea that one member is superior to the other'. This is not to say

---

[53] Roper, Holy Household, 189.
[54] For unruly women in general in this period, see D. Underdown, 'The Taming of the Scold: The Enforcement of Patriarchal Authority in Early Modern England', in Order and Disorder in Early Modern England, ed. A. J. Fletcher and J. Stevenson (Cambridge, 1985), 116–36; for specific evidence from a slightly later period, M. Hunt, 'Wife Beating, Domesticity and Women's Independence', Gender and History, 4 (1992), 10–33.

that the husband's headship is questioned. The argument in Ephesians subtly portrays a difference in the way submission and service are rendered by husband and wife. The gender roles are not interchangeable.[55]

Several of our writers explored the nature of the love men should show their wives, and the duties it involved, at some length. What is loving, said Wing, should be the rule of their actions. Their love 'must be the most dear, intimate, precious and entire that heart can have toward a creature'. It must be immeasurable and its manifestations 'must be universal in everything'.[56] Dod and Cleaver stressed the point that Paul made to the Ephesians about a husband's respect for his wife's personhood. 'The husband must let his wife perceive and know that for the good opinion that he hath of her', they wrote, 'he doth love her simply and faithfully and not for any utility or pleasure.' She was not to be treated either as a drudge or as a sex object.[57] It was just as much the husband's duty to please his wife as vice versa, asserted Whateley: 'the love of the married must be a singular love, causing a man to account his wife the only woman in the world'. They should care for each other's health, watch themselves against destructive suspicions and jealousies, keep each other's secrets and protect each other's credit. Gouge, very much on the defensive as we have seen, was meticulous in matching mutual duties. He wanted to show that if spouses followed his instructions 'the matrimonial yoke will so equally lie on both their necks as the wife will be no more pinched therewith than the husband but that it will be like Christ's spiritual yoke, light and easy'. But when it came to the duties of husbands, Gouge could not avoid the patronising tone which followed an explicit reference to woman as the weaker vessel. Love modified the enforcement of patriarchal authority but we can perceive that Gouge's was a very limited form of mutuality:

His look, his speech, his carriage and all his actions wherein he hath to do with his wife must be seasoned with love: love must show itself in his commandments, in his reproofs, in his instructions, in his admiration, in his authority, in his familiarity, when they are alone together, when they are in company, before others, in civil affairs, in religious matters, at all times, in all things, as salt must be first and last upon the table, and eaten with every bit of meat, so must love be first in a husband's heart and last out of it and mixed with everything wherein he hath to do with his wife.[58]

---

55 B. Witherington III, *Women and the Genesis of Christianity* (Cambridge, 1990), 147–62.
56 Wing, *Crown Conjugal*, 44–6.
57 Dod and Cleaver, *A Godly Form of Household Government*, sig. L6; Witherington, *Women and the Genesis of Christianity*, 161.
58 Whateley, *Bride Bush*, 40; Gouge, *Domestical Duties*, 354–6.

The Puritan clerics, one is left feeling, go so far with St Paul. There is an authentic desire to reform patriarchy in early Stuart England by an insistence upon the husband's duty to love. Yet they do not go by any means all the way with him. None of them grasped or properly expounded the implications of his analogy of the marital relationship with that between Christ and his church. The fact is Paul was too radical for these conservative men. The sticking-point, which prevented them opening their minds to a proper mutuality, was their conviction that women were inferior. This in turn reflected the imprisoning effect of their interpretation of Genesis. He has to begin with the wife's duties rather than the husband's, avowed Gataker in his sermon for Robert and Dorothy Cooke, because it is right to begin with the duty of the inferior partner. 'The wife's duty is as the base or ground that the husband's duty is built upon', he declared, 'it is that must draw duty and respect from the husband.' Within a few minutes of quoting his text, Gataker was reading it in a sense which did little justice to Paul's intentions.[59] Gouge had the same problem. For all his stress on how 'tender respect and provident care' will show a man's high account of his wife, his sense of how things are and should be remained inviolate: 'her place is indeed a place of inferiority and subjection yet the nearest to equality that may be, a place of common equity in many respects, wherein man and wife are after a sort even fellows and partners'.[60] Any surprise one may feel at how deeply this notion of the God-given naturalness of the patriarchal order was embedded in seventeenth-century England is modified by the realisation that there are still some clerics who see it in much the same way nearly four hundred years later.[61]

Much of the prescriptive advice that has been discussed so far was particularly relevant to the behaviour of husband and wife towards each other when they were in the company of others, whether children and servants, or kin and neighbours. Married couples, the conduct book writers knew and expected, lived their daily lives in a throng and this was why setting the right social and moral example was so relevant and requisite. But there was also a private domain inside the chamber door. The very extensive admonitions contained in our sources about sex amount to a radical departure from previous teaching on the subject. There is no question that all these writers valued the physical and

[59] Gataker, *Marriage Duties*, 5–6.
[60] Gouge, *Domestical Duties*, 360–1.
[61] On the day this passage was drafted, 9 September 1992, Rev George Austin, speaking on 'Thought for the Day', made an approving reference to St Paul's household tables and did not point out the basic sexism inherent even in his radical formulation of the duties of married persons to each other.

intimate aspect of marriage very highly indeed. They took their cue from a wholly traditional notion of 'due benevolence', which appears prominently in sixteenth-century tracts such as Bullinger's *The Christian State of Matrimony*, but they made much more of this notion than Catholic or humanist writers had done.[62] The starting-point was Paul's counsel to the Corinthians that it is the husband who has rights over his wife's body and the wife who has rights over the husband's. 1 Corinthians, chapter 7, verse 4, was much cited.[63] The Puritan writers gave an account of sex that was entirely positive.

These married clerics assumed mutual attraction would be a very important consideration for a man in choosing a wife. God, declared Wing, would have men 'choose for sober contentation of their sight that they may have delight and satisfaction that way, that the husband to the wife and the wife to the husband may be the sweetest and most pleasing objects upon earth to take up each other's eyes from all the world besides'. Mutual attraction, he posited, was the best basis for happy and permanent union: his spouse should give a man 'his lawful desire full satisfaction' and remain 'the only delectable object he must desire and behold'.[64] Desire and arousal were seen as natural and spontaneous. They slotted easily into a mental world picture which saw men and women's physiology in terms of 'an economy of fungible fluids' and a state of corporeal flux.[65] Whateley showed his grasp of this economy in a firm prohibition of intercourse during menstruation. Woman, he wrote, was 'more moist and cold of constitution than the man, hence their natural heat not serving to turn their whole nourishment into their own substance yieldeth some overplus for the nourishing and cherishing of their fruit within them'. The monthly menstrual flow, Whateley explained, represented 'an overplus of nourish' which, for women's health, had to find 'its seasonable evacuations'.[66] Orgasm dovetailed so obviously with this economy of fluids that none of our authors thought it necessary to make the point as such. But it is quite clear that they believed, conventionally, that both sexes emitted seed at orgasm and that this release at regular intervals was essential to good health.

Aware that their readers might expect guidance on the matter, several

---

[62] H. Bullinger, *The Christian State of Matrimony* (1541), fol. xxiii; Davies, 'Continuity and Change', 73–4.
[63] E.g. Gouge, *Domestical Duties*, 224; Dod and Cleaver, *A Godly Form of Household Government*, sig. K7.
[64] Wing, *The Crown Conjugal*, 99.
[65] T. Lacqueur, *Making Sex* (1990), 35–52; A. McLaren, *Reproductive Rituals* (1984), 15–22.
[66] Whateley, *Bride Bush*, 21.

of the divines had advice on how much sex was enough. There were no particular limits, said Whateley, what mattered is the spontaneity of desire by one or the other partner. Foreplay – 'mutual dalliances for pleasure's sake' as Whateley put it – was perfectly acceptable when this enabled a spouse to satisfy a partner's need for sexual satisfaction. Emphasising the dangers of natural desires being left to 'tend to unruliness', Whateley enjoined 'the temperate enjoyment of God's ordinance as for a man to drink when labour or other occasion hath made him thirsty'. The rule was for a couple to have intercourse sufficiently regularly that desire 'may not be troublesome to them in the duties of religion and their callings'.[67] Whateley, Rogers and Gouge all promulgated a doctrine of moderation in sexual pleasure which confirms their functional view of intercourse. Excess, declared Rogers, produced 'weakness, diseases, inability of mind and body to calling'. Insatiableness, said Gouge, was an oppression among bedfellows. While moderation bred contentment, insisted Whateley, excessiveness could breed satiety, making partners weary of each other. Rogers, like Whateley, saw getting it right as important, for sexual desire could be a 'distraction and annoyance' to performance of daily religious and secular duties. Couples found the correct measure when 'snaring concupiscence' was prevented and 'fitness of body and mind' was achieved.[68] All this is very straightforward, direct and unrepressive. We can detect a notion of self-discipline, of control of the sexual body, but there is virtually none of that obsessive deployment of sexuality, in Michel Foucault's sense, which became such a marked feature of Restoration and eighteenth-century society.[69]

This functional view of sex was accompanied by a fierce insistence that a successful sexual relationship was an essential preservative against adultery. The notion of marital chastity was at the heart of the Puritan manifesto on marriage. It was the cornerstone, declared Rogers, 'that holds in all the parts of the building'. 'Chastity of the bed', he explained, meant that it was wrong for one partner to defraud the other of sex, using discord between them, religion, conscience or infirmity as pretended excuses.[70] Sex built the strength of the relationship, declared Whateley, reluctance was bad for it: 'man and wife become burdens and vexations each to other instead of comforts'.[71] Gone are the elaborate tables which

---

[67] *Ibid.*, 18–20.
[68] Rogers, *Matrimonial Honour*, 177–8; Gouge, *Domestical Duties*, 225; Whateley, *Bride Bush*, 19.
[69] M. Foucault, *The History of Sexuality*, I: *Introduction* (1981), 92–131.
[70] Rogers, *Matrimonial Honour*, 169, 175–6.
[71] Whateley, *Bride Bush*, 24.

in Catholic marriage doctrine limited the occasions of intercourse besides how it should be performed.[72] There were few limitations. Abstinence for menstruation was a matter of scriptural warrant. But Gouge said there should be no problems in people's minds, given consideration, about sex during pregnancy or while a woman was breast feeding.[73] There were constant warnings in the conduct books against husbands and wives not living together. Wing accepted that there were some, like sailors, who had to be away but in general condemned absence as 'the only opportunity for matrimonial treason and for every ungodly practice whereunto Satan may tempt in such a time'.[74] Gouge believed the only proper exceptions to the rule of cohabitation were weighty state affairs and the necessity of men's callings. He was critical of gentry who sent their wives into the country while they enjoyed the metropolitan season and also of wives who for pleasure 'gad out of their own houses'.[75] Whateley felt so strongly on this issue that he argued that desertion, which he thought almost always implied adultery, was sufficient grounds for divorce, a position he was forced publicly to repudiate.[76]

The quality of a couple's lovemaking was seen as equally important as its regularity, for sex was God's gift to humankind, so that particular men and women could come together in marriage and express and sustain their love for each other. It was 'one of the most proper and essential acts of marriage', said Gouge, because it linked the affections of a couple ever more firmly.[77] Whateley believed that giving each other sexual pleasure made spouses 'dearer and dearer to each other's souls'.[78] Cohabitation, declared Wing, 'is the consolidation and contentation of the husband and wife; it carrieth with it all opportunities of good; it cutteth off all occasions of evil, it nourisheth all entire amity and maketh that house a little heaven where it is carefully observed'.[79] Gataker spoke of the husband's responsibility, when the 'kind of dalliance normal between new married folks' lost its freshness, for preventing the sexual relationship growing lukewarm.[80] Sexual duty, as Dod and Cleaver put it, 'performed godlily, carefully and cheerfully on both sides maketh the marriage yoke light and sweet'. When a man and his wife 'mark one

[72] J. L. Flandrin, *Families in Former Times* (Cambridge, 1979), 161–4.
[73] Gouge, *Domestical Duties*, 226.
[74] Wing, *The Crown Conjugal*, 131.
[75] Gouge, *Domestical Duties*, 232–6.
[76] Whateley, *Bride Bush*, 25–7; *A Care Cloth* (1624), sig. A8; *CSPD 1619–23*, 253; *Birthpangs*, 66 and n. 11.
[77] Gouge, *Domestical Duties*, 224.
[78] Whateley, *Bride Bush*, 25.
[79] Wing, *The Crown Conjugal*, 132–3.
[80] Gataker, *Marriage Duties*, 37.

another and find like heedfulness and buxomness in their duty' they also
enjoyed each other's company more.[81]

What is remarkable about all this is that it shows the Puritan clergy
cutting through the weight of Augustinian objection to sexual pleasure
with apparent ease and rejecting the whole gnostic Manichean strain
of Christianity, which stressed the inherent sinfulness of the flesh.
Following St Paul's precepts in 1 Corinthians, there is a notable lack of
reference to intercourse being solely or primarily for the purpose of
procreation. Indeed their whole account is close to that of St Paul as this
is now read by biblical scholars. Like Paul they saw sexual desire as a
force to be reckoned with, confined its expression to marriage and
interpreted sex in marriage in terms which were at the same time
egalitarian and patriarchal. Their anti-Catholic polemic brought them in
their account of sex to a point somewhere near that of Paul's when he
abandons the notion of female inferiority through a concept of sexual
self-giving.[82] There are times when the sexual union is seen in spiritual
terms. 'By nuptial conjunction', preached Gataker at the Cooke
marriage, 'being joined to him as his wife she becometh not only part of
his flesh as taken from him but sworn flesh conjoined with him . . . here
reciprocally the wife is part of the husband and the husband is part of the
wife, both parts of the same flesh because both making but one flesh.'[83]
But mostly the language remained more earthy than this. They only go
so far with Paul. Yet we may imagine that they went far enough for their
message to be a liberating one for their women readers. We should not
assume, because we know about Gouge's fracas with his discontented
Blackfriars matrons, that the conduct books were in general unwelcome
reading matter if men like Nehemiah Wallington left them around in the
parlour. If the patriarchal stress was conventional and thus predictable,
the clerical approval of real mutuality in bed if not at board was for its
time an immense and radical step forward.

Husband and wife were seen as equal in the sight of God so when it
came to spiritual duties the conduct book writers had the delicate task of
defining an unequal partnership between spiritual equals.[84] Again a
distinction between the public and private aspects of their domestic life
is evident. Whateley saw prayer and singing psalms together as means
towards the cementing the souls of the married.[85] Gouge put emphasis

---

[81] Dod and Cleaver, *A Godly Form of Household Government*, sig. K8.
[82] Witherington, *Women and the Genesis of Christianity*, 161, see also A. West, 'Sex and
Salvation: A Christian Feminist Bible Study on 1 Corinthians 6.12–7.39', in *Feminist
Theology*, ed. Loades, 72–80.
[83] Gataker, *Marriage Duties*, 32.
[84] Amussen, *An Ordered Society*, 46–7.   [85] Whateley, *Bride Bush*, 49.

upon the mutual duty of helping forward the growth of grace in the other.[86] Rogers advised spouses regularly to hear the word, receive the sacrament and pray frequently in each other's company. They should also in private 'confer, read, pray, confess to give thanks'.[87] In these respects there could be an approach to a reality of spiritual equality. But in the hall or parlour it was different. Male authority had to be plainly demonstrated in the conduct of family worship with a wife standing in only if the household head had to be absent. With the gathering of children and servants to hear the Bible, pray and be catechised, the holy household of early Stuart England achieved its most emblematic form. In this sense the conduct books represent one genre among several, like godly tables and printed catechisms, which contributed to the formulation of a particular kind of Protestant consciousness.[88]

This account of the content of the conduct books suggests that the recently fashionable view which sees them as offering little that had not been said before deserves reconsideration.[89] The enthusiastic account of the genre published fifty years ago by William and Malleville Haller has been too much neglected. Their claim that in the warmest of these treatises – especially Whateley and Rogers – Puritan clerics 'suffused marital relations afresh with religious emotion' is warrantable. Their account of the clerics' purpose is surely accurate: they wished 'to set forth an ideal pattern of love and marriage based upon traditional Christian morality, vitalised for popular imagination in terms of the English bible and adapted to the new conditions in which men were having to live'.[90] That ideal pattern probably has its fullest expression in Rogers' treatise, the last of the series. He distinguished conjugal love, desire and passing affection: 'so is this love of couples', he wrote, 'an effect of divine institution not to be dissolved till death'. There was nothing else so precious, 'no joy in any outward union so contentful as this'.[91] That the Puritan scholars also made much of patriarchy need not surprise us. There was much about the times in which they lived that caused them to feel the need to defend it. And the Bible still seemed the obvious source of authority in doing so.

[86] Gouge, *Domestical Duties*, 240–2.
[87] Rogers, *Matrimonial Honour*, 128–9.
[88] T. Watt, *Cheap Print and Popular Piety 1550–1640* (Cambridge, 1991), 217–53.
[89] This view is most clearly expressed in Davies, 'Continuity and Change', 58–80; and in Todd, *Christian Humanism*, 96–117. *Birthpangs*, 90–3.
[90] W. and M. Haller, 'The Puritan Art of Love', *Huntington Library Quarterly*, 5 (1941–2), 235–72. Another neglected article along similar lines is E. Leites, 'The Duty to Desire: Love Friendship and Sexuality in some Puritan Theories of Marriage', *Journal of Social History*, 15 (1982), 383–408.
[91] Rogers, *Matrimonial Honour*, 150.

The conduct book writers must have had some understanding of how they were walking a tightrope. Gouge certainly felt it keenly. But how successful they were nevertheless. All the new editions of the most popular manuals testify to the fact that substantial householders with an ear to the political and social climate wanted to hear both sides of their message. They wanted all the reassurance those vested with clerical authority could give them that social and gender order was, and would remain with their help, fully intact. But they also wanted to hear about love, affection and partnership. The market remained good for the conduct books, until Civil War engulfed the nation and turned the printers' interest to more immediate concerns, because they were readable and plausible. They neatly combined description with prescription, representing mainstream opinion among the godly gentry and middling sort about best practice in marital relations and domestic management.[92] There was much in them that was stereotyped and repetitious yet, in their force and coherence rather than their total originality, they portray a distinctive English version of the Protestant idea of marriage.

When all this is said the writings we have considered in this essay are the product of a particular world which was dissolving before the eyes of those who read them, a relatively uniform religious world in which scripture remained authoritative and the Baconian approach to knowledge had not yet properly made its impact. It is significant that this advice literature is not informed by any depth of analysis about masculinity and femininity. In fact it is at its least original when dealing with gender roles. There is an idealism about patriarchal marriage here, most evident in the lack of any kind of double sexual standard, which could not survive the problematisation of gender that followed the Restoration. That idealism rests on a certain simplicity of view, a certain confidence in the old cosmology, which perhaps explains why these writers might be puzzled at the thought that there could be double messages in what they said. Theirs was a comfortable world which had its certainties. Within those certainties, as married men themselves, they could give advice which was wholly traditional yet at the same time inspirational and true to their own emotions.

[92] Wrightson, *English Society*, 104.

8   James VI and I: furnishing the churches in his two kingdoms

George Yule

In his preface to *The Religion of Protestants* Patrick Collinson wrote, 'The sometimes deceptive advantage of reading history backwards makes it difficult to appreciate that Church' (the Church of England) 'as it appeared to its contemporaries and defenders and even as it evidently . . . was.'[1]

This is undoubtedly true for those who see the Church of England through the nineteenth-century eyes of the Oxford Movement or English nonconformity or the twentieth-century eyes of secular sociologists. By progressing from the Elizabethan Puritan movement to the Jacobean church Collinson has produced a series of splendid tapestries that has helped us see 'the intrinsic merits' of the Jacobean church before the 'post revolutionary history of a Church of England erected on narrower and more exclusive principles deceived historians'.

In his preface to these memorable Ford Lectures Collinson refers to the destruction of 'the archaeological' remains of the Jacobean church interiors due to the 'Victorian restorations'. It is to the reconstruction of these scattered remains that this essay is addressed.[2]

When James VI of Scotland heard that he was also James I of England he was, said the man who brought him the news, 'like a poor man bereft wandering forty years in the wilderness and barren soil and now arrived at to the land of promise'.[3] But he was still king of the wilderness and barren soil, and he brought to his rule of the land of promise the skills and presuppositions he had acquired during his considerable time of rule over Scotland.

To be ruler of two kingdoms was a formidable task[4] and James did his utmost to unite the two by stressing the common ties of 'language,

[1] Patrick Collinson, *The Religion of Protestants: The Church in English Society 1559–1625* (Oxford, 1982), viii.
[2] *Ibid.*, ix.
[3] Roger Aston to the privy council 1603, quoted D. H. Willson, *King James VI and I* (1956), 171.
[4] Conrad Russell, *The Causes of the English Civil War* (Oxford, 1990), 29–39.

religion and similitude of manners'.[5] It was in religion that James achieved real success due in large measure to his own theological perceptions.

James was strictly brought up in the practices of the Reformed Church of Scotland by that learned dominee, George Buchanan, and a younger scholar, Peter Young, fresh from studies in Geneva under Beza.[6] Of his strongly held Protestantism with a Scots face there is no doubt. In his speech to the parliament of 1603 he 'thanked God I sucked the milk of God's truth with the milk of my nurse'.[7] The Reformation in Scotland though marred by 'a popular tumult and rebellion' was 'extraordinarily wrought by God',[8] and until he came to live in England he shared the Scots prejudice against the English liturgy. In 1590, after praising the kirk, 'the sincerest kirk in the world', he attacked the English liturgy as being still too like the Mass.[9] He insisted that 'all my religion professed by me and my kingdom was grounded upon the plain words of Scripture without which all points of religion are superfluous'.[10]

He saw prayer was necessary for right understanding of the Bible and chided those who emphasised the sermon at the expense of prayer.[11] But when Bancroft at the Hampton Court Conference denigrated sermons he asked him 'how people could pray if not taught by preachers'.[12]

He attacked Rome for bringing in beliefs and practices found neither in the Bible nor the early church, transubstantiation 'the elevation of the host for adoration . . . and above all worshipping images',[13] and he set up Chelsea College in 1610 to combat the 'sophistry and novelties' of the Jesuits.[14]

He also strongly objected to the papacy taking away the power of Christian monarchs, for he saw himself very much as the successor of Constantine, custodian of 'both tables of the law' and not as either the

---

[5] James, 'Speech to the English Parliament 1603', in *Works of James I* (reprint 1971), 491.

[6] Willson, *King James VI and I*, 20–7.

[7] James, 'Speech to the English Parliament', in *Works*, 491.

[8] James, 'Basilikon Doron', in *Works*, 160.

[9] *Booke of the Universal Kirk*, II, 771, quoted D. G. Mullan, *Episcopacy in Scotland: The History of an Idea* (Edinburgh, 1986), 75. I am much indebted to Mullan's book with its rich quotations from Scottish sources.

[10] James, 'Basilikon Doron', in *Works*, 149–50.

[11] E. Cardwell, *Documentary Annals of the Reformed Church of England* (2 vols., Oxford, 1839), 191.

[12] BL, Harleian MS 828, in R. G. Usher, *The Reconstruction of the English Church* (2 vols., 1910), II, 347.

[13] James, 'To All Christian Monarchs', in *Works*, 303.

[14] D. E. Kennedy, 'King James I's College of Controversial Theology at Chelsea', in *Grounds of Controversy*, ed. D. E. Kennedy (Melbourne, 1989), 110.

pope or the Presbyterian followers of Andrew Melville saw him in Scotland, 'a mere laicus' in the church.[15]

James also strongly differed with Melville and his followers because they used the Bible as a book of precedents for the worship and polity of the church. As Calderwood, a colleague of Melville, wrote, 'Christ being master of his own house has set down the rules and regiment of his own house and household family which may no more be altered, than Moses might have altered the form of the tabernacle set down to him. Exodus xxv.40.'[16]

James by contrast instructed his son 'wisely to discern points of salvation and indifferent things'[17] and chided the Melvillians with making as great a commotion about church polity as if the doctrine of the Trinity was impugned.[18]

This stance allowed James a genuine tolerance and was the basis of his attempts to reconcile division within and between the established churches of his dominions. 'I am far from being contentious in these things, (which for my part I do ever esteem indifferent), as I do equally love and honour the learned and grave men of either of these opinions.'[19] And especially in England as the Laudian bishop, Buckeridge, admitted he gained his end by persuasion.[20] After 1607, provided the Puritan ministers gave genuine signs of good faith, they were allowed a real latitude. This created a widespread harmony.[21]

It was undoubtedly his choice of bishops, preaching, pastoral, Calvinists, whose judgements the Puritan wing of the church respected that was the basis of James' success. None could accuse Abbot, or King, or Lake, or Mathews of popery, Arminianism or lack of zeal, so their advocacy of conformity, calmed the fears of many Puritans.[22] When Abbot said that he knew of only two or three unreformable nonconformists in the church, he was, by his standards, not exaggerating.[23]

[15] James, 'Basilikon Doron', in *Works*, 150–1. See also Mullan, *Episcopacy in Scotland*, 88–90, for a discussion and further references.

[16] David Calderwood, *The History of the Kirk of Scotland* (Wodrow Soc., Edinburgh, 1845), V, 599.

[17] James, 'Basilikon Doron', in *Works*, 143.

[18] *Ibid.*, 153.   [19] *Ibid.*, 144.

[20] John Buckeridge, 'A Sermon Preached before His Majesty 1617', in K. Fincham, *Prelate as Pastor* (Oxford, 1990), 237.

[21] B. W. Quintrell, 'The Royal Hunt and the Puritans', *Journal of Ecclesiastical History*, 31 (1980), 56–7. Most deprivations were during or before 1605 and only the most recalcitrant suffered after that.

[22] For these, see Collinson, *The Religion of Protestants*, ch. 2; and Fincham, *Prelate as Pastor*, ch. 8.

[23] William Laud, *The Works of William Laud*, ed. W. Scott and J. Bliss (7 vols., Oxford, 1847–60), (1857), V, 310.

Bishop Williams of Lincoln, who himself had an ornate chapel at Buckden, with the table against the east wall, strongly defended the practice of it being set table wise in the midst of the chancels as in the famous Grantham case. Like Abbot, he advocated kneeling to receive and said he had won many over to this view by persuasion.[24]

James' policy succeeded remarkably well, and on the whole both the Puritan and non-Puritan wings of the English church acceded to it. This is reflected in the interiors of Jacobean churches which combined the differing attitudes to worship of George Herbert[25] and even Lancelot Andrewes[26] on the one hand and a strong Puritan, like Henry Burton, on the other.[27]

In Scotland his task was harder but he showed an understanding of the Scots traditions and this was the reason for his reluctance to make William Laud a bishop. Buckingham pressed him to do so but James retorted, 'He hath a restless spirit and cannot leave well alone' and instanced the fact that Laud had urged him to impose the English liturgy on the Church of Scotland despite the fact James had promised not to do so.[28]

James had come of age to govern in Scotland at about the same time the Presbyterians had come to power in the church and had passed the *Second Book of Discipline* which not only established a Presbyterian form of government as a *de fide* matter but had also made the church through its General Assembly supreme in the religious sphere[29] insisting that in the kirk 'James VI was not a lord nor a head nor a king but a member.'[30] The king had a duty to uphold the church but could only act in religious affairs on 'the advice of the prophets' as in the Old Testament.[31] The General Assembly, not the king, judged what matters were religious.

James gradually outmanoeuvred the Presbyterians and by 1609

24 John Williams, *The Holy Table Name and Thing*, facsimile edition, in *The Works of Archbishop John Williams*, ed. Barrie Williams (Sutton Courtenay Press, 1980), 5ff., 135–6.
25 George Herbert, *The Country Parson*, ed. Hugh Martin (1956), ch. 22, where he discusses the two ways of reception at communion. For his design of Leighton Bromswold church, see below pp. 190, 194.
26 Thomas Fuller, *The Church History of Britain*, ed. James Nichols (3 vols., 1868), Book x, §§ 46–50.
27 N. Tyacke, *Anti-Calvinists* (Oxford, 1987), 187–8.
28 John Hackett, *Scrinia Reserata, Being the Life of Archbishop John Williams* (1693), 63–4.
29 *The Second Book of Discipline*, ed. James Kirk (Edinburgh, 1980), Book I, §§ 5 and 6, p. 164.
30 James Melville, *The Autobiography and Diary of Mr James Melville* (Wodrow Soc., Edinburgh, 1842), 370.
31 *Second Book of Discipline*, ed. Kirk, Introduction, 65.

restored episcopacy, but it was a very moderate episcopate which worked with the presbyteries and General Assembly.[32]

James wanted a greater degree of liturgical conformity between his two churches and ordered his bishops to introduce what were to become known as the Five Articles of Perth – kneeling to receive communion, the keeping of the Christian year, private communion and private baptism in special cases and episcopal confirmation.[33]

The bishops urged James to drop them. 'Had it been in our power to have dissuaded or declined them, most certainly we would', said Archbishop Spottiswoode in his sermon to the Perth Assembly. But he continued, 'the evil of novations especially in matters of Rites and Ceremonies is nothing so great as the evils of disobedience'.[34] James would not budge. It was for him both a question of the unity of his churches and his own personal belief for he saw kneeling to receive communion as a matter of reverence, but not of transubstantiation. It was, he said, 'a commemoration only of a sacrifice which differs in predicament from a true sacrifice'.[35] He likened the Presbyterian practice to those who 'sit Jack fellow like with Christ at the Lord's Table' (notice he does not call it an altar) 'as his brethren and comrades'.[36]

Because he was seen as the champion of Protestant orthodoxy, by the middle years of his reign in England the standardised Anglican patterns of worship as reflected in the interior arrangements of the parish churches were seen as an acceptable norm, particularly in placing the table, table wise in the chancel or at the east end of the nave where all could hear, see and partake. It was Laud's attack on this arrangement that stamped him in the eyes, not only of the Puritans, but of many non-Puritans, as a betrayer of Protestantism. The royalist, Lord Falkland, for example, accused the Laudian party of defiling 'our church by adorning our churches'.[37]

The Reformation created a difficult problem for the common worship

[32] Mullan, *Episcopacy in Scotland*, 103–13; W. R. Foster, *The Church Before the Covenants* (1975), chs. 3, 5.
[33] Ian Cowan, 'The Five Articles of Perth', in *Reformation and Revolution*, ed. Duncan Shaw (Edinburgh, 1967), 16off.; P. H. R. Mackay, 'The Reception of the Five Articles of Perth', *Scottish Church History Society Records*, 19 (1975–7), 185ff.
[34] *Spottiswoode Miscellany* (2 vols., Spottiswoode Soc., Edinburgh, 1844–5), I, 66. Mullan has a very full account of the responses of the Scottish bishops, *Episcopacy in Scotland*, ch. 9.
[35] This reference comes from Williams, *The Holy Table*, 105. Williams referred here to James' careful response to Cardinal Peron who had refused him the title of Catholic. On the issue of the sacrifice of the Mass, James wrote, 'hoc sacrificium nihil esse apud contendit nisi Commemorationem ejus quod semel in cruce', *Ep. ad Peron*, 52.
[36] James, 'The Lord's Prayer', in *Works*, 593; see also 578.
[37] John Rushworth, *Historical Collections* (1721), IV, 184.

in the parish churches. In the later Middle Ages the worship of the church was concentrated on the celebration of the Mass by the clergy at the altar in the east end of the chancel. The rood screen, surmounted by the rude, and often with the figures of John and Mary, and adorned with paintings or images of saints, shut off the people from this central action. Said in a tongue which few could understand, at a distance from which indeed few could clearly hear, what was left to the laity, except once or twice a year when they partook of the sacrament, was merely to view the elevation of the host. This medieval arrangement, in the words of Addleshaw and Etchells, was the dramatic altar for the eucharist.[38]

But with the Reformation this view was replaced by the ministerial altar.[39] With the new emphasis on the Bible, as in Calvin's phrase, the mirror of the Word of God, Jesus Christ, the sacrament was seen as being bound up with this as the visible Word.[40] The essential things were for people to see, hear and partake. Word and sacrament ideally should be linked together. This was difficult to practice in the medieval church building where the pulpit was in the nave and the altar far away and separated by the chancel screen.

In Scotland the Reformed Church, as we shall see,[41] resolved the matter simply by dispensing with the chancel in a variety of ways and by placing long tables for the sacrament in what was now a one-roomed church, near the pulpit.[42] The situation was more difficult in England for there almost all of the 10,000 medieval churches had well-defined and often very large chancels.

In the Edwardian Reformation no clear policy emerged. There was a widespread destruction of medieval images, rood screens and altars.[43] The altars were to be replaced by 'the Lord's board', to use Ridley's phrase,[44] but where should the new tables be placed? Hooper was quite clear. He agreed with the Zwinglian reformers and wanted tables which would be placed close to the pulpit around which people would sit. The chancels as in Scotland thus became quite irrelevant.[45] Ridley, on the

---

[38] G. W. O. Addleshaw and F. Etchells, *The Architectural Setting of Anglican Worship* (1948), 15–22.

[39] *Ibid.*, 200.

[40] J. Calvin, 'A Short Treatise on the Lord's Supper', in *Calvin: Theological Treatises*, ed. J. K. S. Reid, Library of Christian Classics, 22 (1954), 142ff.

[41] See below, pp. 204–7.

[42] George Hay, *The Architecture of Scottish Post-Reformation Churches, 1560–1843* (Oxford, 1957), 18–22.

[43] Addleshaw and Etchells, *Architectural Setting*, 22–7.

[44] N. Ridley, *Works* (Parker Soc., 1841), 322–3.

[45] John Hooper, *Early Writings* (Parker Soc., 1843), 488.

other hand, wanted the chancels to be retained as special communion rooms as at Emden, Berne Cathedral and many churches in the Netherlands.[46]

With the advent of Mary the medieval pattern returned, but with her death the problem re-emerged. Again, there was widespread destruction of images, altars and rood screens.

For some reason, which is not quite clear, Elizabeth ordered the retention of the chancel and the chancel screen. The communion tables were to be placed where the old altars stood except in time of communion when they were to be moved into the middle of the chancel or the east end of the nave.[47] Many on the Puritan wing of the church would have preferred the Scots and Zurich model of receiving the sacrament seated at long tables and there are in fact surviving a small number of Elizabethan tables that could be extended at either end to form these long tables as at St Dunstan's, Canterbury, in the south aisle.[48] The injunctions also ordered the Creed, Lord's Prayer and Ten Commandments to be set up in all churches along with the Royal Arms.

Elizabeth's ecclesiastical policies lacked profound religious feeling on her part. In the first dozen years of her reign there was uncertainty about the probable duration of the Protestant settlement. After the dismissal of Grindal, there was militant opposition by the Puritans, and the endeavours of Whitgift and Bancroft to remedy the situation were neither reconciling nor theologically compelling.

But this changed with James to a large extent, and by the middle years of his reign there is basically a united Protestant church that had come of age. This, rather than the Elizabethan church, is the true Anglican *via media*. This confidence is reflected in the furnishings of many Jacobean parish churches.[49]

Owing to the propaganda of the Laudian revolution which has come down to us further advanced by the advocates of the Oxford Movement, the Jacobean church and its buildings have had a very negative reputation. But in fact the Jacobean episcopal records show that attention was

---

[46] Addleshaw and Etchells, *Architectural Setting*, 27–9.

[47] *Visitation Articles and Injunctions of the Period of the Reformation*, ed. W. H. Frere (Alcuin Club, 14–16, 1910), III, 2, 108–9; Addleshaw and Etchells, *Architectural Setting*, 30–4.

[48] Other examples are given in R. H. Murray, 'Arrangements of the Chancel at Deerhurst', *Transactions of the Bristol and Gloucestershire Archaeological Society*, 25 (1902), 290, 291.

[49] It is often difficult to date seventeenth-century church interiors exactly. Many churches built soon after James' death are identical with earlier ones, so there are typical Jacobean interiors right into the 1630s. It was in the chancel areas that a distinctive Laudian pattern developed.

given to repairing and enhancing buildings.[50] There are a number of noteworthy restorations and more churches were built than is usually thought.[51] Both the restorations and the new buildings adhere to a style befitting the worship of this Calvinist episcopal English church, and closely reflect the theological and liturgical insights of James and almost all of his senior bishops, with their emphasis on the centrality of the Bible, the importance of preaching, a reverence for, and the participation of the laity in, the sacraments and, particularly for James, the role of the monarch as supreme governor of the church.

Though there are only three churches which still retain something like the Jacobean arrangements in the chancel, there are many churches where Jacobean communion seats remain in the chancels, commandment boards, texts and Royal Arms on the walls, pulpits, desks and pews in the nave, and Jacobean panelling throughout.

There must be at least 1,000 Jacobean pulpits throughout the country. In Suffolk alone Cautley has noted 117 seventeenth-century pulpits, mainly Jacobean.[52] There must be an equal number or more in both Norfolk and Somerset,[53] but every county possesses some. There are very fine Jacobean pulpits at Wednesbury, Staffs., All Saints, Herefs. (with the text, 'How beautiful are the feete of them that bring glad tidings of peace' around the edge of the sounding board), Moreton Jeffries, Herefs., Mintey, Wilts., Ilminster, Som. There was a spate of pulpit building under James partly in response to Canon 83 of 1604 which ordered pulpits to be 'provided and set in a convenient place, and there be seemly kept for the preaching of God's Word'. As well, it was ordered 'that a convenient seat be made for the minister to read service in' (Canon 82). This, in the context of the two centres of liturgical worship, the chancel and the nave, led to the erection of the three-decker pulpit, for preaching, reading the lessons and for conducting the service. Nothing

---

[50] Jacobean visitations often emphasise the need for repairs and note when these have been done. For example, the bishop of Lincoln conducted a survey of churches in response to an inquiry of Bancroft about the fabric of churches. The majority were in good repair and promises of repair came from many of the others. See C. W. Foster, ed.,'The State of the Church in the Diocese of Lincoln', *Lincolnshire Record Society*, 23 (1926).

[51] Some of these restorations and new buildings are discussed below. Others include Hoveton, Norf., 1624; Groombridge, Kent, 1623; Wyke Champflower, Som., 1623–4; Harthill, Ches., 1607; Minterne Magna, Dors., 1610–20; Arthuret, Cumb., 1609, built by money collected at James' instigation (N. Pevsner, *The Buildings of England: Cumberland and Westmorland* (Harmondsworth, 1977), 61–2).

[52] H. M. Cautley, *Suffolk Churches* (1945), 170–2.

[53] H. M. Cautley, *Norfolk Churches* (1949), and N. Pevsner, *The Buildings of England: North Somerset and Bristol* (Harmondsworth, 1979), for individual churches.

could so visibly point to the close relationship James emphasised between prayer and preaching than these three-decker pulpits which also became common in Scotland. At Salle, Norf., the two lower decks were added in 1611. Kedington, Suff., was built in 1616, Wednesbury 1611, while Ashby St Ledger, Northants., Ashington, Som., Haddon Hall Chapel, Derb., 1624, are among many other fine examples.

The same point was made in a different way by George Herbert in his reconstructed church at Leighton Bromswold, Hunts., 1624, where pulpit and prayer desk of equal size are set at either side of the entrance to the chancel.[54] In the nineteenth century the Camden Society with its insistence that prayers must be said in the chancel either destroyed or dismembered these testimonies to Jacobean piety.[55]

Texts were frequently painted on the pulpit or above on the sounding board to emphasise the importance of preaching. At Yaxley, Suff., are inscribed the words, 'Necessity is laid upon me, ye woe is me if I preach not the Gospel'; at Goadby by Manwood, Leics., 'Here [sic] the Word of God'; at Kidderminster, Worcs., dated 1621, later Baxter's pulpit, are the words, 'O give thanks unto the Lord and call upon his name; declare his worship among the people.'

The canons also ordered the Creed, the Lord's Prayer and Ten Commandments to be placed on boards where people could see them either behind the table or on the chancel screen, together with edifying texts from the Bible. So three central aspects of the Christian life, prayer, obedience and faith, were set out and bolstered up by texts from the Bible.

One fine example is at Lydbury North, Salop., 1615, where they take up the entire width of the screen. An even better example is at Parracombe, Devon, which was saved from destruction by Ruskin. This also includes the Royal Arms. It was repainted in 1758 but undoubtedly is a replica of a much earlier screen.

'Fruitful and profitable texts from Holy Scripture' to instruct the people in the faith were painted around the walls of most churches. At Sherrington, Wilts., is a fine set of eleven texts including the Creed and the Lord's Prayer, 1624, placed in appropriate places of the church. Near the table is a communion text, 1 Corinthians, 11.26, 'For as often as ye eat this bread and drink this cup ye proclaim the Lord's death till he come.' Near the font are two baptismal texts, 'Suffer little children to come unto Me', Matthew 19.4, and from Psalm 34.11, 'Come children hearken unto me and I will teach you the fear of the Lord'. Near the door

[54] Addleshaw and Etchells, *Architectural Setting*, 51, 79 (plan).
[55] *Ibid.*, 207–8.

were several texts about the last judgement. The Lord's Prayer is on the south wall; the Creed on the north. Several texts are indecipherable.

In Witnesham, Suff., is another set of early seventeenth-century texts. The church was restored just prior to the Oxford Movement and so the texts escaped destruction. In the chancel are texts appropriate for communion from First Corinthians 11.27, 28. On the north wall where the pulpit was situated in Jacobean times are two texts, 'We are ambassadors for Christ, God making his appeal through us' and 'Woe to me if I do not preach the Gospel.' By the communion rail there used to be, 'I will wash my hands in innocency O Lord and so will I go to thine altar.' (This text is in a similar position in St Margaret's, Hereford.)

With sermons and bible readings becoming central elements in the services, pews and benches became a necessity. In the later Middle Ages some churches of the preaching friars provided seating, but now every church needed seats and there are many examples of Jacobean seating as at Burneston, N.R. Yorks., Brent Eleigh, Suff., Mudford, Ashington, East Pennard, all in Somerset, Lydbury North, Salop., Ashby St Ledger, Northants.

As well as these standard family box pews, more ornate, not to say sumptuous, pews became common for the leading gentry. They were always placed in prominent positions often between the pulpit and the chancel. There are many Jacobean examples like the Barnardiston pew at Kedington, Suff., 1617, two next to the chancel at Rycote, Oxon., 1625; Breedon on the Hill, Leics., Holcombe Rogus, Devon, and Langley Marish, Bucks.[56]

The leading role Henry, Edward and Elizabeth had played in setting up a Reformed Church ensured that the monarch was a Protestant Constantine. To make the point Henry had ordered the Royal Arms to be placed in churches (there is a fine Henrician one remaining at Rushbrooke, Suff.). This policy was followed by Elizabeth (there is a sumptuous Elizabethan Arms filling the tympanum above the chancel screen at Tivetshall, Norf.).

This ecclesiastical ornament precisely fitted in with James' beliefs of his role in the church. Archbishop Abbot ordered John Sergeant to set up in all churches and chapels 'the King's Majesties Arms in due forme with helme, crest, mantell and supporters as they ought to be together with the

---

[56] Kedington (Addleshaw and Etchells, *Architectural Setting*, 77 plan); Holcombe Rogus, North Devon, N. Pevsner, *The Buildings of England: North Devon* (Harmondsworth, 1952); Langley Marish, Bucks. (N. Pevsner, *The Buildings of England: Buckinghamshire* (Harmondsworth, 1960)); Rycote, Oxon. (N. Pevsner, *The Buildings of England: Oxfordshire* (Harmondsworth, 1974)); and N. Yates, *Buildings, Faith and Worship* (Oxford, 1991), 40 and plate 2.

noble young princes'.[57] (There are two churches where both the king's Arms and the prince's can still be seen, St John's Leeds, with James and Prince Charles, and at Messing, Essex, where the Arms are those of Charles and the prince.)

There are not many surviving Royal Arms of James I, for two reasons. First, during the Commonwealth many were destroyed, a few being replaced with the arms of the Commonwealth (which in turn were destroyed, only a very few surviving).[58] Secondly, to save money later churchwardens merely changed the initials of the monarch on the board. This was a common practice under the Georges changing the C.R. to G.R. and then just altering the numeral for the successive Georges. But it is almost certain some Jacobean boards were similarly changed. The Arms of James frequently had texts under them especially 'Exurgat Deus Dissipentur Inimici'. This text is on the Arms at Troston, Suff., Poslingford, Suff., Hillborogh, Norf., and West Bergholt, Essex. The last three still have J.R.I on them, but the one at Troston has G.R. Jacobean boards are also at Blisland, Cornw., 1604, Winsford, Som., 1615, Wisbech, Cambs., 1605, Friston, Suff., and Basingstoke, Hants., which has the text, 'Beati Pacifici'. The text at Winsford, Som., would have pleased James, 'Curse not the King, no not in thy thought; neither curse the rich in thy bedchamber for the soul of the heaven shall carry thy voice and that which has wings shall declare the matter (Ecclesiastes 10.20, Genevan Bible translation).[59]

These interior arrangements of the naves, though reflecting clearly the Jacobean influence, are not distinctive of the Jacobean age alone. But when we turn to the chancels, although very few have escaped major changes, especially after the mid-nineteenth century with the heavy-handed enthusiasm of the Camden Society, we see distinctive Jacobean characteristics.

The general guideline is set out in the canons of 1604 regarding the communion tables. 'Convenient and decent tables had to be provided' and when the holy communion was celebrated they 'shall be placed in so good order within the church [i.e. the nave] or chancel as thereby the minister may be more conveniently heard in his prayers and ministration and the communicants also more conveniently and in more number may communicate with the said minister'.[60] The Elizabethan injunction that

---

[57] Quoted H. M. Cautley, *Royal Arms and Commandment Boards* (1934), 45–6.
[58] *Ibid.*, 58, for examples of Arms of the Commonwealth at Hythe and North Walsham. H. M. Bloxam, *Principles of Gothic Ecclesiastical Architecture* (11th edn, 1882), III, 117, for Commonwealth Arms formerly at Anstey, Warws.
[59] Cautley, *Royal Arms*, 46–50.
[60] Canon 82, 1604, in J. P. Kenyon, *The Stuart Constitution* (Cambridge, 1966), 142.

at all other times the table should be 'set in place where the altar stood' was omitted. In fact it had been more and more ignored in Elizabethan times as many of the tables were so heavy.

What developed in England fitted in well with James' liturgical perceptions. The screen set the chancel off for a special place of prayer for, as James said, 'no time can be so fit for prayer as is the time for receiving the sacrament',[61] and many screens were rebuilt under James. It became the norm in Jacobean churches. Some are on the grand scale as at Croscombe, Som., St John's, Leeds, Longworth, Berks., over which is set the text, 'Turn yet, turn ye even unto Me saith the Lord', Slaidburn, W.R. Yorks., Washfield, Devon, 1624, surmounted by the Royal Arms, Folke Dors., and many others. Some are simple screens, like Harthill, Ches., 1609, a new church, or Wilsford, Wilts. Two are just low partitions, Wilby, Norf., and, notably, Leighton Bromswold, Hunts.

Inside the chancel were the communion seats. They are now referred to as choir stalls, but it was not till the latter half of the nineteenth century that choirs and the organs were placed here to solve a problem created by the Camden Society insisting that the chancel was the place for the clergy, not the laity. So they robed the choir like medieval clerics and put them here.[62]

But in the Jacobean church the chancel normally served as the communion room and either the old collegiate clergy stalls were retained or else new seats were added for the use of the laity during the communion service where they could hear, see and partake either kneeling or seated in these seats. In his visitation articles of 1603 Bishop Thornborough of Bristol asked whether people received kneeling 'not in their several seats where they usually sit but kneeling in the seats severally appointed in your several churches for the communicants to receive the same'. Many visitation articles of this time asked whether seats were provided in the chancel for communicants and in 1627 the churchwardens of Theydon Garnon, Essex, were fined for not so doing.[63]

There are a number of fine examples of these Jacobean communion rooms. One of the most instructive is Cartmell Priory, Lancs., restored in 1618 by George Preston of Holker Hall, later to become a moderate Royalist. In this large medieval building an elaborate screen was placed around the whole chancel area making a communion room very similar to one erected at Marslius, Holland, in 1626. Both have appropriate

---

[61] James, 'A Pattern for a King's Inauguration', in *Works*, 608.
[62] Addleshaw and Etchells, *Architectural Setting*, 209ff.
[63] *Second Report of the Ritual Commission* (1868), 440; Murray, 'Deerhurst', 289.

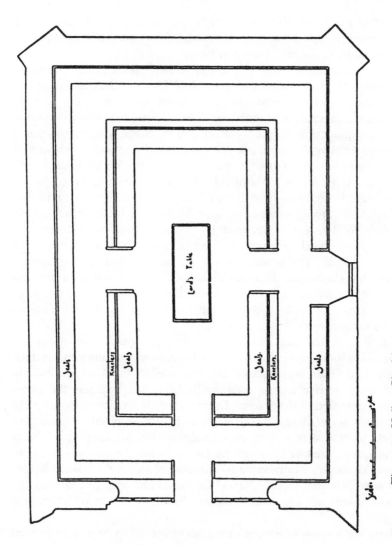

Figure 7   Hailes, Cheshire

communion texts, those at Cartmell being carved over the gates of the screen. On the west face are, 'Enter into his gates with praise', and 'Be thankful unto him and speak good of his name', while on the east face is, 'I would rather be a doorkeeper in the House of the Lord than dwell in the tabernacles of wickedness'.[64]

Leighton Bromswold, Hunts., already mentioned, has a splendid set of forty-eight communion seats in the chancel. Harlton, Cambs., Blore, Staffs., and Ryton, Co. Dur., are examples of old medieval chancels just being taken over for communion seats. Burneston, N.R. Yorks., where the entire nave was reseated, culminating in a three-tiered family seat, in 1627, is entirely in the Jacobean tradition, and has a fine set of communion seats in the chancel, a later addition which replaced earlier seats.[65] Wimborne minster's so-called choir stalls are Jacobean communion seats, as are the two fine rows of Jacobean seats on either side of the chancel in St Mary the Virgin, Oxford. Here, Pusey used to dispense communion to people in these seats which were covered with 'houseling cloths' (shades of the Free Kirk of Scotland!). He thought the doctrinaire changes of the Camden Society missed the real point of the Oxford Movement.[66]

There are many examples of fine Jacobean tables many of which have been relegated to side chapels or vestry tables by the Camden Society which replaced them by cheap deal tables entirely covered with cloths to make them look like altars. (One of the side effects of Vatican Council II has been that a number of Jacobean tables have been restored to a central position.) In East Anglia alone Cautley has counted 405 seventeenth-century tables, many being Jacobean, like Bedingfield, Earl Stoneham, Thorington, Suff., or Besthorpe, Norf.[67]

The crucial issue was where were these tables placed? The answer is that in Jacobean times the vast majority were placed table wise (i.e. with their long sides facing the north and south walls), in the centre of the chancel or in churches where there were small chancels or large congregations at the east end of the nave as in Durham Cathedral. The Laudian revolution consisted, visually speaking, in changing all this, raising the table on steps, setting it altar wise against the east wall, removing all seats from near the table, especially from behind it, and setting it off as a sanctuary by rails at which people had to kneel to receive. As well, the table was often adorned with a reredos and an

64 Addleshaw and Etchells, *Architectural Setting*, 38, 113.
65 *Ibid.*, 44, 45 (plan). I am indebted to Dr Lynn Broughton for information on Harlton.
66 J. F. White, *The Cambridge Movement* (Cambridge, 1962), 32; Addleshaw and Etchells, *Architectural Setting*, 154 n. 1
67 198 seventeenth-century tables in Norfolk, 208 in Suffolk, Cautley, *Norfolk Churches*, 45.

O. JEWITT del & sc

Figure 8   Langley Chapel

emphasis was placed on the visibility of the table and the importance of the chancel as the most fitting place for prayer.[68]

There are to my knowledge only three churches which still retain something like this Jacobean arrangement of the chancels for communion; Hailes, Glos., Deerhurst, Glos., and Langley Chapel, Salop., but right into the early part of the present century there were about twenty more.[69]

Langley Chapel was built about 1600 while the chancels of the other two were reconstructed about the same time. They are almost always described as Puritan survivals, but in fact represent the Jacobean norm, for none of them had a long communion table around which the communicants sat, and all of them have seats where one could receive kneeling. In the case of Langley Chapel one could only so receive.[70] In Deerhurst and Langley Chapel the communicants sit or kneel on the east side as well as on the north and south sides of the table.[71] This was also the case at Hailes until comparatively recently. At Hailes the low table is still set table wise as it was at Deerhurst till the nineteenth century.[72] At Hailes and Deerhurst there are two rows of communion seats around the table while at Langley Chapel the table has kneeling benches along the east, north and south sides, the top being wide enough for book rests. All three allowed for kneeling to receive the sacrament. None had the Puritan long tables though Deerhurst could have had one during the Civil War period.

The normal Jacobean pattern was the table set table wise in the midst of the chancel. Plans of the church at Lower Peover, Ches., 1610, and East Knoyle, Wilts., 1632, show this, while that of Sedlescombe, E. Suss., of 1632, shows seats along the east, north and south walls as at Deerhurst.[73] After the Restoration, 'moderate' Anglicans wished to return to this plan and there is a drawing of a celebration of communion

---

[68] Addleshaw and Etchells, *Architectural Setting*, ch. 4, section 3.

[69] See below, n. 90.

[70] M. Chatfield, *Churches the Victorians Forgot* (Ashbourne, 1979), 38–40; Addleshaw and Etchells, *Architectural Setting*, 78, 111 (plan). The table at Langley now stands in the middle of the chancel with its short ends north and south. But there is an old drawing in *Transactions of the Anastatic Society* (1857) (now defunct) showing the chancel as now except that the table was positioned table wise, i.e. with its short ends east and west. Reproduced in T. M. Tomlinson, 'The Placing of the Lord's Table', in *Collected Tracts on Ritual* (The Church Association, Tract 164).

[71] Murray, 'Deerhurst', 285–93; R. H. Murray, 'The Evolution of Church Chancels', *Transactions of the Birmingham Archaeological Society*, 31 (1905), 79, with photo showing table placed table wise.

[72] Murray, 'Deerhurst'; Addleshaw and Etchells, *Architectural Setting*, 112, plan 114.

[73] Cheshire Records Office P/8/2. Yates, *Buildings*, 35, cites East Knowle, Wilts., 1632, and Sedlecombe, E. Suss., 1632.

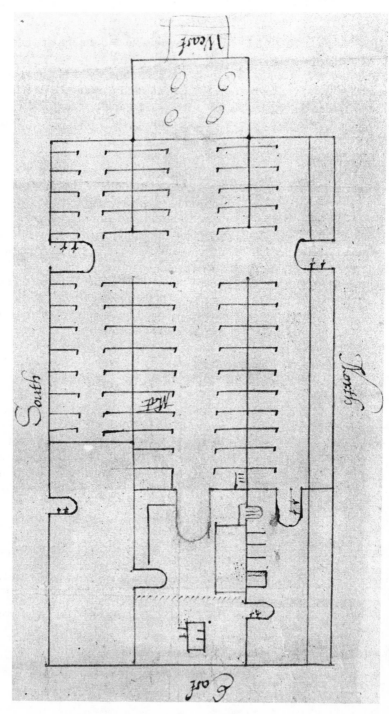

Figure 9   Lower Peover Church, 1610

with the table set table wise in 1674.[74] But the bulk of the evidence comes from Laudian writings wanting change and anti-Laudians protesting at the changes. In his first annual report after becoming archbishop of York, Richard Neile reported, 'It was scarcely found in any place that the communion table was placed in such sort as it might appear in any sense respected.'[75]

In Bath and Wells, William Piers, who had succeeded that outstanding bishop, Arthur Lake in 1632, tried to enforce Laud's policy, yet in 1636 he reported, 'There are in my diocese 469 Churches and Chapels or thereabouts and the communion tables are placed already in about 140 of them as the communion table is placed in our cathedral Church here.'[76] So after four years the large majority of the tables in this diocese were still not placed altar wise against the east wall.

Evidence of a similar state of affairs comes from all over the country. At Rye in 1636 the churchwardens, when challenged, said, 'Our Table standeth where it formerly stood, time out of mind.' The same was true for Udimore and Chiddingly, Suss.[77] A paper found in Laud's study at Lambeth in 1641 stated, 'There are many communion tables in several churches in the city of London that are not railed and some of them are placed in the middle of the church.'[78] D'Ewes speaks of the tables being moved in churches of East Anglia, and how then the communion service could not be heard, 'not one part in five' of the greater churches 'which is unquestionably unlawful'.[79]

To support his policy Laud had said that the altars now stood in this position 'in the royal chapels and most cathedrals'. But most of these changes had been brought about by the Laudian bishops. Even in the chapel royal at St James's Palace, Prynne related how he received communion with the table in the midst of the chapel and 'white linen cloths . . . were spred upon the desks of the seats wherein the communicants sat around in a decent manner, the minister delivering them the sacraments in their seats, and this they certified to me was the custom both in Prince Henry's time and his majesty's time'.[80]

The case was the same with the cathedrals. The table was moved at

---

[74] Addleshaw and Etchells, *Architectural Setting*, 112. Sir Thomas Littleton, Speaker of the Commons 1698, urged that they should return to the Jacobean arrangements for communion, quoted J. S. Howson, *Before the Table* (1878), 41.

[75] Quoted A. Foster, 'Church Policies in the 1630ies', in *Conflict in Early Stuart England*, ed. Richard Cust and Ann Hughes (1989), 203.

[76] William Prynne, *Canterburie's Doome* (1646), 98.

[77] A. Fletcher, *A County Community in Peace and War* (1975), 89, 91–2.

[78] Prynne, *Canterburie's Doome*, 9.

[79] Simonds D'Ewes, *Autobiography*, ed. J. O. Halliwell (1845), 142–3.

[80] William Prynne, *A Quenche Coal* (1637), 161.

Gloucester only with the advent of Laud as dean in 1617, at Durham with the advent of Francis Burgoyne in 1628,[81] at Winchester with the advent of Neile as bishop in 1628, at Chester in 1633, at Carlisle in 1634,[82] at Litchfield in 1636.[83] At Bristol, Exeter, Salisbury and Worcester, the tables were moved to the east end of the cathedrals sometime after 1634.[84]

Placing the table altar wise at the east end and railing it led to two other changes in a considerable number of churches. Where the tables had been placed table wise in the midst of the chancels it became quite common to place the seats for the communicants right around the chancel walls including the east end. This was called by Laud 'seats above the altar', and came under his strongest attack. Abbot too was opposed to it and at Crayford, Kent, he had had them removed.[85] Often they were in quite large churches, St Michael's, Coventry, Wimborne, Hants., Horsham, Suss., as well as many smaller churches like St Martin's, York, or Itchingfield, Suss.[86] Laud complained that the parishioner 'sat above God' at St Augustine's and St Leonard's in London.[87] A cause célèbre was Beckington, Som., which ended up with the churchwardens in gaol as it became a test case.[88]

Deerhurst, Glos., is the only true survival though St Helen's, Norwich, is a little like it with pulpit and seats against the east wall of the nave, and the table against the east wall of the south aisle. There is no chancel. But until 1900 there were many more cases – Shrivenham, Berks., Winchcombe, Glos.,[89] till 1855, Wiggenhall St Mary, Norf., till 1862, Brill, Bucks, Waltham, Leics., Lyddington, Rut., Buckland Monachoram, Devon, Over Winchendon, Bucks.,[90] Puddletown, Dors., which is often referred to as a Laudian church, because of its ornateness but Laud would not have tolerated seats behind the altar.[91]

---

[81] Tyacke, *Anti-Calvinists*, 117–18; Laud, *Works*, IV, 233; VI, 56–7, 239–41.

[82] Tyacke, *Anti-Calvinists*, 214–15.

[83] Prynne, 'A Looking Glass for All Prelates', quoted G. Soden, *Godfrey Goodman, Bishop of Gloucester* (1953), 43.

[84] Tyacke, *Anti-Calvinists*, 215; Prynne, *A Quenche Coal*, 161.

[85] Cardwell, *Documentary Annals*, II, 174–6.

[86] R. Marchant, *The Puritans and the Church Courts in the Diocese of York 1560–1642* (1960), 63–4; Fletcher, *A County Community in Peace and War*, 91; Murray, 'Deerhurst', 287.

[87] *Reports of Cases in the Courts of Star Chamber and High Commission*, ed. S. R. Gardiner (Camden Soc., n.s., 39, 1886), 282–306.

[88] 'Documents of the Laudian Period', ed. T. F. Palmer, *Somerset Records Society*, 43 (1928), 193–8.

[89] Photograph of the chancel in 1885 preserved in the church.

[90] Listed in Murray, 'Deerhurst', 287–8; Murray, 'Evolution of Church Chancels', 82–5; Bloxam, *Architecture*, 173ff.; C. A. Swainson, *The Rubrical Question of 1874* (1875), 24, 25.

[91] Murray, 'Deerhurst', 287.

Laud's altar policy also caused friction with the gentry. At Billingshurst, Suss., the table was set in 'the squire's chancel', and here Mr Goring had his family pew against the east wall.[92] Tombs were an issue as well for often from the sixteenth century, large gentry tombs were placed in the chancel. Laudian bishops often ordered the removal of these and also the removal of family seats not only from the chancel but from central places in the nave if they obscured the view of the altar.[93] Cosin did not believe women should have a place in the chancel so in Durham although the gentry could retain their seats in the chancel, their wives were given special seats in the nave.[94]

James' bishops left well alone for as Collinson has shown there was a real rapport between the ministry and magistrates. In that socially conscious age the position of one's pew in church was a contentious issue. Pews took up so much space that often they could not be fitted into the most favourable positions in the front of the nave or near the pulpit. So gentry had been allowed to put them in the chancel along with their tombs. At Kedington, an entire bay between the pulpit (against the second pillar west of the screen) and the screen is taken up with the Barnardistons' pew and tombs.

It was not only the gentry. At Dartmouth the town council renewed the chancel of their church in 1614 and placed their special seats along the east wall with a specially carved and cushioned seat for the mayor and his wife. They remained there till the late nineteenth century.[95]

There are a number of churches which, except for the rearrangement of their chancels and communion tables, are very much as they were in Jacobean times. Croscombe, Som., was a medieval church, the interior of which was completely refurnished by the Fortescue family in the early 1600s with the blessing of the bishop of Bath and Wells, Arthur Lake, who in 1616 gave the ornate pulpit. Lake was a fine preacher and pastor and in theology was clearly closer to Calvin than to Scholastic Calvinism. Those who think the Laudians had the monopoly of ornate churches should think again. This is a Jacobean church on a grand scale. The screen, a most elaborate design surmounted with the Royal Arms of

[92] Fletcher, *A County Community in Peace and War*, 91.

[93] Laud, 'Annual Accounts of his Province to the King, 1634', in *Works*, V, 324–5; W. W. Palmer, ed., 'Visitation Returns of the Ely Diocese', *Transactions of the Cambridge and Huntingdon Archaeological Society*, 4 (1915–30), *passim*; Prynne, *Canterburie's Doome*, 91.

[94] John Cosin, 'Correspondence', *Surtees Society*, 52 (1868), xxix. Bishop Buckeridge acted in the same way in Rochester. Letter to the mayor, April, 1625: women should not be allowed 'to sit in the chancel which was instituted for clerks', *Archaeologia*, 12 (1809), 103.

[95] *An Historical Record of St Saviour's Church, Dartmouth* (printed Tozer & Co., n.d.), 2; Bloxam, *Gothic Architecture*, III, 177.

James I set above those of the Fortescue family, runs right across the church, not at the chancel arch but one pillar to the west of it. The reason for this is that the small chancel to accommodate the communicants was enlarged by incorporating some of the nave. How this enlarged chancel was furnished is impossible to tell for the Victorians returned to the old medieval arrangements and it is now stepped and filled with a late nineteenth-century reredos. But the nave west of the screen is much as it was in Jacobean times, all centred upon the pulpit around which is the text, 'Blessed are they that hear the word of God and keep it'. The lectern and prayer desk are in the nave on either side of the chancel arch and the seats between them and the pulpit face the pulpit as do the seats on the south aisle. The old Jacobean table is in a side chapel and the whole of the nave is dominated by the Royal Arms of James on top of the screen. Two nineteenth-century texts flank the altar, but they probably copied the earlier ones that were there for they are unusual for a post-Oxford Movement setting. 'Thy Word is a lamp unto my feet' and 'If ye then be raised with Christ seek the things which are above where Christ is'.[96]

A similarly ornate church is St John's, Leeds, built in 1631, but completely in the Jacobean style. The donor, John Harrison, a wealthy woollen merchant, appointed a known Puritan, Robert Todd, curate of the old parish church as its first minister. John Cosin, chaplain to Archbishop Neile, preached at the morning service on the day St John's was consecrated. Todd preached a sermon so radical in the afternoon that the archbishop suspended him and Harrison had to intervene to restore him to his parish. Harrison subsequently fell out with Todd because he had ceased to pray for Harrison as patron of the church. A number of writers have claimed that St John's is a Laudian church whereas it is one that clearly represents what may be loosely called the Jacobean consensus. It is structurally a one-roomed church, but divided into two by a large ornate screen surmounted with the arms of James facing west and of Charles facing east. The fine pulpit, originally a three decker, formerly stood against the north wall half-way down the nave. The Victorian restorers moved it to the north-east corner of the nave. The large communion area was created by the screen being carried right across the whole width of this wide church one and a half bays to the west of the east wall, with chancel seats around the north and south walls and along the screen and possibly on the east wall, except behind the table.[97]

---

[96] *Croscombe Parish Church of St Mary the Virgin* (Wells, 1983); Pevsner, *North Somerset*, 117.
[97] Janet Douglas and Ken Powell, *St John's Church, Leeds, A History* (published by Redundant Churches Fund, London, n.d.); J. E. Stocks, 'The Church of St John the Evangelist, Leeds', *Thoresby Society*, 24 (1919), 190–226.

These are two Jacobean churches on the grand scale. Most of those remaining have more modest furnishings, though with the same general design. One of the best preserved is Kedington, church of the Barnardistons, one of the leading Suffolk families and strongly Puritan. It is a typical East Anglian church and much of the furnishing is eighteenth century. But the plan of the nave is entirely Jacobean. The three-decker pulpit, 1610, the first recorded in England, is set near the centre of the church against the first pillar westward of the chancel arch with many of the pews facing it. On the north side of the aisle nearer the chancel is the Barnardiston family pew and on the south side are the fine family tombs. In the small north chapel is the original Jacobean table. The screen is of 1619, again illustrating the conservative nature of the Jacobean church buildings. In the chancel are two of the original communion pews. The communion setting would almost certainly have gone through four changes from 1630 to the late seventeenth century. Before Laud, the table would have been placed in the centre of the chancel, table wise. With Bishop Wren, it would have been set against the east wall altar wise and raised on steps. During the Civil War it would have reverted to the Jacobean pattern. With the Restoration it returned to the east wall and in 1707 was surrounded on three sides by rails, given by Samuel Barnardiston.[98]

There are a number of churches with their naves still holding to this pattern and many also have communion seats.[99] Many, of course, have eighteenth-century refurnishing, but until the Camden Society restorations, were similar to what they were in the Jacobean period.

Three small churches call for comment. Lewston, Dors., was built as a private chapel by Sir John Fitzjames, 1610, and is virtually unchanged. From time to time it has served as a parish church. It is a single cell building with a two-decker pulpit in the south-east corner next to the table which stands against the east wall. Raised by one step this alone demarks the communion area where the table is against the Jacobean panelling of the east wall.[100]

Dale Abbey, Derbs., is a little two-aisled medieval chapel transformed into a Jacobean church. Most of the furnishings are of 1634, but Laudian it is not. A screen divides the 'nave' consisting of three rows of medieval benches from the chancel where there are three box pews. The pulpit is

[98] Roy Tricker, *St Peter and St Paul Kedington* (1990). Plan on back page.
[99] Many have already been mentioned. Others include Brent Eleigh, Suff.; Wilby, Norf.; Folke and Minterne Magna, Dors.; Barnoldswick and Slaidburn, W.R. Yorks.; Low Ham and Ashrington, Som.; Lower Peover, Ches.; Ashby St Ledger, Northants.; Idlicote, Warws.; Broughton, Staffs.; Wickhamford, Worcs.
[100] Chatfield, *Churches*, 32–4.

in the north-east corner; jammed next to it is the reading desk against the east wall. In front of this and right against it is the small table in which are cupboards for the communion plate. In the south-east corner is the prayer desk while the font is at the east end of the south aisle.[101]

Inglesham, Wilts., is a very small thirteenth-century church consisting of a chancel, short nave with a south aisle of equal length and a shorter north aisle. The immediate impression is one of studied disorder whose charm was seen by William Morris, but is, in fact, a standard Jacobean type with a Jacobean pulpit and desk against the chancel arch, communion seats (incorporated in the eighteenth century into two family pews) along the chancel wall, the Jacobean table now against the east wall on which is a communion text (1 Cor. 11.23), and near the south door is the font with a Jacobean cover. The Commandments are written above the chancel arch while the Apostles' Creed, Lord's Prayer and two other texts are on the walls with the Royal Arms on the north wall.[102] These three illustrate the non-doctrinaire nature of the Jacobean church yet one that was strongly Protestant emphasising both Word and sacraments.

The situation in Scotland was quite different and this created a real problem for James. English commentators are apt to write off Scots kirks when compared with English ones as mere auditoria. This is because they fail to appreciate the central role that communion played in the life of the Scots Reformed Church. It was Calvin who wanted a weekly celebration at least and whose stress on the centrality of the presence of the humanity of Christ in the sacrament was a key part of Scots eucharistic worship, to seal in the hearts of worshippers 'that blessed conjunction, union and society that the elect have with their head, Christ Jesus. And thus we utterly damn the vanity of those that affirm Sacraments to be nothing else but naked and bare signs.'[103]

James, as his writings reveal, adhered to this tradition. Like the English reformers, the Scots wished all to hear, see and partake of the sacrament. But largely through Knox's influence, whose commonest term for the eucharist was the Lord's Board or Lord's Supper, the Scots believed that sitting at tables was the nearest approach to what happened at the Last Supper.

The *First Book of Discipline*, 1560, stated, 'The Table of the Lord is then most rightly ministered when it approacheth most nigh to Christ's

---

[101] *Ibid.*, 20–1.

[102] *Ibid.*, 133–5. W. H. Knowles 'The Church of St John Baptist, Inglesham', *Transactions of the Bristol and Gloucestershire Archaeological Society*, 53 (1917), 191–205, with plan.

[103] 'The Confession of Faith Professed and Believed by the Protestants in the Realm of Scotland', in *John Knox's History of the Reformation in Scotland*, ed. W. C. Dickinson (Edinburgh, 1949), ch. 21.

own action. But plain it is that at that Supper Christ Jesus sat with his disciples, and therefore do we judge that sitting at a table is most convenient to this holy action.' In a later passage, 'tables for the ministration of the Lord's Supper' are included as essential furnishing for a church.[104] They wanted to emphasise the close connection of Word and sacrament so these tables on the communion Sunday were set usually in front of the pulpit. Some of the larger Scots kirks for some time used their chancels as communion rooms as in England, and placed the long tables there as in Crail Culross, Perth, and other churches.[105] Though others, like St Mary's Dundee, or St Nicholas', Aberdeen, made two parish churches, one in the nave, one in the chancel, and so each became a one-roomed church.

But the vast majority of Scots kirks were small rectangular buildings with no structural change between nave and chancel. In the larger ones the chancels were just blocked off or used for the laird's loft or burial aisle. The pulpit was normally placed against the middle of the south wall and the communion tables brought in and placed in front of them. A dish for baptisms was attached to the pulpit.[106] But many of these churches were so small that this imposed very cramped conditions for the sacrament. So there developed a distinctively Scots design, the T-shaped kirk where an aisle was built out at right angles to the nave facing the pulpit. This became almost standard in the eighteenth century and had many advantages. All the congregation was relatively near the pulpit and the long table could be placed either along the nave or along this aisle with the head table near the pulpit.

The first Scots T-shaped kirk was probably at Weem, 1609. Other early ones were Aberdour and Dalmeny, both old Norman churches, Duddingston, Stow, Pentcaitland, Anstruther Easter, 1636, Fowlis Wester and Moneymusk (where the T has been turned into a vestry and a chancel restored).[107] This plan was often copied, especially in the north of England, but was so much disliked by the Oxford Movement that Aldfield, N.R. Yorks., alone remains. In the south, Little Hadham, Herts., possibly the first English church of this design, 1638, Stelling, Kent, Great Elm, Som., and several others, remain.[108]

One Jacobean experiment that is unique is Burntisland. Built in 1592,

[104] *The First Book of Discipline*, ed. James K. Cameron (Edinburgh, 1972), 90–3, 203.
[105] Hay, *Architecture of Scottish Post-Reformation Churches*, 26. W. M. McMillan, *The Worship of the Scottish Reformed Church 1550–1638* (Edinburgh, 1931), 242–3, for other churches.
[106] McMillan, *Worship of the Scottish Reformed Church*, 251–4.
[107] Hay, *Architecture of Scottish Post-Reformation Churches*, 52–4.
[108] Yates, *Buildings*, 93ff.

it predates James' knowledge of English churches. It is a square some sixty feet across whose central tower is supported by four semi-circular arches on square piers. Galleries are on all sides and the seats in these and on the ground floor were assigned to the various guilds marked with their insignia. The pulpit against the south-west pillar faces diagonally across to the north-east against which pillar is the special laird's pew, now the magistrate's. Presumably in the seventeenth century, tables were brought in specially for communion, for Laud, who was there in 1633, saw no obvious place for an altar.[109]

As we have seen, James tried to enforce his liturgical ideas on the Church of Scotland in the Five Articles of Perth. Despite enormous opposition and the reluctance of the Scots bishops, they eventually passed the Perth Assembly, August 1618, and in 1621 were ratified by the Scots parliament.[110] James then ordered the bishops to enforce the articles for the only way to keep down both papistry 'a disease of the mind and Puritanism a disease of the brain . . . was a grave settled and well ordered Church in the obedience of God and their king'.[111]

The most contentious clauses were keeping the Christian year and kneeling to receive communion. James in part combined them both by insisting on Easter and Christmas communions which had 'to be received reverently upon their knees from the hands of the ministers'.[112]

Resistance to the Articles was widespread, especially in Edinburgh and the rest of Lothian and Fife. Many stayed away on communion Sundays or went to other churches where kneeling was not strictly enforced. Some went in for outright disobedience. Richard Dickson, the minister of St Cuthbert's, Edinburgh, celebrated communion before and not during Easter and forbade his congregation to kneel.[113] Calderwood alleges that only about 20 knelt out of 1,600 communicants at the College Kirk, Edinburgh. 'Cold and graceless were the Communions, and few were the communicants' was his assessment.[114] On the other hand, Lord Binning said that though many absented themselves 'neither man nor woman during the space of almost four hours, offered to receive sitting upon the forms, except one only base fellow',[115] and certainly in other parts of Scotland most seemed to have conformed, like the Kirk Session of Perth

---

[109] Hay, *Architecture of Scottish Post-Reformation Churches*, 32–4 (with plan).
[110] See above, nn. 33, 34.
[111] John Spottiswoode, *History of the Church and State of Scotland* (1677), 542.
[112] Mackay, 'The Reception of the Five Articles of Perth', 185.
[113] D. Calderwood, *The True History of the Church of Scotland* (Wodrow Soc., Edinburgh, 1842–9), VII, 353.
[114] *Ibid.*, VII, 438, 359.
[115] *Original Letters Relating to the Ecclesiastical Affairs of Scotland* (Bannatyne Club, 1851), 99.

which agreed unanimously to do so on 25 March 1619. But there was deep unease and Spottiswoode admitted that by 1627 kneeling had been given up in many places.[116]

It is hard to see how kneeling could be the practice along with long tables, but the scant evidence that remains suggests that the long tables continued as shown above in the remark of Lord Binning and by the fact that some ministers, to gain some measure of conformity, said they would allow people to stand, sit or kneel.[117]

One church that conformed to the English Jacobean pattern was Dairsie built by Spottiswoode in 1621, whose family owned the neighbouring castle. It is a small Scots Gothic rectangular building. Its interior is now quite bare, but from investigations by the Synod of Fife in 1641 and 1645, we know that there were sundry crosses within the church, 'which were not thought to be superstitious, various kneeling desks at the raised east end' and 'a glorious partition dividing the body of the Church from the choir, on which were displayed the royal arms of England and Scotland with divers crosses above and about them'. The Synod ordered their destruction in 1645. Spottiswoode wished to be buried here, but in fact was interred in Westminster Abbey.[118] Dairsie was probably the only Scottish church that reflected James' ideal, for despite his desire for a degree of uniformity with England, James was at pains to preserve the integrity of the Scottish church.

But not so with Laud. He 'laboured to have the English liturgy sent them without any omission or addition at all . . . but some of the Scottish bishops prevailed against me',[119] but to not much effect in other respects for Brereton reported from his travels in Scotland that 'now the ceremonies of the Church of England are introduced and conformity is much pressed and kneeling is much pressed'.[120] But the Laudian incursion into Scottish church affairs finished James' attempt at reconciliation. The return to the old system was complete. In April 1638, at Perth, communion was given in the old manner – 'the ministry at the little Table and the elders at the two Boards, there being people at both sides thereof, and everyone took the bread first off the plate with his own

[116] 'Kirk Session Register of Perth', *Spottiswoode Miscellany*, II, 289. George Gillespie, *A Dispute against the English Popish Ceremonies* (1637), 80, in McMillan, *The Worship of the Scottish Reformed Church*, 182.
[117] Calderwood, *The True History*, VII, 359.
[118] M. Ash, 'Dairsie and Archbishop Spottiswoode', *Scottish Church History Society Records*, 19 (1975–7); Hay, *Architecture of Scottish Post-Reformation Churches*, 43–5.
[119] Laud, *Works*, III, 51, quoted in G. Donaldson, *The Making of the Scottish Prayer Book of 1637* (Edinburgh, 1954), 53, the definitive study on this issue.
[120] William Brereton, *Travels in Holland, the United Provinces, England, Scotland and Ireland* (Letham Soc., 1844), 159.

hand and so the cup'.[121] In November, the Glasgow Assembly declared that the episcopal government of the church was 'abjured and removed'.[122] Scotland was in a state of rebellion. How wise were James' words to Buckingham regarding Laud, 'Take him to you but on my soul you will repent it.'

---

[121] Quoted in Mackay, 'The Reception of the Five Articles of Perth', 125ff.
[122] *Records of the Kirk of Scotland*, ed. Alexander Peterkin (1838), 168. See also Mullan, *Episcopacy in Scotland*, 191.

9   A British patriarchy? Ecclesiastical imperialism under the early Stuarts

John Morrill

I

In the summer of 1639, Charles I called upon the resources of all three of his kingdoms to bring the recalcitrant Covenanters in Scotland to heel.[1] Meanwhile, in deepest Norfolk, the antiquarian scholar Sir Henry Spelman was writing with enthusiastic insouciance to his friend, James Ussher (archbishop of Armagh) about 'Justellus the learned Frenchman ... [who] is about a great worke touching the describinge of the ancient Patriarchies in church government and comptinge (as I understande) that of our British Churches to be one of them.'

Spelman sought Ussher's 'advice and approbacon' in assisting Justellus. Two months later he received a very dusty reply in haughty Latin. Ussher's antiquarian enthusiasms clearly did not extend to allowing Ireland to be recognised as historically 'subject to the Church of England'. Scotland, perhaps, said Ussher; but Ireland never.[2]

Several historians have recently argued that the early Stuarts sought to anglicise (or in ecclesiastical terms anglicanise) all three of their kingdoms; that there was a drive towards a unity of the kingdoms through imposing a conformity to English ways. Conrad Russell, speaking for this group, has written that 'Charles and Laud [sought] to construct a new programme of British uniformity. Since their major commitment was to those features of the English Church which were conspicuously absent in Ireland and Scotland, this programme for

---

[1] This essay was first given at a conference on Triple Monarchy in seventeenth-century Britain at the University of Illinois in April 1990. A revised version was given as a James Ford Special Lecture in Oxford in November 1991. The version printed here is the Oxford version with some cuts restored. I am grateful to many scholars for their comments on both occasions; and I wish to single out Peter Lake, the commentator in Illinois, Steven Ellis, David Smith and Anthony Milton for their comments on written versions of the paper.

[2] BL, Add. MS 34600, fols. 172, 173, 179–80, 186 (and cf. fo,. 133).

British uniformity inevitably turned into one for English hegemony.'[3] Yet the striking thing about the Spelman–Ussher correspondence is precisely that it was a private correspondence. As far as I can tell, there was no attempt at the Jacobean court, nor even within the Laudian circle in the 1630s, to discuss these claims for a British patriarchy. In re-examining the extent of English ecclesiastical imperialism in the period between the Union of the Crowns and the War of Three Kingdoms, this is the dog that did not bark in the night.

II

My purpose in this essay is, then, to look at the relations between the Churches of England, Scotland and Ireland in order to establish how far there was a Canterburian plot both to subvert the autonomy of the other churches, and consciously to anglicanise them by what might be termed ecclesial acculturation. In order to gain some perspective for this search, we need to gain some sense of the trajectory of the reformation processes in each of the churches.

The Scottish Reformation can be said to be the half-sister of the English Reformation; and the Irish Reformation the non-identical twin. To stretch that metaphor perhaps too far, after 1603 archbishops of Canterbury became the stepmothers to the Scottish Reformation, and rather impulsive and ineffectual stepmothers at that.

The Scottish Reformation was a Reformation carried through against the will and preference of a queen absent for much of the time in body and all the time in mind. Over the years 1560–1603, it developed first and foremost in accordance with local conditions, in response to the low level of Scottish state formation and in the absence of a godly prince either to shape or obstruct it. It was characterised by a strong parochial discipline, a powerful iconophobia and a clearly defined four-fold ministry of preacher, doctor, elder, deacon. It was the mirror image of the English church: radically decentralised, strong on discipline and preaching, slack in liturgical precision and confused in its relationship to the state.[4]

In all this it developed away from the English model. And yet it owed much to the English Reformation. In the vital early years, most of its clerical leaders and many of its noble supporters were men who had spent

[3] E.g. Conrad Russell, 'The British Problem in the English Civil War', *History*, 72 (1987), 399.
[4] For all this, see especially G. Donaldson, *The Scottish Reformation* (Cambridge, 1960), 177–83, 229–33 and *passim*; D. G. Mullan, *Episcopacy in Scotland: The History of an Idea* (Edinburgh, 1986), esp. chs. 2–3; J. Kirk, *Patterns of Reformation* (Edinburgh, 1989), chs. 3, 6, 9.

formative periods in England in the years before 1553 or in exile in the reign of Mary Tudor. The liturgies in almost every kirk was derived either from the English–Genevan Book of Common Order or was a sort of ASCII-file version of the English Book of Common Prayer. It took English invasions in 1560 and 1573 to secure the Protestant party in power.[5]

For all that, the English were deeply inhibited about interfering too openly in the affairs of the Scottish kirk. Elizabeth spurned the overtures from Morton for a closer association of the two churches;[6] Archbishop Adamson's visit to London in 1583–4 with a view to creating a common front with Whitgift against Presbyterianism was a complete fiasco, as Elizabeth forbad her archbishop to hold formal discussions with him. (He was forced to retreat to Scotland on borrowed money and a borrowed nag.)[7]

When Richard Bancroft, at the time chaplain to the lord chancellor, offered a spirited defence of episcopal government as the subject of his Paul's Cross sermon in 1589, he illustrated the hazards of Presbyterianism by caustic remarks about Scotland in general and John Knox in particular.[8] He had clearly overstepped the mark and the storm of protest from the kirk,[9] especially at a time when Elizabeth still felt that James might take advantage of the Spanish threat to England, caused the English queen to compel Bancroft to make a half-hearted apology and a mealy-mouthed retraction.[10]

The reluctance of Elizabeth or her bishops to get drawn into the internal affairs of the kirk was based in part on English indifference to developing closer cultural and institutional links with Scotland; in part on English fears that once broad strategic objectives in Scotland had been secured, there was danger for England in being felt to be interfering (Elizabeth never seems to have been able to read James' intentions, especially in religious matters); and in part on the queen's instinctive dislike of *active* policies anywhere.

[5] Donaldson, *Scottish Reformation*, 53–76, 149–82.
[6] Mullan, *Episcopacy in Scotland*, ch. 3; J. Kirk, '"The Polities of the Best Reformed Kirks": Scottish Achievements and English Aspirations in Church Government after the Reformation', *Scottish Historical Review*, 59 (1980), 36–43.
[7] G. Donaldson, 'The Attitude of Whitgift and Bancroft to the Scottish Church', *TRHS*, 4th ser., 24 (1942), 97–100; Mullan, *Episcopacy in Scotland*, 56. For conclusive evidence of Adamson's intentions, see his letters to Whitgift in *The Life of Andrew Melville*, ed. T. McCrie (2 vols., Edinburgh, 1819), II, 519–21.
[8] The key passages from his sermon are printed in *Miscellany of the Wodrow Society* (1842), 482–8.
[9] *Ibid.*, 489–520.
[10] Donaldson, 'Attitude of Whitgift and Bancroft', 104–9; Mullan, *Episcopacy in Scotland*, 66–71; S. B. Babbage, *Puritanism and Richard Bancroft* (1962), 29–36.

The Scots did not feel so inhibited about interfering in the internal affairs of the Church of England. As James Kirk has demonstrated, English critics of royal ecclesiastical constipation looked readily to Scotland for inspiration, example and support.[11] English ministers flocked to Scotland to see for themselves and to talk to Knox and his allies; and they appealed (with success) to the General Assembly to speak out against Parker's *Advertisements* which enforced the wearing of (popish) vestments.[12] Later, in 1595, the kirk persuaded James to protest at the imprisonment and punishment of John Udall.[13] What seems likely is that the Scots were particularly interested in seeking the completion of reformation in the English church because they were coming to terms with the prospects of regal union far earlier than the English were (and certainly than Elizabeth was and would allow her bishops to be). Some Scots looked on the bright side. As Arthur Williamson has shown, from Knox onwards, the Scottish apocalyptic tradition was as resolutely *British* as the English Foxeian tradition was resolutely *English*.[14] Others evidently foresaw that the pockmarked English church would be an uncomfortable bedfellow for the unsullied kirk under a Union of the Crowns. The more cosmetic surgery it had received before that date the better. In other words, down to 1603, English churchmen had been irritated by Scots interference in their affairs but had been disinclined to interfere in return. The Scots were the more apprehensive about the prospects of Union, and hypersensitive about what James might do to bring about a renewed quest for a 'conformity of Kirks'.

III

I called the Irish church the non-identical twin of the Church of England. Legislation for the Church of Ireland always closely paralleled English legislation; but it never merely replicated it. Thus the Irish Act of Uniformity of 1560 was 95 per cent but not 100 per cent identical with the English act of 1559. It leaned far more towards accommodating conservative sentiment, permitting the continued use of Latin liturgies, many Catholic practices (reservation of consecrated hosts, requiem eucharists) and rubrics which in effect underwrote the paraphernalia of

---

[11] Kirk, '"Polities of the Best Reformed Churches"', esp. 24–6, 28, 32–5.

[12] D. Calderwood, *The True History of the Church of Scotland* (1678 edn), 41; Mullan, *Episcopacy in Scotland*, 18–19, 33, 36–7, 42–4.

[13] Calderwood, *History*, 265.

[14] A. Williamson, *Scottish National Consciousness in the Age of James VI* (Edinburgh, 1979), esp. 10–12, 42–3.

medieval Catholicism.[15] Yet the Irish *via media* did not wean the people from Catholic recusancy; it nurtured traditional practice until the missionary priests could lead them into recusancy. The Irish church, denied both adequate endowment and at best self-interested colonial elite protection, was in even less good shape than those of England and Scotland to undertake the work of evangelism.[16]

There is no evidence that I have been able to discover that the archbishops of Canterbury in the period before 1603 took any interest in the Irish church. Certainly the surviving correspondence of Parker, Grindal or Whitgift contains little reference to, or concern with, the Irish church. In the mid-1590s, Richard Bancroft intervened to ensure that the Dublin properties earmarked as an endowment for Trinity College, Dublin, were not siphoned off by the lord deputy. But Bancroft was almost certainly acting out of concerns developed as a longstanding prebendary of St Patrick's Cathedral, and even he was not to play an active part in Irish affairs once he was translated to Canterbury.[17] The creation of Trinity College, however, draws attention to another major problem of the Church of Ireland. An effective indigenous clergy was lacking, and yet conditions in Ireland (materially and spiritually) were so unpromising that the idea of migration to positions within the church there can only have appealed to those Englishmen with a thirst to spread the gospel that was out of the ordinary, or with a determination to escape English episcopal surveillance. And there were too few such men in the sixteenth century to garrison more than the cathedral churches. The sparse number of English and university-trained ministers, once in Ireland, thus found themselves caught up in increasingly bitter confessional strife, as an embattled and endangered minority, and as serving embattled and ruthless settler communities. It is no surprise to find such men proving receptive to those Calvinistic ideas forged and fined in the furnaces of the French and Dutch religious wars. The ready acceptance of the 1604 Prayer Book, Archbishop Daniel's 1609 Gaelic translation of that Prayer Book (with its inclusion of changes of the very

[15] On this, see the very important article by H. A. Jefferies, 'The Irish Parliament of 1560: The Anglican Reforms Authorized', *Irish Historical Studies*, 26 (1988).
[16] S. Ellis, *Tudor Ireland* (Harlow, 1985), esp. ch. 7; N. Canny, *From Reformation to Restoration* (Dublin, 1988), chs. 3–4; A. Ford, 'The Protestant Reformation', in *Natives and Newcomers*, ed. C. Brady and R. Gillespie (Dublin, 1986), 50–74; B. Bradshaw, 'Sword, Word and Strategy in the Reformation of Ireland', *HJ*, 21 (1978); N. Canny, 'Why the Reformation in Ireland Failed: *Une Question mal Posée*', *JEH*, 30 (1979); C. Bottigheimer, 'Why the Reformation in Ireland Failed: *Une Question Bien Posée*', *JEH*, 36 (1985). Jefferies, 'The Irish Parliament of 1560'; S. Ellis, 'Economic Problems of the Church: Why the Reformation Failed in Ireland', *JEH*, 41 (1990).
[17] *DNB*, Richard Bancroft.

type the Puritans sought in England – the removal of most Holy Days, the substitution of the word 'minister' for the word 'priest', etc.) and above all the strongly Bezan Irish Articles of 1615 are all testimony to the Irish Protestant community's experience over the previous half-century.

Yet those very changes show that community's readiness to learn from and be subordinated to the English Church. Thus the 1604 changes arising from the English Convocations were accepted as binding in Ireland, without reference to an Irish Parliament or Convocation although they constituted fundamental changes to the *Irish* Act of Uniformity of 1560. Furthermore, the Irish Articles of 1615 were closely modelled on the Lambeth Articles of 1595.[18] What seems clear is that while the strong colonial lobby sought to maintain the legislative supremacy of a separate Irish parliament and a degree of autonomy for the Irish privy council, law courts and a respect for the positive laws of the kingdom of Ireland, there was less likelihood of resistance to the *principle* of Canterburian intervention in the Irish church.

IV

James VI's accession to the thrones of England and Ireland had far more implications for the Church of Scotland than for the Church of Ireland. His ambitions for a Union of kingdoms as well as of Crowns was already known in Scotland. But this did *not* mean that he looked for an early or even an ultimate fusion or institutional union of the two churches. It is striking, for example, that James, in a private communication urging on Cecil in the work of the Union Commission of 1604, expressed the hope that 'this errand shall never be left off till it be fully accomplished, I mean specially by the uniting of both laws and parliaments of both the nations'. The omission of 'churches' is significant.[19] James' assurances to the General Assembly in 1604 that Union of the churches was not on the agenda seems to have been genuine.[20] The rapid movement to restore diocesan episcopacy in Scotland over the next decade can be placed in other contexts.

First, then, Presbyterianism had become associated in James' mind with the political creed of Buchanan and the Melvilles. Sovereign power was as incompatible with their church and state dualism as with the

---

[18] A. Ford, *The Protestant Reformation in Ireland, 1590–1641* (Frankfurt, 1985); J. R. Garstin, *The Book of Common Prayer in Ireland* (Dublin, 1871), 83–100.
[19] HMC, *Calendar of Salisbury at Hatfield MSS*, xvi, 336.
[20] See below, p. 218.

parallel church and state dualism of the Romanists.[21] Furthermore, the structures of church government under the Golden Acts rendered the king impotent to control the most effective institutions of any form outside Edinburgh. Episcopal government would give him eyes, ears and a voice in the regions of Scotland that the privatised civil jurisdictions did not give him. In any case the polity of the Scottish church was in a muddle. Whatever the Melvillians might want to believe, in the 1590s there was still one living pre-Reformation bishop drawing upon the revenues of his see, one Marian Catholic appointee and six tulchan bishops appointed under the Leith formula of 1572, some of them active.[22] James had already moved to regularise the position of this group, and had paid particular attention to the restoration of the clerical estate to the Scottish parliament as a prelude to strengthening royal control of the lords of the Articles.[23] He never attempted, and clearly did not seek, to give his new bishops an autocratic power over their dioceses.[24] They were to be permanent moderators of diocesan synods and presbyteries, and were to ordain ministers in a ceremony in which they and presbyters jointly laid hands on those to be ordained. Ordination into the diaconate was not to precede ordination into the priesthood.[24] James wished to place bishops between himself and the layers of government built up within the Church of Scotland since 1560; and the primary jurisdiction of Kirk Session and the role of the presbytery was not challenged.[26] The Scottish church would retain its distinctiveness. Its conformity with England lay in the reassertion of royal supremacy within the Scottish church, not in its anglicisation or in any strict uniformity of polity.[27]

---

[21] Neatly summarised in 'The Heads and Conclusions of the Church' presented to parliament in 1578, printed in J. Spottiswoode, *History of the Church of Scotland* (3 vols., Edinburgh, 1850), III, 289–90.

[22] G. I. R. McMahon, 'The Scottish Episcopate, 1600–1638' (University of Birmingham PhD thesis, 1972), ch. 1. The last of the superintendents appointed in the 1560s had died in 1592.

[23] See the arguments advanced by James in his address to the General Assembly in 1596, Spottiswoode, *History*, 438-42.

[24] For the continuing differences, see Spottiswoode, *History*, 512-15.

[25] *Miscellany of the Wodrow Society*, I, 591–615; P. Heylyn, *Cyprianus Anglicanus* (1668), 374–5. James' primitive episcopate in Scotland bears striking (and unnoticed) similarities to James Ussher's 'reduced episcopacy' as laid out in his proposals from 1641 on.

[26] The best accounts are in Mullan, *Episcopacy in Scotland*, 106–11; McMahon, 'Scottish Episcopate', ch. 2; M. Lee, *Government by Pen* (Urbana, 1980), 170–89; I. A. Dunlop, 'The Policy of the Scottish Church, 1600–1637', *Scottish Church History Society Records*, 12 (1958), 161–84.

[27] In terms of polity, the greatest innovation resonant of anglicisation was the introduction of the two Courts (soon united) of High Commission in 1610. But even they were reshaped and quite distinct in function and performance from their English

Secondly, as James made clear in his speech to the English parliament in 1604, the Union of the Crowns was but a prelude to the unions of Christian princes and of Christendom itself which the enhanced standing of Great Britain could promote. Brown Patterson and Hugh Trevor-Roper have both explored James' ecumenism, his attempt to bring together liberal and open-minded leaders of Roman and reformed (and Orthodox) churches into a greater mutual respect and recognition. It was central to James' purpose to distinguish the core of teaching and witness that bound Christians together and which was central to all major Christian churches. These were to be distinguished from the particular forms and practices allowed in particular national churches. If James wanted to encourage a greater mutual understanding and respect between the Christian churches throughout Europe, it would actually have been counter-productive for him to fuse the churches of Britain into one church with uniformity of government, confession of faith and liturgy, let alone for him to subordinate the kirk to the jurisdiction of the Church of England.[28]

Thirdly, what James was striving for in the early seventeenth century is perhaps best described as the 'congruity' of the churches.[29] If he admired the reverence and richness of developed Anglican liturgy, he admired (as much as Elizabeth had disparaged) preaching and he sought to make good sermonising as ubiquitous in England as he had left it in Scotland. The tenor of his criticisms of the Church of England as reflected in the undertakings he demanded for reform at the end of the Hampton Court Conference reflect precisely the criticisms of English parish discipline and evangelism which were commonly held in Scotland.[30] Conversely, of course, the Conference saw a decisive rejection of those demands for reform of the polity of the English church which would bring it into conformity with that of Scotland. If the English church had to become more evangelical, the Scottish church had to accept a form of government that was properly apostolic. He sought to provide for each national church all those marks of a true

namesakes. See G. I. R. McMahon, 'The Scottish Courts of High Commission, 1610–38', *Scottish Church History Society Records*, 15 (1966), 195–209.

[28] W. B. Patterson, 'James I's Call for an Ecumenical Council', *Studies in Church History*, 7 (1970); H. R. Trevor-Roper, 'The Church of England and the Greek Church in the Time of Charles I', *Studies in Church History*, 15 (1978).

[29] J. S. Morrill, *The Scottish National Covenant in its British Context* (Edinburgh, 1991), 8–11.

[30] G. Prothero, *Statutes and Constitutional Documents Illustrative of the Reigns of Elizabeth and James I* (4th edn, Oxford, 1913), 416–17. See the highly instructive report written by Patrick Galloway, an observer for the presbytery of Edinburgh, on the conclusions of the Hampton Court Conference, Calderwood, *History*, 474–7.

church which the leaders of each saw to be necessary. The aim therefore was not to subordinate the Church of Scotland to the Church of England, still less to give York or Canterbury jurisdiction over Scotland. James' policies aimed to raise each church in the estimation of the other. Thus many Scots ministers were brought south to strengthen the preaching rosters of the cathedrals, whereas no Englishmen were intruded into the Church of Scotland;[31] and three Scots bishops were brought south to be consecrated by English bishops. This ceremony of consecration perfectly illustrates that it was the restoration of diocesan episcopacy and of an apostolic succession that mattered to James, not the introduction of a carbon copy of English episcopacy. James called three Scottish bishops to London. It is noteworthy that he did not summon the primate, George Gladstanes. He told them that

he had to his great charge recovered the Bishopricks forth of the hands of those that possessed them and bestoed the same upon such as he hoped should prove worthy of their places; but since he could not make them bishops, or could they assume that honour to themselves, and that in Scotland there was not a sufficient number to enter charge by consecration,[32] he had called them to England, that being consecrated themselves they might at their return give ordination to those at home.[33]

Spottiswoode expressed his anxiety that 'the Church of Scotland, because of old usurpations, might take this for a sort of subjection to the church of England'. James replied that 'he had provided sufficiently against that, for neither should the archbishop of Canterbury nor York, who were the only pretenders, have hand in the business, but consecration should be used by the bishops of London, Ely, and Bathe'.[34] The

[31] The details of numbers and purposes are contained in a paper by Mr Robin Angus, delivered to Sir Geoffrey Elton's seminar in 1977 but sadly never published. It should be stressed that the Scots were placed in English deaneries and prebends' stalls, not into bishoprics. Although no Englishmen were established in positions of influence, two groups of English preachers were sent on preaching circuits in Scotland at particular times to exhort the Scots to look more sympathetically at episcopacy. These preaching teams did not contain any English bishops (although they contained men later promoted to English sees). See Mullan, *Episcopacy in Scotland*, 100–1; Calderwood, *History*, 588–9.
[32] In Roman and Anglican eyes, the consecration needed to be performed by three bishops who had themselves been consecrated into the apostolic order.
[33] Spottiswoode, *History*, III, 209.
[34] In fact Bath and Wells (James Montague) could not be present. His place was taken by the bishops of Worcester and Rochester (J. Collier, *Ecclesiastical History of Great Britain* (2 vols., London, 1708–14), II, 702 (citing Abbot's register as bishop of London); T. Hannan, 'The Scottish Consecrations in London in 1611', *Church Quarterly Review*, 71 (1911), 387–413.

consecration did not subordinate the Church of Scotland: it raised its standing in the eyes of its brethren in England.[35]

Not that this allayed the gloomier fears of those Scots who thought that with the Negative Confession of 1581 and the Golden Acts of 1592 the Scottish church had attained a purity of form to match the purity of its teachings. The hypersensitivity of such men to the very fact of James being contaminated by contact with English bishops can be seen in James Melville's response to the reading of the account the presbytery of Edinburgh received of the Hampton Court Conference: 'They would watch and take heed, that no peril, nor contagion come from our neighbour kirk, and give warning, in case there be occasion, to the Presbyteries throughout the Realme, and namely, that they take heed at this Parliament, which is indicted by proclamation, and intended for Union of the two realmes.'[36]

The Synod of Fife called for a General Assembly to be held before the parliament at which it was known James would establish a commission to begin the process of Union of the realms: 'that the realms could not be united, without the Union and Conformitie of the Kirks government and worship; and how could the kirks be united, unless the one gave place to the other'[37] James replied that Union of the churches was not on the agenda and there seems no reason to doubt his word.

Thus there was no formal attempt to create an outward conformity of polity or public witness between the two churches, still less to reassert the ancient claims of the primate of England to a superiority of jurisdiction over the Church of Scotland (a claim last publicly aired in the 1540s).[38] Yet I would not want to overstate this case. For in practice he did become increasingly sloppy about protecting the autonomy and equality of the two churches; nor did it prevent him becoming increasingly drawn to the formalism of Anglican worship, which in turn gave him an itch to modify Scottish practice.

First, James permitted English bishops to become involved in the disciplining of dissident Scottish ministers in 1606–7. This followed the determination of the radicals to hold a token session of the General

[35] Mullen, *Episcopacy in Scotland*, 113; McMahon, 'Scottish Episcopacy', 33–4.
[36] Calderwood, *History*, 478.
[37] *Ibid.*, 479. See also the interesting briefing document drawn up by the Synod of Fife for the commissioners of the Assembly who attended the parliament of 1604, which concluded that 'the essential grounds of the discipline, and Government of the Church and Kingdom of Scotland, is not a thing indifferent, or unalterable, but a substantial part of the Gospel' (*ibid.*, 480–1).
[38] *An Epitome of the Title that the Kynges Maiestie of England Hath to the Sovereigntie of Scotland...* (1548); cf. J. Henrysoun, *An Exhortation to the Scottes to Conform Themselves* (1547).

Assembly at Aberdeen that James had stood down. Eight ministers were summoned to London where they were harangued by four English bishops on the necessity of episcopacy and of obedience to the king. They were quartered on the bishops (where they proved unwelcome guests: as Bancroft told James Melville: 'the bishops would have little pleasure of you . . . for our custome is, after our serious matters, to refresh ourselves an hour or two with cards, or other games after our meale: but ye are more precise').[39] Although James' formal interviews with the ministers about their opposition to him were conducted before the Scottish members of the English Council, one of the sessions was held (against Andrew Melville's protest) in a meeting of the Council attended by some English lords, while 'thrie or four Bisschoppis and Deanes standing in diverse duris behind the tapestries, quho, comeing in now and then, discoverit thame selffes'.[40] Although, formally, judgement was reached by the Scots councillors, procedures had got badly muddled.[41]

Secondly, James largely ignored the Scottish church in 1617 when he was invited to send a delegation to the Synod of Dort. He did send Walter Balcanquhal (a Scot long resident in England) as an afterthought, and the delegates were listed in the Dort canons as 'ex Magna Britannia' (though in their proposals on the fifth head of doctrine they were listed as from 'theologi ecclesiae anglicanae'). An opportunity had been missed.[42]

Thirdly, and most sinister, there was the rash act of Abbott in releasing the marquis of Huntly from an excommunication imposed by his Kirk Session and confirmed at the Scottish High Commission. James was aware of what he was doing. The grounds for the release were that Huntly had shown contrition for his past errors, and had expressed a desire to receive communion from the archbishop of Canterbury. Both James and Abbott stressed that it would have shown less respect for the Scottish church to have disregarded the excommunication north of the Border. They claimed that 'this bruised reed should not be broken, but that so great a personage (whose example may doe much good) should be cherished and comforted in his coming forward to God'. It was, they said, inexpedient to delay the healing process that the reception of holy communion would involve by shipping him back

[39] Calderwood, *History*. 564.
[40] *The Autobiography and Diary of James Melville*, ed. R. Pitcairn (Wodrow Soc., Edinburgh, 1842), 658-9.
[41] The full story can be reconstructed from *ibid.*, 643-5, 652-63, 670-9, 694-701, 748-9. Calderwood, *History*, 537-49, 563-5 (largely a digest of Melville's account).
[42] I am grateful to Peter White for his discussion of this point.

to Scotland. The letters were emollient, but the precedent had been set.[43]

Cumulatively these things constitute a very considerable English subverting of the authority and autonomy of the kirk. Indeed I want to suggest that they may well constitute a greater subversion of that independence of jurisdiction than took place under Charles I.

The final point about Jacobean plans for the Scottish church has to be his aborted schemes for liturgical reform. Here too the evidence is not straightforward. Between 1616 and 1621 he pressed two parallel sets of changes on the Scottish church. One was a new service book; the other was a specific set of 'observances and practices which had been disused since the Reformation'.[44]

James clearly came to like the order and formality of English worship, and to deplore the lack of a single, enforceable liturgy in Scotland. While the Book of Common Order formed the basis of the worship in most kirks, its use was not prescribed, and it was in any case as much a manual for the construction of free liturgies as a full service book. There is little reason to doubt James' sincerity in telling Spottiswoode in 1615 that 'there is lacking in our church a form of divine worship; and whiles every minister is left to the framing of publick prayer by himself, both the people are neglected and their prayers prove often impertinent'. As Donaldson says, his letter 'showed that what he had in mind was the improvement of the existing order'.[45] The revised liturgies drawn up in the following years were all based on existing Scottish forms, not English ones. This is important in evaluating the purpose of the Five Articles of Perth which enjoined kneeling to receive communion, confirmation by the bishop, private baptism and communion under certain circumstances, and the observance of Holy Days. These clearly reflect things that James had come to like about English worship, and, as Conrad Russell recently remarked, the aim seems to have been to enforce subscription rather than to enforce the ceremonies because James was less concerned to make the Scots kneel to receive communion than to prevent the Scots complaining when the English knelt to do so.[46] However, James' lack of interest in imposing the Book of Common Prayer limits the extent to which the Articles represent a residual ecclesiastical unionism. His stated concern – prescribed order in

---

[43] Spottiswoode, *History*, 525–7.
[44] For the probably exaggerated view, see R. G. Usher, *The Reconstruction of the English Church* (2 vols., 1910), II, 154–74; McMahon, 'Scottish Episcopate', 26–35; for a cooler assessment, Mullan, *Episcopacy in Scotland*, 95–7.
[45] G. Donaldson, *The Making of the Scottish Prayer Book of 1637* (Edinburgh, 1954), 31–2.
[46] Conrad Russell, *The Causes of the English Civil War* (Oxford, 1990), 49.

worship – fits better under the heading of congruence. Another mark of a true church could be taken to be due order in worship, for the lack of which the Church of Scotland lost respect in the eyes of her brethren in England.

There was a further aspect of James' 1616–17 reforms, however. The parliament of 1616 was induced to declare that: 'whatsoever his Majesty should determine in externall government of the Church, with the advice of the archbishops, bishops, and a competent number of the Ministry, should have the strength of a law'.[47]

James was attempting to do what Charles attempted to do in 1637: to arrogate to himself and a clique of bishops the power to change the liturgy of the church. But faced by a storm of criticism, James backed off. First he fell back on pushing his reforms through the Assembly and (in the case of the Five Articles) through parliament. Then, when these had been approved (albeit only by intensive gerrymandering), he did not seek to enforce the changes. They could lie on the statute book until a more opportune time. Thus Charles was not to move far from his father's intentions, nor from his preferred means. But whereas James backed off in the face of a fiercer resistance than he had anticipated, Charles was to blunder on to catastrophe.

The overall verdict on James must be that he was preoccupied less with the Union of the Churches than with two other things: one was the reassertion of his authority as king of Scotland within the Scottish church and the other was to begin the process of fostering a 'union of hearts and minds' within the churchmen of both kingdoms in order to generate greater mutual respect and co-operation.

V

The central paradox of the Jacobean Church of Ireland was that it was peopled by the English but developed along rather different lines from the Church of England. Alan Ford has revealed the 'second reformation' that occurred in Ireland from the 1590s to the 1630s. The number of preaching ministers rapidly increased and they were men of a different stamp from the traditionally minded, native reading ministers who had been thinly scattered across Elizabethan Ireland. As Ford puts it, 'the amorphous church of the 1590s was succeeded by [a] tightly-knit, firmly calvinist institution . . . with its own confession and distinct ideological outlook'.[48] This further reformation was wrought principally under the

[47] Spottiswoode, *History*, 531.
[48] Ford, *Protestant Reformation*, 287.

supervision of English-born bishops and tutors at Trinity College Dublin; but it was wrought by men whose experience in Ireland caused them to emphasise and to develop particular aspects of their Calvinist background. The resulting ideology was deeply pessimistic, growing out of a set of strongly millenarian and providentialist concerns, an ideology which came to justify a withdrawal from the evangelisation of the native population (whose hearts God had hardened) and a commitment to serve and to strengthen the faith of the embattled settlers; to create, in a religious sense, garrisons of good order in a world where Antichrist was both immanent and imminent.[49]

The Church of Ireland by the 1620s looked to England for its manpower, and many of its leaders looked to friends in England for support, encouragement, a shoulder to cry on. But it had developed its own sense of identity. It drew in English resources, but it was evolving away from the *ecclesia anglicana*. And there is no evidence to any attempt by James or his archbishops to halt this drift. One occasionally encounters the archbishop of Canterbury being consulted on Irish affairs (as in 1618 when James I told the lord deputy that he had referred a complaint from the bishop of Down on the decayed state of his diocese to the archbishops of Canterbury and Armagh for a report.).[50] On two reported occasions, Lord Deputy Chichester sought the help of Bancroft in the appointment of a bishop; in one case the nominee was appointed, in the other not.[51] But, as far as I can determine from readily available evidence, English bishops were only involved in Irish affairs when their assistance was desired by the authorities in Ireland; and that was not very common.

Nothing in James' reign prepared the Irish Protestant establishment for the onslaught on their church to be mounted by William Laud.

VI

A number of historians have suggested that the aim of Charles I and Laud was to create a narrow conformity and uniformity of the churches in Charles' three kingdoms. In 1640 the Scots, in presenting articles

---

[49] *Ibid.*, 288–92 and *passim*; Ford, 'The Protestant Reformation', 60–74; *A New History of Ireland*, III: *Early Modern Ireland, 1534–1691*, ed. T. W. Moody, F. X. Martin and F. J. Byrne (Oxford, 1976), 227.

[50] *CSPI 1615–25*, 129. For another example, see a report from the bishop of Meath 'in the behalf of the prelacy and clergy of Ireland after consultation with the archbishop of Canterbury and others of the Privy Council', *ibid.*, 375.

[51] *Ibid.*, *1606–8*, 77 (successful plea for the dean of Cashel to be promoted to the see of Down and Connor); *ibid.*, *1608–10*, 390 (unsuccessful plea on behalf of his personal chaplain – a 'Mr Barlowe' – for the see of Ossory).

against Laud to the Long Parliament, had no doubts that he had sought to exercise direct jurisdiction over the Scottish church, for the purpose of introducing into it the very innovations and corruptions he was also introducing into the *ecclesia anglicana*.[52] We shall see that there is plentiful evidence of Laud's direct and flagrant interference into the affairs of the Irish church. But I wish to suggest that we must not over-simplify a complex pattern of ecclesiastical thought and action.

Charles I had a style of government in each kingdom which was similar. It was naturally authoritarian in that it sought out and was prepared to use royal discretionary power not just *in extremis* but whenever he could not get his own way by due process. If he was more naturally authoritarian in Scotland and Ireland than in England it was largely because he lacked the imagination to realise just how impossible were the demands he was making on his ministers and just how much he was alienating opinion in those kingdoms.

But a common *style of government* does not mean that he had common policies in each kingdom. Only in one (or perhaps two)[53] areas can a single, clear policy be seen: his determination to restore much of the wealth and most of the jurisdiction lost by the clerical estate at the Reformation. In England, Scotland and Ireland, Charles sought to re-endow the churches,[54] and put an end to the encroachments of the secular courts into the affairs of the churches. Here Laud was not simply his ally as his instructor. Upon his appointment to Canterbury, Laud found much dilapidation:

You do well [he told Wentworth] to give me good hopes of my new Canterbury wife, but . . . she is a very shrew . . . and which is worse hath been in some things ill dealt withal, so that (as it often falls out with them that marry widows) her worldly estate is nothing near so good as was commonly voiced before I married her. But howsoever, tis now for better for worse.[55]

He set to work to recover his 'wife's worldly estate', waging a steady and relentless war against those in England who had wriggled out of their obligation to pay tithes, or had misappropriated impropriations, and against the 'church cormorants' amongst the judges and lawyers who had

[52] William Laud, *The Works of William Laud*, ed. W. Scott and J. Bliss (7 vols., Oxford, 1847–60), III, 298–378.
[53] A second possible common policy is the revival of feudal claims to forests and to fiscal exactions from those who had 'misappropriated' them.
[54] James had begun, in a modest way, to reverse the trend in Ireland, or at least in Ulster; see the *Valor Beneficiorum in Hibernia* (Dublin, 1741). I am grateful to Steven Ellis for drawing my attention to this document and to written discussion of this point.
[55] Laud, *Works*, VII, 54.

invaded and usurped the church's jurisdiction.[56] And, as he put it to John Bramhall, who had complained of the alienations of church lands in Ulster, 'England hath been badd enough for that, and therfore I may easily conceave Ireland hath been much worse.'[57] Furthermore, the recovery of teinds and the securing of the interests of the church (as well as of the Crown) is what lay behind the Act of Revocation in Scotland (a veritable policy of surrender and regrant).

Ian Atherton has recently suggested that the 1st Viscount Scudamore, a close friend to Laud, and a man much trusted by the king, spent so much on the restoration of churches and support for poor clergy because of his fear that his estates, almost all of them dissolved monastic lands, brought his family under a shadow of sacrilege. It is just possible that Charles shared Scudamore's deep fear, and that his policy was designed to alleviate a deep anxiety about the extent to which the Crown was answerable to God for its plunder of the church over the previous century. Certainly Laud used the term 'sacrilege' to describe the lay appropriation of the wealth of the church in all three kingdoms.[58]

There are a number of occasions when Laud appears to be thinking in terms of a policy for all three kingdoms. He told Ussher that bishops must be aged forty or more (and reiterated this point to Wentworth);[59] later he made it clear to Wentworth that the king would only appoint as bishops those whom he had got to know as his chaplains-in-ordinary, a policy which he implies will extend to all three kingdoms;[60] and that in each kingdom a rule is to be introduced that no bishop is to hold a deanery *in commendam*.[61] As we will see, the Irish bishops were required to don 'bishop's attire' for the sake of conformity with 'the whole Catholic Church of Christ'.[62] In ordering Ussher to see to it, Laud made clear that the king was imposing that which had not been the custom in Ireland since the Reformation.[63] In advising William Bedell how to deal with the abuses of power practised by the civil lawyers who presided over the church courts, Laud spoke of how 'the canon law hath been blasted

[56] C. Hill, *Economic Problems of the Church* (Oxford, 1960), *passim*. For Laud and the common lawyers, see, e.g., Laud, *Works*, VI, 310–12, 330–4; for English impropriations, see, e.g., his comment to Wentworth in March 1635 that now Lord Treasurer Portland was dead 'the impropriations will come no more into Lady Mora's hands' (Laud, *Works*, VII, 114).

[57] Huntington Library (San Marino, California), Hastings MS HA 15172, no. VI, 4 March 1634/5.

[58] I. Atherton, 'Viscount Scudamore's Laudianism', *HJ*, 34 (1991), 567–96. For Laud's use of the term sacrilege in this sense, see, e.g., Laud, *Works*, VII, 67.

[59] Laud, *Works*, VI, 258.

[60] *Ibid.*, VII, 102.

[61] *Ibid.*, VI, 532.

[62] Laud, *Works*, VII, 291–3.   [63] *Ibid.*, VI, 291–3.

in these kingdoms'; and how we live in times in which the church is over-
grown, not only with weeds within it, but with trees and bushes about it,
which, though they were set at first for a fence, yet now they are grown
up they drop sourly upon whatever is good in it.[64]

There was thus a British policy. But I am not so convinced that this
can be extended to deal with other matters of government and religious
practice or even be seen as stages towards an imposed uniformity. For
example, James and Abbott had initiated a tentative policy of involving
Irish and Scottish bishops in the consecration of English bishops.
Thomas Moreton was consecrated in 1616 by three English bishops, by
the archbishop of Armagh and by the bishop of Caithness; and
Theophilus Field was consecrated in 1619 by three English bishops, a
Welsh bishop and by the bishop of Derry. The practice lingered on into
the first two years of Charles' reign and then abruptly halted, just as
Laud's influence became dominant over Abbott's.[65]

Furthermore, if Charles did have it a British policy, it is not one of
straightforward anglicisation. Once more, I will suggest, the notion
of *congruity* seems a better term for his policy than the enforcement of
uniformity between the churches. In my view, Laud most nearly captured
the essence of his vision for the churches of Britain when he told Ussher
that the wearing by the Irish bishops of 'rochets and their bishop's attire'
was to be strictly enjoined, and that Ussher was

to certify the Kind of their obedience and conformity. And while I use the word
conformity, I pray your Grace to understand, that his Majesty's meaning is not
conformity to or with the Church of England, but with the whole Catholic
Church of Christ, which ever since her times of peace and settlement hath
distinguished the habit of the bishop from an inferior priest.[66]

Now it may be that for Laud 'conformity . . . with the whole Church of
Christ' is a hyperbole or rhetorical flourish and what Laud meant was
that this was not *merely* or *capriciously* the practice of the Church of
England. What the church lacked was what the Church of England had
determined to be the practice of the whole church.[67] But I would like

[64] *Ibid.*, VI, 285.
[65] W. Stubbs, *Registrum Sacrum Anglicanum* (Oxford, 1858), 115–17. The consecrations in
question all took place between July 1616 and December 1627. Perhaps Abbott was the
force behind them. Another interesting feature was the involvement of Marc Antonio
de Dominis (Roman Catholic bishop of Spalato before his reception into the Church of
England) in the consecrations of Felton and Montaigne in 1616 – more evidence of
James' universalism?
[66] Laud, *Works*, VII, 291–3 (letter dated 5 Nov. 1634).
[67] This is the interpretation of the letter offered to me by Derek Hirst and Anthony
Milton, and I am loathe to go beyond their interpretation. What I now add is more than
usually speculative and to be treated cautiously (perhaps sceptically!)

to suggest it may mean a bit more than this. The wearing of rochets was not the invariable practice of the English bishops, after all. And Laud certainly did not believe that that church yet conformed to what he believed to be the practice of the primitive church in many particulars.[68] I suspect that what Laud is implying here is that while James had sought out the *highest common factor* of the British churches, the core of essentials which in every church needed to underlie and underpin a host of non-essential detail particular to each church, Laud himself was seeking out a *lowest common multiple*, that ideal to which all churches must aspire. The Church of England came closest to that ideal, but it too had some way to go; the Churches of Scotland and Ireland had to abandon much false practice even before they began to join the English church in the final strivings after perfection.

However this passage is best interpreted, it is important to stress that when it came to Canterburian interference in the affairs of Ireland and Scotland, a sharp distinction quickly becomes apparent between Anglo-Irish and Anglo-Scottish affairs.

VII

Laud interfered shamelessly in the affairs of the Irish church. This was not just a question of fraternal advice. He told Ussher to send him details of the valuations of church lands in Ireland 'that I may be the better able to serve that church'.[69] (Ussher, in congratulating Laud on his translation to Canterbury, stressed that he would not be able 'to put a happy end to that great work . . . of settling the reversion of the impropriations of this kingdom [= Ireland] upon the several incumbents'.)[70] He took a strong personal interest in every aspect of the government, discipline and practice of the Irish church. The reports he received (especially his monthly jeremiads from Bishop Bramhall of Derry) left him in no doubt that there was much to do. Thus Bramhall knew Laud would share his outrage of the condition in which he found the diocese of Down in 1643:

almost the whole resident clergy absolute irregulars, the very ebullition of Scotland, but conformists very rare, and those rather in judgment than practice . . . It would trouble a man to find twelve Common Prayer Books in all their

---

68 For some circumstantial evidence in support of this, see below, p. 231. See also Cosin's annotations on the imperfections of the Prayer Book, and his pleas during the Interregnum that the opportunity be taken to remove imperfections from the Book. I am grateful to Anthony Milton for making this point forcefully to me.

69 Laud, *Works*, VI, 261.

70 C. R. Elrington and J. R. Todd, *The Wole Works of James Ussher* (17 vols., Dublin, 1847–64), XV, 572.

churches, and those only not cast behind the altars because they have none, but in place of it a table ten yards long, where they sit and receive the sacrament together like good fellows.[71]

Laud did not become interested in the affairs of the Church of Ireland as an extension of his responsibilities as archbishop of Canterbury. His concern with them – and interference with them – goes back at least to his appointment to the see of London. As early as 1629, Laud could direct Ussher to let him have copies of the names of all the bishops and deans in Ireland 'that I may be the better able to serve that church'.[72] In 1629, the Fellows of Trinity College could write asking him 'to use your favour with the King to preserve the ancient [sic] liberties of our society' and continue: 'we thank *you* for appointing our provost to the Bishopric of Kilmore'.[73] By 1633 he was openly boasting of his role in the nomination of bishops.[74] In 1630, the bishop of Kilfenora thanked God 'for having stirred you up like another Nehemiah to defend the Church, [for] there is no want of Sanballat to stop the good work'.[75] More striking still is the testimony of Archbishop Ussher in 1631 (before the two men had their major falling out). He wrote: 'You strike such a terror into the hearts of those who wish to despoil the Church, that if I merely mention your name at the [Irish] Council Table, it is like the Gorgon's head to some of them.'[76]

Laud never claimed any formal authority over the Irish church. Whatever Ussher's fears in his correspondence with Spelman about the British patriarchy,[77] Laud never advanced that claim, publicly or privately. Nor did Laud ever act in his capacity as a member of the Irish committee of the privy council at Whitehall to give orders to the Irish Church.[78]

His interest, then, was personal rather than institutional. When he gave orders and expected them to be obeyed, he was acting *ultra vires*, although presumably with the knowledge and assent of the king. What made his involvement with the Irish church immeasurably easier was, however, his close alliance with Lord Deputy Wentworth. In part this

---

[71] E. P. Shirley, *Papers Relating to the Church of Ireland, 1631–1639* (1874), 71–2, 41.

[72] Laud, *Works*, VI, 262.

[73] *CSPI 1625–33*, 452–3.

[74] Laud, *Works*, VI, 52.

[75] *CSPI 1625–33*, 568. Nehemiah was chosen to reconstruct the walls of Jerusalem after the Babylonian Captivity. He also sought to put an end to the worldly and slack practices of the inhabitants, typified by Sanballat, who had appropriated whole areas of the Temple as storerooms for his goods.

[76] *Ibid.*, 622.

[77] See above, p. 236.

[78] See, for example, Laud, *Works*, VII, 66.

in turn rested on Laud's relationship with John Bramhall, who accompanied Wentworth from Yorkshire to Ireland as his chaplain, and who was soon promoted to the bishopric of Derry. Bramhall was to be Laud's eyes and ears in Ireland henceforth, and an important voice too on occasion.[79] But Wentworth had exacted a promise from Charles that he would have a free hand in Ireland and that he would not, as his predecessors had, find himself undermined by the countermanding of his decisions in Whitehall. Laud's influence therefore rested ultimately on his personal rapport with the Lord Deputy. The astonishing flow of correspondence between the two men leaves us in no doubt as to the mutual respect and trust between these two workaholics. Laud was vital to Wentworth in guarding his back at court and warning him of the attempts at court to undermine his authority.[80]

Initially Laud sought to co-operate with the Irish primate, James Ussher. They were on opposite sides of the spectrum (or fence) theologically,[81] but can be found working together against some of the entrenched lay interest in the church and to persuade several energetic men to take up positions in the Irish church (including Vossius).[82] Laud gradually became more and more irritated with Ussher's failure to take firm action, his lack of administrative energy and his outright obstruction over the reform of the practice of the church.[83] By 1635 he could reprimand Ussher over vestments and other matters, but the primate's obstruction of the new canons clearly represented a major breach in their relations which was never to be healed.[84]

Laud thus had a narrow base and considerable ignorance of Irish affairs. He several times explained that he did not know the surname of

[79] This crucial relationship can be traced in *ibid.*, VI and VII, *passim*; *The Works of the Most Reverend John Bramhall*, ed. A.W.H. (5 vols., Oxford, 1842–5); and the series of 23 letters between them in the Huntington Library, Hastings MS HA 15172, nos. I–XXIII.

[80] Laud, *Works*, VI and VII, *passim*; *The Earl of Strafford's Letters and Despatches*, ed. W. Knowler (2 vols., 1799), I and II, *passim*.

[81] For the best recent analysis see the University of New South Wales PhD by Mandy Capern on Ussher (1991), completed after this essay. I am grateful to Mandy Capern for many illuminating discussions about Ussher. For a flavour, see the disparaging remarks about the Durham House Group in Alexander Cook's letter to Ussher of January 1626, Elrington and Todd, *Works of Ussher*, XV, 356.

[82] Laud, *Works*, VII, 114–19, 132, 139, 291–3.

[83] See his acidic and unfavourable comparisons of Abbott and Ussher (Laud, *Works*, VII, 139); and his comment to Wentworth that 'no man can be so easily found more unfit for government than *the Pri*[mate] [so that] you must think of some dry nurse . . . I would recommend you for that office L[ord] B[ishop] of Derrye' (*ibid.*, 387).

[84] E.g. Huntington Library, Hastings MS M553, fols. [16–18, 26–8]. Laud similarly was willing to work with Calvinist conformists like William Bedell and Henry Leslie, but fell out with them too in time (Laud, *Works*, VI, 260–2, 280–8; Huntington Library, Hastings MS HA 15172, nos. IX, 20 July 1635, and XII, 5 April 1637).

a bishop referred to by his see in a letter from Wentworth or Bramhall; he had to ask where certain places were; and admitted to ignorance of the nature of the Irish judicial establishment.[85] This did not stop him having strong views about the failings of the Irish church, nor about the appropriate remedies.

Wentworth was sent to Ireland first and foremost to make it no longer a drain on the English Exchequer. He had to balance the Irish budget which was a seventeenth-century equivalent of making rural bus routes pay for themselves. The more one puts up fares the more passengers one drives away. Wentworth's answer to this conundrum was to make the New English pay disproportionately, for they were in no position to rebel. In his correspondence with Laud no one is so obviously and gleefully in their sights and the butt of their rough humour as the earl of Cork.[86] The Old English and native Irish were not spared, and in the next phase those living in the south and west would have suffered further. Meanwhile they had the novel experience of seeing their recent oppressors oppressed and they found themselves (as Catholics) with greater freedom to organise and practice their religion than they had enjoyed in seventy years or could imagine themselves enjoying under any other English yoke. In the view of Laud and Wentworth, the Irish Protestant church was too weakened to undertake the work of evangelism. It was better not to attempt fruitless religious persecution until that church was recovered, properly endowed and resourced with an educated and effective clerical establishment backed by efficient ecclesiastical regiment. The reform programme of Laud and Wentworth was not primarily intended to bring the Irish church into conformity with England. It was to equip it for the deferred task of bringing the Irish nation to a saving knowledge of and obedience to the will of God. This strategy was sophisticated but flawed – flawed in that the period of grace granted to the Catholics while Protestantism regrouped could also be used by the Catholic hierarchy to evangelise the Catholic population and further secure their immunity to Protestantism.[87]

---

[85] Huntington Library, Hastings MS HA 15172, no. XII, 5 April 1637.

[86] E.g., Laud, *Works*, VI, 396–403; VII, 51–3, 57–9, 138–47. In part, Wentworth's co-operation with Laud over the humiliation of Cork with respect to his ecclesiastical policies was predicated upon Cork's humiliation of Wentworth's predecessors when they had failed in their bid to indict Cork of fraudulent dealings in his acquisition of secular property. See T. Ranger, 'The Career of Richard Boyle, Earl of Cork' (Oxford DPhil thesis, 1951). I am grateful to Ronald Asch for this point.

[87] There were, of course, more secular reasons for Wentworth's espousal of Laud's programme. For example, most of the Irish bishops were closely connected to colonial interests in Ireland, and had proved close allies of Cork on the Irish Council in the 1620s.

Laud set out that programme in a series of letters to Wentworth early in the latter's time as lord deputy. The most authoritative was despatched from Lambeth in April 1634.[88] Laud called for the 'reception and establishment' (by the Irish convocation but not the parliament) of the English Thirty Nine Articles and the English canons of 1604; for the establishment of an Irish High Commission suitable to local conditions; for the punishment of 'some great sacrileges' such as the Boyle family's sequestration of the lands of the bishopric of Lismore and the college at Youghal;[89] and the necessity of moving the family tomb of the earl of Corm from the east wall of Dublin Cathedral.[90]

Unusually for the seventeenth century, this was a reform programme that was realised by 1640: the canons and articles were introduced as was the Court of High Commission;[91] Laud had placed men who thought like him in many key dioceses and was able to bypass the primate;[92] a programme of sustained exhortation and intimidation had yielded spectacular results in the restoration of diocesan funds.[93] The earl of Cork's tomb *was* moved.[94] The church was refurbished, redecorated, cleaned and polished, ready to evangelise the Catholic communities; and then in 1640 the roof caved in.

Two particular points require emphasis. One is to ram home the degree to which Laud went beyond advising the Irish church and issued peremptory orders; and the second is that he was in no way obsessively concerned with conformity and uniformity with England. Laud did not just advise the Irish hierarchy: he commanded it. In 1635, Laud rewrote the draft canons submitted to him by Ussher. His determination to have the final say contrasts with his more discrete, advisory role in the making of the Scottish canons. In 1636, Laud directed Wentworth to investigate a report that Archbishop Hamilton of Cashel had instituted a Sunday fast throughout his province. Wentworth was to investigate, and if necessary to prosecute and admonish him: 'and this your Lordship may not fail to do'. The tone is worth noting.

---

88 Laud, *Works*, VII, 65–71. Cf. the earlier and less systematic letters of April 1633 (*ibid.*, VI, 310–12, 352–8).

89 The section on misappropriated church lands and tithes is by far the longest.

90 Cork's reputation as an avaricious plunderer of the church has been corrected by Nicholas Canny, *The Upstart Earl* (Cambridge, 1983), 9–18 and *passim*.

91 Huntington Library, Hastings MS HA 15172, nos. IV, 1 October 1634, and VI, 4 March 1634/5; Laud, *Works*, VI, 418; VII, 109, 132; Huntington Library, Hastings MS HA 15172, no. V, 16 June 1634/5; Laud, *Works*, VI, 396–403; VII, 97–110, 132.

92 B. Fitzpatrick, *Seventeenth-Century Ireland* (Dublin, 1988), 57–8.

93 Huntington Library, Hastings MS HA 15172, no. I, 16 August 1633; Shirley, *Papers*, 50–1, 52–5.

94 Huntington Library, Hastings MS HA 15172, no. II, 19 February 1633/4; Laud, *Works*, VI, 396–403; VII, 51–3, 57–9, 135.

Laud undoubtedly wished to remove from the Church of Ireland those things which were an affront to order and a challenge to the English church's beliefs and practices. He was not obsessed with a narrow uniformity. Thus he repeatedly commented on the need for a general and not a precise conformity of the English and Irish canons: 'I have pressed the English canons to be received *formaliter*, a little the softer to my Lord Primate [he told Wentworth], becaus you write that the addition of some fewe canons is very necessary for that kingdom[95] . . . tis better haveing them materially and in substance with peace, then formally with heart burning amongst yourselves.'[96] The Irish canons included a requirement for east-end railed altars and allowance of aural confession[97] that went beyond the English canons, though not beyond Laud's aspirations for England. On the other hand the canon that would have required all to bow at the name of Jesus was lost. It was a minor disappointment. But, never one to be magnanimous in victory, Laud was determined to have the last say: 'as for the name of Jesus, since they will have no joint in their knees to honour Him, they may get the gout in the knees not to serve themselves'.[98]

VIII

Laud's involvement with the Scottish church was far more circumspect than this continuous interference in the affairs of the Church of Ireland. By 1640, the Scots had no doubt of his intrusion into their affairs, but the extent to which he took the blame in 1637–8, at the time of the National Covenant, should not be exaggerated.

The Scottish church, unlike the Irish church, was not a rib out of the side of the English church. Nor did it have Englishmen amongst its bishops. Charles I did not attempt to change this. The Church of Scotland would continue to be in hands of Scotsmen. Although Laud was clearly consulted about appointments to Scottish sees,[99] his voice was less dominant than in appointments in the other national churches. Only one appointment (the English-educated and English-domiciled

---

[95] Huntington Library, Hastings MS HA 15172, nos. VI, 4 March 1634/5, and VII, 11 May 1635.

[96] *Ibid.*, fol. [17].

[97] Cf. the letter of James Croxton to Laud on 18 April 1638 in which he says that 'I have prepared the people in my charge here (at a thoroughfare town in Kilkenny) for the sacrament (they kneeling at the altar) by hearing their confessions. My action is opposed. I was censured in Convocation and look for your help and protection' (*CSPI 1633–47*, 186). For Bramhall's earlier commendation of Croxton to Laud for advancement, see *ibid.*, 88.

[98] Laud, *Works*, VII, 132.   [99] E.g. *ibid.*, VI, 434–5.

Wedderburn appointed to Dunblane in 1636) differed from the pattern of appointments made by James.[100]

Laud clearly involved himself more routinely with the affairs of the Scottish church than had his predecessors. Here his visit to Edinburgh for the king's Scottish coronation in 1633 was a turning-point.[101] Thereafter he kept up a regular correspondence not only with the primate but with those he found more of his own mind, especially Maxwell of Ross.[102] His concerns were not with further changes in the polity of the Scottish church: the remaining differences between the English and Scottish episcopates do not seem to have rankled. His concern was principally with ceremonies and forms. As we will see, he was active (in much the same way as Bancroft had been) with *advising* the king and the Scottish bishops on the new canons and the new Prayer Book; but he could argue, and could carry conviction, when accused of interfering in the making of the Scottish Prayer Book, that he was only giving fraternal advice.[103] Here the anomaly of a British king being able to consult English churchmen before declaring his will for Scotland has to be recognised. But ultimately the Scottish Prayer Book was the responsibility of the Scottish bishops.

Only occasionally, however, does Laud seem to me to have exceeded his role as an adviser to the king and to have interfered in the affairs of the Scottish church in ways that implied that he had any jurisdiction there. When Bishop Bellenden used a bowdlerised form of the Book of Common Prayer in the Chapel Royal and preached on the prohibited topic of Grace, Laud issued a firm rebuke behind the back of the Scottish primate.[104] But when Bellenden transgressed again, by ordering a Sunday fast throughout his diocese, Laud wrote to Spottiswoode passing on a royal command that the two Scottish metropolitans command the diocesans not to permit any such fasts, and that a canon be drawn up to prohibit the practice. He also instructed Spottiswoode 'to write a short letter to the Bishop of Aberdeen, to let him understand how he heth overshot himself; which letter you may send *together with mine*'.

Significantly, Laud's reason for this peremptory command to the

[100] McMahon, *Episcopacy in Scotland*, chs. 2 and 7.
[101] For the staging of the coronation and much else in what follows see my article in Morrill, *National Covenant*, 2–4.
[102] Laud, *Works*, VI, 438, 443; VII, 464.
[103] This is the emphasis of the defence he mounted against Scottish charges brought in parliament in 1640–1 (*ibid.*, III, 310, 318, 336–42).
[104] *Ibid.*, VI, 370–1 and cf. *ibid.*, 383–4, 419-20. For Charles' order to the bishops about interim liturgies, pending the preparation of a new service book, see *The Earl of Stirling's Register of Royal Letters . . . from 1615 to 1635* (2 vols., 1885), II, 679.

Scottish primate was that Sunday fasts were 'contrary to the rules of Christianity, and all the ancient Canons of the Church'.[105]

The second, and greater, intervention came in his response to a complaint from James Wedderburn in April 1636. The story tells itself:

And whereas you desire a copy of our Book of Ordination, I have here sent you one. And I have acquainted his Majesty with the two great reasons that you gave, why the book which you had in King James' time is short and insufficient: as first that the Order of deacons is made but a lay office, at least as that book may be understood; and secondly, that in the admission to Priesthood, the very essential words of conferring orders are left out. At which his Majesty was much troubled, as he had great cause, and concerning which he hath commanded me to write, that either you do admit of our Book of Ordinations, or else that you amend your own in these two gross oversights . . . and then see the book reprinted. I pray fail not to acquaint my Lord of St Andrews and my Lord Ross with this express command of his Majesty.[106]

This may or may not have been an order from the king of Scotland. But it was written and sealed by an archbishop of Canterbury to a junior Scottish bishop for action by the Scottish church.

The role of Laud, Wren, Cosin and Juxon in the making of the Scottish Prayer Book has been fully explored by Gordon Donaldson and others.[107] He showed that their role was one of heavy-handed correction to drafts prepared by the Scots. But, at times, something more than fraternal advice was offered. On 20 April 1636 Laud told Wedderburn that 'if you find the book of my Lord Ross's, and this, to differ in anything that is material, there you are to follow this later book I now send, as expressing some things more fully'.[108]

Nonetheless, what mattered most to Charles in relation to Scotland was not to anglicanise its discipline and liturgy as to provide clear rules and to insist on uniformity of practice.[109] If Charles' method of introducing the Prayer Book represented foolhardy authoritarianism, it was based upon an inability to think in terms of Scottish law and custom, not upon a determination to subordinate Scotland to English ways. It showed a sheer lack of imagination and empathy. If he had tried to impose a new prayer book on *England* without consulting parliament, convocation, the privy council and (to quote John Row) 'not even a

---

[105] Laud, *Works*, VI, 443.
[106] *Ibid.*, VI, 456.
[107] Donaldson, *Prayer Book*; and see the additional comments of Mcmahon, *Episcopacy in Scotland*, 194–8.
[108] Laud, *Works*, VI, 456.
[109] Donaldson, *Prayer Book*, remains the best account, superseding and incorporating all others. M. Lee, *The Road to Revolution, 1625–1637* (Urbana, 1985), 184–222, is a useful summary.

conventicle of bishops and doctors', William Laud would have been amongst the first to shriek out at the violation of the rights of the church.[110]

The Scottish canons[111] show the lack of concern with a narrow uniformity of the churches but the preoccupation with order: they may well have maintained an ominous silence about presbyteries and enjoined communion tables 'at the upper end of the chancel',[112] but they also laid down rules for ordination much more respectful of Scottish traditions than English ones, and were clearly not based in any significant way on English models.[113] In their defence, Walter Balcanquhal wrote that:

> because there was no booke extant containing any rules of such governement, so that neither the clergie nor laity had any certaine rule either of the one's power, or of the other's practice and obedience, and considering that the Acts of their General Assemblies were but written, and not printed, and so large and voluminous . . . we had them reduced to . . . such a paucitie of canons and those published.[114]

At least this suggests that there were good reasons for a king obsessed with order to impose canons. But his aim was to improve royal and not English control of the Scottish church.

In Charles' view, sinful man could best be brought to an inner obedience to the Will of God by learning an outer conformity. As William Laud put it: 'No external action in the world can be uniform without some ceremonies; and those in religion, the ancienter they be the better.'[115]

These are sentiments shared in large part by several of the Scottish bishops, including Spottiswoode, who stated that 'In things indifferent

---

[110] Lee, *Road to Revolution*, 201–4, is the most forthright writer on the inanity of Charles' methods. For John Row's comment, see his *History of the Kirk of Scotland from 1558 to 1637*, ed. D. Laing (Wodrow Society, 1842), 394. Charles did, of course, consult what he (disingenuously) referred to as the 'representative body of the church' i.e. *some* of the bishops; but he did so individually and not (Row's point) in conclave; and not all of them.

[111] The canons are in Laud, *Works*, v, 583–607.

[112] This went further than in England where the placing of the communion table in each church was left to the discretion of the ordinary (which led, in many cases, even in Laud's diocese to an order placing it elsewhere than at the east end), see Julian Davies, *The Caroline Captivity of the Church* (Oxford, 1992), ch. 4. It is worth noting that the Scottish canon did not insist on (or mention) the placing of rails around the Holy Table, something Laud was more insistent on in England.

[113] Morrill, *National Covenant*, 14–17, 33–6.

[114] [W. Balcanquhal], *A Large Declaration Concerning the Late Tumults in Scotland* (1639), 44–5.

[115] Laud, *Works*, II, xvi (from the Epistle Dedicatory to *A Relation of the Conference . . . with Mr Fisher the Jesuit*, and cited in W. H. Hutton, *Archbishop Laud* (1900), 69–70).

we must always esteeme to be best and most seemly which seemeth so in the eyes of publike authority; neither is it for private men to control public judgments.'[116] And later that 'for matters of rite and government, my judgment is and hath been, that the most simple, decent, and humble rites should be chused, such as is the bowing of the knee in resaving the holy sacrament, and otheres of that kinde, prophanenesse being as dangerouse to religion as superstition'.[117]

The Scottish church certainly lacked the ordered liturgy that Charles craved. The Book of Common Order lacked statutory force, was a manual of instruction on how to construct a liturgy and not a set form, and was admired by contemporary Scottish ministers precisely because, as Calderwood put it, 'none are tyed to the prayers of that book; but the prayers are set down as samplers'.[118]

Charles' explanation of his Scottish Prayer Book was both unambiguous and convincing. The Preface recalls the words of the Lords of the Congregation in 1559:

Religion was not then placed in rites and gestures, nor men taken with the fancy of extemporary prayers. Sure, the Public Worship of God, being the most solemn action of us his poor creatures here below, ought to be performed by a Liturgy advisedly set and framed, and not according to the sudden and various fancies of men.[119]

Order not uniformity with England was intended. Walter Balcanquhal recalled James' growing concern at 'that diversitie, nay deformitie which was used in Scotland, where no set or publike forme of prayer was used' which had led him to start the process that led to the 1637 liturgy. But Charles had taken special care to ensure such differences from the English Prayer Book

as we had reason to thinke would best comply with the mindes and dispositions of our subjects of that Kingdome: for we supposing that they might have taken some offence, if we should have tendered them the English service book *totidem verbis*, and that some factious spirits would have endevoured to have misconstrued it as a badge of dependance of that church upon this of England.[120]

---

[116] Quoted in G. Gillespie, *A Dispute against the English Popish Ceremonies* (1637), 2.
[117] Quoted in M. Ash, 'Dairsie and Archbishop Spottiswoode', *Scottish Church History Society Records*, 19 (1975–7), 131. This article also describes the crucifixes, east-end altar with kneelers and chancel screen which Spottiswoode installed in the church he built in his home parish.
[118] See the excellent discussion in J. K. Hewison, *The Covenanters: a History of the Church of Scotland from the Reformation to the Revolution* (2 vols., Glasgow, 1908), I, 43–5.
[119] Donaldson, *Prayer Book*, 102.
[120] [Balcanquhal], *A Large Declaration*, 18.

The liturgy was based on the English one, 'so that the Roman party might not upbraid us with any weightie or materiall differences in our Liturgies'.[121]

I see no reason to doubt this description of Charles' intentions. For him, a want of order in worship and a lack of clear authority emanating from the Crown and exercised through the bishops cast doubt upon the catholicity of the Scottish church in the same way that the lack of an apostolic priesthood in the Scottish church or the want of a full preaching ministry in England had troubled his father. Once again a concern with congruity might be a better way of explaining Charles' policy than a concern with uniformity or anglicanisation.

Let me conclude. Despite the discussion in intellectual circles of the patriarchies of the ancient church, and of the patriarchy of Britain in particular, Laud never resurrected the claims of Canterbury to jurisdiction over the church in Ireland, nor of the sees of Canterbury and York to jurisdiction over Scotland. Nor did Charles seek to transform the nature of episcopal authority in Scotland into that held by English bishops. Even if he could not bring himself to enshrine Presbyterian forms in the Scottish canons, the polity of the Church of Scotland remained episcopacy-in-presbytery. When Charles came to provide a liturgy for Scotland, he did not impose the English Prayer Book, but one which both respected many Scottish customs and imposed ceremonies which were not permitted by the English Prayer Book. The published Scots case in 1637–8 (as against that of 1639–40) was not that they were being anglicanised, but that they were being subjected to something worse than the English Prayer Book.[122] The Churches of Scotland and Ireland were not being subordinated to the jurisdiction of the Church of England nor was there a straightforward English acculturation of Scotland. What Scotland and Ireland experienced was nothing as straightforward as a drive for uniformity; rather each was subject to a naked royal authoritarianism that followed overlapping but distinct objectives in each kingdom. This was, indeed, royal supremacy *iure divino*.[123] But it was constrained in each kingdom only by the limits of the king's ignorance of local law and custom.

At the very time that Ussher was begging Spelman not to tell Laud about the researches of the learned Frenchman, Bramhall was writing to Laud begging him not to support the translation to Irish sees of Scots

---

[121] *Ibid.*; Donaldson, *Prayer Book*, 102.
[122] Morrill, *National Covenant*, 16–20.
[123] The phrase is Conrad Russell's: see his *Causes*, 114.

bishops, recently defrocked by the General Assembly. He blamed their 'extreme oscitancy or too imperious a disposition' for their hubris. He also denounced their meddling in politics. 'Since my Lord's coming to the sword, the Councell Table [here] was never troubled with the Jurisdiction of an English Bishop . . . I wish I could say the same of them.' He concluded: 'I have no quarrel with any of that nation, nor they with me. I hope they love me better than one another, yet this much I thought myself bound to represent to your Grace.'[124]

Bramhall here saw the affair of the three churches and the three kingdoms as intimately connected. But I submit that it does not indicate a Laudian or Caroline drive for anglicisation or integration of churches or kingdoms.

[124] Shirley, *Papers*, 71–2.

10 The Anglo-Scottish Union 1603–1643: a success?

Conrad Russell

This title may at first sight provoke a certain amusement.[1] Some readers may be moved to ask: 'The Anglo-Scottish Union a success? It produced four Scottish invasions of England in eleven years, didn't it?' Many people, including myself, have written on the weaknesses and the difficulties of the Anglo-Scottish Union. Those weaknesses patently existed, and were significant. Yet most of the writing on the weakness of the Union has been directed to the task of explaining either the Covenanting Revolution, or the English Civil War, or both. It has therefore had a teleological bias towards concentrating on the weakness of the Union. Yet there is another trend, equally valid if equally teleological, which leads, not towards 1643, but towards 1707. It is necessary to survey the Union of the Crowns from both vantage points before we can get a fix on it, and approach the task of seeing it as it was.

This essay is not intended to unsay what I have already written on the weakness of the Union of the Crowns. It is intended to provide a context in which, in a perfect world, I should have put it in the first place. Neither then nor now has the Union of England and Scotland been free of strains, yet it has one solid achievement to its credit. It survived, and is now 390 years old. In this, as contemporaries in 1603–4 were well aware, it differs from many other imperfect unions. An imperfect union is one which does not integrate the two countries in a single state, but combines two states under a common authority. In 1604, many people regarded the Union of the Crowns, without any further incorporation in a single body politic, as a prescription for impermanence. Yet, when the system was changed after 104 years, it was changed, not for less union, but for more.

In this, it differs sharply from the union which was seen as the closest

[1] This is a revised version of the Andrew Lang Lecture, delivered at the University of St Andrews on 28 January 1993. I would like to thank the University for their invitation to give the lecture and for their hospitality, and the audience, especially Professors David Stevenson and John Guy, for their helpful comments. I would also like to thank Dr Jenny Wormald for reading and commenting on an earlier draft.

parallel in 1603–4, the union of Castile and Portugal. In the climacteric year of 1640, the union of Castile and Portugal was dissolved, but that of England and Scotland was not. When we read Professor Elliott's essay on the dissolution of the union of Castile and Portugal, we are not entitled to a smug confidence that it cannot happen here.[2] We should consider Professor Elliott's reasons why that union broke up in order to see whether they give us any clues to why it did not happen here. In the years immediately after 1603, the parallel between the two unions was widely perceived. Sir Henry Savile, in his union tract of 1604, said it was 'in mine opinion the likest to ours'. An anonymous Scottish tract of the same year said the Anglo-Scottish union was a union without union of laws, like that of Portugal and Spain, 'wherein there can be no great assurance of continuance'.[3] Sir Francis Bacon, in 1607, also made the parallel with the union of Castile and Portugal, 'of which there is not yet sufficient triall'.[4] The Conde Duque of Olivares, commenting on the Covenanting movement in 1638, said: 'this will calm down, like the Portuguese business'.[5]

This sense of the potential impermanence of the Anglo-Scottish union was very deep, and often involved pressure for some measure of closer union, involving some constitutional means of regulating the relations between the two kingdoms. An anonymous tract of 1604, subsequently presented to Robert Cecil, said that 'if people reduced under one government be not therein united; if they be set together, and not into one; they are like sand without lime, subject to dissipation by every winde; they are like stones, heaped but not compacted together, easily severed by their proper weight'.[6] Some realised that James' views on the succession made this risk of impermanence more acute. Under the will of King Henry VIII, which was confirmed by statute, James VI should never have become James I at all: the succession should have gone to the Grey line. James was therefore forced to deny, in his English Act of Recognition, that an act of parliament had power to alter the succession. Since he did so on grounds of divine law, his denial had to be universal in its effect. If this was accepted, it meant that it became *ultra vires* for the parliaments of England and Scotland to pass acts tying their laws of

[2] J. H. Elliott, 'The Spanish Monarchy and the Kingdom of Portugal 1580–1640', in *Conquest and Coalescence*, ed. Mark Greengrass (1991), 48–67.
[3] J. H. Elliott, 'A Europe of Composite Monarchies', *Past and Present*, 137 (1992), 61. *The Jacobean Union: Six Tracts of 1604*, ed. Bruce R. Galloway and Brian P. Levack (Scottish Historical Soc., Edinburgh, 1985), 229, 47.
[4] PRO, SP 14/26/53.
[5] J. H. Elliott, 'The Year of the Three Ambassadors', in *History and Imagination*, ed. Hugh Lloyd Jones, Valerie Pearl and Blair Worden (Oxford, 1981), 167.
[6] PRO, SP 14/9/37.1.

succession together. As Sir John Holles reported in 1604, there was a risk
to the union by 'the mortality of the King's offspring, which though the
King shall by these Parliaments of England and Scotland ty both the
kingdomes to the lynes of the kings of England; yet it is certain this
subject is beyond the power of a Parlament: examples heertofore Henry
the 8 and other his progenitors'.[7]

Yet the dissolution of the Union is another of those historical dogs
which did nothing in the night-time. It is surprisingly hard to find people
who even proposed the dissolution of the Union. My own list, certainly
not exhaustive, now runs to seven people, all but one of them in the first
three years of the Union. All of them are Englishmen. Whether this
measures an objective difference between the nations, or my greater
familiarity with English sources is a question for others to answer. It
should be stressed that most of the English examples are found in types
of source to which there is little or no parallel north of the Border. These
seven are: Bartholomew Ward, tailor, Thomas Browne, yeoman,
Richard Hartopp, labourer, William Fletcher, saddler, John Tydsdale
and Guy Fawkes, papists, and the earl of Leicester, English ambassador
to Paris in 1640.[8]

If comparative history is to be done properly, it should be understood
that no comparisons are exact. Parallels are like wines: some of them
travel much better than others. Nevertheless, with that reservation in
mind, it may be interesting to begin by looking at Professor Elliott's
checklist of the reasons for the dissolution of the union between Castile
and Portugal, and see whether those reasons operated in Britain. It is
instructive to find that the first of Professor Elliott's reasons for the
readiness of the Portuguese nobility to break the union was the
ineligibility of the Portuguese for household offices in Madrid, and their
exclusion from the flow of Castilian patronage.

As every schoolboy knows, this is very different from the policy of
James VI and I, whose readiness to give household offices, and patronage, to Scotsmen has become notorious. To the English, both then and
now, this readiness has appeared to be nothing more nor less than part of

---

[7] *The Letters of John Holles 1587–1637*, ed. P. R. Seddon (Thoroton Soc., 36, 1986), III, 521.
This is a fuller version of Bacon's report of 25 April 1604, on the proposed change of
name to Great Britain or Brittany: *CJ*, I, 184.

[8] PRO, SP 14/2/96, SP 14/21/52; *CSPD 1603–10*, 246: Kent Archive Office, De L'Isle and
Dudley MSS z 47. I am grateful to Blair Worden for bringing this part of the collection
to my attention, and to the late Viscount De L'Isle and Dudley, VC, KG, for
permission to quote from it. William Fletcher identified himself as one of 'some verye
fewe that did mourn for the death of her matie'. The earl of Leicester, by contrast, gave
no reason at all for wishing to break the union.

his famous folly.[9] Perhaps, though if the maintenance of the Union is once recognised as a legitimate policy objective, and one which required some effort, James' readiness to reward Scotsmen is capable of a more serious *realpolitik* justification than it has yet received. It was an essential part of communication between the countries that some Scottish noblemen should live where the king resided, and that they should be able to keep state in a way which kept their heads up among the English. As the earl of Mar remarked, the comparative poverty of the Scottish nobility sometimes made this difficult for them.[10] It was a difficulty it was essential they should overcome. It may be that the need of Scottish noblemen for help arose from more than their objective poverty. The exchange rate mechanism of 1603 fixed the Scottish pound at a parity of twelve to one English pound, which had been vehemently lowered, by James' action, from a parity of some six to one thirty years earlier.[11] If the Scottish pound was indeed fixed at an artificially low parity, this would have been good for the Scottish economy, but particularly tough on noblemen living in England on Scottish rents. Their need for help may have arisen in part from James' own manipulation of the exchange rate.

The institution of the Scottish Bedchamber depended on more than just James' liking for people from his own state, though James had as good a right to that liking as President Clinton. The Bedchamber was a serious constitutional mechanism for dealing with the problem of an absentee king, and probably a more effective solution than the Portuguese, or Irish, alternative of a resident viceroy. In July 1603, Lord Fyvie, lord chancellor of Scotland, wrote to Robert Cecil to remind him that 'the prince's presence and readiness at all occurrences has been the surest band and warrand of the obedience of this kingdome'. He said there was a danger if their 'misordered people' found the hand of authority weaker than before.[12]

It is hard to read the correspondence of the earls of Mar and Kellie, or of the earls of Ancram and Lothian, without seeing the Bedchamber as a vital means open to Scots, and especially to Scots who wanted

---

[9] Neil Cuddy, 'The Revival of the Entourage: The Bedchamber of James I 1603–1625', in *The English Court from the Wars of the Roses to the Civil War*, ed. David Starkey (1987), 199–208.

[10] K. M. Brown, 'Noble Indebtedness in Scotland between the Reformation and the Revolution', *Historical Research*, 62 (1989), 261n.

[11] Jenny Wormald, *Court, Kirk and Community* (1981), 166; J. Kirk, *Patterns of Reform* (Edinburgh, 1989), xxi.

[12] PRO, SP 14/2/57.

something, of bringing the king's will to bear.[13] In providing Scots noblemen with that means, it provided them with a necessary condition for finding the Union acceptable. When, for example, the earl of Lauderdale wanted a place in the Prince's Council, when the bishop of Caithness, who doubled as minister of Jedburgh, was threatened with the dreadful fate of being made to live all the year in Caithness, or when Traquair wanted to be made a baron, they wrote to Robert Kerr, later earl of Ancram, in the Bedchamber.[14] Even the earl of Rothes, in April 1625, wrote to him to complain of 'the imposing of certain novations upon the kirk . . . and the impairing of the libertys of the nobility both in counsell and in Parliament', and did so, remarkably, with some hope of success.[15] The Covenanters were slow to give up hope of this sort of contact, and it was not until fear of English invasion forced them to it that they abandoned what seems to have been their instinctive method of operation.[16] Even in the Covenanter period, when Hamilton and Loudoun developed an excellent political relationship, and in December 1641, when the earls of Lothian and Lindsay, both of whom had their contacts about the king, were given keys for the king's privy garden at Whitehall, the Scottish nobility seem to have instinctively gravitated to the Mar and Kellie pattern.[17] James had taught them that it worked, and, in doing so, had perhaps made a lasting contribution to the survival of the Union.

The first crisis of the Union, whose gravity may be greater than we have yet appreciated, came in the three years after James' death. It is unlikely to be a coincidence that this came with Buckingham's attempt to bring the Scottish Bedchamber under his own control, nor that that attempt was first made immediately after James' death. In these years, Charles and Buckingham replaced such Bedchamber Jacobeans as the earl of Kellie with their own men such as Robert Maxwell earl of Nithsdale, who, according to the French ambassador, had vast designs lightly conceived. The contempt of the earl of Mar, Jacobean lord treasurer of Scotland, for these men still starts off the page today. These changes in counsel coincided with Charles' ill-prepared Revocation scheme, and with the strains caused by war. The Scots were called to

---

13 HMC, *Mar and Kellie* and HMC, *Mar and Kellie Suppl.*: *Correspondence of Sir Robert Kerr First Earl of Ancram and his Son William third Earl of Lothian*, ed. R.D. Laing (Roxburghe Club, Edinburgh, 1875).

14 *Ibid.*, I, 26–7, 29–31, 39–40.

15 *Ibid.*, I, 36–7.

16 Scottish Record Office, GD 406/1, Hamilton MSS 252, 305, 366, 522, 531, 646 and *passim*.

17 Conrad Russell, *The Fall of the British Monarchies 1637–1642* (Oxford, 1991), 417–18: PRO, LC 5/135 (unfol.) Surveyor 6 Dec. 1641.

assist the English war effort, and a regiment led by the earl of Morton sent to fight, symbolically, against the French. We need a full study of the interactions between these strains. Such a study might provide further evidence of the importance of an independent Scottish Bedchamber, not under English control, to the peaceable working of the Union of the Crowns.[18]

Among Professor Elliott's other reasons for the collapse of the union of Castile and Portugal, the failure to defend the Portuguese empire does not give rise to any parallel. The readiness of foreign powers to recognise the independence of Portugal, and if necessary to help to guarantee it, is clearly vital. The Covenanters in 1639–41 enjoyed no such advantage, and I will return later to the reasons why not. Professor Elliott's other reason, the presence of an available king in Portugal, highlights the absence of any such candidate in Scotland. It highlights once again the remarkable strength of the Stuart family, which was their loyalty to each other. There is no sign in 1639–41 that either Lennox or Hamilton would have been willing to pretend if asked, and indeed Lennox would have been most unlikely to have been asked. Hamilton, playing the tempter to Rothes, once mentioned the possibility of a free state on Dutch principles,[19] but it is easy to script the comments Napier and Montrose might have made on such a proposal. For many of the Scottish nobility, it would have created more problems than it solved. There was no substitute for an acceptable pretender.

The questions cannot be answered by parallels alone, and it is necessary to look at the pattern of Anglo-Scottish relations in its own right. The characteristic pattern which at once emerges is much more like the pattern found by Desplat in Béarn than that found in Castile and Portugal.[20] It is a pattern of co-operation across the border with co-religionists, rather than co-operation with fellow-nationals. What is more, this pattern is not the result of the Union, since it clearly predates it. Professor Donaldson, in two illuminating articles, has traced it back to

---

[18] Keith Brown, *Kingdom or Province? Scotland and the Regnal Union 1603–1715* (Edinburgh, 1991), 99–106; *The Wentworth Papers 1597–1628*, ed. J. P. Cooper (Camden Soc., 4th ser. 12, 1973), 248 (on Kellie), Russell, *Fall of the British Monarchies*, 262n (on Nithsdale); Cuddy, 'The Revival of the Entourage', 217–25; Allan I. MacInnes, *Charles I and the Making of the Covenanting Movement 1625–1641* (Edinburgh, 1991), 26–101; Peter Donald, *An Uncounselled King* (Cambridge, 1990), 15–27; HMC, *Mar and Kellie*, 133–55; *Ancram and Lothian*, ed. Laing, I, 44–5; *CSPV 1625–6*, 490, 499–500, 587; *CSPV 1626–8*, 11, 86, 119–20.

[19] John Leslie Earl of Rothes, *Relation*, ed. James Nairne (Bannatyne Club, 37, Edinburgh, 1830), 138.

[20] Christian Desplat, 'Louis XIII and the Union of Béarn to France', in *Conquest and Coalescence*, ed. Greengrass, 68–83.

the 1580s, to the period of the Black Acts and the Scottish Presbyterian exiles in England.[21] Robert Pont, in 1603, was surely right to see this pattern as going back to the Scottish Reformation. He said religion had caused the amity of the past fifty years, 'which seldome before happned'. He was perhaps cutting a corner in speaking of an 'unseparable bande of unchanged and reciprocal amity'.[22] Anglo-Scottish relations were always turbulent and unstable, but because alliances were almost always with co-religionists, they almost never took the form of a straight national quarrel. Dunfermline, writing to Salisbury in 1606, ascribed the breaking of Scottish links with France both to diversity of religion, and to the improvement of Scottish universities.[23] This pattern was instantly reasserted in 1603, when the Synod of Lothian petitioned James 'for releefe of good brethrein of the ministerie of England', and in doing so may have laid some of the groundwork for the Hampton Court Conference.[24] The pamphlet war for and against the ratification of the Five Articles of Perth seems to have been fought between two Anglo-Scottish factions,[25] and the Covenanters, in choosing to work in this pattern in 1639, were following a tradition which went back at least to the 1580s. This is a pattern which rested, not merely on zeal, but on a very clear perception of common interest. Since many people, of whom I am one, have already argued this point at length, there is perhaps no need to labour it now.[26]

The task of preparing this essay has taught me that it is difficult to do counter-factual research: it is hard to know where to go to look for

21 Gordon Donaldson, 'The Attitude of Whitgift and Bancroft to the Scottish Church', *TRHS*, 4th ser., 24 (1942), 95–115, and 'Scottish Presbyterian Exiles in England 1584–8', *Records of the Scottish History Society*, 14 (1960).

22 *The Jacobean Union*, ed. Galloway and Levack, 7.

23 PRO, SP 14/19/88.

24 David Calderwood, *The True History of the Church of Scotland* (Wodrow Soc., Edinburgh, 1842–9), VI, 222. *A Faithfull Report* (Edinburgh, 1606), sig. A2.

25 John Michaelson, *The Lawfulness of Kneeling* (St Andrews, 1620), 50, 62. David Calderwood, *A Defence of our Arguments against Kneeling* (Edinburgh, 1620), Epistle, 35–6, 40. Michaelson, writing for the Five Articles, joined issue with Perkins, who, he claimed, wrote only against 'the idolatrous kneeling of the papists', and claimed the absence of 'bread-worship' in England as proof of the safety of kneeling. Calderwood, answering Michaelson, accused him of borrowing his arguments from Morton. He cited Hooker and Buckeridge as the source of the errors he was attacking, and claimed: 'conformity with England is intended. Therefore kneeling for reverence of the sacrament is intended.' This is surely a cross-border debate. The timing of Buckeridge's *Discourse on Kneeling* (1617) and of Morton's *Three Ceremonies* (1619) suggests an attempt to help James in the debate on the Five Articles.

26 Conrad Russell, *The Causes of the English Civil War* (Oxford, 1990), 32–9 and *passim*; *Fall of the British Monarchies*, 147–205 and *passim*; David Stevenson, *The Scottish Revolution* (Newton Abbott, 1973), 187–8 and other refs.; Donald, *An Uncounselled King*, 191–6, 245–51 and many other refs.

evidence of what is not there. I have decided to look in turn at the three parties who might have chosen to break the Union: the king, the English and the Scots. Of these, the one who undoubtedly suffered most from the Union was the king, since he was the only one who had to live with its problems every day of his working life, and finally lost three Crowns in part because he was unable to solve them. The one advice to break the Union by a serious politician, the earl of Leicester, was designed for Charles. It puts the basic point in a nutshell that we have no evidence that it was ever delivered to Charles, and we know it only from Leicester's private commonplace book. One does not advise kings to throw away their kingdoms, and had Leicester done so, he would probably have brought his political career to an abrupt and inglorious end. Even Burghley had found the task of advising Elizabeth to abandon Calais, which had already gone, extremely difficult and hazardous. By comparison, advising the heir of Fergus I to abandon his native kingdom was well outside the realms of practical politics: it would have been a gross injury to his honour. Thus the one person in whose interest it might have been to break the Union could not contemplate doing it.

Beyond doubt, the most vocal body of discontent at the relationship between the kingdoms came from the English, yet, with the seven exceptions I have listed, they do not ever seem to have proposed breaking the Union. When I ask why, I am tempted to say that they could not propose breaking it until they admitted it had happened. This is not a mere figure of speech. On 8 May 1607, when the English parliament began the committee stage of the bill for abolishing hostile laws, Wilson reported to Salisbury that they set on every word in the title and preamble, objecting to the words 'continuance and preservation' of the union, 'which they said seemd to presuppose an union already made, to which they would not in any wise assent, nor to any naming of the union at all in the title'. Wilson said that 'it seemed they thought the word "union" a spirit, for they shunned the very shaddowe and the name of it'. They drew back only when Bacon and the Attorney General pointed out that the word 'union' was in two of their own recent Acts of Parliament. They still cut out 'the fayre and well-composed large preamble', and discussed instead a preamble reading: 'for the honor weale and good of these two mighty famous and ancient kingdomes and for the furtherance of the happie union already begone in His Majesty's royall person'. Even this was only won a doubtful division, in which the ayes sounded louder because they were called first.[27]

The vital word, for the English objectors, was 'two'. They adhered, in

---

[27] PRO, SP 14/21/17; also nos. 16, 21.

a peculiarly literal form, to the Spanish maxim that the king, who is king of all, should be treated as if he were only king of each.[28] Their concern, encapsulated in the long fight against the name of 'Britain' in 1604, was to deny the suggestion that the Union had created any British body politic, capable of infringing the sovereignty of the English nation-state. For the same reason, it was necessary for them to fight the suggestion of common citizenship in the proposal to naturalise the post-nati, because a common citizenship carried with it the threat of a common state. Crew, in February 1607, argued the central point: 'if ther lawes are severall they are two divided bodies'.[29] Sir Edward Coke, rightly or wrongly (and perhaps more interestingly if wrongly) claimed to have been the first that conceived that the change of name could not be with safety to the king or kingdom, because it would destroy the ancient constitution. He said that in the king's previous dominions, such as Guyenne and Gascony, 'none of any of the native or natural lawes of thes dominions were ever extinguished or altered'. 'The king cannot change the natural law of a nation. This foundacon is a firm foundacon.' Only a conqueror had this power: and we know what Sir Edward Coke thought about conquest.[30]

Bacon, reporting a conference the next day, said there had been concessions on both sides. The Commons had yielded that there was a union in the king's person, and the judges that there was a distinction in separation of the laws. He said the 'oculus quaestionis' was whether one of these drew on or involved the other. Bacon was indeed right in his identification of the question. For Thomas Wilson, 'the end of this union continuall peace, and agreement, as one body under one head'.[31]

For James, like Wilson, it was this idea of a British state as 'one body' which was his central objective. James wanted what, if he shared the common view that an imperfect union was an impermanent union, he should have wanted: a recognition that a British state was more than the sum of its independent parts. Any, and probably all, of the details might be open to negotiation: it seems to have been the symbolism of recognition as 'one body' which was crucial to James. On 31 March 1607, he said he wanted 'such a naturalizing, as may make one body of both kingdoms under me, your king . . . Such an union as was of the Scots and Pickes in Scotland, and of the Heptarchy here in England.' James wished to avoid the problems of governing multiple kingdoms, from which, like

28 Elliott, 'The Spanish Monarchy', 50.
29 PRO, SP 14/26/54.
30 *Ibid.*, 14/26/64.
31 *Ibid.*, 14/23/61 and 62; also 14/26/65, and Ellesmere in 14/26/76.

many Scots, he feared Scotland might suffer, 'for no more possible is it for one king to govern two countries contiguous, the one a greater, the other a less; a richer and a poorer; the greater drawing like an adamant, the lesser to the commodities thereof; then for one head to govern two bodies, or one man to be the husband of two wives; whereof Christ himself said, *ab initio non fuit sic*'. Yet when James spoke of 'one body', he did not mean, as Sandys would have done, a single unitary state with a uniform system of law. James came from an older political tradition, which still thought of liberties, not of liberty, and had no conceptual difficulty with some parts of a kingdom enjoying privileges, laws and customs which were unknown in other parts of it. He thought Britain, as much as France, might enjoy estates and representative institutions which did not cover every part of the kingdom. James was innocent of any 'Tudor Revolution in government'.

He explained: 'when I speak of a perfect union, I mean not confusion in all things: you must not take from Scotland those particular privileges that may stand as well with this union, as in England many particular customs, in particular shires, as the customs of Kent, and the royalties of the County Palatine of Chester, do with the common law of the kingdoms'. James was moved to growing impatience by English inability to understand this distinction. Sir Edwin Sandys, in his 'long, learned speech' of 28 April, was avowedly answering James' speech of 31 March, and thought James' proposals demanded a full unitary state: 'it is not *unus grex* until the whole do ioyne in making laws to governe the whole; for it is fitt and just, that every man do ioyne in makeing that, which shall binde and governe him, and because every man cannot be personally present, therefore a representative body is made to perform that service'. For Sandys, there could not be 'one body' until there was one sovereign parliament able to give uniform law to the whole. It was surely to Sandys' speech that James referred on 2 May, when he objected to the 'hay and stubble' which 'fools' had built upon his speech, and said that 'I propounded ever, and so I crave at your hands, an absolute and full union, but not a perfect union.'[32] For Sandys, such a distinction was totally unintelligible: 'while they continue a distinct bodie from us, it is no reason to communicate all the benefits of our state with them'.[33] Sandys was an adherent of the characteristically rigorous English attachment to the Cromwellian notion of a unitary state. His argument in 1604 that 'a kingdome is in itself indivisible, and can not contayne in it selfe

---

[32] *CJ*, I, 358; *The Parliamentary Diary of Robert Bowyer 1606–1607*, ed. D. H. Willson (repr. New York, 1971), 255–61; *CJ*, I, 366–7. See also PRO, SP 14/7/38.
[33] PRO, SP 14/26/73.

distinct kingdomes' is one which Scotland has heard from Westminster in many centuries.[34]

The English were restrained from recognising England as part of a larger state of Britain by their difficulty in drawing up any form of constitutional agreement capable of restraining the sovereignty of their king in parliament. This was, at least in part, a genuine difficulty. England's major constitutional peculiarity is that it is a state which has no recorded foundation: we do not know for certain when the seven kingdoms of the Anglo-Saxon heptarchy were transformed into the state of England. This means that England's king, and consequently its parliament, which he summons, can enjoy no title to power save prescription. That is why it was argued that it was not possible to create any power capable of controlling it unless 'the alteration of name draws after it an erection of a new kingdom, and extinguishment of the old'. The supporters of the union tried to trump this argument by creating a founder of England, in the form of Egbert king of Wessex, a southern version of King Fergus I. This, though probably textually based in the Anglo-Saxon Chronicle entries for 823 and 827, is almost certainly too early, and is clearly contradicted by the entries for 851 and 853. This line of argument was dangerous to pursue too far, since Egbert's title to be king of England was undoubtedly that of a conqueror.[35]

Back in a situation where they could not create any higher authority to regulate their relations with another state, the English kept returning to the only precedent with which they were comfortable: that of Wales. An anonymous tract presented to Salisbury said there was no way of restoring peace between the kingdoms but by union, as with Wales.[36] Francis Bacon said that 'I wish the Scottish nation were governed by our lawes, for I hold our lawes, with some reducement, worthy to govern, and it were the world.' Just in case any Scot should be dim enough to miss the point, Bacon concluded by praising Edward I's attempt to conquer Scotland, because he was aiming for 'solid strength *at home*'.[37] The Welsh model of union saved the English from all the intellectual problems which followed from admitting that one state could have many parts. This was why Sir Edwin Sandys, from 1604 onwards, was only willing to recognise the union if it were a perfect, incorporating union, and not an imperfect union regulating the relations of autonomous parts. In 1607, Sandys spelt out the conclusion of this approach, saying they

[34] *Ibid.*, 14/7/63.
[35] *Ibid.*, 14/23/62 and 14/7/65.
[36] *Ibid.*, 14/9/37.1.
[37] *Ibid.*, 14/26/53 (my italics).

desired a perfect union, 'when two kingdomes become one in government', 'and that the Scottish nation be ruled by our lawes'.[38] In fact, the only union he could recognise was annexation.

Failing that, the English critics of Union recognised no change in the sovereign, independent character of the English state. That their king happened also to be king of Scots had, in their eyes, no constitutional consequences whatsoever, and their only problem, as they saw it, was to bring this fact home to a misguided king. If their king chose, in his spare time, to be king of Scots, that was nothing to do with them. However, as opponents of Union, they were caught in their own logic. If no Union existed, it could not be dissolved. If there was no constitutional relationship between the kingdoms, it could not be broken. If they recognised no constitutional consequences for England, they recognised nothing they could propose to change. In fact, it is the literal truth that they could not propose to end the Union until they recognised that it had happened.

By contrast, the arguments of English supporters of Union were much more pragmatic, and much more likely to influence those in power. They were cast, essentially, in terms of national security. Lord Howard of Effingham, in 1588 had believed the Spanish armada intended a landing in Scotland or Ireland.[39] This security nightmare, which went back to the threat from the French in 1559, lasted, and it was argued, typically, that the Union had taken away France's first and safest defence. Thomas Wilson, in 1606 listed as one of the arguments for a change of name 'that there is utility in it by rooting up the seeds of war and hate, which hath hindered our victories; opened gates to invasion, wasted the borders and distressed both states'.[40] They were prosaic arguments, but they were ones to which those who held power in the English state were likely to cling with great tenacity. As Ireland, which was the subject of comparable arguments, discovered, these reasons made the English capable of resisting the break-up of Union with quite remarkable determination. This is something the Scots seem to have understood. These arguments were, in fact, validated on the only occasion on which the Anglo-Scottish union has actually been dissolved. This was in 1649, when the English, in a fit of absence of mind, cut off the head of the king of Scots with the crown upon it. Since the Union had rested entirely in the person of the king, and the English had resisted any constitutional relationship between the kingdoms, there was no legal obstacle to the Scots crowning King Charles II, whom even Cromwell, for a while, referred to

[38] *Bowyer*, ed. Willson, 219.
[39] *CSPD 1581–90*, CCXI, no. 17.
[40] PRO, SP 14/10/56, 14/23/61 and 62. Also *ibid.*, 14/9/37.1

punctiliously as 'the King of Scots'. The Scots, on the other hand, aggressively recognised him as king of Britain. The English, of course, found this threatened their security, and responded by restoring the Union by conquest. It is Scottish fear of precisely this response which seems to have been the biggest obstacle to any move to break the Union from north of the Border.

Scottish attitudes to the Union were also influenced by the fact that there has always been a considerable body of Scots, out of line with politically correct sentiment in their own country, who had a vital interest in the Union, and in encouraging any move towards closer conformity with England. Such moves might give them a place in the sun, or at least in a less dark patch of shade. For them, England was always capable of appearing as a liberating force from the thraldom of Melvillian or Covenanter dominion, and England could always rely on their support against any potential move to break the Union. This strand of Scottish opinion caused considerable anxiety to the Covenanters in 1639, and it is to them Baillie was referring when he wrote: 'certainlie our dangers were greater than we might let our people conceave'.[41] In 1639, it proved a damp squib, partly because its Anglophilia stopped short of supporting an English conquest, but its opposition to any attempt at Scottish secession would have been a far from negligible force.

From Patrick Adamson to Montrose and beyond, this is a continuous Scottish tradition. Just as English historiography has tended to paint Catholics, supporters of a Spanish alliance and others for whom there is no room in the Whig pantheon as un-English, so this strand of Scottish opinion has often been regarded as un-Scottish. It is perhaps time we allowed that both groups were an essential part of the identity of their nations. They were not always so recognised at the time. In 1606, James Melville was dismayed to find that the imprisonment of the ministers at the abortive Assembly of Aberdeen 'by many (yea, which is very strange, even of the ministers) is not thought evil of'.[42] In 1637, the immediate response of the ministers of Edinburgh to the new service book was to ask for 'a competent maintenance' for their 'better inducement' to undergo the charge of the service book.[43] The town council of Elgin, taking the Covenant in 1638, wanted a declaration to allow them to kneel at communion, which they were not allowed. When delegates were to be chosen for the Glasgow Assembly, it was decided that 'when the

---

[41] Robert Baillie, *Letters and Journals*, ed. David Laing (Bannatyne Club, Edinburgh, 1841–2), I, 194.
[42] Calderwood, *The True History*, VI, 298.
[43] *Register of the Privy Council of Scotland, 1635–7*, 514.

presbiterie is unsure, as wher the greatest part are episcopall', the ablest gentlemen were to be put on the Kirk Session.[44] This group of Scots has always been denigrated. The earl of Mar's judgement on the bishop of Ross in 1626 is typical of many: 'his judgement was far short of that quhilk the gravitie of his beird did promiss'.[45] We will never understand this judgement without remembering that it is the judgement of one Scot on another. A bishop of Ross, almost *ex officio*, had to be a Unionist.

This may help with one of the most intriguing questions of the whole story, why the Scottish Covenanters never took the nationalist road. There cannot be any doubt that the Covenanters were patriotic Scots, who were resisting, in Baillie's words, a danger of 'our poor country made ane English province, to be disposed on for ever hereafter at the will of a bishope of Canterbury'. *The Intentions of the Army* said the king threatened that 'wee should no more bee a kirk or a nation'.[46] Yet, for all their nationalist language, independence, as Professor Stevenson has pointed out, was 'evidently unthinkable to the Covenanters'.[47] This is a paradox which cries out for explanation.

It is vitally important that, whereas the King of Castile had inherited Portugal, it was the King of Scots who had inherited England. Professor Stevenson has pointed to Scottish loyalty to 'their native Stewart dynasty'. In *An Information*, in 1639, they pledged their loyalty to the line of King Fergus I 'so long as the sun and moone endureth'.[48]

Professor Stevenson has also drawn attention to the even more important point that the Scottish Covenanters wanted not only victory, but a secure peace, which would not be overthrown by another war with England, perhaps this time resulting in defeat.[49] There is no mistaking the fear of defeat in the Covenanter army on the Border in 1639. Johnston of Wariston recorded 'want of all the necessares of warre, men, horses, victual, money, munitions, commanders, order, and dicipline, yet we know in qm we trust'. They warned the committee in Edinburgh that people were ruing what they were doing, and would 'subject their necks to spirituall and bodilie slavery'.[50] The Scots knew how lucky they were in 1639. They were as lucky again in 1640, but it would have been tempting providence to assume they would be as lucky again a third time.

---

[44] Rothes, *Relation*, 109, 169; also 73. PRO, SP 16/539/17.
[45] HMC, *Mar and Kellie*, 139.
[46] Baillie, *Letters*, ed. Laing, I, 66. *The Intentions of the Army of the Kingdom of Scotland* (Edinburgh, 1640), 5.
[47] Stevenson, *The Scottish Revolution*, 132.
[48] *An Information* (1639), 3.
[49] Stevenson, *The Scottish Revolution*, 242.
[50] *Diary of Sir Archibald Johnston, Lord Wariston*, ed. G. M. Paul (Scottish Historical Soc., 26, Edinburgh, 1896), 47, 62.

They needed, not only peace, but a secure peace, which meant, as they said in their negotiating instructions for the Pacification of Berwick that 'both the King and the English must give us assurance that heerafter they will not invade or wrong us any manner of way'.[51] The particular English threat which they most clearly saw as 'able to bring the kingdome of Scotland to be no more a kingdome'[52] was that of the English naval blockade. Twenty-three ships cruising off the Firth of Forth appear to have succeeded in 'stopping all trade and commerce betwixt this and any other natione'.[53] They claimed, at various times during the negotiation of the Treaty of London, that 88 ships had been taken, and about 500 laid up for six or seven months.[54] These were negotiating claims, which they expected to be scaled down, but they could be scaled down a long way and still be formidable losses. In 1640, they stressed that it was the blockade which compelled them to invade England, because they could no longer sustain their losses.[55] In 1640, their negotiating terms for the Treaty of London included a demand that there should be no blockade without the assent of the English parliament.[56] If it was indeed this blockade which made the Covenanters so frightened of a 'nationall quarrel', it might imply that the only achievement of Ship Money was the preservation of the Union.

It is against this background that the Covenanters decided, in Professor Stevenson's words, that what they needed was 'not less union but more',[57] and based their strategy, as many Scots had done before them, on an appeal to their English co-religionists. The Covenanters occasionally talked explicitly of union, and praised James' efforts in this direction. It would be an exaggeration to say they wanted Union, and the demand of their paper of 24 February 1641, for 'nearer union', expresses their views most exactly.[58]

It is hard to know how far the Covenanters intended to achieve the demands set out in their eighth article at the Treaty of London. The article was ideally designed for its immediate purpose, which was to take

[51] *Ibid.*, 72.
[52] BL Stowe MS 187, fol. 27v.
[53] *Johnston of Wariston*, ed. Paul, 41.
[54] BL Harleian MS 457, fol. 46r; BL Stowe MS 187, fol. 31v.
[55] Scottish Record Office, Hamilton MS 1218; Baillie, *Letters*, ed. Laing, I, 207, and many other refs. See also Scottish Record Office, Hamilton MS 326.1 (Hamilton to the king, 27 November 1638) for Hamilton's recommendation of the blockade as a means to 'subdue' Scotland.
[56] PRO, SP 16/471/22.
[57] Stevenson, *The Scottish Revolution*, 132.
[58] National Library of Scotland, Advocates' MS 33.1.1, vol. XIII, no. 72; BL Stowe MS 187, fol. 47v; BL Harleian MS 457, fol. 66r; Scottish Record Office, PA 13/1.

up as much time as might be needed. Yet at the very least it shows a strongly unionist tinge in the Covenanters' daydreams. The key practical demand was that neither kingdom should make war on the other without the consent of its parliament. In addition, they asked for the king and the prince to reside part of each year in Scotland, for Scots to be placed about the king, the queen and the prince and for unity in religion between the kingdoms. They wanted a parliamentary say in the choice of Scottish councillors, no foreign war without the consent of both kingdoms and mutual assistance against invasion. They wanted full mutual naturalisation, complete internal freedom of trade, a common external tariff, equality of coin and Scottish freedom to trade with English colonies. They wanted the keeping of these terms to be entrusted to Conservators of the Peace, who were to report to triennial parliaments in each kingdom. It is not an exaggeration to say this programme had unionist overtones.[59] Yet, if it would be an exaggeration to describe the Covenanters as unionists, their strategy certainly looked rather towards 1707 than towards 1320. There are occasional suggestions of devolutionist inclinations in the Covenanter programme. In the eighth article in the Treaty of London, they said that since the kingdom of England would take up most of the king's time, they desired he might choose his council and officers by the advice of the estates, and statesmen should be 'liable' for the discharge of their duties to the king, and to the parliament's trial and censure.[60] This particular demand was justified by the king's absence in part because of the king's fear that it might be taken as a precedent for England. Yet its effect would surely have been to drive Charles back towards James VI's famous 'stroke of a pen', which was a process of rubber stamping the conclusions of a devolved government. In looking tentatively in this direction, the Covenanters combined an intense desire for greater Scottish autonomy with a programme of guarantees to be based on their allies in the English parliament, and with a realistic recognition that, as Roxburgh wrote to Ancram in July 1638, 'our hapenes under God most cum from where yee are' – in the king's Bedchamber in London.[61] For all the frothy enthusiasm of the religious language used by Johnston of Wariston and others, the programme rested on a very hard-headed series of political calculations.

This approach was not only based on fear of English military and naval power. It was also based on a recognition of the immense pull of English

---

[59] Russell, *Fall of the British Monarchies*, 195–6; BL Stowe MS 187, fols. 40r–v and 34v–48r *passim*.

[60] BL Stowe MS 187, fol. 48v. Also *Johnston of Wariston*, ed. Paul, 73–4.

[61] *Ancram and Lothian*, ed. Laing, I, 99.

cultural influence, which had predated the Union of 1603, and would surely survive its dissolution. This fear of English cultural influence shows all through Covenanter writing. When Rothes was told that the law would recover its force if the service book and canons were taken away, he replied 'that all the ground of our fears lay not in these books, since in Ingland they wer printing books for superstition and idolatrye'.[62] It was only if this infection were controlled at source that Scotland could be free from the risk that it would spread again. Baillie recorded Covenanter proceedings against Dr Panter, Professor of Divinity at the University of St Andrews, because he used English methods of study, beginning with the popish schoolmen and the Fathers, and fell to 'grossest Pelagianisme'.[63] Breaking the Union would not make these dangers go away. As the Scottish Commissioners at the Treaty of London said, the Church of Scotland had been 'vexed and disquieted by the bishops of England' from before the coming in of King James to England'.[64] It had not come with the Union, and it would not go with the Union. If the constant requests sent by the earl of Lothian to the earl of Ancram from Newcastle during 1640 are any guide, the cultural dangers of London might be reinforced by its attractions as a centre for shopping. In April 1641, he asked his father to get him two night caps and two pairs of slippers, one grass green, the other sky colour, with gold or silver or gold and silver gallon lace upon them. 'I can nether gett them heare nor in Edinburgh.'[65] This was the sort of influence the mere breaking of a political relationship could not end, and so long as that continued, the Scottish church would be liable to influences coming from London. That was why, as Johnston of Wariston always argued, it was necessary to attack the prelacy of England, 'the fountaine whence all these Babylonish streames issued unto us'.[66]

This insistent need to have a say in what happened in England was one of the forces which inhibited Covenanter urges to call in foreign help. As Baillie put it, calling in foreign help would have made England their enemy, 'the evill in the world we most declyned, and our adversaries did most ayme at'. It was the same need, he said, which hindered Scottish pursuit of the flying English after Newburn.[67] Again, the high principle

---

[62] Rothes, *Relation*, 78.

[63] Baillie, *Letters*, ed. Laing, I, 148–9.

[64] National Library of Scotland, Advocates' MS 33.4.6, fol. 144v.

[65] *Ancram and Lothian*, ed. Laing, I, 117. For similar, if less drastic, examples, see 113, 109, 118, 122–3.

[66] *The Lawfulnesse of Our Expedition into England Manifested* (Edinburgh, 1640), sig. A3.

[67] Baillie, *Letters*, ed. Laing, I, 190–1, 257. The ministers also opposed asking for help from the Lutheran Danes because it would involve 'too much leaning to the rotten reed of Egypt'.

of Covenanter language on common cause with the English godly covers a very careful calculation of Scottish self-interest.

This brings us back to where we began: the fact that Portugal could enjoy foreign help in breaking away from Spain, but there was no power willing to do for Scotland what France, the Netherlands and even England were willing to do for Portugal. This was not only because the Covenanters did not enthusiastically seek it: it was because there was no foreign power with a clear interest in providing it. The Dutch, it is true, sold the Covenanters arms, yet this is not particularly significant. It would be more significant if we could find any country in Europe to which the Dutch did not sell arms. The Danes, whom some Covenanters viewed with optimism, were not big enough to take on the certain hostility of England without the support of either Sweden or the emperor, either of whose support might embrace Denmark rather too tightly.

Yet the key to Scotland's lack of allies for any bid for independence lies in Whitehall. The most certain rule of politics is that 'my enemy's enemy is my friend', yet Charles' vacillating and ineffectual foreign policy had left him with no certain enemy. For that reason, Scotland had no certain friend. Neither the Dutch nor the Swedes would have been happy encouraging more Englishmen to support Charles' Hispanophile inclinations. Richelieu in 1639 had particular cause to avoid acute English hostility while he was tackling the Norman revolt on the other side of the Channel.[68] Moreover, Richelieu seems to have reached, some time back, the conclusion that the best thing to do with England was to immobilise it and pull it off the road, and this the Covenanters were already doing adequately with no more than the discreetest signs of sympathy.[69]

Perhaps more important, the French were after a bigger prize. On 25 October/4 November 1640, as the Long Parliament met, the French

[68] See Elliott, 'The Year of the Three Ambassadors', 168n, for a report that Richelieu had sent £40,000 to the Covenanters. If true, this is a long way short of the expensive commitment to defend an independent Scotland. Evidence of active French help to the Covenanters is intriguingly thin on the ground.

[69] On 12 December 1625 (NS) the Venetian ambassador in Paris reported that Richelieu 'cannot bring himself to believe that the English will do much. He laughs at Buckingham's journey to Holland and his proposals, and does not expect much help from the English fleet. He says the King is poor without the help of Parliament, and that will never meet because of Buckingham who very nearly came to grief through the last one.' This low assessment of English power, though initially the mood of a moment, seems to have been confirmed by experience. Save in the changed financial and constitutional circumstances of Cromwell's Protectorate, it seems to have been the basis of French policy until Louis XIV guessed wrong by sticking to it in 1688. *CSPV 1625–6*, 245.

ambassador reported that Pym had come to visit him, offering to make the name of Spain odious to all England, and asking, to that end, to be supplied with a list of occasions on which Spain had deceived its neighbours. No French ambassador was equipped to resist so seductive an offer, and he reported a week later that though Pym was a great Puritan, and therefore suspect, their interests appeared to coincide.[70] In their growing co-operation with Pym, the French were slowly led into moves to support increasing Scottish influence in England, and therefore to support closer union. Father Phillips, the Queen's confessor, asked in May 1641: 'can they [Richelieu and Louis XIII] suffer England and Scotland to ioyne in one body or common weale, that seemes to be the present desyne?'[71] The answer seems to have been 'yes'. In playing for the support of a united British state, whose unity might well have been first expressed in a continental campaign for the Elector Palatine, France was playing for a much bigger prize than the support of an independent Scotland, which would inevitably have jolted England firmly into the Habsburg camp. Without the support of France, Scottish independence could not be sustained.

It was thus in no one's interest to break the Union. It was not in the king's interest, because it would have diminished his honour. It was not in the interest of the English anti-Scots, because they would have had to compromise their ideas on English national sovereignty before they could admit that there was anything to break. It was not in the interest of anti-Covenanting Scots, who would have lost their only possible protector, and it was not in the interest of the Covenanters, because it would have diminished, rather than increasing, their security. For once in a blue moon, all parties, with the possible exception of the king, correctly perceived their interest, and acted in it. If only politics were always that simple!

[70] PRO, 31/3/72, 295, 300–1.
[71] PRO, SP 16/480/18.

11 Popery, purity and Providence: deciphering the New England experiment

Susan Hardman Moore

I

In 1636, Thomas Allen, Rector of St Edmund's, Norwich, delivered a ringing affirmation of his work in the Church of England, to protest against a sentence of excommunication imposed on him for refusing to conform to Bishop Wren's Injunctions:

> I neither can nor dare rest from the Exercise of my Ministry . . . I was exhorted and charged by the Bishop . . . to have in remembrance unto how high an Office I was Called . . . A Messenger, a Watchman, a Pastor & Steward of the Lord . . . to feed and provide for the Lord's family . . . and to see that I never ceased my Labor.

Loyalty to the church was at stake. But who had become disloyal? As Allen saw it, the authorities pressed him to accept unlawful innovations, beyond the 'Lawes and Ordinances of the Church by Parliament established'. To Clement Corbet, the bishop's chancellor, Allen and his like took pride in 'sily Inventions', and jeopardised 'the goode foundation of doctryn and disciplyn'. Allen left Norwich for New England in 1638, and soon held office as minister to the church at Charlestown, Massachusetts.[1] In the winter of 1639–40, he crossed the Charles river every Thursday to join the crowds that listened to John Cotton preach at

---

[1] Thomas Allen, 'Humble Remonstrance', Bodleian Library, Tanner MS 68, fols. 116–19; Clement Corbet to Matthew Wren, 17 Feb. 1636/7, Tanner MS 68, fol. 189. For Allen, see *Calamy Revised*, ed. A. G. Matthews (Oxford, 1934). Michael Metcalfe, a parishioner of Allen's who also went to New England, left a letter complaining of popery, Arminianism and Wren's innovations: 'To all the true professors of Christs gospel within the city of Norwich', 13 Jan. 1636/7, *New England Historical and Genealogical Register*, 16 (1862), 279–84. Recent opinions about the character of Wren's activity are as divided as those of Allen and Corbet. Nicholas Tyacke, *Anti-Calvinists. The Rise of English Arminianism c. 1590–1640* (Oxford, 1987), 205–8, points to its novelty. Kevin Sharpe, *The Personal Rule of Charles I* (New Haven, 1992), 369–74, argues for a drive for conformity characterised by patience with nonconformists; see also P. King, 'Bishop Wren and the Suppression of the Norwich Lecturers', *HJ*, 11 (1968), 237–54. Julian Davies, *The Caroline Captivity of the Church* (Oxford, 1992), 250, believes Wren's rigour was exceptional, and has obscured the moderation of Laud. See also John T. Evans,

257

the Boston lecture. Cotton, once of Boston, Lincolnshire, had cultivated the distinctive practices of New England's churches. In the sermons Allen heard, Cotton gave the message that there was no way back to England. If you 'be once incorporated into any of their Parishes', he warned, 'you will finde the body of the Church rent from you, or you will be rent from the body, if you shall walk roundly and sincerely in the ways of God'. He seemed to reject what the settlers had known in England as antichristian. Yet at the same time, New England's ministers sent word to England that seemed to say the opposite, affirming colonists' affinity with the congregations left behind: 'such congregations are true Churches, notwithstanding sundry defects and corruptions found in them . . . we [cannot] judge or speake harshly of the Wombes that bare us, nor of the paps which gave us suck'.[2]

Interpretation of the New England experiment is bedevilled by the puzzling behaviour of the colonists. They protested their loyalty to the English church before and after emigration, yet once in New England made daring innovations in religion. Contemporaries judged their protestations insincere. Even allies turned against them and accused them of schism. They had cut themselves off from the English church, rejected it as no church, whatever they might say. Modern historians have also found it hard to understand the contradiction, and have tended to side with settlers' contemporary critics. Perry Miller called their rhetoric of loyalty 'utterly fantastic', a 'cobweb of sophistry'. Stephen Foster has judged it hollow talk, and reckons colonial leaders consistently underplayed their distance from England.[3]

The problem posed by this self-contradictory conduct is important. From the English side, the question of emigrants' motivation feeds into dispute about the causes of Civil War. From the American side, the terms of their departure are crucial to debate about forces that shaped early settlement. Why did they leave England? It has been argued that emigration was not provoked by a crisis about religious innovation under

Seventeenth-Century Norwich. Politics, Religion and Government 1620–1660 (Oxford, 1979), 84–96; Kenneth W. Shipps, 'Lay Patronage of East Anglian Puritan Clerics in Pre-Revolutionary England" (PhD thesis, Yale University, 1971), 267–99.

[2] John Cotton, *An Exposition upon the Thirteenth Chapter of the Revelation* (1655), 'Epistle to the Reader' [by Thomas Allen], and 20; 'An Answer of the Elders of the Severall Churches of New-England to Two and Thirty Questions', in [Richard Mather], *Church-Government and Church-Covenant Discussed* (1643), 26.

[3] Perry Miller, *Orthodoxy in Massachusetts, 1630–1650* (Gloucester, Mass., 1933), 84, 136–44; Stephen Foster, *The Long Argument: English Puritanism and the Shaping of New England Culture, 1570–1700* (Chapel Hill, N.C., and London, 1991), 165, 169; see also Andrew Delbanco, *The Puritan Ordeal* (Cambridge, Mass., and London, 1989), 99; Avihu Zakai, *Exile and Kingdom: History and Apocalypse in the Puritan Migration to America* (Cambridge, 1992), 226.

Laud in the 1630s: colonists amounted to 'religious extremists whose views few high Calvinists would have tolerated', bent on stricter isolation from the profane; or perhaps economic migrants, accompanied by a few madcap clergy.[4] Furthermore, settlers' radical roots show in the confident rhetoric of purity and mission that shaped their plantations: New England saw itself as a 'city on a hill', it had a divine 'errand into the wilderness'.[5] This kind of approach to emigrants' motivation tends to read the New England experiment back into old England – then draws the conclusion that New England emerged as a consequence of radical tendencies in English Puritanism. And of course such a view can build on a characterisation of English Puritanism that has had a long history: Puritanism inevitably corroded the establishment; gathering the godly together ate away at the fabric of the church, and would end parish religion; Puritanism set itself on the road to the sectarianism of New England and to Civil War.[6]

This perspective on New England comes unstuck, however, if we start with the interpretation Professor Collinson has pioneered. He has argued that Puritanism, left to itself, did not erode the established church, but represented its most vigorous and successful tendencies. He has painted a picture of the Jacobean church, in which New England's settlers grew up, as a church of balanced compromise. Puritan clergy with scruples about ceremonies had leeway to follow their own path because the bishops valued their preaching skills. The godly gathered within and across parishes to practice 'voluntary religion', but strongly resisted the notion of forming exclusive, separated, churches.[7] If, then, Puritanism

---

[4] G. W. Bernard, 'The Church of England c. 1529–c. 1642', *History*, 75 (1990), 199; Zakai, *Exile and Kingdom*, 207–30. D. Cressy, *Coming Over: Migration and Communication between England and New England in the Seventeenth Century* (Cambridge, 1987), 74–106, argues that 'the primacy of puritan concerns in the bulk of the movement' is unproven, and stresses economic betterment; see also Sharpe, *Personal Rule of Charles I*, 751–7. Virginia DeJohn Anderson, however, believes religious motives were paramount: 'Migrants and Motives: Religion and the Settlement of New England, 1630–1660', *New England Quarterly*, 58 (1985), 339–83, with a riposte by D. G. Allen, 'The Matrix of Motivation', *ibid.*, 59 (1986), 408–18; Virginia DeJohn Anderson, *New England's Generation: The Great Migration and the Formation of Society and Culture in the Seventeenth Century* (Cambridge, 1991), 12–46. The significance of the variety of motives for emigration will be discussed below.

[5] Zakai, *Exile and Kingdom*, most recently states the case, which derives from Perry Miller, 'Errand into the Wilderness', in Miller, *Errand into the Wilderness* (Cambridge, Mass., 1956), 1–15.

[6] Christopher Hill, *Society and Puritanism in Pre-Revolutionary England* (1964), 483–92; Sharpe, *Personal Rule of Charles I*, 731–8.

[7] See particularly Patrick Collinson, *The Religion of Protestants: The Church in English Society 1559–1625* (Oxford, 1982), 275–83; Collinson, 'The English Conventicle', in *Voluntary Religion*, ed. W. J. Sheils and D. Wood (Studies in Church History, 23, Oxford, 1986), 223–59; Collinson, 'Towards a Broader Understanding of the Early

was not necessarily corrosive of the establishment, how are we to decipher the apparent sectarianism of New England? This essay outlines an answer to that question.

The rhetoric and behaviour of godly preachers who left for New England will be central to the discussion. This is partly a matter of sources: most of the voices that survive are those of clergy, and the clergy offer a bounded group we can study. Sometimes the actions of ministers are put to one side as atypical, because Puritanism is seen as a radical movement where lay assertiveness threatens clerical control.[8] Without denying the tensions inherent in the Puritan desire for a purer church, I set out here with a less appositional model of relations between preachers and people. The clergy both articulated and shaped the religious experience of the laity, principally through the medium of preaching which formed such a central part of Puritan piety, but also through the intensive attention given to godly life in burgeoning conduct literature and in private counselling about cases of conscience.[9] If we start with this model, the voices and behaviour of the clergy can provide important clues for interpreting New England. In the 1630s ministers created a religious framework for a crisis that was generally felt. Their perception of the way Providence was leading proved a powerful device to structure and bind together motives for emigration.

What made New England turn out as it did? The riddle of the inner dynamic of the New England experiment, rather than the precise development of colonial church order, is the question tackled here. It is important to fathom this dynamic from sources of 1630–40, and not to read later interpretations back into the first decade. The key to understanding New England, I shall argue, lies in understanding the terms of

Dissenting Tradition', in his *Godly People: Essays on English Protestantism and Puritanism* (1983), 527–62. Collinson, 'The Cohabitation of the Faithful with the Unfaithful', in *From Persecution to Toleration: The Glorious Revolution and Religion in England* (Oxford, 1991), 51–76. Professor Collinson's recent approach differs from 'The Godly: Aspects of Popular Protestantism' (written in 1966) which saw the movement as more corrosive, with potential for congregationalism: *Godly People*, 1–18. The inclusive character of the Jacobean church has been confirmed by Kenneth Fincham, *Prelate as Pastor: The Episcopate of James I* (Oxford, 1990).

[8] Christopher Hill, 'Archbishop Laud's Place in English History', in his *A Nation of Change and Novelty: Radical Politics, Religion and Literature in Seventeenth Century England* (1990), 78–9; Foster, *Long Argument*, 99, 115–16, 141–3, 153; Zakai, *Exile and Kingdom*, 219–20; David D. Hall, *The Faithful Shepherd: A History of the New England Ministry in the Seventeenth Century* (Chapel Hill, N.C., and London, 1972), 32–3, 39–40, 90–1, 109–11. David Cressy regards ministers and lay leaders as unrepresentative of the mass of migrants, whose religious opinions must remain obscure: *Coming Over*, 79, 83, 87.

[9] Collinson, *Religion of Protestants*, 231–4, 264–8; John Morgan, *Godly Learning: Puritan Attitudes towards Reason, Learning and Education, 1560–1640* (Cambridge, 1986), 79–94.

emigrants' departure; the terms on which the New England venture was declared legitimate. To justify emigration, the godly who left had to be released from their obligation to stay with the godly at home. The rationale for leaving England, the casuistry that defended it, was born of exceptional circumstances. The logic of the rhetoric that carried settlers away was to stamp a particular character on New England. As we shall see, the terms that were agreed for going over pressed the godly in directions that, despite their intentions, undermined unity with England. The decision to leave, then, became an unexpected watershed.

II

New England's settlers came from godly circles in English parishes where loyalty to the Church of England ran deep. Opposition to popery on the one hand, and to separatism on the other, played a crucial part in defining the character of their allegiance. The English church might be blemished, but it remained God's own. The fragile and incomplete nature of the reformation made it urgent to witness against popery. Yet traces of Catholicism could not mar the church to the point where it was lawful to renounce it as antichristian and step outside it.[10]

Preaching stood at the centre of their strategy to uphold the Church of England. Future defenders of New England played their part, as godly preachers, in warding off the threat posed by recusant Catholics and radical separatists. In 1629, Richard Mather preached a series of sermons against Catholics in Liverpool: the Corporation believed there were 'many papists who might be converted by hearing the preaching of the Established Church'. In the early 1620s, John Cotton told his congregation that the presence of godly preachers, and the gathering of the faithful to hear the Word, proved separatists were wrong to turn their backs on the Church of England: 'where the faithfull hearing Christs voice resort, and will not heare any voyce but Christs, follow those'; and 'where you find faithfull ministers Priests . . . Thither carry your kids, there plant your families to bee fed under such shepheards.' Both Mather and Cotton affirmed their loyalty to the church through preaching. Mather agreed to his bishop's condition that only ministers who would

---

10 Collinson, *Religion of Protestants*, 270–83; Collinson, 'English Conventicle'; Peter Lake, *Moderate Puritans and the Elizabethan Church* (Cambridge, 1982); Peter Lake, 'Anti-Popery: The Structure of a Prejudice', in *Conflict in Early Stuart England: Studies in Religion and Politics 1603–1642*, ed. R. Cust and A. Hughes (1989), 72–106; Peter Lake, 'The Significance of the Elizabethan Identification of the Pope as Antichrist', *Journal of Ecclesiastical History*, 31 (1980), 161–78; Peter Lake, 'William Bradshaw, Antichrist and the Community of the Godly', *ibid.*, 36 (1985), 570–89.

not 'prejudice the doctrine or discipline of the Church' could participate in the Liverpool campaign. Cotton gathered his godly parishioners together by a covenant, and became notorious for evading ceremonies, but warned his hearers constantly of the serious error of separating from the Church of England.[11] In assessing the activities of preachers like these, it is important not to overplay differences between them in use of ceremonies and overlook the strength of their common opposition from the pulpit to popery and separatism: to do so distorts the emphasis of their commitment to the English church. Such preachers ensured a market for their sermons by stressing the high cost of resisting God's Word. The spiritual journey of a Puritan became a journey from sermon to sermon. What the clergy said in public lay people repeated in private, reading sermon notes to one another. On the eve of emigration, ministers still held the 'sovereignty of exposition'. Their preaching provided structure and expression for the religious aspirations of the laity.[12] By the time the 1630s came, the godly had invested heavily in preaching over several decades. If antipathy to popery and separatism set the boundaries of their loyalty to the Church of England, preaching sat at its heart.

Because so much had been staked on preaching, the threat Laudian policies posed to Puritan preachers inevitably appeared to endanger the English church. When the authorities set conditions Puritan clergy could not accept – ceremonies, the Book of Sports, prohibition of preaching about predestination – the godly perceived a regime intent on crippling the faithful ministry by imposing a 'new conformitie'.[13] 'Silenced'

---

[11] R. J. Coffman and M. F. Rhinelander, 'The Testament of Richard Mather and William Thompson: A New Historical and Genealogical Document of the Great Migration', *New England Historical and Genealogical Register*, 140 (1986), 5; John Cotton, *A Brief Exposition of the Whole Book of Canticles* (1642), 34–5 (the 1642 edition is to be distinguished from that of 1655, which contains sermons Cotton preached in New England); Larzer Ziff, *The Career of John Cotton* (Princeton, N.J., 1962), 46–9.

[12] Collinson, *Religion of Protestants*, 267; see also Collinson, 'Lectures by Combination: Structures and Characteristics of Church Life in 17th Century England', in *Godly People*, 467–98. The spiritual testimonies of New England colonists, recalling English experience, witness to the importance of sermons: *Thomas Shepard's Confessions*, ed. George Selement and Bruce C. Woolley (Publications of the Colonial Society of Massachusetts, *Collections*, 58, Boston, 1981). Nehemiah Wallington once heard nineteen sermons in a week: Paul Seaver, *Wallington's World: A Puritan Artisan in Seventeenth-Century London* (Stanford, 1985), 37.

[13] Robert Stansby, rector of Westhorpe, Suffolk, distinguished between the old conformity and 'the new conformitie as they call it': Stansby to John Winthrop, 17 March 1636/7, *The Winthrop Papers, 1498–1649*, ed. Allyn B. Forbes, *et al.* (Boston, Mass., 1929–47), III, 380–1. The protestations of Allen and Metcalfe (see n. 1) alleged that Laudian policies brought unwarranted innovations, and support Tyacke, *Anti-Calvinists*, ch. 8.

preachers could not deliver the means of building and safeguarding reformation. David Cressy underplays the fears church policies of the 1630s aroused when he contends that Puritans 'told of suspensions and harassments, but . . . did not normally see them as catastrophic'. The suspension of Thomas Hooker, lecturer at Chelmsford in Essex, caused a local furore. His followers clamoured against Laud 'as a man indeavouring to suppres good preaching and advance Popery.' When Thomas Allen and other Norwich ministers were prevented from preaching, the citizens immediately protested that the number of papists had increased. Rumours flew fast and furious about 'lights' likely to be 'eclipsed'.[14] In his farewell sermon, Hooker warned 'the gospel is going . . . Christ is departing'. The despisers of preaching would have their day: 'Thou, man or woman, that canst not abide so much preaching, but standest on thorns, to have the sermon done . . . Thou sayest, "Depart, preaching." And so it shall.' The preaching England had known 'this twenty, thirty, forty, fifty, nay sixty years and upwards' seemed to be coming to an end. Popery would follow. Like many other preachers, Hooker saw the crisis that had befallen Protestants in the Palatinate as a vivid warning of what might happen. If Catholicism could reassert itself in the best of reformed churches, why not in England?[15]

In the context of the 1630s, the logic of the rhetoric that had been built up to defend the English church suddenly pointed in more than one direction, and generated uncertainty about how to react to the situation. Cotton's arguments against separatism in the 1620s, for example, had relied on the presence of godly preachers. Now his earlier sermons started to look like arguments for separation, not against it, as here:

When Christ goes, let all his faithfull spouses goe with him . . . but are there these causes now? doth not Christ dwell here in the simplicity of his ordinances? As long as Christ is here in England, let us not goe away . . . As long as Christ is pleased to feed us, to drop milke and honey into our soules, let us not depart.[16]

[14] Cressy, *Coming Over*, 236; Tyacke, *Anti-Calvinists*, 189–92; Bodleian Library, Tanner MS 68, fols. 160–1. Samuel Ward of Ipswich reported rumours of 'lights' eclipsed: PRO, SP 16/278, fol. 150. For examples of concern among John Winthrop's correspondents about suppression of preaching, see *Winthrop Papers*, ed. Forbes et al., III, 243, 305, 370, 380–1.
[15] Hooker, 'The Danger of Desertion' (1631), in *Thomas Hooker: Writings in England and Holland, 1626–1633*, ed. G. H. Williams, N. Pettit, W. Herget and S. Bush (Cambridge, Mass., 1975), 232–3, 242–5; see also Cotton, *Canticles*, 32, 61. Tom Cogswell, 'England and the Spanish Match', in *Conflict in Early Stuart England*, ed. Cust and Hughes, 113–14, 120, discusses the impact of the crisis in the Palatinate.
[16] Cotton, *Canticles*, 127.

Yet resistance to separatism remained sharp. New England, significantly, presented an alternative way out of the dilemma: a colonising venture could offer shelter abroad, without the taint of separatism. But if the logic of the old rhetoric pressed the godly to go, it pressed hard for them to stay. Disaster had not happened yet. The godly must stay to witness against popery. Whatever happened, God could be relied on to protect his own, just as he had preserved the elect during the centuries of Roman domination. Emigration to New England threatened to deprive England of large numbers of godly citizens, at a time when England could ill spare them: it had implications altogether different from private, temporary, flight.[17] Strategic retreat to the Low Countries, a well-established refuge in storms over conformity, might be better than a godly exodus to the New World.[18] For ministers, the careers of Jacobean Puritans like John Dod and Arthur Hildersham proved that conflict with church authorities need not mean separatism or an end to pastoral work. Another veteran, William Bradshaw, had set down the principle that faithful ministers should guide their people 'to the death', even if prevented from preaching.[19] The crisis might soon pass, or prove less drastic than feared. Samuel Ward, lecturer at Ipswich, challenged by the authorities about promoting emigration, declared he was 'not of soe melancholly a spirritt, nor looked through soe blacke spectacles as to write that Religion stands on tiptoe in this land, lookinge Westwards'; nor did he share the fear of 'an imminent departure of the Gospell'. For the moment, he 'commended such as stayd in their native Country and mother Church', though uncertain about his own conduct if it came to a 'time of triall'.[20] In the new circumstances of the 1630s, the old rhetoric of loyalty delivered an ambiguous message: except that it was clear that to desert England without good cause meant falling into the pernicious error of schism.

Pressure for the Laudian 'new conformitie', far from being tangential

---

[17] The issues are rehearsed in 'Arguments for the Plantation of New England', *Winthrop Papers*, ed. Forbes *et al.*, II, 106–49; Richard Mather, 'Arguments Tending to Prove the Removing from Old England to New . . . to Be Not Onely Lawful, but Also Necessary . . . ' (1635) in [Increase Mather], *The Life and Death of . . . Richard Mather* (Cambridge, Mass., 1670); John Cotton, *God's Promise to his Plantations* (London, 1634, preached 1630). Theodore Dwight Bozeman, *To Live Ancient Lives: The Primitivist Dimension in Puritanism* (Chapel Hill, N.C., and London, 1988), 93–8, surveys reasons colonists gave for going over, but includes later texts from New England: to avoid adding emphases from ex-post rationalisations for emigration, I have restricted myself to motive statements that predate arrival in the New World.

[18] Cressy, *Coming Over*, 89–90; and see n. 24.

[19] Fincham, *Prelate as Pastor*, 213–31; W. Bradshaw, *English Puritanisme* (1605), 9.

[20] 'Answers of Samuel Ward to Articles Objected against Him', 19 Dec. 1634, PRO, SP 16/278, fols. 149–50.

to the Great Migration, became the catalyst that detached an unlikely cast of characters from their homeland. Emigration went against the grain of Puritan commitments to the English church, precipitated by a mounting sense of crisis. The departure of godly ministers illustrates this. They left only in the wake of the drive for conformity.[21] New England's preachers came not from an underworld of sectaries, but mostly from parish pulpits. Very few fit the category of irregular clergy, long 'liberated from parochial obligations', that Stephen Foster believes turned English Puritanism in a sectarian direction and prepared the way for New England. His picture of a 'nicodemite Puritan ministry', a 'tenebrous domain . . . in which lecturers on the run or tucked away in quiet corners ministered intermittently to a floating collection of self-certified saints', does not square with the origins of colonial clergy-to-be. Most left parishes they had served for years. Cotton had been in Boston, Lincoln-shire, over twenty, and Thomas Allen's neighbour Robert Peck left Hingham, Norfolk, after thirty-two.[22] Avihu Zakai has argued that the crisis was not particular to the 1630s: emigration provided an escape from the profane, and meant the surrender of a long struggle to reform England. But the character of clerical emigration suggests otherwise. Seventy-nine clergy took the decision to leave between 1629 and 1640. The precise circumstances of a number remain obscure, but at least fifty-two had been in conflict with the authorities. Twenty-five had been deprived or suspended from their ministry. A further seventeen resigned or left under

21 The conclusions of this and the next paragraph derive from research for my forth-coming book on return migration from New England. The following sources have been particularly useful in identifying emigrant clergy: Thomas Lechford, *Plaine Dealing or Newes from New England* (1642; reprinted in Massachusetts Historical Society, *Collections*, 3rd ser., 3 (Boston, 1833); Cotton Mather, *Magnalia Christi Americana: Or the Ecclesiastical History of New England*, ed. T. Robbins (Hartford, Conn., 1853); Frederick L. Weis, *The Colonial Clergy and the Colonial Churches of New England* (Lancaster, Mass., 1936); Samuel E. Morison, *The Founding of Harvard College* (Cambridge, Mass., 1935), Appendix B; Norman C. P. Tyack, 'The Humbler Puritans of East Anglia and the New England Movement: Evidence from the Court Records of the 1630s', *New England Historical and Genealogical Register*, 139 (1984), 79–106; Norman C. P. Tyack, 'Migration from East Anglia to New England before 1660' (PhD thesis, University of London, 1951); Richard Waterhouse, 'Reluctant Emigrants: The English Background of the First Generation of the New England Clergy', *Historical Magazine of the Protestant Episcopal Church*, 44 (1975), 473–88.
22 Foster, *Long Argument*, 99–106; in contrast, Fincham, *Prelate as Pastor*, 212–31, 323–6, emphasises the comprehensiveness of the English church before 1625. Unbeneficed clergy who were working as schoolmasters, chaplains or lecturers before emigration constituted a negligible element among those who became colonial ministers; some had turned to such posts only in the changed climate of the 1630s. Recent graduates of Oxford and Cambridge filled up the New England ministry before Harvard produced home-grown candidates. For Peck, see J. Browne, *A History of Congregationalism in Norfolk and Suffolk* (1877), 103–4.

the threat of imminent action in High Commission, or in anticipation of being unable to conform to requirements put to them by diocesan or metropolitical authorities. At least ten more went as pressure in their locality tightened.[23] The timing of emigration, diocese by diocese, is striking. The diocese of London saw the earliest and greatest concentration of departures, from among those under scrutiny in the Laudian campaign of 1629–30, though several took refuge in the Low Countries before leaving for New England. Archbishop Neile's campaigns for conformity in the diocese of Chester and in the West Riding triggered emigration.[24] In the diocese of Norwich, Wren's Injunctions of 1636 provoked departures, reinforced by the vigilance of his chancellor, Clement Corbet. A night-time raid masterminded by Corbet, to bring Thomas Allen before the Court of High Commission, is the last we hear of Allen before he appears in New England.[25] Wren later tried to disassociate emigration from episcopal pressure, and pointed to the prevalence of emigrants from the lenient diocese of Lincoln. But Lincoln, a haven under Bishop John Williams for those who scrupled at

---

[23] Zakai, *Exile and Kingdom*, 136–7, 207–30. Waterhouse, 'Reluctant Emigrants', identifies seventy-six emigrants, of whom forty-seven had been in trouble with the authorities. Cressy, *Coming Over*, 87, plays down religious tensions by stressing that *only* forty-seven had clashed with their ecclesiastical superiors: however, this figure represents those for whom evidence is available, not a final total. Virginia Anderson claims over 200 clergy emigrated before 1660, but mistakenly relies on Harry Stout's figures for 'university men', which include lay and ordained emigrants, and Harvard graduates: Anderson, *New England's Generation*, 18n, citing Stout, 'University Men in New England, 1620–1660: A Demographic Analysis', *Journal of Interdisciplinary History*, 4 (1974), 377. David Grayson Allen, *In English Ways: The Movement of Societies and the Transferal of Local Law and Custom to Massachusetts Bay in the Seventeenth Century* (Chapel Hill, N.C., and London, 1981), 13–14, reckons 129 ministers came over, but has inflated the numbers by including young men who entered the ministry later, in New England.

[24] William Hunt, *The Puritan Moment: The Coming of Revolution in an English County* (Cambridge, Mass., 1983), 253–60. Thomas Hooker, John Davenport, Thomas Weld and Hugh Peter went to the Low Countries: Keith L. Sprunger, 'William Ames and the Settlement of Massachusetts Bay', *New England Quarterly*, 39 (1966), 69–70; Keith L. Sprunger, *Dutch Puritanism: A History of English and Scottish Churches in the Netherlands in the 16th and 17th Centuries* (Leiden, 1982), 103–20, 166–8, 172, 285, 347. On the character of Neile's administration, see R. A. Marchant, *The Puritans and the Church Courts in the Diocese of York 1560–1642* (1960), 54–6 and *passim*; John A. Newton, 'Puritanism in the Diocese of York (excluding Nottinghamshire), 1603–1640' (PhD thesis, University of London, 1955), 83–94, 108–9.

[25] Bodleian Library, Tanner MS 68, fol. 120; Tanner MS 220, fols. 1–3; King, 'Bishop Wren and the Norwich Lecturers', 242; Tyack, 'Humbler Puritans', 83. Corbet's rigour was matched by that of Laud's commissary in Suffolk, Henry Dade: Cressy, *Coming Over*, 140–1; King, 'Bishop Wren and the Norwich Lecturers', 239n. Ferdinando Adams, a warden at Samuel Ward's church in Ipswich, left for New England after being illegally excommunicated by Dade: PRO, SP 16/302, fols. 320–2; *Winthrop Papers*, ed. Forbes *et al.*, III, 439–40.

ceremonies, saw emigration by parochial clergy only after Laud started to use the High Commission to intervene directly. The court's sentence against John Vicars of Stamford in 1631 sounded a warning: deprived, and suspended from the ministry for seven years. John Cotton, though heavily involved in the discussions that led to the sailing of the Winthrop Fleet in 1630, left his parish only when his own activities came under investigation.[26] There was no eager rush to New England: these were not willing migrants.

The impression that ministers were reluctant to depart is reinforced by the hesitancy of emigration, and the small number who took the decision to go. Those who left formed only a fraction of those who felt under stress and considered New England. David Cressy believes the modest numbers show how irrelevant pressure on Puritanism was to emigration.[27] It is more likely, however, that the low tally reflects the difficulty of the decision to leave. With hindsight, the gathering momentum of the 'Great Migration' is evident. But it was not at the time. New England was not the only option. Ministers worked through an old repertoire of choices before resolving on New England. Thomas Allen protested against his sentence, and tried legal action against those responsible for the communion rail and chancel steps in his church. He went to Holland for a few months, but returned to Norwich until Corbet's raid flushed him out. His parishioners continued to support him financially.[28] Many followed a similar path, staying in or near their parishes for a time, though unable to preach, before resorting to emigration.[29] Ezekiel Rogers of Rowley, Yorkshire, prohibited from

---

[26] Bodleian Library, Tanner MS 314, fol. 153v; Ziff, *Career of John Cotton*, 65–70. For Vicars, see *Reports of Cases in the Courts of Star Chamber and High Commission*, ed. S. R. Gardiner (Camden Soc., n.s., 39, 1886), 198–238, 273–4; C. Holmes, *Seventeenth Century Lincolnshire* (Lincoln, 1980), 42–3, 62. Efforts had been made in 1629 to recruit Cotton: *Winthrop Papers*, ed. Forbes *et al.*, II, 177–8. Samuel Skelton, chaplain to the earl of Lincoln, left before any of the parochial clergy, accompanying the group that settled at Salem, Massachusetts. As a member of the earl's household, he was readily released to take part in the earl's plans to promote New England: Richard Cust, *The Forced Loan and English Politics, 1626–1628* (Oxford, 1987), 171–2. Cressy, *Coming Over*, 90, echoes Wren's claim that emigration was unrelated to episcopal pressure. Allen, *In English Ways*, 173–4, 179, makes the same point with reference to migration from Hingham, Norfolk. However, though some left Hingham before pressure tightened on the minister, Robert Peck, two-thirds of the emigrants left in 1638, when Peck himself went: Tyack, 'Humbler Puritans', 98n.

[27] Cressy, *Coming Over*, 87; see also Sharpe, *Personal Rule of Charles I*, 752.

[28] Bodleian Library, Tanner MS 68, fols. 3v, 115–20, 205v, 230, 234, 242; Tanner MS 220, fols. 1–3.

[29] For example, Henry Whitfield of Ockley, Surrey; Richard Mather of Toxteth, Lancashire; Robert Peck of Hingham, Norfolk. Peck, like Allen, received financial support from his parishioners: Bodleian Library, Tanner MS 68, fol. 234. Allen, 'Matrix of Motivation', 415–16, believes that because Peck did not leave England until

preaching in December 1634 for (as he later put it) 'Refusing to Reade that accursed Booke that allowed sports on Gods holy Sabbath', stayed on until 1638, with a curate occupying his pulpit. He believed ' ''Tis possible the times may alter, and I may againe be capable of my place.'[30] Thomas Shepard only decided to emigrate after he had tried without success to escape episcopal attention by moving from Essex to Northumberland: 'seeing I had been tossed from the south to the north of England and now could go no farther, I then began to listen to a call to New England'.[31] Like Shepard, Charles Chauncy attempted evasion. He left the diocese of London for the diocese of Peterborough in 1633, claiming he had been driven out of Ware, Hertfordshire, by an order to rail in the communion table. High Commission investigated his activities in his new parish of Marston St Lawrence, Northamptonshire, and allowed him to continue his ministry only after extracting a damaging public submission: in words provided by the Court, Chauncy endorsed communion rails and kneeling to receive the sacrament. A message sent to Laud in 1637, however, observed that Chauncy 'mends like sour ale in summer', and would be in trouble at the next visitation. He took ship for New England that year, leaving behind a fierce recantation of his compliance.[32] As we have seen, several clergy, like Thomas Allen, went to the Low Countries before New England; John Cotton considered this.[33] Some no doubt hoped New England would prove a temporary exile: a safe haven from which the godly could 'returne after the storme', to 'be of better use to their mother Churche'.[34] Nathaniel Ward, once of

1638, and returned in 1641, his motives for emigration were not religious. In my view, Peck's case proves just the opposite.

[30] *The Probate Records of Essex County, Massachusetts*, ed. G. F. Dow (Salem, Mass., 1916–20), I, 332; Marchant, *Puritans and Church Courts*, 96–102, 274; Rogers to Sir Thomas Barrington, 2 Nov. 1636, BL, Egerton MS 2646, fol. 104v. Barrington, Rogers' patron, refused to accept the situation and insisted on presenting another man to the living. This precipitated Rogers' resignation and emigration. Foster, *Long Argument*, 29, 93, 158, 165, suggests Rogers had deserted the Church of England before he set sail: the case is discussed further below.

[31] *God's Plot: The Paradoxes of Puritan Piety, Being the Autobiography and Journal of Thomas Shepard*, ed. M. McGiffert (Amherst, Mass., 1972), 55.

[32] PRO, SP/16/261, fols. 298v–9; SP16/312, fols. 113r–v; SP16/324, fol. 5; SP16/361, fol. 128; Charles Chauncy, *The Retraction of Mr. Charles Chauncy* (1641). He was suspended on 26 November 1635, and made his submission on 11 February 1635/6.

[33] Ziff, *Career of John Cotton*, 66–9.

[34] *Winthrop Papers*, ed. Forbes et al., II, 125; see also 147. Thomas Allen's brother later claimed Allen had been 'compelled to live in forreigne parts'; Robert and Martha Peck of Hingham were said to have been made 'exiles in their old age': Bodleian Library, Tanner MS 220, fols. 1–3. Bozeman, *To Live Ancient Lives*, 96–8, discusses exilic language before and after emigration. Those who could afford to keep property in England did so: Anderson, *New England's Generation*, 48–50; Cressy, *Coming Over*, 180.

Essex, then of Ipswich, Massachusetts, later put into the mouth of his satirical character, the simple cobbler of Agawam, an 'American creed': 'no man ought to forsake his owne countrey, but upon extraordinary cause, and when that cause ceaseth, he is bound in conscience to return if he can'.[35]

To understand the emigrants' dilemma about whether to go or to stay, we need to grasp how deeply they worried about being on the right side of Providence, and what a corporate, social, process discerning Providence had to be. Without God's blessing, a venture to New England courted disaster. The ungodliness, poverty and disorder of other colonies exemplified the potential for ruin. To identify the hand of God, the godly who stayed and the godly who left had to have the same view of emigration. Just as saints become saints because their sanctity is recognised by others, so the leading of Providence had to be recognised not only by the emigrants themselves, but also by the peers they left behind. Only public scrutiny and acceptance of their 'grounds' could free them to go without schism. Defending emigration later, John Allin and Thomas Shepard pointed to the conversations which had validated their enterprise, 'with the admirable workings of Gods Providence first and last about it': 'Yea, how many serious consultations with one another, and with the faithfull Ministers, and other eminent servants of Christ, have been taken about this worke, is not unknowne to some; which cleares us from any rash heady rushing into this place, out of discontent'. In the summer of 1629, meetings in Lincolnshire, Bury St Edmunds and Cambridge thrashed out the prospects for settlement. John Winthrop sent papers setting out the issues to interested parties like John White of Dorchester. John Cotton sought the approval of the nonconformist John Dod for his own decision to leave. Richard Mather wrote down his deliberations about it for fellow-ministers to scrutinise.[36] The diary of young Samuel Rogers, who aspired to be a preacher, reveals fervent heart-searching about the matter between 1635 and 1637. 'Poor Suffolk and Norfolk lying desolate by that cursed, wretched, Wren . . . Oh Lord some way for preaching; oh my soul is in New England', Rogers wrote; but was persuaded to stay on in England by his

---

[35] Nathaniel Ward, *The Simple Cobler of Agawam in America*, ed. P. M. Zall (Lincoln, Neb., 1969; originally published London, 1647), 25. For Ward, see *DNB*.

[36] John Allin and Thomas Shepard, *A Treatise of Liturgies* (1653), 3, 6; *Winthrop Papers*, ed. Forbes *et al.*, II, 110–52; Cotton Mather, *Magnalia*, I, 263; Richard Mather, 'Arguments', in [Increase Mather], *Life . . . of . . . Richard Mather*, 57–68. David Underdown, *Fire from Heaven: The Life of an English Town in the Seventeenth Century* (1992), and Frank Thistlethwaite, *Dorset Pilgrims: The Story of West Country Pilgrims who Went to New England in the Seventeenth Century* (1989), provide recent discussions of John White's role.

father.[37] The extent of the deliberations, private and public, underscores the crisis of conscience that emigration posed. The intensely collaborative character of the process reflects a determination to leave with godly consent. The blessing of the godly and the blessing of Providence went together.

How, in the end, could emigrants overcome their ambivalence about leaving England? Only by claiming exceptional circumstances, and by pitting popery against purity, threat against opportunity. The polarity between popery at home and purity abroad, in the special context of the 1630s, is crucial: overlook that dynamic and the New England experiment is misunderstood. The resurgence of Catholicism in old England posed an 'extraordinary' threat. The empty landscape of New England presented a Providential opportunity to begin again from 'first beginnings'. Emigrants weighed old England against New: popery, persecution, danger and hindrances to enjoying 'pure ordinances', versus purity, peace, liberty and opportunity. Theodore Bozeman has shown how the desire for 'refuge' and 'pure ordinances' dominates migrants' motive-statements, and how the ideal of primitive biblical purity shaped their outlook. Emigration was a flight from human invention. His case is compelling, but underestimates just how far heightened concern for purity was an effect of the threat of popery. Fear of popery sharpened the desire for purity. Anxiety about the return of Catholicism, which showed itself in the language of refuge, released emigrants from inhibitions about leaving England. The popish threat ran like a thread through deliberations about emigration, and had the strength and elasticity to tie together a multiplicity of concerns. In the debate between Winthrop and his correspondents, the stain of popery lay across the decay of justice, economic troubles and the corruption of 'the fountains of learninge and religion'. At the same time, the chance to begin again from first principles in New England was a vital counterpart to the threat in England. Providence had provided a new plantation: escape from popery need not mean separation, yet a godly society could be built from scratch.[38] However, this is not to say that godly settlers left England

---

[37] Diary of Samuel Rogers, 5 Dec. 1636, Queen's University, Belfast, Percy MS, fol. 184; cited by Kenneth W. Shipps, 'The Puritan Emigration to New England: A New Source on Motivation', *New England Historical and Genealogical Register*, 135 (1981), 90–1. Samuel's father was Daniel Rogers (*DNB*), lecturer at Wethersfield, Essex; Ezekiel Rogers was his uncle, and Nathaniel Ward and Nathaniel Rogers (*DNB*), clerical emigrants from Essex, were also relatives.

[38] Bozeman, *To Live Ancient Lives*, 95–8, 111–14. A letter from Robert Ryece to John Winthrop, [1629], illustrates the importance of the threat from popery: *Winthrop Papers*, ed. Forbes et al., II, 127–30; see also Robin Clifton, 'Fear of Popery', in *The Origins of the English Civil War*, ed. C. Russell (1973), 144–67. The historical basis for

convinced they had an eschatological 'errand into the wilderness'. The notion that such an 'errand' inspired the first migrants promotes the idea of America's special origins, but has little substance. Avihu Zakai has recently restated the argument for an errand in stark terms: emigrants thought God had 'desacralised' England for her sins, and that salvation history had shifted to the wilderness of New England. But Zakai misreads Thomas Hooker's pulpit rhetoric when he contends that Hooker in 1626 praised 'this little England' as the elect nation, whereas by 1631 he was ready to 'cut all ties with corrupt England and fly into the wilderness of America'. The themes of the sermons Zakai cites are in fact remarkably similar. Neither casts England off. Both balance the favours England has received against the judgement imminent if she does not repent. However, conflict between preacher and prelate in the 1630s sharpened the message. Hooker, who said of Noah in 1626 'every nail he drove was a sermon', warned in 1631 'God begins to ship away his Noahs, which prophesied and foretold that destruction was near'.[39] Emigration was a prophetic sign, a warning. Bozeman, rightly, characterises emigrants' religious motives as a retreat to biblical patterns rather than a militant millenarian errand.[40] They turned to primitive purity in reaction against the Catholicism that might overwhelm the English church. The threat of popery at home defined the prospect of purity in New England.

The assortment of motives emigrants put forward to rationalise leaving England cannot diminish the importance of the particular crisis of the 1630s.[41] A true calling to join the venture proved itself by the sheer variety of signs that pointed towards New England. To discern the hand of Providence, the godly looked for a concurrence of motives, personal and general, religious and secular. For this reason, it is misleading to play off economic and godly motives against each other. Michael Metcalfe,

---

belief in a Laudian conspiracy to restore Catholicism has been investigated by Anthony Milton, 'The Laudians and the Church of Rome, c. 1625–1640' (PhD thesis, University of Cambridge, 1989). On the importance of raising a 'new' church, from 'infancy', *Winthrop Papers*, ed. Forbes *et al.*, II, 112, 128.

[39] Zakai, *Exile and Kingdom*, 120–206; *Thomas Hooker: Writings*, ed. Williams *et al.*, 86, 246. Zakai adopts William Haller's view of England as the 'elect nation', a view questioned by Patrick Collinson, *Birthpangs*, 11–17.

[40] Bozeman, *To Live Ancient Lives*, 238–62. For critiques of Perry Miller's essay 'Errand into the Wilderness', *Errand into the Wilderness* (Cambridge, Mass., 1956), and the literature it has generated, see Bozeman, *ibid.*, 80–90; Andrew Delbanco, 'The Puritan Errand Re-Viewed', *Journal of American Studies*, 18 (1984), 343–60. Francis J. Bremer, 'To Live Exemplary Lives: Puritans and Puritan Communities as Lofty Lights', *The Seventeenth Century*, 7 (1992), 27–39, is more sympathetic to Miller's case.

[41] Cressy, *Coming Over*, 74–106, plays down the importance of the crisis because of the 'mixture of motives'; see also Sharpe, *Personal Rule of Charles I*, 751–7.

one of Thomas Allen's parishioners, would be one more weaver pushed to New England by the slump in the textile industry if his letter to the people of Norwich had not survived, lamenting unprecedented innovations in religion – 'never heretofore urged upon any man's conscience, by any Bishop of the see of Norwich since the Reformation'.[42] 'Religion and profit do jump together' said Edward Winslow of Plymouth Plantation. John Frederick Martin's recent study, the nicely titled *Profits in the Wilderness*, demonstrates the significance of entrepreneurship in New England, in the industry, creativity and acquisitiveness of early settlers. To recognise the tug of Providence in the call to emigrate, those who left England had to be certain they could make a living. However, the Great Migration is marked out from other contemporary ventures by its family-based character, and its settlers were not fortune-hunters. Colonists just hoped Providence would provide 'competency': 'nothing sorts better with piety than competency', as John White of Dorchester put it.[43] Thus in the process of choosing whether to go or to stay, many motives came into play, and the viability of life in New England was a critical factor. However, within the framework of godly mentality, the variety of motives cannot be taken to show that religion, in the context of the 1630s, played a minor role: in order to see their way to the difficult decision to leave, potential emigrants were encouraged to count up the ways Providence led down the same path.

By setting popery against purity as they did, emigrants twisted the old rhetoric of loyalty to the English church to a new purpose. But they refused to cast off its other element, opposition to separatism. As we have seen, a concern for unity among the godly balanced the rhetoric of popery and purity. Moreover, to show they left lawfully, they set a high premium on making right use of the liberty of New England. Purity must

---

[42] Timothy Breen and Stephen Foster make this point, in an article which remains influential for its refusal to accept a dichotomy between religious and economic concerns: 'Moving to the New World: The Character of Early Massachusetts Immigration', *William and Mary Quarterly*, 3rd ser., 30 (1973), 203; see also Foster, *Long Argument*, 345. For Metcalfe, see n. 1.

[43] Edward Winslow, *Good Newes from New-England* (1624), 52, 64; John Frederick Martin, *Profits in the Wilderness: Entrepreneurship and the Founding of New England Towns in the Seventeenth Century* (Chapel Hill, N.C., and London, 1991); John White, *The Planters Plea* (1630), in Peter Force (comp.), *Tracts and Other Papers, Relating Principally to the Origin, Settlement, and Progress of the Colonies in North America* (Washington, DC, 1836), II, 18. The notion of 'competency' is explored by Daniel Vickers, 'Competency and Competition: Economic Culture in Early America', *William and Mary Quarterly*, 3rd ser., 47 (1990), 3–29; Anderson, *New England's Generation*, 123–7, and *passim*. Delbanco, *Puritan Ordeal*, argues that emigrants left England to escape the acquisitiveness they had created: their 'tough entrepreneurship' was tempered by a critique of capitalism.

be matched with peaceful, orderly settlement. William Ames, the eminent nonconformist, offered no direct advice to Governor John Winthrop as Winthrop prepared to set out, 'being ignorant of special difficulties'; however, he assumed 'the general care of safetie, libertie, unitie, with puritie, to bee in all your mindes and desires.'[44] Winthrop knew emigrants could not afford to forfeit the good opinion of the godly at home. To do so would threaten the view that the venture had the blessing of Providence. Concern for the reputation of New England lay at the heart of his famous words to fellow-passengers on the way:

wee shall be as a Citty upon a Hill, the eies of all people are upon us; soe that if we shall deale falsely with our god in this worke wee have undertaken . . . wee shall be made a story and a by-word through the world, wee shall open the mouthes of enemies to speake evill of the wayes of god and all professours for gods sake; we shall shame the faces of many of gods worthy servants, and cause theire prayers to be turned into Cursses upon us.[45]

Winthrop's 'city upon a hill' was not the 'world-redeeming beacon', the 'hub of the universe', the 'New Jerusalem' it has been taken for by followers of Perry Miller.[46] The context betrays an altogether more defensive, anxious theme: a caution against the godly experiment becoming a by-word for error, a cause of shame, the object of curses.

Godly settlers left England arguing that Providence approved their departure. To rationalise the decision to go, opposites had been set against each other: popery and purity; persecution and peace; danger and liberty; hindrance and opportunity; no ordinances against all ordinances; old England and New. Spurred by the threat to preaching, ministers provided a message that could harness a wide variety of concerns to promote emigration. The familiar rhetoric against popery and separatism defined the legitimacy of leaving England, just as it defined loyalty to the English church. Yet although arguments had been amassed to justify New England, ambivalence remained. Far from being a confident, assertive, 'errand', the Great Migration was reactive, a response to pressure. Emigrants still craved the approbation of the godly left behind. The cost of their gesture against popery marks the evolution of New England: the terms on which they set sail proved crucial in shaping the new venture.[47]

---

[44] Ames to Winthrop, 29 Dec. [1629], *Winthrop Papers*, ed. Forbes *et al.*, II, 180.

[45] Winthrop, 'A Modell of Christian Charity', *Winthrop Papers*, ed. Forbes *et al.*, II, 295.

[46] Loren Baritz, *City on a Hill* (New York, 1964), 17; Sacvan Bercovitch, *The Puritan Origins of the American Self* (New Haven, 1975), 97; and for Miller, see n. 40.

[47] Bercovitch, *Puritan Origins of the American Self*, 102–3, identifies 'psychic uncertainty and rhetorical self-assertion' in early New England, but gives his theme a decidedly triumphalist, millenial, cast: New England was the 'New Jerusalem' that would

III

If keeping the good opinion of the godly in England was so important, why did New England go beyond the familiar patterns of Puritan voluntary religion? Why bring in innovations like church covenant that proved controversial with the godly back home? Interpretation of the English experience of colonists influences the answer. If we begin with a model of English Puritanism spinning in a separatist direction, with lay initiatives threatening to usurp clerical control, it is tempting to see the influence of radical separatism in the formation of New England. Stephen Foster emphasises the influence of separatism on the laity and argues that as the 1630s progressed, ever-more embittered Puritans arrived to press the settlers further in the direction of *de facto* separatism.[48] However, if we recognise a powerful resistance to separatism in colonists' English experience, and take a less appositional view of relations between preachers and people, New England looks different. The idea of radical laity pressing the clergy in new directions may not be the right way to account for colonial innovations. James F. Cooper has recently questioned the role attributed to lay assertiveness, and studies of lay religion have stressed the part the clergy continued to play in providing the framework for piety.[49] Undeniably, the call to New England recruited Puritans of a radical temper. But radicalism and separatism did not inevitably go hand in hand. Emigration went against the grain and was pressed by a mounting sense of crisis. English experience radicalised people into emigration, not necessarily into rejecting their mother church. Foster's case that emigrants of the late 1630s were more radical than those who came earlier is attractively

'harbour the elect plucked out of the final conflagration'. In my view, Bercovitch's contention that the emigrant 'had to justify himself by justifying America' needs to be read in a quite different way.
48 Foster, *Long Argument*, 138–44, 151–66; Hall, *Faithful Shepherd*, argued in 1972 for the influence of lay initiatives.
49 James F. Cooper, Jr, '"A Mixed Form": The Establishment of Church Government in Massachusetts Bay, 1629–1645', *Essex Institute Historical Collections*, 123 (1987), 233–59; 'The Confession and Trial of Richard Wayte, Boston, 1640', *William and Mary Quarterly*, 3rd ser., 44 (1987), 310–32; 'Ann Hutchinson and the "Lay Rebellion" against the Clergy', *New England Quarterly*, 61 (1988), 381–97. For lay religion and the clergy, see George Selement, 'The Meeting of Elite and Popular Minds at Cambridge, New England, 1638–1645', *William and Mary Quarterly*, 3rd ser., 41 (1984), 32–48; David D. Hall, 'Toward a History of Popular Religion in Early New England', *ibid.*, 49–55; David D. Hall, *Worlds of Wonder, Days of Judgment: Popular Religious Belief in Early New England* (Cambridge, Mass., 1989), 11–20, 240–1; Charles Hambrick-Stowe, *The Practice of Piety: Puritan Devotional Disciplines in Seventeenth-Century New England* (Chapel Hill, N.C., 1982), 86–9; Charles Cohen, *God's Caress: The Psychology of Puritan Religious Experience* (New York and Oxford, 1986), ch. 6.

argued, but not compelling. If anything, the reverse is true. To support his belief in a contrast between the 'original, broadly based Puritanism of the early migration and its more militant, more sectarian successor', he compares John Davenport, who arrived in 1637, with Richard Mather, who emigrated in 1635: Davenport, the moderate Puritan conformist, turned out 'harder and meaner' in New England than the nonconformist Mather, because of the sharp reversal entailed in his disillusionment with England.[50] But this line of reasoning presents problems. The extent of Mather's nonconformity in England is hard to determine, as Foster admits; and in any case, as we have seen, attitudes to ceremonies were not necessarily the heart of Puritanism. What is more, Davenport fled England before Mather, going to Amsterdam in 1633. Thus although Davenport arrived in New England later than Mather, his 'disillusionment' reached emigration pitch earlier, and Amsterdam gave him greater radical experience than Mather before New England, not less. In the late 1630s both took a common stand to defend the validity of English churches, as we shall see. The difficulties of Foster's case are compounded when other emigrants are brought into the picture. What, in terms of time of emigration and English experience of nonconformity, are we to make of John Cotton and Roger Williams? Both emigrated early in the 1630s with a clear record of nonconformity. Cotton stands behind some of New England's most controversial innovations and advised the 'hard and mean' Davenport about framing church and state in New Haven; Williams became New England's 'sectarian' *par excellence*. And though some late arrivals in the 1630s turned out to be radicals, such as Hanserd Knollys, who soon returned to England and became a Baptist, other late emigrants stand out for their conservative disposition: like the Boston lawyer, Thomas Lechford, a supporter of William Prynne; or Richard Sadler of Lynn; or Mary Oliver of Salem, who came over from Thomas Allen's Norwich parish.[51] Foster admits that 'New England's settlers were recruited from a spectrum of progressive Protestantism

[50] Foster, *Long Argument*, pp. 156–65, 348 n. 39.

[51] For Mather and Davenport, see Coffman and Rhinelander, 'Mather–Thompson Testament'; Tyacke, *Anti-Calvinists*, 186–7; Sprunger, *Dutch Puritanism*, 112–19; I. M. Calder, *The New Haven Colony* (New Haven, 1934), 44, 51. For Cotton, see Ziff, *Career of John Cotton*; for Williams, *Dictionary of American Biography*, ed. A. Johnson and D. Malone (20 vols., London and New York, 1928–36); for Knollys, *DNB*; for Lechford, see his *Plain Dealing: Or, Newes from New England* (London, 1642) and *Dictionary of American Biography*, ed. Johnson and Malone; for Sadler, 'Richard Sadler's Account of the Massachusetts Churches', ed. R. C. Simmons, *New England Quarterly*, 42 (1969), 411–25; for Oliver, Breen and Foster, 'Moving to the New World', 202, and John Winthrop, *The History of New England from 1630 to 1649*, ed. J. Savage (2nd edn, Boston, 1853), I, 281–2.

broad enough to run from a Roger Williams to a Mary Oliver and beyond', but presses the significance of Puritan volatility, of radical tendencies. Yet the increase of pressure late in the decade, and the variety of reasons put forward to convince people that the call to New England came from Providence, tended to recruit more widely, more indiscriminately, than Foster makes out. Emigrants reflected the breadth of English Puritan opinion, united by opposition to popery.[52] Colonial leaders faced the task of welding this company into a viable plantation. They had to accomplish this in a bewildering environment, under astonishingly hard conditions, without many of the landmarks of English society. In such circumstances innovation in religion became inevitable. However, to read it as a lurch into separatism distorts the picture.

The reasons for the path New England took lie in the need to be true to the terms on which the New England venture was undertaken. Settlers needed to convince the godly back home, and not least themselves, that leaving England had been justified. To witness against popery, they had to establish purity. To show themselves no separatists, they had to keep order and unity. For the blessing of Providence to shine clear, New England must make a profit, or at least not be an economic catastrophe. Ironically, colonists' efforts to prove themselves right would put them in the wrong with England. But that comes later. First, we need to look more closely at the imperatives of order, viability and purity that came from the rhetoric used to legitimise emigration.

To create an orderly, successful plantation, New England's leaders wrestled with the task of stabilising settlement. Conditions shocked new arrivals. The need to brace settlement became particularly acute in the late 1630s after immigrants poured in at the height of the Great Migration. Virginia Anderson speaks of a 'Great Reshuffling', as people moved to new towns and into new patterns of work.[53] From the start, some colonists questioned whether Providence had intended to bring them to New England. A surgeon called John Pratt wrote home complaining of 'the improbability or impossibility of subsistence for ourselves or for our posterity without tempting God'. To ask for stones

---

[52] Stephen Foster, 'New England and the Challenge of Heresy, 1630 to 1660: The Puritan Crisis in Transatlantic Perspective', *William and Mary Quarterly*, 3rd ser., 38 (1981), 641–2. Carla Gardina Pestana, *Quakers and Baptists in Colonial Massachusetts* (Cambridge, 1991), 7–11, 13, notes the wide spectrum of opinions in the Salem church (which is usually cited for inclinations to separatism), and argues that both Philip Gura, *A Glimpse of Sion's Glory: Puritan Radicalism in New England, 1620–1660* (Middletown, Conn., 1984), and David S. Lovejoy, *Religious Enthusiasm in the New World* (Cambridge, Mass., 1985), overestimate the agitation of radicals in early Massachusetts.

[53] Anderson, *New England's Generation*, ch. 3; her findings support those of Breen and Foster, 'Moving to the New World', 208–16.

to be turned into bread, in a barren land of 'rocks, sands and salt marshes', was to listen to the devil's promptings. He feared the spiritual cost of hardship would be high: 'the gospel would be as dear here as in England'; he saw danger of 'decaying here in our first love'. Reprimanded by the magistrates for sending back such a negative report, he argued that material difficulties caused spiritual trouble: 'how hard it is to keep our hearts in that holy frame which sometimes they were in, where we had less to do in outward things'. After all the talk in advance, New England was a disappointment, materially and spiritually.[54] John Winthrop feared what would happen if settlers got away from the eyes of the ministers and magistrates, and at first wanted all settlements clustered close round Boston. When some proposed to go to Connecticut, opinion was so split that the Massachusetts General Court called a fast-day to seek God's will. Back in England, the godly were judging that 'a kingdom divided against itself cannot stand'.[55] To those responsible for guiding the new plantation, the survival of the infant communities hinged on steadying settlement.

Stability, and indeed New England's reputation, depended on putting in place the familiar structures of godly religion. Continuities between Puritanism in the old world and the new can be overlooked in the quest to search out the distinctiveness of New England, but are massive and important. Sermons played a central part, as in England. The heavy-handed didacticism of early New England tried to teach the 'right story' about the colonial experiment. Each town had its church, and the magistrates required every resident to hear the sermon, church member or not. In 1635 the General Court ruled that all houses must be built within half a mile of the meeting house. Just as the godly gathered in England for lecture-days, fasts and thanksgivings, and met in private to repeat sermons, so too in New England. Preachers delivered sermons to encourage those come newly ashore.[56]

---

[54] 'Pratts Apology', Nov. 1635, Massachusetts Historical Society, *Collections*, 2nd ser., 7 (Boston, 1818), 126–8; see Luke 4:3–4. Winthrop's answer to objections against emigration tackled precisely the matter Pratt raised of 'tempting God': *Winthrop Papers*, ed. Forbes *et al.*, II, 137–8. Pratt's disappointment is echoed in the testimonies of members of Thomas Shepard's Cambridge church, which will be discussed below.

[55] Martin, *Profits in the Wilderness*, 117; Darrett Rutman, *Winthrop's Boston: A Portrait of a Puritan Town, 1630–1649* (Chapel Hill, N.C., 1965), 280–3; Winthrop, *History of New England*, I, 167–9; Robert Stansby to John Winthrop, 17 April 1637, *Winthrop Papers*, ed. Forbes *et al.*, III, 390.

[56] Hambrick-Stowe, *Practice of Piety*, chs. 4, 5; Harry S. Stout, *The New England Soul: Preaching and Religious Culture in Colonial New England* (New York and Oxford, 1986), chs. 1–3; *Records of the Governor and Company of Massachusetts Bay*, ed. N. B. Shurtleff (Boston, 1853–4), I, 157. Susanna Bell, an emigrant of the late 1630s, could remember in 1672 the text of 'the first sermon that I heard after I came ashore': 'The

The need to be settled may also explain unfamiliar aspects of New England's religion: in particular, the controversial innovations of church covenant, and the profession of faith and repentance, or conversion narratives, that most churches required of settlers who wished to become members. Half-consciously at the start, church covenants emerged as a strategy to keep people put. Church covenants stood alongside town covenants and conditional land grants as ways of securing commitment.[57] Constituting churches by covenant was a separatist practice, and New England's opponents accused colonists of adopting separatist ways. But covenants and vows also played an important part in mainstream Puritan piety in England, as a means of strengthening and stabilising godly lives. It is likely that the momentum for New England's church covenants came from this source. John Cotton had gathered the godly by a covenant in old Boston, yet firmly rejected separation. Writing from England in 1630, before he took the decision to emigrate, he rebuked the church of Salem, Massachusetts, for its covenant: 'an explicit . . . covenant is rather a solemne vow to bind the members of the church together in nearer fellowshipe with god and one another, than any such essential cause of the church without which it can not be'. Coming over, he admitted to the Salem congregation that his criticism of their covenant had been a mistake. However, it is vital not to overlook the fact that Cotton's 'recantation' began a sermon very precisely aimed against separation.[58] Stephen Foster has argued that the more extensive and

---

Legacy of a Dying Mother to Her Mourning Children', in *The Complete Works of Thomas Brooks*, ed. A. B. Grosart, VI (Edinburgh, 1867), 453; see also *Shepard's Confessions*, ed. Selement and Woolley, 98.

[57] Martin, *Profits in the Wilderness*, 139–48, 310–15. Martin shows that in the 1630s, the formation of land corporations and church-gathering happened more or less at the same time, though this changed later; this is confirmed by B. C. Daniels, *The Connecticut Town: Growth and Development, 1635–1790* (Middletown, Conn., 1979), 95. For a complaint about conditions attached to a land grant, see Giles Firmin to John Winthrop, 26 Dec. 1639, *Winthrop Papers*, ed. Forbes *et al.*, IV, 164. Stephen Foster has explored the importance of covenant in relation to the imperatives of order and love: *Their Solitary Way: The Puritan Social Ethic in the First Century of Settlement in New England* (New Haven, 1971), 11–64.

[58] Collinson, *The Religion of Protestants*, 269–73; David D. Hall, 'John Cotton's Letter to Samuel Skelton', *William and Mary Quarterly*, 3rd ser., 22 (1965), 483; John Cotton, 'A Sermon at Salem, June 1636', in *John Cotton on the Churches of New England*, ed. Larzer Ziff (Cambridge, Mass., 1968), 41–68. Cotton's sermon refuted the views of Roger Williams, defining the just grounds for separation from a church very narrowly: Cotton insisted 'sinful pollutions', due to ignorance or weakness, were not sufficient reason; separation could only be legitimate where there was wilful, knowledgeable defiance, 'when . . . the church doth separate [itself] from . . . known Christ . . . in cool blood' (p. 59). Similar themes appear in a letter to Williams, early in 1636, where Cotton defends his refusal to pray for separatist churches in England – 'we cannot pray in faith for a blessing upon their separation, which we see not to be of God': *The Correspondence*

rigorous use of covenants as the 1630s progressed resulted from the heady influence of separatism. But the need to stabilise the rapidly growing new communities provides a better explanation. English critics quickly spotted that the binding character of covenants meant 'none are to be admitted as set Members, but they must promise not to depart or remove, unlesse the Congregation will give leave'. Defending the necessity of covenant, John Davenport argued, first, that the vow represented nothing new, but a commitment to 'review and renew our purpose afresh' to watch over each other out of love; and, secondly, he stressed

the necessarie Ruine that may fall upon the Body, if every particular member should depart at his own pleasure . . . If one man may . . . depart, why may not another also, though never so usefull in that Body . . . And if one, why not 2.6.10.12 as well as one? For where will you stop, seeing all may plead the same libertie? And if members may so do, why may not the Pastor and Teacher also . . . ? And so . . . the whole building must fall down. And if that may be so in one Church, why not all? And so Christ should have no certain setled Church on earth.[59]

The practice of asking for conversion narratives, adopted in most churches from 1634–5, formed part of the drive to nurture community. On the eve of emigration, English Puritans were increasingly pre-occupied with examining their experience for signs of God's work. This self-scrutiny played into the process of decision about emigration. In New England, conversion narratives acquainted the godly with one another. Patricia Caldwell has shown how powerful a vehicle the testimonies could be for expressing disappointment in New England. Speakers told not the assured stories ministers hoped for, but tales of confusion and bewilderment; signs of the need to settle people down. The practice of covenant and conversion narratives might make New England's churches seem exclusive and divisive, but in the early years, membership embraced a high proportion of the

of Roger Williams, ed. G. W. Lafantasie (Hanover and London, 1988), I, 43. Lafantasie, ibid., 31–3, gives a bibliography of the Cotton–Williams controversy.

[59] Foster, Long Argument, 159–60; [John Davenport], 'An Answer of the Elders . . . unto . . . Nine Positions', in [Mather], Church-Government and Church-Covenant, 75–6; see also Thomas Weld, An Answer to W[illiam] R[athband] His Narration (1644), 48–9; Winthrop, History of New England, II, 87. A Bristol alderman opposed his son's move from Maine into Massachusetts because he had heard that church covenant 'bindeth a man from removing uppon any ocation to uld england': Winthrop Papers, ed. Forbes et al., IV, 274. The Cambridge Platform of 1649 preserves Davenport's emphasis: W. Walker, The Creeds and Platforms of Congregationalism (New York, 1893), 224–5. Larzer Ziff has argued that by 1640 covenant had created a new, American, cultural identity: 'The Social Bond of Church Covenant', American Quarterly, 10 (1958), 454–62.

population.⁶⁰ As J. F. Martin's study of the process of settlement observes, 'one habit of community is exclusiveness'. These innovations were devices to cope with what William Ames called the 'special difficulties' of a new plantation.⁶¹

Behind the desire to stabilise settlement lurked fear of breaking into religious fragments, of becoming disorderly separatists. Ames had commended 'safetie, libertie, unitie, with puritie' as the guiding principles for New England. Conrad Russell has described New England as a 'very controlled experiment', and indeed it was. Magistrates and ministers worked together, after the prototype of Moses and Aaron, to nip unruly dissent in the bud. The debate between John Cotton and the separatist Roger Williams in 1636, and the dispute about grace in the Antinomian Controversy of 1637, provided opportunities to demonstrate to the godly back home that the freedom of New England need not lead to religious anarchy. The terms of their departure from England dictated tight control: Providence would not smile on schism or factious behaviour. As Cotton put it to Williams, 'the way of separation is not a way that God hath prospered'.⁶²

Just as this drive for order and unity attempted to meet the terms on which colonists left England, so too the quest for purity. Popery and purity had been pitted against each other to legitimate the decision to emigrate. As a consequence, New England must set new standards. On the journey over, John Winthrop expressed this conviction to his fellow-travellers:

wee must not content our selves with usuall ordinary meanes whatsoever wee did or ought to have done when wee lived in England, the same must wee doe and

---

⁶⁰ Patricia Caldwell, *The Puritan Conversion Narrative: The Beginnings of American Expression* (Cambridge, 1983), chs. 1–3; also Hambrick-Stowe, *Practice of Piety*, 76–89; Cohen, *God's Caress*, 137–61; Delbanco, *Puritan Ordeal*, 177–9. R. P. Stearns and D. H. Brawner, 'New England Church "Relations" and Continuity in Early Congregational History', *Proceedings of the American Antiquarian Society*, 75 (1965), 13–45, have argued that the intention of the test was not exclusive but inclusive; likewise, J. S. Coolidge, *The Pauline Renaissance in the Church* (Oxford, 1970), 65–6. Baird Tipson, 'Samuel Stone's "Discourse" against Requiring Church Relations', *William and Mary Quarterly*, 3rd ser., 46 (1989), 786–99, has shown that Stone and Thomas Hooker refused to require narratives.
⁶¹ Martin, *Profits in the Wilderness*, 303; Ames to Winthrop, 29 Dec. [1629], *Winthrop Papers*, ed. Forbes et al., II, 180.
⁶² Conrad Russell, *The Causes of the English Civil War* (Oxford, 1990), 9; Pestana, *Quakers and Baptists*, 1–4; Cotton to Williams [c. early 1636], *Correspondence of Roger Williams*, ed. Lafantasie, I, 42; and see n. 58. Foster, 'New England and the Challenge of Heresy', 629, argues that the Antinomian crisis was a measure of the rising sectarian temperature and another instance of 'lay initiatives in sharp conflict with the New England clerical order'; this view is challenged in Cooper, ' Ann Hutchinson'. Fear of separatism exaggerated the spectre of radicalism.

more allsoe where wee go: That which the most in theire Churches mainteine as a truthe in profession onely, wee must bring into familiar and constant practise.[63]

This is not the place to work through the detail of their pursuit of pure ordinances.[64] What we need to be alert to here, in order to grasp the dynamic motivating Puritan activity in New England, is the extent to which reaction against England's popery shaped colonial ideas of purity. Settlers arrived without a fully fledged church polity. Their experience in godly circles of local, voluntary, religion set an agenda. Beyond that, Jacobean and Elizabethan theorists provided muddled guidance: crucial aspects of ideal church order, such as the role of synods and the relation between minister and people, had been left unresolved.[65] Wrestling to work out theory in practice, settlers consistently resolved ambiguities in a direction that made New England the antithesis of all they saw as popish in England. Thus New England's churches became autonomous, local, voluntary, consensual; in contrast to the hierarchical, national, mandatory, autocratic English church. Though this might seem separatist, they themselves insisted that their drive for purity should not be read that way.[66] It is better understood as a furious campaign against popery, necessary to rationalise leaving England. A parallel with Puritan behaviour back home is pertinent. Ministers who wanted to gather the godly within their parish had to be much more publicly preoccupied with defining the nature of godliness than out-and-out separatists. Separatists, prepared to turn their backs on the rest of the church, drew the boundaries of the godly community simply by their act of separation.[67]

---

63 Winthrop, 'A Modell of Christian Charity', *Winthrop Papers*, ed. Forbes *et al.*, II, 293.
64 Bozeman, *To Live Ancient Lives*, chs. 4, 5, shows how pursuit of purity shaped New England's institutions.
65 S. Brachlow, *The Communion of Saints. Radical Puritan and Separatist Ecclesiology 1570–1625* (Oxford, 1988); Carol Geary Schneider, 'Godly Order in a Church Half-Reformed: The Disciplinarian Legacy, 1570–1641' (PhD thesis, Harvard University, 1986). Both studies stress the common ground in Puritan ecclesiology, and its congregationalist emphases, and contest Perry Miller's view that 'non-separating congregationalists' were distinct from 'Presbyterians'. Details of the 'New England Way' were clarified in debates with Presbyterians in the 1640s.
66 See, for example, Cotton, *Exposition upon . . . Revelation [13]*, 13–16, 57–9, 254–5; John Cotton, *A Coppy of a Letter from Mr. Cotton of Boston* (1641) [written *c.* 1636]. Timothy Breen has argued that colonists' experience of resistance to Stuart centralisation meant New England was shaped by 'localism': 'Persistent Localism: English Social Change and the Shaping of New England Institutions', *William and Mary Quarterly*, 3rd ser., 32 (1975), 3–28. The character of the polarity they perceived between the true and false church gives this notion an ecclesiological dimension. Repudiation of hierarchy, of course, allowed New England simultaneously to recognise true 'sister' churches in England, and yet move away from English practices to achieve 'pure ordinances'.
67 Collinson, 'The Cohabitation of the Faithful with the Unfaithful', 58–63.

Colonial leaders, keen to prove emigration anything but a private, schismatic, separation, made much of New England's purity to show how legitimate it had been for them to withdraw from the struggle against popery in England.

It was inevitable that this strategy put a distance between New England and old; and yet at the same time colonists wanted to affirm their continuing affection for the godly left behind. A letter from John Cotton illustrates how defending emigration compelled settlers to cry up the contrast between colony and homeland. Writing back to friends in old Boston in 1635, he told them 'were I again with you, I durst not take that liberty which some times I have taken: I durst not joyn in your Book-Prayers . . . I durst not now partake in the Sacraments with you, though the Ceremonies were removed.' The Presbyterian Robert Baillie later seized on this to prove how far Cotton had strayed into separation. But Cotton set up a distance between himself and his former neighbours to justify leaving England at a time of crisis, and to encourage them to follow.

While you and some of my other friends continue . . . [in Boston], I fear the rest will settle upon their Lees with more security. The wise-hearted that left their Stations in Israel . . . were some of them, if not all, useful and serviceable men in their places; yet they did themselves and their Brethren more good service in going before their Brethren, as the Goats before the Flocks, Jere. 50.8, then if they had tarried with them to the corrupting of their own wayes. 2 Chro. 11.14, 16.

The text from Jeremiah endorsed the legitimacy of flight under pressure. The text from Chronicles pressed home the assault on the Puritan ministry as an incentive for emigration: when the Levites fled, rejected as priests by Jereboam, they were followed by 'those from every tribe of Israel who set their hearts on seeking the Lord'.[68] Like Cotton, Thomas Weld, once of Terling, Essex, played up the superior purity of New England to his former parishioners to urge them to come over.[69] Emigrants' sense of the distance they had travelled left its stamp on New England church practice. The godly bewailed their share in England's corruption. However, formal abjurations of England played no part in

---

[68] R. Baillie, *A Dissuasive from the Errours of the Time* (1645), 66–7. Cotton cited 2 Chronicles 11:13–15 in his sermon to the Winthrop fleet, drawing attention to its use by the Marian exiles to justify flight in anticipation of persecution: *God's Promise*, 9–10. It was often cited to distinguish lawful secession from unlawful schism, as in *Golden Apples* (1659), 32–5, a tract by the Presbyterian Samuel Clarke.
[69] Weld to his former parishioners in Terling, June/July 1632, *Letters from New England: The Massachusetts Bay Colony, 1629–1638*, ed. E. Emerson (Amherst, Mass., 1976), 94–8.

the new church order.[70] Typically, marking the distance between New England and old was balanced by a declaration of affection. Baillie cited only the fragment of Cotton's letter that suited him, but we might hazard a guess that the rest contained Cotton's warm reassurance of his regard for England. Weld told his ex-parishioners: 'I assure you we look at our dear native country as the place where the Lord showed us mercy and to His Holy ordinances there as the holy means of God. If ever we had it, we had it there.' Ezekiel Rogers of Rowley might call the English hierarchy 'wholly antichristian', but he prefaced this with an endorsement of England's 'soundness of doctrine', 'excellency of ministerial gifts' and 'power of religion', 'in all which there appeared more . . . in England than in all the known world besides'.[71] Putting distance between New England and old was part of the strategy to legitimise emigration to themselves and to the godly back home. It came out of the logic of their rhetoric for leaving England, but did not tip them over into casting England off.

Rather than seeing New England's innovations and rhetoric of purity as signs of inherent radicalism, then, we can interpret them as tactics to shore up the grounds for leaving England. Paradoxically, however, the New Englanders' anxiety to show the legitimacy of their experiment led to it being judged illicit. By the late 1630s, the godly back home looked askance at the financial and spiritual standing of New England. Backers, seeing too little profit, wondered whether Providence wanted settlers to move to the Caribbean instead.[72] As news of church practices filtered home, godly ministers sent letters accusing New England of turning separatist. Former allies became critics. This is particularly evident in

---

[70] Cotton to Williams, c. early 1636, *Correspondence of Roger Williams*, ed. Lafantasie, I, 35–41; Cotton, *Coppy of a Letter*, 1–2; Richard Mather to William Rathband and 'Mr. T', 25 June 1636, *Letters from New England*, ed. Emerson, 202.

[71] A later letter from Cotton to the corporation and church of old Boston shows this balance: *Of the Holinesse of Church Members* (1650), preface. Weld: *Letters from New England*, ed. Emerson, 97; Rogers: as recalled by John Winthrop, *History of New England*, I, 335. At a critical point in his case for the colonists' sectarianism, Foster quotes only Rogers' criticism, not the balancing affirmation: *Long Argument*, 158. Winthrop's report that Rogers and his flock had 'of a good time, withdrawn themselves from the church communion of England, and that for the many corruptions which were among them', need not be read as a declaration of forthright separatism, particularly in light of the circumstances of Rogers' departure.

[72] Winthrop, *History of New England*, I, 399–401; Lord Say and Sele to Winthrop, 9 July 1640, *Winthrop Papers*, ed. Forbes *et al.*, IV, 263–7; see also John Endecott to Winthrop, *ibid.*, 314–16. Karen Ordahl Kupperman discusses the Caribbean schemes: 'Errand to the Indies: Puritan Colonisation from Providence Island through the Western Design', *William and Mary Quarterly*, 3rd ser., 45 (1988), 70–99. Cotton had replied in 1636 to a critical letter from Say and Sele on church and state: *The Puritans*, ed. Perry Miller and Thomas Johnson (New York, 1938), I, 209–12.

questions from a group that included the respected nonconformist John Dod.[73] In 1632, Dod had supported Cotton's flight to America. But in the late 1630s he was 'utterly averse' to the plans of George Hughes to emigrate:

if such as you, & all the Godly of the Land because of persecution should presently leave the Land, as Lot did Sodom, what doe you think will become of our poor native Country? It will be even as Sodom and Gomorrah. I pray you lay by these thoughts. Our case is not desperate at home. The Lords arm is not shortened but that he can retrieve and save us . . . Let's wait a while upon our God . . . he will not totally lay you by, but open a doore for you in some other place.[74]

Dod's group represented ministers under pressure who now eschewed New England. They admitted the need for innovation to deal with the special circumstances of new settlements, but believed colonists had gone beyond this. Similar criticism came from Lancashire ministers associated with Richard Mather, and from Richard Bernard of Batcombe, Somerset (father-in-law to Roger Williams), who had earlier retreated from an experiment with covenant in England.[75] So the stratagems to legitimate New England had backfired. In the attempt to be true to the terms on which they left England – opposition to popery, in a spirit that was not separatist, on a venture guided by Providence – colonists backed themselves into a corner where they could not succeed.

The suspicions of the godly in England confirmed restlessness and anxiety in New England, and heightened the need to defend being there.

---

73 Dod sent questions over in 1637, with John Ball, Simeon Ashe, Robert Cleaver, Ralph Shearard, Timothy Dod, William Bourne, Thomas Paget, Julines Herring, Thomas Langley, John Winston, Nathaniel Cotton and Ephraim Huitt: Boston Public Library, Prince Collection, Cotton Papers, part 2, no. 9; later printed in *A Letter of Many Ministers in Old England*, ed. Simeon Ashe and William Rathband (1643). Ball carried the debate further in *A Friendly Triall of the Grounds Tending to Separation* (1640). For links between the signatories and the significance of the divide with New England, see N. Tyacke, *The Fortunes of English Puritanism, 1603–1640* (Friends of DWL, 44th Lecture, London, 1989), 18–19; Schneider, 'Godly Order in a Church Half-Reformed', 230–7, 337–407. Of this group, only Huitt emigrated to New England.

74 Cotton Mather, *Magnalia*, I, 263; DWL, transcript of Quick, 'Icones Sacrae Anglicanae', fols. 494–5. For Hughes, see *Calamy Revised*, ed. Matthews. After two months Dod found him a place as chaplain to Lord Brooke at Warwick Castle.

75 *Letters from New England*, ed. Emerson, 201–8; B. R. Burg, 'A Letter of Richard Mather to a Cleric in Old England', *William and Mary Quarterly*, 3rd ser., 29 (1972), 81–98. Bernard's critique does not survive, but the reply appears in [Mather], *Church-Government and Church-Covenant*. The '32 Questions' printed in the same work were attributed to Lancashire ministers by Thomas Edwards, *Reasons against the Independent Government of Particular Congregations* (1641), 32. However, the reply from New England refers back to the answer sent to Dod and Company, which suggests the thirty-two questions also came from them: *Church-Government and Church-Covenant*, 83–4.

Giles Firmin, of Ipswich, Massachusetts, reported to John Winthrop in 1639 a disconcerting rumour:

I have heard a Conclusion gathered against these Plantations, because the Lord hath so sadlye afflicted the founders of them in their estates; that therefore it was not a way of God, to forsake our Countrye, and expose ourselves to such temptations, as wee have done, so long as we might have enjoyed God in any comfortable measure in the place whence wee came, alledginge that it is scarcely knowne that any church in a way of Separation as wee are did ever yet thrive in grace.

The reasons woven together to legitimate emigration were unravelling. The godly at home reckoned that Providence disapproved of New England. By leaving England unlawfully, settlers courted ruin; their dire straits now confirmed them as separatists. This was the verdict colonial leaders had tried hard to avoid. The great influx of immigrants exacerbated unsettledness, and with the first whiff of change in England, immigration dried up, values of property slumped. There was a serious risk settlers would scatter west or south, or return to England.[76]

By the time Thomas Allen sat listening to John Cotton in the first months of 1640, the preachers of New England had a double task: to refute the charge of separatism from the godly back home; and to reassure colonists about the purpose of settlement. They adopted a variety of strategies. To show England how far they stood from separatism, John Davenport and Richard Mather argued that England's churches might be blemished, but had been truly constituted by the covenants implicit in the gathering of the godly. Where England continued practices New England had abandoned, England's corruption was excused by ignorance. New England's so-called 'innovations' arose from a legitimate call to scriptural purity. Davenport and Mather bolstered their case by appeal to an armoury of arguments from the common past.[77] Taking a different tack, Thomas Shepard tried to reassure colonists about the hand of Providence on New England by redefining the relationship between Providence and hardship. He acknowledged the settlers' plight:

Their estates decay, they run into debt . . . they secretly repent themselves of the fellowship of God's people . . . [and] account their course, and hazards they have

---

[76] Firmin to Winthrop, 12 Feb. 1639/40, *Winthrop Papers*, ed. Forbes *et al.*, IV, 191 (for Firmin, see *Calamy Revised*, ed. Matthews). Winthrop, *History of New England*, I, 399–401; II, 25; *Winthrop Papers*, ed. Forbes *et al.*, IV, 205; J. Cotton, *The Churches Resurrection* (1642), 21.

[77] This summary is based on the replies to questions from England, sent back in 1639–40, and printed in [Mather], *Church-Government and Church-Covenant*.

run, either madness or rashness . . . The Israelites brought to the wilderness, they would go back: why? They questioned whether God was with them: why? Because they wanted water, bread and a variety of blessings.

But hardship could not discredit New England. On the contrary, Providence meant adversity to serve a special purpose. 'New England's peace and plenty of means breeds strange security', he argued. 'There are no enemies to hunt you to heaven, nor chains to make you cry . . . here are no sour herbs to make the Lamb sweet'. Hardship took the place of popery and persecution to sharpen Puritan piety.[78] John Cotton, in the sermons Thomas Allen heard, shared Shepard's concern to reassure colonists that Providence supported the New England experiment. Cotton's tactic, however, was to impress on his hearers the distance between New and old England in terms of purity:

You shall have many poore creatures that came hither to this Country, and will be ready to go back againe, they looke at things as mean and poor here . . . If you goe thither, you will have much adoe to escape the paw of the Bear, If you be once incorporated into any of their Parishes, you will finde such beastly work in Church Government . . . you must worship the beast or the Image of the beast; a Diocesan or Nationall Church, is but an Image of the great beast . . . you will finde the body of the Church rent from you, or you will be rent from the body, if you shall walk roundly and sincerely in the ways of God.

New England released settlers from England's compromises with corruption: 'We have here cause to praise God for our present liberties, and therefore you are to be wary of what you do . . . turn not againe to that from which the Lord by his stretched out arme hath delivered you.'[79] Thus, as in his earlier letter to old Boston, he defended New England by its special purity.

Cotton's warnings might sound as if he has rejected England. But that is to ignore the context in which he spoke: he was desperate to defend the future of New England's churches in the face of rumblings about return. In fact, Cotton still balanced his strong words against England's corruption with recognition of the godly back home. Even as he asked his hearers 'will you be gone back againe to Egypt?' he added 'God forbid I

---

[78] Thomas Shepard, *The Parable of the Ten Virgins Opened and Applied*, in *The Works of Thomas Shepard*, ed. J. A. Albro (Boston, Mass., 1853), II, 626, 170, and *passim*. Keith Thomas, *Religion and the Decline of Magic* (Oxford, 1971), 95–6, discusses attempts by Puritan clergy to persuade their flocks to see affliction as a sign of God's affection.

[79] Cotton, *Exposition upon . . . Revelation [13]*, 20. The image of the 'paw of the bear' for God's judgement comes from Hosea 13:7–8; the 'outstretched hand', delivering Israel from Egypt to a land of milk and honey, from Deut. 26:8. Thomas Allen, in the 'Epistle to the Reader', states Cotton preached the sermons between January and April 1640.

should count all our native country as Egypt'; the sermons culminated in an appeal for prayer for England and the Short Parliament.[80] An intriguing document from around the same time, written by Cotton 'some yeares before the suppressing of the Bishops', confirms that his attitude to England does not contradict the stance of Davenport and Mather. It shows Cotton trying to apply the principles of New England to English parishes in a surprisingly subtle and undogmatic way. In proposals for reform that predate later Presbyterian–Congregationalist disputes, he drew attention to godly instructions, albeit obscure or ill-used, in the 'publick Service-booke', the Book of Common Prayer. Adults, for example, could affirm the Catechism before coming to the Lord's Table for the first time, which 'if it be seriously done, and not perfunctorily, is somewhat of like nature with our receiving of members into the Church, and joyning them by Covenant'. His ideas were framed by loyalty to English churches:

wee cannot but conceive the Churches in England were rightly gathered and planted according to the Rule of the Gospel; and all the corruptions found in them since, have sprung from Popish Apostasie in succeeding ages . . . all the worke now, is not to make them Churches which were none before, but to reduce and restore them to their Primitive Institution.

Giles Firmin, who later endorsed Cotton's sentiments, explained the contrast between colony and homeland thus: 'You must put a difference between Churches new erecting and these in England . . . when I raise a house new from the ground, I may then doe as I please, but if I be mending of an old house, I must do as well as I can, repaire by degrees.'[81] Perhaps in that perception lies a solution to the puzzle of New Englanders' behaviour. To take rhetoric like Cotton's as a sign of rejecting the Church of England is to look at New England through the eyes of its opponents. This fails to do justice to the colonists' intentions.

By 1640, the preachers' message ran in different directions for different audiences, but provided a vigorous, consistent defence of the terms on which emigrants had left England. All the old opposites

---

[80] Cotton, *Exposition upon . . . Revelation [13]*, 20, 262. Foster, *Long Argument*, 158–9, takes Cotton's comments as a sign of *de facto* separatism, of a break with the objectives of the first emigrants.

[81] John Cotton, *The Way of the Churches of Christ in New England* (1645), 111–16; G. Firmin, *Separation Examined* (1652), 20, 82. Cotton's tract was published without his consent, but he did not repudiate it: he thought his *Keys of the Kingdom* (1644) more authoritative; but discrepancies were of 'logicall notion', not of doctrine or practice. His comments on the composition and date of *Way of the Churches* can be found in John Owen, *A Defence of Mr. John Cotton from the Imputation of Selfe Contradiction* (Oxford, 1658), second pagination, 36–41.

appeared: popery and purity, persecution and peace, danger and liberty, hindrance and opportunity. At the same time, preachers professed unity with the godly back home. The rhetoric had not changed, even if it had been displaced to New England: to call for reform in England, they witnessed against popery; to affirm loyalty to the godly back home, they railed against separatism. This rhetoric, derived from Puritan defences of the Church of England, had provided the logic for leaving England and shaped the new venture. That England could not recognise it at such a distance was hardly New England's fault.

IV

Starting from New England's roots among Professor Collinson's godly Protestants, and understanding emigration in terms of the casuistry that framed it, colonists' behaviour seems less of a conundrum. Their reasoning was subtle, but no more subtle than Puritans had been using for a long time. The episode illustrates the character and cost of a separation driven by circumstance, separation for an 'extraordinary cause'.[82] The logic that justified emigration had a momentum about it that backed New England into a tight spot. Because fear of popery catalysed the experiment, settlers had to play off popery and purity, old England and New, in a way that led old England to take them for the separatists they had not intended to be. Their casuistry also made the hardship of New England a difficult issue. Spiritual and material causes alike fed ambivalence about whether being in New England was right. From all this, the 'errand into the wilderness' can be judged a consequence, not a cause, of the Great Migration. A later generation carved the 'errand' out of the themes of hardship, purity and Providence that ministers began to use when the consensus with England about the Providential meaning of emigration broke down.

Richard Saltonstall, one of Massachusetts' leading magistrates, illustrates the impact of Cotton's strategy to defend New England by pure ordinances. 'In the times of the unsetled Humyrs of many mens spirits to Returne for England', Saltonstall explained to Cotton, he had 'made a vow to God not to leave the countrey, whilest the Ordinances of God continued here in purity.'[83] But though New England survived, Cotton's success was not as straightforward as the onward march of American history might suggest. The advent of pure ordinances in

---

[82] See the comments of Collinson, 'English Conventicle', 246.
[83] Cotton to Richard Saltonstall Jr [c. 1648–9], Boston Public Library, Prince Collection, Cotton Papers, part 3, Appendix, no. 5. The date is ascribed by S. Bush, 'John Cotton's Correspondence: a Census', *Early American Literature*, 24 (1989), 103.

England put doubts in many minds about why they were in New England. Saltonstall went back. So did Thomas Allen, invited to become preacher to Norwich Corporation. In fact hundreds of colonists returned, including twenty-eight of the seventy-nine godly preachers. Among their number was Nathaniel Ward, who coined the maxim 'divers make it part of their American creed, that no man should desert his country but upon extraordinary cause, and when that cause ceaseth he is bound in conscience to return if he can'. A layman, William Cutter, who returned to Newcastle-upon-Tyne after more than a decade in Cambridge, Massachusetts, wrote back to New England in 1654 to say how much he missed his family and friends there: 'I often wish I could se[e] them again . . . butt it is not like[ly] . . . truly the sad discouragements in comeing by sea is enough to hinder: unles it were as formerly: that we could not injoy the ordinances of God.'[84]

---

[84] Ward, *Simple Cobler*, 25; William Cutter to Henry Dunster, 19 May 1654, Massachusetts Historical Society, *Collections*, 4th ser., 2 (Boston, 1854), 196. The details on return migration are derived from my forthcoming book.

12 Provincial preaching on the eve of the Civil War: some West Riding fast sermons

William Sheils

I

When Charles I entered the city of York on the afternoon of Saturday 17 March 1642 he was met by the corporation, but despite reports that 'the streets were embroidered with people on both sides' in welcome the reception did not go well.[1] Immediately prior to the king's arrival the corporation had expressed concern that a number of aldermen would absent themselves on the day, and the speech of the mayor, Edmund Cowper, was not well received.[2] After the usual introductions the mayor compared the present circumstances unfavourably with those of the previous royal visit in 1639, he continued with an expression of those pieties customarily addressed to a monarch but then recalled the current dispute with the following advice: 'Howsoever (most gracious Sovereign) remember Parliament, forget not them that always remember you: concur with them in their sedulous consultations, that so by that meanes your Imperiall dignity may be the more advanced.'[3] These were hardly words which Charles wished to hear from his loyal subjects, and the king's displeasure was widely reported. The mayor's speech was not the only public pronouncement in the city on that day, however, and it may be that Charles' subsequent irritation arose more from knowledge of the other public criticism being voiced by the civic preachers.

Having been met by the mayor outside Micklegate Bar the royal entourage would have proceeded down Micklegate and over Ousebridge on its way to the house of Sir Arthur Ingram in the cathedral close.[4] In the course of this progress it passed the church of St Michael, Spurriergate, where the rector, Samuel Wintour, chose to preach a sermon on

---

[1] Sir Nathaniel Rigby, *The Kings Noble Entertainment at York with the Lord Maior of York his Worthy Speech to the King* (1641).

[2] York City Archives, House Book 36, fols. 68–9; A. J. Fletcher, *The Outbreak of the English Civil War* (1981), 231.

[3] Rigby, *Noble Entertainment*.

[4] F. Drake, *Eboracum* (1736), 147. On his 1639 visit Charles had stayed at the King's Manor and not in the Minster Yard.

that very day. Wintour had recently been appointed rector of the church and was also one of the four civic preachers maintained by the corporation.[5] He was a graduate of Emmanuel College, Cambridge, who had started his ministry in the 1620s under John Cotton at Boston, whence he moved north to the renowned centre of East Riding Puritanism at Rowley, serving as curate to Ezekiel Rogers. When Rogers, with considerable numbers of his parishioners, emigrated to the New World in 1638 Wintour stayed behind taking up his post in York in 1641.[6] Wintour's text on 17 March was Judges 10:14; 'Go and cry unto Gods which ye have chosen; let them deliver you in the time of your tribulation', from which he drew the forceful but unexceptional moral that the nation required an urgent return to the proper worship of God, and a speedy renewal of His covenant with His people. Such preaching was commonplace among Puritan divines, but with the king in such close proximity, the series of accounts of the violent fates of rulers such as Ahaz and Saul, who had refused to listen to the word of God, lent the sermon an immediacy reinforced by the account of 'the chiefs of all the people, even of all the tribes of Israel [who] presented themselves in the assembly of God' on the eve of the Civil War with Benjamin which occupied a large part of the sermon. The identification of parliament with 'the assembly of God' was not made explicit, but the parallel would not have escaped the hearers.[7] The sermon, therefore, went beyond the more cautious statements of the civic authorities whose words, whilst acknowledging the disagreements between king and parliament, reflected the tone of the pamphlet literature in which hopes of reconciliation, however faintly held, seemed to dominate.[8]

This difference in temper was revealed again on the following day by the recorder of York, who reiterated the words of the mayor, in asking Charles to 'hearken unto and condescend unto Parliament',[9] whilst more

---

[5] For the civic preachers, see *VCH City of York*, ed. P. M. Tillot (1961), 201–2.

[6] J. and J. A. Venn, *Alumni Cantabridgienses*, IV, 440; R. A. Marchant, *The Puritans and the Church Courts in the Diocese of York 1558–1642* (1960), 293 and for Rowley, see 96–102.

[7] Otley parish church, Otley parish records, book of sermon notes, 1–6. I am grateful to the Rev. I. T. Rodley, vicar of Otley for permission to use this document. For discussion of parliament as a representative assembly at this time see J. Wilson, *Pulpit in Power* (Princeton, N.J., 1969), 55–6, and J. Sanderson, *'But the People's Creatures': The Philosophical Basis of the English Civil War* (Manchester, 1989), 19.

[8] C. S. R. Russell, *The Fall of the British Monarchies 1637–1642* (Oxford, 1991), 458–65, 486–7.

[9] Fletcher, *The Outbreak of the Civil War*, 231. The recorder was Sir Thomas Widdrington, formerly MP for York and a son-in-law of Ferdinando, Lord Fairfax, M. F. Keeler, *The Long Parliament, 1640–41: A Biographical Study of its Members* (1954), 393.

forceful views came from another city church, St Cuthbert's, where the preacher chose as his text of the day Genesis 3:17, the account of God's judgement on Adam for hearkening unto Eve. The text of the sermon rehearsed by implication the well-established distrust of the intentions of the king in respect of Catholicism, and the role of the queen in this matter, and contemporary reference was made explicit when the present state of England was likened to Eden after the Fall. This was a common theme in contemporary Puritan preaching, and the person of Henrietta Maria, by this time on the continent, had long been a focus for popular godly fears.[10] This was combustible material and knowledge of it placed the civic authorities in a difficult position.[11] Not only were their own preachers showing open defiance to Charles but an inflammatory pamphlet, purporting to be a petition to the king by the citizens, was circulating in the city. The text of the pamphlet highlighted the plight of the Irish Protestants, asking Charles to ensure that a similar fate should not befall his English subjects;

which miseryes present and dangers imminent cann neither be prevented or redressed if theise distances of place and differences of Counsells doe continue betweene youre Majestie and your Majesties great Councell the Parliament. And therefore your Majesties petitioners doe humbly Implycate that your Majestie will be pleased to reconcile the displeasures conceived against your Loyall subjectes of the Realme represented by the Parliament, into whose Religious and Faithfull Councells as we have referred ourselves so we doe most humbly desire your Majestie to vouchsafe your princely care and personall presence.

The corporation were deeply embarrassed by the document and, on 4 April, passed a resolution denying any responsibility for its composition. This was followed three days later by a 'Humble Declaration' of their own, framed in conciliatory tones but nevertheless expressing the hope that 'your Majesties greate and assiduous endevours may tend to effect a true understanding betweene your Majestie and your parliament'.[12] It is perhaps significant, in the light of the known Puritan leanings of many of the members of the corporation, that very few of them were present at this meeting which sought to establish its good name with the king, and that the civic authorities continued to

---

[10] Otley sermon notes, 6–11; for the role of the queen in anti-Catholic fears, see R. Clifton, 'Fear of Popery', in *The Origins of the English Civil War*, ed. Conrad Russell (1973), 144–67, esp. 152, 155–7. More generally C. Hibberd, *Charles I and the Popish Plot* (Chapel Hill, 1983), esp. 168–226.

[11] R. Davies, 'An Episode in the Municipal History of the City of York', *Yorkshire Archaeological Journal*, 5 (1879), 52–62.

[12] York City Archives, House Book 36, fols. 70–1.

express concern at the absence of some of their colleagues from meetings.[13]

II

As the official records and the pamphlet literature indicate, the days following the king's arrival at York were difficult ones, but it is not our purpose to trace how those difficulties were resolved. Instead our attention will focus on the role of the preachers during this critical summer. Looking back on events in these months Clarendon was clear that the pulpit, and especially its use by Pym in parliament, was an essential tool of policy in the conflict with the king,[14] and his view from the centre was echoed by observers of the provincial scene. In Shropshire the Puritan minister Stanley Gower complained that the royalists had stolen the propaganda initiative so that 'the pulpit is made a stage' whereby the preachers set out to 'work a hatred in the hearts of the people against Parliament'.[15] Puritans were no less active elsewhere and John Hacket, writing in the 1650s about events at Hull in April 1642, singled out the preachers as the means by which the people were turned from subjects into rebels.[16] Such direct evidence is rare and both Gower and Hacket were party to the conflict and thus likely to exaggerate the activities of their opponents at this critical time, but there is a broad measure of agreement that religion, or the maintenance of true religion, was a central plank in the platform of both parties. Professor Fletcher has identified the fear of popery as the most prominent theme running through the petitions sent up from the counties to parliament in the early months of 1642, the work of Dr Morrill has led him to conclude that the Civil War represented not so much a political or social revolution as 'the

---

[13] *Ibid.*, fol. 72, order of 2 May. Attendances at other meetings when important business was transacted were generally larger, see meetings 17 March and 4 April for example. For the Puritanism of the corporation see D. Scott, 'Politics and Government in York, 1640–1662', in *Town and Countryside in the English Revolution*, ed. R. C. Richardson (Manchester, 1992), 46–69, esp. 48–9. Later that summer royalists raided the house of the Puritan Alderman Vaux who had issued a warrant for the arrest of a soldier, *A Most True Relation of the Laste Weekes Passages in Yorke and Hull* (23 June 1642), 3–4.

[14] Edward, earl of Clarendon, *History of the Great Rebellion*, ed. W. D. Macray (Oxford, 1888), IV, 194.

[15] J. Eales, *Puritans and Roundheads: The Harleys of Brampton Bierlow and the Outbreak of the English Civil War* (Cambridge, 1990), 129; Stanley Gower, the writer of the letter, had previously been a minister in York diocese. R. A. Marchant, *The Puritans and the Church Courts in the Diocese of York 1560–1642* (1960), 169–70; and J. A. Newton, 'Puritanism in Yorkshire 1603–1640' (unpub. PhD thesis, London Univ., 1964), 104.

[16] J. Hacket, *Scrinia Reserata* (1693), 186.

last of the wars of religion',[17] and most recently Professor Russell has shown that a long tradition of godly preaching was the common factor in those communities which raised volunteers for parliament.[18] The fundamental importance given to religion by both parties in their public pronouncements does not mean, however, that it was always the determining factor in the decisions of individuals or communities about whether, or for whom, to take up arms, and its role in the formation of local loyalties remains elusive because we know next to nothing about the preaching which took place in parochial pulpits in 1641 and 1642.

Fortunately this gap in our knowledge can be filled for one locality through the survival of a volume of extensive notes from sermons preached in the summer of 1642 in a few chapelries in the West Riding. The volume is currently to be found among the parish records of Otley,[19] where most of the sermons recorded were preached, but was formerly among the manuscripts of Charles Fairfax of Menston, son of Ferdinando, Lord Fairfax.[20] The authorship of the document remains unknown, but it was almost certainly produced for a member of the Fairfax household and with a very specific purpose in mind. Beginning as it does on the very day that Charles entered York, the volume is unlikely to have formed part of a larger collection of sermon notes of the sort associated with private study by an individual or repetition within a household, as was common among the godly.[21] The date on which the volume opens and the fact that the last sermon recorded was preached on 31 July, shortly before the king left the county on his way to Nottingham where he raised his standard on 22 August, reinforces the identification of the document with the Fairfax family suggested by its provenance. Several members of the family were closely involved in various ways with the response of the Puritan gentry of the county to the royal presence in their midst.[22] Between those dates the volume records, in 375 pages of notes, closely written in an execrable, if consistent, hand,

[17] Fletcher, *The Outbreak of Civil War*, 200; J. S. Morrill, 'The Religious Context of the English Civil War', *TRHS*, 5th ser., 34 (1984), 155–78 and his, 'The Attack on the Church of England in the Long Parliament, 1640–1642', in *History, Society and the Churches*, ed. D. Beales and G. Best (Cambridge, 1985), 105–24.

[18] Conrad Russell, *The Causes of the English Civil War* (Oxford, 1990), 21–2.

[19] Otley parish church, Otley sermon notes.

[20] W. J. Connor, 'The Fairfax Archives: A Study in Dispersal', *Archives*, 11 (1973–4), 76–85, esp. 83. I am grateful to Mr Connor for discussing this document with me.

[21] Newton, 'Puritanism in Yorks', 381–8.

[22] Fletcher, *The Outbreak of the Civil War*, 314–17, 389; *The Fairfax Correspondence: The Reign of Charles I*, ed. G. W. Johnson (1848), II, 406–9.

the content of forty-four sermons preached at nine locations in York and the West Riding.[23] The notes for each sermon are detailed and suggest, from extensive biblical references in the margins and the divisions of some sermons into text, cases and conclusions, that they are fair copies, made soon after the event, of notes made at the time of delivery by someone both well versed in the style and structure of contemporary preaching and sympathetic to its content.

The principal pulpit recorded in the volume was that at Otley, the parish church of the Fairfaxes, and the great majority of the sermons were preached by the two curates in the parish, David Ellison, who served the parish church and also as schoolmaster in the town, and John Cooper, curate in the chapelry of Burley.[24] The parish of Otley comprised an extensive area of Wharfedale, with twelve townships ranging in size from the small farming community of Timble to the six principal villages in the parish, at Otley, Baildon, Hawkesworth, Burley, Farnley and Bramhope, each of which contained between forty and sixty-five households. The Easter books for the period 1639 to 1642 suggest that there were 432 households, or almost 2,000 people, living in the parish.[25] The presence of various branches of the Fairfax family, at Denton and at Menston, meant that the leadership of the community was active in the political debate. Other substantial landholders, such as the Vavasour family of Stead, also shared these concerns and a sympathy for godly religion,[26] which they demonstrated as trustees of the recently founded grammar school in the town.[27]

In so far as the debate about godly religion was concerned with the power and responsibilities of the established church in secular affairs, local circumstances at Otley gave the arguments added point, for the lord of the manor was the archbishop of York. As such, his authority impinged on most of the householders of the parish to a greater or lesser extent. In Otley and Farnley the manor had twenty-one leasehold tenants, occupying about 700 acres of land, and a further thirty-three

---

[23] Sermons were preached at four different locations in York, though these have not been counted separately. The other locations were Otley parish church and its chapels at Burley, Denton and Weston, at Calverley, south-west of Otley and at Morley to the south of Leeds.

[24] BIHR, v.1640/Exh. Bk fol. 26; CB fol. 49v.

[25] Yorkshire Archaeological Society, Leeds, DD 146/12/1/6 tithe book, Otley rectory 1633-43.

[26] BIHR, Bp. Dio. 3, p. 111 Leeds Archives Dept, 2RL/109, refers to an endowment of Burley chapel by William Vavasour.

[27] F. Cobley and L. Padgett, *Chronicles of the Free Grammar School of Prince Henry at Otley* (Otley, 1923), 73–80; Ferdinando Lord Fairfax was the principal governor and the archives of the school were held in his study at Denton, *ibid.*, 94.

tenants holding copyhold lands.[28] Within the town itself the market and burgage tenures were part of the manor, and ancient dues, known as 'Bishop's Bounds', were payable to the lord by landholders in nine of the parochial townships.[29] The manor also had frankpledge jurisdiction and was part of the archiepiscopal liberty of Sherburn, in which the archbishop had the right of appointment of magistrates within the town to administer justice independent of the county institutions.[30] There existed therefore, in this rural region, an extensive ecclesiastical liberty with the same potential for conflict between secular and ecclesiastical authority as raged between corporations and chapters in cathedral cities during the 1630s.[31] Moreover, that liberty abutted on to the estates of one of the principal Puritan magisterial families in the West Riding, the Fairfaxes,[32] whose close connection with the corporation of York would have made its members familiar with the acrimonious disputes between mayor and chapter which took place in the city during the previous decade.[33]

Paradoxically, the authority which the archbishop had locally in secular affairs was not reflected in the ecclesiastical institutions. The patronage of the living was in Crown hands and, as such, open to local lobbying, which was responsible for the appointment of the Puritan William Harrison in 1608.[34] Harrison was a veteran of West Riding Puritanism, being closely involved with the exercises of the 1620s, and remained as vicar in 1642.[35] He was in his seventies by this date, and

---

[28] G. E. Kirk, 'Two Rentals of the Manor of Otley', *Publications of the Thoresby Society*, 37 (1945), 202–24.

[29] *Ibid.*, 207–17, 220–4; BIHR, CC.Ab. 8/3, the parliamentary survey of the archbishopric estate, fols. 144–80, covers Otley, and though the survey dates from 1647, most of the leases referred to were effective in 1642.

[30] *Ibid.*, CC.Ab. 9, Cawood and Wistow, Otley contains some records of the Liberty for the 1740s, but none survive from this date.

[31] See, for example, A. Fletcher, *A County Community in Peace and War: Sussex 1600–1660* (1975), 235–7; P. Clark and P. Slack, *English Towns in Transition, 1500–1700* (1976), 151. For York, see below, n. 33.

[32] J. T. Cliffe, *The Yorkshire Gentry from the Reformation to the Civil War* (1969), 239, 248. The surviving Quarter Sessions records for the early seventeenth century were kept among Fairfax Muniments, Connor, 'The Fairfax Archives', 84, and have been printed by the Yorkshire Archaeological Society.

[33] For these see M. C. Cross, 'From the Reformation to the Restoration', in *A History of York Minster*, ed. G. E. Aylmer and R. Cant (Oxford, 1977), 211–12. The Fairfax family owned property in the Bishophill area of the city, and houses in that area conveyed by Thomas Lord Fairfax to his son Charles, of Menston, in 1630, Connor, 'The Fairfax Archive', 76; Leeds Archives Dept, 2RL/126. Sir Thomas was resident there during the summer of 1642, C. R. Markham, *A Life of the Great Lord Fairfax* (1870).

[34] G. Lawton, *Collectio Rerum Ecclesiasticorum . . . diocesi Eboracensi* (1842), 98; BIHR Inst. AB. 3 fol. 382.

[35] Marchant, *Puritans and Church Courts*, 49–50.

appears to have handed over the preaching ministry to others, for he is not named in the volume.[36] There were six chapelries within the parish; at Burley, Baildon, Pool, Farnley, Denton and Bramhope, and though not all of them were sufficiently well endowed to sustain a minister we know that at least four of them were being served by curates in 1640.[37] These curates were either appointed directly by the vicar or by local trustees with his agreement. Thus there was considerable local control of the character of the parochial clergy, which sometimes expressed itself in co-operation between magistrate and minister over the exercise of godly discipline.[38] That lay support and co-operation placed a high value on preaching, and in earlier decades of the seventeenth century many of the local clergy were members of the exercise which nurtured and sustained that preaching tradition in a number of venues in the county, some of them close to Otley. This exercise had received the tacit support of Archbishop Matthew, support not given by Archbishop Neile who adopted a more confrontational approach in the 1630s.[39] In the context of the conflicts of the 1630s and 1640s, therefore, Otley exemplified many of the contradictions facing the established church; it was a community whose secular and agrarian life was under the authority of the archbishop, but one in which the oversight of religious provision rested with the principal inhabitants. In the view of the godly the essential element in such provision was the preaching of the word of God.

III

The exercise had, by the 1630s, established a godly preaching tradition in the towns and parishes around Halifax, Leeds and Bradford. Otley, equidistant from both Leeds and Bradford, was well placed to benefit from this activity which also penetrated parishes in the Craven district of Upper Wharfedale. The character of the preaching in those exercises can be recovered in part from the extensive notes made by the secretary, Elkanah Wales. These have been studied by J. A. Newton whose work has stressed the pastoral and exhortatory emphasis in the sermons; they contained little criticism of ecclesiastical authority, were vigorously

[36] *Ibid.*, 253, for his ordination date; BIHR, PRTs Otley, 1635-9.
[37] Lambeth Palace Library, MS Comm/x11a 331-8; BIHR, v.1640/CB, fols. 49v-50; Exh. Bk fols. 10, 25v-6.
[38] Newton, 'Puritanism in Yorks', 320-5.
[39] Marchant, *Puritans and Church Courts*, 30-1, 52-68; for an assessment of these meetings in the early Stuart church see P. Collinson, 'Lectures by Combination: Structure and Characteristics of Church Life in 17th-Century England', *Bulletin of the Institute of Historical Research*, 48 (1975), 182-213.

opposed to separatist views, and were not too condemnatory of the failings of the people. Though preaching was at the heart of religion, and repetition and meditation upon sermons was encouraged among the godly, the sacraments still had an important place in the church and, in one sermon at least, the benefits of frequent communion were urged. Dr Newton has noted the moderate tone of the preachers in the matter of ceremonies and the absence of political reference in the sermons, but identifies a more vigorous stance in opposition to Catholicism, warning people to 'watch, else theire blood shalbe required at your handes'.[40] All this is typical of the Jacobean churchmanship revealed to us by Professor Collinson,[41] but its moderation was tested in the 1630s when Archbishop Neile pursued a more rigorous standard of conformity on the clergy. Unfortunately, no texts survive for that period so the response of the exercise can only be seen through the less revealing records of the church courts.[42] Clearly relations deteriorated and tensions were such that some laity of the area emigrated, a course of action considered and rejected by Elkanah Wales.[43] Wales was still active at Pudsey in 1642, as was another patriarch, Robert More, at Guiseley, but though Wales preached one of the sermons recorded in the book, the evidence of the Otley material is that preaching was now in the hands of a younger generation of clerics, educated at Cambridge in the 1620s and many of them still unbeneficed in 1642.

The two main preachers, David Ellison and John Cooper, were both Cambridge graduates, of St John's and Jesus respectively.[44] Before coming to Otley Ellison had been curate and schoolmaster at Bradford, where he had probably come to the notice of the Fairfaxes;[45] Cooper was a local man who had assisted Robert More at Guiseley before taking up the curacy at Burley where he was to remain until his death in 1644.[46] These two provided the weekly diet of preaching in the parish and were responsible for thirty-two of the forty-four sermons recorded in the volume. Others were invited to preach at Otley, including another local

---

40 This paragraph is heavily indebted to Newton, 'Puritanism in Yorks', 315–88.
41 P. Collinson, *The Religion of Protestants: The Church in English Society 1559–1625* (Oxford, 1982), *passim*.
42 Marchant, *Puritans and Church Courts*, 52–68, 106–30.
43 Newton, 'Puritanism in Yorks', 323.
44 J. and J. A. Venn, *Alumni Cantabridgienses*, I, 390; II, 98.
45 Marchant, *Puritans and Church Courts*, 245, describes his troubles with the diocesan authorities; for Fairfax involvement with church affairs in Bradford in 1633 and 1642, see *Fairfax Correspondence*, ed. Johnson, I, 334; II, 381–2. Thomas Fairfax subsequently got good support in the war from Bradford, Markham, *Life of Fairfax*, 59.
46 Marchant, *Puritans and Church Courts*, 241; *Leeds Parish Register 1639–67* (Thoresby Society, 7, 1897), 184.

man, John Furness, who had been born in the parish at Menston and had gone to Magdalen College, Oxford, taking his MA in 1636. He preached on two occasions.[47] Two other local clergy shared the preaching on Easter Sunday; Philip Tandy preached in the morning and was followed by Robert Hitch, the incumbent of the neighbouring parish of Adel, in the afternoon. Hitch was rather older than the others recorded in the volume, having entered Trinity, Cambridge, in 1611, and was unusual in being beneficed.[48] His subsequent career and that of his fellow-preacher could hardly have been more different: Hitch remained at his living throughout the wars and Interregnum and at the Restoration was granted a prebendal stall in York Minster, being appointed dean in 1665; Tandy became a Baptist, was charged with being a 'great sectary' and was one of those provided by the government for ministry to the garrisons in Ireland in the 1650s.[49] Another special occasion was the visit of Bulstrode Whitelocke to Otley on 3 April when Ellison shared the pulpit with a 'Mr Hirne', probably one of the Hieron brothers who subsequently served in their native Derbyshire and were ejected from the ministry in 1662.[50] In addition to the Sunday sermons preached at Otley, the volume also records one sermon preached by Ellison away from the parish church at Denton, where the pulpit was occupied on another Sunday by Richard Clarkson, curate of Illingworth near Halifax and presently serving the neighbouring parish of Bingley. Clarkson was another Cambridge graduate of the 1620s who had been in trouble with the diocesan authorities for nonconformity in the 1630s.[51] The remaining Sunday sermon recorded in the neighbourhood was preached at Weston on 3 June by Josias Bellwood, master of Otley Grammar School, a graduate of St John's, Cambridge, and the son of Roger Bellwood, one of the civic preachers at York. Fairfax's influence in the City, and Lord Ferdinando's position as governor of the school no doubt secured Josias' appointment to Otley.[52] Bellwood and Furness were younger than the other preachers mentioned, but shared their strong local connections. Such connections

---

[47] J. Foster, *Alumni Oxonienses 1500–1714*, p. 523; Otley sermons, 170–6, 188–95.

[48] J. and J. A. Venn, *Alumni Cantabridgiensis*, II, 376; Otley sermons, 77–88.

[49] D. M. Smith, *Le Neve, Fasti Ecclesiae Anglicanae: Diocese of York, 1547–1858* (1975), 6, 17 for Hitch. T. C. Barnard, *Cromwellian Ireland, English Government and Reform in Ireland, 1649–1660* (Oxford, 1975), 102n, and *The Sabbath Observer* (New York, 1844), I, pt II, 5, for Tandy. I am grateful to Dr B. W. Ball for this reference.

[50] *Calamy Revised*, ed. A. G. Matthews (Oxford, 1934), 261–2. Whitelocke's visit may have led to the appointment of John Furness to the living of Great Marlow in Bucks. that year for Whitelocke was MP for that town, R. Spalding, *The Improbable Puritan* (1975), 73.

[51] Marchant, *Puritans and Church Courts*, 111, 239, his case was linked to that of Ellison.

[52] J. and J. A. Venn, *Alumni Cantabridgiensis*, I, 131.

were crucial to the ability of all these clergy to sustain themselves adequately within the ministry for a period of years whilst remaining unbeneficed.

Local contacts were also important to the preachers of the remaining sermons. On 1 May our scribe was once again in York where he heard two sermons, one preached at All Saints Pavement by John Shaw, a native of Sykehouse who went up to Christ's in 1623 and who, in the later 1630s, emerged as the leader of the Puritan party in the city.[53] The remaining sermons were preached at less public occasions, reserved to the godly. One provides a direct link to the earlier West Riding exercises, for the preacher was Elkanah Wales and his text, from Acts 8 on planting the church in Samaria, was appropriate to the occasion, the baptism of a child of one of his younger clerical colleagues, John Furness.[54] The other occasion was the exercise held on 13 July at Calverley, where the preachers were described as two beneficed clergy, the vicars of Batley and Bradford respectively.[55] The volume thus comprises a collection of sermons preached by experienced ministers whose careers remained, for the most part, on the periphery of the established church but within it, and whose local origins and connections saw them rooted in the tradition of godly piety which had arisen in the exercises of the early seventeenth century. Such 'godly connections', like the circle of friendships, clerical and lay, revealed in the diary of the Warwickshire schoolmaster Thomas Dugard, were a feature of provincial religious life throughout the 1630s in several localities.[56] These sermons, therefore, represent a unique source derived from a not untypical Puritan context and, as such, can stand as a localised expression of the response to crisis of a godly tradition rooted in the churchmanship of the early seventeenth century.

IV

Most of the texts in the volume represent the weekly preaching in the parish church on Sundays, from which the unsurprising themes of

---

[53] For Shaw see *DNB* and *Yorkshire Diaries and Autobiographies of the 17th and 18th Centuries* (Surtees Soc., 65, 1877), 128–40. For he and Neile at York, see, Newton, 'Puritanism in Yorks', 88.

[54] Otley sermons, 252–62.

[55] The vicar of Batley was Roger Awdsley, but the document wrongly identifies a Mr Cocker as vicar of Bradford at this date. There is no evidence for a beneficed cleric of this name and may be a scribal error for Jeremy Collier, who was lecturer in the town and had preached at the Halifax exercise, Marchant, *Puritans and Church Courts*, 239.

[56] A. Hughes, *Politics, Society and Civil War in Warwickshire, 1620–1660* (Cambridge, 1987), 71–80.

repentance and renewal emerge. Constant reference was made to the need for the people, and specifically the people as a nation rather than as individuals, to renew their covenant with God, a covenant which had seen England once hold the pre-eminent position among the reformed nations, a position which it had now lost. That eminence, which looked back to the days of Elizabeth, had been lost by a sinful generation which had failed to heed God and, by its negligence, had brought great affliction on the nation and upon those people of God who lived there. Thus the Calvinist doctrine of election reinforced in the words of the preachers the division within society between the godly and the multitude, whose sins were responsible for the difficulties with which the godly were confronted at this time.[57] Such preaching was commonplace in the Puritan pulpits of early seventeenth-century England, but the tone was given sharper focus when the preachers warned their congregations that the sufferings of God's people would eventually rebound to the disadvantage of their persecutors, upon whom God's vengeance would be poured. It was not clear whether this would happen in this world or the next, but several sermons returned to the career of Saul as a warning to kings who failed to follow God's path. In contrast to Saul the career of Paul provided counter-examples of the ways in which suffering would bring increase to the church.[58] Such concentration on the need for repentance left little room for the pastoral preaching for which the earlier exercise has been noted, especially so in the light of the sermons which had been preached at Otley on the parliamentary fast days. It is these sermons which command our particular attention.

The parliamentary fast sermons have been identified as an important tactical instrument of policy in which radical proposals were first announced and through which dramatic episodes were prepared by the preachers who 'already knew their parts'. Chief among them was the Essex Minister Stephen Marshall, whose sermon of February 1642 'Meroz Cursed' was later said by some soldiers to have been the reason why they took up arms against the king. This sermon which earned

[57] The idea of 'the nation' and of 'God's people' in the parliamentary sermons are discussed in Wilson, *Pulpit in Power*, 168–74. This division is itself a subject of intense historical debate, and the records do not survive to test whether the local community at Otley was polarised in the way that seems to have been the case at Terling, K. Wrightson and D. Levine, *Poverty and Piety in an English Village: Terling 1525–1700* (1979). It is clear that, at this time of crisis, such polarisation was perceived to be the case, and that this view overlaid the earlier pastoral tradition of the area, which may have reflected the alternative view to Wrightson and Levine's and which has been documented by E. Duffy, 'The Godly and the Multitude in Stuart England', *The Seventeenth Century*, 1 (1986), 31–55.
[58] See, for example, the sermons of 17, 24 April, Otley sermons, 88–112.

Marshall the title 'the great incendiary of this unhappy war' from his opponents, was preached by him on no less than sixty occasions up and down the country.[59] No doubt some of these took place in country pulpits to coincide with the parliamentary fast days, for from February 1642 a new and regular system of monthly fasts, formally linked to the Irish Rebellion, were appointed to be observed on the last Wednesday of each month. They were to prove an important tool of propaganda at the centre, and they were designed to be preached also in 'all cathedrals, collegiate and parish churches and chapels' thus uniting the nation with the parliamentary cause.[60] The evidence for such sermons is sparse and Cornelius Burges, one of the parliamentary preachers, on 30 March berated the members present for their slackness in seeing the proclamation enacted in the localities: 'But is there any care taken to see how these Fasts are performed? Which of you have made enquiry how they are observed, in the severall Countries and Places for which you serve? Should you do it you would receive a sad return from many places.'[61] It has been suggested that in the country these fasts were resented, and the regular orders for enforcement and penalties for their omission confirm Burges' criticism.[62] But this did not apply to Otley where, from March at least, the monthly fast day was observed by the preaching of two sermons, one in the morning and one in the afternoon, by the curates Cooper and Ellison.

The morning sermon of 30 March took Deuteronomy 10:12 as its text: 'And now Israel, what doth the Lord thy God require of thee, but to fear the Lord thy God, to walk in his ways, and to love him and serve the Lord thy God with all thy heart and with all thy soul.'[63] Israel, of course, was England, whose present disorders resulted from the neglect of spiritual duty – 'Now is England to feare, above other nations; doth not the Lord justly expect it, it being the field wherin he hath plentifully sown, and where much is given, much is required.' This text returned again to the consequences for the nation of falling away from the trust which God had placed in it through the early preachers of reform, and the present state of the country was likened to the humiliation of Job, its past greatness

---

59 H. R. Trevor-Roper, 'The Fast Sermons of the Long Parliament', in his *Religion, Reformation and Social Change* (1967), 294–344, esp. 294–308; Christopher Hill, *The English Bible and the Seventeenth-Century Revolution* (Harmondsworth, 1993), 79–108, esp. 79–92; Collinson, *Birthpangs*, 127.

60 Trevor-Roper, 'The Fast Sermons', 306.

61 C. Burges, *Two Sermons Preached to the Honourable House of Commons* (1645), 'The Necessity and Benefit of Washing the Heart', 33; the text of this sermon is available in *The Fast Sermons to Parliament*, ed. R. Jeffs, II (1970), 255–309.

62 Trevor-Roper, 'The Fast Sermons', 310.

63 Otley sermons, 47–53.

forgotten. That greatness was identified with the reign of Elizabeth, England's Deborah, the fruits of which had been dissipated by later generations. The sermon then moved to recent events in Ireland, and to the dire situation of the Protestants there where 'fair countries' were laid waste and 'poor cities burned to heaps'. These events were to serve as a warning about the enemy close at hand, and of the danger from Catholics. This danger was internal also and England was likened to the flourishing state of the Jews, among whom the Lord had 'planted a fruitful soil to raise bread without scarcity and with great variety, peace and plenty within our walls', and yet the people persisted in idolatry and were thrown into bondage. The preacher, John Cooper, then moved to more contemporary affairs, talking of the recent plots and confusions in the realm which had been brought on by bad advice, and warning the congregation that 'God hath not his due, and keeps back his hand from those who do not do his will.' Chief among these, and the object of bad advice, was the king and, in reference to Charles, Cooper warned of the fate of Saul whose failure to carry out God's law meant that 'God rends his kingship from him and gives it to David, one that will execute all his wills.' This argument recalls one of the chief ways in which Puritans, faced with the example of a king supporting an ungodly church polity, resolved their difficulty. The declared resolution was a providential one, with God intervening to shorten the rule of an ungodly monarch, and in this respect the sermon reflected 'the most commonly expressed political principle in early Stuart England' that subjects could never justifiably use force against the king.[64] This was an issue which the preachers of Otley never quite confronted, despite the increasing seriousness of the situation facing their godly congregation.

The morning sermon, concentrating as it did on the theme of a neglectful nation labouring under an ungodly, or ill-advised magistrate, was matched in the afternoon by one which concentrated on the sufferings of the church, taking as its text Hebrews 13:3 'Remember them that are in bonds; as bound with them; and them which suffer adversity, as being yourselves also in the body.'[65] The threat from Ireland, and the sufferings there, dominated the sermon:

You christians in England if you lend them not a lift under their burden you are never His friends nor any members of our Church forsaken; the feare of God's

[64] J. P. Sommerville, *Politics and Ideology in England 1603–1640* (1986), 35. The development of resistance theories 1640–2 is discussed in Sanderson, *'But the People's Creatures'*, 10–37, where most of the texts post-date the outbreak of hostilities.
[65] Otley sermons, 63–4, the pattern throughout the summer was for Cooper to preach in the morning and Ellison in the afternoon.

church calls for it, and the state. In this the antichristian hierarchy are said to afflict England even more than Ireland and that, if the Church is not defended against them it will be deprived of public assemblies, bibles taken, children murdered, and wives ravished.

To Ellison the dangers from the papists in Ireland could easily be transferred to the English scene, and with many Catholic families in the area around Otley this was more than a theoretical analysis.[66] The Catholics were likened to the Philistines at the gate and the example of Saul who 'though a valiant man, when the enemy came into the land, full of fear in his heart greatly trembled' was used to demonstrate that lack of strong leadership would lead to disaster as 'on the day of affliction they [the enemy] turne rebels to King and State, to God's own people'. Charles and England, therefore, had a duty, following the example of Abraham, to befriend the suffering church and 'to entertain strangers and be kind and open hearted to such as suffer for Christ's sake, driven and forced to fly from houses for religion'. Failure to do so was not only to ignore the demands of Christian charity, but also placed the whole church in danger, for 'mihi hodie, tibi cras' was the warning. The dangers to the church from both Catholics and 'the antichristian hierarchy' were great, and brought great suffering on God's people, but such was, and always has been, the lot of the church: 'It is the duty of Christians to have a fellow feeling of the sufferings and afflictions which many of God's people shall meet with in this world.' Suffering was a sign in itself and like that of Paul 'did cause the inlargement of the Church', so that in these difficult days the godly shared Christ's pains and should be glad to do so. But there were limits to the demands of such suffering for 'it is noe holy matter to suffer imprisonment, [to] lay in bonds, see your houses burnt, wives deflowered and slayn . . . as in Ireland'. The call to action, however, was a generalised one demanding assistance to the Irish Protestants and encouragement to the king to provide the same. The dangers of failing to act were also expressed in general terms, and the implications behind the limitation placed on the church's suffering were not spelled out.

The month of April had seen the king declare his intention of going to Ireland, and also the meagre response of the Yorkshire gentry to his plea for support. The attempt by Charles to enter Hull on 23 April, and his humiliating rebuff and retreat from there, had also polarised opinion in

---

[66] For the impact of the Irish Rebellion on English attitudes, see K. J. Lindley, 'The Irish Rebellion of 1641 in England and Wales 1641–45', *Irish Historical Studies*, 18 (1973), 144–75. Local recusant families are identified in H. Aveling, 'The Catholic Recusants of the West Riding of Yorkshire', *Leeds Philosophical and Literary Society*, 10, pt 6 (1963), 191–306, recusants were noted at Burley, Baildon, Denton and Otley between 1603 and 1642 (pp. 287–9).

the county.[67] The fast sermons on 27 April took prayer as their theme, and both preachers filled their texts with examples of its efficacy. Reference to the benefits wrought by David, a king who prayed 'morn, noon, and eventide' for his people, were scattered liberally through the sermons, and the case of Peter and his miraculous escape from prison was used by both preachers to show how constancy in prayer, even in the darkest of circumstances, brought release to the godly from oppression. Cooper, in the morning sermon,[68] made specific reference to the 'recent breaches and factions' at home and, more directly, spoke of parliament as embodying the will of the nation: 'God now shakes his sword; let us meet him in the way of his judgement, with tears and repentance, our enemyes plott to subvert and undermine all proceedings of Parliament, pray that He will be their safeguard and give them success.' This was the first explicit mention of parliament, and the identification of its opponents as 'our enemyes' made the discussion of domestic issues both more specific and, by implication, more partisan, but those enemies were never named directly. Ireland remained a central concern of the preachers but there was an important shift in emphasis, expressing mistrust of Charles' intentions in going there. Whereas earlier sermons had stressed the dangers of events in Ireland spilling over into English politics, there was no sense that such an outcome had been planned. Now, however, the warning was made clear: 'Ireland may be our looking glasse, see the ruins and bloodshed; yet England is the object of all ther plotts for mischief and desolation. The Lord take them in their own traps.'[69] By the end of April, therefore, the rhetoric of the preachers was more partisan and more directly contemporary, but each remained committed to a providential solution; Cooper reminding his hearers that the way to ensure a godly triumph was 'through prayer, for a non praying Christian is an idolator', and Ellison ending the day with this exhortation; 'Truly this is thy duty, pray for [the] king, pray for parliament.'[70]

---

[67] Fletcher, *The Outbreak of the Civil War*, 232–3.

[68] Otley sermons, 112–17; the text was from 1 Thessalonians 5:17, 'Pray without ceasing'.

[69] Suspicion of royal motives were responsible for the poor response of the Yorkshire gentry to Charles' plea. Moreover, rumours circulated that Charles was in collusion with some of the rebels, and though one would not want to make too much of this, it may be significant that, when those rumours were published, it was by Edward Bowles, who had been one of the York civic preachers. The importance of the rumours must not be underestimated, and their impact on Richard Baxter's decision to take up arms against the king has been elegantly demonstrated in W. Lamont, *Richard Baxter and the Millennium* (1979), 76–123.

[70] Ellison's text was from Psalms 28:9, 'Save thy people and bless thine inheritance: feed them also and lift them up forever', and is found in Otley sermons, 117–26.

During May Charles had increased the billeting of soldiers in York, and the continuation of the parliamentary garrison at Hull had interfered with the export of cloth, thereby threatening the prosperity of the towns near Otley.[71] In response to these deteriorating circumstances fasting and humiliation were the themes adopted by Cooper and Ellison on 25 May, when they preached on successive verses of the epistle of St James.[72] The way to return to God was 'by lamentation and bitter weeping' and though God wept over Jerusalem 'for her hardness, yet they relented not'. The nation was sunk in idolatry so that 'God be dishonoured and his servants disgraced', but 'the Lord now calls for mourning in these times, the wound of godly sorrow should never be soe skined but that it should bleed affresh'. The days were dark, and the warning of the Passover angel who did not 'spare anie but those marked for mercy' was placed before the enemies of the godly. For the godly themselves, however, the only courses of action were the spiritual ones commended in the chosen themes of the day, but they would ensure the ultimate victory 'for they that sowe in tears shall reape in Joy. When heaven rules the earth, a great increase; but when earth rules heaven (as nowe present) God will refuse Joy to such her . . . , and will give beauty for ashes.' The sermon ended with the reassurance that those currently suffering under the regime 'shalbe comforted, ther is greater joy in heaven for this sorrow, more then the pleasure in sinne'. At this fast Cooper and Ellison were joined by John Furness, who preached on Jehosaphat 'a good man and a good King, he walked in the ways of David, God established his kingdom, his heart was lifted up in the ways of the Lord, he brings the people to God'.[73] This example of godly kingship was also used in the parliamentary sermons on that day,[74] and further examples of the redemptive power of such kingship were scattered throughout Furness' text. Kings had a heavy responsibility in this matter, for it was their trust in God which protected the nation from its enemies. Failure to act meant that 'this nation will be subject to nationall judgement' in which it would find 'sinne is the cause of all woe'. The way to avoid this was to follow the example of Judah and resolve upon a fast, 'So are our fasts, in these days, a means for the nation to seek God.' The godly, therefore, had a duty to pray, but the king had a responsibility to act, and the consequences of failing to do so

---

71 Fletcher, *The Outbreak of the Civil War*, 223, 315; *The Humble Petition of The Clothiers Inhabiting in the Parish of Leeds, Vicaridge of Halifax, and Other Parts Adjoyning . . . Presented . . . at Yorke the 14 of April 1642* (1642).

72 Otley sermons, 184–8, 195–206: the texts were from James 4:9–10.

73 *Ibid.*, 188–95: his text was 2 Chronicles 20:3.

74 See the sermon of R. Harris, *A Sermon* in *Fast Sermons*, ed. Jeffs, II, 9–67, esp. 62.

would seem to be increasingly stark for those who failed to hear God's voice.

A pamphlet published at the end of May referred to 'the greate dissension here in this our county' with 'many Feares and Jealousies entering into the hearts of true hearted Protestants in the Northerne parts of England, and especially in the County of Yorkshire'. It went on to mention the 'great preparations for warre made in this county' which struck terror into the hearts of Protestants who suspected the royalists, and especially 'the blood thirsty Papists', of believing 'that the world will never be good till there be some bloud of the Puritans shed'.[75] Such foreboding was increased further after the muster on Heworth Moor outside York in early June when the freeholders' petition was presented and rebuffed.[76] The morning text for the fast on 29 June was taken from Jeremiah: 'Be thou instructed, O Jerusalem, lest my soule depart from thee: lest I make thee desolate',[77] and confronted the congregation with the consequences of war. The country had failed to heed the warnings of the prophets, and had ignored the examples of the recent desolations in Germany and Ireland, so that 'as a Physician gives over his patient as incurable, so will God give us some fearfull judgement' and the 'sword will be sheathed in blood'. The cruel discords within the nation were spelt out, 'city against city, town against town, neighbour against neighbour', so that the malady had infected the whole body 'from the Crown of the Head'. Whereas in earlier sermons the king had had the responsibility to act in order to protect the nation against spiritual ills, many of which emanated from outside the realm, by this date he was seen to be, if not the source, an integral part of these ills. This was a major shift in emphasis, but one made in passing and not expanded upon, except in the increasingly pessimistic tone of the preachers. The only hope was in the oft-repeated call to enter 'a covenant with God for the better to submit to his hand'. According to the afternoon text that covenant was like a marriage, which could only be broken by adultery, a crime of which England, like Israel in the days of Saul, had been guilty.[78] The nation, therefore, had driven God from itself, despite the pleas of parliament to the people 'not to lett God depart from amongst us'. The consequences of such adultery were grievous, 'Is not our estate woeful? Then let not God goe out of England. Will we part with him on any terms

[75] *The King's Maiesties Resolution Concerning Yorkshire* (26 May 1642).
[76] Fletcher, *The Outbreak of the Civil War*, 317; Markham, *Life of Fairfax*, 47–8.
[77] Otley sermons, 285–90.
[78] *Ibid.*, 290–302: the text was Hosea 9:12, 'Woe also to them when I depart from them.' Hosea was used as a text by many preachers warning of God's judgement on a neglectful people, Collinson, *Birthpangs*, 3, 20–3.

and conditions? Shall we drive him out of the Kingdom, and out of our assemblies and congregations? . . . If war and confusion are at hand, and God farr off, we are miserable.' The imminent prospect of civil war was the result of the nation's rejection of God's love: 'we know not how sone God may take us by the hand and bidd us farewell', but it was not yet too late to restore the covenant, 'Let us fetch him and have love for him.' Despite this hope, however, the afternoon sermon on this day, unlike those on previous occasions, did not place before the congregation the spiritual consolations of suffering, but continued the usual morning stress on the judgement likely to befall an ungodly and ungrateful nation. The bleakness of the situation was expressed in Ellison's sombre, and by this date essentially rhetorical, question with which his sermon ended, 'Is God departed from our brethren in Ireland, and from many believers in England? Is he already gone or going?'

Parliament voted to raise an army of 10,000 volunteers on 9 July and it was in the course of this month, probably for the first time in the view of Professor Russell, that 'one of the vital conditions of a civil war had been achieved, in that both sides believed that they were strong enough to be able to win'.[79] The fast sermons at the end of the month, however, resumed their usual format with the morning text, from Jeremiah this time, stressing the hardness of the nation's heart in failing to listen to the voice of God, who had therefore put the people to silence and given them waters of gall to drink. The afternoon sermon took up the usual theme of suffering, based on the normally comforting verse from the beatitudes, 'Blessed are they that mourn, for they shall be comforted',[80] but the conventional consoling lesson to be drawn from this text was obscured by the gravity of the dangers confronting a people faced 'with the desolation of Ireland and Germany, and at home rumours of warrs. Hou soone may our stately buildings be laid level, our children killed, wives deflowered before our eyes? Our standing is slippery, and dangers at hand look on.' The wilfulness of the people had left the nation friendless so that, like Jerusalem, England 'hath no friends to bewail her miseries'. Neither of the preachers denied that sorrows were shortly to engulf the godly in their daily lives, but in this provincial pulpit, the only resorts left to them were the spiritual ones of prayer, fasting and repentance. Sorrow, like repentance, had its own reward, for 'godly sorow mends the heart and makes him better when humbled and fell', and thus God's people, in these mournful days, were to welcome the tears they would shortly have to face in this world, secure in God's promise that 'they will not be spilt'.

---

[79] Russell, *Fall of the British Monarchies*, 518.
[80] Otley sermons, 360–2 for Cooper, 362–72 for Ellison.

Thus at the end of July the message of the preachers to the congregation at Otley was that its members should put their trust in God's providence, but within that message it was made clear to the people that responsibility for the present woes of the nation lay with the king and his advisers and not with parliament. Nevertheless, and despite the imminent catastrophe about to engulf the nation, the preachers remained within the conventions of early seventeenth-century thought, recognising the central place given to civil authority in the religion of Protestants, and did not urge the people to resist the authorities.[81] In one sense this looked like a retreat from an earlier position. In the fasts of March and April Ellison and Cooper appeared to support more active military involvement on the part of the godly and were more directly critical of the king, but both of these positions were taken at a time when the danger seemed to come from outside the realm and the need was to support suffering fellow-Protestants. In such circumstances the call of the preachers was consistent with the long-stated demand that England should come to the aid of other endangered co-religionists, and was very far from a call to resist authority. It was more a call for the king to recognise the national responsibility, and to fulfil it.[82] Failure to do so would have dire consequences for the nation, but these did not include rebellion. Once it became certain that the king could not be trusted to act against the Irish rebels and that conflict would break out within the realm then the criticism remained, but the issue of resistance by the people was not raised. The context may have been important here; the fast days did indeed unite the provinces with the cause of parliament, and the preachers left no doubt on that score, but the fast was an essentially spiritual exercise to renew the people's covenant with God. Moreover, unlike those of their ministerial colleagues preaching before parliament, the Otley sermons were directed to the people and not to a politically sophisticated audience; it was one thing for Stephen Marshall to preach resistance to the assembled body of MPs, but quite another for Cooper or Ellison to place the same arguments before the yeomen or artisans of Otley. They may themselves have held such views, and Ellison's subsequent involvement with Puritan activists in Bradford are consistent with this,[83] but held back from public advocacy. We do know that such

---

[81] Sommerville, *Politics and Ideology*, 207–23, esp. 223.

[82] See S. L. Adams, 'Foreign Policy and the Parliaments of 1621 and 1624', in *Faction and Parliament: Essays in Early Stuart History*, ed. K. Sharpe (Oxford, 1978), 139–71; P. Collinson, 'England and International Calvinism 1558–1640', in *International Calvinism 1541–1715*, ed. M. Prestwich (Oxford, 1985), esp. 201–10.

[83] For Bradford's resistance see Markham, *Life of Fairfax*, 81–2 and notes. For Ellison at Bradford in 1643, see *Bradford Antiquary*, 10 (1960), 292.

views were being expressed by clergy associated with these sermons. At the exercise held at Calverley on 13 July, a more private affair restricted to ministers and, perhaps, selected leading lay supporters, the morning sermon was preached by Roger Awdsley, vicar of Batley, in which, at the end of a long plea for repentance, the lesson was drawn out that the followers of the Lord, in imitation of David and the Amalekites, should not stay from waging war on His enemies.[84] Awdsley was himself no radical[85] and the fact that he could express such views and that they were current and being discussed among the clergy of the area, albeit in their more private meetings, shows the extent of alienation from the king in these quarters. That alienation rarely led to public exhortation to resist his authority and did not do so at Otley, but those members of the congregation who had listened to their preachers would have had no difficulty, once formal hostilities were declared, in knowing where to lay the blame for the calamities of the time. In that respect Cooper and Ellison prepared their congregation for armed resistance without publicly espousing that course, and the evidence of the exercise suggests that they understood precisely what they were doing.

V

These sermons raise issues of both text and context. The context was both local and national. Locally Otley revealed all the contradictions of early Stuart England, ecclesiastical authority in secular affairs, lay control of ecclesiastical patronage and a godly tradition in close proximity to substantial recusant families. Yet the town does not appear to have been the scene of one of those petty 'wars of religion' identified as a feature of this period by Professor Collinson.[86] Just as did the place so did the preachers reflect those same contradictions; many of them shared a common godly education, both locally and at Cambridge, which encouraged them to feel at ease in each other's pulpits in these months of crisis, but their responses to the conflict ultimately diverged and were to lead some to dissent and one to a deanery. The sermons they preached were designed for local consumption but were also part of a national

---

[84] Otley sermons, 319–30; this example had been used in Marshall's parliamentary sermon, *Meroz Cursed*: Trevor-Roper, 'The Fast Sermons', 308.

[85] Awdsley was subsequently ejected by the Commonwealth in favour of a chaplain in Fairfax's army, but was reinstated at the Restoration and died in possession of the living in 1666; A. G. Matthews, *Walker Revised* (Oxford, 1948), 389; M. Sheard, *Records of the Parish of Batley* (Dewsbury, 1894), 144.

[86] See the essay in *Birthpangs*, 125–55, and D. Underdown, *Revel, Riot and Rebellion: Popular Politics and Culture in England 1603–1660* (Oxford, 1985), 44–72.

programme, to which the presence of the monarch in the locality gave added point. Their survival owes much to the uniqueness of the location, but their origin owed everything to the uniqueness of the time, and in this lies their chief value. The texts reveal, if not contradictions, a mixture of conviction and confusion; conviction about who was responsible for the current difficulties, confusion about the practical remedies available. Above all they show how the crisis of the summer of 1642 came to dominate the pulpits in this part of West Yorkshire to the exclusion of almost everything else. By such concentration on the difficulties of the time the preachers invested contemporary conflict with fundamental religious concerns, making them inseparable in the eyes of their godly parishioners. As the situation deteriorated over the summer so the sermons became more gloomy in tone, but the preachers stopped short at support for armed resistance. They stopped short at little else, however, and when the moment of choice arrived they had armed their congregation with a clear view of where both right and responsibility lay so that, when the Fairfaxes summoned the West Riding to rise against the royalists, one of the local godly could say 'When I put my hand to the Lord's work . . . I did it not rashly, but had many an hour or night to seek God, to know my way.'[87] That degree of considered conviction was the result of such preaching, and was the hallmark of the often reported independence of the West Riding tenantry and townsmen,[88] many of whom were, according to Clarendon, 'so notoriously disaffected, especially in matters relating to the church, that they wanted only conductors to carry them into rebellion'.[89] Clarendon's view of the Yorkshire godly was unfair and, if the sermons are to be trusted, it was not rebellion but the defence of the Protestant religion that the people sought. It was only when the king seemed incapable of providing that defence that the ministers began to articulate notions of resistance, and even then not in the public pulpit. Nevertheless, the preaching which had gone on during the summer months had prepared the people for the catastrophe of civil war and, once hostilities started, they showed themselves more zealous for the fray than their leaders.[90] In this respect

---

[87] 'Memoirs of Captain John Hodgson' in *Original Memoirs Written during the Great Civil War* (Edinburgh, 1806), 95–6.
[88] See B. Manning, *The English People and the English Revolution* (1976), 184, 210–15.
[89] Clarendon, *Great Rebellion*, II, 285.
[90] See, for example, letter from Sir Thomas Fairfax to his father on 9 January 1643 in which he forcibly makes this point, and asks his father's permission 'to join with the readiness of the people' in attacking the royalists; discussed by Manning, *English People*, 215–16, where the social context is stressed. The evidence of the sermons discussed here is that the religious issues were those most forcibly placed before the people; see also Morrill, 'Religious Context', 174.

both Cooper and Ellison were among the 'conductors' mentioned by Clarendon and, just as the preachers at York had complicated the king's arrival in the city in March, so their preaching, and that of their colleagues in and around Otley, provided the people with the spiritual and intellectual arguments to enable them to decide for themselves where their loyalties lay when the king forced the issue in August. For most of them, if not a war of religion, it was a war for religion, and no other cause could justify the reluctant breaking of God's peace, a peace which had been cast aside by the wilful governors of an ungrateful nation and was the only guarantee of the people's liberties.[91]

[91] See the comments in Hill, *The English Bible*, 34, on religious language and political action.

13   Popular form, Puritan content? Two Puritan appropriations of the murder pamphlet from mid-seventeenth-century London

Peter Lake

I

At about four o'clock on the morning of 6 August 1657 one Nathaniel Butler, an apprentice of a London silkman, Arthur North, took a knife and cut the throat of his fellow-apprentice John Knight. Knight died and Butler was arrested, convicted and executed.[1] On the face of it this was an event of no particular significance (except for Butler and Knight, of course). However, it became the subject of a number of printed pamphlets.[2] That, too, was not particularly unusual; bloody or shocking crimes were often the subject for short, sensationalist pamphlets written in a hurry and printed for profit.[3] Only some of the pamphlets prompted by Butler's deed answered this description. One written and attested to by a number of prominent Presbyterian ministers, co-ordinated by Stephen Yearwood, the lord mayor's chaplain, and provided with a preface by the mayor himself, dwelt not so much on the gory details of the murder as on the subsequent spiritual development and deportment of the murderer in prison and on the scaffold. Here was a rather striking amalgam of two distinct genres, the Puritan conversion narrative and the murder pamphlet. Taken together with a very similar account of another apprentice murder committed by Thomas Savage in 1668, these pamphlets represent a curious meeting of the popular, the profane and the Puritan, at a time when conventional accounts of the failure of godly

[1] City of London Record Office Sessions Files 140, indictment of Nathaniel Butler for the murder of John Knight. I owe this reference to the kindness of Michael Bowman.
[2] *Heaven's Cry against Murder. A True Relation of the Bloody and Unparalleled Murder of John Knight* (1657); *Blood Washed Away by Tears of Repentance* (1657); *A Full and the Truest Narrative of the Most Horrid, Barbarous and Unparalleled Murder Committed on the Person of John Knight* (1657).
[3] J. A. Sharpe, '"Last Dying Speeches": Religion, Ideology and Public Execution in Seventeenth Century England', *Past and Present*, 107 (1985); P. Lake, 'Deeds against Nature; Cheap Print Protestantism and Murder in Early Seventeenth Century England', in *Culture and Politics in Early Stuart England*, ed. K. Sharpe and P. Lake (1994).

313

314   Peter Lake

reformation in the 1650s picture the cultural gap between 'the people' and 'the godly' as a yawning chasm of mutual incomprehension and antipathy.[4]

To pursue the point we need to set these particular pamphlets into two contexts. Of these the first is the highly charged atmosphere surrounding the gallows demeanour and last dying speeches of notorious murderers and other felons. As Jim Sharpe, amongst others, has observed public executions could attract large crowds and the choreography of these occasions could provide the rulers of church and state with ample opportunity to assert the majesty of the law and to bolster the cause of social and moral order. Moreover, the capacity to bring the convicted murderer to a genuine and publicly convincing repentance was a source of considerable charisma and reputation for any minister and in the right circumstances could be mobilised for overtly polemical purposes.[5]

Helping both to frame and to exploit the theatre of the gallows were the murder pamphlets themselves, a genre or sub-genre within the category of cheap print to be found amongst the providentialised news and crime pamphlets of the period after 1570. In an earlier paper I argued that the murder pamphlet was an inherently mixed genre both titillating and admonitory, moralised and exploitative, even at times pornographic. On the one hand its appeal lay in the graphic scenes of violence, sex and moral outrage around which many of the narratives turned. Similarly sensational were the providential, indeed at times frankly miraculous, means whereby the foul deeds described in the pamphlets were revealed and their perpetrators brought to book. But these same providential elements provided the terms whereby many of the pamphlets were legitimated as moral lessons about the wages of sin in murder and murder's consequences on the gallows. Moreover, many of the pamphlets contained some demonic presence, explaining the origins of the deed and often the tale was told as a struggle between a demonically personified sin and a providentialised divine judgement. Nearly all the murder narratives at least gestured at the repentance of the murderer but, in some, considerable attention was given to that repentance, and the

[4] Randolph Yearwood, *The Penitent Murderer, Being an Exact Narrative of the Life and Death of Nathaniel Butler* (1657); Robert Franklin, Thomas Doolittle, Thomas Vincent, James Janeway and Hugh Baker, *A Murderer Punished and Pardoned or a True Relation of the Wicked Life and Shameful-Happy Death of Thomas Savage* (1668). For the failure of godly reformation, see D. Hirst, 'The Failure of Godly Rule in the English Republic', *Past and Present*, 132 (1991).
[5] Sharpe, '"Last Dying Speeches"', and P. Lake, 'Puritanism, Arminianism and a Shropshire Axe Murder', *Midland History*, 15 (1990), 37–64.

consequent salvation, of the murderer achieved, as often as not, under the auspices of the godly ministry.[6]

While all these elements can be found in most examples of the genre, they were mixed together in different combinations and in pamphlets of rather different lengths. Indeed, by examining the relative prominence of one theme against another it is almost possible to construct a spectrum of pamphlets, ranging from the most overtly titillating, indeed sub-pornographic, examples, at one end, to the most heavily moralised and openly edifying, at the other.

At one end of the spectrum we can locate the relatively unvarnished accounts of particularly tragic or curious crimes. *Page of Plymouth* tells the story of an arranged marriage which went badly wrong. Mistress Page continued to see her own choice as husband even after her marriage, at her father's insistence, to the older and richer Page. She and her lover plotted and compassed Page's death. Discovered, they confessed their guilt, but went unrepentant to their deaths; Mistress Page professing that she would rather die with her lover than live with her husband. Save for a brief appearance by the devil, who was presented as having been instrumental in arranging the marriage, the pamphlet was almost devoid of moralising rhetoric. The only comment was provided by three omens which were appended to the narrative as a commentary on the tragic and unnatural acts described in the main body of the tract and by a brief prayer to the effect that 'we may avoid the danger of shedding of innocent blood and fear the judgement of God which continually followeth wilfull murderers'. The moralising commentary in a very short pamphlet about a fisherman of Rye who poisoned his wife with ratsbane and powdered glass was limited to an opening statement on the prevalence of Satan and his desire to lead humanity to perdition and a closing prayer that God would help us 'withstand satan's temptations and eschew his subtleties'.[7]

Spare narratives like this, in so far as they were moralised at all, stood, like prodigy pamphlets, as illustrations of a rather cloudy providential-ism, dreadful signs of the sinful times, warnings of moral decline and of the judgements of God likely to be visited upon it. Thus in Anthony Munday's *A View of Sundry Examples* various murder stories were recounted along with other prodigies and natural disasters (a monstrous

6 Lake, 'Deeds against Nature', and 'Puritanism, Arminianism and a Shropshire Axe Murder'.

7 *The Murder of Page of Plymouth*, from *Sundry Strange and Inhumane Murders Lately Committed* (1591), reprinted in *Blood and Knavery*, ed. J. Marshburn (Rutherford, N.J., 1973), 58–64, esp. 64; *The Examination, Confession and Condemnation of Henry Robson, Fisherman of Rye* (1598), sigs. A3r, B2r.

birth in Gelderland, the London earthquake of 1582, a freak storm in Prague) all of them designed to show that the times were bad and God's judgement imminent.[8]

The next spot on the titillation/edification dial was occupied by pamphlets in which the moralising message was made rather more explicit. Sometimes this occurred in the prefatory material or in a coda at the end. A 1595 pamphlet, which recounted the story of a miner who stabbed his wife to death, contained in the narrative only a bare mention of the demonic inspiration of the deed and a short closing statement on the inevitable punishment visited upon the sin of murder. The epistle to the Christian reader, however, contained an elaborate, highly moralised vision of a world turned upside down by sin and murder, and a plea for moral reform in all classes of society.[9] In other pamphlets the moralising elements were inserted directly into the narrative. Which of the various available themes or motifs carried the moral freight varied according to the whim of the author and the narrative opportunities provided by the crime in question. In two pamphlets concerning a peculiarly disgusting series of murders in early seventeenth-century Hertfordshire the pseudo-miraculous testimony of a tongueless little girl provided the opening through which a morally legitimating providentialism entered a narrative otherwise mostly concerned with recounting the bilious details of the crimes in question.[10] In *News from Perrin*, a fairystory-like account of the murder of a long lost son returning incognito to his parents' house, the overt moralising was transposed on to the figure of the returning prodigal, his picaresque adventures as an Algiers pirate, his providential escapes from both ship wreck and the galleys, his consequent repentance and return home as a solid citizen earning an honest living as a ship's doctor. In the scenes concerned with the murder, the devil was prominently displayed tempting the stepmother to kill and rob the rich young stranger (who was in fact her stepson). When the identity of the victim was revealed the next morning, the father, followed in quick succession by his wife, committed suicide in remorse. At this point, the pile of bodies littering the stage was left by the author to speak for itself.[11] Clearly, authors felt free to respond to the opportunities and constraints inherent in the stories they were telling.

---

[8] A. Munday, *A View of Sundry Examples* (1580), *passim*.

[9] *A Most Horrible and Detestable Murder Committed by a Bloody Minded Man upon his Own Wife* (1595).

[10] *The Most Cruel and Bloody Murder Committed by an Innkeepers Wife called Annis Dell and her Son George Dell* (1606) and *The Horrible Murder of a Young Boy of Three Years of Age* (1606).

[11] *News from Perrin of a Most Bloody and Unexampled Murder* (1618).

Most of the pamphlets made some mention of the repentance of the murderer. Certainly, where repentance was absent some comment was called for. One author, describing a murderer who had yet to appear in court, virtually repented for him, with a prayer that God would 'pour down the grace of his holy spirit into the heart of . . . the prisoner, that by the virtuous working thereof he may spend this long time which God hath lent him in hearty sorrow and true repentance'. Where repentance could not even be imputed to the felon, authors felt almost compelled to consign the persons in question to hell. However, by no means all the pamphlets dwelt on the demeanour of the felon on the scaffold or on the nature or authenticity of his or her repentance. Some authors passed over such matters in a sentence or two tossed off at the end of the narrative. One particularly brutal wife murderer and drunkard, having resisted various attempts to bring him to repentance, was somewhat airily described as having looked 'into the foulness of his offence' and asked 'the forgiveness both of God and the world'. Other pamphlets, of course, made far more fuss about both the means which brought the malefactor to repentance and the forms which that repentance took.[12]

And it is those pamphlets which we can place at the end of the spectrum marked edification. In the most heavily Protestantised of the murder pamphlets published before 1640 by authors like Arthur Golding, Gilbert Dugdale, Henry Goodcole and Thomas Cooper all the elements described above were present but they were explicitly glossed and tightly organised around recognisably Protestant, even Puritan, themes, perspectives and doctrines. Thus Thomas Cooper produced a heavily providentialist and predestinarian gloss on the genre in his pamphlet of 1620. Other authors followed suit, switching the emphasis on to the conversion and repentance of the felons involved – indeed, a Goodcole pamphlet of 1618 actually had the word conversion in its title. Golding's effort of 1577 and Dugdale's of 1604 both described the prison visits that lead to the murderer's repentance and dwelt on the outward devotional forms which that repentance took, printing *in extenso* what purported to be the confessions read from the gallows by the condemned. On one view the Butler and Savage narratives with which we started can be seen as the culmination of this trend of appropriation. They represent the logical outcome of that process of glossing murder narratives, a

---

[12] *A Brief and True Report of Two Most Cruel, Unnatural and Inhuman Murders Done in Lincolnshire* (1607), reprinted in *Reprints of English Books 1475–1700*, ed. J. Foster (Claremont, Ca., 1948), I, no. 4, 10–11, 20; for an example of a murderer going unrepentant to her death, see *The Apprehension, Arraignment and Execution of Elizabeth Abbot* (1608) where it was concluded that 'the devil whom she served had fully hardened her heart'.

commercial literary form, whose saleability almost certainly resided in its most titillating, even pornographic aspects, in terms of certain central Protestant or Puritan doctrines and attitudes.[13]

For all the Puritan credentials of the authors – respectable Presbyterian divines in the case of the Butler narrative, notable nonconformists in the case of the Savage pamphlet – both accounts retained many of the central characteristics of the average murder pamphlet. Both seemed designed to exploit the buzz of notoriety and rumour surrounding peculiarly unpleasant murders. Both Savage and Butler attracted more than one author; in the case of Butler there were a number of rival accounts, one of which, written by 'a lover of truth', explicitly denounced the falsehoods spread about the crime by 'pot pamphlets and paper murderers' and 'sheet pamphleteers' who wrote only to make money from the credulity of the public. Savage's crime and execution also seems to have attracted much contemporary attention. Not only the brutality of the crime but also the fact that Savage appears to have survived the first attempt to hang him seems to have aroused considerable public interest and rumour and his crime, too, produced a more or less conventional murder pamphlet, complete with a crude woodcut of the gallows.[14]

Moreover, even the accounts of the event produced by the ministers retained many of the central, overtly titillatory elements of the murder pamphlet format. Butler was described as 'a very lewd young man', 'addicted to divers sins', among them company keeping, gaming, petty theft, fornication and 'frequenting the company and the houses of harlots'. Here, then, was the chain of sins starting with commonplace faults and lapses but culminating, under Satan's influence, in murder that lay at the heart of many of the murder pamphlets. Typically, then, Butler was quoted as admitting that 'the very sin of whoredom did draw him on to that of shedding blood'. This occasioned one minister to comment 'following harlots will lead thee to hell'.[15] This was a notion

---

[13] H. Goodcole, *A True Declaration of the Happy Conversion, Contrition and Christian Preparation of Francis Robinson* (1618), which was concerned with a Catholic executed for counterfeiting the great seal, whose 'conversion' was from popery to Protestantism; T. Cooper, *The Cry and Revenge of Blood* (1620); Arthur Golding, *A Brief Discourse of the Late Murder of Master George Sanders* (1577); G. Dugdale, *A True Discourse of the Practices of Elizabeth Caldwell* (1604).

[14] *A Full and the Truest Narrative of the . . . Murder . . . in Milk Street*, sig. A2v, p. 14; for similar remarks in a rival account, see *Blood Washed Away by Tears of Repentance*, 2; for the illustrated account of the Savage case, see *God's Justice Against Murder or the Bloody Apprentice Executed* (1668).

[15] Yearwood, *The Penitent Murderer*, section headed 'An exact narrative of the life and death of Nathaniel Butler', 1–2, 50.

amply confirmed by the case of Thomas Savage, who was addicted to the company of 'that vile strumpet Hannah Blay' at whose house he used regularly to spend the Sabbath and at whose instigation, desperate to meet her demands for payment, Savage had killed the maidservant who stood between him and his master's money. Blay's injunctions to 'knock her brains out and I will receive the money', the description of Savage's subsequent murder of the maid with a hammer or the account of Butler's botched and protracted half-hour-long attempt to cut the throat of his fellow-apprentice were all reminiscent of the gory, titillating details which were such a marked feature of many murder pamphlets.[16] Here, therefore, were all the crucial elements for a standard low-life murder pamphlet, with the figure of the evil and depraved prostitute personifying the inverted sinful values of the wicked city and acting as the devil's agent in leading the young, the unsuspecting and the averagely sinful into damnation. Unsurprisingly, it was upon these aspects of the case that the short, illustrated and anonymous account of the Savage murder dwelt.

II

However, in addition to these traditional elements, both the Puritan accounts featured long conversion narratives, in and through which we can glimpse something of the emotional interactions, the spiritual transactions between the young felons and their clerical mentors in the condemned cell. The accounts of the conversions of both men followed roughly the same, stereotyped course, a course dictated by the dialectic between the law and the gospel, or, from the sinner's point of view, between presumption and desperation. At the outset, when one of the young men, Thomas Savage, expressed the hope that he might be saved despite his crime because he repented, he was asked whether he could give an account of any 'experience of a gracious change wrought in him'. When he could not and yet still hoped to be saved it became clear that he needed first to be brought 'to a sight and sense of the corruption of his nature and of the sinfulness of his heart'. Confronted with the depth of his own sin he would have to acknowledge that his own puny tears and sighs of repentance counted for nothing. Only then could he be brought wholly to rely on Christ. To that end his clerical mentors applied a healthy dose of the law, that he be 'caste down' and made truly sensible of his lost estate. Once that had been done, lest he despair, the ministers left him with three examples of dreadful sinners (one of them a

---

[16] James Janeway *et al.*, *A Murderer Punished and Pardonned*, 4–5.

murderer) who had also been elect saints of God. They chose Manasseh, Mary Magdalene and St Paul. In 1657 David and Manasseh had been the examples set before Nathaniel Butler. Paul was now singled out for Savage as a 'pattern of free grace toward great sinners' in order to convince him that only Christ and not any amount of his own prayers and tears could save him. At first Savage could not comprehend how he could perform the religious duties of repentance and yet place no final or absolute value on them. Savage only put these doubts behind him as he came to see that rather than any works of his, his prayers and tears of repentance were Christ's works in him. This conviction was accompanied by a lively sense that it was not his murder but his own corrupt and sinful nature which had deserved damnation and death. It was only after he had achieved these two crucial conceptual breakthroughs that he began to display the tell-tale signs of a true faith.[17]

Nathaniel Butler's conversion followed almost exactly the same course. Unlike Savage he had brought himself to a sense of his own desperate spiritual condition. Alone in chains after his condemnation he saw himself 'in the glass of God's law and under the judgement of eternal death'. In that condition his clerical advisers found him and were able to lead him first to 'as right a notion of the state of unregeneracy as ever I found in a new convert'.[18] Thence, having warned him about the dangers of a false and hypocritical repentance, they led him between the Scylla of presumption and the Charybdis of desperation. At first, struggling against the threat of presumption, he made 'very diligent and frequent search into his soul concerning the sincerity of his sorrow and would not easily believe that his repentance was true'. Accordingly, he could not immediately 'come up to that full assurance of hope and confidence as he desired and we also desired heartily on his behalf'. Gradually, however, he came to see that 'the design of God in the scriptures is not to give some feeble, weak hope of pardon but a lively hope and a firm expectation of salvation to all that mourn and really repent'. In the end, therefore, 'he was so satisfied concerning the favour and mercy of God towards him in Jesus Christ that he rather now desired death then feared it, as seeing death through Jesus Christ without a sting'. In short, Butler's growth in grace was held up as an almost perfect example of the 'orderly gradual' spiritual progress, from the threats of

---

[17] *A Murderer Punished and Pardoned*, 9–10, 13–15; for Butler's experience see Yearwood, *The Penitent Murderer*, section headed 'an exact narrative', 5, 16.

[18] Yearwood, *The Penitent Murderer*, section headed 'a brief account of a visit given to Nathaniel Butler . . . by Thomas Case', sig. BV–B2r and the section headed 'an exact narrative', 70–1.

the law to the promises of the gospel, to which all Christians should aspire.[19]

Savage, too, at the end achieved a lively sense of his own salvation through Christ. Of course, the authenticity of the young men's conversions could scarcely be tested in the conventional Puritan manner, through the godliness of their lives and Christian profession. There was scarcely enough time for all that. Instead, it was validated through the charisma of conversion, that is, through the ravishing effects of the young men's spiritual transformation both on themselves and on those around them. Both pamphlets were suffused with the baroque emotionalism of late Puritan piety. Savage's speech at his trial brought tears to the eyes of both judge and jury. After his condemnation his private devotions brought him such sweetness as to give him a foretaste of heaven; when he prayed with others the spiritual temperature rose until the sighs and groans of the participants echoed around the room: 'a mighty presence of the spirit poured out upon him and on those that joined with him'. Those present wondered how one so young and so sinful could have had 'such a spirit of prayer poured out upon them'. As the author concluded, 'the nearer he came to his end the more we perceived God was ripening him for glory'. That spiritual ripeness found expression in Savage's utter conviction of his own salvation. Now he was able to affirm with perfect confidence that 'when my body is upon the gibbet my soul shall be carried by angels into heaven'. 'I know God loveth me and that I am going to the kingdom of heaven.' Butler, too, gave off the tell-tale glow of Puritan spiritual enthusiasm and assurance. One witness remarked on the young man's 'breathing panting ecstasy', at the prospect of God's mercy and his own salvation. Yearwood himself reported how at five in the morning before his execution 'he [Butler] fell into such a rapture and ecstasy of consolation as I never saw nor (I believe) any of my fellow spectators for he would shout for joy that the lord should look on such a poor vile creature as he was'.[20]

Here and throughout these pamphlets we can see these young felons being coached by their clerical mentors in the distinctive rhetoric and behaviour patterns of the godly and observe the ministers' almost proprietorial surveillance, monitoring and display of their protégés' burgeoning command of the conventions of Puritan self-fashioning. Both pamphlets show the young men being visited repeatedly in prison by

---

[19] *Ibid.*, section headed 'an exact narrative', 10–12; from the section headed 'Certain observations of Thomas Parson, minister of Michael Wood Street, London', sig. B6v.

[20] *A Murderer Punished and Pardoned*, 28–30, 33, 38; for Butler see Yearwood, *The Penitent Murderer*, section headed 'an exact narrative', 77, 17.

various ministers. In part the Butler pamphlet took the form of a series of accounts by different ministers and the lord mayor himself of their visits to Butler in prison, reproduced by Yearwood like so many certificates of spiritual authenticity. One minister told of a sermon he had preached before Butler, which had been attended by a large crowd of people, come to 'see a poor reed shaken with the wind, staring him in the face as a condemned malefactor'. The minister carefully noted Butler's demeanour throughout this ordeal; he was, he claimed, oblivious to the attentions of the crowd and focused entirely on 'the pardon I, in the name of God, offered him'. In short, he concluded, Butler's 'deportment did in my judgement . . . speak a well mixed and compounded sense of his own deserts and divine mercy which also did his words'.[21]

As death approached this ministerial surveillance became even closer. On the last night before his execution, Stephen Yearwood, Butler's chief counsellor and the compiler of the pamphlet stayed with him in his cell, withdrawing only for two or three hours to let Butler sleep in preparation for his performance on the scaffold the next day, when he would, they all hoped, 'declare what the lord had done for him'. After this nap Yearwood and his friends returned to the cell both to prompt and to observe Butler's conduct throughout the night. At 7 o'clock he was led to the place of execution, where, 'having passed through many thousands of people many of whom prayed for his soul and showed compassion otherwise to him', he addressed the crowd in a long speech, which was subsequently printed verbatim in the pamphlet.[22]

The same odd mixture of anxious surveillance, careful recording of the condemned man's demeanour, words and actions and an awed and emotional admiration of his spiritual accomplishments can be found in the Savage pamphlet. Both Butler and Savage were intermittently asked trick questions, put through their spiritual paces, in order to confirm and display their spiritual condition as elect saints of God. Thus when toward morning on his last night before execution Butler kept anxiously asking the time, Yearwood 'demanded why he enquired so concerning the time of the day? Would you gladly die?'; to which rather heavy-handed prompt Butler perhaps predictably replied 'yes, yes I desire to be dissolved and to be with Christ which is best of all'. A similar trap was laid for Savage.

We spoke to him concerning his coffin that was by him, whether it did not trouble and amaze him to have it in his sight; he replied with all my soul I could

---

[21] Yearwood, *The Penitent Murderer*, section headed 'certain observations of Thomas Parson, minister', *passim*.

[22] *Ibid.*, section headed 'an exact narrative', 12–13, 18–19; for the purported text of Butler's speech, see 19–33.

go into my coffin, oh, it is a comfortable place. (He spake it with joy.) I can comfortably die. I have found such a deal of joy and comfort that I would not for a world have been without it.[23]

One last visit to Savage was squeezed in just before he left for the gallows

the rather because one minister that had not yet been with him was desirous to visit him: and then again after some few words with him we asked him to go to prayer again, once more saying now this will be the last time that we shall pray with you in this place. And he did perform this duty with great liveliness that now he excelled himself and the nearer he came to his end the more fervently we perceived he prayed but we took notice that in the last duty in Newgate he was much in praising God and blessing God for his mercy to him, to our great astonishment.[24]

By this point Savage had attained the status of a self-validating spiritual prodigy, a genuine adept in the arts of Puritan godliness, whom his counsellors and trainers were anxious should be seen by as many people as possible, so that they too could testify to the genuineness of his conversion and tell others of this staggering proof of the reality of God's grace as a creative and transformative force in the world.

Throughout these pamphlets there was a strong sense of the salvation of these young men as the product of the collective endeavour of the godly. In Butler's case God was presented as responding to the young man's despair 'by the hand of one that visited him'. Butler himself acknowledged 'the prayers, compassion and care of so many of his precious servants both ministers and others' as a crucial element in the manifestation of God's goodness and mercy towards him. According to one minister, Thomas Parsons, 'the sermons, visits, general pity of God's people in the importunate enlarged fervency of ministers and Christians in praying for him [was] scarcely to be paralleled in the memory of men'.[25]

Over against these efforts of the godly was ranged the power of Satan and of his agents, the profane. To compass his purposes Satan used two main instruments; the first the young men's own doubts and fears in the face of death and, the second, the blandishments of the papists and the ungodly. Both Butler and Savage experienced doubts about the authenticity of their own repentance and in both cases these doubts were

---

[23] *Ibid.*, section headed 'an exact narrative', 18; *A Murderer Punished and Pardoned*, 33.
[24] *A Murderer Punished and Pardoned*, 38.
[25] Yearwood, *The Penitent Murderer*, section headed 'a brief account of a visit given to Nathaniel Butler . . . by Thomas Case', sigs. B1r, B2r; *ibid.*, section headed 'certain observations of Thomas Parson', sig. B7r.

attributed to the promptings of Satan. Savage's difficulties in performing the duties of repentance without placing any final or absolute value on them were thus laid at Satan's door, who 'was loath to loose such a prey . . . when he had brought him to the very mouth and gates of hell to have him snatched out of his hands by the free grace of God'. 'The devil was very busy with him and did solicit him grievously with his temptations, persuading him to have thoughts of escaping' or filling him 'with drowsiness that I can neither pray nor read nor perform any duty'. On other occasions the devil tempted Savage to delay; there was time enough to repent, after he was condemned; God was merciful, there was no hurry. Sometimes he tempted him to despair but his greatest fear was that the devil would appear personally to him,

which did so exceedingly trouble me in prayer so that I could say nothing when I kneeled down but was fain to set the candle down before me and durst not look one way nor other for fear I should see him and my thoughts have been so vain many times when you have been reading to me that I have scarce heard a word of what you said.[26]

Against these internal temptations and diabolic machinations the godly struggled manfully. But they had other external enemies as well. Satan sent Savage's erstwhile friends and they twice tempted him into drunken forgetfulness of his sin. His fellow-prisoners alienated by his denunciation of his fellow-culprit Hannah Blay also plied Savage with drink in the hope of casting doubt on the genuineness of his conversion. This prompted some to conclude that Savage had only ever enjoyed 'some common workings of the spirit'. Later rumours took up the theme of drink; one claimed that Savage had been too drunk to plead in court; the other that he had got so drunk the night before his execution that the whole thing had to be rescheduled. These charges were refuted in the pamphlet describing Savage's fate. There the claim about his conduct on the eve of his execution was simply denied but the accusation concerning his demeanour in court was rather uncomfortably explained away as the result of both an accident and a plot. It was an accident because although Savage had indeed had a drink he had not consumed enough, under normal circumstances, to get him drunk. The plot was that of his fellow-prisoners explained above. However, after all this extenuation the author was forced to concede that Savage's binge had cast 'a blemish upon the profession that he had made after he came to Newgate'.[27] In this pamphlet the palpable demonic presence which

[26] *A Murderer Punished and Pardoned*, 17, 20; for the devil and Butler, see, for instance, Yearwood, *The Penitent Murderer*, sig. A8r.
[27] *A Murderer Punished and Pardoned*, 17–18, 23–4, 29.

suffused many of the murder pamphlets was diffused and distributed throughout the narrative in interesting ways. On the one hand it was construed internally, in terms of the young man's subjective doubts and fears as he confronted his sin and his maker in prison. On the other, it was given external social form in the malign and corrupt attentions of the profane as they sought both to lead Savage astray in prison and to spread rumours about the hypocrisy of his profession to the wider world. The godly were presented in both pamphlet narratives as pitting their collective spiritual wits against this satanic onslaught; as Satan tried to suck the young offenders down to hell so they endeavoured to yank them up into heaven.

There was thus a transaction or exchange taking place here between the felon and his or her godly mentors and well-wishers. The felon gained from his conversion a certain charisma, a glow of spiritual potency. He or she became a living example of the autonomous action in the world of the Holy Spirit. For a brief incandescent moment between capture and execution the converted felon could bask in the glamour of the dying. Trapped in that liminal space between life and death, their every word, deed and gesture was invested with a heightened significance. No longer were they condemned murderers, the objects of the obloquy, disgust and craning curiosity of the mob. Rather they became objects of interest, admiration, even awed wonder, living proof of the miracles of which God's free grace was capable. Some sense of the existential benefits which this sudden change in status could confer on the condemned can be gleaned from the case of Elizabeth Caldwell. For Caldwell's conversion allowed her to turn the tables on her neglectful and profane husband almost completely. He was the putative victim of a murder plot concocted by Caldwell and her lover; the 'murder weapon' was some 'oaten cakes' poisoned with ratsbane which merely made the husband sick but which killed a little girl from next door. Now, for a brief but delicious interval between her capture and execution, Caldwell's new-found role as an elect saint of God allowed her to lecture her intended victim on the need for repentance and religious conversion.[28] All this, plus the hope of eternal salvation, offered to a sixteen-year-old apprentice, alone in prison and facing certain death, was rather too good to turn down. Small wonder that Butler and Savage proved so receptive to the idioms of Puritan godliness.

On their side of the bargain the godly gained a powerful confirmation of their own vision of true religion. The converted felon and the godly audiences who flocked to the prison to instruct, watch and pray with

---

[28] Dugdale, *A True Discourse of the Practises of Elizabeth Caldwell, passim.*

him were thus bound together in an emotionally collusive cycle; each presented the other with a mirror in which they could see their own self-images magnified and confirmed. When Savage looked at the godly he saw his new-found status as an elect saint and his consequent certainty of salvation reflected in their acceptance of him as one of their own; when the godly looked at Savage they saw the truth of their own view of true religion and the purity and potency of their profession demonstrated by the miraculous change wrought in this young sinner by the free grace of God. Savage claimed that

he could not but love the ways of God and the people of God. O it is so sweet to be in company with them, praying and conversing with them . . . that I account it as great a mercy as any almost that I may be in their company. Oh methinks it is a heaven to me to be with God's ministers and people and prayer now is so sweet that I grudge the time always when I am off my knees.[29]

In making that statement Savage was at once providing evidence of his own spiritual condition and confirming the godly in their good opinion of themselves, as 'the people of God' amongst whom the grace of God could be seen making and remaking the sinful souls of fallen humanity into spiritual temples, fit habitations for his spirit in the midst of a corrupt and fallen world.

III

At the most obvious level the pamphlets were celebrations of the power of Puritan godliness. As such they represented an attempt both to control and to exploit the buzz of rumour and popular interest surrounding the murders. The plethora of pamphlets describing both cases itself provides convincing evidence of that interest and of the existence of a number of contradictory rumours surrounding each murder. The exchanges between the young men and their would-be mentors took place in semi-public. One author of a pamphlet about Butler describes first writing an exhortatory letter to the young man and then turning up at the gaol, paying his admission fee and meeting him in person. The resulting pamphlet claimed to represent the text of the original missive together with Butler's reply.[30] We have already seen accounts of the press of godly visitors surrounding both young men and of the crowd attending one set piece sermon preached before Butler. Gilbert Dugdale claimed that up to 300 people a day visited Elizabeth

---

[29] *A Murderer Punished and Pardoned*, 25.
[30] *Blood Washed Away by Tears of Repentance* (1657).

Caldwell in gaol and in Yearwood's formulation alternatively 'thousands' and 'a multitude of people' attended Butler's execution.[31] Moreover, as we have seen in the case of Savage's prison drinking bouts, not all of the rumours surrounding the case fitted in with the godly's reading of it. Their struggle in the spiritual hot house of the condemned cell for the souls of these young men was replicated in a parallel struggle in the pamphlets to impose a satisfyingly godly reading on the event. Once, however, the murderer had been brought to a safely pious end on the scaffold and a suitably edifying closure had been imposed on the printed narrative, the event and the pamphlet in which it was encapsulated became available for all sorts of polemical and political purposes.

Socially, as the struggle for Savage and Butler's souls could be presented as one between God and his people, on the one hand, and the devil and the profane, on the other, so it could be made to stand, in microcosm, for the wider political, cultural and spiritual struggles being waged, during this period, around the issue of further reformation. That connection was rendered explicit in the Butler pamphlet, which, of course, emanated from a group of divines very close to the centre of secular authority in 1650s London.[32] There Butler's crime and eventual fate was directly linked to a rhetoric of public as well as private reformation. Butler's sin, the judgement upon it and his ultimate repentance were generalised into metaphors for the condition of London and the judgement of God looming over it. Butler's sinful life was taken as a symbol for the sins of the city. In the sermon preached by Yearwood at a service after Butler's execution his murder was transmuted into the far more common sin of hatred of one's fellow-citizens; the youthful sins which set Butler on the road to murder – lust, drunkenness, adultery, covetousness, theft – were taken as standing for the sins for which the whole city was notorious. More particularly, the neglect shown for Butler's upbringing in true religion by his master served as an occasion for a diatribe against cruel and negligent heads of households and a plea

---

[31] Dugdale, *A True Discourse of the Practises of Elizabeth Caldwell*, sig. B2r; Yearwood, *The Penitent Murderer*, section headed 'an exact narrative', 18, 53.

[32] In addition to Yearwood's narrative *The Penitent Murderer* contained accounts by Thomas Case and Thomas Parson and the *Serious Advice to the Citizens of London by Some Ministers of the Gospel in the Said City* which was both appended to the pamphlet and separately printed under the names of Edmund Calamy, Arthur Jackson, James Nalton, Thomas Jacomb, Robert Hutchison, Thomas White, Thomas Parson, Thomas Doolittle, Simeon Ashe, Thomas Case, William Taylor, Roger Drake, George Griffith, Matthew Poole, Daniel Batchelor. Doolittle provides a personal link between the ministers involved with the Butler case and those who produced the pamphlet about Savage.

for the restoration of proper standards of discipline and religious observance by which Yearwood meant family prayer, catechising, the repetition of sermons, austere and punctilious observance of the Sabbath – in short a plea for the enforcement, amongst the young, of a full-scale Puritan definition of religious observance. While in Yearwood's sermon the heads of houses were called upon to fulfil their religious obligations towards their dependants, in Butler's own speech from the scaffold and a separately printed appeal to 'the citizens of London . . . upon the occasion of the horrid murder and dreadful death of Nathaniel Butler' by the ministers who had attended him in prison, the magistrate was exhorted to put down the ale and bawdy houses which had set the young man on the road to murder and to repress the papists who had tempted him with soul-destroying errors when he was in prison.[33] Indeed, this public aspect of the rhetoric deployed about the Butler case represents the culmination of a series of official attempts to stage manage his conviction and execution in the interests of a certain (Puritan?) view of order. It was the lord mayor himself who had granted a two-week stay of execution so that Nathaniel could be prepared to meet his maker; Yearwood, Butler's primary spiritual counsellor, was the mayor's chaplain; he not only presided at Butler's execution (arranged symbolically opposite the scene of the crime in Milk Street) and at his funeral, he also announced, at the latter event, the imminent publication of an official account of the affair which he himself edited. The pamphlet itself was preceded by an attempt to stop other, unofficial and presumably less accurate, accounts of the affair being published and appeared with a preface and endorsement by the lord mayor, who had himself conferred at length with Butler in prison on more than one occasion.[34]

Nor were the polemical uses of such material limited to the realm of politics. Doctrinally, the story of the salvation of such unregenerate and utterly undeserving young sinners as Butler and Savage could be presented as stark and irrefutable refutations of all popish and Arminian notions of merit or free will. The Butler pamphlet actually contained an account of Butler's temptation in prison by a group of Catholic women. His response, apparently, was immediate; 'that is the saddest religion in

---

[33] Yearwood, *The Penitent Murderer*, 19–80, and the separately paginated *Serious Advice* appended at the end of Yearwood's pamphlet.

[34] Yearwood, *The Penitent Murderer*, 30, also see the epistle dedicatory to Sir Robert Tichborne, the lord mayor, *ibid.*, sigs. A3r–A4v, Tichborne's own account of his meetings with Butler, *ibid.*, sigs. A6r–8v, and his official endorsement of Yearwood's account published 'by my appointment' which was printed opposite the title page; also see *A Full and the Truest Narrative of the . . . Murder . . . in Milk Street*, 11, 15, and *Blood Washed Away by Tears of Repentance*, 23.

the world for me, I shall never be of that religion, . . . for I am the vilest wretch that lives, I have not a good thought to trust to. I must be saved only by the merits of Christ, if ever I be saved.' On this view, there could scarcely be a clearer example of the impotence of Catholic works theology to offer succour to a poor, repentant Christian trapped in the toils of sin.[35]

Rather Butler's faith was presented as due entirely to the autonomous action of God's grace; it was 'a great and extraordinary passage of divine providence'. That providence could be discerned working in and through the act of murder itself. For, on one level, 'this great sin was clearly a judicial sin, the punishment of former sins.' But on another it was also a blessing, since it was precisely Butler's foul deed that provided the grounds for his subsequent repentance and conversion; 'the lord over-shooting satan in his own bow and by what means he took to make sure of him, God startled and roused conscience which would not with the noise of less guilt be awaked and humbled the sinner'. There was, of course, nothing in either Butler's or Savage's earlier lives which could possibly have deserved or attracted God's mercy. Thus, it was observed of Savage that

no motive from this young man's person or any previous good disposition (he being so exceedingly vitiated by such defiling sins) could in the least incline God to have mercy upon him, but the motive was taken from himself and his own bowels. He had mercy on him only because he would have mercy and compassion on him because he would have compassion . . . It is through free grace that any are saved but in the salvation of such a one God hath demonstrated the exceeding riches of his grace towards him through Jesus Christ.

It was only the 'distinguishing grace of God', wrote Yearwood, that had snatched Butler 'as a firebrand' from the fires of hell.[36]

If God could save such unregenerate and desperate sinners he could save anyone. Weighed in the balance against the blood of Christ, the blood of even the most violently despatched murder victim counted for nothing. It was, therefore, never too late for God to reclaim a sinner be he or she never so sunk in sin and iniquity. Thus concluded Robert Tichburne the lord mayor of London in his preface to the Butler volume

[35] Yearwood, *The Penitent Murderer*, section headed 'a brief account of a visit . . . by Thomas Case', sig. B3r–v; *ibid.*, section headed 'some passages between Nathaniel Butler and a friend of his that came to visit him', sigs. B7v–B8r; *ibid.*, section headed 'an exact narrative', 79.

[36] Yearwood, *The Penitent Murderer*, epistle to the reader, sig. A5v; from the section headed 'certain observations of Thomas Parson', sig. B6r–v; *A Murderer Punished and Pardoned*, 45–6.

I am truly persuaded . . . that though his [Butler's] former life was full of all wickedness, his soul exceeding ignorant of God and his own sinful nature all that time and his repentance and faith in Christ very late, yet that the free grace of God (who is not bounded in time) did make both his faith and repentance true.[37]

Such cases were, therefore, a powerful corrective against hopelessness for all Christians languishing in despair at the enormity of their own sins. But the sheer arbitrariness of God's intervention to save these seemingly damned and damnable young sinners could also be used as a powerful argument against delaying repentance. 'May not God cut you off in the act of some of your sins and not give you time for repentance? And if life doth continue may not he deny you the grace of repentance? Doth not custom and continuance in sin harden your heart and fasten you in satan's chains?' These were exceptional cases, sent by God precisely to rouse ordinary secure sinners into a true faith. It was, therefore, courting disaster to delay repentance in the hope that a similar last-minute conversion might bring home the bacon. Nor should the sight of the apparent salvation of such grievous sinners serve to reassure those whose sins were less spectacular or overt. All Christians were sinners who owed their freedom from extreme sin to 'the restraining grace of God'. Yet because 'they live free from such gross and scandalous crimes they think themselves in a good estate and that they shall be saved'. In that they were sadly mistaken, for 'until their natures are changed and renewed they are accounted as guilty of all sins before God and as uncapable of heaven and salvation as if they had committed them in the greatest act'.[38] Such people who slept soundly in their beds, untroubled with thoughts of judgement, death and damnation were in greater spiritual peril than convicted murderers like Butler and Savage, who, for obvious reasons, found a genuine soul-shattering repentance rather easier to come by. Here, then, the attempt to use the extreme example of the convicted murderer as an ideal type or symbol for the spiritual condition of the averagely sinful and secure Christian, which had been a marked feature of some of the earlier murder pamphlets, has been brought to its highest and purest form.

---

[37] Yearwood, *The Penitent Murderer*, from the section headed 'three conferences held with Nathaniel Butler by . . . the Lord Mayor', sig. A8r–v.

[38] Yearwood, *The Penitent Murderer*, from the section headed 'a brief account of a visit given to Nathaniel Butler . . . by Thomas Case', sig. B3r; *A Murderer Punished and Pardoned*, 46.

IV

In short, in these two pamphlets we can see the genre of the murder pamphlet and the assumptions and polemical opportunities surrounding the 'last dying speeches' of notorious malefactors being taken up and exploited for explicitly Puritan ends. The authors of the two groups of pamphlets were all Puritan divines – in the first instance London Presbyterian ministers, in the second respectable nonconformists. Moreover, as we have seen, the purposes, both public and private, for which the young men, their stories and conduct, were being enlisted, were explicitly Puritan. The style of piety, of personal religion and godliness, which suffused the pamphlets, and which was written into the very structures of the conversion narratives that dominated both publications, was distinctively Puritan. The doctrinal tone and polemical thrust of both were typical of the evangelical Calvinism which underpinned so much of the piety of Presbyterian Puritanism and respectable dissent. Moreover, as ever with Puritan piety, the internal was inextricably connected to the external, the private, interior world of spiritual introspection, linked to the external world of public policy and godly reformation.

Here, then, is perhaps the culmination of a process of appropriation, whereby, in the period after 1570, an inherently mixed and popular genre – the murder pamphlet – had been taken up and glossed in a number of providentialist, indeed predestinarian and Puritan, ways. In the accounts of the Butler and Savage murders described above this process has arguably reached its logical conclusion, its highest and purest form. The outlines of the murder pamphlet genre may still be discernible here but they have been all but crowded out by the conversion narratives which dominate the pamphlets. The overtly titillating concern with the details of the crimes themselves and of the sins which produced them has been crammed into something like five pages out of over fifty. The demonic presence has been largely spiritualised into the epic struggle for the soul of the murderer taking place between God and the godly, on the one hand, and the devil, the profane and the papists, on the other. There is no pseudo-miraculous providentialism at work in these narratives; the only miracles here are the miracles of free grace converting and reclaiming a young Christian seemingly hopelessly lost in sin.

It would be tempting, therefore, to construe chronologically the thematic spectrum, running from the sparest and least moralised of the pamphlets to the most explicitly theological and providential examples of the genre outlined above. On this view that formally defined, and at least potentially synchronic, spectrum could be taken to represent a diachronic and cumulative process of Protestantisation, through which a genuinely popular form was gradually taken over by the godly and earlier pre-Protestant, pseudo-magical and superstitious beliefs about the devil, the cry of the victim's blood for revenge, direct and miraculous divine intervention in the world, were grafted on to ever more sophisticated, spiritualised, Protestant notions of providence, conscience or pre-destination.

There are, however, difficulties with an interpretation that sees the pamphlets as agents in the Protestant assault on traditional superstition, bit players in the decline of magic and the rise of religion. To begin with, such a view does not fit with the basic chronology of the genre; some of the most moralised and Protestantised pamphlets were relatively early; Golding's dated from 1577 and Dugdale's from 1604. Again, some of the most highly moralised later narratives, like those written by Goodcole, were suffused with the voyeurism that characterised the entire genre.[39]

Again at the level of thematic development, Keith Thomas has rendered familiar the notion that the providentialism of the godly played a crucial role in the demystification, the disenchantment, of the world that is so central to his account of the early modern period. In many of the murder pamphlets providence certainly played a crucial role in vindicating the claim that murder will out and God's justice will prevail no matter how clever or cruel the criminal. And yet in many of the pamphlets the line between the properly providential and pseudo-miraculous is very hard to draw. The authors themselves scarcely distinguished between the different means through which God could reveal a hidden or forgotten murder. Indeed, they tended to run them together in order to play up God's omnipotence and the reach of his justice. As one remarked 'though men see ye not, God doth; though men betray ye not birds may. If birds do not beasts may; if neither do your consciences shall, but if they be seared up God certainly will find out a mean.' Even in Thomas Cooper's pamphlet of 1620, where the theological underpinnings of Puritan providentialism were laid bare and their predestinarian consequences fully developed, Cooper was at pains to insist that the accidental discovery of the crucial *corpus delicti* in a pond confounded any natural or rational explanation. Rather, it was explicable only in terms of the direct intervention by divine providence which cut across the wills, intentions and interests of the human agents involved. Here, then, was no smooth progress from the pseudo-miraculous and magical to the religious and the proto-rational, by way of a Protestant or even Puritan providentialism. Indeed, whether such providentialism led

---

[39] Lake, 'Deeds against Nature'.

to a decrease in the sorts of magical or superstitious beliefs contained in the pamphlets seems doubtful. In some murder narratives at least the one fed off the other, and it might be argued that, particularly during moments of crisis, when the hand of God was being sought most urgently in events, the prevalence of Puritan providentialism helped to stimulate rather than to suppress such beliefs. On this view there might well be a straight line to be drawn from say Munday's *Sundry Examples* to the prodigy pamphlets provoked by the Civil War.[40]

Thus, rather than a straightforward process of appropriation or take-over, whereby a genre from the repertoire of cheap print, an inherently sensationalist, titillating even sub-pornographic form, was adopted and adapted by godly authors for their own purposes, we have an on-going dialogue or dialectic between the Puritan and the popular, in which, at various points and according to the exigencies of a variety of immediate local and national circumstances and political conjunctures, godly authors, indeed in the cases of Butler and Savage leading London, Puritan divines, could dip into the repertoire of cheap print and the canons of popular taste to get their case across to 'the people'. It is, of course, not without significance that the Savage and Butler narratives, as well as Thomas Cooper's elaborate predestinarian gloss on the genre of 1620, were all over fifty pages in length. Thus at the very moments at which the predestinarian Protestant appropriation of the genre reached its peak, the pamphlets in which that appropriation was taking place swelled to such a size as virtually to exclude themselves from the category of cheap print altogether. This, of course, is precisely what we should expect from a genuinely dialectical relationship between the 'popular' and 'the Protestant', as Puritan and Protestant authors dipped into popular genres and concerns, and subtly changed or transformed those forms and concerns in the process of appropriating them. On this view, then, instead of ossifying into a simple antipathy or opposition in the period after 1580, the relations between 'the popular' and 'the Protestant or Puritan' remained problematic. Both categories remained open to contest and negotiation. They were subject to a continual process of mutual definition and redefinition throughout the early seventeenth

[40] K. V. Thomas, *Religion and the Decline of Magic* (Oxford, 1971), ch. 4 and *passim*; *Two Notorious Murders. One Committed by a Tanner . . . the Other on a Grazier near Aylesbury* (1595), 5; Cooper, *The Cry and Revenge of Blood*, 37–42. Of course, the category in need of interrogation, if not deconstruction, here is 'providentialism' itself. This process is currently in the safe hands of Ms Alex Walsham of Trinity College, Cambridge, who is engaged in important research on the theological provenance of the doctrine of providence itself and on its deployment in the cheap news and prodigy pamphlets of the period (of which the murder pamphlets under discussion here were but a relatively small subset).

century and the dialogue or dialectic between them, so brilliantly analysed by Professor Collinson for the later sixteenth century,[41] must remain at or near the centre of any attempt to explain the religious changes and conflicts of the seventeenth century.

[41] *Birthpangs*, ch. 4.

14   The two 'National Churches' of 1691 and 1829

William Lamont

Puritanism has a natural tendency to fragment into ever smaller units. That is what their opponents said about the movement, and, just because Samuel Parker and Roger L'Estrange said so, does not make it wrong. The dissidence of dissent is indeed one of the great historical platitudes. Patrick Collinson has never been one to let sleeping platitudes lie, however, and in a notable recent paper he has pointed to the resilience of a contrary strain within Puritanism; of what we might call a centripetal, rather than a centrifugal, tendency. He argues that the voluminous anti-separatist literature did have its effect, individuals could be pulled back from the brink (like Robert Browne himself, the man who gave a name to a tendency), the seceders were in any case less set apart from the rest of the community than was once supposed, combination lectureships strengthened not weakened the established church, and so on. It adds up to a formidable case for taking seriously the possibility of writing a different script for Puritanism, in which it becomes the ally, not the enemy, of a comprehensive national settlement.[1]

Collinson wants historians to maintain an open-endedness: to recognise that by the end of the early years of the seventeenth century (where his analysis stops), it was by no means a foregone conclusion that the evolution of Puritanism would be synonymous with the triumph of the sects. Now this may be true, but once we move forward in time to the end of the seventeenth century it becomes harder to sustain that open-endedness. The three Edmund Calamys may speak for generational changes within Old England Puritanism, as the three Mathers did for New England Puritanism.[2] The first two Calamys exhibit that strain of what Collinson calls 'unitive Protestantism': anti-separatist, respectful of the magistrate, upholders of order and conformity. With the

---

[1] Patrick Collinson, 'Sects and the Evolution of Puritanism', unpublished paper presented to Conference on *Puritanism in Old and New England*, Millersville University, Pennsylvania, 4–6 April 1991.
[2] R. Middlekauff, *The Mathers: Three Generations of Puritan Intellectuals, 1596–1728* (New York, 1971).

third Calamy we breathe a different air. He *says* that he is defending 'moderate Nonconformity' in 1704, but it is what most of those who defended that shibboleth in previous generations would have recognised as its opposite. Calamy, it is true, denied that he was an advocate of 'a Brownisticall Separation', which still had a fatal ring even in 1704, but a separation 'managed with Charity and Moderation', on the other hand, was no more than a recognition of political facts. The Clarendon Code had destroyed for ever the Puritan dream of 'further reformation' within a national structure. At the same time it had opened up the possibility of new alignments. John Owen and his Independents had been quicker off the mark than the first two Calamys in recognising this change of status. But the third Calamy at least could see by 1704 that it was better for 'each worshipping Congregation in the Land, to manage it self in an entire Independency, than to have a National Church of one sort or another with Penal Laws'. With Calamy's treatise, English Presbyterianism had come of age. His Presbyterian colleagues stood him a supper. Congratulations came to him from John Locke and John Howe. The long Puritan love-affair with the idea of a 'National Church' was over.[3]

I do not believe that it *was* over, I want to show in the rest of the essay why Collinson's 'unitive Protestantism' did not die out with the Clarendon Code, and why it would flower – in vastly different political circumstances, of course – in two extravagant declarations on behalf of 'National Churches' in 1691 and in 1829.

The first of these was made by Richard Baxter. That was the supreme embarrassment for Calamy, who wanted to pass himself off as Baxter's spiritual heir. It was not lost on an opponent like Benjamin Hoadly. When Calamy asked men to 'separate from a National Church' whose bottom is unscriptural, Hoadly's devastating reply was that 'no man has loaded it with more Aggravations than Mr. Baxter'. Calamy's counter seems weak in comparison: ''tis now no new thing for Persons to represent that Good Man as inconsistent with himself, when it seems for the Interest he should be tho't so'.[4]

But the truth was that Baxter *was* inconsistent with himself. We are back with Collinson's point, that centrifugal and centripetal impulses were both present within individuals themselves as well as within groups, and which of the two impulses prevailed in the end was more dependent upon outside events than is commonly recognised. At the age of

---

[3] Edmund Calamy, *A Defence of Moderate Nonconformity* (1704), II, 86, III, 112.
[4] *Ibid.*, III, 112; Roger Thomas, 'Presbyterians in Transition', in *The English Presbyterians*, ed. C. G. Bolam, Jeremy Goring, H. C. Short and Roger Thomas (1968), 127–9.

eighteen, Baxter had attended secret conventicles. This did not mean that he was a separatist in the making. Baxter had read his Collinson, and knew that to belong to a group, half of whose members were conformists, whose functions were simply edificatory (praying and repeating sermons) and whose secrecy was not sought but imposed by outside persecution, did not put him outside the national structure. Six years later he found himself at Bridgnorth as a curate. The parish was in discord. The minister Cross, a 'thorough Conformist' in Baxter's book, had a year earlier preached a provocative sermon. Widows, he told his congregation, were like a Banbury cheese; remove the rind and there's little left. Warming to his theme, he equated the search for a wife of virtue to a dip into a barrel of snakes. A hundred-to-one she would not be caught, and if she were, she would prove a slippery handful. The Bridgnorth women were not having this. They boycotted the minister's sermons. Were they right to do so? No, argued Baxter, because for all his faults Cross was an orthodox licensed preacher. In separating from him, the women separated from the Catholic Church.[5] Women were prone to such errors. Their body fluids made them ripe for separation. As Samuel Parker put it, 'all this sort of Religion floats in the Blood, and rises and falls with the Ebbs and Tides of the Humours'.[6] Parker in 1671 was attacking, not just separatists, but all those who were ejected as a result of the Clarendon Code. Baxter shared the prejudice, though not the conclusion drawn from it by Parker. It was 'women and weak young Men', in Baxter's view, who had formed the bulk of the separatists before the Civil War; he loathed 'silly women who cant out against their Teachers [Antichrist] and [popery] upon words or actions not understood'; the woman-on-top was a nightmare spelt out in the pages of Thomas Edwards' *Gangraena*, the anti-sectarian diatribe to which Baxter himself had made some anonymous contributions in the mid-1640s.[7]

But it was not only women and radicals who were infected with the separatist virus. Take a conformist man, like Martin of Walsall. He had a minister in Lapthorne, whom Baxter likened to Latimer as 'a rustic thunderer'. When the pulpit thunder got too much for Martin, he would up and leave. He did this one time too often, 'the ground opened and swallowed him for good', and he was never seen again. However, he provided Lapthorne with a ready moral: 'when any one would goe out

[5] Richard Baxter, *Catholick Communion Defended Against Both Extreams* (1684), II, 55–6; *Catholick Theologie* (1675), preface.

[6] Samuel Parker, *A Defence and Continuation of the Ecclesiastical Politic* (1671), 341–2.

[7] Baxter, *An Account of the Reasons . . .* (1684), 26; *Catholick Theologie*, 294; *The True History of Councils Enlarged and Defended* (1682), 190.

of Church at a blustering passage, Mr. Lapthorne would call to him *Remember Martin*.[8]

From 1660 to 1676 Baxter remembered Martin. In the face of Samuel Parker and the Clarendon Code this took some doing. He could rejoice, in a letter in May 1666 to a correspondent at Kidderminster, that he had left no separatists among his flock.[9] His influential *Christian Directory* of 1673 expresses that philosophy: anarchy was worse than tyranny; the magistrate must be upheld.[10] But even in the earlier letter he had acknowledged strains in sustaining that line when contemplating the 'deseases or ulcers' of the church. And as early as 1660 he had been aware of the attractions of an alternative course. St Martin was a figure from ancient history, who had been visited by angels and *told* to avoid communion with the bishops. Baxter admitted that the story unsettled him 'concerning my Communion, the Reader may easily know with whom'. He had ways (just) to rationalise his compliance at that time: the angels might have only been a dream; St Martin's separation was only a *temporary* withdrawal 'from those individual persons, whom he supposed to be scandalous'.[11]

After 1676, however, one might say that Baxter stopped remembering *Martin*, and learned to remember *St Martin*. By this time Baxter had written off the majority of the bishops as partners in a 'Grotian' coalition with French papists; as such they were *worse* than the synods of Ithacius and Idacius, from which St Martin had separated.[12] The Emperor Constantine, the model for godly rule in the pages of Foxe's great history, was now seen as a tarnished figure: a man (like Charles II?) who could be pushed around by strong-minded prelates. Baxter even apologised for his earlier excursion into sect-bashing with Thomas Edwards: what were the excesses of a few sects when put in the balance against the 'Muscovy' tyranny of the bishops?[13]

If Baxter had died in 1684 his career would have provided a perfect exemplar of the power of Puritan centrifugalism. The man offered a

---

[8] Baxter, *Catholick Communion*, 32–3.
[9] DWL, *Baxter Correspondence*, I, fols. 94–5.
[10] Baxter, *A Christian Directory* (1673): the work drawn upon both by Weber and Tawney, when they identified Baxter as the spokesman for the Protestant Ethic, as if it stood for his philosophy of a lifetime and not (as here argued) for a transient response to particular political circumstances.
[11] Baxter, *The Successive Visibility of the Church* (1660), p. 317.
[12] Baxter, *The Nonconformists Plea for Peace* (1679), dedicatory epistle.
[13] Baxter, *The True History*, 190. Cf. his comment in the unpublished *A Political Catechise* of 1689/90: 'In Muscovy all preaching is forbidden lest the Ministers should preach sedition, and only Liturgies and Homilies allowed, and so an ignorant ministry set up': DWL, *Baxter Treatises*, VI, fol. 286v.

bishopric in 1660, and who would quote his friend Lord Chief Justice Hale on the need for a *new* Act of Uniformity,[14] ended up as an apologist for 'the world turned upside down'. Except that is not how he ended up, there were seven years of life left to him, and he would use that time not merely to recapitulate earlier themes of 'unitive Protestantism', but to come up with some wholly fresh ideas of why men should find salvation in 'National Churches'. These were the arguments which one of our greatest literary figures would find so compelling 140 years later.

The catalyst for change was Baxter's friend and fellow-minister, John Humfrey. He encouraged Baxter to write a paraphrase on the Epistle to the Romans. The work widened in scope, and Baxter ended up by paraphrasing the whole of the New Testament, including the Book of Revelation. Hitherto Baxter had steered clear of apocalyptic speculation; now he was forced to engage with it. The authorities read sedition in his paraphrase of the New Testament, and he was sent to gaol. Friends were no less alarmed than enemies, however, by his denial in that work that the Bible revealed that the pope was Antichrist. Over the years he had grown sceptical of this thesis – hitherto seen as the rock of the Protestant faith – but his researches in the Apocalypse only confirmed these doubts. As he went on investigating the Apocalypse in prison, his secret notes show two important revaluations: the pope was not Antichrist *in a scriptural sense*, but as the *usurper* of the magistrates's legitimate authority the identification was now actually closer than ever; the Book of Revelation demonstrated the truth of Foxe's argument, that the Christian emperor as head of a 'National Church' had begun the past millennium. Only ignorance of history blinded the millenarians of his own day to the scope of what Christian emperors had achieved in the past. What Constantine had done, Elizabeth I and (fleetingly) Richard Cromwell had done. The omens were not good in 1686, with Baxter in prison and James II on the throne, but two years later the Glorious Revolution made the idea of a 'National Church' practical politics again. In 1691 Baxter hailed William III as the new Constantine to head a National Church.[15]

By 'National Church' Baxter did not mean diocesan episcopacy. That was the mistake made by his friend, John Humfrey, who had set him on his paraphrasing of the New Testament in the first place, and who had suggested 'Of National Churches' as the title for Baxter's work of 1691

---

[14] DWL, *Baxter Treatises*, II, fol. 392.
[15] Among the publications of Baxter in 1691 in which these views are set out: *Of National Churches*; *Against the Revolt to a Foreign Jurisdiction*; *The Glorious Kingdom of Christ*.

which would ensure a good sale.[16] But Humfrey was an Erastian, like William Prynne. Both men had argued against Baxter earlier in favour of common admission to the sacrament of the Lord's Supper.[17] This was too lax for Baxter, who favoured an outward profession of holiness in those who came to the Table, although that, in its turn, fell short of the 'deeper discoverie' required by John Owen (and his fellow-Independent architects of the Savoy Declaration of 1658).[18] Humfrey thought that Baxter's 'National Church' was a concept vitiated by overambition.[19] Baxter had thought that it was possible to have the minister's pastoral care over his congregation extended on a national canvas, for England to become Kidderminster writ large. Thus it would be a national settlement even acceptable to Independents – or at least to those of them of the right sort.[20] This did not seem fantastic to Baxter, even if it did to Humfrey; indeed if it were not possible to have such ministerial discipline, Baxter was not interested in a national programme. He laughed at Humfrey's idea of a 'National Church' which would be wide enough even to include papists. Here was the Erastian *reductio ad absurdum*: Judge Jeffreys ordaining ministers alongside Archbishop Sancroft in Humfrey's 'National Church'![21]

But did not the very act of widening the field to national dimensions necessarily entail the inclusion of hypocrites? Not so, argued Baxter, because of the precious institution of 'catachumens'. The church in ancient times had kept men in this state of readiness long enough to prevent them from lying, and fitting them to covenant with sincerity and understanding. Baxter called it a 'cruell mercy' to open the gates of a 'National Church' before the candidate was ready; on the other hand to leave him among the catachumens without the prod of discipline was spiritual sloth. Catechising thus avoided the twin evils of promiscuity on the one hand, and elitism on the other. Baxter attached the greatest importance to what he saw as this 'ripening' process.[22] Since Baxter

[16] DWL, *Baxter Correspondence*, I, fol. 72.
[17] See Humfrey's defence of Prynne's views on free admission in his letter to Baxter in October 1657: DWL, *Baxter Correspondence*, I, fols. 196–7.
[18] A traumatic blow for Baxter, as revealed in his anguished contemporary comment in his personal papers: 'How low then hath this laid our hopes of Reconciliation': DWL, *Baxter Treatises*, VI, fol. 203.
[19] John Humfrey, *Union Pursued* (1691), 12–13.
[20] In 'A Political Primer for Nationall Churches', a manuscript which Baxter wrote in 1691 against John Humfrey, he appealed to what he called 'Intelligent Independency'. The Dr Owen who tried to establish 'godly rule' in Oxford at the beginning of the 1650s was singled out by Baxter as an 'intelligent Independent', but the Dr Owen who drafted the 1658 Savoy Declaration presumably was not: DWL, *Baxter Treatises*, VI, fol. 302.
[21] DWL, *Baxter Treatises*, VI, fol. 297.
[22] DWL, *Baxter Correspondence*, I, fol. 199.

believed that 'Popery is built on the Ruines of Nationall Churches' there was only one form of separatism which *was* allowable, and that was from a professed 'National Church' which, in reality, revolts to a foreign jurisdiction.[23] He did not like the 'deseases or ulcers' of the Restoration church but that had not in itself then excused separatism; after 1676, however, the take-over of that church by a conspiracy of 'Grotian' divines altered the situation. But not for good. There were Anglican supporters with the root of the matter in them – men like Tillotson and Isaac Barrow – and 1688 was as much *their* triumph, as it was William III's. Calamy, like Owen earlier, had therefore set his sights too low when, in 1704, he urged his fellow-Presbyterians to think of reform only at the level of parish, and not at the level of nation.

To see Baxter's advocacy of 'National Churches' in 1691 as a simple restatement of that 'unitive Protestantism' described by Collinson, and which had indeed served him between 1660 and 1676, is, in the light of this analysis, wrong. What is now apparent is that this apocalyptic solution synthesised two different elements in Baxter's make-up: the side of him which responded to unity and deference to the authority of the magistrate, and the side of him which responded to ministerial discipline. The first element was honoured in Sylvester's posthumous edition of Baxter memoirs 1696, the *Reliquiae Baxterianae*; the second, in Calamy's abridgements of that work in successively 1702, 1713 and 1727. With judicious selectivity Sylvester gives us a 'Tory' Baxter (omitting material in it which reflected on the Stuart magistrates' loyalty to Protestantism), and Calamy responds with a 'Whig' Baxter (highlighting the bits that Sylvester left out, and for his part playing down Baxter's stress upon uniformity and comprehension); both as self-serving editorially as John Toland, who had turned Ludlow, the Puritan saint, into a Whig republican.[24] Far wider than perhaps the special case, it might appear, of Baxter in its implications is the more general proposition of Collinson that the essence of Puritanism is to contain both elements – the centrifugal *and* the centripetal – and that the magic of Baxter's 'National Churches' was therefore to offer a formula which synthesises the two.

Two further case-studies may reinforce this point. They are sources neglected by historians for different reasons, despite the voluminous quantity of material in each. The first – the diary of the countess of

---

[23] The aphorism comes from Baxter's manuscript defence in April 1691 of the pamphlet he published in that year under the title, *Against the Revolt to a Foreign Jurisdiction*: DWL, *Baxter Treatises*, VII, fol. 99v.

[24] For the different editorial distortions of Sylvester and Calamy, see my *Richard Baxter and the Millennium* (1979), 79–88; for the editorial distortions of Toland, see *A Voyce from the Watch Tower*, ed. Blair Worden (Camden Soc., 4th ser., 21, 1978).

Warwick between the years of 1666 and 1677 (crucial for Baxter's evolution) – is accessible enough in manuscript form to historians. What puts them off is probably not so much the size – though it runs to more than 40,000 pages – but its lack of specific detail. In the words of one, it 'mentions little about anything except prayers and thanks to God', and this from the historian who turned the unpromising devotional diary of Ralph Josselin into a rewarding anthropological arsenal.[25] Now it is true that the lady will tease us, time and again, by recording the 'profitable discourse' which she had with various figures, and then will *not* go on to tell us what that discourse was, but the company she keeps is itself an education. She will read Baxter, dine with him, give him discreet charity, but she will also sup with his enemies, Archbishop Sheldon, Bishop Ward and even Baxter's pet hate, Bishop Morley, and derive no less pleasure from *their* discourse.[26] The Puritan courtier is a familiar enough figure, and it could be argued that she too is a special case. But her diary does document in a rich way the tensions in Baxter and his peers.

The lady is a loyalist. She attends court, even if it only provides her with thoughts afterwards of the vanity of earthly pleasures.[27] She prays for the Crown constantly, and faithfully keeps the anniversary days (and records the sermon notes) of Charles I's execution and Charles II's restoration.[28] She blames her near-death from smallpox on hearing the news of 'that barbarous and unheard of wicked action of beheading King Charles The First'.[29] But she is also a Puritan, reading Samuel Rutherford, desolated by her husband's oaths, seeing the Dutch Wars as the engine for the advance of French popery.[30] Above all, she has an intensity of devotion to the sacrament of the Lord's Supper which goes beyond, not only the formalism of Erastians like Prynne and Humfrey, but even the professed holiness, demanded of communicants by Baxter. In her anxiety that the sacrament be not polluted she comes closest of all to John Owen and to his insistence on a rigorous scrutiny of com-municants. A typical entry for Christmas Day 1667, on the effect of communion, reads: it 'set my heart a panting and breathing after Christ, longing to embrace him in the armes of my faith . . . I did there enjoy such sweet and ravishing Communion with God.'[31] For the sacrament on

---

25 Alan Macfarlane, *The Family Life of Ralph Josselin* (Cambridge, 1970), 8.
26 BL Additional MS 27351, fols. 39, 43v, 44v, 47v, 48, 68v, 80v, 82v, 91, 96, 113v, 163v, 169, 286v.
27 *Ibid.*, fol. 71.
28 *Ibid.*, fols. 58, 159v; BL Additional MS 27354, fol. 158.
29 *The Autobiography of Mary Countess of Warwick*, ed. T. Crofton Croker (1848), 25.
30 BL Additional MS 27351, fols. 11v, 53, 94–5.
31 *Ibid.*, fol. 150.

22 November 1668 preparations take on the mantle of a military campaign. Ten days beforehand, a whole afternoon is spent in catechising her maids: 'God was pleased to make some of them much moved'. On 13 November another entire afternoon is spent on the preparation of her servants for communion. On 14 November her stepdaughters repeat to her the Sunday sermon: 'and when they had done, I did indeavour by all the most moveing awakening arguments I could use to persuade them to a searious diligence in the examining their own heartes before the Sacrament which we were to Receive the next Sunday ... I wepte much as I talked to them, and they too seemed much afected.' A week later, on 21 November, the attack was resumed: 'after diner the two young ladies being to receive I did with all the awakening considerations I would stir them up to selfe examination and to try whether they weare yet regenerate'.[32]

Baxter could hardly quarrel with this piety, unless it toppled over into such intensity that separatism – always a snare for women especially, as we have seen – became the goal. But the intensity of that experience, 'breathing and panting after Christ to that love feast' in her own words,[33] carried just such dangers, which were only too familiar to a pastor whose correspondence – let alone his ministerial duties – seems to be inordinately taken up with female overscrupulousness. 'Hindred by company and business from being retired', the countess with relief flees from company in the afternoon to enjoy two hours of solitary meditation.[34] One of Baxter's most tenacious correspondents, Katherine, Lady Gell, wrote to him in just such terms: 'many a time I goe about my house and amongst my servants when I had rather locke my self up in a roome alone amongst my books for meditation'.[35] Baxter had to jolly her out of this introspective melancholia, as he did the countess. In her diary the countess records Baxter cajoling her to 'keepe up a cheerful frame', and on another occasion, warning her that, while it was prudent to separate from evil persons as bosom friends, it was not right to cut herself off from ordinary civil commerce and neighbourly offices.[36] Her chaplain, Gifford, followed up his Restoration anniversary sermon on the duty to pray for kings and those in authority with another five days later on the theme that 'some heresies and corruptions in a Church were not a sufficient ground for separation'.[37] Perhaps the sister of Robert Boyle was

[32] *Ibid.*, fols. 258v, 259, 260, 262v.
[33] *Ibid.*, fol. 150.
[34] *Ibid.*, fol. 34v.
[35] DWL, *Baxter Correspondence*, v, fol. 3.
[36] BL Additional MS 27354, fols. 95, 110.
[37] *Ibid.*, fols. 158, 159v.

not an obvious Brownist-in-embryo, but the diary shows even so that she needed some stiffening counter-pressure from men like Gifford and Baxter (who himself at the time was sensitive to the very same temptations) to keep her piety within centripetal bonds.

A second case-study is equally profuse: the thirty-four volumes of sermon notes of John Pointer, rector of Alkerton in Oxfordshire between 1663 and 1710. This manuscript is now lodged in the Folger Library at Washington, and deserves to be more widely known. Pointer was very much in the Baxter mould. He quoted frequently from Baxter, shared his belief that Antichrist would fall but, like him, disliked those who gave a date to it, and both men read providence in witches, lightning and thunder claps.[38] With the same concern as the countess that the sacrament must not be polluted, he would go so far in 1689 as to invoke the model of St Ambrose who would bar the blood-stained Emperor Theodosius from the Lord's Supper.[39] Yet, like Gifford and Baxter, he held to the line that 'so long as the worship I go into, is for the substance of it, pure and according to gods ordinance, the corruptions and sins which another brings into it, cannot defile it unto me, or shall be imputed unto me at all, so long as I show my dislike into them'.[40] Thus the command to separate from heathen and idolaters is justification for 'warrantable separation', but not from a true church. And 'corruption of manners in matters not notoriously scandalous',[41] where Baxter also drew *his* line, does not disqualify the Church of England from being a true church. A universal toleration is bogus because it takes in 'libertines, Antinomians, Arians, Socinians and Quakers', and these are not 'Churches of God' but 'conspiracies of Monstrous Hereticks'. As for the papists, 'if we were in their hands as they are in ours we shall not soon escape as they do'.[42]

And if the sovereign were to be a papist? Pointer's sermon on the anniversary of the king's execution in 1687 cannot rest with a celebration of the virtues of the Royal Martyr or even, as with the countess, be an excuse for tears. If Pointer gives the final prayer 'for those whom God sets over us especially Kings and Princes', the meat in the sermon is his reminder to his parishioners that 'no Magistrates can hinder the Saints

---

[38] FL, Pointer MS XVII, II, IV, XII, no foliation (in these, and all subsequent references).

[39] *Ibid.*, V. For the significance of St Ambrose-versus-Theodosius, see P. Collinson, 'If Constantine, then also Theodosius: St. Ambrose and the Integrity of the Elizabethan *Ecclesia Anglicana*', *Godly People: Essays on English Protestantism and Puritanism* (1983), 109–35.

[40] FL, Pointer MS XVII.

[41] *Ibid.*, VIII.

[42] *Ibid.*, XVII.

being godly, as to the embracing of the truth in their hearts and secret performance of prayer'.[43] True, the authority of the secular magistrate may be upheld, as in a 1683 sermon, since 'better is it to bear one Tyrant than many',[44] (Baxter's favourite comfort between 1660 and 1676), but this is not a blank cheque for the ruler, any more than it was for the Emperor Theodosius in the past. In another sermon in 1687 Pointer went back to Mary Tudor's days as a reminder that princes 'are limited and stinted by their Lord, how far they should goe'.[45] Protestants like Pointer and Baxter could accommodate a Nero more easily than they could a Mary Tudor.[46] Pointer can draw on Romans XIII for an unambiguous sermon on non-resistance, but the date is then 1695 and by then a Protestant sits on the English throne.[47] The countess' diary is less forthcoming, but even so when she celebrates the anniversary of the regicide in 1674 it is coupled with despair at 'the sinnes of the King and Kingdom', not merely of the kingdom, and the entry closes with the prayer 'that popery might be kept out'.[48] Again it is 'the King and Kingdomes angry sinnes' which comes to her mind when she makes her private fast to commemorate the Great Fire in 1675.[49]

These two contemporary sources – the countess's diary and the minister's sermons – with their curious amalgam of centrifugal and centripetal drives are a good context for Baxter's prison researches in 1686. These would end in the discovery of 'National Churches' which would synthesise both of these tendencies: a nation with the discipline of a well-run ministry like Kidderminster. But, while a papist sat on the throne, this model was non-realisable. The Glorious Revolution changed all that, and the secret manuscript notes of 1686 become the basis for the public propaganda of 1690 and 1691.

The 'National Church' of 1691, given this background, is intelligible in a way that its revival in 1829 is not. The argument in this essay is that it was a conscious revival by a man whom we know to be steeped in *Baxteriana*, Samuel Taylor Coleridge. The evidence for this connection is admittedly indirect. Professor Morrow's study of Coleridge's political thought draws attention to a notebook entry as early as April–May 1802, in which Coleridge refers to a projected study of church government with a tantalising allusion to 'Presbyterians and Baxterians in the time of

[43] *Ibid.*, XII.
[44] *Ibid.*, XXII.
[45] *Ibid.*, XII.
[46] Cf. Baxter, *The Glorious Kingdom of Christ* (1691), 7.
[47] FL, Pointer MS XVI.
[48] BL Additional MS 27353, fol. 274.
[49] *Ibid.*, 27354, fol. 58.

Charles 1 and 2'. This leads Professor Morrow to the cautious conclusion that 'it is possible that Baxter provided part of the basis for his revised views on the legitimacy of religious establishments'.[50] Even if the proof is in the end circumstantial, the case for the indebtedness of Coleridge to Baxter can be put more strongly than that.

It was late in 1829 that Coleridge published his last work in political philosophy, *On the Constitution of the Church and State, According to the Idea of Each*. A revised version of the book appeared in 1830 together with a piece entitled 'Aids toward a Right Judgment of the late Catholic Bill'. It was the prospect of Catholic Emancipation in fact which triggered off Coleridge's advocacy of 'National Churches'. And so the mood of the later writings is totally different from the earlier. In 1691 Baxter had been confident that, with a constitutional settlement which put Protestants on the English throne, the success of National Churches was assured. Coleridge agreed: he called it a period of 'little less than a century and half' when 'Englishmen have collectively, and individually, lived and acted with fewer restraints on their free-agency than the citizens of any knowne Republic, past or present.'[51] The prospect of Catholic Emancipation threw that achievement in jeopardy.

To oppose Catholic Emancipation, however, was to find oneself in dubious company (even, among them, a Mitford ancestor).[52] Coleridge wanted to separate himself from the bigots: 'in seceding from Burkes, Cannings and Lansdownes, I did not move a step nearer to the findings and opinions of their antagonists': a 'National Church' was not the same thing as Henry VIII's Reformation; rather, it stood for what Henry VIII 'might and should have done'.[53] The loot from the monasteries should have been diverted to social ends. We are back with the programme of Edward VI's 'Commonwealth' preachers: the need for funding for schools and universities, for pastoral control in the parishes, for school-masters' discipline over their pupils. Or, indeed, back with Richard Baxter's 'Holy Commonwealth' programme of 1659, with his plans for a new University elaborated in correspondence with John Lewis, his advancement of ministerial discipline through the Worcestershire Association and his legislative reforms outlined in letters to the MP, John

[50] John Morrow, *Coleridge's Political Thought* (New York, 1990), 63–4.
[51] S. T. Coleridge, *On the Constitution of the Church and State*, ed. J. Barrell (Everyman's University Library, 1972), 80.
[52] Lord Redesdale, *A Political View of the Roman Catholic Question Especially Regarding the Supremacy Usurped by the Church of Rome* (1829); I owe this reference to my former Sussex colleague, Dr Valerie Cromwell.
[53] Coleridge, *Constitution of the Church*, iv, 39, 41, 42.

Swinfen.[54] For Coleridge, the enemy of a National Church was a body which had 'the poor withdrawn from the discipline of the church' and the 'education of the people detached from the ministry of the church'.[55] So, too, Baxter's test for a National Church was whether it advanced the 'common welfare'.[56] Popery opposed National Churches because it commanded 'allegiance to a foreign Power';[57] a restatement of Baxter's aphorism that 'Popery is built on the Ruines of National Churches'.[58] Coleridge wanted to separate this reasoned case from 'fanatical and puritan cant'. He had in mind those bizarre commentators on the Apocalypse who identified a Nero or a Napoleon with Antichrist.[59] So too Baxter wanted no truck with separatist women incanting 'Antichrist' and 'Popery', and he had his own bit of fun with a millenarian contemporary who identified the German emperor with the Beast of Revelation.[60] Coleridge thought that the seventeenth century had been overzealous in the scriptural identification of the pope with Antichrist, but the danger of his day lay in *'the twaddle* of human charity'. The twaddle had allowed a new airing for old 'principles and language of Laud and his faction'. Hugo Grotius was back in fashion: he who had 'yearned for a conciliatory settlement of the differences between the Romish and Protestant churches'.[61] Baxter, also no friend of *scriptural* identification of Rome with Antichrist, likewise saw as the great enemy of National Churches the 'Grotian' (as he called it) fifth column of the church under Laud and his clique.[62] But both Coleridge and Baxter agreed that Rome *was* Antichrist, although not in the biblical sense, but as a usurping power of magisterial rights. As Coleridge said, 'if the papacy, and the Romish Hierarchy as far as it is papal, be *not* Antichrist, the fault of schism, in its most aggravated form, lies on the authors of the Reformation'.[63] Both men found their way out of this impasse in the same, relatively obscure, source: Henry More's *A Modest Enquiry* of

---

[54] See respectively: DWL, *Baxter Correspondence*, I, fol. 127; G. F. Nuttall, *Richard Baxter* (1965), 68–73; R. B. Schlatter, *Richard Baxter and Puritan Politics* (New Brunswick, 1957), 61–6.

[55] Coleridge, *Constitution of the Church*, 49.

[56] *The Reverend Richard Baxter's Last Treatise*, ed. F. J. Powicke (Manchester, 1926), 53.

[57] Coleridge, *Constitution of the Church*, 65.

[58] DWL, *Baxter Treatises*, VII, fol. 99v.

[59] Coleridge, *Constitution of the Church*, 116.

[60] Baxter, *Catholick Theologie*, 294; DWL, *Baxter Treatises*, VII, fol. 302v.

[61] Coleridge, *Constitution of the Church*, 115.

[62] DWL, *Baxter Treatises*, VII, fol. 277; Baxter, *The Grotian Religion Discovered* (1658).

[63] Coleridge, *Constitution of the Church*, 116; DWL, *Baxter Treatises*, II, fol. 112v. In his sermon of 2 February 1701, Pointer follows the same *nonapocalyptical* identification of Antichrist as an usurper: FL, Pointer MS XII.

1664.[64] More had known that 'Antichrist', even then, was debased coinage – 'smells as strong as of Onions and Garlicks'. He advocated a different methodology: start with the concept and then turn to scripture, and not the other way round. Then all the qualities one would expect of an Antichrist – most telling of which was the pride which *usurped* the power of emperors – would be found when one went back to the Holy Word.[65] Pointer, Baxter and Coleridge all agreed on this identification of Rome with Antichrist as an usurper. Coleridge pointed out that Luther had got there before them on this, also without recourse to the Book of Revelation. Actually Coleridge claimed to have more regard for the Apocalypse than Luther had had: it was 'the most perfect specimen of symbolic poetry'.[66] Until his paraphrase of the New Testament, and his investigations of the Apocalypse in prison, Baxter had been as tentative about Revelation as Coleridge had.[67] His researches worked in two directions: to reinforce his agnosticism about Antichrist in scripture, but also to reinforce his awe of Christian empire (and, therefore, to make the Antichrist-as-usurper tag for Rome the more compelling). In the margin of Coleridge's personal copy of Baxter's autobiography, he had scribbled down the classic objection to a 'National Church': 'where there is Law, there can be no discipline'.[68] It is the Humfrey objection: National Churches *cannot* be congregations. But both Baxter and Coleridge believed the opposite: that a National Church which was not holy was not worth having. They agreed on how it could be made holy, even if their expression of that agreement was different. One found in Revelation the key to history (even if only at the end of his life);[69] the other found only symbolic poetry. One found in Oliver Cromwell's earlier non-involvement in matters of religion cause for regret[70] (cancelled out by later stirrings, and the promise of his son's Protectorship); the other welcomed it as 'one among a thousand proofs of Cromwell's attachment to the best interests of human nature'.[71] One smelt conspiracy where the other denounced twaddle. These made for

---

[64] Coleridge, *Constitution of the Church*, 107; Baxter, *The Cure of Church-Divisions* (1670), dedicatory epistle.
[65] Henry More, *A Modest Enquiry* (1664), preface, 44, 54, 59, 207.
[66] Coleridge, *Constitution of the Church*, 121.
[67] Among many examples: Baxter, *Christian Concord* (1653), 69; *Richard Baxter's Admonition to William Eyre* (1654), 8; *A Key for Catholicks* (1659), 301.
[68] BL Additional MS 32568, fol. 9.
[69] See especially: Baxter, *The Glorious Kingdom of Christ* (1691), *passim*.
[70] DWL, *Baxter Correspondence*, III, fols. 272–3.
[71] Morrow, *Coleridge's Political Thought*, 151. Pointer was at one with Baxter, not Coleridge, on this: 'Take heed of that rotten principle that Magistrates have nothing to do with Religion – they are called in Scripture phrase Lords of restraint' (FL, Pointer MS XVII).

important differences of language, but on the whole it is the *convergence* of views, across 150 years of British history, which astonishes.

What weight should we give to that convergence? Perhaps it should lead us to be more cautious in associating Protestantism with 'opposition' ideology. What Protestants *were* opposed to in the seventeenth century was the Catholic or crypto-Catholic tendencies of their Stuart kings (we saw it surfacing in the reservations of Pointer, Baxter and the countess of Warwick). But it was not absolutism *per se* that most of them objected to; it was the uses to which it was put: to advance the cause of popery. Pointer, like Baxter, an imperial Protestant reared on Foxe, looked back with nostalgia to the rule of Elizabeth, 'our English Deborah',[72] and to its recrudescence in the reign of William III. After 1688 'popery' and 'arbitrary government' were issues which would never again be united within the nation to tear it apart; and so Pointer could approve of an expansionist foreign policy, which actually *advanced* the powers of the executive (but in a Protestant, not papist, direction)[73] to the extent that the whole of one sermon of 1706 could be taken up simply with a resumé of Marlborough's military campaigns. Pointer revived the language of Oliver Cromwell in telling his parishioners then that 'we have many and great Mercies to praise God for this day'.[74] In the same year, another of his sermons would be devoted to an attack upon the separatist arguments of his fellow-nonconformist, Stephen Lobb.[75] Lobb had swallowed James II's bait of Indulgence in 1687 and thus had turned his back on Protestant imperial traditions. Pointer not only rehearsed the old arguments of non-separatism in reply, but expanded them into a defence of the 'Commonwealth' concept. Pointer said that 'peace and prosperity are bound up in the publick, in the same bundle: you are like to have a common share in weale or in noe so that in seeking the public good you seek your own'. This was Baxter's 'Holy Commonwealth' of 1659, as well as his 'National Church' of 1691. To belong to a 'Commonwealth', in

---

[72] In a sermon in January 1671: FL, Pointer MS xxviii. And over thirty years later, in December 1701, he is still recounting an affecting passage on the deathbed scene of Elizabeth I, 'that Queen of women and Maid of Heaven': *ibid.*, xxix.

[73] Jonathan Clark, *Revolution and Rebellion* (Cambridge, 1986), 80, argues that the apogee of monarchical power in the reign of the first two Georges, which is what he believes it was, was acceptable to English subjects precisely because it was *Protestant* power, and that one had to go back, behind the Stuarts, to Elizabeth I before one could make a similarly unambiguous assertion. Unless the Cromwells (father and son) were brought into the calculation, that is, and then the question (as for Baxter) was whether their Protestantism redeemed their origins.

[74] FL, Pointer MS xxxi.

[75] The object also of a detailed refutation by Baxter in manuscript on 20 April 1684: DWL, *Baxter Treatises*, ii, fols. 83–4.

this sense, made a member a 'citizen of the new Jerusalem', according to Pointer.[76]

Professor Hirst has shown that the idea of 'godly rule' had been abandoned by many English Protestants before the Restoration.[77] But, thanks to the Baxters and Pointers, it never quite died out. These ministers faced a formidable enemy in sustaining this case in the contradictory Puritan impulse to separate, to keep the wheat apart from the tares. The countess of Warwick's desire to withdraw into meditation, to keep the sacrament from pollution – what could be more venial? Yet her chaplain, Gifford, and Baxter himself, had to keep her from straying into separatist paths by constant reminders of *community* responsibilities. Could personal holiness be imposed in a national setting? The case against was never better put than in Roger Williams' *The Bloody Tenent of Persecution* and Milton's *Areopagitica*. Both defended a pluralist society in which imposed conformity was renounced, and the civil magistrate did no more than keep the peace. But both still wanted the tares to be forcibly separated from the wheat; by God, though, not by the civil magistrate; and in the hereafter, not now. And both thought that the hereafter was soon, because both wrote their books out of a millenarian conviction. Milton's vision of 'a knowing people, a nation of prophets, of sages, and worthies' would become anyway a reality within five months; with effort the time-table could be reduced to a mere five weeks.

In its upbeat tone it sounds like Baxter's 'Holy Commonwealth' or 'National Church'. But with this crucial difference: the millennium and the magistrate were, by Milton, kept resolutely apart. In the interim period, the magistrate was to confine himself to keeping order, and nothing more. Neither Williams nor Milton was put off by the consequence of this: a society with 'much arguing, and writing, many opinions'.[78] Plurality of views was simply knowledge in the making. John Owen would emerge, in the latter half of the seventeenth century, as the spiritual heir of Williams and Milton in his advocacy of religious toleration, but it was from a different base. He was not sanguine, as they were, about the virtues of pluralism. Near the end of his life, he would lament the multiplicity of thoughts in men's minds: 'what a hell of horror and confusion it must needs be!' And he would argue that 'the

---

[76] FL, Pointer MS xxix. Pointer also has a long analysis, in a sermon on 5 May 1709, of what the term 'commonwealth' means, going back to Aristotle, and it is there that the term, 'new Jerusalem', appears: *ibid.*, XVII.

[77] Derek Hirst, 'The Failure of Godly Rule in the English Republic', *Past and Present*, 132 (1991).

[78] John Milton, *Areopagitica* (1644), in *John Milton, Paradise Lost and Selected Poetry and Prose*, ed. Northrop Frye (New York, 1965), 496.

design of conviction' was 'to put a stop unto these thoughts, to take off from the number, and thereby to lessen their guilt'.[79] Earlier in his career, as chaplain to Oliver Cromwell, he had hoped in a magistrate who would put a stop to such pluralism; these hopes did not survive the end of that Protectorate or the rule of the son. By 1658 he was committed to the requirement of an 'inner discoverie' in communicants to the Lord's Supper which Baxter rightly saw as antithetical to an imposed national settlement. What Owen did have in common with Milton and Williams was lack of faith in the historical basis for such an imposition by the magistrate; they all knew that the 300 years before Constantine was emperor was the best time for the church.[80]

John Foxe had drawn, from Revelation, a quite different interpretation. With Constantine, the millennium had begun. Baxter had not always thought as highly as this of the first Christian emperor; there was a time in the late 1670s when he and Marvell even offered an alternative view of Constantine as a good man mugged by bishops.[81] And that was the time when he felt most strongly in himself these rival separatist temptations. But magistrate and millennium, however, came together again indissolubly in his 1686 rediscovery of Foxe in prison, and in his subsequent advocacy of 'National Churches'. That advocacy was, in its inspiration, millenarian, not Utopian, and therefore escaped the Miltonic derision for those who thought that 'all in a Church is to be expected *gold and silver and precious stones*'.[82] That was why, for Baxter, 'catachumens' were essential. Milton's 'nation of prophets' was not to be postponed (five weeks or five months), *until* the millennium; it was achievable *on earth* with the right induction and preparation. The requirements for membership of a 'National Church' were neither impossibly stringent (Owen) not indecently lax (Humfrey). Nor did the magistrate have to be a saint, although experience proved that he could not be a papist (James II) or even a 'Grotian' half-papist (Charles I and Charles II). In their different ways, Elizabeth I, Richard Cromwell and William III had shown what could be done with a Protestant sovereign on the throne. This achievement was secured by the terms of the Revolutionary

---

[79] John Owen, *The Grace and Duty of being Spiritually Minded* (1681), 299.
[80] John Owen, *An Enquiry into the Original, Nature, Institution, Power, Order and Commerce of Evangelical Churches* (1681), 116. His objection in that pamphlet to the Donatist heresy, interestingly enough, is not the conventional one, that the sect stood for disruptive purity, but that it flouted Calvinist beliefs in the perpetuity of the regenerate (p. 311).
[81] See my 'The Religion of Andrew Marvell: Locating the "Bloody Horse"', in *The Political Identity of Andrew Marvell*, ed. C. Condren and A. Cousins (Aldershot, 1990), 135–57.
[82] Milton, *Aeropagitica*, in *Milton*, ed. Frye, 502.

Settlement, until the issue of Catholic Emancipation cast its permanency in question, and provoked once again the appeal to 'National Churches'.

The Puritan is more often cast in history as foe, not friend, of magistracy. When John Updike, that marvellously acute intelligence who brings Barthian theology to the problems of wife-swapping in New England, explains why he was a Vietnam 'hawk' he draws on his Protestant inheritance.[83] When he goes beyond the sentimentalism which makes him melt at the sight of President Johnson and Dean Rusk hugging each other at a dinner – 'two broad-backed Southern boys, trying to hold the fort' – it is what Tillich called Luther's 'positivistic authoritarianism' which he draws on for his inspiration. This surprises us. The 'protest' politics of his former wife (which, he acknowledges, he was in part reacting against) was rooted in her own Unitarian beliefs, and this is something on the other hand we can recognise at once. But the persistence of the 'National Church' aspiration is a reminder of the dual nature of the Protestant legacy.

John Humfrey had mocked that aspiration. He said that 'Law' and 'Discipline' could not be combined. Protestants had to choose between them. The Muggletonians were one small seventeenth-century sect which made that choice, and after the Restoration plumped for 'Law' rather than 'Discipline'. Quietism for them, as for other burnt-out Protestants after 1660, would be their path to survival. This was a marked contrast to their temper in the Protectorate. Then they had hailed Oliver Cromwell as the fulfilment of prophecy: 'a spiritual Lion of the Tribe of Israel'. It was phrases like that which were eliminated by Lodowick Muggleton in the revised edition in 1661 of the original work of 1656, *The Divine Looking-Glass*. What could not be eliminated from the hearts of his followers was the aspiration the words embodied: the conviction that England could become a holy commonwealth. There would be Muggletonians in the nineteenth, and even the twentieth, century who still held out for the authenticity of the 1656 text.[84] The Muggletonian influence on William Blake had set E. P. Thompson off on a detective trail which would culminate in the discovery of the lost archive.[85] When today, in parish churches of a Sunday, elderly ladies pledge to build Jerusalem in England's green and pleasant land, do we, straining to hear, catch the faintest echoes of the ghosts of 1691 and 1829?

---

[83] John Updike, 'On Not Being a Dove', *Self-Consciousness: Memoirs* (1989), 107–55.

[84] See my 'Lodowick Muggleton and "Immediate Notice"', in Christopher Hill, Barry Reay and William Lamont, *The World of the Muggletonians* (1983), 111–62.

[85] E. P. Thompson, *Witness against the Beast: William Blake and the Moral Law* (Cambridge, 1993), 115–19.

Bibliography of the published writings of Patrick Collinson, 1957–1992

Compiled by

Susan Wabuda

I BOOKS, ARTICLES AND LECTURES

1957

'The Puritan Classical Movement in the Reign of Elizabeth I', unpublished London PhD dissertation, 2 vols.

1958

'The Authorship of *A Brieff Discours off the Troubles Begonne at Franckford*', *JEH*, 9, pp. 188–208. (Reprinted in *Godly People* (1983), pp. 191–211.)

1960

Letters of Thomas Wood, Puritan, 1566–1577. Bulletin of the Institute of Historical Research, Special Supplement no. 5. (Reprinted in *Godly People* (1983), pp. 45–107.)

1961

'John Field and Elizabethan Puritanism', in *Elizabethan Government and Society: Essays Presented to Sir John Neale*, ed. S. T. Bindoff, J. Hurstfield, and C. H. Williams (London: Athlone Press), pp. 127–62. (Reprinted in *Godly People* (1983), pp. 335–70).

1964

'The Beginnings of English Sabbatarianism', in *Studies in Church History*, 1, ed. C. W. Dugmore and Charles Duggan (London: Thomas Nelson and Sons Ltd), pp. 207–21. (Reprinted in *Godly People* (1983), pp. 429–43.)

'The Elizabethan Puritans and the Foreign Reformed Churches in London', *Proceedings of the Huguenot Society of London*, 20, pp. 528–55. (Reprinted in *Godly People* (1983), pp. 245–72.)

A Mirror of Elizabethan Puritanism: The Life and Letters of 'Godly Master Dering'. Friends of DWL, Seventeenth Lecture, 1963 (London: Dr Williams' Trust. (Reprinted in *Godly People* (1983), pp. 289–324.)

'The "Nott Conformytye" of the Young John Whitgift', *JEH*, 15, pp. 192–200. (Reprinted in *Godly People* (1983), pp. 325–33.)

1965

'The Role of Women in the English Reformation Illustrated by the Life and Friendships of Anne Locke', in *Studies in Church History*, 2, ed. G. J. Cuming (London: Thomas Nelson and Sons Ltd), pp. 258–72. (Reprinted in *Godly People* (1983), pp. 273–87.)

1966

'Episcopacy and Reform in England in the Later Sixteenth Century', in *Studies in Church History*, 3, ed. G. J. Cuming (Leiden: E. J. Brill), pp. 91–125. (Reprinted in *Godly People* (1983), pp. 155–89.)

1967

The Elizabethan Puritan Movement (London: Cape; Berkeley: University of California Press). (Reprinted London and New York: Methuen, 1982; Oxford: Clarendon Press and New York: Oxford University Press, 1989; Oxford, Oxford University Press, 1990.)

1971

'The Reformer and the Archbishop: Martin Bucer and an English Bucerian', *Journal of Religious History*, 6, pp. 305–30. (Reprinted in *Godly People* (1983), pp. 19–44.)

1975

'Lectures by Combination: Structures and Characteristics of Church Life in 17th-Century England', *Bulletin of the Institute of Historical Research*, 48, pp. 182–213. (Reprinted in *Godly People* (1983), pp. 467–98.)

'Towards a Broader Understanding of the Early Dissenting Tradition', in *The Dissenting Tradition: Essays for Leland H. Carlson*, ed. C. Robert Cole and Michael E. Moody (Athens, Ohio: Ohio University Press), pp. 3–38. (Reprinted in *Godly People* (1983), pp. 527–62.)

1977

' "A Magazine of Religious Patterns": An Erasmian Topic Transposed in English Protestantism', in *Renaissance and Renewal in Christian History*, ed. Derek Baker (Studies in Church History, 14, Oxford: Basil Blackwell), pp. 223–49. (Reprinted in *Godly People* (1983), pp. 499–525.)

'Magistracy and Ministry; a Suffolk Miniature', in *Reformation Conformity and Dissent: Essays in Honour of Geoffrey Nuttall*, ed. R. Buick Knox (London: Epworth Press), pp. 70–91. (Reprinted in *Godly People* (1983), pp. 445–66.)

1979

Archbishop Grindal 1519–1583: The Struggle for a Reformed Church (London: Jonathan Cape; Berkeley: University of California Press).

'Calvinism with an Anglican Face: The Stranger Churches in Early Elizabethan London and their Superintendent', in *Reform and Reformation: England and the Continent c. 1500–c. 1700*, ed. Derek Baker (Studies in Church History, subsidia 2, Oxford: Basil Blackwell), pp. 71–102. (Reprinted in *Godly People* (1983), pp. 213–44.)

'The Downfall of Archbishop Grindal and its Place in Elizabethan Political and Ecclesiastical History', in *The English Commonwealth 1547–1640: Essays in Politics and Society*, ed. Peter Clark, Alan G. R. Smith and Nicholas Tyacke (New York: Barnes and Noble), pp. 39–57. (Reprinted in *Godly People* (1983), pp. 371–97.)

'If Constantine, then also Theodosius: St Ambrose and the Integrity of the Elizabethan *Ecclesia Anglicana*', *JEH*, 30, pp. 205–29. (Reprinted in *Godly People* (1983), pp. 109–33.)

1980

'A Comment: Concerning the Name Puritan', *JEH*, 31, pp. 483–8.

'Cranbrook and the Fletchers: Popular and Unpopular Religion in the Kentish Weald', in *Reformation Principle and Practice: Essays in Honour of Arthur Geoffrey Dickens*, ed. Peter Newman Brooks (London: Scolar Press), pp. 171–202. (Reprinted in *Godly People* (1983), pp. 399–428.)

'Sir Nicholas Bacon and the Elizabethan *Via Media*', *HJ*, 23, pp. 255–73. (Reprinted in *Godly People* (1983), pp. 135–53.)

1982

The Religion of Protestants: The Church in English Society 1559–1625, Ford Lectures 1979 (Oxford: Clarendon Press). (Paperback edn 1984, reprinted 1985, 1988, 1992.)

'Popular Prelates: Elizabethan and Jacobean Roots of the Low Church Tradition', *Friends of Lambeth Palace Library Annual Report*.

1983

English Puritanism (London: Historical Association), general series 106 (revised edn 1987).

'The Godly: Aspects of Popular Protestantism', printed for the first time in *Godly People*.

Godly People: Essays on English Protestantism and Puritanism (London: Hambledon Press).

'The Jacobean Religious Settlement: The Hampton Court Conference', in *Before the English Civil War: Essays on Early Stuart Politics and Government*, ed. Howard Tomlinson (New York: St Martin's Press), pp. 27–51.

1984

'The Elizabethan Church and the New Religion', in *The Reign of Elizabeth I*, ed. Christopher Haigh (London: Macmillan), pp. 169–94.

'England 1450–1603', in 'Recent Works (1977–1982) on Early Modern British History: A Review Essay', with Aidan Clark, John Morrill and Geoffrey Parker, *Tijdschrift voor Geschiedenis*, 97, pp. 517–54.

1985
'The Church: Religion and its Manifestations', in *William Shakespeare: His World, his Work, his Influence*, ed. John F. Andrews (New York: Charles Scribner's Sons), I, pp. 21–40.
'England and International Calvinism 1558–1640', in *International Calvinism 1541–1715*, ed. Menna Prestwich (Oxford: Oxford University Press), pp. 197–223.
'Truth and Legend: The Veracity of John Foxe's Book of Martyrs', in *Clio's Mirror: Historiography in Britain and the Netherlands*, ed. A. C. Duke and C. A. Tamse (Zutphen: De Walburg Pers), pp. 31–54.
'What is Religious History?', *History Today*, 35, pp. 45–6.

1986
'A Chosen People? The English Church and the Reformation', *History Today*, 36, pp. 14–20.
'The English Conventicle', in *Voluntary Religion*, ed. W. J. Sheils and Diana Wood (Studies in Church History, 23, Oxford: Basil Blackwell), pp. 223–59); and the Introduction to *Voluntary Religion*, pp. xi–xvi.
From Iconoclasm to Iconophobia: The Cultural Impact of the Second English Reformation, Stenton Lecture 1985 (Reading: University of Reading).

1987
The English Captivity of Mary Queen of Scots (Sheffield: Sheffield History Pamphlets).
'Episcopacy and Quasi-Episcopacy in the Elizabethan Church', in *L'Institution et les pouvoirs dans les églises de l'antiquité a nos jours: Colloque de Strasbourg Septembre 1983*, ed. Bernard Vogler, Bibliothèque de la Revue d'Histoire Ecclesiastique Fasc. 72, pp. 229–38.
'The Monarchical Republic of Queen Elizabeth I', *Bulletin of the John Rylands University Library of Manchester*, 69, pp. 394–424.

1988
The Birthpangs of Protestant England: Religious and Cultural Change in the Sixteenth and Seventeenth Centuries, The Third Anstey Memorial Lectures in the University of Kent and Canterbury, 12–25 May 1986 (Basingstoke: Macmillan; New York: St Martin's Press). (Paperback edn 1990.)
'Puritans, Men of Business and Elizabethan Parliaments', *Parliamentary History*, 7, pp. 187–211.

1989
The Puritan Character: Polemics and Polarities in Early Seventeenth-Century English Culture. A paper presented at a Clark Library seminar, 25 April 1987 (Los Angeles: William Andrews Clark Memorial Library, University of California).
'Shepherds, Sheepdogs, and Hirelings: The Pastoral Ministry in Post-Reformation England', in *The Ministry: Clerical and Lay*, ed. W. J. Sheils and Diana Wood (Studies in Church History, 26, Oxford: Basil Blackwell), pp. 185–220.

1990

De Republica Anglorum: Or, History with the Politics Put Back, inautural lecture, delivered 9 November 1989 (Cambridge: Cambridge University Press).

A sermon preached as part of the Faith in History series at King's College Chapel, Cambridge, 11 February 1990, published as 'God will put aside his masks at last' in the Faith and Reason column of *The Independent*, 7 April 1990, p. 15.

'The Late Medieval Church and its Reformation 1400–1600', in *The Oxford Illustrated History of Christianity*, ed. John McManners (Oxford: Oxford University Press), pp. 233–66. (Paperback edn 1992, Italian translation 1993.)

1991

'Andrew Perne and his Times', in Patrick Collinson, David McKitterick and Elisabeth Leedham Green, *Andrew Perne: Quartercentenary Studies* (Cambridge Bibliographical Society Monograph, no. 11, Cambridge: Cambridge University Library), pp. 1–34.

'Clifford Dugmore 1910–1990 Editor: *Journal of Ecclesiastical History, 1950–1979*', *JEH*, 42, pp. 175–7.

'The Cohabitation of the Faithful with the Unfaithful', in *From Persecution to Toleration: The Glorious Revolution in England*, ed. Ole Peter Grell, Jonathan I. Israel and Nicholas Tyacke (Oxford: Clarendon Press), pp. 51–76.

'Godly Preachers and Zealous Magistrates in Elizabethan East Anglia: The Roots of Dissent', in *Religious Dissent in East Anglia*, ed. E. S. Leedham-Green (Cambridge: Cambridge Antiquarian Society), pp. 5–27.

'Publication of the Truth: Religion and the Printed Book in Early Modern England', *Publishing History*, 29, pp. 89–91.

1992

'Thomas Cranmer', in *The English Religious Tradition and the Genius of Anglicanism*, ed. Geoffrey Rowell (Oxford: Ikon Productions Ltd), pp. 79–103.

II REVIEWS

1961

H. C. Jackson, *Pastor on the Nile: Being Some Account of the Life and Letters of Llewellyn H. Gwynne. C.M.G., C.B.E., D.D., LL.D., Formerly Bishop in Egypt and the Sudan and Deputy Chaplain-General in France in the First World War (JEH, 12, p. 259)*.

John Penry, *Three Treatises Concerning Wales (History: The Journal of the Historical Association, 46, pp. 54–5)*.

John Henry Primus, *The Vestments Controversy: An Historical Study of the Earliest Tensions within the Church of England in the Reigns of Edward VI and Elizabeth (JEH, 12, p. 129)*.

1962

V.J.K. Brook, *A Life of Archbishop Parker (JEH, 13, pp. 244–5)*.

Edwin Doernberg, *Henry VIII and Luther: An Account of their Personal Relations* (*History: The Journal of the Historical Association*, 47, p. 66).

Lord Stanley of Alderley, trans. (1881), C. F. Beckingham and G. W. B. Huntingford, rev. and ed., *The Prester John of the Indies. A True Relation of the Lands of the Prester John: Being the Narrative of the Portuguese Embassy to Ethiopia in 1520 written by Father Francisco Alvares* (*JEH*, 13, pp. 241–2).

1963

Charles H. George and Katherine George, *The Protestant Mind of the English Reformation, 1570–1640* (*History: The Journal of the Historical Association*, 48, pp. 69–71).

S. J. Knox, *Walter Travers: Paragon of Elizabethan Puritanism* (*History: The Journal of the Historical Association*, 48, pp. 69–71).

1964

Stuart Barton Babbage, *Puritanism and Richard Bancroft* (*JEH*, 15, pp. 119–20).

Leland H. Carlson, *The Writings of Henry Barrow, 1587–1590* and *The Writings of John Greenwood, 1587–1590, Together with the Joint Writings of Henry Barrow and John Greenwood, 1587–1590* (*JEH*, 15, pp. 261–2).

William Haller, *Foxe's Book of Martyrs and the Elect Nation* (*JEH*, 15, pp. 255–6).

J. P. Hodges, *The Nature of the Lion: Elizabeth I and our Anglican Heritage* (*JEH*, 15, p. 132).

A. L. Rowse, *Ralegh and the Throckmortons* (*English Historical Review*, 79, pp. 601–2).

Paul A. Welsby, *George Abbot, the Unwanted Archbishop, 1562–1633* (*JEH*, 15, pp. 120–1).

1965

John E. Booty, *John Jewel as Apologist of the Church of England* (*English Historical Review*, 80, pp. 591–2).

Charles C. Butterworth and Allan G. Chester, *George Joye, 1495?–1553. A Chapter in the History of the English Bible and the English Reformation* (*History: The Journal of the Historical Association*, 50, pp. 79–80).

John F. H. New, *Anglican and Puritan: The Basis of their Opposition, 1558–1640* (*English Historical Review*, 80, pp. 592–3).

1966

V. H. H. Green, *Religion at Oxford and Cambridge* (*JEH*, 17, p. 272).

Joan Simon, *Education and Society in Tudor England* (*Cambridge Review*, 88, pp. 407–9).

R. C. Strong and J. A. van Dorsten, *Leicester's Triumph* (*JEH*, 17, pp. 272–3).

1967

H. S. Bennett, *English Books and Readers, 1558 to 1603: Being a Study in the History of the Book Trade in the Reign of Elizabeth I* (*JEH*, 18, pp. 104–5).

F. W. B. Bullock, *Evangelical Conversion in Great Britain, 1516–1695* (*JEH*, 18, p. 280).

Arthur C. Cochrane, ed., *Reformed Confessions of the 16th Century* (*Theology*, 70, pp. 321–4).

G. E. Duffield, ed., *John Calvin* (*Theology*, 70, pp. 321–4).

Donald J. McGinn, *John Penry and the Marlprelate Controversy* (*JEH*, 18, p. 134).

Thomas F. Merrill, ed., *William Perkins, 1558–1603; English Puritanist* (*English Historical Review*, 82, pp. 835–6).

James E. Oxley, *The Reformation in Essex to the Death of Mary* (*JEH*, 18, pp. 103–4).

P. G. Rogers, *The Fifth Monarchy Men* (*Theology*, 70, pp. 321–4).

Robert Stupperich, *Melanchthon*, trans. Robert H. Fischer (*Theology*, 70, pp. 321–4).

1968

C. F. Allison, *The Rise of Moralism: The Proclamation of the Gospel from Hooker to Baxter* (*William and Mary Quarterly*, 25, pp. 504–6).

Leland H. Carlson, ed., *The Writings of Henry Barrow, 1590–1591* (*JEH*, 19, p. 128).

Philip McNair, *Peter Martyr in Italy: An Anatomy of Apostasy* (*JEH*, 19, pp. 120–2).

Jasper Ridley, *John Knox* (*Spectator*, 221, pp. 586–7).

1969

Josef L. Altholz, *The Churches in the Nineteenth Century* (*JEH*, 20, p. 184).

E. G. W. Bill, ed., *Anglican Initiatives in Christian Unity: Lectures Delivered in Lambeth Palace Library 1966* (*History: The Journal of the Historical Association*, 54, p. 481).

C. G. Bolam, Jeremy Goring, H. L. Short and Roger Thomas, *The English Presbyterians* (*Theology*, 72, pp. 122–3).

H. Outram Evennett, *The Spirit of the Counter-Reformation*, ed. John Bossy (*History: The Journal of the Historical Association*, 54, pp. 272–3).

Henry Kamen, *The Rise of Toleration* (*History: The Journal of the Historical Association*, 54, pp. 97–8).

Charles J. Lees, ed., *The Poetry of Walter Haddon* (*English Historical Review*, 84, p. 842).

T. H. L. Parker, ed., *English Reformers* (*History: The Journal of the Historical Association*, 54, pp. 93–4).

Steven Runciman, *The Great Church in Captivity: A Study of the Patriarchate of Constantinople from the Eve of the Turkish Conquest to the Greek War of Independence* (*Spectator*, 222, p. 786).

Edward Surtz, *The Works and Days of John Fisher: An Introduction to the Position of St. John Fisher (1469–1535), Bishop of Rochester, in the English Renaissance and Reformation* (*English Historical Review*, 84, pp. 841–2).

1971

H. G. Alexander, *Religion in England, 1558–1662* (*JEH*, 22, pp. 282–3).

Everett H. Emerson, *English Puritanism from John Hooper to John Milton* (*JEH*, 22, p. 283).

Roger B. Manning, *Religion and Society in Elizabethan Sussex: A Study of the Enforcement of the Religious Settlement, 1558–1603* (*JEH*, 22, pp. 268–9).

John W. Packer, *The Transformation of Anglicanism, 1643–1660, with Special Reference to Henry Hammond* (*JEH*, 22, pp. 269–70).

Paul S. Seaver, *The Puritan Lectureships. The Politics of Religious Dissent 1560–1662* (*History: The Journal of the Historical Association*, 56, pp. 445–6).

1972

Ian Breward, ed., *The Work of William Perkins* (*JEH*, 23, pp. 283–4).

H. C. Porter, *Puritanism in Tudor England* (JEH, 23, pp. 282–3).

1973

B. R. White, *The English Separatist Tradition from the Marian Martyrs to the Pilgrim Fathers* (*History: The Journal of the Historical Association*, 58, pp. 99–100).

C. H. Williams, *William Tyndale* (*Journal of Religious History*, 7, pp. 260–1).

1974

'Das Opium des Volkes', a review of G. J. Cuming and Derek Baker, eds., *Popular Belief and Practice: Papers Read at the Ninth Summer Meeting and the Tenth Winter Meeting of the Ecclesiastical History Society* (Studies in Church History, 8); and Derek Baker, ed., *Schism, Heresy, and Religious Protest: Papers Read at the Tenth Summer Meeting and the Elegenth Winter Meeting of the Ecclesiastical History Society* (Studies in Church History, 9) (*Journal of Religious History*, 8, pp. 105-11).

1976

G. R. Elton, *Studies in Tudor and Stuart Politics and Government: Papers and Reviews, 1946–1972. I: Tudor Politics/Tudor Government; II: Parliament/ Political Thought* (*JEH*, 25, pp. 318–19).

A. B. Emden, *A Biographical Register of the University of Oxford, A.D. 1501 to 1540* (*JEH*, 27, pp. 441–3).

R. C. Richardson, *Puritanism in North-West England: A Regional Study of the Diocese of Chester to 1642* (*Journal of Religious History*, 9, pp. 321–3).

Martin A. Simpson, *John Knox and the Troubles Begun at Frankfurt, Comprising a Critical Commentary on 'A Brieff Discours off the Troubles Begonne at Franckford . . . A.D. 1554'. John Knox's Narrative of his Expulsion from the City, with Annotations and an Analysis of Rudolf Jung's 'Englische Flüchtlings-gemeinde' (1910)* (*JEH*, 27, pp. 443–4).

D. F. Wright, trans. and ed., *Common Places of Martin Bucer* (*Journal of Religious History*, 9, pp. 207–9).

1977

'Between the Tables', a review of J. Sears McGee, *The Godly Man in Stuart England: Anglicans, Puritans and the Two Tables, 1620–1670* (*Times Literary Supplement*, 7 January, p. 14).

'Polemical Texts', a review of Peter Milward, *Religious Controversies of the Elizabethan Age* (*The Times Literary Supplement*, 2 September, p. 1056).

1978

Claire Cross, *Church and People 1450–1660: The Triumph of the Laity in the English Church* (English Historical Review, 93, p. 176).

Geoffrey de C. Parmiter, *Elizabethan Popish Recusancy in the Inns of Court* (*JEH*, 29, pp. 247–8).

W. J. Sheils, ed., *Archbishop Grindal's Visitation, 1575: Comperta et Detecta Book* (*JEH*, 29, p. 248).

1980

Peter Clark, *English Provincial Society from the Reformation to the Revolution: Religion, Politics and Society in Kent 1500–1640* (*JEH*, 31, pp. 229–32).

'Experimental Predestinarians', a review of R. T. Rendall, *Calvin and English Calvinism to 1649* (*Times Literary Supplement*, 16 May, p. 561).

Winton U. Solberg, *Redeem the Time: The Puritan Sabbath in Early America* (*JEH*, 31, pp. 261–2).

1981

'The Significance of Signatures', a review of David Cressy, *Literacy and the Social Order: Reading and Writing in Tudor and Stuart England* (*Times Literary Supplement*, 9 January, p. 31).

'Denominational Distinctions', a review of Richard L. Greaves, *Society and Religion in Elizabethan England* (*Times Literary Supplement*, 11 December, p. 1436).

1982

'The Elizabethan Cold War', a review of Wallace T. MacCaffrey, *Queen Elizabeth and the Making of Policy, 1572–1588* (*Times Literary Supplement*, 22 January, p. 71).

Bruce Mansfield, *Phoenix of His Age: Interpretations of Erasmus c. 1550–1750* (*Journal of Religious History*, 12, pp. 94–6).

1983

'Outsize Egos', a review of A. L. Rowse, *Eminent Elizabethans* (*Times Literary Supplement*, 13 May, p. 484).

W. D. J. Cargill Thompson, *Studies in the Reformation: Luther to Hooker* (*History: The Journal of the Historical Association*, 68, p. 151).

1984

A. G. Dickens, *Reformation Studies* (*JEH*, 35, p. 312).

Anthony Fletcher, *The Outbreak of the English Civil War* (*JEH*, 35, pp. 152–5).

'God's Tightrope', a review of Mary Fulbrook, *Piety and Politics: Religion and the Rise of Absolutism in England, Württemberg and Prussia* (*History Today*, 34, pp. 56–7).

J. S. Morrill, *Seventeenth-Century Britain 1603–1714* (*JEH*, 35, p. 169).

Jean Dietz Moss, *'Godded with God': Hendrik Niclaes and his Family of Love* (*JEH*, 35, pp. 316–17).

Willem Nijenhuis, *Adrianus Saravia (c. 1532–1613): Dutch Calvinist, First Reformed*

Defender of the English Episcopal Church Order on the Basis of the 'Ius Divinum' (*JEH*, 35, pp. 149–51).

'The Old Faithful', reviews of J. J. Scarisbrick, *The Reformation and the English People*, and Robert Ashton, *Reformation and Revolution 1558–1660* (*Times Literary Supplement*, 1 June, p. 605).

1986

'Resisting the Renaissance', reviews of *Godly Learning: Puritan Attitudes Towards Reason, Learning, and Education, 1560–1640* by John Morgan, and *Reflections on the Puritan Revolution* by A. L. Rowse (*Times Literary Supplement*, 15 August, p. 884).

1987

Derek Beales and Geoffrey Best, eds., *History, Society and the Churches, Essays in Honour of Owen Chadwick* (*JEH*, 38, pp. 107–11).

'Parliaments without Politics', a review of G. R. Elton, *The Parliament of England 1559–1581* (*History Today*, 37, p. 53).

'Ardently Protestant', a review of Alan Hayes, *The White Bear: The Elizabethan Earl of Leicester* (*Times Literary Supplement*, 13–19 November, p. 1256).

'The Story of Everyday Things', a review of Christopher Hibbert, *The English: A Social History 1066–1945* (*Times Literary Supplement*, 11–17 September, p. 991).

1988

E. S. Leedham-Green, ed., *Books in Cambridge Inventories: Book-Lists from Vice-Chancellors' Court Probate Inventories in the Tudor and Stuart Periods, I: The Inventories; II: Catalogue*, and Sargent Bush, Jr, and Carl J. Rasmussen, eds., *The Library of Emmanuel College, Cambridge, 1584–1637* (*JEH*, 39, pp. 278–81).

1989

'Fundamental Objections', reviews of Margaret Aston, *England's Iconoclasts: Volume One: Laws Against Images*, Kenneth L. Parker, *The English Sabbath: A Study of Doctrine and Discipline from the Reformation to the Civil War*, and David S. Katz, *Sabbath and Sectarianism in Seventeenth-Century England* (*Times Libterary Supplement*, 17–23 February, pp. 155–6).

1991

'Smelling the Gospel', a review of Susan Brigden, *London and the Reformation* (*London Review of Books*, 13, 7 March, pp. 15–16).

G. R. Elton, *The Parliament of England, 1559–1581* (JEH, 42, pp. 488–90).

'Laudable Lying in the Age of Dissimulation', a review of Perez Zagorin, *Ways of Lying: Dissimulation, Persecution and Conformity in Early Modern Europe* (*Times Literary Supplement*, 1 March, p. 23).

1992

'Elton at Seventy', a review of G. R. Elton, *Return to Essentials: Some Reflections on the Present State of Historical Study* (*London Review of Books*, 14, 11 June, pp. 14, 24–5).

Professor Patrick Collinson has also published other reviews in the *Times Literary Supplement*, *London Review of Books* and the *Observer*.

Index

DATE DUE

OCT 1 4 2014

Printed
in USA